SUPERVISION FOR TODAY'S SCHOOLS

EIGHTH EDITION

SUPERVISION FOR TODAY'S SCHOOLS

GEORGE E. PAWLAS
University of Central Florida

PETER F. OLIVA
Author, Developing the Curriculum

1807
⊗WILEY
2007
BICENTENNIAL

JOHN WILEY & SONS INC.

ACQUISITIONS EDITOR   Robert Johnston
SENIOR PRODUCTION EDITOR   Patricia McFadden
MARKETING MANAGER   Emily Streutker
CREATIVE DIRECTOR   Harry Nolan
SENIOR DESIGNER   Kevin Murphy
PHOTO EDITOR   Sheena Goldstein
EDITORIAL ASSISTANT   Eileen McKeever
MEDIA EDITOR   Sasha Giacoppo
PRODUCTION MANAGEMENT SERVICES   Hermitage Publishing Services

COVER PHOTO   © PhotoDisc, Inc.
COVER DESIGN   David Levy

This book was set in 10/12 New New Times Roman by Thomson Press and printed and bound by
RR Donnelley. The cover was printed by Phoenix Color.

This book is printed on acid free paper. ∞

To order books or for customer service please, call 1-800-CALL WILEY (225-5945).

ISBN-13   978- 0-470-08758-9
ISBN-10   0-470-08758-7

Printed in the United States of America
10 9 8 7 6 5 4 3 2 1

To Sharon and Ruth

PREFACE

The eighth edition of this book remains an overview of the field of instructional supervision specifically designed for an introductory course.

This textbook was planned to acquaint the student not only with the authors' views on supervision but with those of other specialists in the field as well. Although we have sought to integrate theory and practice, the book continues to lean toward practice, with heavy emphasis on the supervisor's responsibilities as instructional leader.

We present in these pages not only what we believe to be the most promising and proven practices but also what we see as the prevailing practices in the schools. We owe a debt to the mountains of research conducted on instruction, curriculum, and supervision over the past thirty years. We have not attempted to present a new, idiosyncratic, philosophical, or theoretical approach to instructional supervision. Nor is the book a treatise on principles of educational leadership in general or managerial supervision. Rather, our focus is on the instructional supervisor; hence, there is special emphasis on the supervisor's role in helping teachers improve instruction.

We subscribe to the belief that instructional supervision remains a necessary and viable function in school systems. We adhere to the belief that supervisors should look at teaching before looking at the teacher. We focus on generic instructional skills that we believe can be learned and improved. We believe the supervisor should look at the classroom and school environment within the context of instruction. We continue to believe that supervisors should strive to assess teacher performance as objectively as possible, minimizing subjective judgment.

You will note that we have made frequent use of the terms *help* and *helping*. We are aware of a school of thought that objects to these terms. That school holds that help and helping imply condescension toward and distrust of teachers. On the contrary, we view these terms as positive, as do many others. We take the position that the relationship between the supervisor and teachers is a helping one, the purpose of which is to improve instruction and thereby improve students' achievement. Presumably, supervisors possess—or should possess—superior skills and knowledge that enable them to assist teachers. Any time a supervisor observes a class and provides feedback to the teacher, offers suggestions for improving lesson plans, advises on available curriculum materials, and arranges staff development activities, that supervisor is providing help. It is no secret that teachers welcome help from supervisors when they possess the necessary professional skills and personal attributes.

The text introduces the reader to three domains of supervision: instructional development, curriculum development, and staff development. Training programs for instructional supervisors normally follow the overview course with one or more specialized courses in each of the three domains.

Although the text describes and discusses many promising and proven practices, we do not intend to imply that all practices are applicable with all teachers. As a general rule, supervisors will work more closely and more frequently with new, inexperienced teachers. We can, of course, all cite those cases of new graduates from teacher education institutions who excel without many years of experience. However, these are the exceptions to the rule. Teacher education programs barely scratch the surface. Thus, new teachers generally will need more assistance than experienced teachers. By the same token, many outstanding teachers may be self-directive and may become skilled through trial and error. A competent supervisor, however, may help shorten the trial-and-error learning curve. Of course, some dynamic, experienced teachers may need little more than positive reinforcement. Supervisors must use their own good judgment as to which techniques and programs, if any, fit the needs of an individual teacher or a particular faculty group.

GOALS OF THE TEXT

We would like students to achieve the following goals as a result of reading *Supervision for Today's Schools*:

1. To develop a concept of supervision compatible with the needs of students, teachers, the community, society at large, and their own personalities.
2. To find suggestions for measures that can be taken to improve areas of supervision discussed in the text.
3. To become sensitive to the instructional needs of teachers.
4. To confront recent developments, thought, and research within the domains of supervision discussed in this text.
5. To gain ideas for training programs for teachers.
6. To feel the need for becoming proficient in areas discussed in the text and to take what measures are needed to improve their own competence in each of the areas.
7. To become aware of some of the trends and issues in the field of supervision.
8. To become familiar with the work of some of the specialists in the field, both past and present.

UNIQUE FEATURES OF THIS TEXT

- Clear model of instructional supervision in three domains: instruction, curriculum, and staff development
- Integration of the three domains with tasks of the supervisor
- Integration of theory with practice, emphasizing promising and proven practices from actual school situations

- Treatment of instructional supervision as a helping relationship between supervisors and teachers
- Chapter on the difficult area of classroom management
- Material on research concepts and methods
- Objectives and summaries with each chapter
- Ample references for graduate research

NEW FEATURES OF THE EIGHTH EDITION

- Increased attention to diversity, technology, inclusion, and reading
- Attention to effects of national and state academic standards and testing programs

HOW THIS TEXT IS ORGANIZED

The structure of this text is rather simple. It describes ways in which supervisors work with teachers in three domains: instruction, curriculum, and staff development. We integrate these domains with the tasks of the supervisor. It is true that whole books are available on each of these domains. We feel that an introductory text that incorporates the domains and shows their relationship to the supervisory process is a good jumping-off point for further study.

This textbook is organized into six parts. Part I sets forth the role of the supervisor and raises a number of issues in supervision. Part II discusses the instructional process and ways the supervisor can help teachers in the planning, presentation, and evaluation of instruction. Part III presents ways in which supervisors engage in curriculum development. Part IV describes the supervisor's role in working with teachers both in groups and individually. Part V discusses summative evaluation of teacher performance. Part VI considers the evaluation of both the supervisor and the supervisory program and future directions in supervision.

Early in the textbook we present a model of instructional supervision consisting of three domains, four roles, and twelve foundations. At the beginning of each chapter we have specified desired objectives. Objectives are of two types: cognitive, specifying intellectual tasks; and affective, designed to bring out the reader's personal positions and attitudes. We have consciously tried to provide examples of all the major points discussed in the text. In so doing, we have made a special effort to provide illustrations from actual school systems whenever possible.

At the end of each chapter, you will find not only several questions suitable for class discussion but also a generous number of activities for further study. Some are simple cognitive exercises. Others are complex, calling for research and considerable thought. These activities have two purposes: (1) to clarify and review the content of the chapter, and (2) to extend study beyond the chapter. Instructors and students can select the activities that are most pertinent to them and to their courses.

We have rather arbitrarily classified end-of-chapter activities into two groups: *Reflective* and *Application*. We realize that these classifications may overlap. However, the intent is to classify those activities that are more theoretical, or of a self-inductive nature, as Reflective and those that are more action-oriented as Application. Both categories of activities are designed to expand understanding.

At the conclusion of each chapter, we have assembled ample bibliographies for those wishing to do further research on the topics presented in the chapter. Whenever possible, we have included media other than books that may help instructors illuminate the topics presented in the chapter. Pertinent Web sites for organizations are cited throughout the book.

Throughout this text, as well as in the notes and bibliographies, we have cited both old and new references. Older references in the chapters provide a sense of history to the field, acknowledging our debt to those who have contributed to the field; the newer references reflect current thought. With the end-of-chapter questions, exercises, and bibliographies, the instructor has the equivalent of an instructor's manual.

This text, which has found wide acceptance among trainers of supervisors and practitioners in its previous editions, reflects positions held by many (perhaps the majority of) practicing supervision specialists. The book reflects the status of instructional supervision as it currently functions in school systems throughout the United States and as it is practiced by many dedicated, experienced individuals at local school, district, and state levels.

We want to thank all of the professors, students, and practitioners who have used previous editions of this text. We are indebted to the following reviewers of this edition for their helpful suggestions for revising the textbook: Janet Alleman, Michigan State University; Lynn Beckwith, Jr., University of Missouri, St. Louis; Ronald Hyman, Rutgers University; Kenneth Johnson, Lindenwood University; Linda K. Lemasters, George Washington University; Iren Maduakolam, Winston Salem State University; Xavier McClung, Valdosta State University; Gary L. Reglin, University of West Florida; Amany Saleh, Arkansas State University; Olusegun Sogunro, Central Connecticut State University; Kip Sullivan, Sul Ross State University; Donald Wise, California State University at Fresno; and Flora Wyatt, University of Kansas. We would also like to thank Gerri Spinella for her hard work on the accompanying PowerPoint slides.

We would like to extend special thanks to the Wiley/Jossey-Bass team, Robert Johnston, Patricia McFadden, Eileen McKeever, Len Neufeld, Laura Poole, and Larry Meyer, for making this eighth edition possible.

ABOUT THE AUTHORS

George E. Pawlas is a Professor in the College of Education at the University of Central Florida (UCF). Currently he teaches courses in supervision, contemporary issues in educational leadership, school–community relations, and organization and administration of schools. Prior to joining the faculty at UCF in 1991, Pawlas gained experience in public education as an elementary school teacher in Rocky River, Ohio, a suburb of Cleveland. He also was an elementary school principal there and in Columbia, South Carolina. He added other experiences at the South Carolina State Department of Education and as the principal of the lab school at Georgia Southern University in Statesboro, Georgia. Pawlas is an active member of many professional organizations and maintains positions on several editorial committees. *The Administrator's Guide to School/Community Relations* was his first book; a second edition was published in 2005. He co-authored the fifth, sixth, and seventh editions of *Supervision for Today's Schools* with Peter Oliva. He is a co-author of *The Adjunct Professor's Guide to Success* and has contributed chapters to several other books. A regular book reviewer for AASA, Pawlas has more than forty articles published in professional journals and magazines.

Peter F. Oliva is a retired Professor from Florida International University and Georgia Southern University. He has served on the faculties of the University of Mississippi, the University of Florida, Indiana State University, Southern Illinois University, and the University of Hawaii. As adjunct instructor, he has supervised interns at the University of Central Florida. He has published numerous articles in education journals and is author of several textbooks in the fields of instruction, supervision, and curriculum, including *Developing the Curriculum*. He has traveled extensively in Europe, Latin America, and the Middle East. He is a member of the Association for Supervision and Curriculum Development, Phi Delta Kappa, the National Education Association, and Phi Beta Kappa. He holds an A.B. degree from Cornell University; an M.A.T. from Harvard University; and an Ed.D. from Teachers College, Columbia University.

CONTENTS

PREFACE   vi

PART I

NATURE OF SUPERVISION   1

CHAPTER 1   *ROLES OF THE SCHOOL SUPERVISOR*   3

Supervision Defined   3
Historical Approaches   4
Varying Interpretations   10
Problems That Complicate the
   Supervisory Role   11
      Continuing Diversity of Conceptions of
         Supervision   11
      Differing Conceptions of Effective Teaching   12
      Mandates from the State and National
         Levels   13
      Tensions between Teachers and Administrators/
         Supervisors   13
Who Are the Supervisors?   14
      Types of Supervisors   15
Tasks of Supervision   19
A Model of Supervision   20
      Domains of Supervision   22
      Varying Roles   23
      Foundations of Supervision   24

CHAPTER 2   *ISSUES IN SUPERVISION*   32

Numerous Unresolved Issues   32
      Issues in Supervision   35
   ISSUE 1: Is Supervision Necessary?   37
      Limitations of Teaching   38
      Need for the Supervisor   38

ISSUE 2: For Whom Should Supervision
      Be Provided?   40
      Teacher Experience and Teacher Effectiveness   40
      Subject-Centered Teachers versus Learner-Centered
         Teachers   41
      Teachers Who Are Ineffective and Know It   42
      Teacher Burnout   42
      Supervision for All Teachers   43
ISSUE 3: Should the Supervisor's Authority Be Based on
      Expertise and Interpersonal Relationships
      or on Conferred Status and Decision-Making
      Responsibilities?   44
ISSUE 4: Should the Supervisor Be an Administrator?   46
ISSUE 5: Is Supervision Staff Development?   50
ISSUE 6: Is Supervision Curriculum Development?   51
ISSUE 7: Is Supervision Evaluation?   53
ISSUE 8: Should Supervisors Work with Groups of Teachers or
      with Individual Teachers?   55
ISSUE 9: Should Supervision Be Carried Out by Supervisors
      Based in the Central Office or in the Individual
      School?   57
      State Level   57
      Intermediate Level   58
      Local School Districts   61
ISSUE 10: Should the Supervisor Use a Directive or
      Nondirective Approach?   65
ISSUE 11: Should School Systems Organize for Supervision
      by Employing Generalists or Specialists?   68
      Characteristics of Generalists and Specialists   69
      Need for Specialists   71
      Some Parallels   72
ISSUE 12: Should There Be National Professional Standards
      for Teachers?   72
ISSUE 13: What Should Be the Role of Technology in the
      Supervisory Process?   74
ISSUE 14: Should Multiculturalism Be a Focus of
      Supervision?   76

PART II

LEADERSHIP IN INSTRUCTIONAL DEVELOPMENT   85

CHAPTER 3   *HELPING TEACHERS PLAN FOR INSTRUCTION*   87

Models of Instruction   **87**
   Simplified Model   **89**
Classroom Planning: A Six-Point Program   **89**
   Following a Systematic Approach to Instructional Design   **90**
   Following a Model of Instruction   **92**
   Writing Instructional Goals and Objectives   **93**
   Applying Taxonomies of Instructional Objectives   **99**
   Describing and Analyzing Learning Tasks   **105**
   Multiple Intelligences   **113**
   Organizing Instructional Plans   **114**

CHAPTER 4   *HELPING TEACHERS PRESENT INSTRUCTION*   125

What Is Effective Teaching?   **125**
Steps in Implementation   **127**
Selection of Resources   **128**
Selection of Strategies   **130**
Lesson Presentation   **137**
   Beginning the Lesson   **138**
   Moving through the Middle of the Lesson—Teaching to the Objectives (T$_2$O)   **142**
   Closing the Lesson   **154**
A Checklist   **156**
   A Checklist for Lesson Presentation   **156**

CHAPTER 5   *HELPING TEACHERS WITH CLASSROOM MANAGEMENT*   164

Discipline: A Serious Problem   **164**
Causes of Behavior Problems   **167**
   Causes Originating with the Child   **169**
   Causes Originating with the Child's Group   **171**
   Causes Originating with the Teacher   **172**
   Causes Originating with the School   **174**
   Causes Originating with the Home and Community   **177**
   Causes Originating in the Larger Social Order   **178**
Preventing Behavior Problems   **179**
   Analyze Attitudes   **179**
   Analyze Teaching Styles and Students' Learning Styles   **180**
   Analyze the Classroom Environment   **182**
   Analyze the Curriculum Continuously   **182**
   Analyze the Methods of Instruction Employed   **182**
   Gather as Much Information as Possible about Individual Learners   **183**
   Analyze the Disciplinary Models Used   **184**
   Set and Enforce Minimum Expectations of Behavior   **186**
Correcting Behavior Problems   **187**
   Ten Reasonable Punishments   **192**
   Corporal Punishment   **197**

CHAPTER 6   *HELPING TEACHERS EVALUATE INSTRUCTION*   208

Evaluation: An Essential Phase   **208**
Preassessment   **209**
Continuing Assessment   **210**
Norm-Referenced and Criterion-Referenced Measurement   **212**
   Norm-Referenced Measurement   **213**
   Criterion-Referenced Measurement   **215**
Relation of Evaluation to Objectives   **216**
Formative and Summative Evaluation   **218**
Testing   **219**
   State Assessments   **222**
   National Assessments   **222**
   Teacher-Made Tests   **223**
Evaluating Affective Objectives   **239**
Other Evaluation Techniques   **240**
   Observation of Class Participation   **240**
   Oral Reports   **240**
   Written Assignments   **242**
   Portfolio Assessment   **242**
   Creative Assignments   **243**
   Group Work   **243**
   Self-Evaluation and Joint Evaluation   **243**
Marking Student Achievement   **246**
Reporting Student Achievement   **249**

PART III

LEADERSHIP IN CURRICULUM DEVELOPMENT 259

CHAPTER 7 *HELPING TEACHERS PLAN AND IMPLEMENT CURRICULA* 261

A Model for Curriculum Development **261**
The Supervisor in Curriculum Development **265**
Approaches to Curriculum Development **266**
    Planning **266**
    The Comprehensive Approach **266**
    The Problem-Centered Approach **278**
    Design of the Plan **280**
    Involvement of Others **281**
Continuing Problems of Curriculum
   Development **281**
    Scope of the Curriculum **282**
    Sequence of the Curriculum **286**
    Balance in the Curriculum **288**
    Organization of the Curriculum **290**
    Curricular Reform **291**
    Controversial Problems **291**
    Implementation and Evaluation **292**

CHAPTER 8 *HELPING TEACHERS EVALUATE CURRICULA* 298

Curriculum Evaluation: Essential and
   Difficult **298**
The Supervisor's Role in Evaluation **301**
    Research Orientation **302**
Basic Research Concepts **303**
Types of Research **307**
Teacher Participation in Research **308**
Types of Evaluation **309**
    Evaluation Models **309**
Conducting a Curriculum Needs Assessment **312**
    The Delphi Technique **315**
Evaluative Criteria **316**
Curriculum Mapping **318**
Evaluation of Materials and Studies **318**
State Assessment Programs **321**
Local Assessment Programs **322**

PART IV

LEADERSHIP IN STAFF DEVELOPMENT 329

CHAPTER 9 *HELPING TEACHERS THROUGH IN-SERVICE PROGRAMS* 331

Supervision and Staff Development **331**
    Purposes of Staff Development **332**
    The Supervisor's Role in In-Service Education **334**
Assumptions about In-Service Education **338**
Characteristics of Effective In-Service Programs **340**
A Model for In-Service Education **341**
    Planning **341**
    Implementation **345**
    Evaluation **351**
    Post-Training Application and Evaluation **351**
Control of In-Service Education **356**
    Teacher Education Centers **356**

CHAPTER 10 *HELPING TEACHERS ON A ONE-TO-ONE BASIS* 365

Formative Evaluation **365**
Clinical Supervision **366**
The Supervisor's Role in Clinical Supervision **368**
Models of Clinical Supervision **370**
    Preobservation Conference **373**
    Observation **375**
    Postobservation Conference **382**
Problems in Clinical Supervision **384**
    Who Will Do the Supervising? **384**
    Collegiality in Supervision **385**
    Do We Have the Necessary Resources? **388**
    For Whom Should Clinical Supervision Be
      Provided? **388**
    Are There Models Other Than the Clinical? **389**

CHAPTER 11 *HELPING TEACHERS WORK TOGETHER* 399

Living in Groups **399**
The Supervisor as Group Leader **403**
    Definition of Leadership **403**

Traits of Leaders **404**

Styles of Leadership **406**

Decision Making **407**

Effecting Change **409**

Organizational Development **412**

Communication **419**

Group Process **423**

Group Process versus Group Counseling **426**

Training in Group Interaction **428**

Practice in Interaction Skills **430**

Record of Behavior of Individuals in Groups **430**

Provision of Group Therapy-Type Sessions **430**

National Staff Development Council **433**

CHAPTER 12 *HELPING TEACHERS EVALUATE THEIR OWN PERFORMANCE* **441**

Three Faces of Evaluation of Teacher Performance **441**

Competencies to Be Evaluated **449**

Evaluation of Instructional Skills **451**

Evaluation of Personal and Professional Attributes **462**

Using Evaluation Instruments **463**

Student Evaluations **471**

Parent Evaluations **473**

PART V

THE SUMMATIVE DIMENSION OF TEACHER EVALUATION **479**

CHAPTER 13 *SUMMATIVE ASSESSMENT OF TEACHER PERFORMANCE* **481**

Summative Evaluation **481**

Who Should Be Evaluated? **483**

Who Should Evaluate Teachers? **484**

What Should Be Evaluated? **486**

How Should the Evaluations Be Done? **489**

How Should the Data Be Used? **502**

Problems in Summative Evaluation **507**

PART VI

INSTRUCTIONAL SUPERVISION: EVALUATION AND CHANGE **515**

CHAPTER 14 *IMPROVING INSTRUCTIONAL SUPERVISION* **517**

Role of the Supervisor: A Reprise **517**

Evaluation of the Supervisor **519**

Evaluation by Superordinates **519**

Self-Evaluation **520**

Evaluation by Teachers **523**

Evaluation of the Supervisory Program **524**

Evaluation by Objectives **525**

Evaluative Questioning **525**

Future Directions in Supervision **526**

Domains of Supervision **526**

Clarification of Approaches, Functions, and Roles **527**

Balanced Supervision **528**

Teacher Empowerment **529**

School-Based Supervision **530**

Peers, Coaches, and Mentors **531**

Teacher Incentives, Career Ladder, and Merit Pay **532**

Emphasis on Observable Teaching Competencies **534**

Clinical Supervision **535**

Goal-Oriented Supervision **535**

Supervisory Teams **535**

Increased Use of Technology **536**

Needed Research **536**

Professional Education **537**

CREDITS **545**

NAME INDEX **551**

SUBJECT INDEX **555**

PART 1

NATURE OF SUPERVISION

Lawrence Migdale/Stock, Boston

CHAPTER 1

ROLES OF THE SCHOOL SUPERVISOR

OBJECTIVES

After studying Chapter 1 you should be able to accomplish the following objectives:

1. Outline the historical development of the field of supervision.
2. Formulate a working definition of supervision.
3. Describe a conceptual model of supervision.
4. Identify supervisors in a school system.
5. List common tasks of supervision.
6. Describe various roles of supervisors.
7. State what you believe to be the minimal qualifications of a supervisor.
8. Discuss your thoughts about supervision as a career.

SUPERVISION DEFINED

One of the best-kept secrets outside the education profession and, to a degree even within the profession, is the existence of a large shadow army of school personnel known by the collective title of supervisors. Parents and sometimes teachers profess not to know of the presence of these specialists in the school systems of the nation. Although laypersons may be aware that school systems employ a variety of personnel, such as custodians, secretaries, cafeteria workers, and counselors, the concept of school personnel held by a typical layperson is that of a teacher in every classroom and a principal in every school. Were members of the community asked to identify a school supervisor, they would probably indicate the principal, who may or may not be the sole supervisor. Or they might refer to the superintendent, who plays a relatively small part in the type of supervision discussed in this book, namely, instructional supervision.

Yet as the alien watchers say about extraterrestrial beings, supervisors are "out there." In fact, they are all around us. We could discover to what degree they are present if we had the power to equip every supervisor with a coal miner's hat and to turn on all the light beams. If we could then photograph the light trails, we would trace a pattern of motion as astounding as any graphics drawn by a computer. We'd see almost endless movement as supervisors journey from class to class, school to school, and school system to school system. Whereas teachers are usually place-bound, supervisors are in periodic motion. A distinguishing feature of true supervisors is that they leave their offices frequently for the purpose of helping other school personnel—namely, teachers—do their jobs better.

Considering the veritable army of supervisors on local and state levels of schooling throughout the country, it is surprising to find that the role of the supervisor in education remains rather ill defined. Business and industry are not troubled by this same malady. The position of commercial or industrial supervisor is highly visible and well defined in the managerial structure of the organization. Educational supervisors may or may not be a part of the managerial structure of school systems. The question of whether they should be part of management is, as we will discover later, a storm center among specialists in supervision.

Responsibilities of educational supervisors are not at all clear from locality to locality and from state to state. Even within localities, supervisory roles are often poorly delineated. To compound the problem, the titles of supervisors are almost as varied as their roles.

Ben M. Harris attributed the variations in roles to differing theoretical perspectives:

> Supervision, like any complex part of an even more complex enterprise, can be
> viewed in various ways and inevitably is. The diversity of perceptions stems not
> only from organizational complexity but also from lack of information and absence
> of perspective. To provide perspective, at least, the total school operation must be
> the point of departure for analyzing instructional supervision as a major function.[1]

To varying degrees, many occupations outside education use the services of supervisors, whether as office boss, telephone supervisor, floor manager, construction supervisor, department store head, or assembly-line supervisor. These individuals carry out the task of supervision in the original sense of the Latin word *supervideo*, "to oversee." They demonstrate techniques, offer suggestions, give orders, evaluate employees' performance, and check on results (products).

HISTORICAL APPROACHES

Supervision has gone through many metamorphoses. If we look at some of the changes that have occurred in this field since the early days, we can a bit arbitrarily establish historical time frames for the evolution of instructional supervision. In analyzing the development of most aspects of education, we should keep in mind what we might call axioms.[2] Applied to curriculum development, these could include "School curriculum not only reflects but is a product of its time" and "Curriculum changes made at an earlier period of time can exist concurrently with curriculum changes at a later period of time." The same axioms are valid if we substitute the word *supervision* for *curriculum*.

Supervisory behaviors and practices are affected by political, social, religious, and industrial forces existent at the time. Furthermore, traces of supervisory behaviors and practices that existed in the earlier days of our nation can be found even today among highly divergent practices and behaviors. History is forever with us. However, supervision has come a long way since colonial days, as we can see in Table 1.1, which outlines the major periods in the historical development of supervision.

Not until the establishment of organized schools did the need for specialized school supervisors materialize. When parents, "dames," and tutors instructed youngsters in the home, these people were, in effect, both teacher and supervisor, but as the population grew, early

TABLE 1.1 Major Periods in the Historical Development of Supervision

Period	Type of supervision	Purpose	Persons responsible
1620–1850	Inspection	Monitoring rules, looking for deficiencies	Parents, clergy, selectmen, citizens' committees
1850–1910	Inspection, instructional improvement	Monitoring rules, helping teachers improve	Superintendents, principals
1910–1930	Scientific, bureaucratic	Improving instruction and efficiency	Supervising principals, principals, general and special central-office supervisors, superintendents
1930–1950	Human relations, democratic	Improving instruction	Principals, central-office supervisors
1950–1975	Bureaucratic, scientific, clinical, human relations, human resources, democratic	Improving instruction	Principals, central-office supervisors, school-based supervisors
1975–1985	Scientific, clinical, human relations, human resources, collaborative/collegial, peer/coach/mentor, artistic, interpretive	Improving instruction, increasing teacher satisfaction, expanding students' understanding of classroom events	Principals, central-office supervisors, school-based supervisors, peer/coach/mentor
1985– present	Scientific, clinical, human relations human resources, collaborative/collegial, peer/coach/mentor, artistic, interpretive, culturally responsive, ecological	Improving instruction, increasing teacher satisfaction, creating learning communities expanding students' classroom events, analyzing cultural and linguistic patterns in the classroom	School-based supervisors, peer/coach/mentor, principals, central-office supervisors

colonists realized that they needed some formal structure for the education of their young. The Commonwealth of Massachusetts passed the famed Old Deluder Law of 1647, which required communities with 50 or more families to provide instruction in reading and writing and communities with 100 or more families to establish a grammar school. Thus, educated young people would not be led astray by the Old Deluder, Satan. Note the powerful effect of the church on early education in the colonies. Although church and state are more or less separated today, strong controversy still exists about the role of religion in the public schools.[3]

As schools became established, local school committeemen fulfilled the function of supervisors by giving directions, checking for compliance with teaching techniques, and evaluating results of instruction by the teachers in their charge. In an authoritarian mode, early supervisors set strict requirements for their teachers and visited classrooms to observe how closely the teachers complied with stipulated instructions. Departure from these instructions was cause for dismissal.

Even in the eighteenth century, school people were anxious to appear at their best when visited by the town selectmen. Walter Herbert Small observed that as early as 1733 schools provided a dinner for schoolmasters, selectmen, and certain public officials on the occasion of the selectmen's visit to their schools.[4] Taking a cue from their eighteenth-century predecessors, today's school faculty, administrators, and board members commonly extend the hospitality of an initial breakfast or dinner meeting to visiting teams from regional accrediting associations.

Limited schooling, primarily for boys, was the prevailing pattern through most of the seventeenth and eighteenth centuries. Benjamin Franklin's Philadelphia Academy and Charitable School, which opened in 1751, extended the curriculum and provided opportunities not found in the earlier Latin grammar schools. A growing population necessitated more schools, and an expanding curriculum revealed the need for specialists in instructional supervision.

Universal public education for boys and girls, poor and rich, was a phenomenon of the nineteenth century. The common elementary school grew rapidly in the first half of the nineteenth century, imitating Prussian and military models of graded organization. Horace Mann, secretary of the Massachusetts State Board of Education from 1837 to 1848, pushed the cause of public schools and created the first normal school in the United States for training teachers. He defined the state's responsibility for public education. During the same period, Henry Barnard, first secretary of the Connecticut State Board of Education, was also promoting public education.

The number of high schools in the country grew rapidly, spurred by political, social, and educational developments of the time. Among these developments were the creation of the first high school in Boston in 1821, the Massachusetts law of 1827 requiring a high school with a two-month program in towns of 500 or more families, and the famous Kalamazoo, Michigan, case of 1874 that affirmed the right of communities to levy taxes for secondary education. New institutions, new programs, expanded student bodies, and increased population called for new ways of supervising instruction. Selectmen, citizens' committees, clergy, and parents gave way to trained educators.

In the nineteenth century, local committees began looking to professionally trained persons to administer and supervise the schools. As early as 1837, Buffalo, New York, and Louisville, Kentucky, employed school superintendents. By 1870, some twenty-nine school systems were headed by superintendents.[5] Superintendents in the early nineteenth century spent considerable time visiting and supervising schools, although their focus changed from looking for deficiencies meriting dismissal of teachers to helping teachers overcome difficulties.

Inspection, often derided as "snoopervision," was the prevailing approach in the nineteenth century. The appeal to authority was very evident in the widely reproduced set of instructions to teachers in Harrison, South Dakota, in 1872, shown in Figure 1.1. To some extent school supervisors, or inspectors as they are called in other countries, continue to fulfill their tasks with an authoritarian approach. The classic illustration—although not entirely accurate—is France, of which it has often been said that on any given day the Minister of Education can tell exactly where each teacher is in any textbook anywhere in the country. Such a situation implies a highly structured form of instruction and a very centralized system of supervision.

In the United States, we have no instructional inspectors in the foreign sense of the word. There are no inspectors from the U.S. Department of Education whose duty it is to check on teachers and schools. Some states do provide or have provided a limited type of inspection of teachers prior to full certification in a subject or grade level, but this is not

1. Teachers will fill lamps, clean chimneys and trim wicks each day.

2. Each teacher will bring a scuttle of coal and a bucket of water for the day's use.

3. Make your pens carefully. You may whittle nibs for the individual tastes of children.

4. Men teachers may take one evening each week for courting purposes or two evenings a week if they go to church regularly.

5. After ten hours in school, the teacher should spend the remaining time reading the Bible and other good books.

6. Women teachers who marry or engage in other unseemly conduct will be dismissed.

7. Every teacher should lay aside from every pay a goodly sum of his earnings for his declining years so that he will not become a burden on society.

8. Any teacher who smokes, uses liquor in any form, frequents pool or public halls, or gets shaved in a barber shop will give good reasons to suspect his worth, intentions, integrity and honesty.

9. The teacher who performs his labors faithfully without fault for five years will be given an increase of $25^\cent$ a week in his pay—providing the Board of Education approves.

FIGURE 1.1 1872 Instruction to the Teacher. *Source*: Board of Education, Harrison, South Dakota, and Leo W. Anglin, Richard Goldman, and Joyce Shanahan Anglin, *Teaching: What It's All About* (New York: Harper and Row, 1982), p. 11. Reprinted by permission of Board of Education, Harrison, South Dakota.

particularly common. Even today, however, some individuals behave like inspectors, although their job specifications do not call for such behavior.

Our system of education does not begin to approach foreign systems in degree of centralization, but during the 1970s and 1980s we saw pronounced centralization at the state and school district levels. Some states either recommended or mandated minimal competencies or standards that students were (and to an increased degree still are) expected to achieve in certain subjects at each grade level. Some school districts, engaging in a process called curriculum alignment, specified detailed objectives that students were expected to master during each marking period in each subject. Learning activities and test items based on the objectives were designed for each marking period. In states that conducted student-assessment programs, local curriculum guides were keyed into the objectives assessed on the states' examinations. In the early 1990s, the movement toward centralization slackened somewhat, resulting in a degree of decentralization and empowerment of teachers and laypeople.[6] At the beginning of the twenty-first century, however, we see a strong revival of centralization efforts, especially in the form of state and national standards and assessment programs.

As the population grew and schools increased in number, the superintendent could no longer supervise individual schools closely. In the late nineteenth century, principals and central office supervisors shared a major part of the burden of everyday supervision.

With the advent of the Industrial Revolution and the influence of people like Frederick W. Taylor and Max Weber in the late nineteenth and early twentieth centuries, scientific and bureaucratic approaches to supervision replaced inspection. Scientific management and efficiency were buzzwords of the new approach. The assumption of these strategies was that if organizations followed established principles for efficiency, production would presumably be high. Supervisors had only to ensure the rigorous application of the principles.

While Taylor was expounding on scientific management, Weber was promoting the concept of bureaucratic management of organizations as the ideal model for achieving efficiency and productivity. The model provided for a hierarchy of authority and responsibility—from the chief executive officer at the top of the pinnacle to the lowliest worker at the bottom. The bureaucratic model became the pervasive organizational structure in all human institutions—business, industry, government, social organizations, church, and schools. In fact, the bureaucratic model has become so entrenched in our lives that *bureaucracy* has become, under some circumstances, a derogatory term.

Thus, in the early part of the twentieth century, the bureaucratic model of organization became firmly rooted in our school systems with the superintendent at the top and the teacher at the bottom. In between came a whole echelon of generalist and specialist personnel. Although philosophies, attitudes, and operating procedures have changed since the early twentieth century, the bureaucratic model remains the dominant form of school organization despite predictions of an "emerging, pluralistic, collegial" concept of administrative organization[7] and despite sporadic efforts by some organizations to apply principles of shared management as advocated by W. Edwards Deming.[8]

Describing the attitude of scientific managers during the early 1900s, William H. Lucio and John D. McNeil said that "teachers were regarded as instruments that should be closely supervised to insure that they mechanically carried out the methods of procedure determined by administrative and special supervisors."[9] "Scientific" supervisors look for fixed principles of teaching, drawn from research, that can be prescribed for teachers. The teachers' performances can then be judged on how well they follow the instructional principles in their teaching. To supervisors of this persuasion, teaching is a science rather than an art, and they believe that by following a prescribed set of rules, teachers are bound to be successful. Does this sound familiar to you in the new millennium?

Following research on instruction carried out through the 1960s and 1970s, many educators still perceive teaching as a science whose component skills—generic competencies—can be identified, learned, and mastered.

Under the influence of people like Elton Mayo, Mary Parker Follett, Kurt Lewin, Ronald Lippitt, Ralph K. White, Kenneth D. Benne, Paul Sheats, and Warren G. Bennis in the mid-twentieth century, supervision turned in the direction of human relations and group dynamics. Stress on the democratic process and the application of the behavioral sciences commanded the attention of supervisors. No longer did supervision constitute handing down methods to teachers and then monitoring their performances. Collaboration and partnership between supervisors and teachers became important. Supervisors began to realize that their success was dependent more on interpersonal skills than on technical skills and knowledge; they had to become sensitive to the behavior of groups and individuals within groups. They became more aware that they must respond to needs as determined by the people they served—the teachers—as opposed to satisfying their own needs based on their supposedly superior judgments. The prefix *super-* of supervision declined in importance. The word *supervision* itself became modified by such words as *collaborative*, *cooperative*, *democratic*, and *consultative*. This change of focus has continued and intensified into the present.

What we are seeing today is an amalgamation of practices and attitudes. True, we can find holdovers of the inspection mentality and we can still encounter the boss–employee mind-set, but we are experiencing more cases of cooperation and collaboration between supervisors and teachers than in the past. We find a definite acceptance of the idea that instructional supervisors are employed to help teachers build on their strengths, improve, and remain in the profession instead of probing teachers' deficiencies and seeking their dismissal.

We are finding principles of scientific supervision within a clinical yet supportive context. Even within a scientific framework, supervisors place heavy reliance on human relations. We also note that teachers themselves are acting as instructional supervisors to their peers. We are also experiencing newer focuses of supervision—human resources, artistic, interpretive, and ecological approaches. We will return to these later in the text.

Before exploring the newer directions in instructional supervision, it is helpful to note that of the three older approaches mentioned, today's supervisors would reject the first two and minimize the third.

- **The Authoritarian-Inspectorial Approach.** Professional supervisors realize that teachers, as professionals, can be persuaded but not coerced; many times, they have better answers to their own problems than do the supervisors.

- **Laissez-faire.** To some, supervision is a laissez-faire task. Supervisors who are thus inclined agree with many teachers that in the case of supervision, less is better. Nondirective in their approach, they may visit the teachers' classrooms or stop by the teachers' lounge for a cup of coffee. They tend to consider a classroom visit and an appearance in the teachers' lounge as equally important; some might rate the chat in the lounge as more important. They see their task as giving the teacher a benevolent pat on the back now and then.

- **Group Dynamics.** To others, supervision is a never-ending exercise in group process. They see improvement of instruction as a continuing exercise in human relations. Viewing themselves as resource persons to the group, they spend considerable time fostering a positive group climate, using social affairs to establish a happy, cooperative frame of mind among teachers. They hope that after a period of deliberation, groups will reach consensus on points under discussion.

Neither an authoritarian nor a laissez-faire approach is adequate or suitable for today's schools, nor is an exclusively group-process approach. Supervisors may favor group processes, but they will be called on to work with both groups and individuals. They must be mindful that many of the innovations in schools are products of experimentation by one or two individuals rather than groups.

VARYING INTERPRETATIONS

This discussion, however, still leaves us unsure of what supervision is or should be. To create a sharp, clear-cut definition of supervision is extremely difficult, as acknowledged by Ralph L. Mosher and David E. Purpel:

> The difficulty of defining supervision in relation to education also stems, in large part, from unsolved theoretical problems about teaching. Quite simply, we lack sufficient understanding of the process of teaching. Our theories of learning are inadequate, the criteria for measuring teaching effectiveness are imprecise, and deep disagreement exists about what knowledge—that is, what curriculum—is most valuable to teach. ... When we have achieved more understanding of what and how to teach, and with what special effects on students, we will be much less vague about the supervision of these processes.[10]

Looking at the way specialists in supervision have defined the term may help us in our quest for a viable definition. Let's sample some past and present definitions. William H. Burton and Leo J. Brueckner gave supervision a broad interpretation, viewing it as a technical service requiring expertise, the goal of which is improvement in the growth and development of the learner.[11]

Stressing the helping nature of supervision, Jane Franseth early on stated, "Today supervision is generally seen as leadership that encourages a continuous involvement of all school personnel in a cooperative attempt to achieve the most effective school program."[12] Ross L. Neagley and N. Dean Evans pointed to the democratic nature of modern supervision in their definition:

> Modern supervision is considered as any service for teachers that eventually results in improving instruction, learning, and the curriculum. It consists of positive, dynamic, democratic actions designed to improve instruction through the continued growth of all concerned individuals—the child, the teacher, the supervisor, the administrator, and the parent or other lay person.[13]

Contemporary definitions of supervision stress *service*, *cooperation*, and *democracy*. In this book, you will find the emphasis placed on *instructional* supervision. Harris wrote: "Supervision of instruction is what school personnel do with adults and things to maintain or change the school operation in ways that directly influence the teaching process employed to promote pupil learning."[14] Robert J. Alfonso, Gerald R. Firth, and Richard F. Neville offered a slightly different definition: "Instructional supervision is herein defined as: Behavior officially designated by the organization that directly affects teacher behavior in such a way as to facilitate pupil learning and achieve the goals of the organization."[15]

John T. Lovell, in revising the earlier work of Kimball Wiles, looked at instructional supervisory behavior as behavior that "is assumed to be an additional behavior system formally provided by the organization for the purpose of interacting with the teaching behavior system in such a way as to maintain, change, and improve the design and actualization of learning opportunities for students."[16] Don M. Beach and Judy Reinhartz, rejecting the use of the word *help* in defining supervision, see "supervision as a complex process that involves working with teachers and other educators in a collegial, collaborative relationship to enhance the quality of teaching and learning within schools and that promotes the career-long development of teachers."[17]

Note how many definitions focus on (1) the behavior of supervisors (2) in assisting teachers (3) for the ultimate benefit of the student. Robert D. Krey and Peter J. Burke offered a comprehensive definition of supervision:

> Supervision is instructional leadership that relates perspectives to behavior, clarifies purposes, contributes to and supports organizational actions, coordinates interactions, provides for maintenance and improvement of the instructional program, and assesses goal achievements.[18]

Thomas J. Sergiovanni and Robert J. Starratt advised understanding supervision today as both a role performed by formally designated supervisors and a function carried out by designated supervisors and others, including teachers.[19]

John C. Daresh and Marsha A. Playko offered a concise definition, viewing supervision as "the process of overseeing the ability of people to meet the goals of the organization in which they work."[20]

Jon Wiles and Joseph Bondi viewed supervision as "a general leadership role and a coordinating role among all school activities concerned with learning."[21]

Emphasizing process and function of supervision rather than title or position for the purpose of improving student learning, Carl D. Glickman, Stephen P. Gordon, and Jovita M. Ross-Gordon pictured those in supervisory roles as involved in assistance to teachers, curriculum development, professional development, group development, and action research.[22]

You will note recurring themes, some similarities, and some differences in emphasis or perspective among the many definitions of supervision.

Supervision, as presented in this text, is conceived as a service to teachers, both as individuals and in groups. To put it simply, supervision is a means of offering to teachers, in a collegial, collaborative, and professional setting, specialized help in improving instruction and thereby student achievement. The words *service* and *help* should be underscored, and they are used repeatedly in this text.

PROBLEMS THAT COMPLICATE THE SUPERVISORY ROLE

Definitions by themselves do not reveal the complexities of the supervisory role. Supervision today is complicated by a number of factors, including diversity of conceptions of supervision and good teaching, mandates from the state and national levels, and tensions between teachers and administrators/supervisors.

Continuing Diversity of Conceptions of Supervision

Realizing that the term *supervision* by itself is subject to many different interpretations, some specialists in the field have found it expedient to add modifiers. Thus, in the literature we encounter *administrative, clinical, consultative, collaborative, developmental, differentiated, educational, general, instructional,* and *peer.* Each of these adjectives offers a special interpretation of the term *supervision.*

Administrative supervision covers the territory of managerial responsibilities outside the fields of curriculum and instruction. *General supervision* is perceived by some as synonymous with *educational supervision* and by others as that type of supervision that takes place outside the classroom. *Differentiated supervision* allows teachers to choose the types of developmental activities in which they will engage.

Whereas *educational supervision* suggests responsibilities encompassing many aspects of schooling, including administration, curriculum, and instruction, *instructional supervision* narrows the focus to a more limited set of responsibilities, namely, supervision for the improvement of instruction. *Clinical, consultative, collaborative, developmental,* and *peer supervision* are subsumed under *instructional supervision.*

Whether the supervisor perceives teaching as a science or as an art further colors the supervisor's role. The supervisor who follows a scientific approach believes that generic teaching skills can be identified and that all teachers at all levels should be able to demonstrate them. Such a supervisor believes that those skills can be described, observed, and analyzed. The supervisor who follows an artistic approach believes that teaching is a highly individualized activity that bears the stamp of the teacher's unique personality. This type of supervisor believes that the entire setting for instruction, the persons involved in the teaching act, and the general atmosphere of the classroom must be considered.

Some specialists would maintain that supervisors should devote all or most of their emphasis to a single approach or type of supervision. Others, including ourselves, see room for a more eclectic approach. We return to varying conceptions of supervision in later chapters of the book.

Differing Conceptions of Effective Teaching

Some specialists ascribe difficulty in defining *supervision,* as did Mosher and Purpel, to a lack of understanding of the teaching process, impreciseness of the criteria for assessing teacher performance, and lack of agreement on what should be taught.[23] Those who follow an interpretive or hermeneutic approach to supervision look at the unique characteristics of a particular learning situation and, with the teacher, seek to interpret the events that have taken place during a lesson. Some supervisors look at *process,* that is, the demonstration of teaching skills. Some focus on *product,* such as test scores of students. Others include the teacher's personal and professional attributes in their description of effective teaching. Certain supervisors are partial to particular models and styles of teaching. Some smile, for example, on discovery learning and frown on lecturing. Some favor direct instruction of entire groups, others champion cooperative learning, and still others advocate individualized instructional techniques.

These differing conceptions of what constitutes effective teaching make the supervisory process difficult for both the teacher and the supervisor. Many research studies on effective teaching have been conducted in recent years. These studies furnish partial answers to some of the pedagogical questions. They do not, however, provide answers to differing philosophical premises held by supervisors. We will discuss some of that research in Chapter 4.

Mandates from the State and National Levels

Over the past three decades, many state legislatures have passed laws calling for sweeping reforms in public education. They have raised teacher salaries, mandated state testing of teachers, instituted on-the-job assessment, established student-assessment programs, prescribed aspects of the curriculum, and ordered annual evaluations of all school personnel. State departments of education have implemented and administered the many reforms mandated by their legislatures and state boards of education.

Although room has remained for some local decision making, increased direction from the state and federal levels has certainly reduced the flexibility of local school systems to make decisions based on their assessment of local needs and on their own philosophies of education. Local school systems have had to give priority to state mandates and federal requirements. After meeting state requirements, they may and often do go beyond the mandated directives.

The supervisor's role is heavily affected by state mandates: by state tests for both teachers and students, by state model instruments for evaluating teachers, by state-developed curriculum guides, by state specification of teaching competencies, and by federal legislation, especially the No Child Left Behind Act of 2001. Supervisors who are in disagreement with state and national reforms are faced with intrarole conflicts. State assessments of student achievement, for example, are almost exclusively cognitive in nature, especially reading and mathematics. The supervisor who has a commitment to affective and psychomotor as well as cognitive learning will feel uncomfortable with testing restricted to only the cognitive domain. Nevertheless, the supervisor owes it to the teachers to help them produce high student test scores. State and federal mandates have established priorities for local school personnel, including supervisors. For a brief period, state mandating peaked, and the responsibility for administration, supervision, curriculum, and instruction shifted more to the local schools. Movements toward decentralization, including site-based or school-based management, teacher empowerment, and parental participation in decision making, placed more responsibility and authority on the individual schools and less on the district and state levels. However, as the first decade of the twenty-first century unfolds, we are seeing renewed stress (in both its meanings of "emphasis" and "tension") on setting standards and testing coming from the district and state levels, and, as is the case of the No Child Left Behind Act, the national level.

Tensions between Teachers and Administrators/ Supervisors

The public and, to an increasing degree, the profession have expressed dissatisfaction with student achievement and with incompetent teaching. Increased emphasis on student achievement, accountability of teachers, and teacher competence have brought about increased pressure for evaluation of teacher performance. Consequently, evaluation of teaching has loomed large in recent years.

Teachers, especially through their organizations, have not wholeheartedly embraced current processes of evaluation. They have raised valid questions concerning the competencies on which they will be judged, who will do the evaluating, how the evaluation will be conducted, and what use will be made of the results.

Teachers question the reliability of the data collected on their performances and the competence of the administrators or supervisors in making assessments. Furthermore, they want to be involved in the creation of the evaluation process.

The inability to separate supervisory service from evaluation, an issue addressed in Chapter 2, adds to the tensions. Teachers, as a rule, welcome real supervisory help. Yet many of them view supervisors with contempt, feeling, sometimes rightly and sometimes wrongly, that teachers are more capable than supervisors or that supervisors have nothing of value to offer them. Many teachers simply ignore supervisors, choose not to ask for their help, and avoid opportunities to work with them.

Many years ago, Arthur Blumberg pictured the tensions between supervisors and teachers as a "private cold war."[24] To some extent progress in empowerment of teachers, human relations skills, and principles of collegiality and collaboration have reduced conflicts between supervisors and teachers but have not completely eliminated them.

Negative, fearful, or hostile attitudes are symptoms of the malaise brought on by uncertainties about the role, function, and effectiveness of the supervisory profession. Great needs exist to clarify the duties and responsibilities of supervisors, to discover the most effective techniques and skills, and to identify who the supervisors are.

WHO ARE THE SUPERVISORS?

In the traditional meaning of supervision, anyone who oversees the work of another is a supervisor. Hence, every administrator is ipso facto a supervisor. If we limit the concept of supervision to management of resources and personnel, we are on firm ground in labeling the administrator a supervisor. But if we delimit supervision to the means of improving the curriculum and instruction, we may not conclude that every administrator is an instructional supervisor.

Logically, it would seem that any school official who assists teachers in improving curriculum and instruction is a supervisor. In practice, however, some individuals in the school system are charged with the management of resources and personnel as their primary task, whereas others are assigned the improvement of curriculum and instruction as their major function.

Many arguments are waged over whether the building principal, for example, is a supervisor. Although principals have responsibility for the curriculum and instruction of the school, supervision of those aspects is only one of their many tasks. Unfortunately, instructional supervision is often a secondary task for many school principals, who commonly lament that they do not have time to devote to curriculum and instructional leadership because they are too busy with the day-to-day operation of the school.

We hasten to add that in those small schools throughout the country that employ several teachers and a principal with no assistant, the principals do, by necessity if not by desire, perform the function of instructional supervisor. We might more accurately refer to those principals by a title used in earlier days, *supervising principals*, to distinguish them from *instructional supervisors*. We are witnessing, however, a desire for change, if not change itself, in the role of the building principal—from manager to instructional supervisor. The profession has begun to recognize the individual school as the locus of change, placing responsibility for instructional leadership squarely on the principal. Although some principals will continue to devote less time to instructional supervision than to other duties and may, if possible, delegate much of the task to others, more principals are accepting responsibility for the role of instructional supervisor. Developments, such as state-mandated curricula, evaluation systems, merit pay, and career ladder programs, further push the principal into fulfilling instructional supervisory responsibilities.

"By their fruits ye shall know them" is more pertinent in the world of supervision than "by their titles ye shall know them." Controversy swirls around the issue, which we examine in Chapter 2, concerning whether supervisors should assume administrative responsibilities. We should note at this point that the issue is not ordinarily reversed—that is, there is seldom discussion of whether administrators should assume supervisory responsibilities. For both legal and practical reasons, administrators already have these responsibilities.

As we try to identify supervisors, it might be helpful to depict the degree to which administrators and supervisors take on the role of guiding instructional improvement. Figure 1.2 illustrates how we can chart varying degrees of supervisory responsibility.

A full-time administrator (e.g., superintendent of schools; many principals, especially of large schools) is deep into budgeting, transportation, staffing, pupil personnel services, and public relations. He or she devotes little or no time to curricular and instructional supervision but delegates that duty to others. Some administrators, however, though preoccupied with managerial problems, expend some time and energy on instructional supervisory activities. They may visit—and in many cases they are required by law to visit—teachers in their classrooms, observe their teaching, make judgments, and offer advice. When they behave in this fashion, administrators become supervisors, if only for a portion of their time.

Some school personnel whose job description classifies them as supervisors are charged with or assume on their own initiative administrative duties such as annual assessments of teacher performance. When they accept managerial tasks, they join the ranks of the administrators. Finally, those personnel who spend all of their time and efforts in helping teachers directly with the improvement of instruction may be called full-time instructional supervisors. Thus, with a nod to Izaak Walton, we have the Compleat Administrator on one side of the spectrum and the Compleat Supervisor on the other.

Types of Supervisors

The American system of education is a confusing diversity of systems that confounds people from abroad who attempt to study it. In fact, at times our system even perplexes Americans. This confusion extends to the provision of special services such as supervision.

In this book, we talk about a person whom we call the supervisor. Unless otherwise specified, we are talking about the *instructional supervisor*. In agreement with many specialists, we include curriculum supervision within the context of instructional supervision.

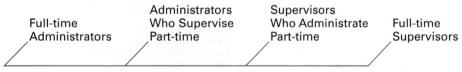

FIGURE 1.2 Continuum of Supervisory Responsibility.

Because of the great diversity in roles and duties of supervisors, we urge the reader to keep in mind the distinction between the *supervisor*, with *supervisor* emphasized, and *the* supervisor, with *the* emphasized. In discussing the supervisor, we make the assumption that principles and practices of supervision may apply *generally, to most but not all situations and not to all persons* who wear the hat of supervisor. This book concentrates on the *supervisor.* Were we to talk about *the* supervisor, we would be conveying the erroneous notion that there is a single, accepted role that supervisors can, do, or should play. The effort to identify a single role applicable under all circumstances is akin to searching for that elusive will-o'-the-wisp, the best model of teaching. A more detailed discussion about the roles that the school administrator plays—as a supervisor and as an administrator—appears in Chapter 2.

Supervisors are special service personnel to be found on the staffs of administrators at the state, district, and school levels. In administrative parlance these service personnel are *staff* employees, whereas the administrators, equipped with the mantles of status and authority, are *line* employees. Staff employees are hired by and responsible to the line employees. Line employees below the top position (e.g., superintendent) are hired by and responsible to other line employees higher up in the chain of command.

Supervisors are often referred to as auxiliary personnel or staff. Although the titles and responsibilities of these auxiliary personnel differ from state to state and from school district to school district, we can identify the major types of supervisors. Figure 1.3 shows some of

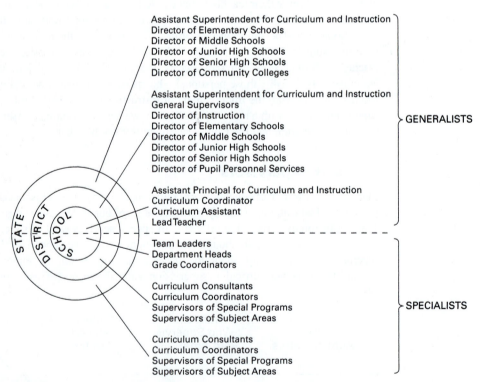

FIGURE 1.3 Types of Supervisors.

the varieties of supervisors on different levels. Included among the types of supervisors are administrators who spend a portion of their time in supervising instruction as well as full-time supervisors. Figure 1.3 also distinguishes generalist supervisors, whose duties cut across disciplines and grade levels, from specialist supervisors, whose responsibilities fall within a subject or grade level.

State Supervisors   The chief supervisor on the state level is the assistant super-intendent for curriculum and instruction. Although this position may bear other titles, this person's responsibility is to supervise the entire curricular and instructional program of the public schools in the state, with the help of staff members. The assistant superintendent interprets state department of education and state legislative mandates concerning educa-tion and is directly responsible to the state superintendent of public instruction. The assistant superintendent's office frequently directs teachers in the preparation of certain curricular materials and often supervises textbook adoptions. That office also provides consultant service to the schools, sponsors conferences on curriculum and instruction, and acts as liaison with the federal government in the preparation of proposals for grants for federal projects. This office encourages experimentation in curriculum design and instructional techniques.

The assistant superintendent for curriculum and instruction is aided by a staff of specialists who may be designated supervisors, directors, consultants, or coordinators. Frequently, these include specialists in curriculum and instruction, such as directors or supervisors of elementary, middle, and secondary education. These staff members aid in fulfilling the assistant superintendent's tasks. They generally confine themselves, however, to providing leadership at their own levels.

Well-developed state departments of education provide a variety of specialists in particular areas or disciplines, such as exceptionalities, reading, mathematics, science, and social studies. These supervisors operate throughout the state in their own areas of specialization, assisting teachers, suggesting materials, giving advice, and demonstrating effective methods of teaching their specialties. They are generally responsible to the director of elementary education or director of middle schools, junior high schools, or senior high schools, depending on their level of responsibility. We sometimes find, for example, a supervisor of elementary language arts and a supervisor of secondary language arts on the assistant superintendent's staff.

Local Supervisors   The presence and effectiveness of the supervisor are felt more keenly on the local than on the state level. The state supervisors' areas are so large and their responsibilities are so numerous that they cannot possibly make the rounds of all the schools and teachers demanding services. Consequently, local supervisors become key people in the school system.

District Level   On the school district level, supervisors are on the staff of the local school superintendent. They are referred to in the literature and in practice as central-office personnel, a designation that distinguishes them from school-based personnel employed to serve in particular schools.

On the central-office staff, customarily an assistant superintendent for curriculum and instruction or sometimes a director of instruction provides curricular and instructional leadership throughout the local district. This key local official aids teachers in developing materials, encourages experimentation and research, provides schools with up-to-date materials and consultants, leads the district in the continuous task of curriculum development, and meets with teachers and administrators on problems of curriculum and instruction.

Helping the assistant superintendent are personnel of various types. Often these include one or more general supervisors, responsible for supervision from kindergarten through twelfth grade. They are frequently in the schools assisting individual teachers and groups of teachers in a variety of fields. These persons are familiar with learning theory, adolescent psychology, methods of handling groups and individuals, and new ways to organize for instruction. Some of the smaller school districts limit their central-office personnel to positions of this type.

Larger school systems employ supervisors or directors of elementary, middle, and secondary education. Whereas the general supervisor must be spread thin over the entire school system, these three specialists may concentrate on their individual levels.

Large school districts often provide a variety of supervisors or consultants in special fields, such as reading, guidance, foreign languages, and vocational education. Some of the special-area supervisors divide their time between the elementary, middle, and secondary levels as, for example, in art, music, and physical education; others confine their work to one level. These specialists are in a strategic position for effecting change in individual classrooms. They have expertise in a particular field and may devote their full time and energies to the development of curriculum and instruction in their specialties. They can be knowledgeable about the latest content, materials, and methods in their fields.

School Level   Within the individual schools of a district are people who could be labeled supervisors. Often a school will employ an assistant principal whose main duty is the supervision of curriculum and instruction. This person devotes full energies to developing the curriculum of his or her own school and helping teachers improve instruction.

Curriculum coordinators or lead teachers are sometimes found in the individual schools either as assistants to or replacements for the assistant principal for curriculum and instruction. Their task is to assist teachers with curricular and instructional problems and to give leadership to the development of the curriculum and the improvement of instruction.

Team leaders, grade coordinators, and department heads in the individual schools can, should, and sometimes do serve as supervisors. With the team-staffing patterns followed by many schools, the person who heads an instructional team plays a significant role as supervisor for that team. The department head in middle, junior high, and senior high schools fulfills for a department a supervisory function similar to that fulfilled by the team leader. Because elementary schools are ordinarily not departmentalized, the grade coordinators for all sections of a grade level and the team leaders for each section of a grade level serve as quasidepartment heads who carry supervisory responsibilities. In middle, junior high, and senior high schools, we may find both team leaders and department heads, with team leaders within departments responsible to the department heads.

School-based supervisors should lead in curriculum development, assist teachers in the production of instructional and curricular materials, arrange for staff development, and help teachers improve their teaching methods. Principals have the obligation of freeing their coordinators and leaders so that they will not become bogged down, as so often happens, with either administrative details of running their grades, teams, or departments or with full-time teaching schedules. These activities can prohibit them from giving adequate time to instructional and curricular leadership. Newer practices in supervision enlist the services of peers, coaches, and mentors in the process to help avoid this overload.

Unlike state supervisors, whose interaction with district-based and school-based supervisors is infrequent, central-office supervisors work frequently and collaboratively with school-based supervisors and teachers to assist in achieving district goals.

You may question whether those personnel shown in Figure 1.3 who hold line or administrative positions are truly supervisors—for example, the assistant superintendents and directors on both state and district levels who often work only minimally with teachers. The assistant superintendent for curriculum and instruction and frequently the directors on the local district level occupy line rather than staff positions. Depending on the school district, line personnel may or may not work directly with teachers. In Figure 1.3, however, these line officials are classified as supervisors because they devote at least part of their time to supervisory duties. Whereas some specialists in supervision restrict their concept of a supervisor to those staff persons who work full time directly with teachers, others include within their concept line officers who have responsibilities for curriculum and instruction. Because many line administrators do engage in supervision, they should be trained in supervision, as are those who pursue full-time careers in supervision. It is an unfortunate commentary on the licensing process in many states that the requirements for preparation of administrators and supervisors, which are often minimal, are identical. By taking a handful of college courses in educational administration and supervision, a person can become certified in both administration and supervision.

However delightful such an arrangement is for prospective administrators and supervisors, as one preparation program opens up two job markets, differentiation in training programs for administrators and supervisors remains a serious need of the profession. The training requirements of these two related careers are not identical.

TASKS OF SUPERVISION

We can gain a clearer insight into the field of supervision by focusing our attention on what supervisors actually do. As long ago as 1922, William H. Burton listed the tasks he saw as relevant to the supervisor. These tasks, which some might label *arenas*, are shown here:

1. The improvement of the teaching act.
2. The improvement of teachers in service.
3. The selection and organization of subject matter.
4. Testing and measuring.
5. The rating of teachers.[25]

Burton's listing has been viewed as "the first modern statement and concept" of supervision.[26] This list looks surprisingly current when we examine the numerous tasks that today's supervisors actually perform.

Writing a half century later, Harris enumerated ten tasks of supervision in the following rather detailed list:

Task 1. Developing curriculum.

Task 2. Organizing for instruction.

Task 3. Providing staff.

Task 4. Providing facilities.

Task 5. Providing materials.

Task 6. Arranging for in-service education.

Task 7. Orienting staff members.

Task 8. Relating special pupil services.

Task 9. Developing public relations.

Task 10. Evaluating instruction.[27]

Harris classified tasks 1, 3, and 4 as preliminary; 6 and 10 as developmental; and the others as operational.[28] You will note both similarities and differences in the Burton and Harris listings. We can find supervision specialists who would be willing to accept either compilation of supervisory tasks. On the other hand, we can find experts in the field who would reject both lists. Those who view supervision as a one-to-one, clinical relationship between the teacher and supervisor would eliminate many of the tasks from both lists. Those who view supervision as a field distinct from administration would delegate administrative tasks such as scheduling, staffing, and public relations to the administrator rather than to the instructional supervisor.

Holding that "traditional supervisory practices of helping and evaluating individual workers" are "no longer useful except with respect to contract decisions," Karolyn J. Snyder viewed the supervisor's task in the following light:

> The primary supervisory task is to develop professional learning communities, in work teams, that not only acquire new knowledge and skills but also learn how to study and respond exceptionally well to their natural work and learning environments.[29]

Snyder perceived "the new work of the supervisor" as "building the energy mass, school by school and team by team."[30]

What is more revealing about the roles and functions of supervisors are the statements of expectations as shown in the job descriptions of various school personnel. Were we to compare job descriptions across school systems, we would inevitably discover differences in the duties assigned to personnel with the same titles. What is universally true throughout school systems, however, is that much is expected of all supervisors.

A MODEL OF SUPERVISION

The supervisor plays a variety of roles within certain domains, and the expertise demonstrated in the particular domains is derived from a number of bases or foundations. One way to explain the dimensions of supervisory behavior is in the form of a conceptual model. Figure 1.4 depicts the concept of supervision followed in this text.

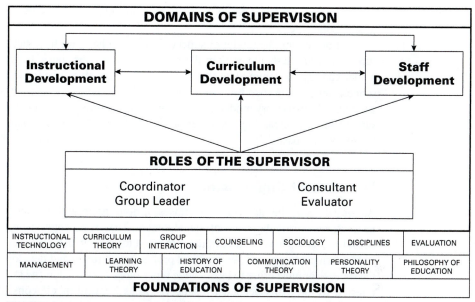

FIGURE 1.4 A Conceptual Model of Supervision.

The model shows three large domains or territories within which supervisors work (*instructional development*, *curriculum development*, and *staff development*) and the four primary roles of the supervisor within those domains (coordinator, consultant, group leader, and evaluator). The domains and roles rest on a foundation—the supervisor's knowledge and skills.

The model conveys the notion that supervision is both service-oriented and dynamic. The supervisor serves teachers dynamically by playing all or any of the roles within all or any of the domains. The two-headed arrows connecting the three domains show that all are interrelated. For example, a supervisor who works as a group leader in curriculum development (say, in mathematics) may at the same time work in the domain of instructional development (e.g., by helping teachers try out new techniques of presenting geometric concepts) and/or the domain of staff development (e.g., by conducting seminars on new techniques).

A conceptual model can clearly reveal the concepts held by the person who designs it. Thus one could take this same basic design but follow a different set of assumptions. Some people, for example, might take issue with the three domains, cut them into one or two, or expand them beyond three. They might eliminate supervisory duties in curriculum development, leaving only instructional development and staff development. They might restrict supervision to instructional development and limit it to clinical supervision. They might remove instructional development as well as curriculum development, allowing only staff development to remain (e.g., if they feel that staff development means assistance to teachers in improving both personal and professional qualities, then instructional development becomes a by-product or part of staff development). In restricting the domain of supervision to staff development alone, these people might perceive the roles of the supervisor as dual: consultant to individual teachers and consultant to groups of teachers. Some might go even further and restrict the supervisor to one role: consultant to individual teachers, or simply trusted colleague.

In presenting the model of supervision shown here, we have taken the position that supervisors do and should work in all three domains and carry out at least the four roles. This model can also accommodate the required administrative functions of supervisory personnel, through the four roles already charted. In contrast, whereas this text presents a generalized supervisory model, Bernadette Marczely offered a differentiated conception of supervision encompassing a number of models from which supervisors may choose on a "case-by-case basis."[31]

Domains of Supervision

As we've seen, the supervisor exercises various roles within each of three domains: instructional, curricular, and staff development. That is, the supervisor acts as coordinator, consultant, group leader, and evaluator to assist teachers in the improvement of instruction, curriculum planning, and personal and professional growth and development. In doing so, the supervisor must bring to bear a wide repertoire of knowledge and skills. Floyd C. Mann referred to the skills needed by supervisors as a "skill-mix," consisting of technical, managerial, and human relations skills.[32]

Edward Pajak headed a study on identification of supervisory proficiencies sponsored by the Association for Supervision and Curriculum Development. By reviewing the literature on supervision and surveying instructional leaders, Pajak affirmed twelve domains, with relevant knowledge, attitudes, and skills in each domain.[33] These domains and their definitions are as follows:

- Community Relations—Establishing and maintaining open and productive relations between the school and its community.
- Staff Development—Developing and facilitating meaningful opportunities for professional growth.
- Planning and Change—Initiating and implementing collaboratively developed strategies for continuous improvement.
- Communication—Ensuring open and clear communication among individuals and groups through the organization.
- Curriculum—Coordinating and integrating the process of curriculum development and implementation.
- Instructional Program—Supporting and coordinating efforts to improve the instructional program.
- Service to Teachers—Providing materials, resources, and assistance to support teaching and learning.
- Observation and Conferencing—Providing feedback to teachers based on classroom observation.
- Problem Solving and Decision Making—Using a variety of strategies to clarify and analyze problems and to make decisions.

- Research and Program Evaluation—Encouraging experimentation and assessing outcomes.
- Motivating and Organizing—Helping people to develop a shared vision and achieve collective aims.
- Personal Development—Recognizing and reflecting on one's personal and professional beliefs, abilities, and action.[34]

Eleven of these twelve domains—essentially ways of working with individuals and groups within the schools—are discussed in this volume. The external aspects of the supervisor's job—that is, community relations, which is an important domain not only for supervisors but also for administrators, teachers, and other school personnel—find less treatment here. For help in the domain of community relations, the reader should consult some of the literature on public relations, building community support, and power structure.[35] Building positive community relations is extremely important for every school person. However, the designated administrator should assume the primary task of leadership in community relations and allow the instructional supervisor to concentrate on the task for which he or she is uniquely equipped: service to teachers.

Varying Roles

The roles supervisors play vary from locality to locality and from state to state. They are defined by the superintendents or principals to whom the supervisors are responsible and, as happens in most positions of leadership, by the supervisors themselves. Although some variation will be found in the roles supervisors may fulfill, more than likely the service-oriented supervisor will perform at varying times each of the four roles shown in the model.[36]

Coordinator The supervisor serves as a coordinator of programs, groups, materials, and reports. It is the supervisor who acts as a link between programs and people. He or she knows the disparate pieces of the educational process and directs the actions of others to make the pieces blend. As a director of staff development, the supervisor plans, arranges, evaluates, and often conducts in-service programs with and for teachers.

Consultant The supervisor serves in a consulting capacity as a specialist in curriculum, instructional methodology, and staff development. In this capacity, he or she renders service to both individual teachers and groups. At times, the supervisor may simply furnish necessary information and suggestions. At other times, he or she may help teachers define, set, and pursue goals. The supervisor should be a prime source of assistance to teachers wishing to improve either their generic or specialized teaching skills. Although some will disagree with us, we believe the supervisor–consultant should be able to demonstrate a repertoire of teaching strategies.

Group Leader The supervisor as group leader works continuously to release the potential of groups seeking to improve the curriculum, instruction, or themselves. To perform this role the supervisor must be knowledgeable about group dynamics and must demonstrate leadership skills. The supervisor assists groups in consensus building, in moving toward group goals, and in perfecting the democratic process. As a group leader, the supervisor seeks, identifies, and fosters leadership from within the group.

Evaluator As an evaluator, the supervisor provides assistance to teachers in evaluating instruction and curriculum. The supervisor helps teachers find answers to curricular and instructional problems, identify research studies that may have a bearing on their problems, and conduct limited research projects. In addition, the supervisor helps teachers evaluate their classroom performance, assess their own strengths and weaknesses, and select means of overcoming their deficiencies.

Foundations of Supervision

The foundations of supervision (see Figure 1.4) are areas of learning from which the supervisor derives expertise. The large number of areas from which a knowledgeable and skilled supervisor must draw suggests the need for a broad training program in preparation for work as a supervisor.

When we study the conceptual model of supervision, with its domains, roles, and foundations, we can deduce competencies that supervisors should be able to demonstrate. Supervisors should possess (1) certain personal traits and (2) certain types of knowledge and skills.

Personal Traits The literature on supervision is remarkably silent on what personal characteristics are necessary for successful supervisory behavior. Perhaps this silence can be attributed to one or more of the following reasons.

1. Personal characteristics can be inferred from the skills supervisors should possess. Thus, if supervisors are expected to demonstrate a high degree of skill in human or interpersonal relations, they should exhibit human and humane traits like empathy, warmth, and sincerity.

2. Educational research has been notably unsuccessful in identifying personal qualities common to all successful administrators and supervisors. The presence of generally valued personal traits in a leader does not guarantee success on the job, nor does the absence of these traits ensure failure. Because the search for universal traits has been unproductive, the experts have concentrated on the more certain requisite knowledge and skills.

3. Personal traits necessary for success in positions of leadership appear so obvious that they need no elaboration. Some specialists in the field may feel that a compendium of supervisory traits is similar to the oath that Boy Scouts take, promising to be trustworthy, loyal, helpful, friendly, and so on.

4. The search for personal traits is a somewhat dated activity at a time when researchers are attempting to identify competencies that school personnel should demonstrate.

Despite these encumbrances, let's briefly consider the question of personal characteristics needed by supervisory personnel. The successful supervisor is in constant contact with people and should possess those personal traits of warmth, friendliness, patience, and a sense of humor that are essential not only to supervision but also to teaching. As a service-oriented agent for improvement, the supervisor must be imbued with the spirit counselors refer to as "the helping relationship," the desire to give of oneself to be of assistance to others. Beyond this, the supervisor needs the kind of persuasiveness and infectious enthusiasm that inspires teachers to want to make changes for the better.

The supervisor should be an "idea person," one who leads people to think about new and improved ways of doing things. He or she needs to convey the attitude of valuing and seeking the ideas of others while not appearing to have answers to all the problems teachers face.

The supervisor who is a helper to teachers is able to effect a democratic environment in which the contributions of each participating member are valued. Above all, the supervisor needs to possess a predisposition to change and must constantly promote improvement. If supervisors, whose chief responsibility is to bring about improvements, are satisfied with the status quo, they can be sure that the teachers will be, too. The supervisor must be able to live with change and help teachers adapt to the changing needs of society and of children and youth. To accomplish this mission, the supervisor should be able to work effectively in both one-to-one relationships and in groups.

Knowledge and Skills   Although personal traits of supervisors are not often discussed, we can find an abundance of statements about the knowledge and skills successful supervisors need. There is general agreement that supervisors should have

- A sound general education program.
- A thorough preservice professional education program.
- A major field of study.
- A solid graduate program in supervision.
- Three to five years of successful teaching at the elementary, middle, or secondary school level.

In preservice and in-service training programs, supervisors should develop a grounding in

- Learning theory and educational psychology.
- Philosophy of education.
- History of education, especially of curriculum and instructional development.
- The role of the school in society.
- Curriculum development.
- Instructional design and methods.
- Group dynamics.
- Conferencing and counseling.
- Assessment of teacher performance.

Lovell and Wiles pointed to necessary knowledge and skills when they wrote that supervision is

- Releasing human potential.
- Leadership.
- Communications.
- Coordinating and facilitating change.
- Curriculum development.
- Facilitating human development.[37]

Alfonso, Firth, and Neville drew implications for instructional supervisory behavior from organization leadership, communication, decision making, and change theories.[38]

Read the table of contents of any textbook on supervision and you will see the broad knowledge and special skills demanded by the profession. To identify the knowledge and skills required for effective supervision, we may also turn to Figure 1.4 and analyze the domains, roles, and foundations presented in the conceptual model. To perform effectively, the supervisor must possess broad knowledge of both a general and professional nature and be able to translate that knowledge into skillful practice. At appropriate points in this book, you will encounter further discussion of the knowledge and skills essential to instructional supervisors.

People considering the job of supervisor might begin by taking a look at themselves. They should decide whether they possess the fund of knowledge and skills required by the job. Prospective supervisors should ponder whether they have the personality for dealing with teachers in a supervisory capacity. They should know whether they enjoy working intimately with people in a helping relationship. A beginning point in supervision is the determination by the prospective supervisor of his or her adequacy to fill the roles demanded.

SUMMARY

The roles and titles of supervisory personnel vary among the school systems of the nation. *Supervision* is defined in this text as help and service to teachers, both as individuals and in groups, to improve instruction and thereby improve student achievement.

A supervisor is a trained auxiliary or staff person whose primary function is the provision of service according to a conceptual model. The model presented in this chapter portrays the supervisor as fulfilling the roles of coordinator, consultant, group leader, and evaluator within the domains of instructional, curricular, and staff development.

The supervisor should possess personal traits that will enable him or her to work harmoniously with people and sufficient knowledge and skills to perform all functions effectively. Leadership, interpersonal, and communications skills appear to be especially important to successful supervision. Supervisors should possess a judicious mix of technical, managerial, and human relations skills.

Supervisors perform a wide variety of tasks, which may or may not include administrative duties. The focus of this book is on instructional supervision, which is an inclusive term that signifies service to teachers in developing the curriculum, instruction, and themselves.

QUESTIONS FOR DISCUSSION

1. Are there other domains of supervision besides those shown in Figure 1.4 or cited from the Pajak study?

2. Do supervisors have roles besides the four shown in Figure 1.4?

3. Are there other foundations of supervision besides those shown in Figure 1.4? If so, what are they?

4. How would you describe the current state of instructional supervision in your school/district?

5. Discuss how the three domains of supervision interrelate and impact each other.

ACTIVITIES FOR FURTHER STUDY

REFLECTIVE

1. Cite at least four definitions of supervision to be found in the bibliography of this chapter, show their similarities and differences, state whether you agree or disagree with each definition, and give reasons for your position.

2. Formulate your own definition of supervision.

3. State your position on the following questions:

   a. Is the principal a supervisor? Why or why not?

   b. Would our system of education be better if the U.S. Department of Education employed inspectors to check on instruction throughout the country? Give reasons for your answer.

   c. Would our system of education be better if state departments of education regularly sent out inspectors to check on instruction throughout their states? Why or why not?

   d. How much teaching experience is essential for a person to be an effective supervisor?

4. Write a short paper, using references in the bibliography at the end of this chapter, expanding on the list of qualifications of supervisors discussed in the chapter.

5. Write a short paper, using references in the bibliography at the end of this chapter, expanding on the functions, roles, or tasks of supervisors discussed in the chapter. See, for example, Don M. Beach and Judy Reinhartz, pp. 16–18 (see bibliography) on roles of the supervisor.

6. Following the concept of a "skill-mix," list specific (a) technical, (b) managerial, and (c) human relations skills that you believe are needed by a supervisor.

7. Write an analysis of your own knowledge, skills, and personal traits as they bear on the role of the supervisor. Describe your strengths and indicate areas in which you feel you need improvement.

APPLICATION

1. Examine the staffing pattern of a school system you know well and list as many different types of supervisors as you can discover.

2. Design your own conceptual model of supervision.

3. Poll a sample of teachers and inquire (a) whether they know what supervisory help is available to them and (b) how they perceive the functions of each supervisor.

4. Identify at least two improvements in curriculum and/or instruction that have been made in a particular school system in the last three years and determine what role, if any, a supervisor played.

5. Inquire of several teachers how often supervisors visited them in their classrooms during the past school year. Identify the supervisors by title, such as assistant principal for curriculum, supervisor of language arts, and so on.

6. Interview and obtain a job description, if available, for one or more of the following supervisors and write a brief description of their chief duties based on the interview:

   a. Assistant superintendent for curriculum and instruction.

   b. Director of elementary, middle, junior, or senior high schools.

   c. General supervisor.

   d. Team leader.

   e. Grade coordinator (grade chairperson).

   f. Lead teacher.

   g. Department head.

7. Describe supervisory assistance available to teachers in your field from the following sources:

   a. State department of education.

   b. Cooperative (regional) educational service agencies (intermediate school district level).

   c. School superintendent's office.

8. Outline a desirable university training program for supervisors and compare it with a training program with which you are familiar.

9. Tape an interview with a supervisor on the central-office staff and write a summary covering the following points: (a) How does the supervisor perceive his or her role? (b) What are major problems in supervision as he or she sees them? (c) What training is required for the job?

10. Outline the state requirements for certification as (a) a school principal and (b) a supervisor. Write a brief summary contrasting the differences, if any, and comparing the similarities.

NOTES

1. Ben M. Harris, *Supervisory Behavior in Education*, 3rd ed. (Englewood Cliffs, N.J.: Prentice Hall, 1985), pp. 1–2.
2. Peter F. Oliva, *Developing the Curriculum*, 6th ed. (Boston: Allyn and Bacon, 2005), p. 28.
3. See ibid., pp. 547–53.
4. Walter Herbert Small, *Early New England Schools* (Boston: Ginn and Company, 1914), p. 340. Reprinted by Arno Press and *New York Times*, New York, 1969.
5. Ellwood P. Cubberley, *Public School Administration* (Boston: Houghton Mifflin, 1922), pp. 58–59.
6. See G. Alfred Hess Jr., *Empowering Teachers and Parents: School Restructuring through the Eyes of Anthropologists* (Westport, Conn.: Bergin and Garvey, 1992).
7. Edgar L. Morphet, Roe L. Johns, and Theodore L. Reller, *Educational Organization and Administration*, 4th ed. (Englewood Cliffs, N.J.: Prentice Hall, 1982), pp. 79–82.
8. See W. Edwards Deming, *Out of the Crisis: Productivity and Competitive Position* (Cambridge: Massachusetts Institute of Technology Press, 1986). See also Chapter 11.
9. William H. Lucio and John D. McNeil, *Supervision: A Synthesis of Thought and Action*, 2nd ed. (New York: McGraw-Hill, 1969), p. 3.
10. Ralph L. Mosher and David E. Purpel, *Supervision: The Reluctant Profession* (Boston: Houghton Mifflin, 1972), p. 3.
11. William H. Burton and Leo J. Brueckner, *Supervision: A Social Process*, 3rd ed. (New York: Appleton-Century-Crofts, 1955), p. 11.
12. Jane Franseth, *Supervision as Leadership* (Evanston, Ill.: Row, Peterson, 1961), p. 19.

13. Ross L. Neagley and N. Dean Evans, *Handbook for Effective Supervision of Instruction*, 3rd ed. (Englewood Cliffs, N.J.: Prentice Hall, 1980), p. 20.
14. Harris, *Supervisory Behavior*, pp. 10–11.
15. Robert J. Alfonso, Gerald R. Firth, and Richard F. Neville, *Instructional Supervision: A Behavioral System*, 2nd ed. (Boston: Allyn and Bacon, 1981), p. 43.
16. John T. Lovell and Kimball Wiles, *Supervision for Better Schools*, 5th ed. (Englewood Cliffs, N.J.: Prentice Hall, 1983), p. 4.
17. Don M. Beach and Judy Reinhartz, *Supervisory Leadership: Focus on Instruction* (Boston: Allyn and Bacon, 2000), pp. 8–9.
18. Robert D. Krey and Peter J. Burke, *A Design for Instructional Supervision* (Springfield, Ill.: Charles C. Thomas, 1989), p. 22.
19. Thomas J. Sergiovanni and Robert J. Starratt, *Supervision: A Redefinition*, 8th ed. (Boston: McGraw-Hill, 2007), p. 5.
20. John C. Daresh and Marsha A. Playko, *Supervision as a Proactive Process: Concepts and Cases*, 2nd ed. (Prospect Heights, Ill.: Waveland Press, 1995), p. 26.
21. Jon Wiles and Joseph Bondi, *Supervision: A Guide to Practice*, 6th ed. (Upper Saddle River, N.J.: Merrill/Prentice Hall, 2004), p. 15.
22. Carl D. Glickman, Stephen P. Gordon, and Jovita M. Ross-Gordon, *SuperVision and Instructional Leadership: A Developmental Approach*, 6th ed. (Boston: Allyn and Bacon, 2004), pp. 10–11.
23. Mosher and Purpel, *Supervision*.
24. Arthur Blumberg, *Supervisors and Teachers: A Private Cold War* (Berkeley, Calif.: McCutchan, 1980).
25. William H. Burton, *Supervision and the Improvement of Teaching* (New York: D. Appleton-Century, 1922), pp. 9–10.
26. A. S. Barr, William H. Burton, and Leo J. Brueckner, *Supervision: Democratic Leadership in the Improvement of Learning*, 2nd ed. (New York: Appleton-Century-Crofts, 1947), p. 5.
27. Harris, *Supervisory Behavior*, pp. 10–12.
28. Ibid., p. 13.
29. Karolyn J. Snyder, "What Is the New Supervisory Role in an Age of Complexity?" in Jeffrey Glanz and Richard F. Neville, eds., *Educational Supervision: Perspectives, Issues, and Controversies* (Norwood, Mass.: Christopher-Gordon Publishers, 1997), p. 306.
30. Ibid. See also Robert H. Anderson and Karolyn J. Snyder, "Functions of School Supervision," in Gerald R. Firth and Edward F. Pajak, eds., *Handbook of Research on School Supervision* (New York: Macmillan, 1998), pp. 341–73.
31. Bernadette Marczely, *Supervision of Education: A Differentiated Approach with Legal Perspectives* (Gaithersburg, Md.: Aspen Publishers, 2001), pp. 23–33.
32. Floyd C. Mann, "Toward an Understanding of the Leadership Role in Formal Organization," in Robert Dubin, ed., *Supervision and Productivity* (San Francisco: Chandler, 1965), pp. 773–77.
33. Edward Pajak, *Identification of Supervisory Proficiencies Project* (Athens: College of Education, University of Georgia, 1989).
34. Ibid., pp. 4–5.
35. See, for example, George E. Pawlas, *The Administrator's Guide to School-Community Relations*, 2nd ed. (Larchmont, N.Y.: Eye on Education, 2005); Ralph B. Kimbrough and Michael Y. Nunnery, *Educational Administration: An Introduction*, 3rd ed. (New York: Macmillan, 1988); and Don Bagin, Donald R. Gallagher, and Leslie W. Kindred, *The School and Community Relations*, 8th ed. (Boston: Allyn and Bacon, 2005).
36. For descriptions of nine roles of the supervisor, see Beach and Reinhartz, *Supervisory Leadership*, pp. 16–18.
37. Lovell and Wiles, *Supervision for Better Schools*, pp. 3–6, 8, 10.
38. Alfonso, Firth, and Neville, *Instructional Supervision*, part II.

BIBLIOGRAPHY

ALFONSO, ROBERT J., GERALD R. FIRTH, and RICHARD F. NEVILLE. *Instructional Supervision: A Behavior System*, 2nd ed. Boston: Allyn and Bacon, 1981.

ANDERSON, ROBERT H., and KAROLYN J. SNYDER. "Functions of School Supervision." In GERALD R. FIRTH and EDWARD F. PAJAK, eds., *Handbook of Research on School Supervision*, pp. 341–73. New York: Macmillan, 1998.

BARR, A. S., WILLIAM H. BURTON, and LEO J. BRUECKNER. *Supervision: Democratic Leadership in the Improvement of Learning*, 2nd ed. New York: Appleton-Century-Crofts, 1947.

BEACH, DON M., and JUDY REINHARTZ. *Supervisory Leadership: Focus on Instruction*. Boston: Allyn and Bacon, 2000.

BLUMBERG, ARTHUR. *Supervisors and Teachers: A Private Cold War*, 2nd ed. Berkeley, Calif.: McCutchan, 1980.

BOBBITT, FRANKLIN. *The Supervision of City Schools*. Chicago: University of Chicago Press, 1913.

BURTON, WILLIAM H. *Supervision and the Improvement of Teaching*. New York: D. Appleton, 1922.

BURTON, WILLIAM H., and LEO J. BRUECKNER. *Supervision: A Social Process*, 3rd ed. New York: Appleton-Century-Crofts, 1955.

CUBBERLEY, ELLWOOD P. *Public School Administration*. Boston: Houghton Mifflin, 1922.

DARESH, JOHN C., and MARSHA A. PLAYKO. *Supervision as a Proactive Process: Concepts and Cases*, 2nd ed. Prospect Heights, Ill.: Waveland Press, 1995.

DEMING, W. EDWARDS. *Out of the Crisis: Productivity and Competitive Position*. Cambridge: Massachusetts Institute of Technology Press, 1986.

FIRTH, GERALD R., and EDWARD PAJAK, eds. *Handbook of Research on School Supervision*. New York: Macmillan, 1998.

FRANSETH, JANE. *Supervision as Leadership*. Evanston, Ill.: Row, Peterson, 1961.

GALLAGHER, DONALD R., DON BAGIN, and LESLIE W. KINDRED. *The School and Community Relations*, 8th ed. Boston: Allyn and Bacon, 2005.

GLANZ, JEFFREY, and RICHARD F. NEVILLE, eds. *Educational Supervision: Perspectives, Issues, and Controversies*. Norwood, Mass.: Christopher-Gordon Publishers, 1997.

GLATTHORN, ALLAN A. *Differentiated Supervision*, 2nd ed. Alexandria, Va.: Association for Supervision and Curriculum Development, 1997.

GLICKMAN, CARL D., ed. *Supervision in Transition*. 1992 Yearbook. Alexandria, Va.: Association for Supervision and Curriculum Development, 1992.

GLICKMAN, CARL D., STEPHEN P. GORDON, and JOVITA M. ROSS-GORDON. *SuperVision and Instructional Leadership: A Developmental Approach*, 7th ed. Boston: Allyn and Bacon, 2007.

GORDON, STEPHEN P., ed. *Standards for Instructional Supervision: Enhancing Teaching and Learning*. Larchmont, NY: Eye on Education, 2005.

HARRIS, BEN M. *Supervisory Behavior in Education*, 3rd ed. Englewood Cliffs, N.J.: Prentice Hall, 1985.

HESS, G. ALFRED JR. *Empowering Teachers and Parents: School Restructuring through the Eyes of Anthropologists*. Westport, Conn.: Bergin and Garvey, 1992.

HOY, WAYNE K., and PATRICK B. FORSYTH. *Effective Supervision: Theory into Practice*. New York: Random House, 1986.

KIMBROUGH, RALPH B., and MICHAEL Y. NUNNERY. *Educational Administration: An Introduction*, 3rd ed. New York: Macmillan, 1988.

KOSMOSKI, GEORGIA J. *Supervision*, 3rd ed. Mequon, Wis.: Stylex, 2006.

KREY, ROBERT D., and PETER J. BURKE. *A Design for Instructional Supervision*. Springfield, Ill.: Charles C. Thomas, 1989.

KYTE, GEORGE C. *How to Supervise: A Guide to Educational Principles and Progressive Practices of Educational Supervision*. Boston: Houghton Mifflin, 1930.

LOVELL, JOHN T., and KIMBALL WILES. *Supervision for Better Schools*, 5th ed. Englewood Cliffs, N.J.: Prentice Hall, 1983.

LUCIO, WILLIAM H., and JOHN D. MCNEIL. *Supervision: A Synthesis of Thought and Action*, 3rd ed. New York: McGraw-Hill, 1979.

MAEROFF, GENE I. *The Empowerment of Teachers: Overcoming the Crisis of Confidence*. New York: Teachers College Press, 1988.

MANN, FLOYD C. "Toward an Understanding of the Leadership Role in Formal Organization." In ROBERT DUBIN, ed., *Supervision and Productivity*, pp. 773–77. San Francisco: Chandler, 1965.

MARCZELY, BERNADETTE. *Supervision in Education: A Differentiated Approach with Legal Perspectives*. Gaithersburg, Md.: Aspen Publishers, 2001.

MARKS, JAMES R., EMERY STOOPS, and JOYCE KING-STOOPS. *Handbook of Educational Supervision: A Guide for the Practitioner*, 3rd ed. Boston: Allyn and Bacon, 1985.

MORPHET, EDGAR L., ROE L. JOHNS, and THEODORE L. RELLER. *Educational Organization and Administration*, 4th ed. Englewood Cliffs, N.J.: Prentice Hall, 1982.

MOSHER, RALPH L., and DAVID E. PURPEL. *Supervision: The Reluctant Profession*. Boston: Houghton Mifflin, 1972.

NEAGLEY, ROSS L., and H. DEAN EVANS. *Handbook for Effective Supervision of Instruction*, 3rd ed. Englewood Cliffs, N.J.: Prentice Hall, 1980.

OLIVA, PETER F. *Developing the Curriculum*, 6th ed. Boston: Allyn and Bacon, 2005.

PAJAK, EDWARD. *The Central Office Supervisor of Curriculum and Instruction: Setting the Stage for Success*. Boston: Allyn and Bacon, 1989.

———. *Identification of Supervisory Proficiencies Project*. Athens: College of Education, University of Georgia, 1989.

PAWLAS, GEORGE E. *The Administrator's Guide to School-Community Relations*, 2nd ed. Larchmont, N.Y.: Eye on Education, 2005.

SERGIOVANNI, THOMAS J., ed. *Supervision of Teaching. 1982 Yearbook*. Alexandria, Va.: Association for Supervision and Curriculum Development, 1982.

SERGIOVANNI, THOMAS J., and ROBERT J. STARRATT. *Supervision: A Redefinition*, 8th ed. Boston: McGraw-Hill, 2007.

SMALL, WALTER HERBERT. *Early New England Schools*. Boston: Ginn, 1914. Reprinted by Arno Press and *New York Times*, New York, 1969.

SNYDER, KAROLYN J. "What Is the New Supervisory Role in an Age of Complexity?" In JEFFREY, GLANZ and RICHARD F. NEVILLE, eds., *Educational Supervision: Perspectives, Issues, and Controversies*, pp. 299–314. Norwood, Mass.: Christopher-Gordon Publishers, 1997.

Sullivan, Susan, and Jeffrey Glanz. *Supervision that Improves Teaching: Strategies and Techniques*, 2nd ed. Thousand Oaks, Calif.: Corwin Press, 2005.

TANNER, DANIEL, and LAUREL N. TANNER. *Supervision in Education: Problems and Practices*. New York: Macmillan, 1987.

WILES, JON, and JOSEPH BONDI. *Supervision: A Guide to Practice*, 6th ed. Upper Saddle River, N.J.: Pearson, 2004.

ZEPEDA, SALLY J. *Instructional Supervision: Applying Tools and Concepts*. Larchmont, N.Y.: Eye on Education, 2003.

———. *The Instructional Leader's Guide to Informal Classroom Observations*. Larchmont, N.Y.: Eye on Education, 2005.

ZEPEDA, SALLY J., and R. STEWART MAYERS. *Supervision Across the Content Areas*. Larchmont, N.Y.: Eye on Education, 2004.

CHAPTER 2

ISSUES IN SUPERVISION

OBJECTIVES

After studying Chapter 2 you should be able to accomplish the following objectives:

1. Identify several issues in supervision.
2. Explain various positions on each issue.
3. Choose a position on each issue and defend it.

NUMEROUS UNRESOLVED ISSUES

The educational world seems to attract unresolved issues. Whether we are talking about learning theories or curriculum or methodology, there are no certainties to which we can subscribe. Take, for example, the specification of behavioral objectives. This procedure is roundly attacked by its opponents and strongly supported by its adherents. As with many issues, a polarity has developed, with vocal camps on both sides. Extremists in one camp hold that the writing of behavioral objectives is a complete waste of time; those in the opposite camp feel that teaching can scarcely survive unless teachers design behavioral objectives.

At various places between these poles are groups who champion portions of a position and reject other aspects. For instance, some educators encourage behavioral objectives in the cognitive and psychomotor domains but not the affective; others insist on behavioral objectives in all three. Some claim that it is impossible to write behavioral objectives in the affective domain; others assert that affective objectives can and must be specified. Some advocate a formulaic approach to writing objectives; others are willing to be more flexible. Some accept general goals in place of specific objectives; others accept only objectives that can be observed and measured. When we discuss helping teachers plan for instruction, we will return to the issue of behavioral objectives. We introduce it at this point solely as an illustration of one controversial issue in professional education, of which there are many. A quick list of current controversies in education relative to curriculum or instruction would surely include the following:

- Corporal punishment.
- Behavior modification.
- Mainstreaming handicapped children (i.e., full inclusion).

- Charter schools.
- Multicultural education.
- Inquiry learning.
- Character education.
- Bilingual education.
- Integration of subject matter.
- Minimal competencies for graduation.
- Alternative assessment options.
- State assessment of student achievement.
- Methods of teaching reading.
- Alternative scheduling.
- Placement of subject matter.
- Grouping learners.
- Role of vocational education.
- Home schooling.
- Vouchers.
- IDEA special education.
- Standards and high-stakes testing.
- School violence.
- Parental involvement.
- Grading of schools.
- Teacher certification.
- Distribution of funds.
- ESE and EDHD students.
- No Child Left Behind (NCLB).

This list, far from being a complete set of issues in education, illustrates unresolved problems with which supervisors must contend. Like its companion disciplines, sociology and psychology, education is besieged with unresolved problems because by their very nature, education, sociology, and psychology are imprecise sciences. These social and behavioral sciences lack precision primarily because they deal with human beings. Unlike machines, people are notoriously unpredictable. Whereas natural scientists may manipulate elements and equipment in laboratories, social and behavioral scientists have difficulty manipulating people. People, especially in a literate, democratic environment, tend to reject manipulation. Of course, we can all point to exceptions, as studies of mob behavior, demagoguery, and totalitarianism readily show. People living in a democracy, however, prefer to think through answers to problems themselves. As a result, we often find that there are multiple answers to specific problems. The presence of multiple answers causes consternation for many people in education who are seeking *the* definitive answers to particular problems.

We cannot even be sure, for example, that 5 plus 4 equals 9. If we are working with a base of 6 instead of 10, 5 plus 4 equals 13. Perhaps John Dewey and his progressive followers were right after all when they declared that truth was relative.

To know whether 5 plus 4 equals 9 or 13, we must know, as they say in that esoteric language called psychobabble, "where you're coming from." If you're working in base 6 and trying to communicate with a person who thinks in base 10—and who believes 10 is the only base possible—the message does not get through. Thus, for those who see a supervisor only as a specialist who works with individual teachers, many of the issues in the field are either nonexistent or spurious.

Because supervision, along with teaching, counseling, and administration, is one of the subsystems of the enterprise of education, we should not be surprised to find it struggling with a number of unresolved problems. Supervision may even be confronted with more issues than the other subsystems because the role of the supervisor is defined in so many different ways. Teachers, counselors, and administrators usually have a clearer perspective of their behavior systems and the roles they are expected to fill than do supervisors. Figure 2.1 shows the relationships among these four major behavior systems.

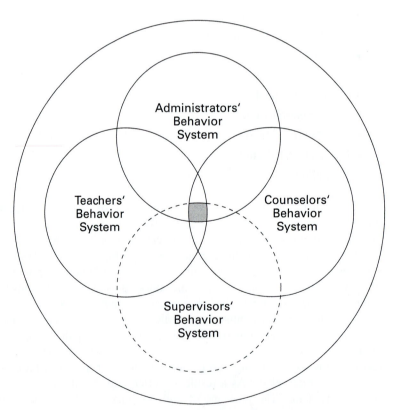

FIGURE 2.1   Relationships among Four Major Behavior Systems.

All systems interact with each other. The four behavior systems shown here meet, relate, reinforce each other, and sometimes lock horns. The educational commons where the four come together (shaded area in Figure 2.1) is both bedecked with roses and replete with thorns. The supervisory behavior system is in a broken circle to indicate that its borders are less rigid than those of the other three systems. The uncertainty of the supervisor's role creates some problems, but at the same time it has the saving grace of giving specialists the opportunity to refine the role. In this respect, supervision is more malleable than the other systems.

Issues in Supervision

In 1975, the executive council of the Association for Supervision and Curriculum Development (ASCD) created the Working Group on Supervisory Practices, which identified issues in supervision. The Working Group surveyed 163 public school supervisors and others associated with colleges and universities, all of whom were members of the ASCD. The public school personnel made up 70 percent of the respondents.

The seventeen issues identified by the ASCD Working Group as problems that members of the profession considered important are all still with us, along with many other issues. Some persons may be inclined to say that the either/or dichotomy of these issues is unrealistic. They would assert that supervisors must be occupied with both sides of these issues. For example, they would take the position that one cannot evaluate instruction without evaluating teacher performance.

Yet affirming that supervisors must fulfill responsibilities on both sides of every issue is as simplistic as rejecting one side or the other out of hand. We do find supervisors devoting energies to both sides of some issues. In a few cases, they expend equal energy on the two tasks. In contrast, other supervisors put greater effort into one side of an issue than into the other. Generally, supervisors tend to at least lean toward one side of an issue; even if only slightly past the midpoint, they lean far enough to show their preference.

An even larger question than where supervisors actually spend their time is where they *should* spend their time. To answer the *should* question, we must bring to bear not only a knowledge of prevailing practice but also the philosophical assumptions we hold about supervision. We find so many conflicting views on what supervision is because the viewers start with conflicting sets of assumptions. This textbook, of course, is no exception. We present here certain positions for your consideration and analysis. We would be the last to say that every position—yes, and bias—in this book represents *the right* answer. "Right" answers are hard to come by. We need to think in terms of *situational supervision* in much the same way we think of *situational leadership*. Leadership is a function both of the characteristics of the leader and of the situation in which the leader demonstrates his or her abilities. Successful supervision is the judicious application of the supervisor's knowledge and skills in a particular setting at a particular time.

Practitioners therefore must exercise professional judgment in determining what is right in a given situation. To do this, however, practitioners must know what the options are, and if they reject a practice that has been found to be generally effective elsewhere, they should be able to explain their reasons.

In this chapter, we examine what we see as some of the more pressing issues in supervision. The first eleven issues reflect the Working Group's findings, and the last three have been included as a result of current issues present in schools:

1. Is supervision necessary?

2. For whom should supervision be provided?

3. Should the supervisor's authority be based on expertise and interpersonal relationships or on conferred status and decision-making responsibilities?

4. Should the supervisor be an administrator?

5. Is supervision staff development?

6. Is supervision curriculum development?

7. Is supervision evaluation?

8. Should supervisors work with groups of teachers or with individual teachers?

9. Should supervision be carried out by supervisors based in the central office or in the individual schools?

10. Should the supervisor use a directive or nondirective approach?

11. Should school systems organize for supervision by employing generalists or specialists?

12. Should there be national professional standards for teachers?

13. What should be the role of technology in the supervisory process?

14. Should multiculturalism be a focus of supervision?

Issues are problems whose answers are not fully clear and on which specialists may disagree. At the beginning of our discussion of each issue, we've placed a figure representing a scale.

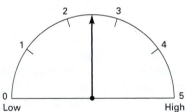

The reading on the scale shows graphically the position we take on the issue—that is, which way we lean. The indicator on the scale can point to any value from 0 to 5. The labels under 0 and 5 indicate the two sides of the issue. If we lean completely to one side or the other, the indicator will point to 0 or 5; if our position on an issue is less strongly held, the indicator will point somewhere between 0 and 5.

In the following pages, the positions we have taken apply to the instructional staff supervisor, the protagonist of this book. Our positions may or may not be the same for line supervisors (administrators), and when there are differences of this nature, we note them in the narrative. It is not the purpose of these discussions to persuade supervisors and prospective supervisors to accept our positions but rather to help them think through the issues and reach their own decisions.

ISSUE 1: Is Supervision Necessary?

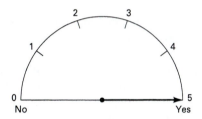

The question "Is supervision necessary?" may seem out of place in a text on supervision. The mere fact that there are supervisors and a body of literature on supervision would seem to indicate its necessity. Yet this fundamental question has probably not been given enough consideration. Teachers, administrators, and supervisors assume the necessity for supervision as a given. In their memory, supervisors have been like the firmament; they have always existed and so presumably they will always exist.

We might phrase the question in another way. Can we do without supervisors? As the system now operates, the answer is apparently that we cannot. Supervisors meet a need in our current educational structure and will undoubtedly continue to do so for a long time to come. Theoretically, however, we could dispense with the services of supervisors *if*—a very improbable if—all teachers were dynamic, knowledgeable, and skillful. Because not all teachers have reached a state of perfection, the need for supervision remains.

An assumption in our discussion of this issue is that preservice programs do not turn out finished teachers. The typical training program consists of general education, concentration in a teaching field, and professional education. In a time of rapid development in all fields of knowledge, prospective teachers cannot begin to learn in college all that they will need to know when teaching. Nor can they gain a full mastery of techniques of instruction; study of curriculum and teaching constitutes only a beginning point. In many college programs, the work in curriculum and instruction occurs in a hypothetical context, which students may translate into practice only in limited participation programs and in student teaching. Student teaching gives the preservice teacher merely a taste of teaching—ten to twelve weeks in a school under the direction of a supervising teacher. To the limited programs must be added the differences among individuals themselves. Teachers develop their capacities at different rates. Some are ready to move into the classroom with a sense of confidence and demonstrable ability at the end of—sometimes even before—the student-teaching experience. Others will need a few years to develop their potential; some, unfortunately, will never become really good teachers. The assumption can be made, then, that teachers need the help of supervisors because they have not been fully prepared by their teacher education programs and because there are great differences among their abilities and needs. The increasingly large numbers of teachers who have participated in alternative certification programs will also be candidates for the need of a supervisor's insight and suggestions. Many of these individuals are proficient in their knowledge of the subjects they will teach but lack the pedagogy presented in traditional teacher preparation programs.

Limitations of Teaching

By providing supervision, the educational system is declaring, in effect, that teachers are not completely free to run their own classrooms as they see fit. Limitations are imposed by school regulations, state legislative regulations, types of students, and types of communities. A supervisor is often more aware of or more sensitive to these limitations than teachers and can help teachers work within the restrictions.

Supervision skirts dangerously close to the issue of academic freedom, teachers' right to teach as they deem appropriate within their particular realm of competence. The doctrine of academic freedom, however, raises many questions. Do teachers have the right to teach topics that have been explicitly forbidden by the school board or administrators? Can teachers reject textbooks that have been adopted by a state textbook commission or by colleagues in their own grade or department? May a teacher follow a curricular program that disrupts the sequence from one grade level to another?

Academic freedom has its limitations, and more so on the public school level than in institutions of higher education. For a number of reasons, public schools are more susceptible to pressures from the community than are colleges and universities. This means that a public school teacher must work within certain limitations and seek individuality within the context generally accepted in the school system. The supervisor helps teachers understand that context and find their own ways of teaching within it. A simple illustration is the case of the teacher who does not like a particular textbook used in the school. The teacher cannot simply ignore the school's investment in the textbook or arbitrarily declare that pupils must buy a different textbook. If the textbook is part of a sequence, the teacher cannot disrupt this sequence without upsetting the previous planning of colleagues and confusing students. However, the supervisor can help the teacher find ways to use the textbook; expand on it; provide supplementary, original activities that go beyond it; locate additional text materials; and make use of the Internet.

When the teacher and supervisor discuss the thorny issue of academic freedom, they should not ignore a dimension that some teachers overlook, namely, that academic freedom does not exist for the teacher alone. Not only should academic freedom provide an environment in which a teacher is free to teach—within established parameters—but it should also provide a climate in which the learner is free to learn—within the same parameters.

Need for the Supervisor

Providing a program of supervision reflects the assumption that change is desirable, necessary, and indeed, inevitable. School programs and methods of instruction must keep pace with changing times. The number of new teachers entering the profession each year is significant and continues to rise. Supervisors will play an important role in the induction of these new teachers. Helping monitor these new teachers or preparing experienced teachers to become effective mentors will be a major responsibility of many supervisors. At the same time, supervisors' time may be consumed with helping experienced teachers maintain their enthusiasm and interest in teaching. Individuals choose to go into teaching for a number of reasons. Some are dedicated to teaching and over the years become devoted teachers. Others enter teaching because they have majored in a particular field and, by adding some professional education courses, can be certified to teach. They may have no great interest in teaching but reason that teacher training will equip them for the job market. Still others in teaching are just marking time until they can move into another profession. Some are in teaching because it gives them a sense of power over the lives of young people. For these reasons, teachers will need a considerable degree of supervision.

One assumption in supervision is that without assistance, some teachers will not make changes. This implies that supervisors are able to help teachers bring about changes. Whether this implication is translated into fact depends on the supervisor, the teacher, and the interaction between them. Possibly, if existing patterns of educational organization were changed, means other than the presence of a live supervisor *might* help teachers effect change. Dissemination of professional literature from the central office or other teacher/administrator and self-evaluation techniques, including the use of media and technology, also might help teachers change. So far, however, the evidence seems to point to the need for supervisors to facilitate change.

Educators agree that there should be some internal consistency to sequences of subject matter and that there should be articulation between grades of a school and levels of the school system. Supervisors are the school system personnel who can help achieve these goals. The district supervisor, for example, moving from school to school, knows what materials are being used in each class and what the objectives of teachers are in the various schools. The supervisor of language arts in the elementary school, for example, helps teachers coordinate their sequences, avoid duplication of content, define goals, and work cooperatively.

The district supervisor is concerned with sequences across levels—that is, with the problem of articulation. The supervisor of language arts in the elementary school works with the supervisor of language arts in the middle or secondary school to develop coordinated, sequential programs between the elementary and middle or secondary levels. The provision of coordinated sequences of subject matter between levels—elementary and middle school or junior high, middle school or junior high and senior high, senior high and college—is a problem in need of a solution in many communities. Solution requires joint planning by teachers at the various levels. The supervisor can act as a catalyst in getting teachers together so they can cooperatively work out sequences whose parts will bear some relationship to one another.

At the individual school level, the principal, assistant principal, lead teacher, curriculum coordinator, or curriculum resource teacher can oversee the planning for continuous sequences among courses or grades, with help from team leaders, curriculum resource teachers, grade coordinators, and department heads. Students should be able to go through an orderly progression of study from elementary school through high school. This orderly progress is founded on a well-planned, well-formulated sequence in each area of study. Achieving this sequence requires the cooperation of teachers at all levels. The supervisor brings these teachers together and acquaints them with the problems of sequence and articulation.

Ross L. Neagley and N. Dean Evans explained the need for supervision in the following way:

> Supervision, then, seems destined to be essential to deciding the nature and content of the curriculum, to selecting the school organizational patterns and learning materials to facilitate teaching, and to evaluating the entire educational process. Effective coordination of the total program, kindergarten through high school, has never been achieved in most school systems, although this is one of the most pressing needs in American public education today.[1]

Supervision is therefore a necessary service to teachers for a number of reasons. The stage has not yet been reached when the services of these specialized personnel may be eliminated. In fact, there is a pressing need for more supervisors who are better trained and more highly skilled in the performance of their tasks.

ISSUE 2: For Whom Should Supervision Be Provided?

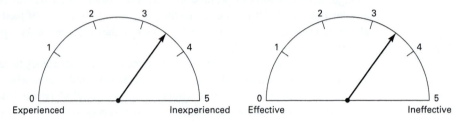

Teacher Experience and Teacher Effectiveness

Should supervision be provided for new teachers only? for older as well as newer teachers? for the experienced as well as the inexperienced? Ostensibly, supervision is made available to all teachers, and supervisors make choices about where they will spend most of their time and energies.

Naturally, most effort is devoted to those who seem to need most help: the new, the inexperienced, and the less able teachers. Teachers who are new to a school system need help in learning how the system operates. The supervisor introduces them to the resources of the school and community and helps them understand the types of students and parents in the system. The teacher new to a school system has special needs, different from the needs of those who have been in the system a while. A supervisor must be tuned in to these special needs and must make an effort to help new teachers become familiar with the system.

The supervisor will spend more time assisting teachers who are inexperienced. He or she knows that an inexperienced teacher is not a finished product. Although those who are in their first years of teaching are often uncertain of themselves, they usually make up in enthusiasm what they may lack in experience. They will probably be eager to receive whatever help is extended to them. They are often more approachable and more receptive to suggestions than more experienced teachers, who are more likely to be convinced that they know all the answers because of their years of service. It is understandable that many supervisors choose to put most of their efforts into helping new and inexperienced teachers.

The less able teacher requires particular help from the supervisor. This teacher may or may not be new or inexperienced and may or may not seek help from a supervisor. There are, of course, both more and less competent teachers among the new and inexperienced. In many cases, the supervisor can help the less effective new or inexperienced teachers improve their teaching. Along with this help, familiarity with the school system and a few years of teaching experience often resolve the problems of some teachers who were initially ineffective.

Similarly, we find both more and less able teachers among those who are experienced and have been in a school system for years. Susan Trimble, Ed Davis, and Marsha T. Clanton interviewed a variety of middle school and high school principals about their practices with marginal teachers. Three types of ineffective teachers were identified: the contrite, the cocooner, and the coaster.[2] In addition, they offered approaches for working with teach type of teacher. Less able teachers fall into several categories. There is first the teacher who is ineffective in the supervisor's judgment but sees himself or herself as effective. This teacher is identified by the poor progress of his or her students, lack of rapport with students, lack of knowledge of the material being taught, lack of skill in presenting the material, and lack of classroom control. A supervisor can help this type of individual take an inventory of personal strengths and weaknesses. In this type of case, the supervisor is usually supported in his or her judgment of the teacher because the teacher is considered ineffective by the school principal and by colleagues as well. A much more difficult problem for the supervisor is the teacher who the supervisor considers ineffective but who is not so considered by either the principal or the teacher's colleagues. Such a teacher considers himself or herself to be effective, maybe even superior. To put it simply, such a teacher does a great job of teaching the wrong things in the wrong way, but only the supervisor recognizes that fact.

Subject-Centered Teachers versus Learner-Centered Teachers

In the opinion of some teachers and some principals, rigid discipline is a virtue. Strict disciplinarians keep all learners under their thumbs, allowing no freedom for childhood or adolescent exuberance. Some teachers and principals believe that the subject matter is king and that the learner should be adjusted to the subject matter rather than the reverse. Some feel that the "old ways" of teaching are better than the "new ways," if we may so distinguish between subject-centered and learner-centered approaches to presenting content. Thus, a teacher who is a stern disciplinarian, subject-centered, and a follower of tradition is often labeled effective or even superior. But if the supervisor believes that some allowance should be made for young learners, this same teacher is considered ineffective. The supervisor would consider an authoritarian, regimented classroom inappropriate, a type of educational climate more suitable to a totalitarian than a democratic society.

If the supervisor believes that the learner should take precedence over subject matter and that subject matter ought to be tailored to fit the learner rather than vice versa, he or she will consider the subject-centered teacher ineffective. The supervisor will work with such a teacher to bring about an understanding of the motivations of learners and to review learning theories, some of the principles of educational psychology, and their application in the classroom.

In working with a strictly subject-centered teacher, the supervisor may find the route to change in behavior slow going, for the weight of tradition is on the side of the teacher. Tradition is a powerful block, especially when it is supported by school administrators and other teachers who resist change. Experienced teachers are often in greater need of supervision with respect to rigidity and subject-centeredness than are inexperienced teachers. Inexperienced teachers who have just recently completed their preparation programs know some of the latest methods and strategies in education and in their teaching field and are not set in their ways. They are still flexible and have not developed particular techniques, plans, and procedures to which they are committed and which they repeat from year to year, nor have they as yet become tainted by the cynicism that some experienced teachers develop. The supervisor will have less difficulty working with inexperienced teachers who have open minds than with experienced teachers who might not.

Teachers Who Are Ineffective and Know It

A third category of ineffective teachers includes those who are clearly ineffective and know it. They are usually the most difficult for supervisors to deal with because these teachers know their shortcomings but are often not willing to accept suggestions for improvement, even when supervisor, principal, and colleagues all agree that the teacher is ineffective. A willingness on the part of the teacher to improve is a first step. Yet ineffective teachers who recognize their ineptness are often defensive about their instruction and refuse to seek the help of the supervisor or other resource people. Declining to participate in teachers' workshops or institutes for fear of revealing their own inadequacies, they develop defensive excuses for their lack of competence. Often they blame the students, claiming they are unmotivated. Or they blame uncooperative administrators for their difficulties. They claim that they are placed in the wrong grade, in their minor teaching field, or in the wrong school. But deep inside, they know they lack the preparation or other qualifications to be effective teachers. They see improvement in their instruction as an insurmountable barrier and often exhibit the same lack of motivation that they ascribe to their learners. Tenure regulations and lifetime certificates make it difficult to correct situations like this, no matter how hard a supervisor tries, unless the teacher is willing to be helped. The documentation required to substantiate a teacher's ineffectiveness remains the responsibility of the school principal, but the supervisor may be involved in the development of this documentation.

The supervisor can work with any teacher who is willing to cooperate, but first he or she must develop a trusting relationship in which the teacher will not be fearful of disclosing inadequacies. The teacher must know that no retribution will result from revealing problem areas. Because retribution can be harsh—a change of grade level or school or even dismissal—no teacher will willingly make personal inadequacies known if punishment is expected to follow.

Teacher Burnout

Numbered among the ineffective teachers are those who are "burned out." Such teachers may or may not be aware of their ineffectiveness or be willing to admit that they are suffering from burnout. Some of those who confront the problem resolve it by leaving teaching. Others stay on and mark time.

Teacher burnout is characterized by disenchantment with teaching, fatigue, frustration, impatience, rationalization, decreased motivation, cynicism, a day-to-day mode of existence, and alienation from the system, especially from administrators and supervisors, who are perceived as additional burdens. A 1990 study on teaching conditions by the Carnegie Foundation for the Advancement of Teaching revealed widespread dissatisfaction on the part of teachers. Forty-five percent of the more than 21,000 elementary and secondary public school teachers surveyed expressed a feeling of lack of control over their own professional lives. Whereas 75 percent had reported satisfaction with the degree of control they felt they had over their professional lives in 1987, that figure had dropped rather significantly to 55 percent—slightly over half of the teachers—by 1990.[3] The results from *The MetLife Survey of the American Teacher, 2006: Expectations and Experiences* revealed that 27 percent of the 1,001 teachers who were surveyed said they were likely to leave teaching because they were not satisfied with their careers. A similar MetLife study conducted in 1986 revealed that 33 percent of the teachers reported career satisfaction.[4] Such dissatisfaction is bound to spill over into the classroom.

Teacher burnout arises from stressful situations brought on by a variety of conditions: unruly and, in some cases, unmanageable students; students for whom English is not the primary language; massive amounts of paperwork and record keeping; low pay; inadequate budgets; high teacher–pupil ratios; uncaring (or perceived as uncaring) administrators and supervisors; school facilities in need of repair; parental demands; a major focus on meeting academic standards imposed by individual states; restrictions on freedom to plan and teach; and overemphasis on student test scores.

Supervisors have attempted to combat teacher burnout by providing staff development activities on management of time and stress or by suggesting that teachers get involved in employee assistance programs. Administrators can help alleviate some of the pressures on teachers by ensuring reasonable class size, helping teachers with discipline problems, keeping required paperwork to a minimum, and providing a variety of other forms of help and service.

Supervision for All Teachers

Civility and positive reinforcement from administrators and supervisors go a long way toward making the job more satisfying to the teacher. Teaching must be made to appear attractive if young people are to enter the profession. Teachers' ego needs, like the administrators' and supervisors' ego needs, must be fulfilled if teachers are to do an effective job and remain in the profession.

Supervisors must not act surprised at whatever low level of preparation or skill is shown by teachers they supervise. Supervisors can work with teachers only after developing a trusting relationship and then allaying all the teachers' fears that exposure of their difficulties will have unpleasant repercussions.

Supervision should be available to all teachers, not just the new, the inexperienced, and the ineffective. Supervisors can be of help to experienced and effective teachers, too. Those who are capable and see themselves as capable tend to welcome suggestions and advice and go out of their way to seek new ideas. These are the teachers who urge supervisors to drop in to watch them teach and discuss teaching. These teachers are completely at ease when supervisors, administrators, and colleagues step into their classrooms and observe. Some enjoy the experience of demonstrating to others that they are effective teachers. These teachers can serve as demonstration models for others to observe and might form a corps of mentor teachers who can be asked to work with new teachers just entering the profession.

Supervisors should be concerned with helping teachers not only overcome their deficiencies but also grow, develop, and build on their strengths. Supervisors can help the better teachers by offering suggestions about proven practices drawn from visits to other classrooms and personal experiences. They can assist more able teachers by introducing them to new publications and materials that feature promising practices these teachers have not had a chance to examine. In some ways, supervisors may get "better mileage" from suggestions they make to more able teachers than from those they offer to the less able. Because they possess the self-confidence to surmount failures, more able teachers do not fear failure of a new plan or technique. Cooperative, able teachers are a joy to the supervisor.

The supervisor has to prioritize. One priority—to concentrate on troubleshooting—yields short-term results but does little over the long term. If leadership is to be given in improving instruction, the supervisor must do more than troubleshoot; he or she must work with individuals and groups in developing the curriculum and improving instruction. Supervisors and teachers together must study goals, means of reaching the goals, and ways of evaluating what they have accomplished, a process that requires considerable time. The supervisor must achieve some balance between short-term and long-term projects. There must also be balance in workload between helping teachers individually and working with them in groups. The supervisor cannot give complete attention to one individual who has a problem but rather has to devise ways to handle both individuals and groups. Just as the teacher cannot follow a single strategy and expect all learners to be successful as a result, the supervisor cannot use the same approach with every teacher or group of teachers but must work in keeping with the strategies of situational supervision.

Ideally, supervisors should provide help to all teachers, experienced and inexperienced, effective and ineffective, although, of course, they will need to spend more time with the inexperienced and ineffective.

ISSUE 3: Should the Supervisor's Authority Be Based on Expertise and Interpersonal Relationships or on Conferred Status and Decision-Making Responsibilities?

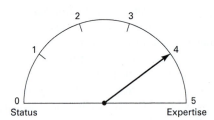

Authority is derived from various sources. Although we tend to think of conferred power as the only source of authority, many leaders actually derive their authority from an ability to influence other people. A role is prescribed either directly or indirectly for each position in an organization. With each role go certain expectations. Power to varying degrees undergirds positions so that leaders may fulfill their role expectations. Thus, role expectations are often met because of the power attached to them.

Some leaders, however, fulfill their roles without resorting to the use of power. These leaders, by the force of reason, persuasiveness, and personality, can achieve their goals without exerting power and flaunting status. They would be able to perform their duties even if the props of power and status were removed.

Other leaders, lacking the ability to reason, to demonstrate vision, or to relate to other people must fall back on bestowed power to get their tasks done. Some of these leaders spend more time preserving the authority of their office than solving the problems of the organization.

Robert J. Alfonso, Gerald R. Firth, and Richard F. Neville posited that the status and power conferred on the supervisor by the organization are necessary if he or she is to be effective.[5] In considering this issue, we must distinguish between line supervisors (administrators) and staff supervisors. Line supervisors, like the assistant superintendent, the principal, and the assistant principal, possess certain powers conferred on them through law and state and local regulations; staff supervisors possess only those powers narrowly prescribed by regulation and by the administrator. The staff supervisor's power is greatly circumscribed. One need only look at a school system's table of organization to realize that supervisors are not high in the power structure; as a result, their jobs are not high-status positions. We believe, however, that the staff person who serves as instructional supervisor needs neither conferred power nor exalted status. Supervision, like teaching, has an importance of its own.

Line supervisors (administrators) can fall back on power and status if they need to enforce their orders. The staff supervisor cannot command nearly as much power. That is not to say that the supervisor has no power. In fact, supervisors work in the delegated power of the administrator and the organization. Teachers may follow a supervisor's direction because they perceive supervisors to possess powers that, in reality, the supervisors do not have.

In the next section, we will examine the issue of whether the supervisor should be an administrator. At this point, however, we need to decide whether supervisors should seek to use the limited powers they may have, call on the administrator's power, or convey the impression of possessing derived administrative powers in fulfilling their roles.

William H. Lucio and John D. McNeil maintained that the authority of office and influence cannot be separated and that there are times when supervisors must use the authority of their position.[6]

Resorting to authority of office, however, can interfere with helping teachers. If the teacher fails to respond to the supervisor's directions and the supervisor resorts to using power, this action implies punishment of some kind and creates a threatening climate. Like most human beings, teachers perform more effectively in a nonthreatening environment.

Wayne K. Hoy and Patrick B. Forsyth saw formal authority and status as getting in the supervisor's way:

> Supervisors are staff—master teachers. They are expected to provide advice and support to colleagues, not to discipline them. The staff position has little formal authority; authority is primarily informal and earned—arising from the supervisors' expertise and personal skills. Teachers must have confidence in those to whom they turn for help, and trust can more readily be built when status distinctions among supervisors and teachers are limited. In fact, formal authority and status can be dysfunctional for supervisors as they seek to establish colleague relationships. Such status distinctions are likely to curtail authentic interactions and productive problem solving because they hinder social support and restrict and distort communication of information.[7]

Numerous studies have shown that if teachers seek help at all—and many do not[8]—they want the supervisor to demonstrate the type of expertise that will help them in the classroom.[9] They also expect the supervisor to be able to develop rapport with them and to work with them in a cooperative way.

It probably does not matter to teachers whether the supervisor possesses power if he or she is able to help them do their jobs better. If the supervisor is able to provide teachers with the help they need, he or she will not find it necessary to call on power. Of course, in the case of the hopelessly incompetent teacher, as contrasted with the ineffective teacher, the supervisor will not be able to help. In this situation, then, the supervisor should use whatever power he or she has to remove the incompetent teacher from the classroom.

ISSUE 4: Should the Supervisor Be an Administrator?

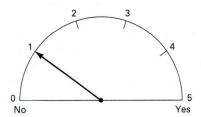

In Chapter 1, we noted the uncertainty and ambiguity surrounding the question of whether the supervisor should be an administrator and vice versa. Administrators by the very nature of their positions have supervisory responsibilities, and in recent years those responsibilities have increased because of the decrease in the number of staff supervisors. Unfortunately, many administrators are not able to give primary attention to the main purpose for which schools have been established—instruction of the students. They are too busy with meeting state standards, record keeping, plant maintenance, personnel management, scheduling, auxiliary services, public relations, and other assigned responsibilities.

On the surface, we can distinguish between administration and supervision. William H. Burton and Leo J. Brueckner described the difference in the following way:

1. Administration is *ordinarily* concerned with providing material facilities and with operation in general.

2. Supervision is *ordinarily* concerned with improving the setting for learning in particular.

3. Administration and supervision considered *functionally* cannot be separated or set off from each other. The two are coordinate, correlative, complementary, mutually shared functions in the operation of educational systems.[10]

Although administration may be distinguished from supervision, an ongoing controversy centers on whether supervision *should* be an arm of administration. In a small school, where the principal has no assistants and no supervisory help from the central office, the principal *must* serve as both administrator and supervisor. On the other hand, where additional supervisory resources exist, distinctions in roles and functions can be made. Still, the question remains of whether supervisors should be administrators. On one side of the issue are those who view supervision as a fundamental appendage of administration. On the other side are those who would divorce supervision from administration. Some fifty years ago, Harold Spears stated the issue clearly, pointing out the lack of success in resolving the problem:

> Ever since supervisors were added to school management, there has been a concerted attempt to draw a line of demarcation between administration and supervision, between the job of administering and that of supervising. But this campaign for strict interpretations is still far short of its goal, for those who have dared to set the stakes have reached no common agreement.[11]

The issue remains with us. Historically, supervision has been part of administration. In the first edition of their textbook titled *Supervision of Instruction: A Phase of Administration*, Glen G. Eye and Lanore A. Netzer defined supervision as "that phase of administration which deals primarily with the achievement of the appropriate selected instructional expectations of educational service."[12]

James P. Esposito, Gary E. Smith, and Harold J. Burbach have created a four-part taxonomy of the supervisor's role that encompasses both administrative and supervisory responsibilities. Their taxonomy is reproduced in Table 2.1.

Only in recent years has supervision branched out from its parent, administration. In the early years of our country, supervision was decidedly one of the functions of the administrator—the person with status and power. Thus, the administrator was the person with superior vision about education and it was he (early administrators were universally males) who hired, directed, demanded, inspected, examined, and dismissed.

From the mid-1950s to the present, specialists in supervision have been inclining toward reducing the supervisor's administrative roles—some on philosophical grounds, some on the basis of role definition, and some for the very practical reason that supervisors have too much to do when they take on administrative as well as supervisory duties.

Underscoring the conflict and tension between administrative and supervisory functions, Hoy and Forsyth proposed a differentiated model of supervision in which administrative and supervisory roles are distinct but complementary.[13]

The problem might be resolved if the administrator would assume more of a supervisory role and turn over to assistants some managerial aspects of running a school system. However, most administrators are unwilling to relinquish management responsibilities. They may, therefore, concentrate on administrative and operational matters and delegate responsibilities for curricular and instructional leadership to a subordinate. Or they may call in outside help—specifically, staff members who are able to perform the supervisory roles the supervisors cannot fill.

The question is not so much whether administrators should assume supervisory tasks, because they already do this to one degree or another and they already possess responsibility for supervision—especially the summative part of the supervision process. Rather, the question is whether supervisors should assume administrative tasks and responsibilities. Should the administrator require or permit a person charged with leadership in curriculum and instructional development to perform administrative duties? Should teachers recognize the supervisor as one who has direct line authority over them, determines promotions, passes

TABLE 2.1 Taxonomy of the Supervisory Role

Helping role		Administrative role	
Factor I indirect service to teachers	**Factor IV direct service**	**Factor II administrator**	**Factor III evaluator**
• Plan and arrange in-service education programs and workshops	• Assist in the orientation of new and beginning teachers	• Coordinate instructional programs	• Plan and arrange in-service education programs and workshops
• Participate in in-service education programs and workshops	• Assist teachers in the location, selection, and interpretation of materials	• Assist in the evaluation and appraisal of education programs	• Participate in in-service education programs and workshops
• Coordinate instructional programs	• Visit and observe in the classroom	• Perform routine administrative duties	• Assist in the evaluation and appraisal of school programs
• Assist in the orientation of new and beginning teachers	• Teach demonstration lessons	• Participate in the formulation of policy	• Arrange intersystem visitations to observe promising practices
• Assist teachers in the loacation, selection, and interpretation of materials	• Hold individual conferences with teachers	• Engage in public relations	• Arrange intrasystem visitations to observe promising practices
• Collect and disseminate current curriculum materials		• Work with citizens' or lay groups	
• Collect and disseminate current curriculum materials		• Arrange intersystem visitations to observe promising practices	
• Develop curriculum designs and coordinate curriculum improvement efforts			
• Assist in the development of curriculum guides and other publications			
• Assist textbook selection committees			
• Develop and prepare new instructional media			
• Assist in the evaluation and appraisal of school programs			

Source: James P. Esposito, Gary E. Smith, and Harold J. Burbach, "A Delineation of the Supervisory Role," *Education* 96, No. 1 (Fall 1975): 66. Reprinted with permission of *Education*.

on salary increments, decides on retention, makes decisions on expenditures for materials and equipment, and determines specifications for construction of new facilities teachers will use?

Should supervisors think of themselves as administrators? If administrative authority is not delegated to the supervisor per se, should the supervisor act as the agent of the administrator who reports back to the administrator? Are the supervisor and administrator in cahoots, so to speak? Is the supervisor the administrator's alter ego when setting foot in the teacher's classroom?

If we conceive of supervision as service, it is difficult to see how supervisors can maintain rapport with teachers if teachers perceive them as people who control their destinies. For supervision to be successful, teachers must want the services of the supervisor and value the *trusting relationship* that must exist between them. They must feel that the supervisor is there to serve them and to help them become more effective teachers.

We find ourselves in a real dilemma with respect to rating teacher effectiveness, an issue discussed more fully in Chapter 13. Should the supervisor rate teachers and, having rated them, report to the administrator? What does this do to the trusting relationship? When this happens, what does it do to the teachers' willingness to call on the supervisor for help and to reveal their inadequacies?

Central-office administrators often require staff supervisors to perform administrative tasks, such as rating teachers. By their close proximity to the superintendent (frequently sharing office space in the same building), they fall heir to administrative duties they might not have if they were housed away from the center of administrative power. The supervisor, as a subordinate, cannot refuse to accept assigned administrative duties. The fact that supervisors must accept such tasks prompts the suggestion—perhaps impractical—to house central-office supervisors away from the administrator's headquarters.

Teachers would understand such a move as affirming that staff supervisors are really employed primarily to help them and not to assist the administrator. Although such a move might not appeal to supervisors who see themselves as administrators, those who see themselves as service-oriented people might welcome it. We might hypothesize that supervisors who maintain they have no time to visit schools and are unduly loaded with paperwork see themselves as administrators rather than as supervisors. They have become involved in administrative decision-making activities assigned to them by the administrator or assumed on their own initiative.

To take the extreme position that the supervisor must never accept administrative tasks would be unrealistic. Sometimes the administrator requires the supervisor to fulfill administrative duties. At other times, as in the case of teacher evaluation, the supervisor is in the most advantageous position to assess performance and to suggest remedial measures to teachers.

Today's supervisors need to emphasize supervisory behavior and to deemphasize administrative behavior. Unfortunately, some supervisors enjoy being near the center of power without sharing the responsibilities borne by the administrator, just as there are also supervisors who seek to join the ranks of the administrators. Like many teachers, some supervisors are administrators-in-waiting, looking forward to the day when they might be able to trade in their staff job for a line position. In contrast, those supervisors who view instructional leadership as their career will try to keep their administrative responsibilities to a minimum.

ISSUE 5: Is Supervision Staff Development?

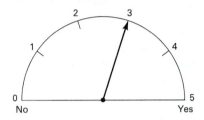

In this book, staff development is conceptualized as one of the three domains of supervision (refer back to Figure 1.4). It is not, however, as it appears to be in some school systems, the sole domain. As was shown in Figure 1.4, the role of the supervisor involves instructional development, on which there is little or no controversy; curriculum development, on which there is disagreement; and staff development, on which there is also argument.

In large school systems, more than one person may be employed to carry out the multiple tasks of supervision. Their responsibilities may range across all three domains, or individuals may devote themselves entirely to one or two domains. There are, for example, directors of staff development, directors of curriculum development, and directors of both staff and curriculum development. These directors are often subordinate to an assistant superintendent for curriculum and/or instructional development.

If supervision is a service designed to help teachers become more effective so that their students will benefit, then staff development is an important domain of supervision. Staff development should focus on the professional growth of those involved in the activities.

Many people equate staff development with in-service education. Lloyd W. Dull, for example, used the terms *in-service education* and *staff development* synonymously. He defined in-service education as "the sum of all activities designed for the purpose of improving, expanding, and renewing the skills, knowledge, and abilities of staff personnel."[14]

Ben M. Harris took the position that a distinction should be made between staff development and in-service education. He divided staff development into two aspects: staffing and training. The staffing aspect he viewed as the assignment of the best qualified person to a task. The training aspect he separated into in-service education and advanced preparation. By *in-service education* he meant "any planned program of learning opportunities afforded staff members of schools, colleges, or other educational agencies for purposes of improving the performance of the individual in already assigned positions."[15] Advanced preparation, according to Harris, is training for a different and higher position.

Donald C. Orlich also saw staff development as subsuming in-service education. Explaining the difference, Orlich said:

> Whereas in-service education is oriented toward immediate training objectives, staff development implies persistent and personally significant activities. In essence, staff development subsumes in-service education projects and also addresses the larger issue of developing organizational problem-solving capacities and leadership skills. The totality of building human and institutional resources in the organization becomes the goal of staff development.[16]

Not only is *staff development* often equated with *in-service education*, it is also sometimes used interchangeably with *instructional development*. We would address this notion by saying that instructional development or improvement is one hoped-for result of staff development. Although we concede that *staff development* is a somewhat broader term than *in-service education*, we still view the terms as virtually synonymous. We define in-service education as a program of organized activities for both groups and individuals, planned and carried out to promote the personal and professional growth of staff members—in this case, teachers. (In Chapter 9, we discuss the supervisor's role in staff development.)

Instructional development is part of staff development; it consists of those staff-development activities that focus directly on the improvement of instruction—for example, perfecting testing techniques. Instructional development focuses on *instructional* design, implementation, and evaluation. We do not include within the concept of instructional development those staff-development activities that aim primarily at the personal growth of the teacher, such as helping teachers learn to demonstrate empathy, to be more cooperative in group settings, and to treat parents courteously and professionally.

Because we are examining the specialized field of supervision, our discussion emphasizes activities that are organized and planned by the supervisor. We would be remiss if we did not note that a good deal of staff development is much less structured; it is planned and engaged in by individual teachers for their own self-improvement.

As we shall see when we consider issue 6, we encounter a question with curriculum development similar to the question of distinguishing between staff development and instructional development. Staff-development activities relate to curriculum development when they consist of organized, planned activities for groups or individuals that focus on curriculum design, implementation, and evaluation.

In effect, staff development, instructional development, and curriculum development flow into each other. To paraphrase Gertrude Stein, we might say that staff development is instructional development is curriculum development is staff development . . . ad infinitum. Each pair of domains is like a pair of conjoined twins; it is very difficult and sometimes impossible to separate them. Perhaps we need not separate them if we are aware of the general extent and limitations of each. In any case, supervisors should have staff development high on their agenda.

ISSUE 6: Is Supervision Curriculum Development?

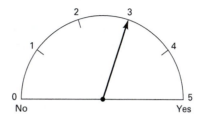

When supervisors help teachers, either individually or in groups, make decisions about programs as opposed to methods, they are working in the domain of curriculum development. As curriculum leaders, supervisors direct teachers in the study of scope and sequence, of balance, and of articulation.[17] When they chair curriculum councils or serve as resource persons to them, supervisors engage in curriculum development. When they direct a curriculum needs assessment involving students, teachers, administrators, and parents, they are exerting curriculum leadership. Supervisors are in the curriculum arena when they help faculties try out innovative programs such as learning centers, integrated thematic instruction, remedial laboratories, increased use of technology, and continuous progress or nongraded.

Helping teachers make decisions about programs can be a full-time job. The scope of curriculum development is so vast that supervisors once committed to the domain may never leave. There is constant need for review and revitalization of the curriculum to keep it current with rapidly developing knowledge.

Those who feel that people who direct or coordinate curriculum are not really supervisors point out that these staff people spend so much time in curriculum development, running from school to school and group to group, that they never have time to get into the classrooms where the real action is. In that situation, teachers who desperately need help with improving instruction go without assistance. Because some supervisors put all their eggs in the curriculum basket, those who believe that students would benefit more if supervisors worked in a clinical setting, on a one-to-one basis with classroom teachers, may reject curriculum development as a domain of supervision.

Yet programmatic decisions must be made daily and continually, and those decisions are usually difficult and complex. They call for knowledge of the research and intelligent deployment of human and physical resources. They require a match between the school's philosophy and its practice, and they must be accompanied by an appropriate evaluation plan.

Groups must be assembled to study ramifications of curriculum problems, make recommendations, and translate plans into operation. Leadership is essential for successful completion of these tasks.

We could argue about whether it would be better for school systems and for education in general to limit supervision exclusively to one domain or to provide attention to two or three domains. But in the absence of conclusive evidence that doing so would yield a better product, we would risk the result of doing a respectable job in one area while neglecting the other areas. Consequently, we believe supervision must be provided in all three domains. Whether we would assign supervisors to each one or whether all supervisors would work in all domains is not the major question. Supervision becomes questionable when the supervisory staff, no matter how large or how small, restricts itself to one area, whether it is staff development, instructional development, or curriculum development.

The supervisory job can be done in all three domains by (1) choosing priorities carefully, (2) managing time wisely, (3) placing energies where they will be of most benefit, and (4) making better use of personnel, even if they have to be trained on the job. School systems are making better use of assistant principals, department heads, curriculum resource teachers, team leaders, grade coordinators, and teachers themselves in the roles of coaches and mentors. In addition, many teachers who have achieved certification from the National Board for Professional Teaching Standards are serving as coaches and mentors. These people could be of enormous help to administrators, curriculum directors, and other instructional supervisors.

Supervisors must set their objectives, manage their time, and direct their energies to enhance their efficiency. Some supervisors, because of the scope of their responsibilities, make the mistake of moving frantically at top speed from one problem to another without asking whether the problem is serious, without delegating authority and responsibility for its resolution, and without completing one task before they leap to the next.

A review of the literature on supervision reveals many specialists who include curriculum development within the responsibilities of the supervisor. John T. Lovell and Kimball Wiles asserted that "supervision is curriculum development ... an important function of instructional supervisory behavior."[18] Kathryn V. Feyereisen, A. John Fiorino, and Arlene T. Nowak stressed curriculum change in their book *Supervision and Curriculum Renewal: A Systems Approach.*[19] Lucio and McNeil assigned a large leadership role in curriculum development for the supervisor. In a chapter on curriculum planning and change titled "Strategies and Tactics for Program Improvement," they wrote, "the public relies on supervisors who possess certain professional competencies to present to the elected representative body definite recommendations for improving the curriculum for children and youth."[20] Morris Cogan, however, narrowed the definition of supervision to clinical supervision, which focuses on ways of helping teachers improve their performances in the classroom. Cogan labeled all supervisory activities that occur outside the classroom as "general supervision."[21] However desirable it might seem to throw all of the supervisory forces into staff development and/or instructional development, we believe the supervisor must continue to function in curriculum development, too.

ISSUE 7: Is Supervision Evaluation?

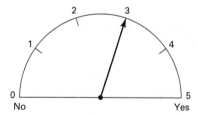

Whenever one individual makes a judgment of any kind about another individual, he or she is engaging in evaluation. It makes little difference whether that judgment is called *assessment, appraisal,* or *evaluation.* The issue of whether supervision is evaluation touches on four questions that you have already encountered: What is the purpose of supervision? Is supervision administration? Who should carry out supervisory functions? What is the role of the principal in supervision?

Those who maintain that supervision is not evaluation are thinking in terms of a process involving observation of the teacher's classroom performance for the purpose of helping the teacher improve instruction without the necessity for making personnel decisions. We would call this type of supervision *consultative* or *formative evaluation.*

In contrast, those who see supervision in terms of evaluation have in mind administrative assessments based on data obtained both within and outside the classroom for purposes of making personnel decisions, such as contract renewal, tenure, merit pay, teaching assignments, and placement on a career ladder. We would call this type of supervision *administrative* or *summative evaluation*. Whether consultative or administrative, evaluation is always present.

Gary Embretson, Ellen Ferber, and Terry Langager drew a clear line between supervision and evaluation:

> Supervision and evaluation are quite distinct from one another and this distinction is recognized. Supervision is a developmental process which promotes continuing growth and development of staff members in the art of teaching; continued and increased staff motivation; and an improved instructional program. Evaluation on the other hand is a management function designed to maintain organizational efficiency; establish standards for staff performance; and appraise staff performance.[22]

They described a process wherein the supervisor would "*observe* performance in order to improve it (supervision) and *judge* performance on the basis of accepted criteria of good teaching (evaluation)."[23]

G. H. Fredrich, too, saw supervision and evaluation as different concepts. "Too often the terms *evaluation* and *supervision* are used synonymously when, in fact, they represent different concepts. Supervision is a formative, supportive approach to improving teaching competence: evaluation is a summative process that should culminate a period of supervision."[24] Fredrich added that the responsibility for supervision and evaluation should rest with different personnel; that department heads, supervisors, consultants, and colleagues should take primary responsibility for supervision, whereas the principal should handle evaluation. Using secondary school principals as an example, Fredrich commented:

> The principal's role as evaluator is well established, but what about his role in supervision? In many jurisdictions one of the stated primary expectations of a principal is to be a curriculum leader. If this role description were consistent with the practice, then the principal would play a primary part in teacher supervision. However, whether by choice or time restrictions, few principals at the secondary school level can claim that their primary function is to act as curriculum leaders.
>
> Nor is this undesirable. I believe that the principal would be much more effective as a *coordinator of supervision*.[25]

Thomas A. Petrie, on the other hand, maintained that contemporary practice in schools refutes the belief that supervision and evaluation are incompatible. He believed that principals do and should have the responsibility for supervision and evaluation: "The principal is the person in the best position to orient new teachers to the needed instructional skills, observe instruction, provide information about the instructional repertoire, arrange opportunities to improve, and to make evaluation judgments."[26]

If the purpose of supervision is to help teachers improve their performance and if the data collected are not used for making personnel decisions, supervision is less an evaluation process. We say "less" because supervision can never be completely free of this dimension.

If the purpose of supervision is the collection of data for making decisions about a teacher's career, supervision is an administrative evaluation process. If a staff supervisor carries out the supervisory task and does not supply the data for personnel decisions, supervision is a consultative evaluation process. If a line supervisor (administrator) performs the supervisory function, the element of administrative evaluation is always there, for the data can, will, and should be used in making personnel decisions. However, if a trusting relationship has been developed between the school administrator and the teachers, they can expect to only see comments and observations written on the formative evaluation forms or the summative evaluation form.

If a staff person serves as the supervisor, the evaluation can be formative in nature—that is, assessment of progress for the purpose of diagnosing difficulties and suggesting remediation during the course of the year. If a line administrator, such as a school principal, serves as the supervisor, the evaluation may be formative as well as summative, culminating in an annual written evaluation of the teacher's performance. In many school systems this appears to be the trend. What disturbs some people—and rightfully so we believe—is that supervision is sometimes perceived as summative evaluation only, with little or no effort at formative evaluation.

John C. Daresh spoke to this point when he said,

> Educators often assume that *educational supervision* is virtually synonymous with *evaluation*—that supervisors do little more than evaluate teachers and curricular programs. ... To be sure, a strong relationship exists between supervision and evaluation. Supervisors *do* have a responsibility to carry out evaluation ... evaluation is simply one important aspect of the effort to match individual human abilities with organizational goals, objectives, and priorities, and we will try to defuse the notion that educational evaluation automatically and necessarily involves evaluation of the teaching staff for the purpose of making employment decisions.[27]

Evaluation, then, is an integral part of supervision, because supervisors will unavoidably collect data on teacher performance. The key is what is done with the data. Supervisors, being human, do more than process data; they analyze and interpret it and render judgments, which is the essence of evaluation. When a supervisor decides, for example, that a teacher needs help with certain skills, he or she is engaging in evaluation.

Those who argue that supervision is not evaluation would have us separate the helping relationship from the administrative dimension. As discussed later in this book, certain approaches to supervision do emphasize the helping relationship and deemphasize the administrative function.

ISSUE 8: Should Supervisors Work with Groups of Teachers or with Individual Teachers?

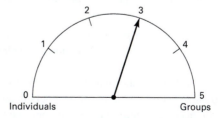

Supervisors must decide repeatedly whether their time is best spent with groups of teachers or with individual teachers who need and want their help. As much as our sentiments lean to the individual side of the scale, our judgment counsels us that such an orientation is not practical. Individualization of supervision cannot imply assisting all or even most teachers in a school system on a one-to-one basis, because very few school districts have either the funds or the personnel to do so.

Traditionally, supervisors have worked with groups of teachers in an in-service mode with workshops, conferences, and the like. In Edward Pajak's analysis of the role of the central-office supervisor of curriculum and instruction, it is striking how often supervisors, at least at the central-office level, work in and with groups of one kind or another.[28]

The work of a number of specialists in recent years in the field of clinical supervision has brought this issue to the forefront. These specialists encourage us to move the pendulum toward the individual side of the scale, but both group and individual work have advantages, as shown in the lists that follow.

Working with groups has the following merits:

1. It is less costly in terms of the supervisor's time and effort (e.g., it eliminates excessive travel from classroom to classroom).
2. It is a more efficient use of resources. For example, it would be foolish to offer individual teachers training in the classroom use of computers and other types of technology.
3. Supervisors will be less likely to experience burnout if they do not have to repeat learning experiences for teachers individually.
4. Some activities necessitate group decisions, as in the case of curriculum proposals.
5. Some activities require the efforts of more than one person, as in conducting a curriculum needs assessment for a school system.
6. Some activities are inherently group-oriented and cannot achieve their objectives if attempted on an individual basis, such as training in group dynamics.

Individualized supervision also has advantages:

1. It meets the special needs of the individual teacher (i.e., it is tailor-made supervision).
2. It demonstrates the supervisor's personalized interest in the teacher.
3. If it meets the teacher's needs, it overcomes some of the hostility teachers often feel toward group sessions.
4. If conducted properly, it permits teachers to reveal inadequacies without fear of exposure.
5. It allows more trusting, personal relationships to build between the supervisor and teacher—relationships that cannot develop in a group setting.

Unless we are talking about very small schools with a handful of teachers, adequate individualized supervision for all teachers is unlikely to occur. As a result, some compromises are necessary. Supervisors can continue to spend more than half their time working with and through groups. They can provide individualized help to those teachers who call for it, those teachers for whom administrative assessments reveal deficiencies, and inexperienced teachers who need help initially. Although effective, experienced teachers would often welcome individual help that would contribute to their professional development, time in most school systems does not permit supervisors to render a great deal of that aid. We may lament that fact, but it is perhaps fortunate that not all teachers seek help, for if they did the demand would exceed the supply of helpers.

Therefore, supervisors must plan for a judicious mixture of both group and individual activities. They can often plan training that combines both features—for example, group instruction in learning about a particular subject or teaching strategy followed by observation and advisement in the classrooms of those teachers who participated in the group training session. This type of follow-up usually has good results. From the standpoint of cost-effectiveness, school administrators show partiality to group-oriented supervisory activities, because they want as much "bang for the buck" as possible.

We laud school systems that have effective programs of supervision that are completely or predominantly individualized. But recent trends in supervisory practices and available financial resources make it clear that supervisors will have to devote most of their time to working with groups and only the balance to helping teachers on an individual basis. Even if this weren't the case, an effective program of supervision would still consist of a combination of both group and individualized activities.

ISSUE 9: Should Supervision Be Carried Out by Supervisors Based in the Central Office or in the Individual School?

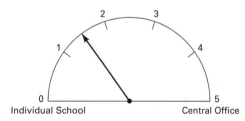

In practice today, supervisory services to the local schools are furnished by supervisors who are headquartered at one of four locations: (1) the state level, (2) an intermediate level between the state and local school, (3) the school district (central-office) level, or (4) the individual school level.

State Level

Education is one of the powers reserved to the states by the Tenth Amendment to the U.S. Constitution. In principle, the state has the authority to manage and supervise all public schools within its boundaries. For practical and political reasons, however, with the notable exception of Hawaii, states choose not to oversee the daily operations of their school systems. Though some may disagree, state education officials largely restrict their roles to activities they can handle with a degree of efficiency.

State Departments of Education Instructional supervision from the state level is extremely limited. Leaders from the state department of education may direct research studies, supervise state assessments of student achievement, and help define statewide educational goals. They may assemble groups to work on statewide curricular and instructional issues and problems. Examples of such activities include reviewing and recommending textbooks and related materials, identifying minimal competencies for high school graduation, and specifying important generic teaching competencies. State-level supervisors may organize groups to write curriculum guides, which unify the scope and sequence of disciplines and which can be (though are not necessarily required to be) used throughout the state. Some state departments of education offer limited consultative help to local school systems.

State supervision is often of an administrative rather than an instructional nature, as in checking compliance with state-mandated programs. Instead of being broadly based, if it is provided at all, state supervision concentrates on the concerns of the moment indicated by the state legislature, the state board of education, or the state department of education. Examples of these issues might be prekindergarten programs, early childhood education, language arts, mathematics, and NCLB proficiency standards.

Learning Resource Systems The various states, through federal funding, have created agencies known as learning resource systems. These are part of a nationwide network of special education resource centers.

Each state network, made up of a number of centers, is a teacher support system for people working with children who have special needs. Georgia, for example, maintains sixteen centers within its network. These centers, which come under the jurisdiction of the Georgia Department of Education, provide a number of services to special educators, including the ones listed here:

1. Maintenance of instructional materials, which may be borrowed on a short-term basis for diagnosis, teacher training, and children's use.
2. In-service training of teachers.
3. Sponsorship of innovative projects.
4. Dissemination of information.
5. Help with diagnosis and referral.

Practically speaking, the state level is too far removed from the scene to be of significant supervisory help to teachers and schools directly and consistently. We must look to lower levels for the more important types of supervisory services.

Intermediate Level

The intermediate level of school organization and administration is a veritable maze. No other organizational structure within American education so vividly shows the effects of decentralization as this level, with its multifarious permutations and commutations.

Most of us are aware that responsibility for education in America rests with the states. The prevailing pattern of school administration within a state has, at the highest level, some type of state board of education to which an appointed or elected state commissioner or superintendent is responsible. Local school districts are under the direction of this commissioner or superintendent. Each local school district has a local school board and is administered by a superintendent who is responsible to the local board. Both the superintendent and the local board may be elected by the people or appointed. (When superintendents are appointed, it is generally by the local board; if the local board is appointed, it may be by a grand jury or other such body.) Both the superintendent and the local board serve as agents of the state.

As noted, however, this basic pattern may be expressed in a variety of ways, some of which are described in the following two sections ("County Superintendents" and "Cooperative Educational Service Agencies").

County Superintendents   Thirteen states administer schools (K–12) through the county-unit system. In those states, the school district is congruent with the political entity called a county. County-unit school systems are governed by a county school board and administered by a county school superintendent. The models for the county-unit system vary state by state. Florida, for example, is divided into sixty-seven counties, each of which has a county superintendent and board who exercise jurisdiction over all public schools in the county. One of these is Dade County, the largest county in Florida. With more than 20 incorporated communities within its borders (including populous Miami), close to 400 schools, some 20,000 teachers, and more than 350,000 students, this county gets along with only one school board and one superintendent of schools. Holmes County, in the rural panhandle of Florida, likewise has one board and one superintendent to govern its 8 schools, some 250 teachers, and more than 3,000 students. Each Florida county is a single school district. County-unit school systems of this type are local school districts, not intermediate units.

The pattern in Georgia, another county-unit state, is slightly different. In Georgia, there are 180 school districts, of which 156 are county units and 24 are city districts. The city districts operate independently from the county units.

Outside the county-unit states, the patterns of school organization vary widely. Hawaii forms a single school district. Illinois has close to 893 school districts (out of some 14,559 nationally). In an Illinois community you can find an elementary school district and a secondary school district, each with its own board, administrators, faculties, and facilities.

We must explore the positions of county superintendents to understand the county unit. County superintendents come in three main varieties. First, there is the *county* county superintendent. These are the superintendents of schools in the thirteen states that have the county-unit system. They are elected by the people or hired and fired by the local school board, and they are responsible to the local board. We have little difficulty understanding this species of county superintendent: he or she heads a local school district whose boundaries are coterminous with those of the county.

Second, there is the *state* county superintendent. The state of New Jersey has complicated the picture of the intermediate unit with county superintendents appointed by and responsible to the state commissioner.[29]

Third, there is the *intermediate* county superintendent, once a plentiful but now a dying species. The intermediate county superintendency has a long history. This official functions somewhere between the state level and the local school level. His or her jurisdiction, as in the case of New York State, may not be coterminous with the county boundaries. In cases where these administrators' territories expanded beyond the confines of a county, they were often called *intermediate district superintendents*. (In other cases, the intermediate units were smaller than the counties and were called *townships*; these formed intermediate units prior to the establishment of the county superintendency.)

What is important for our purposes is to remember that the intermediate county superintendent has fewer powers than the *county* county superintendent or the *state* county superintendent. The intermediate units are by-products of a rural society. Although the functions of the intermediate unit are undergoing study and change in the states where they exist, the typical intermediate unit does not manage schools or programs; it does not hire and fire teachers; it does not mandate curricula, provide transportation to students, or handle disciplinary problems. Its traditional mission is to furnish the local districts with services they cannot afford or choose not to perform themselves. Among these services are centralized purchasing of supplies, pupil testing, school health, reporting, research, and what interests us most, curriculum development, staff development, and instructional supervision.

Cooperative Educational Service Agencies   Over the years, the intermediate units have undergone transformation. The intermediate unit in New York State, for example, evolved from deputy superintendent appointed by a county board of supervisors to town superintendent, to elected county superintendent, to supervisory district superintendent, to district superintendent hired by a district board of school directors, to district superintendent selected by a board of cooperative educational services (i.e., a cooperative educational service agency).

Cooperative educational service agencies encompass wide service areas. In New York, the Board of Cooperative Educational Services (BOCES) provides service through some 38 centers to most of the over 700 local school districts of the state.

Cooperative educational service agencies are funded by the state or through a combination of state and local money. In New York, the BOCES unit is administered by a district superintendent who serves as executive officer of the district board of cooperative educational service. At the same time, the BOCES superintendent reports to the state commissioner of education.

Emery Stoops, Max Rafferty, and Russell E. Johnson suggested that local school districts could look to the intermediate units for the following services:

1. Direct supervision of classroom teachers (which diminishes as school districts grow larger).
2. Coordination of area programs among districts.
3. In-service education of certificated and classified personnel.
4. Preparation of communication and publication aids.
5. Adoption and preparation of courses of study.
6. Provision of audiovisual, library, educational TV, and other materials or programs.
7. Consultant help with pupil personnel services.
8. Operation of federal programs, such as Title III (Elementary-Secondary Education Act [ESEA]), and assistance to districts that apply for federal programs under the several titles of ESEA.
9. Cooperation with business and industry to improve vocational education.
10. Scoring, interpreting, and summarizing standardized testing.

11. Furnishing leadership toward innovations such as flexible scheduling, programmed instruction, team teaching, Head Start and preschool education, collective bargaining or professional negotiation, continuing education in business and industry, citizenship, and skills in human relations.

12. Coordination and cooperation with problem departments, law enforcement agencies, legislative committees, character-building organizations, and community support groups.[30]

The intermediate level provides a considerable amount of instructional supervision. What we have said about supervision from the state and intermediate levels is a prologue to consideration of the heart of issue 9: whether local school districts should make use of central-office supervisors or assign supervisors full time to individual schools.

A related issue, which time and space do not permit us to discuss, is whether supervision should be provided by the intermediate unit or by the local school districts. Is service from the intermediate unit the only way small school systems can conduct supervisory programs? Can only the larger and wealthier local school districts establish their own staff, curriculum, and instructional development programs?

Local School Districts

An example of the organization of a large urban school district is shown in Figure 2.2. This figure depicts the organization of the public school system in Brevard County, Florida. Each of the four area superintendents supervises a large number of administrators/coordinators in a variety of disciplines and specialties (i.e., subject areas). These administrators/coordinators assume leadership for program development in their assigned fields. As such, they represent a typical staffing pattern for a large school system.

The effective central-office supervisor must be an itinerant staff member, which means that he or she cannot spend a great deal of time with any one teacher or in any one school. He or she will more likely concentrate on working with groups than with individual teachers.

Neagley and Evans outlined the major duties of the K–12 central-office subject-area coordinator:

1. Visits classrooms and works with teachers from K–12 on instructional and curricular matters peculiar to the discipline or subject area.

2. Includes teachers in decision making and change.

3. Works with the principals and coordinators of elementary and secondary education in a staff relationship and shares particular knowledge and competence as needed.

4. Reports to the assistant superintendent and informs this person of the developing curriculum and new trends and research in the area of specialization.

5. Chairs the district curriculum committees in the discipline or subject area.

6. Makes recommendations to the appropriate officials of instructional and curricular materials and resources.

7. Works closely with the appropriate curriculum consultants in the intermediate unit office or the regional curriculum center, and keeps abreast of the latest research and trends in the field.

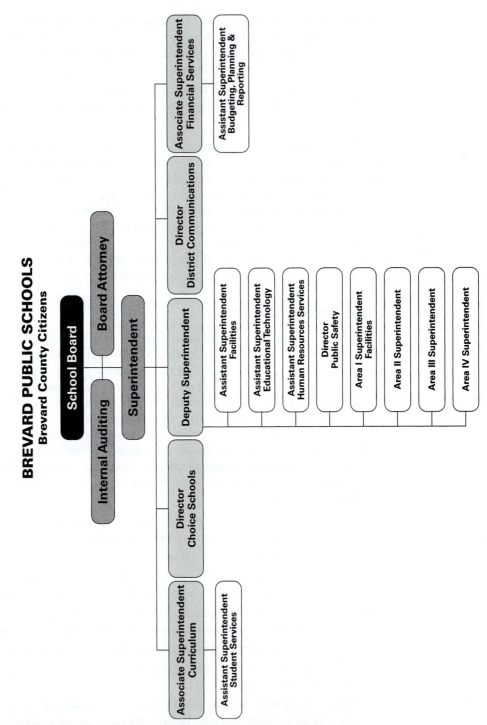

FIGURE 2.2 Table of Organization, Brevard County, Florida, Public Schools. *Source:* Brevard County Public Schools, Viera, Florida. Reprinted with permission of the Brevard County Public Schools.

8. Conducts parent and community meetings for the lay public and interprets the latest methods and content in the subject area.

9. Prepares written materials for the lay public on topics related to the discipline.

10. Participates actively in the sessions of the curriculum council, especially when the coordinator's area of concern is on the agenda.

11. Meets and works with the other subject-area coordinators, under the leadership of the assistant superintendent in charge of instruction, in order to develop a balanced curriculum.[31]

In his study, Edward Pajak confirmed the variety of responsibilities of the central-office supervisor. He noted that

> the responsibilities of central office supervisors, curriculum coordinators, and directors of instruction may be described without exaggeration as being extremely diverse and global. ... While no two job descriptions are exactly the same, those associated with supervisory positions typically include instruction-related tasks, such as coordinating the educational program, ensuring continuity in the kindergarten-through-twelfth-grade curriculum, supervising curriculum planning and development, coordinating program evaluation at the district level, coordinating staff supervision and evaluation, identifying staff development and in-service needs of teachers, planning for staff meetings and workshops for the improvement of instruction, and selecting and recommending textbooks and other teaching materials.[32]

Pajak observed that many other duties required of central-office supervisors go beyond instructional responsibilities into administrative and management activities: collecting information, writing reports, managing budgetary tasks, and engaging in public relations.[33]

Historically, instructional and curricular supervision at the individual building level has generally been very limited throughout the country. Most supervisory service within school systems has come from the central office. Until recent years, the small amount of supervision that can be identified as an individual school activity has been carried out by the principal or assistant principal, occasionally with the help of lead teachers, curriculum resource teachers, team leaders, grade coordinators, and department heads.

The lead teacher is a newer position roughly equivalent to a school-based curriculum coordinator. Many schools are employing lead teachers, curriculum coordinators, and resource personnel as members of the staff.

Team leaders, grade-level coordinators, and department heads are, as a rule, allocated so little released time for supervisory duties that their roles in supervision become meaningless. As noted earlier, these leaders represent a reservoir of talent that should be developed and put to use in a supervisory capacity. Some Florida elementary principals have added curriculum resource teachers (CRTs) to their faculties. Teachers in these assignments generally are certified to be administrators but fill a major role in helping teachers improve instruction or in assisting with other classroom concerns.

Arthur J. Lewis and Alice Miel proposed a solution to the central-office versus individual school issue by separating responsibilities for curriculum leadership and instructional leadership. They suggested that central-office supervisors should carry heavy responsibility for curriculum development, whereas the staff of the individual school should concentrate on instructional development:

> The separation of curriculum and instruction lends itself well to this view of a useful sharing of responsibility and authority between central office and semi-autonomous individual schools. Certain kinds of curricular decisions may be made at the school system level in the interests of a broad range of young people. The decisions may be refined and implemented or greatly modified at the building level where those to be educated can be known quite well.
>
> Initiative for curriculum change can be exercised by anyone at any level and provision for coordination makes it more likely that innovative ideas will be shared. Responsibility for instruction clearly belongs in the individual school.[34]

John T. Lovell observed that if we separate curriculum leadership from instructional leadership we might designate the two categories of personnel "curriculum supervisors" and "instructional supervisors."[35] Although the notion of separating curriculum from instruction may be appealing and can be done for purposes of analysis, we find it extremely difficult to do in practice.

Decentralization of authority and responsibility for the operation of schools has gained in popularity in recent years. State direction and power over local schools have increased in recent years as states have mandated student promotion and graduation standards. For example, the state legislature of Florida considered a proposal made by the commissioner of education and endorsed by the governor to suspend some state mandates for a period of three years and allow local schools to devise their own plans for meeting state goals. Florida public schools have seen their destinies controlled by decisions made at the school level but designed to meet state standards and expectations.

In a similar vein, in keeping with the philosophy of such influential educators as John I. Goodlad, who saw the school as the unit for improvement, more responsibility has shifted from the school district level to the individual school level.[36] The movement toward allowing parents to choose their children's schools, whether public or private, may well impel schools further toward school-based management, as competition among schools increases and faculties strive to make their schools more effective. At the same time, pressures are growing for "empowering" teachers—that is, granting them the right to share in decision making.[37] If empowerment is to become reality, shared decision making will need to take place at the individual school level.

In recent years, administrators have recognized the value of school-based management. School-based supervision is a necessary result of school-based management, with the individual school staff accepting responsibility for bettering the school's programs and for helping teachers improve instruction. In this approach, school principals, supporting staff, and teachers all join forces to promote the school's goals.

Although figures documenting an increase in the number of school-based supervisors are not available, figures do reveal that many schools are supplementing their administrative staff with resource persons, consultants, coordinators, and teachers on special assignment as instructional supervisors. This decrease at the district level does not necessarily mean that the increase in school-based supervisors has come about at the expense of central-office supervisors. Central-office supervisory positions are often the first to be terminated when school systems must make budget cuts. The public prefers to see more resources where their children are—in the individual schools.

Lack of clarity about the central-office supervisor's role also creates problems. Pajak observed, "The absence of a clear conception of the role makes the position of central-office supervisor vulnerable when resources are scarce, but it is tenuous even in prosperous times."[38]

The use of school-based supervisors—in recent years, the school principal or assistant principal—offers several advantages. They are on duty in the school building full time. They can devote all of their energies to assisting teachers or to delegating that helping responsibility to someone else at the school. They can respond to teachers when they are needed, and they can serve as the schools' designated leaders in curriculum and instruction.

Although schools cannot and should not duplicate the kinds of supervision the central office can provide, school systems do need to find additional ways for individual schools to create their own supervisory programs in conjunction with central-office assistance. What is needed is a well-planned team approach that carefully divides supervisory responsibilities between central-office and individual school staff, with a somewhat heavier share of the responsibility falling on the supervisors of the individual school. Both central-office and individual school personnel should work in all three domains of supervision: instructional development, curriculum development, and staff development.

In passing, we should observe that the department head of the secondary school is in a precarious position. The department head is often perceived as a member of the administrative team even though he or she is also a teacher. Despite contractual limitations, department heads can still be available to assist teachers at their request and can work with them on an informal basis. Such an approach might be even more productive in the long run than the traditional department head function.

Significant developments that can greatly and effectively expand supervisory services on the local school level are the movements toward use of teachers as coaches to their peers and of experienced mentors to assist less experienced teachers. These collegial practices in supervision are discussed later in Chapter 10.

ISSUE 10: Should the Supervisor Use a Directive or Nondirective Approach?

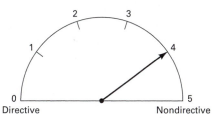

Should the supervisor adopt a directive or a nondirective approach to working with teachers? Is it the supervisor's mission to tell teachers how to go about their tasks, or does the supervisor attempt to effect change through persuasion and example?

Some supervisors see their role as highly directive and so prescribe content, materials, and techniques for teachers to follow. Others prefer more indirect methods of helping teachers come to their own decisions.

A nondirective approach in supervision is similar to the nondirective approach followed by guidance personnel and psychologists. The nondirective counselor refrains from claiming to know the answers, thereby allowing the client to express his or her own concerns and ideas. Often the teacher merely wants the reassurance that the supervisor is in a position to give. The teacher wants help in thinking through problems and wishes to try out solutions on a person whose judgment can be trusted. An effective supervisor is ready with suggestions for a teacher to consider, knowing that it is up to the teacher to accept the suggestions and incorporate them into his or her behavior.

Of course, teachers expect the supervisor to be of help and to have some answers. But they do not always expect to receive the "right" or "approved" or "only" answers; they want the freedom to feel that their own solution to an instructional problem can be as good as or better than the supervisor's solution.

Teachers can argue with the nondirective supervisor who serves as a sounding board but not with the directive supervisor, the one who tells them what and how they must teach. We are raising a basic question in human relations: Are people motivated to change, cooperate, and work effectively by being told what to do? In the case of supervision, can we tell highly trained professionals how to teach and expect effective change?

Even the administrator who possesses legal or other authority to tell, demand, or order finds that in dealing with people a cooperative approach is far more effective in most cases than a hard-nosed approach.

A hard-nosed administrator says, "You must do this because I say so," and may fall back on status and legal authority for enforcing compliance. Individuals commonly react to this type of highly directive approach in one of several ways: (1) They may comply with the administrator's wishes because they happen to be in accord with them and choose to ignore the manner in which they have been made known. (2) If they take issue with the directive manner of an administrator, they may (and probably will) still comply, though in a sullen, resentful way. (3) They will do just enough to meet the minimal requirements of the administrator's edict. (4) They will be superficially cooperative and deeply uncooperative.

Still another type of individual may simply throw in the towel and withdraw from teaching in body or spirit. The creative teacher who feels compelled to accept the administrator's or supervisor's prescribed methods down to the last detail may despair and give up teaching entirely. Others silently ignore edicts, remain in teaching, and resign themselves to the knowledge that their reluctant behavior will lead to penalties for them in assignments, recognition, salary, and promotions.

Of course, administrators should have the authority to be directive when they need to be. If a teacher proposes an activity that might be dangerous to the bodies or minds of students, the administrator has not only the right but the duty to be directive. Teachers recognize this authority as necessary to the administrator's job. It is more often the manner of the administrator than the actual requests that antagonize teachers.

Those supervisors who behave in a highly directive fashion are more likely to perceive supervision as a function of administration than are those who behave in a nondirective fashion. Directive supervisors tend to see themselves as line administrators rather than as staff service personnel.

If a supervisor is not an administrator, he or she does not have the implied sanction of status and legal position to be prescriptive. To effect change, the prescriptively oriented supervisor must then appeal to the administrator to make teachers see things the supervisor's way. If the supervisor frequently appeals to the administrator's authority to effect change, the supervisor then becomes aligned in the teachers' minds with the administrator and is no longer perceived as a service-oriented person whom they can count on, confide in, and trust. The supervisor has destroyed what needs to be maintained—rapport with the persons to be served and assisted.

"Have you ever thought of . . .?" "Why don't you try . . .?" and "What would you think of . . .?" are much better ways to phrase suggestions to a teacher than "Do it this way," "Never mind your way," and "It is required." It is a basic psychological principle that individuals will go out of their way to comply with a directive they feel they have helped formulate, about which they have made a choice. Whether they indeed had a choice is not nearly as significant as whether they feel that they did. They need to feel also that it is not just the beliefs of one individual that necessitate their compliance with requirements in curriculum and instruction, but that compliance is in the best interest of all concerned— the students, the community, and colleagues.

Blumberg contrasted direct and indirect approaches in supervision, noting the effects of each style:

A supervisor using predominantly direct behavior might well be assuming that:

- The control of a situation is based on the authority of one's position in an organizational hierarchy.
- People in higher organizational positions have more expertise.
- People in lower organizational positions can best be evaluated by those who are higher.
- The most important external rewards of a job come to a person primarily from a person who holds a higher position.
- Empathic listening to the teacher is not a necessary dimension of helping.
- People learn best by being told what to do by someone in a higher organizational position.
- Work is rational; there is little place in supervision for discussion of feelings or interpersonal relationships.
- Collaborative problem solving between supervisor and teacher is not a critical concern in supervision.
- Teaching as a skill can generally be separated into the right and wrong ways of doing things.

The assumptions about people that appear to accompany a supervisor's heavily loading indirect behavior are that:

- Control of the situation depends on the demands of the problem. The problem determines the direction that events take.
- Expertise is a function of knowledge and experience, not necessarily of organizational position.

- The product of a teacher's work is the best evaluative tool to use in measuring his performance.
- The important rewards of teaching are intrinsic to the job, but they need to be supplemented by external rewards.
- People learn best by being confronted with a situation and, with help, finding their own solution.
- It is important for teachers to feel that they have been listened to and understood.
- Work is both rational and emotional; that discussion of feelings and interpersonal relations may be as important as discussion about the job.
- Collaborative problem solving between supervisor and teacher is an important concern of supervision.
- Teaching is a complex process and what works well for one person may not for another, so that most of what goes on in a classroom needs to be viewed experimentally.[39]

Supervisors who follow a nondirective approach treat teachers as intelligent, professional, and valued persons. Room must be left, however, for a directive approach under two circumstances: (1) when a teacher's actions may be detrimental to students, to other faculty, to the program, or to the school; and (2) when the teacher wants or responds only to directive supervisory behavior. Some teachers prefer the direct approach. They want to be told what to do. They feel that a nondirective approach wastes their time and the supervisor's. Furthermore, some teachers believe that a nondirective approach is a subtle way of manipulating them.

Carl D. Glickman referred to a third approach, which he termed *collaborative*. This approach is neither directive nor nondirective, or conversely, it is *both* directive and nondirective, on the parts of both the teacher and the supervisor. In collaborative supervision, the supervisor and teacher work together and take turns at listening, analyzing, and making suggestions.[40] It is the supervisor's task to use an individual approach adapted to each teacher's style. We examine directive, collaborative, and nondirective approaches more closely in Chapter 10.

ISSUE 11: Should School Systems Organize for Supervision by Employing Generalists or Specialists?

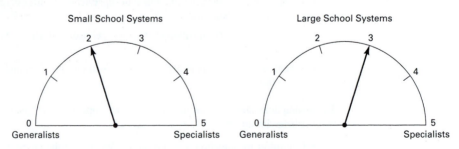

The chief school administrator—the superintendent—must make some difficult decisions on what qualifications to look for in hiring supervisors and on how to use personnel.

The superintendent must decide how many supervisors and what kind will be needed and develop a plan for organizing supervision in the district.

Because the employment of specialized personnel will have to be justified to the public, the administrator will have to offer strong reasons for adopting supervisory programs, particularly if they entail a sizable staff. The patterns of organization that are adopted will have to conform to the available resources and other limitations of the school district.

Granted the freedom to adopt whatever pattern of organization seems wisest, the superintendent must decide on the kinds of personnel desired: director of instruction, consultants, coordinators, and so forth. But perhaps more basic than the kinds and titles of supervisory personnel is a question that has been debated inside and outside supervision circles for many years: Should the superintendent employ generalists or specialists to perform the supervisory functions?

Characteristics of Generalists and Specialists

The generalist may be described as a supervisor who has responsibilities for supervising teachers in a number of grades or in a variety of subjects. Possessing expertise and experience in at least one teaching field, the generalist may (and usually does) supervise in areas in which he or she has not had special training or has had no training at all. A generalist should be an expert at teaching who knows what constitutes good general teaching methods. Each generalist, for example, can recognize a good classroom environment, knows when a teacher is presenting a lesson well, and can judge the effectiveness of planning.

The generalist understands learning theory, is conversant with principles of evaluation and measurement, understands the use of audiovisual materials, has a good background in resources and materials, and knows how and where to locate additional sources.

The generalist has a broad view of curriculum and can compare what teachers in various grades, classes, subjects, and schools do. The generalist supervisor can assist the teacher with problems of discipline and may be able to help the teacher develop counseling techniques. The able generalist also has a good overall knowledge of curriculum and instruction. By helping teachers of different grades and subjects work together, this leader can serve as a unifying force.

Generalist supervisors possess such titles as assistant superintendent of curriculum and instruction, director of instruction, director of elementary education, director of middle schools, director of secondary education, and general supervisor. In recent years, school principals and assistant principals have been viewed as part of this group.

The specialist supervisor has depth of preparation and experience in a particular level or subject. Each such supervisor not only knows the level or subject thoroughly but also is abreast of modern techniques and the latest trends in teaching.

A specialist possesses some of the same knowledge and skills as the generalist. He or she understands learning theory and can help a teacher with discipline, classroom climate, and guidance. The specialist's forte lies in his or her ability to relate principles and techniques to a particular grade level or subject area.

The specialist can help a teacher apply techniques of evaluation to a particular subject or can discuss the use of audiovisual materials with the teacher in relation to a specific grade

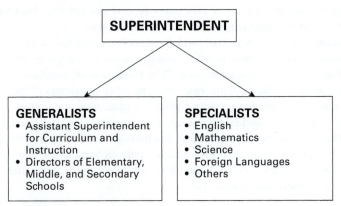

FIGURE 2.3 Generalist and Specialist Supervisors at the District Level.

or field. Planning is considered with the teacher in relation to a specific field rather than in relation to abstract principles of planning.

The specialist knows sources of specific materials useful to teachers and can help them detect and correct mistakes made in teaching particular topics. The specialist has a more limited view of curriculum and instruction than the generalist, because he or she works within one area and provides narrow, in-depth supervision. Specialist supervisors bear such titles as supervisor of language arts, supervisor of science, coordinator of foreign languages in the elementary school, consultant in social studies, and English resource teacher.

A typical arrangement for generalist and specialist supervisors at the district level appears in Figure 2.3. At the school level, a typical arrangement might show the principal administering a supervisory staff composed of one or two generalists, with team leaders, grade coordinators, or department heads performing the roles of specialist supervisors (see Figure 2.4).

Should teachers be supervised by generalists or specialists? Which type of supervision is the most effective? This is one of the more difficult questions to answer.

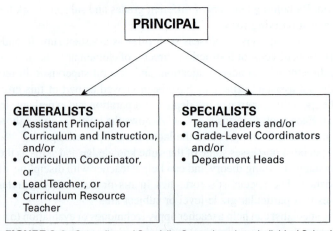

FIGURE 2.4 Generalist and Specialist Supervisors in an Individual School.

Both types of supervision are found throughout the country. Although some school systems provide the services of both generalists and specialists, others must limit their choice to one or the other.

Because they normally have limited financial resources, small school systems tend to employ generalists who can work in a number of areas and across grade levels. Thus the general supervisor is a common position in those small school districts that can afford the services of a supervisor. In a large school system with greater financial resources, however, the choice may be open to the superintendent, and the chief school officer must decide whether to provide supervisory help through general supervisors or special supervisors, or both. As fiscal resources continue to become more limited, the decision is generally in favor of hiring more generalists.

There are certainly roles for both generalists and specialists in school supervision. A school system that can afford the services of a full staff of both generalists and specialists is fortunate.

The critical problem arises when a school system must choose one type or the other. The superintendent's philosophy and the wishes of teachers will loom large in solving this problem. At the elementary level, because most elementary classrooms are self-contained, the superintendent may wish to begin a supervisory program by using generalists, who can work very effectively at the elementary school level. They have a breadth of knowledge that corresponds to that of training provided for elementary school teachers.

Need for Specialists

Even elementary teachers, however, are increasingly in need of help from specialists. Mathematics, science, and reading programs have posed problems both for teachers and for general supervisors who are not trained in the latest techniques of these programs. Instructing exceptional children, along with including these children in regular classrooms, teaching foreign languages, and implementing programs of bilingual and multicultural education, have created the need for specialized supervision. General supervisors often lack the depth of training to help teachers write objectives, select appropriate methods, and evaluate results in these specialized fields. They may work effectively in the more generic phases of the program, such as language arts, social studies, or humanities. Probably they feel more at home supervising in fields for which they have had preparation and experience, and this may lead them to minimize or omit assistance to teachers in some critical areas of the school's program.

As school systems move into newer programs and patterns of curriculum organization, the need for special supervisors becomes increasingly clear. Whereas an elementary school might get along satisfactorily with the use of generalists, we believe it is imperative today to provide specialists in supervision at the middle and secondary levels. Content and methods have changed—and will continue changing—so rapidly that no generalist can possibly keep up with the changes in all fields.

What school systems really need are specialists who are, in effect, generalists, or conversely, generalists who are, in effect, specialists. A specialist who is well trained should have had at least the usual preparation in principles of effective teaching. Each will ordinarily have had work in the foundations of education and should be able to identify a suitable learning environment as readily as a generalist. The specialist should recognize the necessity for teachers to maintain rapport with their students. From prior training and experience, the specialist should know principles of discipline, evaluation, and counseling.

Most generalists are also specialists. They have responsibilities in a number of areas and have depth in one or two. They can fulfill the coordinating function of generalists while at the same time providing skillful supervision in one or two fields.

Generalists such as the director of instruction may assume some responsibilities for coordinating the work of specialists. They may devote their energies to working with groups of specialists from different fields. The specialists may then work with individual teachers and groups of teachers in the same field.

Little (if any) solid research exists on the relative merits of using generalist or specialist supervisors. In any case, both kinds of supervisors must be competent and easy to work with as they help teachers achieve the goal of improving instruction.

Some Parallels

The issue of generalist versus specialist is encountered in other situations within and outside the profession of education. Universities continue to wrestle with this problem in providing faculty supervision of student teachers. Some teacher-training institutions have set up their programs in such a way that more generalists than specialists supervise student teachers at all school levels.

It is easier to employ generalists than specialists, and it is easier for a university to administer a student-teaching program in which supervision is conducted by generalists. Generalists are in larger supply, are easier to schedule, and can be used more flexibly.

Outside the field of education, medicine has long since resolved the question of generalist versus specialist in favor of specialists over general practitioners. With the mighty strides made in medicine, it has become extremely difficult for the general practitioner to keep up to date in all fields of specialization. Medicine, however, has preserved a role for the generalist. The medical profession's solution to the generalist versus specialist dilemma parallels to some extent the education profession's answer, using generalists who refer particular problems to specialists.

How then shall we organize for supervision? Shall we provide wide-sweeping supervision or supervision in depth?

ISSUE 12: Should There Be National Professional Standards for Teachers?

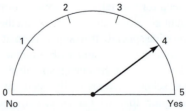

If we are to raise the level of school performance, one important action we can take is to strengthen classroom teaching. That is the purpose of the National Board for Professional

Teaching Standards (NBPTS). NBPTS is a private, nonprofit organization formed in 1987 as a result of a recommendation from the Carnegie Forum on Education and the Economy. The sixty-three-member governing board oversees the program to establish high and demanding standards for what accomplished teachers should know and be able to do as they teach. The NBPTS also wants to develop and operate a voluntary national system to assess and certify teachers who meet those standards.

The philosophy behind NBPTS certification is expressed in five core propositions:

- Teachers are committed to students and their learning.
- Teachers know the subjects they teach and how to teach those subjects to students.
- Teachers are responsible for managing and monitoring student learning.
- Teachers think systematically about their practice and learn from experience.
- Teachers are members of learning communities.

Standards that cover subject matter and the developmental age of students have been developed by committees of teachers and other experts. The standards serve as the basis for the twenty-four certification areas for National Board Certification.[41]

Increasing support for the NBPTS mission is coming from federal legislation, the Council of Chief State School Officers, state and local school districts, and contracts negotiated between teachers and local school boards. The negotiated contracts allow reimbursement for NBPTS fees and/or a salary increase or special endorsement as lead teacher based on this national certification. Major education organizations, including the National Education Association, the American Federation of Teachers, the National Association of Elementary School Principals, the National Association of Secondary School Principals, and the American Association of School Administrators, are supporting the NBPTS's efforts. Financial support from private corporations and foundations has been increasing in recent years.

The first group of eighty-one teachers from twenty-three states to pass the Early Adolescence/Generalist certificate field test was announced in January 1995. They were among the larger group of 290 teachers who completed the rigorous national assessment exercises for that specific certificate.[42]

In August 1995, a second group of ninety teachers from twenty-three states received NBPTS certification in Early Adolescence/English Language Arts. These English language arts teachers of middle-grade students started as part of a larger group of 230 teachers seeking the certification. Additional certificates issued by the NBPTS focus on Exceptional Needs/Generalists in Early and Middle Childhood and Early Adolescence through Young Adulthood.[43] As of fall 2006, nearly 55,300 teachers held national certification in several areas.[44]

In 1998, the Florida legislature passed the Excellent Teaching Program Act of 1998. The act stipulated that the state would pick up 90 percent of the application fee for NBPTS certification. The law also provided teachers who achieved national certification with a 10 percent raise in salary as long as their certificate remained active, plus an additional 10 percent bonus if they mentored newly hired teachers or another teacher seeking NBPTS certification.

To be considered a candidate for NBPTS certification, a teacher must have a baccalaureate degree from an accredited institution; have three years of early childhood, elementary, middle, or high school teaching experience; and have held a valid state teaching license for each of those years. NBPTS certification differs from state licensure, sometimes referred to as certification, because a state license focuses on entry-level requirements for teaching in a state. NBPTS certification is designed to recognize experienced and accomplished teachers who practice at a superior level. Teachers are evaluated on knowledge of their subjects, understanding of students and teaching, and actual classroom practice.[45]

We believe the heart of education is teaching. Providing each student in our schools with the best teacher should be the focus of every supervisor working in those schools. Ensuring that the professionals working with the students are committed to the students and their learning is essential. It appears that one way of realizing the goal of developing a truly excellent educational system is through the NBPTS's efforts. Supervisors, school principals, school board members, and the general public need to continue to unify their efforts to support NBPTS in raising teaching standards to improve the quality of instruction in America's classrooms. The support can be financial (helping pay the board's fee, providing salary supplements, allowing the teacher participants paid professional leave) or can take the form of sharing information about the NBPTS standards, encouraging teachers to seek NBPTS certification, and offering incentives to participate in the process. Shapiro noted that Nettie Webb, a school principal and former NBPTS board member, observed that

> traditionally, the principal has been viewed as the instructional leader. But in today's schools, with their complex array of problems and diverse student body, this must be a shared role. Our promise to the community is to improve student learning. With a National Board Certified Teacher on the faculty, that promise can become a reality.[46]

ISSUE 13: What Should Be the Role of Technology in the Supervisory Process?

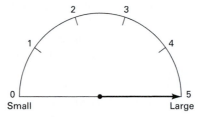

A case can be made for increasing or for excluding technology in the supervisory process. Just as it was not possible twenty years ago to predict the impact that the microcomputer would have on schools, it is probably impossible to predict what the most significant technologies will be ten years from now. It appears that technology to assist educators will continue to evolve at a rapid pace, offering educators an increasing variety of options for use in their instruction and their students' learning. Some teachers have reported that students of different abilities can be more easily paired up to use educational software on a computer to go beyond or reinforce classroom learning. Teachers who make the transition to using technology will become the "guide on the side" in the classroom rather than the "sage on the stage."

Supervisors' roles will change as they work with teachers who make this transition. First, they should initially encourage teachers to use technology to strengthen learning in the curriculum areas they are most comfortable teaching.[47] Teachers will need training in the basics of the technology, followed by ongoing one-on-one instruction in using the technology's more advanced features. The train-the-trainer approach to professional development has yielded significant changes in instruction in some school districts. The South Huntington Union Free School District on Long Island, New York, first trained the teachers who were most interested in technology.[48] These teachers held workshops at their schools and also worked one-on-one with their colleagues, activities that came about because of the leadership and continued support from the district's administrators and supervisors.

Supervisors will have to be aware of, and willing to support, teachers as they take time to rework their lessons to use technology effectively and experiment with new teaching styles. This is where the "service" and "help" aspects of the supervisor's role become prominent and where supervisory success will be dependent on the level of trust that has been established in the relationships with teachers.

"Integrated education works best," said Bernie Poole. "Computer-based teaching and learning is constructed on eight pillars of success." Poole's eight pillars are:

1. Active support must come from the top.
2. A nondictatorial approach is best.
3. Every school should have a core of teacher-computerists.
4. User-friendly technical support must be available, ideally onsite and on demand.
5. Teachers must come first.
6. Parents and students must be involved in the evolutionary process.
7. An ongoing technology training program must be in place.
8. Teachers must be given the time and freedom to restructure the curriculum around the technology.[49]

Supervisors will need to be actively involved in the process, advocates Poole.

Another important aspect of the supervisor's role with regard to the use of technology will be the support given to teachers who want to share what they are trying in the classroom with other teachers. The goal of administrators and supervisors should be to help teachers integrate technology into their teaching more than to help them teach students technology skills. Supervisors should support teachers who teach technology skills but within the context of academic lessons rather than as a separate subject.

Technological support for teachers should be available at the building level as well as the school district level. Teachers will react positively to the idea of using technology in their teaching if they know they will have the necessary equipment and overt support from administrators and supervisors. The supervisor's responsibility will be to advocate the use of technology in all the schools. Support must be mustered to get others to see that technology is changing and will have an expanding impact on how information is located and processed. Technology is increasing the number of sources that can be consulted beyond the textbook, the media center, or the immediate community to a network of worldwide resources that all students must be trained to access and use effectively. Helping teachers prepare to deal with these facts will be the supervisor's task. Technology and its many forms of media will assume a greater role in teaching, learning, and supervisory processes. Making these tools available to meet the needs of the teachers and students who must use them is the challenge supervisors face.

It is axiomatic that today's supervisors must themselves possess a high degree of proficiency in computer skills so that they can assist teachers who are less proficient, make professional staff development presentations, and carry out their own office tasks.

ISSUE 14: Should Multiculturalism Be a Focus of Supervision?

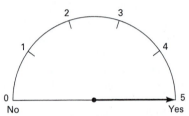

Few would argue against paying attention to multiculturalism or cultural diversity in the classroom. The increase in numbers and influence of minorities mandates recognition of the language, contributions, and cultures of children of varying ethnic and national origins. Demographic data show that the present white majority will in the not-too-distant future become a minority, as is now the case, for example, in Chicago, Miami, Los Angeles, Orlando, and other large cities; the numbers of minority students are growing in many other parts of the country.

Multiculturalism becomes controversial when the question includes the word *central*: Should multiculturalism become the *central* focus of teaching and therefore supervision? We can find advocates on each side of this issue because it evokes numerous curricular and instructional questions, such as:

1. Shall we offer bilingual education?
2. Shall we offer academic subjects in the students' native language?
3. Shall we give equal time to Christmas, Hanukkah, Kwanzaa, and other religious days?
4. Shall we stop overemphasizing the contributions of Western Europeans to American civilization?
5. Shall schools seek to preserve distinctions among ethnic and national groups at the expense of what used to be called "Americanization"?

The last question results, perhaps, in the greatest disagreement among the public. Into the early twentieth century, immigrants largely sought to adapt to American culture. Recent immigrants, in contrast, have sought to preserve their cultural roots both at home and in school.

For education, the issue of cultural diversity is often posed as: Should the curriculum of the public schools promote a vision of America as an assemblage of diverse cultures, sometimes referred to as a "salad bowl" concept, or should the curriculum strive to perpetuate the idea of America as a "melting pot," which blends cultures into a unified whole without diverse ethnic and national distinctions?

The melting pot concept has been the traditional approach of society and schools, but it presumes adoption of unifying behaviors and values, including the now-controversial predominance of the English language and subscription to the principles of the Declaration of Independence and the U.S. Constitution. The language issue has become polarized between the extreme of English only and the extreme of continuous instruction in a foreign language in academic subjects for speakers of other languages. Both the public and curriculum planners must ask for whom bilingual education should be offered. On the surface, the answer is simple: for those whose native language is not English. Beneath the surface, however, lies the problem of providing for the wide diversity of students whose native language is not English: Vietnamese, Chinese, Eastern Europeans, Central and South Americans, and so on. In practice, bilingual education has become to a large extent a Hispanic phenomenon, perhaps because Spanish speakers constitute by far the most numerous non-English-speaking minority.

Beyond bilingual education we can find dissension over supposed American values. For example, the once-hallowed documents, the Declaration of Independence and the U.S. Constitution, have themselves been under attack as racist (white Founding Fathers, some of whom were slaveowners), sexist and chauvinistic ("all *men* are created equal"), and ethnocentric (the Founding Fathers were primarily of Anglo-Saxon descent). The discoveries of Columbus have been decried as leading to exploitation of Native Americans, as an encroachment of Western Europe on the New World, and Columbus's achievements have been characterized as exaggerations.

Whereas Jeannie Oakes viewed the melting pot concept as "conformity to white Anglo-Saxon mores,"[50] Arthur M. Schlesinger Jr. cautioned that abandonment of George Washington's concept of *e pluribus unum* ("out of many, one") could result in "disintegration of the national community, apartheid, Balkanization, tribalization."[51]

Our position will not satisfy proponents of either extreme—that is, those who believe that multiculturalism must *dominate* the entire curriculum and those who believe there is no place for attention to cultural diversity. We would reject an either-or position. Certainly, increased attention must be paid to cultural diversity in the classroom. Emphasis on multiculturalism, however, shouldn't mean sacrificing attention to the overarching, unifying aspects of American culture.

Through staff development, the supervisor must help teachers demonstrate an awareness of cultural diversity and acceptance of this diversity as a positive value. They must help teachers develop curricula and instructional plans that accommodate the diversity represented in their particular classrooms. Perhaps the major challenge of multiculturalism lies in the fact that most of us have grown up in a single cultural environment with its own values and traditions and are in effect inexperienced and unschooled in the culture of other ethnic and national groups. Consequently, supervisors must involve members of various cultural groups to assist in the development of materials and experiences designed to educate teachers and to be used in the classroom.[52]

SUMMARY

In this chapter, we have explored fourteen issues in supervision:

- First, supervision is seen as a continuing and necessary service to teachers.
- Second, the supervisor can provide help to all teachers, whether they are experienced or inexperienced, effective or ineffective; but more time should be allocated to the inexperienced and the ineffective.
- Third, the supervisor's authority should be derived from expertise and interpersonal relationships.
- Fourth, the supervisor is likely to maintain a higher degree of rapport with teachers and render more effective service if he or she is not perceived as an administrator and does not perceive him-or herself in that role.
- Fifth and sixth, staff development and curriculum development are legitimate domains of supervision.
- Seventh, supervision encompasses two types of evaluation: formative, for the purpose of helping the teacher; and summative, for the purpose of making personnel decisions.
- Eighth, supervisors should work with both individuals and groups of teachers, with a somewhat greater allocation of time to working with groups.
- Ninth, supervision is best carried out by a judicious combination of central-office and individual-school supervisors, with greater weight given to the supervisory program of the individual school.
- Tenth, supervisors should, as a rule, use a nondirective approach in working with teachers.
- Eleventh, supervision requires the services of both generalists and specialists, with a slightly greater preponderance of specialists in the larger school systems that can afford them.
- Twelfth, supervisors should encourage teachers to achieve certification from the National Board for Professional Teaching Standards to assume the responsibility of mentoring new teachers.
- Thirteenth, supervisors should help teachers incorporate technology into the teaching/learning process.
- Fourteenth, as the cultural diversity of the students attending schools continues to increase, supervisors should help teachers incorporate multiculturalism into their approach to meet the needs of their students and to treat different cultures equitably in their teaching.

QUESTIONS FOR DISCUSSION

1. Which of the fourteen issues in supervision has the greatest impact on supervision in your school and school district?
2. Should a supervisor work primarily with inexperienced teachers or with experienced teachers? Defend your choice.
3. Should a supervisor work primarily with ineffective teachers or effective teachers? Why?
4. Should supervisors have had administrative experience? Why?
5. Should a supervisor spend the majority of time working with groups of teachers or with individual teachers? Explain.

ACTIVITIES FOR FURTHER STUDY

REFLECTIVE

1. For each of the fourteen issues discussed in this chapter, draw a scale similar to the one shown with each issue and draw an arrow that shows your position.

2. Find out what Ben M. Harris (*Supervisory Behavior in Education*, 3rd ed.) means by *tractive* and *dynamic* supervision.

3. Find out what Carl D. Glickman (see the chapter bibliography) means by developmental, directive, collaborative, and nondirective supervision.

4. Study the objectives of local chapters of the National Education Association and the American Federation of Teachers. How many of these objectives concern curriculum and instruction? How would the actions of these organizations affect the status and duties of supervisors?

5. Describe characteristics of ineffective teachers and state how you would work as a supervisor with ineffective teachers.

6. Select one characteristic of an ineffective teacher (identified in activity 5) and describe how you would help the teacher improve with regard to that characteristic.

7. Write a brief paper on one of the following questions:
   a. Should the supervisor of elementary education be a specialist or generalist? Why? Is there an area of specialization called elementary education?
   b. Should the supervisor of secondary education be a specialist or generalist? Why? Is there an area of specialization called secondary education?

8. Participate in small-group discussions in class on each of the fourteen issues examined in this chapter. Try to reach consensus on which issue is the most important, first in the small group and then with the class as a whole.

9. Cite one or more issues other than those discussed in this chapter and state your position on each.

APPLICATION

1. Interview several practicing supervisors and determine the types of teachers with whom they spend most of their time: new, inexperienced, experienced, effective, or ineffective.

2. Poll a group of teachers at the school level in which you are most interested and ask them whether they prefer help from generalists or specialists.

3. Poll a group of teachers to learn whether they believe that supervisors in their school system are directive or nondirective and ask them which approach they prefer.

4. Conduct a limited research study in a local school system to confirm or negate the hypothesis that experienced teachers are more effective than inexperienced teachers.

5. Talk with a sample of school principals and learn what percentage of their time is devoted to supervision of instruction. Determine whether they would prefer to spend more or less time on this task and why they gave the answers they did.

6. Interview one of the top administrators of the school system you know best and tape his or her comments and views on the role of supervisors on the staff. Among other things, ask how the administrator rates supervisors.

7. Obtain and analyze the staffing pattern of a school system you know well and write a critique of its strengths and weaknesses.

8. Learn whether your state has intermediate units and report on their organizational structure and the services they provide to local schools.

NOTES

1. Ross L. Neagley and N. Dean Evans, *Handbook for Effective Supervision of Instruction*, 3rd ed. (Englewood Cliffs, N.J.: Prentice Hall, 1980), p. 4.
2. See Susan Trimble, Ed Davis, and Marsha T. Clanton, "Working with Ineffective Teachers," *Principal Leadership* 4(3), 36–41.
3. Carnegie Foundation for the Advancement of Teaching, *The Conditions of Teaching, 1990* (Princeton, N.J.: Carnegie Foundation for the Advancement of Teaching, 1990), p. 12.
4. MetLife, Inc., *The MetLife Survey of the American Teacher, 2006: Expectations and Experiences* (New York: Metropolitan Life Insurance Company, 2006), p. 2.
5. Robert J. Alfonso, Gerald R. Firth, and Richard F. Neville, *Instructional Supervision: A Behavior System*, 2nd ed. (Boston: Allyn and Bacon, 1981), pp. 124–25.
6. William H. Lucio and John D. McNeil, *Supervision in Thought and Action*, 3rd ed. (New York: McGraw-Hill, 1979), pp. 26–27.
7. Wayne K. Hoy and Patrick B. Forsyth, *Effective Supervision: Theory into Practice* (New York: Random House, 1986).
8. Arthur Blumberg, *Supervisors and Teachers: A Private Cold War*, 2nd ed. (Berkeley, Calif.: McCutchan, 1980), pp. 19–20.
9. A. W. Sturges, *The Roles and Responsibilities of Instructional Supervisors* (Alexandria, Va.: ASCD Working Group on the Roles and Responsibilities of Supervisors, Association for Supervision and Curriculum Development, 1978).
10. William H. Burton and Leo J. Brueckner, *Supervision: A Social Process*, 3rd ed. (New York: Appleton-Century-Crofts, 1955), p. 85. Emphasis in original.
11. Harold Spears, *Improving the Supervision of Instruction* (Englewood Cliffs, N.J.: Prentice Hall, 1953), p. 27.
12. Glen G. Eye and Lanore A. Netzer, *Supervision of Instruction: A Phase of Administration* (New York: Harper and Row, 1965), p. 12.
13. Hoy and Forsyth, *Effective Supervision*, pp. 9–16.
14. Lloyd W. Dull, *Supervision: School Leadership Handbook* (Columbus, Ohio: Merrill, 1981), p. 110.
15. Ben M. Harris, *In-Service Education for Staff Development* (Boston: Allyn and Bacon, 1989), p. 18.
16. Donald C. Orlich, *Staff Development: Enhancing Human Potential* (Boston: Allyn and Bacon, 1989), pp. 5–6.
17. See Peter F. Oliva, *Developing the Curriculum*, 6th ed. (New York: Longman, 2005).
18. John T. Lovell and Kimball Wiles, *Supervision for Better Schools*, 5th ed. (Englewood Cliffs, N.J.: Prentice Hall, 1983), p. 143.
19. Kathryn V. Feyereisen, A. John Fiorino, and Arlene T. Nowak, *Supervision and Curriculum Renewal: A Systems Approach* (New York: Meredith, 1970), p. 15.
20. Lucio and McNeil, *Supervision in Thought and Action*, p. 155.
21. Morris Cogan, *Clinical Supervision* (Boston: Houghton Mifflin, 1973), p. 9.
22. Gary Embretson, Ellen Ferber, and Terry Langager, "Supervision and Evaluation: Helping Teachers Reach Their Maximum Potential," *NASSP Bulletin* 68 (February 1984): 27.
23. Ibid. Emphasis in original.
24. G. H. Fredrich, "Supervision and Evaluation: Recognizing the Difference Can Increase Value, Effectiveness," *NASSP Bulletin* 68 (November 1984): 12.
25. Ibid., p. 13. Emphasis in original.
26. Thomas A. Petrie, "Ideas That Hinder Education—Debunking the Myths," *NASSP Bulletin* 64 (December 1982): 53–54.
27. John C. Daresh, *Supervision as a Proactive Process* (White Plains, N.Y.: Longman, 1989), p. 195. Emphasis in original.

28. Edward Pajak, *The Central Office Supervisor of Curriculum and Instruction: Setting the Stage for Success* (Boston: Allyn and Bacon, 1989).

29. See Roald F. Campbell et al., *The Organization and Control of American Education*, 6th ed. (Columbus, Ohio: Merrill, 1990), p. 136.

30. Emery Stoops, Max Rafferty, and Russell E. Johnson, *Handbook of Educational Supervision* (Boston: Allyn and Bacon, 1975), pp. 72–73. See also Ralph B. Kimbrough and Michael Y. Nunnery, *Educational Administration: An Introduction*, 3rd ed. (New York: Macmillan, 1988), pp. 209–17.

31. Neagley and Evans, *Handbook for Effective Supervision of Instruction*, p. 107; adapted from Ross L. Neagley and N. Dean Evans, *Handbook for Effective Curriculum Development* (Englewood Cliffs, N.J.: Prentice Hall, 1967), pp. 137–38.

32. Pajak, *The Central Office Supervisor*, pp. 4–5.

33. Ibid., p. 5.

34. Arthur J. Lewis and Alice Miel, *Supervision for Improved Instruction: New Challenges, New Responses* (Belmont, Calif.: Wadsworth, 1972), p. 47.

35. John T. Lovell, "Instructional Supervision: Emerging Perspective," in Sturges, *Roles and Responsibilities*, p. 32.

36. John I. Goodlad, *A Place Called School: Prospects for the Future* (New York: McGraw-Hill, 1984), p. 31. Emphasis in original.

37. See Gene Maeroff, *The Empowerment of Teachers: Overcoming the Crisis of Confidence* (New York: Teachers College Press, 1988).

38. Pajak, *The Central Office Supervisor*, p. 3.

39. Blumberg, *Supervisors and Teachers*, pp. 88–89.

40. Carl D. Glickman, Stephen P. Gordon, and Jovita M. Ross-Gordon, *SuperVision and Instructional Leadership: A Developmental Approach*, 7th ed. (Boston: Allyn and Bacon, 2007), chap. 10.

41. National Board for Professional Teaching Standards Web site, www.nbpts.org, retrieved September 12, 2006.

42. Joanne Kogan Krell, Press Release: "National Board Recognizes First 81 Teachers Who Meet National Certification Standards" (Detroit, Mich.: National Board for Professional Teaching Standards, January 5, 1995).

43. National Board for Professional Teaching Standards Web site, www.nbpts.org/nbpts/nbct/index.html, retrieved September 12, 2006.

44. Ibid.

45. Joanne Kogan Krell, Press Release: "90 Teachers Nationwide Join Elite Group of Top Honorees" (Detroit, Mich.: National Board for Professional Teaching Standards, August 21, 1995).

46. Barbara Shapiro, *National Standards for Teachers: Streamlined Seminar* (Alexandria, VA.: National Association of Elementary School Principals, February 1995), vol. 13.

47. See Mary Ann Zehr, "Changing the Way Teachers Teach Away from the Chalkboard," *Education Week—Technology Counts '98* 18 (October 1, 1998): 41–43.

48. Ibid.

49. Bernard J. Poole and Lorrie Jackson, "The Eight Pillars of Successful Technology Implementation," retrieved August 2, 2006, from http://www.educationworld.com/a_tech/tech/tech188.shtml.

50. Jeannie Oakes, *Keeping Track: How Schools Structure Inequality* (New Haven, Conn.: Yale University Press, 1985), p. 26.

51. Arthur M. Schlesinger Jr., *The Disuniting of America: Reflections on a Multicultural Society* (New York: North, 1992), p. 118.

52. For fuller discussion of multicultural education, see James A. Banks and Cherry A. McGee Banks, *Handbook of Research on Multicultural Education* (New York: Macmillan, 1995). See also Peter F. Oliva, *Developing the Curriculum*, 6th ed. (New York: Longman, 2005), chap. 14.

BIBLIOGRAPHY

ALFONSO, ROBERT J., GERALD R. FIRTH, and RICHARD F. NEVILLE. *Instructional Supervision: A Behavior System*, 2nd ed. Boston: Allyn and Bacon, 1981.

ANTONELLI, GEORGE. "The Educational Warranty: Refocusing Teacher Education." *Kappa Delta Pi Record* 23 (Fall 1986): 16–19.

ASCD Working Group on Supervisory Practices. "Issues in Supervisor Roles: What Do Practitioners Say?" *Educational Leadership* 34 (December 1976): 217–20.

Association for Supervision and Curriculum Development. "Instructional Supervision: Trends and Issues." *Educational Leadership* 34 (May 1977): 563–618.

BANKS, JAMES A., and CHERRY A. McGeeBANKS. *Handbook of Research on Multicultural Education*, 2nd ed. San Francisco: Jossey-Bass, 2004.

BISHOP, LESLEE J. *Staff Development and Instructional Improvement: Plans and Procedures*. Boston: Allyn and Bacon, 1976.

BLUMBERG, ARTHUR. *Supervisors and Teachers: A Private Cold War*, 2nd ed. Berkeley, Calif.: McCutchan, 1980.

BURTON, WILLIAM H., and LEO J. BRUECKNER. *Supervision: A Social Process*, 3rd ed. New York: Appleton-Century-Crofts, 1955.

BUSHWELLER, KEVIN. "Other Voices: Listening to What Fellow Teachers, Parents, and Students Have to Say in Teacher Evaluation." *American School Board Journal* 185 (September 1998): 24–27.

CAMPBELL, ROALD F., LUVERNE L. CUNNINGHAM, RAPHAEL O. NYSTRAND, and MICHAEL D. USDAN. *The Organization and Control of American Schools*, 6th ed. Columbus, Ohio: Merrill, 1990.

Carnegie Foundation for the Advancement of Teaching. *The Condition of Teaching: A State-by-State Analysis, 1990*. Princeton, N.J.: Carnegie Foundation for the Advancement of Teaching, 1990.

CASWELL, HOLLIS L. "The Generalist—His Unique Contribution." *Educational Leadership* 24 (December 1966): 213–15.

COGAN, MORRIS. *Clinical Supervision*. Boston: Houghton Mifflin, 1973.

DARESH, JOHN C. *Supervision as Proactive Leadership*, 3rd ed. Prospect Heights, Ill.: Waveland Press, 2001.

DULL, LLOYD W. "Supporting New Teachers." Theme Issue. *Educational Leadership* 56 (May 1999): 7–95.

EMBRETSON, GARY, ELLEN FERBER, and TERRY LANGAGER. "Supervision and Evaluation: Helping Teachers Reach Their Maximum Potential." *NASSP Bulletin* 68 (February 1984): 27.

ESPOSITO, JAMES P., GARY E. SMITH, and HAROLD J. BURBACH. "A Delineation of the Supervisory Role." *Education* 96 (Fall 1975): 63–67.

EYE, GLEN G., and LANORE A. NETZER. *Supervision of Instruction: A Phase of Administration*. New York: Harper and Row, 1965.

EYE, GLEN G., LANORE A. NETZER, and ROBERT D. KREY. *Supervision of Instruction*, 2nd ed. New York: Harper and Row, 1971.

FEYEREISEN, KATHRYN V., A. JOHN FIORINO, and ARLENE T. NOWAK. *Supervision and Curriculum Renewal: A Systems Approach*. New York: Appleton-Century-Crofts, 1970.

FIRTH, GERALD R., and EDWARD F. PAJAK, eds. *Handbook of Research on School Supervision*. New York: Simon and Schuster Macmillan, 1998.

FREDRICH, G. H. "Supervision and Evaluation: Recognizing the Difference Can Increase Value, Effectiveness." *NASSP Bulletin* 68 (November 1984): 12.

GLANZ, JEFFREY, and RICHARD F. NEVILLE, eds. *Educational Supervision: Perspectives, Issues, and Controversies*. Norwood, Mass.: Christopher-Gordon, 1997.

GLICKMAN, CARL D. *Developmental Supervision: Alternative Practices for Helping Teachers Improve Instruction*. Alexandria, Va.: Association for Supervision and Curriculum Development, 1981.

GLICKMAN, CARL D., STEPHEN P. GORDON, and JOVITA M. ROSS-GORDON. *SuperVision and Instructional Leadership: A Developmental Approach*, 7th ed. Boston: Allyn and Bacon, 2007.

HARDY, LAWRENCE. "A Good Teacher Is Hard to Find." *American School Board Journal* 185 (September 1998): 20–23.

———. "Why Teachers Leave." *American School Board Journal* 186 (June 1999): 12–17.

HARRIS, BEN M. *In-Service Education for Staff Development*. Boston: Allyn and Bacon, 1989.

———. *Supervisory Behavior in Education*, 3rd ed. Englewood Cliffs, N.J.: Prentice Hall, 1985.

HASSER, WILLIAM J. *Predicting the Need for Newly Hired Teachers in the United States to 2008–09*. Washington, D.C.: National Center for Education Statistics, 1999.

HOY, WAYNE K., and PATRICK B. FORSYTH. *Effective Supervision: Theory into Practice*. New York: Random House, 1986.

KIMBROUGH, RALPH B., and MICHAEL Y. NUNNERY. *Educational Administration: An Introduction*, 3rd ed. New York: Macmillan, 1988.

KRELL, JOANNE KOGAN. Press Release. "National Board Recognizes First 81 Teachers Who Meet National Certification Standards." Detroit, Mich.: National Board for Professional Teaching Standards, January 5, 1995.

————. Press Release. "90 Teachers Nationwide Join Elite Group of Top Honorees." Detroit, Mich.: National Board for Professional Teaching Standards, August 21, 1995.

LANGDON, CAROL A. "The Fifth Phi Delta Kappa Poll of Teachers' Attitudes Toward the Public Schools." *Phi Delta Kappan* 80 (April 1999): 611–18.

LEWIS, ARTHUR J., and ALICE MIEL. *Supervision for Improved Instruction: New Challenges, New Responses.* Belmont, Calif.: Wadsworth, 1972.

LOVELL, JOHN T. "Instructional Supervision: Emerging Perspective." In *The Roles and Responsibilities of Instructional Supervisors*, chairman A. W. STURGES. Alexandria, Va.: ASCD Working Group on the Roles and Responsibilities of Supervisors, Association for Supervision and Curriculum Development, 1978.

LOVELL, JOHN T., and KIMBALL WILES. *Supervision for Better Schools*, 5th ed. Englewood Cliffs, N.J.: Prentice Hall, 1983.

LUCIO, WILLIAM H., and JOHN D. MCNEIL. *Supervision in Thought and Action*, 3rd ed. New York: McGraw-Hill, 1979.

MAEROFF, GENE. *The Empowerment of Teachers: Overcoming the Crisis of Confidence.* New York: Teachers College Press, 1988.

MARKS, JAMES R., EMERY STOOPS, and JOYCE KING-STOOPS. *Handbook of Educational Supervision: A Guide for the Practitioner*, 3rd ed. Boston: Allyn and Bacon, 1985.

MetLife, Inc. *The MetLife Survey of the American Teacher, 2006: Expectations and Experiences.* New York: Metropolitan Life Insurance Company, 2006.

MITCHELL, ROSALITA. "World Class Teachers: When Top Teachers Earn National Board Certification, Schools— and Students—Reap the Benefits." *American School Board Journal* 185 (September 1998): 27–29.

MOSHER, RALPH L., and DAVID E. PURPEL. *Supervision: The Reluctant Profession.* Boston: Houghton Mifflin, 1972.

National Board for Professional Teaching Standards Web site, www.nbpts.org/nbpts/nbctindex.html.

NEAGLEY, ROSS L., and N. DEAN EVANS. *Handbook for Effective Supervision of Instruction*, 3rd ed. Englewood Cliffs, N.J.: Prentice Hall, 1980.

OAKES, JEANNIE. *Keeping Track: How Schools Structure Inequality.* New Haven, Conn.: Yale University Press, 1985.

OLIVA, PETER F. *Developing the Curriculum*, 6th ed. Boston: Allyn and Bacon, 2005.

ORDOVENSKY, PAT. "National Certification Sounds Sweet All Right, but Will It Fly?" *Executive Educator* 12 (January 1990): 18–20, 30.

ORLICH, DONALD C. *Staff Development: Enhancing Human Potential.* Boston: Allyn and Bacon, 1989.

PAJAK, EDWARD. *The Central Office Supervisor of Curriculum and Instruction: Setting the Stage for Success.* Boston: Allyn and Bacon, 1989.

PETRIE, THOMAS A. "Ideas That Hinder Education—Debunking the Myths." *NASSP Bulletin* 64 (December 1982): 53–54.

SCHLESINGER, ARTHUR M. Jr. *The Disuniting of America: Reflections on a Multicultural Society*, rev. ed. New York: Norton, 1998.

SERGIOVANNI, THOMAS J., ed. *Supervision of Teaching*, 1982 Yearbook. Alexandria, Va.: Association for Supervision and Curriculum Development, 1982.

SERGIOVANNI, THOMAS J., and ROBERT J. STARRATT. *Supervision: A Redefinition*, 8th ed. Boston: McGraw-Hill, 2007.

SHAPIRO, BARBARA C. *National Standards for Teachers. Streamlined Seminar.* Alexandria, Va.: National Association of Elementary School Principals, vol. 13 (February 1995).

SPEARS, HAROLD. *Improving the Supervision of Instruction.* Englewood Cliffs, N.J.: Prentice Hall, 1953.

STOOPS, EMERY, MAX RAFFERTY, and RUSSELL E. JOHNSON. *Handbook of Educational Administration: A Guide for the Practitioner*, 2nd ed. Boston: Allyn and Bacon, 1981.

STURGES, A. W., chairman. *The Roles and Responsibilities of Instructional Supervisors.* Alexandria, Va.: ASCD Working Group on the Roles and Responsibilities of Supervisors, Association for Supervision and Curriculum Development, 1978.

Subcommittee on National Security and International Operations. Specialists and Generalists, a Selection of Readings. Washington, D.C.: U.S. Government Printing Office, 1968.

TURNER, HAROLD E. "The Department Head: An Untapped Source of Instructional Leadership." *NASSP Bulletin* 67 (September 1983): 25–28.

U.S. Department of Education. *America's Teachers: Profile of a Profession*. Washington, D.C.: U.S. Department of Education, 1993.

VAIL, KATHLEEN. "Raising the Bar." *American School Board Journal* 182 (April 1995): 48–49.

WEASMER, JERIE, and AMELIA MAYS WOODS. "Facilitating Success for New Teachers." *Principal* 78 (November 1998): 40–42.

WILES, JON, and JOSEPH BONDI. *Supervision: A Guide to Practice*, 6th ed. Upper Saddle River, N.J.: Prentice Hall, 2004.

ZEHR, MARY ANN. "Changing the Way Teachers Teach Away from the Chalkboard." *Education Week—Technology Counts '98* 18 (October 1, 1998): 41–43.

PART II

LEADERSHIP IN INSTRUCTIONAL DEVELOPMENT

ArthurTilley/Taxi/Getty Images

CHAPTER 3

HELPING TEACHERS PLAN FOR INSTRUCTION

OBJECTIVES

After studying Chapter 3 you should be able to accomplish the following objectives:

1. Describe your own preferred model of instruction.
2. Demonstrate skill in following a systematic approach to instructional design.
3. Demonstrate skill in following a model of instruction.
4. Demonstrate skill in writing instructional goals and objectives.
5. Demonstrate skill in applying taxonomies of instructional objectives.
6. Demonstrate skill in describing and analyzing learning tasks.
7. Demonstrate skill in organizing instructional plans.

MODELS OF INSTRUCTION

A postcard once arrived at the university address of one of the co-authors of this volume. The card came from an elementary school teacher who requested that a plan for the year's work be sent to her for use with her first graders. It apparently had not occurred to her, despite whatever preservice training she had had, that planning for instruction was her own responsibility. She sought a ready-made, complete year's plan—to be given to her—by someone with no knowledge of her school, her community, her pupils, and her own objectives.

Surprisingly, given the scope of state and district mandates on curriculum over the past several decades, we almost reached that point. As a matter of fact, we have gone through a period when curriculum and instructional planners have sought to create curricula that would be "teacher-proof."

With varying degrees of success, every teacher education institution provides instruction in planning, primarily in its preservice training program. Students learn basic techniques of planning and usually experience opportunities for demonstrating their plans and putting them into practice.

The teacher education institution, however, can only offer an introduction to instruction, providing a foundation and limited practice in demonstrating teaching skills. These skills become refined as a teacher gains experience on the job. Central to this book is the belief that all teachers, no matter how long they might have taught, can develop new skills and improve old ones.

We must add to the picture today that facing a shortage of qualified teachers, some schools, both public and private, are employing persons as teachers who have little or no formal teacher training. The burden of assisting these teachers falls squarely on the shoulders of the instructional supervisor. As more becomes known about the instructional process with every passing year, newer and better ways of providing instruction continuously develop. The supervisor's function is to assist teachers in becoming familiar with promising and proven approaches to instruction and in developing and improving instructional skills.

The alert supervisor becomes aware of the extent of planning and the degree of proficiency in this skill shown by teachers who are to be supervised. For example, supervisors encounter some teachers with no written plans for instruction. Given the complexities of education today, surely some sort of written plan should be expected for each lesson a teacher presents.

Supervisors might begin to examine the problem of planning as they try to ascertain what kinds of plans teachers are making. The authors are mindful that it is standard practice for teachers regularly to submit their lesson plans for review by their school supervisors. As supervisors spot deficiencies in planning, they may work with individuals or groups in devising better ways to go about this fundamental task.

The supervisor may encounter resistance to planning in a variety of forms. Some teachers fully believe that they need not write anything down because they have sufficient mastery of the content of the program. They overlook the value of a written plan as a communication device that allows the *learner* to know what to expect from subsequent instruction.

Some teachers view their role in the Socratic tradition, hoping that young people will flock around them to gather unorganized bits of wisdom. Other teachers will readily admit that they realize the value of planning but rationalize that they do not have sufficient time to write plans. The supervisor needs to show teachers that planning is a much more complicated and important phase of instruction than many believe. Conscientious teachers will have to consider many variables as they begin to plan. Each class has pupils of varying backgrounds, abilities, needs, and interests.

The teacher must adapt subject matter to the physical, mental, emotional, and educational differences among learners. Entering into the complexities of planning are newer emphases and challenges, among which are the increasing linguistic and cultural diversity among students, the practice of including children with exceptionalities in the regular classroom, the incorporation of new technologies into instruction, and, with the pronounced stress on reading skills, the recognition that every teacher is ipso facto a teacher of reading.

A seemingly inexhaustible pool of content exists from which teachers can draw. Certain parameters, such as the school's schedule and budgetary limitations, must be considered, as well as expectations of other teachers, the public, school administrators, and even the state legislature. Faced with many possible methods or strategies for presenting a given lesson, the teacher must make choices, knowing that some of these strategies are likely to be more effective than others for certain purposes, with certain groups, with certain individuals, in certain settings, and for the teacher's particular personality. Consequently, when the teacher jots down a reference to a particular chapter or exercise or topic and views that as an adequate lesson plan, he or she is ignoring many significant variables. Teachers at all levels can improve their planning skills, and one of the supervisor's tasks is to help them do so.

Simplified Model

Planning is the first stage of a continuum, followed by the implementation or presentation stage and then the evaluation stage. Some specialists in instruction would diagram the phases of the continuum as follows:

Planning → Presentation → Evaluation

They would refer to the diagram as a simplified model of instruction, a pattern that teachers can follow. The model indicates simply that the teacher begins the instructional process with initial planning, proceeds through the strategies of presentation, and moves finally to evaluating the results in terms of what the plan set out to achieve.

CLASSROOM PLANNING: A SIX-POINT PROGRAM

In practice, teachers become involved in planning on a school, district, state, regional, and national level—and on rare occasions, on an international level. The present text stresses planning that relates to curriculum and instruction at the classroom, school, and district levels and highlights the supervisor's role in fostering curricular and instructional planning at those levels. This chapter considers techniques for the improvement of instruction in the individual teacher's classroom. Chapter 7 discusses faculty involvement in curriculum development on the various levels.

Effective classroom presentation requires a great deal of thought and preparation by teachers. To assist them with the task of planning, the supervisor may provide training in the development of six competencies, discussed shortly. These competencies are derived from decades of research on instruction. They are as follows:

1. Skill in following a systematic approach to instructional design.
2. Skill in following a model of instruction.
3. Skill in writing instructional goals and objectives.
4. Skill in applying taxonomies of instructional objectives.
5. Skill in describing and analyzing learning tasks.
6. Skill in organizing instructional plans.

The supervisor should begin by surveying the degree to which the various teachers possess these skills. Some teachers may have a high level of expertise in all these competencies. If that is the case, the supervisor, after verifying the fact that the teachers demonstrate these skills, would encourage them to continue their good work and give more attention to teachers who need assistance in perfecting one or more of the skills. The supervisor may use the skilled teachers as models and may call on them to serve as resource persons to those who need assistance.

Following a Systematic Approach to Instructional Design

A systematic approach to instruction is guided by four questions: What do you wish to achieve? What resources do you have and need to achieve your objectives? How will you go about achieving your objectives? How well have you accomplished your objectives?

Whenever a teacher creates a course outline or lesson plan, he or she engages in instructional design. The teacher can make the design process more efficient and more effective by approaching the task systematically. A systematic approach replaces haphazard planning by requiring a careful examination of all the parts of a plan and how the parts relate to each other.

The basic principles of a systematic approach are simple. The approach must yield a planned, integrated, complete design for the use of materials, media, and personnel to accomplish certain predetermined objectives; and each of the component parts must interrelate with the others, providing continuous feedback for modification of the design. Thus, a systematic approach to instruction is the process of creating a learning design in which all the component parts are specified, assembled, and interrelated.

There are eight steps in the process. Let us suppose that we wish to design a year's program in a particular subject or for a particular grade level. We might equally well illustrate the process with a sequence of a particular curriculum extending over several years—for example, the language arts curriculum; we could plan for a portion of a program—a unit—extending over a few weeks; or in abbreviated form, we could plan for a day or a class period. The steps that follow will give us a global look at the process. We have singled out steps 1, 2, 3, and 5 for more extended treatment in this chapter. Because of their complexity, steps 6 and 7 need greater attention and are covered separately in Chapter 4, and steps 4 and 8 are in Chapter 6. The process of systematic planning entails the following steps:

1. *Taking stock of the present program.* The teacher reviews the present program, analyzes what has been covered in the past, and reexamines the current goals and objectives. He or she examines the procedures for presenting the content, the varied resources that have been available, and the existing limitations. The teacher must decide whether the program fits into the total scheme of the curriculum and whether it meets the needs of the learners for whom the program is intended. Before redesigning an old program or designing a new program, the teacher must consider the past and the present.

2. *Specifying the goals of instruction.* The teacher decides on the general purposes of the program. The goals provide a sense of direction for subsequent instruction and help the teacher define the specific objectives.

3. *Specifying the objectives of instruction.* One of the most important phases of systematic design is the specification of objectives, the specific outcomes of instruction. The objectives state what the learner is expected to learn, accomplish, or do; under what conditions; and with what degree of mastery. They serve as the source of the evaluation process.

4. *Designing an evaluation plan.* The instructor must determine whether the presentations have been successful, that is, whether students have mastered the content and whether they have reached the objectives set out at the beginning. The teacher may choose from a variety of quantitative and qualitative evaluation techniques to learn how well students have achieved.

5. *Describing and analyzing the learning tasks.* If the learning tasks are complex, the teacher must break them down and describe the sequence in which instruction is to be presented. He or she must know what skills the learners must bring to the tasks to achieve the objectives; the teacher must analyze the tasks and decide whether they are appropriate for the particular group of learners who will be confronted with the material. The teacher must call on his or her knowledge of learning theory and decide what types or conditions of learning are involved in the pursuit of the tasks.

6. *Designing instructional procedures.* The teacher makes decisions about the strategies of instruction to be employed, choosing the instructional procedures that appear to have the best chance for success given the nature of the program, any constraints that have been imposed, and the nature of the learners. Techniques of instruction must be compatible with the teacher's own abilities and personality.

7. *Implementing the instructional procedures.* At this stage, the design moves from thinking and planning to the actual process of instruction. The instructor meets with the learners and leads them in study of the content, then enters into a process of interaction—the learners interacting with the teacher and with each other and both the learners and the teacher interacting with the content.

8. *Implementing the evaluation plan.* Both during implementation of the instructional procedures and at the end of implementation, the teacher puts the evaluation plan into operation and seeks continuous feedback concerning whether the students are indeed learning the material and mastering the tasks. We must discover whether students are successful not only for traditional purposes of evaluation but also for the purpose of modifying the instructional process.

The teacher uses feedback from evaluation in making revisions in the design and modifying the program. If the objectives are inappropriate for any reason, they must be redesigned. If the data show that instructional procedures have been ineffective, different procedures must be tried. A systematic approach permits—in fact, mandates—continuous redesigning.

If we were to contrast older approaches to planning with a systematic approach, we could note the following differences:

Systematic Approach	*Older Approaches*
Focus on learner's objectives, what the learner does	Focus on teacher's objectives, on what the teacher does
Objectives apparent before instruction begins	Objectives not apparent or apparent only during or after instruction
Continuous feedback	No feedback or feedback at the end of instruction
Continuous redesign	Redesign after instruction and for the next group of learners
Evaluation of all objectives	Evaluation of selected objectives
Achievement of the learner related to mastery of the objectives	Achievement of the learner related to achievement of other learners

The supervisor may wish to offer an in-service training program that takes teachers through the eight steps of a systematic approach to instruction.

Following a Model of Instruction

Instructional designers follow a sequence of steps that they refer to as a model of instruction. A model is a pattern that provides a logical progression from one step to the next. Earlier in this chapter, you became acquainted with a simplified model of instruction consisting of three components: planning, presentation, and evaluation. The literature on instruction normally shows models as charts or schematic representations using a series of boxes, lines, or arrows. The preceding simplified model of instruction can be diagrammed as shown in Figure 3.1. Note the line showing feedback from Evaluation to Planning and Presentation; this makes the model a cyclical plan for continuous improvement.

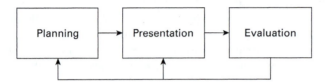

FIGURE 3.1 Simplified Model.

A model serves as a guide to the teacher for instructional design. It reveals both the essential elements of the instructional process and the sequence in which these elements are put into practice.

Although the simplified model of instruction outlines essential phases, we could make the model clearer if we were to expand it by making explicit some phases that are only implicit in the simplified model. For that reason we propose the use of a five-part model (see Figure 3.2).[1]

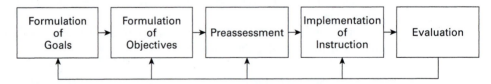

FIGURE 3.2 Five-Part Model.

The five-part model of instruction calls for the formulation or specification of the goals and objectives of instruction. It also calls for an assessment of learners' skills prior to initiating study of the subject matter. Evaluation of student achievement follows implementation or presentation of instruction and feeds back to the preceding stages.

Models found in the literature show many similarities in essential elements. They differ mainly in their details and in the choice of components they emphasize. Some vary the sequence of components slightly. Others attempt to sketch every instructional act in the model itself.

The differences in models are not so great that we would recommend one over another. The important responsibility of the teacher is to select a model compatible with his or her style of teaching or create such a model and follow it in the design of instruction.

The teacher could combine components of various models and even recast the eight steps in the process of systematic planning discussed earlier in the form of a model of instruction, as we have done in Figure 3.3. Note that feedback from evaluation can lead to modification of other component parts of the design.

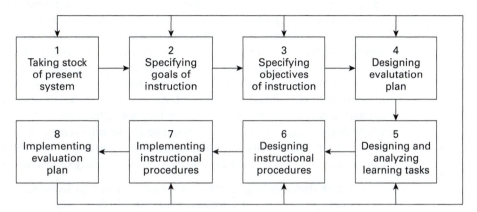

FIGURE 3.3 Alternative Systematic Model.

Which model of instruction a teacher follows does not matter greatly, but for perfecting the skill of following a model, the teacher should select one carefully and stick with it for a period of time. In this way, he or she can develop an easy familiarity with the model, and this familiarity will simplify the planning process.

If supervisors are going to help teachers work with models of instruction, they should try out various models for themselves to see how they work in the actual process of instructional design. After analyzing models of instruction, supervisors should help teachers become acquainted with various ones, assist them in selecting models compatible with their own needs, and encourage them to try their own hands at creating a model.

Writing Instructional Goals and Objectives

Instructional Goals Educational literature is peppered with the words *aims, purposes, goals,* and *objectives.* We hear and read about "the aims of education," "the purposes of American education," "goals of education for the twenty-first century," and "objectives of secondary education." The terms are used interchangeably and loosely. Although the dictionary equates *objective* with *goal,* in instructional planning *goal* and *objective* are not necessarily the same; in our opinion they should not be used interchangeably. For purposes of instructional design, the words *aims* and *purposes* should be avoided. These terms should be confined to philosophical discussions of education on a broader scale.

When some people speak of goals, they mean the broad aims or purposes of education, which we might also refer to as *educational goals.* In this chapter, we are not concerned with broad educational goals but with more limited instructional goals. Whereas educational goals may apply to the whole process of education and schooling, instructional goals apply only to particular content. We make a sharp distinction between goals and objectives in instructional design, though both relate to the instructional process and both are concerned with specific content.

Instructional goals are general statements of hoped-for learning on the part of the student. Goal statements contain such language as "The student should become familiar with ... ," "The student should become aware of ... ," "The student should gain an understanding of ... ," and "The student should develop an appreciation for ... " The extent to which such goals are met cannot be evaluated with any degree of precision. In fact, goal statements may refer to outcomes that are not even observable, such as "to develop an appreciation for ... " It may not be possible for a teacher to discover whether a student has truly developed an appreciation for the particular subject matter.

Goals provide the teacher with a general sense of direction. They are rough indicators of where instruction is taking the student. As such, they are written in terms of the learner, not the teacher. The teacher's goals may or may not be the same as the learner's goals. The whole thrust of instructional design should be on the achievement of the learner. For this reason, statements of goals of instruction are in the form of expectations of the learner. We can illustrate this with some goal statements from a variety of disciplines:

- The student should appreciate the music of Mozart by listening to recordings of his works performed by the London Philharmonic Orchestra.
- Through study of Darwin's *Origin of Species,* the student should better understand the basic principles of Darwin's theory of evolution.
- The student should understand the citizen's role in a democratic society.
- When encountering persons of an ethnic group different from his or her own, the student should have empathy for them.
- The student should become acquainted with a variety of linguistic pattern drills.
- The learner should understand the system of checks and balances written into the U.S. Constitution.
- The student should become familiar with several Web search engines.
- The pupil should learn the nines multiplication table.
- The child should enjoy reading Dr. Seuss's books.
- The student should develop an understanding of his or her role as a member of a family.
- The learner should recognize the hazards of cigarette smoking.
- The student should develop the ability to solve mathematics problems.
- The student should comprehend the necessity for conservation of natural resources.
- The pupil should learn to take responsibility as a member of a committee.
- The pupil should understand why it is necessary to wash his or her hands before eating.
- The student should know the differences between goals and objectives.

The verbs used in these statements—*understand, know, learn, appreciate,* and *recognize,* for example—are nonbehavioral. They do not tell exactly what the learner must demonstrate or do to show the teacher that he or she has accomplished what was expected. Goals serve the useful purpose of giving direction to instruction, but their breadth, lack of specific learner behavior, and vagueness do not permit evaluation of the learner's mastery of content. Writing instructional goals, however, is an important exercise, for it aids the teacher in deriving instructional objectives.

After pointing out the general direction of instruction by specifying the goals, the teacher turns to the task of deciding on instructional objectives—the specific outcomes of learning.

Instructional Objectives   Instructional objectives, alternatively known as behavioral or performance objectives, clearly state expected behavior on the part of the learner. Having undergone research and development from the late 1950s through the early 1980s, instructional objectives have become a standard element in today's educational planning.

Instructional objectives differ from goals in that they are written in terms of student performance that can usually be observed and measured. We say *usually* advisedly, for when we enter the affective domain, it is not always possible to observe or measure expected student behavior. Most instructional planners recommend that instructional objectives possess three characteristics:

1. *Expected behavior on the part of the learner.* The teacher must answer the question, "What will the student actually do to show that he or she has learned the material?" The teacher decides on the expected behavior by examining the goals, describing and analyzing the learning task, and considering the world outside this class where the expected behavior may be applied. (Following the discussion of writing objectives, we will examine the process of describing and analyzing learning tasks. A description and an analysis of a learning task may cause a teacher to revise the instructional objectives already specified.)

The teacher should give some thought to the applicability of the behavior in situations outside the classroom in both the present and the future. We are talking here about the transfer of training. We must ask ourselves in what way the expected behavior may be of value to the learner either in other school situations or outside the school.

Whether the objectives are in the *cognitive* domain (the area of knowledge), the *affective* domain (the area of feeling), or the *psychomotor* domain (the area of perceptual-motor skills), the teacher should consider their usefulness beyond the walls of the classroom. Many objectives, particularly those of a cognitive nature, are useful at the next higher levels of education. They are useful in the next grade, in an advanced sequence, or in a higher institution of learning. As such they are preparatory to additional and continuing education. Other objectives are useful in the learner's day-to-day life in the school, in the home, and in the community. Still others are useful in part-time jobs while the learner is in school or in a full-time career after he or she finishes school. You can easily see the transferability of instruction in auto mechanics, for example. Provided the instruction in auto mechanics has been adequate, the learner can leave school, accept a job as an auto mechanic, and apply the skills learned in school. More difficult to explain to many learners is the transferability—or relevance—of the study of Pizarro's conquest of Peru or of Giuseppe Verdi's opera *Rigoletto*.

Whenever possible, verbs used in statements of instructional objectives should reflect some overt behavior on the part of the learner. The words chosen should be action verbs, such as list, define, interpret, draw, analyze, compare, construct, organize, write, explain, produce, decide, classify, synthesize, type, summarize, and report. While writing the objectives, the teacher should be thinking of ways to determine whether the learners achieve them. The teacher's evaluation plan should begin to take shape in his or her mind when selecting the objectives.

The supervisor can help individual teachers and groups of teachers write goals and objectives by collecting and showing the teachers examples of nonbehavioral goals and behavioral objectives and asking teachers to distinguish between goals and objectives. The supervisor should demonstrate ways in which nonbehavioral goals can be translated into behavioral objectives by means of action words.[2]

2. *Conditions under which the learning takes place.* A complete instructional objective stipulates the conditions in which the learner works to fulfill the objective. The teacher specifies the tools the learner will use and/or the setting in which the learning occurs. For example, a mathematics teacher might decide on the following instructional objective: "Given a pencil, ruler, paper, and compass, the student will construct an isosceles triangle in five minutes." The pencil, ruler, paper, and compass, the tools with which the learner performs the task, are the conditions necessary for accomplishing it. A business education teacher might wish the learners to be able to process forty-five words per minute using a specific word-processing program with a maximum of two errors. The word-processing program is the condition written into this objective. A science teacher may write the following objective: "In the science laboratory, using paper, matches, a small ashtray, and a glass tumbler, the student will demonstrate that oxygen is necessary for combustion to take place."

Some experts in constructing instructional objectives show a preference for expressing conditions by starting with the word *given.* Thus, you find such statements as "Given a set of problems . . . ," "Given a list of authors . . . ," and "Given a paper-and-pencil test . . ." Although use of the word *given* followed by the conditions is one satisfactory way of stating conditions, it is by no means the only way. Following this pattern exclusively can make the construction of instructional objectives border on writing formulas rather than creative ideas. Indeed, when the conditions are obvious, there is no need to state them. For example, it is not necessary for the teacher to state, "Given a paper-and-pencil test . . ." If the teacher prepares a test and distributes it, that is obviously the condition imposed. Behavioral statements should include conditions that are not readily apparent. The supervisor should avoid dogmatically insisting that all instructional objectives contain written statements of conditions. Belaboring the obvious turns off teachers and discourages them from writing instructional objectives.

3. *Level of mastery.* An instructional objective should show or imply a level of mastery of the behavior sought. The teacher should determine what quality of performance is expected of the learner. The teacher needs to specify the standard of performance unless it is obvious. Standards of performance may be expressed in the form of time to complete a task, number of correct responses, number of errors permitted, or percentage of correct demonstrations of the behavior. For example, the earlier illustration, "Given a pencil, ruler, paper, and compass, the student will construct an isosceles triangle in five minutes," contains a time standard—five minutes. The illustration from the business education curriculum, "The student will process forty-five words per minute using a specific word-processing program with a maximum of two errors," contains a two-part standard—forty-five words per minute and a maximum of two errors. The following example calls for a degree of mastery in terms of number of correct responses and percentage: "On this test of twenty-five items, the student will achieve a score of at least twenty (80 percent)." The teacher could make the objective more demanding by adding a time element, such as "On this test of twenty-five items the student will achieve a score of at least twenty (80 percent) in ten minutes."

When the standard is implied or obvious, there is no need to write it into the objective. Take the following example from the field of Spanish: "The student will be able to write with correct spelling the names of the months of the year." The statement includes two levels of mastery, one specified (correct spelling) and one implied (all twelve months). No standard need be written into this objective: "Define the word *ethnic*." The student's answer is either right or wrong. It would be superfluous or artificial to tack on "with 100 percent accuracy." Unless a teacher indicates differently, 100 percent mastery is expected, as in the example, "Given a series of measures in miles, the student will convert them to kilometers." The teacher is requiring the correct conversion of all items in the series.

Some objectives are so complex that it is a difficult or forced procedure for teachers to stipulate levels of mastery. It would require a rather lengthy description to write a standard for this objective: "Draw a graph showing the growth of the population of California for the past decade." To spell out a standard for this objective, the teacher would have to say something about the accuracy of figures used, the learner's skills in graphing, and even the learner's artistic ability. There comes a point of diminishing returns in terms of the time it would take a teacher to refine an objective to the point of including all standards. We must rely on the teacher's judgment for determining whether this objective has been achieved. A similar problem exists in a typical social studies learning task: "The student will present to the class his or her views on welfare payments." This objective involves personal views, informational content, and skills of oral presentation.

Sometimes it is not possible to write a level of mastery. This is particularly true of objectives in the affective domain. The impression is often given that writing affective objectives is analogous to writing objectives of a cognitive or psychomotor nature. Both conditions under which behavior is demonstrated and those with a level of mastery can elude the teacher in the affective domain. What level of mastery might be required from the objective, "Respond to an appeal from fellow students by helping collect food and clothing for needy families of the community"? This could be a very important learning opportunity. The appeal might be seen as the condition, but how much help and what kinds of help should be expected? You could say simply that any degree of help would fulfill this objective. A teacher of environmental studies might want students to "appreciate the consequences of actions that pollute the air and water supplies." Under what conditions should this appreciation take place? What degree of appreciation is required?

The affective domain, in which attitudes, feelings, and values are paramount, begs the question of indoctrination. Whose values should be taught? the learners'? the teacher's? the community's? the nation's? the world's? Are all values of equal worth? Supervisors need to help teachers identify those values that are generally accepted in American society and that can be safely promoted. Writing affective objectives is much more difficult than writing cognitive and psychomotor objectives. The expected behavior of the learner cannot always be observed when we are dealing with affect. We cannot always be sure of the learner's feelings and attitudes. You cannot always know under what conditions or to what degree he or she may show the desired behavior. The expected behavior, if it takes place at all, often takes place outside the classroom and outside the school. Sometimes the expected behavior does not occur until a long time after the learning experiences that sought to produce the behavior. These conditions should not dissuade teachers from writing affective objectives, but the conditions should make teachers realize that they need not strain to write conditions and levels they can neither control nor predict with accuracy.

Components of Instructional Objectives   Most of the specialists who have written on the subject of instructional objectives have recommended the three components described already: (1) the expected, or terminal, behavior; (2) the conditions under which the learning takes place; and (3) the level of mastery the learner is expected to demonstrate. Robert H. Davis, Lawrence T. Alexander, and Stephen L. Yelon suggested a fourth component.[3] They distinguished between performance standards—that is, level of mastery—and performance stability. They believed that a stability standard or criterion should be included to indicate the number of times the learner must perform the behavior at or above the performance standard. They provided examples of objectives that contain both a performance standard and performance stability—for example, "The student will run the 100-yard dash in fifteen seconds, three out of five times." The expected behavior is "run the 100-yard dash." The performance standard is one of time—"in fifteen seconds." The stability criterion is "three out of five times." The conditions under which the behavior is to be performed, incidentally, have been left out of the statement. It is assumed that the student will have a place to run and will probably have to dress properly for the activity. A supervisor may wish to acquaint teachers with the distinction between performance standard and performance stability and suggest that they write a stability criterion into an objective when doing so seems plausible.

Planning for instruction begins with the writing of instructional objectives. Because objectives are often detailed and numerous, setting them down on paper is essential to avoid overlooking important ones and thereby omitting significant learnings. Writing objectives is essentially a creative and thought-provoking activity. In similar situations, different teachers will decide on different objectives. Each teacher brings to this task all he or she knows about the learners, the subject, instruction, and society. Writing instructional objectives is not a simple task. It is extremely important, however, because all subsequent steps of the instructional process hinge on the objectives that have been specified.

To help teachers with the planning process, the supervisor might institute an in-service program on the writing and use of instructional objectives. He or she might consider dividing this program into two distinct phases: (1) writing objectives based on criteria described in this text or in other sources, and (2) using objectives already developed elsewhere.

Some practice in writing objectives would be desirable to help teachers perfect the skill. Teachers have probably had some exposure (and in some cases overexposure) to writing instructional objectives in their preservice training. If they are already familiar with the technique, they may apply it and develop objectives for their particular courses and grade levels. The objectives they develop may be retained to build a local bank of objectives from which they may later draw. As a group activity, the process of writing objectives can be beneficial when teachers examine, exchange, and present critiques of objectives written by their peers.

Because teachers, state departments of education, and organizations in various parts of the country have long been involved in developing instructional objectives in a variety of disciplines, the supervisor should acquire and share with teachers curriculum materials containing objectives that have already been written. The teachers could examine objectives in their fields of interest to see whether they meet the criteria for instructional objectives and to decide whether specific objectives would be useful in their own programs. This activity would be essentially a process of selecting objectives from a pool of objectives that has already been prepared. We should note that some state- and district-mandated curricula prescribe instructional objectives to be mastered by students in various disciplines and grades. For those disciplines in which mandated curricula exist, the teacher's opportunities to specify objectives are reduced. However, teachers would still have the freedom to go beyond the prescribed curricula and, indeed, should do so.

Applying Taxonomies of Instructional Objectives

Earlier in this chapter we used the terms *cognitive domain*, *affective domain*, and *psychomotor domain*. Each domain consists of a large area of related learnings. The cognitive domain encompasses learnings of a factual and intellectual nature; cognitive tasks are mental exercises leading to knowledge. The affective domain takes in learnings of an emotional nature; affective tasks produce feelings and attitudes toward things and people. The psychomotor domain comprises learnings that may require some cognition but are primarily skills that demand movement of parts of the body. Because psychomotor learnings involve both mental and bodily activity, they are often called perceptual-motor skills.

A task description and analysis, discussed later in this chapter, will reveal whether the learning tasks are primarily in the cognitive, affective, or psychomotor domain. The content of a particular course may include learnings from all three domains. The supervisor should encourage teachers to write objectives in all three domains whenever all are applicable. Because cognitive and psychomotor objectives are the most apparent, affective objectives are often overlooked. Of course, not all content will lead to outcomes in all three domains. On the other hand, much of the content studied in school is of such a nature that learnings in at least two and often all three of the domains should be sought.

An experienced teacher soon learns that not all learnings within a given domain are equal. Some learnings are more complex than others. Some are more important than others in terms of their significance to the learner and their permanence. Some learnings clearly reflect a lower level of competence than other learnings.

The three domains have been subjected to study for the purpose of answering these two questions: "What categories of learnings belong in each domain?" "What is the order of importance among the categories?" As long ago as 1956, Benjamin S. Bloom and his associates published a classification system—a taxonomy—of educational (that is, instructional) objectives in the cognitive domain.[4] David R. Krathwohl, Bloom, and

Bertram B. Masia produced a system in 1964 for classifying objectives in the affective domain.[5] A taxonomy of objectives in the psychomotor domain by Elizabeth Jane Simpson appeared in 1972.[6] Widely cited and implemented, these taxonomies are still useful in helping teachers plan for instruction.

In the following discussion of these taxonomies, we describe each domain and give three examples of instructional objectives in each major category. The "a." example in each category of all three domains is drawn from the same learning unit, so you can trace objectives on one theme through all levels of all three domains. To make this possible, we chose a unit from a discipline in which psychomotor as well as cognitive and affective learnings are sought—a unit at the secondary school level on Impressionist painters.

The "b." examples in the Bloom and Krathwohl taxonomies illustrate a theme through all levels of two domains: the cognitive and affective. For this we selected the topic of federal income tax applicable to a course in consumer education at the junior or senior high school level. (Psychomotor objectives are of little importance in filling out a federal income tax return, other than learning how to cope with the headaches attached to this stressful activity.) In Simpson's psychomotor taxonomy, we use a unit on tumbling in physical education at the elementary, middle, or senior high school level as the "b." examples of psychomotor objectives.

In all three taxonomies, the "c." examples are taken from many disciplines of the elementary, middle, and secondary school; there is no relationship among the "c." examples across domains or at any levels within a domain; they constitute a miscellaneous collection of objectives that serve as additional illustrations.

The Bloom Taxonomy   The Bloom taxonomy of the cognitive domain sets forth a hierarchy of six major categories.[7] From the lowest level to the highest, these categories are:

1. Knowledge
2. Comprehension
3. Application
4. Analysis
5. Synthesis
6. Evaluation

The taxonomy further subdivides each of the categories into subcategories according to levels of complexity and importance, but it serves our purposes to confine discussion to the six major categories. The taxonomy says, in effect, that those instructional objectives designed to seek only the acquisition of knowledge are at the lowest level of both complexity and importance. Most laypersons feel that the cognitive domain is or should be what schools are all about. It is no secret to anyone who has gone to school that most of the learnings sought have been, still are, and will likely continue to be in the cognitive domain and that most of those learnings hover around the low end of the taxonomy despite efforts to raise the level. All a supervisor needs to do to verify this point is to examine several tests given by teachers; he or she will see how frequently learners are asked to recall specific factual information as opposed to interpreting, applying, analyzing, synthesizing, and evaluating information. A supervisor needs to help teachers write higher-level objectives. We illustrate what instructional objectives look like at each level of the Bloom system of classification.

1. Knowledge
    a. The student will name four Impressionist painters.
    b. The student will give the number of the short form used for filing his or her federal income tax statement.
    c. On an outline map of the United States showing the Great Lakes, the student will print the name of each lake in its proper location.

2. Comprehension
    a. The student will explain what is meant by *Impressionism*, citing the chief characteristics of this school of painting.
    b. The student will tell the difference between an *exemption* and a *deduction* as applied to the federal income tax.
    c. Given a graph showing the increase in population of the state of Arizona over the past thirty years, the student will interpret to his or her classmates the facts shown by the graph.

3. Application
    a. From a series of prints of classical and modern paintings, the student will select those that are the works of Impressionist painters by applying characteristics studied in class.
    b. Given a set of data, the student will correctly calculate the income tax due the federal government by using the appropriate tax table.
    c. The student will correctly solve eight out of ten problems in long division.

4. Analysis
    a. The student will examine prints of one painting of an Impressionist painter and one of a non-Impressionist painter and contrast the differences in the styles.
    b. Given a completed 1040 tax form, the student will determine whether there are any errors in filling out the form and whether the tax due or refund has been calculated correctly.
    c. The student will watch several commercials on television and decide whether they meet the standard of "truth in advertising."

5. Synthesis
    a. The student will write a biography of an Impressionist painter.
    b. The student will fill out a 1040A tax form using data furnished by the teacher.
    c. The student will produce a documented research paper on the effects of certain drugs on the human body.

6. Evaluation
    a. The student will examine a print of a painting by a lesser-known Impressionist artist and evaluate the quality of the work, applying characteristics studied in this unit.
    b. From background data about a fictitious taxpayer and a completed income tax return, the student will evaluate the deductions taken by the taxpayer and decide

whether he or she was entitled to all the deductions claimed. The student will give reasons for all decisions.

   c. The student will read a short story by Edgar Allan Poe and evaluate it in respect to (1) mood, (2) vocabulary, and (3) impact on the reader.

Although we have used the style "The student will—" in each of the preceding examples, teachers may prefer an abbreviated style that is equally acceptable. "The student will" can simply be omitted, leaving, for example, "Name four Impressionist painters" and "Given a graph showing the increase in population of the state of Arizona over the past thirty years, interpret to your classmates the facts shown by the graph."

A teacher or group of teachers can develop their own classification system. They might create, for example, a simplified system consisting of two levels: low-order objectives and high-order objectives. However, because the Bloom taxonomy has been with us for many years and has been widely followed with considerable success, it provides a ready-made guide that teachers might well choose to follow. In either case, the object is to raise the level of instructional objectives to a higher order than is commonly found in many classrooms. Curricular efforts today place great emphasis on thinking skills. If teachers are ever to develop learners' ability to think, they must move instruction to the higher levels of learning. Parenthetically, we must note that thinking skills cannot be demonstrated in a vacuum. The thinker must possess a knowledge base to use those skills effectively.

We should point out that in all three taxonomies discussed in this chapter, objectives may overlap levels within a domain. Each level within a domain builds on the preceding level, adding a degree of complexity with each ascending step in the hierarchy. It is difficult, sometimes impossible, and generally not necessary for a given objective to fit precisely and clearly within one level. The important understanding we should hold is that the thrust of the objectives should be upward in each hierarchy.

The Krathwohl Taxonomy   Krathwohl and his colleagues enumerated five levels in their classification of objectives in the affective domain:

1. Receiving
2. Responding
3. Valuing
4. Organization
5. Characterization by value or value complex[8]

Like the Bloom taxonomy, the Krathwohl classification breaks each major category into subcategories in a hierarchy from low to high level. As in our discussion of the Bloom taxonomy, we illustrate by referring only to the major categories and rely on the reader to consult the taxonomies themselves for the detailed subdivisions of each category. Following are examples of objectives for each of the five categories.

  1. Receiving
    a. The student will demonstrate in conversation an awareness of Impressionist art that he or she encounters in daily life.

    b. The student will evince an awareness of the need for paying one's federal income tax and the consequences of not filing when required to do so.

    c. The student will show an awareness that Native Americans have suffered at the hands of white settlers in America.

2. Responding

    a. The student will choose and read a book on Impressionism.

    b. The student will observe the deadline for filing his or her tax return.

    c. The student will volunteer to serve on a committee for a class project.

3. Valuing

    a. The student will express an appreciation for the contributions of the Impressionists to our aesthetic life.

    b. The student will support the income tax system by pointing out worthwhile government expenditures financed by tax revenues.

    c. The student will defend physical fitness exercises.

4. Organization

    a. The student will decide whether he or she likes Impressionist painting and what the characteristics are that cause him or her to like or dislike it.

    b. The student will analyze the reasons some people cheat on their income tax returns and decide whether he or she approves of this behavior.

    c. The student will state his or her reasons for subscribing to a particular moral value.

5. Characterization by value or value complex

    a. The student will express a positive predisposition toward the fine arts as an enrichment of our lives.

    b. The student will consistently demonstrate honesty in paying his or her income tax.

    c. The student will develop the habit of collecting facts before making a decision.

These examples show some of the inherent problems of affective objectives. As we noted earlier, objectives in the affective domain are often both unobservable in school and unmeasurable. We cannot know for sure whether the student in example 2b, for instance, will indeed file an income tax return. The student can tell the teacher that he or she is aware of the laws requiring the filing of income tax returns and can express agreement with the need for a federal income tax and measures to enforce the relevant laws. We have no way of knowing, however, whether the student has complied with the law. We do know, of course, that there is often a discrepancy between what people profess and what they actually do. (For some of us, the affective domain may dwarf the cognitive in regard to payment of income taxes. It was tempting to give such examples as "The student will refrain from groaning when income tax time comes around.")

Few people would argue the importance of such learnings as those illustrated in the five categories of the affective domain. Affective objectives can point the way toward hoped-for ends. Because students may achieve the affective objectives, if not immediately, then perhaps in the future, these types of objectives are worth writing. We do raise a flag of caution at this point, however, and will return to it in the discussion of evaluating instruction in Chapter 6. Because it is difficult and often impossible to structure affective objectives in such a way that they can be both observed and measured, and because they reflect values, opinions, and attitudes, they cannot be evaluated and scored in the same way as cognitive and psychomotor learnings.

The Simpson Taxonomy More recent than the taxonomies of the cognitive and affective domains is the Simpson classification of instructional objectives in the psychomotor domain. Simpson recommended a classification system consisting of seven categories.[9] Her major categories from lowest to highest are

1. Perception
2. Set
3. Guided response
4. Mechanism
5. Complex overt response
6. Adaptation
7. Origination

Anita J. Harrow, who also created a taxonomy of the psychomotor domain, suggested that Simpson's categories could be thought of in different terms: perception, as interpreting; set, as preparing; guided response, as learning; mechanism, as habituating; complex overt response, as performing; adaptation, as modifying; and origination, as creating.[10]

The following examples illustrate the Simpson scheme for classifying psychomotor objectives.

1. Perception
   a. The student will perceive the visual impact (blurred effect, dots) of Impressionist painting.
   b. The student will recognize the mat as appropriate equipment for demonstrating skill in tumbling.
   c. The student will identify the sound of the piano.
2. Set
   a. The student will demonstrate how to hold a paintbrush.
   b. The student will demonstrate the correct stance from which to begin tumbling.
   c. The student will demonstrate the proper way to hold the clarinet.
3. Guided response
   a. The student will imitate the teacher's demonstration of mixing watercolors.
   b. The student will imitate the teacher's demonstration of tumbling.
   c. Following directions on the box, the student will mix a batch of batter for pancakes.
4. Mechanism
   a. The student will mix watercolors to prepare the shades he or she will use in copying a print of an Impressionist landscape or seascape.
   b. The student will perfect proper form by practicing several tumbles, each of which the teacher will critique.
   c. The student will manually sand the top of a small wooden table.

5. Complex overt response
   a. The student will copy (paint) a print of an Impressionist landscape or seascape.
   b. The student will do a triple tumble, demonstrating proper form at the beginning, while tumbling, and in regaining standing position.
   c. The student will scan and send a photo via e-mail.

6. Adaptation
   a. The student will paint a copy of a classical landscape or seascape, converting it to Impressionist style.
   b. The student will introduce a variation on the tumbling exercise taught by the teacher.
   c. The student will convert a popular ballad or classical theme to a disco beat (using any musical instrument).

7. Origination
   a. The student will do an original painting in watercolor or in oils in Impressionist style.
   b. The student will create a new tumbling exercise using the mat without additional props.
   c. The student will create and build a model house of original design and of unusual building materials.

Each succeeding category from perception to organization demands a higher degree of skill, from the simplest to the most complex. Some of the psychomotor objectives—mainly in the category of perception—are mastered during the preschool years. With psychomotor skills as with cognitive learnings, it is somewhat easier to write conditions and levels of mastery into these objectives than it is to do so into affective objectives. Some of the examples specify conditions; others merely imply them. Many of the examples imply a level of mastery—right or wrong, correct or incorrect.

When you examine all three taxonomies, you can readily see that they are not discrete and mutually exclusive. Learnings often cut across all domains. All perceptual-motor skills contain elements of cognition and often of affect. Affective objectives require mastery of cognitive and often psychomotor learnings. The cognitive domain may reach into the affective and, many times, the psychomotor. The whole area of language learning, for example, may bounce back and forth among the three domains. When the student completes a sentence correctly, whether written or oral, he or she may be in all domains at the same time: knowledge of the correct grammatical form and sentence structure places the student in the cognitive domain; pleasure at giving the right response and being rewarded for it by the teacher's approval leads the student into the affective domain; and the physical action of writing or of moving the vocal cords, tongue, and lips puts the student in psychomotor territory.

The teacher should therefore classify instructional objectives under the domain that seems to be the primary nature of the task. A workshop on the classification of instructional objectives and the application of a system of classification to instructional planning could be a valuable in-service program for a supervisor to organize.

Describing and Analyzing Learning Tasks

A task description and an analysis of each instructional objective (i.e., each task) are helpful to the teacher in refining planning. Some instructors combine the concepts of task description and task analysis and think in terms simply of task analysis; others distinguish between them. Davis, Alexander, and Yelon clearly separated description of a task from analysis.[11] A task description is a determination of the steps or sequence in which a learning task is studied. A task analysis, according to Davis and colleagues, is the identification of characteristics of the learner, the types of learning involved, and the conditions or constraints imposed. This distinction between description and analysis is a useful one.

Task Description   Certain tasks must be taught in a step-by-step procedure, with each step dependent on successful accomplishment of the preceding step. The teacher should describe that procedure before attempting to present the content. The concept of task description is more useful in some content areas than in others, being particularly helpful in developing competencies in the psychomotor domain. Complex perceptual-motor skills must often be taught in a particular sequence of steps. For example, there are generally accepted sequences for teaching activities such as the ones shown here:

- Cooking an omelet.
- Refinishing a tabletop.
- Making a tuna fish sandwich.
- Repairing a gasoline-powered lawnmower.
- Drawing a blood specimen.
- Making a papier-mâché figure.
- Laying ceramic tiles.
- Painting a living room.
- Operating a DVD recorder.
- Cutting a piece of lumber with an electric circular saw.

These tasks involve both mental and manual skills. To accomplish the tasks correctly the learner must follow a particular, fixed sequence of steps. For example, consider the task of driving a car.

Suppose for a moment that the car is parked in the driveway and that we wish to give our child—who has a learner's permit—a real test before going for the driver's license examination by having our driver-to-be drive to the testing site. He or she would have to demonstrate several series of steps in a fixed order:

1. Start the car.
2. Back out of the driveway.
3. Turn the car in the intended direction.
4. Drive straight ahead.
5. (Possibly) Pass a car.
6. Make right and left turns.
7. Respond to signal lights and road signs.
8. Park the car in a designated area.
9. Shut off the engine, lock the car, take the keys.

Each of these skills requires its own particular sequence of steps. A driver-training instructor would need to describe each sequence.

Task descriptions are less common, less necessary, and less readily apparent in the cognitive and affective domains. The task description is obvious when a student is called on to "list the names of the five leading oil-producing nations of the world." There is no sequence involved in a simple cognitive task of this type. (An element of sequence might be provided by asking the student to list the nations in the order of number of barrels of oil they produce annually, but that is not a sequence of steps in the same sense as previously described.)

In the affective area of learning, it is almost impossible to describe a fixed sequence of steps. What would be the sequence of steps for the affective objective that seeks to have a student "demonstrate empathy for an ethnic group different from his or her own by writing an essay that supports the ethnic group's desire for improved economic and political opportunities"? Students will approach this task in a variety of ways.

Some of the more complex cognitive tasks may lend themselves to task description if there is a generally accepted sequence that most experts follow. Solving various mathematical problems is an illustration of a complex cognitive task that can be described. For example, suppose that we wish to teach pupils to multiply one factor (the multiplicand) by another factor (the multiplier) of three digits. We might ask the student to demonstrate ability to perform this task by requiring him or her to multiply 2326 by 247:

$$
\begin{array}{r}
2326 \\
\times\ \ 247 \\
\hline
16282 \\
9304 \\
4652 \\
\hline
574522 \\
\end{array}
$$

Although the operation can be done mechanically, the learner should be taught that a particular sequence of steps is being followed:

Step 1: Multiply 2326 by 7 $2326 \times 7 = 16282$

Step 2: Multiply 2326 by 40 $2326 \times 40 = 93040$

Step 3: Multiply 2326 by 200 $2326 \times 200 = 465200$

Step 4: Add 16282, 93040, and 465200   574522

Mathematicians are likely to agree that these four steps are the proper ones in teaching this learning task. If there is no agreed-on correct sequence for performing a learning task, the teacher can still make his or her own task description that would show the learner a sequence to follow.

A foreign language specialist in a teacher education institution, for example, might wish students in a methods class to teach some principles of grammar by means of a selected number of oral pattern drills. Although there is no particular sequence to this task, and variations in sequence might occur from instructor to instructor, the specialist would undoubtedly want the students to begin the study of this task with the simpler kinds of drills and proceed to the more complex.

The instructor might phrase the performance objective like this: "In the methods class before peers, the student will demonstrate during one class period four different types of pattern drills for teaching points of grammar." For students to reach this stage, the instructor must teach them the various types of pattern drills and break the task down into four steps:

Step 1: Work on simple analogy drills.

Step 2: Work on item-substitution mutation drills.

Step 3: Work on fixed-increment drills.

Step 4: Work on paired-sentence drills.

The instructor next recasts the steps of the description into behaviorally stated subobjectives, which are often referred to as *enabling objectives* or simply *enablers*. They are the subcompetencies that must be mastered before the major objective, the *competency*, is attempted. In behavioral terms, enabling objectives in this case may be stated as shown here:

1. The student will construct and present orally in class a simple analogy drill.

2. The student will construct and present orally in class an item-substitution mutation drill.

3. The student will construct and present orally in class a fixed-increment drill.

4. The student will construct and present orally in class a paired-sentence drill.

Specifying the steps in a learning task makes it easier to identify the subobjectives that must first be achieved by the learners. The description also helps refine the major learning task.

Although a teacher may often write task descriptions even if the experts in the discipline disagree on the order in which learning should be presented, it is not always possible or desirable for the teacher to attempt a task description. For example, it is questionable whether there can be or should be a fixed progression of steps in such activities as suggesting ways to solve the nation's environmental problems, designing a Web site, writing a poem, designing the floor plan of a house, doing an original painting in water-colors, or composing a song. These learnings appear to be of a creative nature, cutting across the cognitive, affective, and psychomotor domains. To try to establish a fixed sequence of steps in which learnings of this type should be undertaken could squelch the very creativity the learnings are designed to foster.

Task Analysis Task analysis follows task description. After the steps of the task have been determined, the teacher examines the nature of the task, seeking answers to such questions as these: "What is the background of the learners who will encounter the task?" Do they have the requisite skills for beginning study of the topic? "What skills do learners really need to be successful in mastering the content?" In this regard, the supervisor should help teachers develop the ability to assess prerequisite (entry) skills, a topic considered in Chapter 6 when we discuss evaluation of instruction.

The teacher's analysis proceeds by identifying the kind of learning involved in the task so that the best choice of teaching procedures for presenting the content can be made. Some preservice or in-service training in learning theories and their application in the classroom is essential for this task. In this regard, learning theory would be a very appropriate topic for an in-service program arranged by a supervisor. To help the supervisor recognize types of learning, Robert M. Gagné's categories might be used as a guide.[12] Gagné classified what he referred to as conditions of learning from simplest to most complex types. His classification includes the following eight types of learning:

1. *Signal learning.* This is *classical conditioning*—the formation of conditioned responses to planned or unplanned stimuli. Experiments of the Russian scientist Ivan Pavlov, in which he trained a dog to salivate at the ringing of a bell, are the classic illustrations of this type of learning. Fear of thunder is a conditioned response. Somewhere in the past the individual heard a sudden clap of thunder that was followed by a fright reaction—perhaps a scream—of another person, which provoked a fear reaction in the individual. Although teachers need to be aware of both positive and negative kinds of conditioning that may be going on in school, signal learning has little place in planned school instruction.

2. *Stimulus-response learning.* This type of learning, also known as *operant conditioning*, appears to be particularly relevant to the development of motor learning of animals and young children. Gagné illustrated this type of learning with examples of a person teaching a dog to shake hands and someone teaching a child to say "mama." He pointed out that reinforcement of the desired response is an important feature. Gagné observed that it is difficult to find pure examples of this type of learning in humans. What appears to be stimulus-response learning in humans is more likely to be chaining (type 3) or verbal association (type 4).

3. *Chaining.* Gagné limited chaining to motor learning and described it as connecting a series of stimulus-response links. To perform a complex motor skill successfully, the learner must complete the individual stimulus-response links—or subskills—in a particular order. Applying a tourniquet to stop bleeding is a good illustration of chaining. To stop the bleeding, each of the stimulus-response links must be followed in the order given:

Stimulus	*Response*
Sight of person bleeding	Desire to stop the bleeding.
Pad and strip of cloth or piece of cloth alone if no pad available	Place pad over artery that is bleeding; put cloth over pad and around limb between wound and body; tie cloth over pad.
Stick	Slip stick under the cloth next to the limb and turn stick, tightening cloth until bleeding stops.
Bleeding stopped	Note time tourniquet was applied and take person to doctor.

4. *Verbal association.* This type of learning is similar to chaining but differs in that it applies to verbal learning. Verbal association involves the connecting of a series of verbal links—a verbal chain. The naming of objects and the memorization of passages are examples of verbal association. A two-link verbal chain illustrates teaching students the name of the geometric figure called a rectangle:

Stimulus	*Response*
Picture of a rectangle or an actual rectangular object	Observation of the picture or object
Teacher says the word *rectangle*.	Pupils repeat the word *rectangle*.

The test of the pupils' learning would be to determine whether they recognize rectangles when these are next presented.

A three-part verbal chain can be illustrated in teaching both a noun and its definite article in Spanish:

Stimulus	*Response*
Picture of a church.	Pupils observe picture.
Teacher says *iglesia.*	Pupils repeat *iglesia.*
Teacher says *la iglesia.*	Pupils repeat *la iglesia.*

If the pupils have mastered the noun and the article, they will be able to repeat *la iglesia* when the teacher next shows them a picture of a church.

5. *Discrimination learning.* Human beings master a large number of motor and verbal chains, many of which, though distinct, are at the same time similar. Learners discriminate, for example, when they learn to distinguish the different skills required in driving a car with an automatic transmission, a car with a standard transmission, and a tractor-trailer. Pupils who have learned separate verbal chains for *rectangle*, *square*, and *triangle* must learn to discriminate among these figures. Pupils who have been taught that *iglesia* means *church* and *la iglesia* means *the church* must distinguish churches from other buildings, must recognize churches as a class even though each church may be architecturally different, and must repeatedly use *la* with the noun and not *el*, which they have seen in other verbal chains. They must further recognize that "la" when used as an article means "the" and not something else. Even though they have been exposed to hundreds of other verbal chains for other words, they must always remember that the word *iglesia* means *church*.

6. *Concept learning.* We get into a higher order of learning when we seek to teach concepts to learners. Concepts are abstractions—some more abstract than others—that require the medium of language for their learning. The property of a rectangle—its rectangularity—is a concept. The color blue and the number three are concepts. Office building is a concept that differs from the concept of a school building. First, last, and always are concepts, as are north and south, up and down, large and small, left and right. Concepts may refer to concrete objects, such as a football, to properties of objects, such as the color red, and to ideas, such as democracy. Brotherhood, excellence, and honesty are concepts. Students must have the necessary mastery of language to be able to understand concepts. The beauty of language is that it permits us to talk about concepts and communicate these abstractions to others. We do not need the football to talk about it. We do not have to be in the presence of an office building to discuss it. We cannot even see the concept of honesty, but we know what traits an honest person exhibits and can communicate those traits to others. Much of the instruction in school involves teaching concepts.

7. *Rule learning.* A rule is a chain of concepts. The learner grasps the relationship between concepts and formulates a rule or principle. We are constantly teaching rules in school. The science instructor teaches learners that litmus paper turns red when dipped into an acid. This rule involves three concepts: litmus paper, acid, and red. The relationship between the litmus paper and the acid is the action of turning red. We teach the principle that yellow plus blue makes green. We teach that $a^2 + b^2 = c^2$. Students learn that life insurance is a way of protecting one's family. We teach that some drugs have a harmful effect on one's health. Rule learning brings out the relationships and applications of the concepts that are linked together to form the rule.

8. *Problem solving.* This is the highest-order and most complex type of learning. Problem solving represents the development of the ability to think. The learner puts to use all of the rules learned that have a bearing on a particular problem in order to seek a solution to it, and in the process generates new rules and new knowledge. Problem solving is the process of reasoning. In other contexts, problem solving is equated with the scientific method. Each attempt at problem solving reveals new ideas and adds to the store of knowledge, which may in turn be applied to the solution of subsequent problems. The various disciplines teem with illustrations of both successful and unsuccessful attempts to solve problems, such as the discovery of vaccines for life-threatening diseases, the search for ways to convert garbage into energy, more effective means of providing for the nation's housing needs, combating crime, growing disease-resistant grain, communicating worldwide, and piecing together the origin of the human species.

We have reviewed these eight types of learning to help teachers recognize the different types of learning evident in their learning tasks. A supervisor should study a classification system of types of learning, such as that of Gagné, to help teachers make task analyses.[13]

In addition to a review of the learners' characteristics and identification of type of learning, a task analysis should include an appraisal of any special conditions or constraints under which the learning tasks will occur. The teacher should ask, Do the tasks require special equipment or other resources? Can the tasks be performed in the space provided? Are there time constraints? Are there limitations imposed by the school, the community, or the state? If we may go back to the example of parking a car and place it as a topic in a driver education course (either in school or outside of school), we might analyze this task in the following manner:

1. *Nature of the learners.* The learners must be of age to obtain a learner's permit to drive. They must possess sufficient physical coordination skills to handle an automobile. They must know the rules of the road and recognize road signs.

2. *Type of learning.* This task is primarily chaining, the development of a series of perceptual-motor skills.

3. *Special conditions and constraints.* The learners must have obtained their learners' permits. In a group of twenty-five learners, the instructor can allot only a brief period of actual practice in driving a car to each. An automobile that is fully insured and equipped with dual controls must be available for use.

By understanding the nature of the task, the teacher is more likely to realize the goal of instruction—mastery of the content by the learners. Task description and analysis aid the teacher in designing enabling objectives and perfecting the main objective. The supervisor can serve as a consultant to teachers who wish to develop the skills of task description and analysis.

The professional literature of the 1980s and 1990s abounds with articles and books advocating the development of thinking skills as the primary goal of education. Not since 1961, when the Educational Policies Commission declared that the central purpose of education is the development of the ability to think, has there been such a flurry of interest and research into thinking skills.[14] Certainly, problem solving—or, as some people call it, "reflective thinking" or "the scientific method"—is one dimension of the thinking process.

Some educators lump all thinking skills under the rubric of problem solving or critical thinking. Barry K. Beyer distinguished critical thinking from other thinking skills, describing critical thinking as "the process of determining the authenticity, accuracy, and worth of information of knowledge claims."[15]

Research has delved into the functioning of the brain and into metacognition, which Arthur L. Costa defined as "being conscious of our own thinking and problem solving while thinking ... a uniquely human ability occurring in the neocortex of the brain."[16] Costa elaborated on metacognition when he said: "Metacognition is our ability to formulate a plan of action, monitor our own progress along that plan, realize what we know and don't know, detect and recover from error and reflect upon and evaluate our own thinking processes."[17] In one sense, metacognition is thinking about thinking.

Study of the brain and research into the functions of the right and left hemispheres have fascinated people for a long time. As Patricia Wolfe pointed out, "The functions and roles of these two halves, known as the right and left hemispheres, have been debated for centuries. As early as 400 B.C., Hippocrates wrote about the possibility of the duality of the human brain."[18] Some evidence seems to indicate that one side of the brain predominates in individuals. This evidence appears to indicate that when the left side is dominant, people learn best through logical and linear thinking processes; when the right side is paramount, the individual learns best through creative and intuitive processes. Assuming the validity of the left-brain/right-brain research, we can note that most of the school's curriculum is designed for left-hemisphere learners.

Interpreting the left-brain/right-brain research, educators have concluded that the right hemisphere has been neglected, that teachers should determine, through checklists and other means, learners' hemispheric predominance, that teachers should tailor the curriculum to the means by which individuals learn best, and that the curriculum should include more content and experiences oriented to right-brain learning. One goal would be the development of both halves of the brain.

Susan Dobbs cautioned, however, against oversimplification of the concept of hemispheric dominance. She called attention to evidence that complex mental functions are not necessarily symmetrically divided between the brain's hemispheres. She observed that "the terms 'left and right brained' are largely metaphoric, based on an overextension of available data," and warned against "interpreting this metaphor literally in the classroom."[19] Dobbs advocated developing many types of thinking skills, especially higher-order ones, following both logical and creative processes without concern for the location of the processes within the brain. Writing in a similar vein, Wolfe noted, "None of these theories and ideas about the roles of the hemispheres are totally inaccurate, or totally accurate ... the more we study any part of the brain, the more we learn just how complex it is. ... The specializations of each hemisphere develop to their fullest when informed by the opposite hemisphere. The two halves of your brain work together in a beautifully coordinated partnership."[20]

Identification of thinking skills is germane to development of the ability to think. Many researchers have developed lists of thinking skills. Bloom's taxonomy of the cognitive domain is only one of these. Robert J. Marzano presented a useful model of basic thinking and reasoning skills identified by a study conducted by the McREL Institute (see Figure 3.4).[21]

General Information Processing Skills

Identifying Similarities, Dissimilarities, and Patterns

1. Comparing and contrasting

2. Analyzing relationships

3. Classifying

Logic

4. Argumentation

5. Making inductions

6. Making deductions

Knowledge Utilization Skills

7. Experimental inquiry

8. Investigation

9. Problem solving

10. Decision making

FIGURE 3.4 Thinking and Reasoning Skills for Classroom Use Identified by the McREL Study. *Source*: Robert J. Marzano, *Transforming Classroom Grading*. Copyright © by McREL. Published by Alexandria, Va.: Association for Supervision and Curriculum Development, 2000, p. 36. Used by permission of McREL, Aurora, CO.

Knowledge about thinking and strategies for encouraging thinking can go only so far. The teaching of thinking is as much an attitude on the part of the teacher as it is a set of skills. Thinking can only be taught when pupils are placed in a posture of thinking. Simple recall learning, which makes up the major part of a typical school curriculum, cannot elicit thinking. Thinking is encouraged when probing questions replace recall; when divergent questions substitute for convergent; when *why* and *how* replace *who, what, where*, and *when*; when alternative answers are sought in place of single responses; when originality is stressed over conformity; when intuition is fostered; and when higher-order learning displaces lower-order cognition.

We need to remind ourselves that thinking does not occur in a vacuum. Albert Einstein did not pull the formula $E = mc^2$ out of thin air. He had to have mastered a large store of knowledge from which to derive the facts presented in the formula. Therefore we cannot play down the necessity for students' mastery of cognitive learnings, which provide the tools for thinking.

Multiple Intelligences

We sometimes hear the slang term *brainy* used as a synonym for *intelligent*. In fact, popular usage treats intelligence as a global concept. Current thinking views intelligence not as global but as multiple intelligences. Some people excel in one type of intelligence, whereas others excel in another type. For example, Einstein and Mozart, both "brainy," reflected different types of intelligence. Thomas Jefferson exhibited a very different type of intelligence from that of Leonardo da Vinci. Howard Gardner has specified eight intelligences, which we discuss in Chapter 4.[22]

Organizing Instructional Plans

At some point the teacher must assemble the various products of planning, putting them all together in some form of comprehensive plan. In the rest of this chapter we are concerned with types of plans that will be put to immediate use in the classroom; we defer discussion of broader plans (such as curriculum guides) to Chapter 7.

To begin to organize his or her plans, the teacher looks at the content: knowledge, skills, and affective outcomes as a whole and the time available for presenting that content to the students. A year, a semester, nine weeks, or possibly six weeks may be available for dealing with the particular subject matter. The next step is to break that content into its primary topics. A teacher may need the entire time to treat one topic. If the period of time is long, however, several topics can most likely be covered. The teacher should estimate the amount of time necessary for most—and hopefully all—students to master the material.

Unit Plans   After identifying the topics and the time available for each topic, the teacher proceeds to create a type of plan known as a unit, learning unit, or teaching unit. A unit is a segment of an instructional program. If mastery of one unit depends on mastery of previous units, the units must be put into sequence. The unit could follow a number of formats. Drawing on the earlier discussion of models of instruction, we can devise a functional format such as the following:

1. *Goals.* At the beginning of each unit the teacher should state the nonbehavioral instructional goals.

2. *Objectives.* Following the goals should come the instructional objectives. The objectives and subobjectives should be stated behaviorally, classified, and grouped by domain.

3. *Preassessment.* The teacher should indicate what procedures are to be used to answer this question: Do the students already possess the knowledge and skills that the teacher plans to develop in the unit? This information is needed so that the teacher may alter the content or choose different content if the pupils demonstrate they have already sufficiently mastered the content to be studied. The teacher must also specify the entry skills (if any) needed to begin study of the unit and the means by which possession of the prerequisite skills would be determined.

4. *Instructional procedures.* In this part of the unit the teacher should detail the learning strategies to be used to present the material and the human and material resources needed. Chapter 4, on presentation of instruction, is designed to help the supervisor work with teachers in the selection of instructional procedures.

5. *Resources.* The teacher should list the physical and human resources that will be used in the unit.

6. *Evaluation.* The final section of the unit is devoted to evaluation techniques. The teacher chooses assessment techniques most appropriate to the content and the learners and writes whatever tests are to be used to measure student achievement.

The unit outline suggested here is general enough to be adaptable to a broad range of the curriculum: elementary and middle school content; segments of a high school discipline; minicourses (e.g., Purchasing Life Insurance); interdisciplinary topics (e.g., Homes of the Colonial Period); and even phases of the extra-class program of the middle, junior high, and senior high schools.

Although the six points covered in the suggested unit format may apply to planning in most fields and at most levels of learning, there will be variations in the substance, extent, and complexity of plans from teacher to teacher and from program to program. Although a unit plan in social studies, for example, would be quite different from a unit plan in skill areas, such as word processing, gymnastics, or instruction in playing the clarinet, and in creative areas, such as art, writing, and other crafts, teachers in all areas need to spell out goals, objectives, preassessment techniques, instructional procedures, resources, and evaluation techniques on more than a day-to-day basis. A unit plan requires the teacher to look at instruction on a longer-range basis than the next day's work. The supervisor should help teachers find a planning format compatible with their own disciplines or grade levels.

If the unit is primarily for the teacher's use and is not to be put into the hands of the pupils, the teacher has the choice of incorporating tests under the appropriate section—preassessment or evaluation—or placing them in appendixes or keeping them separate from the unit itself.

Some instructors who teach mature learners, particularly at the college level, like to give an entire unit plan to the students. In that case, tests cannot be made a part of the unit. The students do not need a copy of the entire unit but instead may receive an abbreviated version that outlines goals, objectives, entry skills needed, and resources to be used. Whether or not students receive a copy of the plan, the teacher must be certain to communicate the goals and objectives of the units.

Lesson Plans   The unit serves as a basis for day-to-day planning and as a document that can be used to substantiate that specific concepts have been taught. This is an important concept, as many students have to be taught certain concepts based on their Individual Educational Plans (IEPs). From the unit the teacher derives daily lesson plans. The word *daily* should be stressed. If study of a particular unit in a high school course is to last six weeks, a course that meets five days per week will require thirty lesson plans. The elementary school teacher in a self-contained classroom will find it necessary not only to outline the work of an entire day but also to develop mini lesson plans for each subject area or topic studied during the day.

A lesson plan need not be lengthy. The supervisor must remember that planning is a continuing activity of teachers and that the demands on teachers' time are many. Each lesson plan should include at least the following elements:

1. *Objectives of the particular lesson plan.* Not all objectives can necessarily be accomplished in one day's time. Some will carry over to the next day or for several days. In practice, some daily plans will require more than one day's presentation. The teacher must review the plan at the conclusion of the day and make whatever revisions are needed for the next day. That teachers must make a plan for every class every day does not mean that each plan must be totally new; it may legitimately be a revised plan based on the accomplishments of the preceding day.

2. *Instructional procedures and resources.* The teacher will select from the unit plan those procedures pertinent to the particular day's activities and will use those resources applicable for that day.

3. *Evaluation.* The teacher should employ some evaluation techniques, no matter how simple, to reveal whether the day's lesson has "gone over."

Note that the lesson plan does not include goals, which normally apply to the entire unit, or to preassessment, which is conducted before beginning the unit and also relates to the whole unit.

The formats of a unit and lesson plan can be seen in the following abbreviated unit and lesson plan titled "The Use of the Dictionary" for a middle school class.

ILLUSTRATIVE UNIT PLAN: THE USE OF THE DICTIONARY

Goals

The student should become familiar with the kinds of help that can be found in a dictionary.

The student should gain an appreciation of the dictionary as a useful tool in language learning.

(For classes that have access to the Internet) The student should acquire the ability to use an online dictionary to check the spelling and meaning of words.

Objectives

Cognitive and Psychomotor Using a dictionary supplied in class, the student will look up words given orally by the teacher and will write the correct spelling of those words.

Using a dictionary supplied in class, the student will look up words given in written form by the teacher or encountered in books or magazines and will write definitions of the words.

Using a dictionary supplied in class, the student will look up words given in written form by the teacher or encountered in books or magazines and will pronounce them correctly.

Using a dictionary supplied in class, the student will look up words given in written form by the teacher or encountered in books or magazines and will find synonyms for those words.

Using a dictionary supplied in class, the student will look up words given in written form by the teacher and will tell the language origin of those words.

Given words in written form that cannot be found in the dictionary supplied in class, the student will go to the library and look up the definition and pronunciation and verify the spelling in *Webster's Unabridged Dictionary.*

Given three different dictionaries, the student will state the differences in systems for noting division of words into syllables, differences in marking pronunciation, and differences in preferred definitions.

(For classes that have access to the Internet) Using an online dictionary, the student will demonstrate the ability to look up the spelling and definition of words.

Affective When asked by their parents to look up the spelling, meaning, pronunciation, or origin of words not familiar to them, the students will find pleasure in carrying out this task.

On encountering a new word while reading, the student will find satisfaction in being able to find out what the word means.

Preassessment

A pretest [not included in this illustrative unit] will be administered that requires the students to look up the spelling, meaning, pronunciation, and origin of selected words. A mastery level of 90 percent accuracy will indicate that a student already possesses the competencies to be learned in the unit.

The student will be able to read most of the materials of the fifth grade, will be able to write the letters of the alphabet in sequence, and will be able to alphabetize a word to four letters (as, d i c t i o n a r y).

Instructional Procedures

The students will take a spelling test of words dictated by the teacher and will look up in the dictionary words they misspell.

The students will read passages from a book, identify words whose meanings they do not know, and look up the dictionary definitions of those words.

The students will be taken on a tour of the school media center by the media specialist, who will show them various kinds of dictionaries, discuss the value of dictionaries, and demonstrate how to use *Webster's Unabridged Dictionary*.

The students will listen to a presentation by the teacher on how to read the pronunciation of words in the dictionary. The teacher will use computer equipment or an overhead projector for explanations and will distribute a copied sheet that shows words broken into syllables and marked for sounds and stress.

The student will look up the same word in three dictionaries supplied in class and compare differences in noting syllables, indicating pronunciation, and preferred definitions.

(For classes that have access to the Internet) Students will practice looking up the spelling and meaning of words in an online dictionary.

Resources

Dictionaries such as the latest edition of *Merriam-Webster's Collegiate Dictionary*, paperback dictionaries, *Webster's Unabridged Dictionary*, computers and Internet access, and overhead projector and transparencies.

Time allotted for the unit: forty-five minutes per day for five days.

Evaluation

The students will attempt to achieve a 90 percent mastery level on a performance test [not included in this illustrative unit] that requires them to look up words in the dictionary and give their correct spelling, definition, pronunciation, and origin. Students who score less than 90 percent will need individualized help in mastering the content of the unit.

Given the availability of computers with online capability, the teacher will assess students' skills in determining the spelling and meaning of several words using an online dictionary.

ILLUSTRATIVE LESSON PLAN

Objectives

The students will write twenty words dictated by the teacher, look up the correct spelling of the words in a dictionary supplied in class, and verify their spelling of the words.

Instructional Procedures and Resources

Set Induction:[23] The teacher will ask students whether they have ever used the dictionary, whether they have ever wanted to know how to spell words correctly, whether recieve or receive is the correct spelling of the word, and why it is important to know the correct spelling of words. (5 min.)

The students will write words dictated by the teacher. (10 min.)

The students will use a dictionary supplied in class to verify the spelling of each word and correct misspelled words. (20 min.)

Closure:[24] (last 2 min.) The teacher will summarize the students' success in finding and correcting words they had misspelled and will stress the usefulness of the dictionary for helping them with spelling unfamiliar words.

Resources: dictionaries; copied sheet with correct spellings.

Evaluation

The students will double-check the correct spelling of the words from a sheet distributed by the teacher giving spellings they should have found in the dictionary and will report to the teacher how many words they had written correctly after looking them up. (8 min.)

The foregoing outlines of two types of instructional plans—the unit plan and the lesson plan—offer ways to organize products of the planning process into a logical and intelligible form. A great deal of thought and creativity go into constructing instructional plans. Plans may and should differ from teacher to teacher even when topics are the same; no two teachers approach the task of planning the same way, a fact that makes the planning process such a highly creative endeavor.

The supervisor may aid teachers in developing unit and lesson plans by showing them models of well-constructed plans. In so doing, he or she should make clear to them that plans are not written to please the administrator or supervisor but to enable the teachers to carry out instruction more effectively.

SUMMARY

Instructional planning is perceived as the first step in a continuum whose subsequent steps are presentation and evaluation of instruction. Plans must be continuously revised as feedback from learner achievement shows modifications that should be made.

The supervisor can implement a six-point program to help teachers develop and improve skills in following a systematic approach to instructional design, using a model of instruction as a guide to planning, writing nonbehavioral goals and behavioral objectives, describing and analyzing tasks, applying taxonomies of instructional objectives, and organizing instructional plans.

A major goal of schooling is the development of the ability to think. Among the main thinking skills are problem solving, decision making, critical thinking, and creative thinking. Teachers should select content and plan activities using higher-order processes. Two types of instructional plans are recommended: the lesson plan, which shows the planning for one day, and the unit plan, which shows the planning for longer periods of time and from which the lesson plans are derived. Planning requires a good deal of thought and time, but it is an essential process with the ultimate aim of enhancing student learning.

QUESTIONS FOR DISCUSSION

1. What knowledge and skills are necessary for teachers to plan effectively?
2. Is any one of the three taxonomies more important than the others? If so, which one and why?
3. What effect should the presence of exceptional students in the regular classroom have on planning?
4. How would you evaluate a teacher's planning for instruction?
5. Should administrators review teachers' lesson plans? If so, when and how often?
6. What are the major differences between the systematic approach to planning and older approaches?

ACTIVITIES FOR FURTHER STUDY

REFLECTIVE

1. Define the following terms:

instructional design
model of instruction
instructional goal
instructional (behavioral) objective

taxonomy of instructional objectives
cognitive domain
affective domain
psychomotor domain

2. Select a learning task; describe and analyze it.

3. Describe ways teachers can develop thinking skills.

4. Locate and report on a list of thinking skills that differ from those mentioned in this chapter.

5. Review and critique one or more research studies on functions of the left and right hemispheres of the brain.

6. Describe the relationship between brain hemispheres and hand domination.

7. Locate one model of instruction that is different from any model in the text and compare it to the five-part model of instruction described in this chapter.

8. Describe the differences between task description and task analysis.

9. Describe the following types of learning and give one illustration of each:

    chaining   rule learning
    concept learning   problem solving

10. List two behavioral terms (verbs) that might be used in stating cognitive objectives in each of the six categories of the Bloom taxonomy.

11. List two behavioral terms (verbs) that might be used in stating affective objectives in each of the five categories of the Krathwohl taxonomy.

12. List two behavioral terms (verbs) that might be used in stating psychomotor objectives in each of the seven categories of the Simpson taxonomy.

13. State three components of complete instructional objectives.

14. Distinguish a performance standard from a stability standard in writing an instructional objective.

15. Describe ways in which a supervisor can decide whether teachers are doing adequate planning.

APPLICATION

1. Diagram a model of instruction and explain its parts.

2. Apply the taxonomies of the three domains of learning by writing one instructional objective for each of the major categories of each domain.

3. Locate definitions of the following terms and document the sources:

    problem solving   intuitive thinking
    decision making   logical thinking
    critical thinking   cognition
    creative thinking   metacognition
    linear thinking   hemisphericity
    holistic thinking

4. Give examples of low-order questions and high-order questions in your subject field or grade level.

5. Construct one unit plan and one lesson plan.

6. Write one instructional goal for a particular topic that you might teach in school and three instructional objectives derived from the instructional goal.

7. Compare the Bloom taxonomy as revised in Lorin W. Anderson and David R. Krathwohl, eds. (see Chapter 6 bibliography) with the original Bloom taxonomy.

8. Compare Robert J. Marzano's taxonomy of educational objectives (see chapter bibliography) with the Bloom taxonomy.

9. Compare Harrow's taxonomy of the psychomotor domain (see bibliography for this chapter) with the Simpson taxonomy in (a) categories and (b) use.

10. Compare the taxonomy of the psychomotor domain found in Kibler, Barker, and Miles, *Behavioral Objectives and Instruction*, Chapter 3 (see bibliography for this chapter), with the Simpson taxonomy in (a) categories and (b) use.

11. Observe two teachers in their classrooms and try to determine from their presentations whether there is evidence of planning. If you believe there is such evidence, attempt to judge the quality of planning that went into the presentation.

12. Talk with the teachers you selected for Application 11 and report to the class on planning procedures they use. Determine whether the teachers follow planning procedures discussed in this chapter or other techniques.

13. Classify the following instructional objectives as to domain and category within the domain (answers follow). The student will

   a. Evaluate and compare the nutrition value of six breakfast cereals.

   b. Demonstrate how to hold a tennis racket and ball in order to serve.

   c. Listen to a native speaker of a foreign language that he or she is studying and summarize what the speaker has said.

   d. Respond to a call for a contribution to a leading charity.

   e. Assemble a kite following instructions on the wrapper.

   f. Using a twelve-inch ruler, measure and record in inches and fractions of inches the lengths of several straight lines on a handout distributed by the teacher.

   g. Regularly demonstrate sensitivity in relationships with other people.

   h. Write a biography of a famous political or military leader on either side in World War II.

   i. Practice cutting chunks of raw cabbage into pieces for cole slaw.

   j. Name the president and vice president of the United States.

   k. Express admiration for the fine work that has been put into a handmade afghan.

   l. Identify basil leaves by their smell.

   m. Demonstrate an awareness that vandalism is hurting the school's image.

   n. Create an original fruit punch.

   o. Decide whether a proposed solution to a community problem is likely to work.

   p. Change the front left tire (leaving it on the rim) by substituting the spare for it.

   q. Decide whether or not saving money "for a rainy day" is worthwhile.

   r. Refinish in antique white a dresser that has been painted a solid color.

ANSWERS TO ACTIVITY 13

   a. cognitive evaluation

   b. psychomotor set

   c. cognitive comprehension

   d. affective responding

   e. psychomotor guided response

   f. cognitive application

g. affective characterization by value or value complex

h. cognitive synthesis

i. psychomotor mechanism

j. cognitive knowledge

k. affective valuing

l. psychomotor perception

m. affective receiving

n. psychomotor origination

o. cognitive analysis

p. psychomotor complex overt response

q. affective organization

r. psychomotor adaptation

14. For each of the following behaviors identify the type of learning with Gagné's classification of types (answers follow):

    a. Defining charity.

    b. Repeating a sound. (Baby repeats *Da-Da* on hearing his or her father say *Da-Da*.)

    c. Choosing the right computer for the needs of the office.

    d. Showing fear of high places.

    e. Learning that smoking may be hazardous to your health.

    f. Learning a word. (An adult points to an animal in a zoo and says to a child "elephant." When seeing an elephant again, the child says "elephant.")

    g. Pitching a baseball.

    h. Distinguishing oak from other woods.

ANSWERS TO ACTIVITY 14

a. concept learning

b. stimulus-response learning

c. problem solving

d. signal learning

e. rule learning

f. verbal association

g. chaining

h. discrimination learning

NOTES

1. Robert J. Kibler, Donald J. Cegala, David T. Miles, and Larry L. Barker (see bibliography) discussed a four-part model of instruction that they referred to as the "General Model of Instruction." W. James Popham and Eva L. Baker (see bibliography) described a four-part model that they labeled a "Goal-Referenced Instructional Model."
2. For additional help in writing instructional objectives, consult Benjamin S. Bloom, J. Thomas Hastings, and George F. Madaus, *Handbook on Formative and Summative Evaluation of Student Learning* (New York: McGraw-Hill, 1971); Benjamin S. Bloom, George F. Madaus, and J. Thomas Hastings, *Evaluation to Improve Learning* (New

York: McGraw-Hill, 1981); Norman E. Gronlund, *How to Write and Use Instructional Objectives*, 6th ed. (Upper Saddle River, N.J.: Merrill, 2000); Robert F. Mager, *Preparing Instructional Objectives*, 2nd ed. (Belmont, Calif.: Fearon, 1975); Newton S. Metfessel, William B. Michaels, and Donald A. Kirsner, "Instrumentation of Bloom's and Krathwohl's Taxonomies for the Writing of Educational Objectives," *Psychology in the Schools* 6 (July 1969): 227–31; W. James Popham and Eva L. Baker, *Establishing Instructional Goals* (Englewood Cliffs, N.J.: Prentice Hall, 1970).

3. Robert H. Davis, Lawrence T. Alexander, and Stephen L. Yelon, *Learning System Design: An Approach to the Improvement of Instruction* (New York: McGraw-Hill, 1974), p. 41.

4. Benjamin S. Bloom, ed., *Taxonomy of Educational Objectives: The Classification of Educational Goals: Handbook I: Cognitive Domain* (White Plains, N.Y.: Longman, 1956).

5. David R. Krathwohl, Benjamin S. Bloom, and Bertram B. Masia, *Taxonomy of Educational Objectives: in The Classification of Educational Goals: Handbook II: Affective Domain* (White Plains, N.Y.: Longman, 1964).

6. Elizabeth Jane Simpson, "The Classification of Educational Objectives in the Psychomotor Domain," *The Psychomotor Domain*, vol. 3 (Washington, D.C.: Gryphon House, 1972), pp. 43–56. See also Anita J. Harrow, *A Taxonomy of the Psychomotor Domain: A Guide for Developing Behavioral Objectives* (White Plains, N.Y.: Longman, 1972).

7. Bloom, *Taxonomy*, p. 18.

8. Krathwohl, Bloom, and Masia, *Taxonomy*, p. 35.

9. Simpson, "Classification of Educational Objectives."

10. Harrow, *A Taxonomy*, p. 27.

11. Davis, Alexander, and Yelon, *Learning System Design*, chaps. 5 and 7.

12. Robert M. Gagné, *The Conditions of Learning*, 2nd ed. (New York: Holt, Rinehart and Winston, 1970).

13. For a useful discussion of three types of learning (humanistic, cognitive, and behavioral), see Carl D. Glickman, *Developmental Supervision: Alternative Practices for Helping Teachers Improve Instruction* (Alexandria, Va.: Association for Supervision and Curriculum Development, 1981), pp. 3–5.

14. Educational Policies Commission, *The Central Purpose of American Education* (Washington, D.C.: National Education Association, 1961).

15. Barry K. Beyer, "Critical Thinking: What Is It?" *Social Education* 49 (April 1985): 276.

16. Arthur L. Costa, "Teaching for, of, and about Thinking," in *Developing Minds: A Resource Book for Teaching Thinking*, ed. Arthur L. Costa (Alexandria, Va.: Association for Supervision and Curriculum Development, 1985), p. 21.

17. Costa, "The Principal's Role in Enhancing Thinking Skills," in *Developing Minds*, p. 31.

18. Patricia Wolfe, *Brain Matters: Translating Research into Classroom Practice* (Alexandria, Va.: Association for Supervision and Curriculum Development, 2001), p. 43.

19. Susan Dobbs, "Some Second Thoughts on the Application of Left Brain/Right Brain Research," *Roeper Review* 12 (December 1989): 121.

20. Wolfe, *Brain Matters*, pp. 44, 47.

21. Robert J. Marzano, *Transforming Classroom Grading* (Alexandria, Va.: Association for Supervision and Curriculum Development, 2000), p. 36. See also Barbara Z. Presseisen, "Thinking Skills: Meanings and Models," in *Developing Minds: A Resource Book for Teaching Thinking*, Arthur L. Costa, ed. (Alexandria, Va.: Association for Supervision and Curriculum Development, 1985), pp. 43–48.

22. Howard Gardner, *Multiple Intelligences: The Theory in Practice* (New York: Basic Books, 1993) and Kathy Checkley, "The First Seven . . . and the Eighth: A Conversation with Howard Gardner," *Educational Leadership* 55 (September 1997): 8, 9.

23. See Chapter 7 for discussion of this term.

24. See Chapter 4 for discussion of this term.

BIBLIOGRAPHY

ANDERSON, LORIN W., and DAVID R. KRATHWOHL, eds. *A Taxonomy for Learning, Teaching, and Assessing: A Revision of Bloom's Taxonomy of Educational Objectives.* New York: Longman, 2001.

ARMSTRONG, ROBERT J., TERRY O. CORNELL, ROBERT F. KRANER, and E. WAYNE ROBERSON. *The Development and Evaluation of Behavioral Objectives.* Worthington, Ohio: Charles A. Jones, 1970.

ARMSTRONG, THOMAS. *Multiple Intelligences in the Classroom*, 2nd ed. Alexandria, Va.: Association for Supervision and Curriculum Development, 2000.

BAKER, EVA L., and W. JAMES POPHAM. *Expanding Dimensions of Instructional Objectives*. Englewood Cliffs, N. J.: Prentice Hall, 1973.

BANATHY, BELA H. *Instructional Systems*. Palo Alto, Calif.: Fearon, 1968.

BECKER, WESLEY C., SIEGFRIED ENGELMANN, and DON R. THOMAS. *Teaching 2: Cognitive Learning and Instruction*. Chicago: Science Research Associates, 1975.

BEYER, BARRY K. "Critical Thinking: What Is It?" *Social Education* 49 (April 1985): 276.

———. "Improving Thinking Skills—Defining the Problem," *Phi Delta Kappan* 65 (March 1984): 486–90.

BLOOM, BENJAMIN S., ed. *Taxonomy of Educational Objectives: The Classification of Educational Goals: Handbook I: Cognitive Domain*. White Plains, N.Y.: Longman, 1956.

BLOOM, BENJAMIN S., J. THOMAS HASTINGS, and GEORGE, F. MADAUS. *Handbook on Formative and Summative Evaluation of Student Learning*. New York: McGraw-Hill, 1971.

BLOOM, BENJAMIN S., GEORGE F. MADAUS, and J. THOMAS HASTINGS. *Evaluation to Improve Learning*. New York: McGraw-Hill, 1981.

BRIGGS, LESLIE J., and WALTER, W. WAGER. *Handbook of Procedures for the Design of Instruction*, 2nd ed. Englewood Cliffs, J. J.: Educational Technology Publications, 1981.

CAMPBELL, LINDA, and BRUCE, CAMPBELL. *Multiple Intelligences and Student Achievement: Success Stories from Six Schools*. Alexandria, Va.: Association for Supervision and Curriculum Development, 1999.

CHECKLEY, KATHY. "The First Seven . . . and the Eighth: A Conversation with Howard Gardner." *Educational Leadership* 55 (September 1997): 8, 9.

COHEN, JOZEF. *Thinking*. Chicago: Rand McNally, 1971.

COOPER, JAMES M., ed. *Classroom Teaching Skills*, 8th ed. Boston: Houghton Mifflin, 2006.

COSTA, ARTHUR L. *Developing Minds: A Resource Book for Teaching Thinking*, 3rd ed. Alexandria, Va.: Association for Supervision and Curriculum Development, 2001.

———. *Developing Minds: A Resource Book for Teaching Thinking*, rev. ed., vol. 1. Alexandria, Va.: Association for Supervision and Curriculum Development, 1991.

———. *Developing Minds: Programs for Teaching Thinking*, rev. ed., vol. 2. Alexandria, Va.: Association for Supervision and Curriculum Development, 1991.

———. "The Principal's Role in Enhancing Thinking Skills." In *Developing Minds: A Resource Book for Teaching Thinking*, ed. ARTHUR L., COSTA. Alexandria, Va.: Association for Supervision and Curriculum Development, 1985.

———. "Teaching for, of, and about Thinking." In *Developing Minds: A Resource Book for Teaching Thinking*, ed. ARTHUR L. COSTA, Alexandria, Va.: Association for Supervision and Curriculum Development, 1985, pp. 20–23.

DAVIS, ROBERT H., LAWRENCE T. ALEXANDER, and STEPHEN, L. YELON. *Learning System Design: An Approach to the Improvement of Instruction*. New York: McGraw-Hill, 1974.

DOBBS, SUSAN, "Some Second Thoughts on the Application of Left Brain/Right Brain Research," *Roeper Review* 12 (December 1989): 119–21.

Edelman, Paul. TeachersPayTeachers.com, 2006.

Educational, Policies Commission. *The Central Purpose of American Education*. Washington, D.C.: National Educational Association, 1961.

GAGNÉ, ROBERT M. *The Conditions of Learning*, 3rd ed. New York: Holt, Rinehart and Winston, 1977.

GARDNER, HOWARD. *Multiple Intelligences: The Theory in Practice*. New York: Basic Books, 1993.

GRONLUND, NORMAN E. *How to Write and Use Instructional Objectives*, 6th ed. Upper Saddle River, N. J.: Merrill, 2000.

HARROW, ANITA J. *A Taxonomy of the Psychomotor Domain: A Guide for Developing Behavioral Objectives*. New York: D. McKay, 1972.

HUNTER, MADELINE, and DOUGLAS, RUSSELL. "How Can I Plan More Effective Lessons?" *Instructor* 87 (September 1977): 74–75f.

KIBLER, ROBERT J., LARRY L. BARKER, and DAVID T. MILES. *Behavioral Objectives and Instruction*. Boston: Allyn and Bacon, 1970.

KIBLER, ROBERT J., DONALD J. CEGALA, DAVID T. MILES, and LARRY L. BARKER. *Objectives for Instruction and Evaluation*, 2nd ed. Boston: Allyn and Bacon, 1981.

KRATHWOHL, DAVID R., BENJAMIN S. BLOOM, and BERTRAM B. MASIA. *Taxonomy of Educational Objectives: The Classification of Educational Goals: Handbook II: Affective Domain.* White Plains, N.Y.: Longman, 1964.

MAGER, ROBERT F. *Preparing Instructional Objectives*, rev. 2nd ed. Belmont, Calif.: Pitman Management and Training, 1984.

MARZANO, ROBERT J. *Designing a New Taxonomy of Educational Objectives.* Thousand Oaks, Calif.: Corwin Press, 2001.

————. *Transforming Classroom Grading.* Alexandria, Va.: Association for Supervision and Curriculum Development, 2000.

METFESSEL, NEWTON S., WILLIAM B. MICHAELS, and DONALD A. KIRSNER. "Instrumentation of Bloom's and Krathwohl's Taxonomies for the Writing of Educational Objectives." *Psychology in the Schools* 6 (July 1969): 227–31.

MOORE, KENNETH D. *Classroom Teaching Skills*, 6th ed. Boston: McGraw-Hill, 2007.

POPHAM, W. JAMES. "Practical Ways of Improving the Curriculum via Measurable Objectives." *Bulletin of the National Association of Secondary School Principals* 55 (May 1971): 76–90.

POPHAM, W. JAMES, and EVA L. BAKER. *Establishing Instructional Goals.* Englewood Cliffs, N. J.: Prentice Hall, 1970.

————. *Systematic Instruction.* Englewood Cliffs, N.J.: Prentice Hall, 1970.

PRESSEISEN, BARBARA Z. "Thinking Skills: Meanings and Models." In *Developing Minds: A Resource Book for Teaching Thinking*, ARTHUR L. COSTA, ed. Alexandria, Va.: Association for Supervision and Curriculum Development, 1985, pp. 43–48.

————. "Thinking Skills: Meanings and Models Revisited." In *Developing Minds: A Resource Book for Teaching Thinking*, rev. ed., vol. 1, ARTHUR L. COSTA, ed. Alexandria, Va.: Association for Supervision and Curriculum Development, 1991, pp. 56–62.

SIMPSON, ELIZABETH JANE, "The Classification of Educational Objectives in the Psychomotor Domain." *Psychomotor Domain* 3 (1972).

STRONGE, JAMES H. *Qualities of Effective Teachers*, 2nd ed. Alexandria, Va.: Association for Supervision and Curriculum Development, 2007.

"Thinking Skills in the Curriculum." *Educational Leadership* 42 (September 1984): 3–87.

TOMLINSON, CAROL ANN. *The Differentiated Classroom: Responding to the Needs of All Learners.* Alexandria, Va.: Association for Supervision and Curriculum Development, 1999.

TYLER, RALPH W. *Basic Principles of Curriculum and Instruction: Syllabus for Education 360.* Chicago: University of Chicago Press, 1950.

WOLFE, PATRICIA. *Brain Matters: Translating Research into Classroom Practice.* Alexandria, Va.: Association for Supervision and Curriculum Development, 2001.

VIDEOTAPES

A Visit to a Differentiated Classroom. 2001. A sixty-minute videotape with an Online Viewer's Guide. *At Work in the Differentiated Classroom*. Video Series. 2001 Three 28- to 48-minute programs on DVD with a Facilitator's Guide. Association for Supervision and Curriculum Development, 1703 North Beauregard Street, Alexandria, Va. 22311–1714. (800) 933–2723. www.ascd.org.

CHAPTER 4

HELPING TEACHERS PRESENT INSTRUCTION

OBJECTIVES

After studying Chapter 4 you should be able to accomplish the following objectives:

1. Describe characteristics of effective teaching.
2. Select resources by applying appropriate criteria.
3. Select teaching strategies by applying appropriate criteria.
4. Demonstrate set induction.
5. Demonstrate appropriate lecturing techniques.
6. Demonstrate skill in conducting a class discussion.
7. Demonstrate nonverbal cues.
8. Demonstrate oral questioning techniques.
9. Provide for variation of stimuli.
10. Provide for variation of learning activities.
11. Demonstrate closure.
12. Apply a checklist for observing lesson presentations.
13. Express a desire to master skills of presentation so that in your capacity as a supervisor you can help teachers become more effective at lesson presentation.

WHAT IS EFFECTIVE TEACHING?

An observation was made in Chapter 1 that educators disagree on what constitutes effective teaching. A number of studies conducted primarily in the 1970s sought to identify characteristics of effective teaching. Known collectively as the "effective teaching research," these studies made clear that some long-held beliefs about effective teaching are indeed correct and that practices based on those beliefs do make a difference in student achievement. Though stated in different ways by different researchers, the research says to the teacher that student achievement is likely to be higher when the teacher:

- Sets clear goals for the class.
- Holds high expectations of students.
- Focuses on the academics.
- Maintains an orderly classroom.

- Uses suitable materials for instruction.
- Monitors student performance.
- Provides feedback to students about their performances.
- Uses positive reinforcement.
- Continues his or her own personal development.

We can view these findings as generic (i.e., generally accepted principles of effective teaching applicable to all teachers at all levels). In fact, the research affirms strategies that many teachers have followed for many years.

Research describes an effective teacher as one who uses class time wisely and keeps learners engaged in purposeful activities. Time on task has become recognized as an important dimension of instruction. Effective teachers pay close attention to the factor of academic engaged time, that is, the time during which students are occupied with learning activities.

Donald M. Medley summarized almost 300 studies of teacher effectiveness and concluded that the following variables are positively related to student achievement: an orderly and supportive learning environment, time on task, instruction in large groups, and, surprisingly, the use of low-level questioning.[1] Barak V. Rosenshine identified engaged time, content covered, and direct instruction as factors in teacher effectiveness.[2] Other researchers have affirmed the importance of direct instruction and academic focus for student achievement.[3]

Some educators are disturbed by the findings that student achievement is higher when teachers use direct instruction, teach whole groups, engage in low-level questioning, and follow a teacher-centered approach. Direct instruction (that is, techniques such as the teacher's lecturing to the class, questioning limited to a factual basis, and focusing only on subject matter) and teaching an entire class as a group run counter to widely espoused beliefs about individualizing instruction, forming subgroups, involving students more actively in the learning process, and paying heed to the affective and psychomotor domains of learning as well as the cognitive area. Use of low-level questioning clashes with notions about the importance of higher-order questioning and the development of thinking skills. A teacher-directed approach conflicts with teaching methods that are basically student-centered. Nevertheless, it seems clear that direct instruction, teaching the whole class as a group, the use of low-level questioning, and teacher-centeredness can raise student achievement in some areas of the curriculum. We emphasize the word *some*, observing that some school districts have misapplied the effective teaching research.

Effective teaching research has also pointed to some basic principles on which most teachers can agree, such as setting goals, having high expectations, monitoring, giving feedback, and keeping students on task. Other principles—such as direct instruction, teaching whole classes, and teacher-centeredness—can follow under certain conditions and for certain instructional purposes. However, teachers should not rule out strategies such as cooperative learning, discovery learning, small-group discussion, individualized techniques, higher-order questioning, and student-centered activities for other instructional purposes.

Effective teaching principles are based on what is known as *process-product* research. The instructional strategies that teachers employ are the process; the product is student achievement as measured by standardized tests. You can immediately see the limitations of this type of research. Some instructional objectives—for example, higher-order cognition, creative activities, and affective and psychomotor skills—do not lend themselves readily or at all to standardized testing.

Within its process-product parameters, the effective teaching research demonstrates well certain principles of instruction that apply generally. What it does not reveal are those characteristics idiosyncratic to individual effective teachers. Ascertained only by observation of particular teachers, those traits may or may not offer clues generalizable to other teachers.

Part of the difficulty of identifying characteristics of effective teaching lies in the fact that educators and indeed the public are not in agreement on the goals of education. Is the purpose of schools to enable students to pass state and national tests? to turn out literate young men and women? to provide character training? to equip students with vocational skills? to prepare students for college? to solve social problems? Without agreement on goals, we cannot know whether teaching is effective.

Effective teaching research has apparently reached a plateau and leveled off. Perhaps this particular research emphasis has gone as far as it can go, or perhaps we are in a period during which its principles are being digested and incorporated into teaching practice. If effective teaching research accomplished nothing else, it confirmed the effectiveness of didactic teaching under certain conditions and for certain purposes. It also affirmed commonsense principles, such as the importance of time on task and holding pupils to high expectations. Most educators believe that the basic findings of the effective teaching research, which pointed to important generic teaching skills, still hold; others feel that those findings are too simplistic and fail to identify and validate other essential characteristics of contemporary education, such as the concept and practice of schools as learning communities, the existence of a culturally diverse student population, the omnipresence of technology, and the differences from teacher to teacher, class to class, grade to grade, and subject to subject.

Similar to the research on effective teaching, a body of studies known collectively as effective schools research has identified schoolwide characteristics like those demonstrated by effective teachers—namely, maintenance of an orderly school climate, high expectations of students and staff, emphasis on academics, monitoring of student progress, and one additional, very important ingredient—strong leadership by the principal.

STEPS IN IMPLEMENTATION

An old saw prescribes the steps for presenting a lesson. It directs the teacher to

1. Tell them what you are going to tell them.
2. Tell them.
3. Tell them what you told them.

Like old wives' tales, old saws sometimes have a ring of truth. Today we couch our ideas in more technical language, but this prescription is not completely off target. We talk now of *set induction* instead of the more pedestrian "tell them what you're going to tell them," of *explaining* instead of the pointed "tell them," and of *closure* instead of the mundane "tell them what you told them."

To initiate the discussion of ways to help teachers present instruction, we can use the five-part model of instruction discussed in Chapter 3 (Figure 3.2) as our reference point. Recall that the fourth part of the model is implementation of instruction. In the following discussion, implementation of instruction is seen as including the selection of resources and the selection and implementation of teaching strategies.

The selection of resources and the decisions about strategies are parts of the planning phase, whereas implementation of the resources and strategies is the actual presentation phase. The task of selecting resources and strategies prior to presentation reinforces a concept discussed in the previous chapter, namely, that the instructional process is a continuum. There are no sharp divisions between planning and presentation, between planning and evaluation, or between presentation and evaluation. The components of a model of instruction glide into and double back on each other.

SELECTION OF RESOURCES

The great disparities in school financing are nowhere more readily visible in a school system than in the case of instructional resources. The resources at the teacher's command vary considerably from state to state, from community to community, and even from school to school within a community. Some schools have only the barest essentials, whereas others have an overabundance of materials and equipment, some of which lie unused in media storage rooms. A few fortunate schools are blessed with an instructional materials center that produces audiovisual aids in support of instruction throughout the school.

At the top of today's list of desired resources is arguably the most potent learning resource—the computer. Schools are engaged in efforts to obtain sufficient hardware and software at all grade levels and to take advantage of the infinite learning opportunities offered by going online. There is no question that today's teacher must be computer-literate and trained in the effective use of computers in instruction.

A major task of the teacher is to identify whatever resources are available for instructional purposes. A central task of the supervisor is to assist the teacher in locating, obtaining, and creating instructional aids. There are very few teachers who would not like additional resources and who do not feel that they would be more effective if these resources were available to them. The task of selecting resources is dual. First, teachers must make effective use of the resources they do have; second, they must uncover resources that are available but untapped.

Generally, even the most poorly financed classrooms possess some instructional resources. Most classrooms contain a chalkboard or white board, a bulletin board, text-books, a dictionary, and often maps and a globe. In some classrooms these time-honored aids could be put to more effective use.

One of the first jobs of teachers new to a school system is to learn what instructional materials and equipment are available, not only in the school itself but also from the central office. A supervisor can speed up this initial orientation process by providing written lists of available resources, their locations, and how to obtain them.

Teachers must develop the habit of thinking beyond the confines of the school for obtaining aids in instruction. Some communities are rich in educational resources. To varying degrees, all communities can provide significant educational experiences for young people. We must get away from the old notion that the only educational experiences that are important are those that take place within the walls of the school; we need to develop the broader notion that the community is the school's campus. A supervisor can do much to break down the traditional barriers between the school and the community by suggesting sources of aid and by encouraging teachers to make full use of what is available. One helpful technique for promoting the use of community resources is an organized tour of the community for teachers who are new to the system. This would give them an early chance to see the neighborhoods from which their students come and to pinpoint people and places that might be of future help to them in instruction.

Teachers must think in terms of human as well as physical resources. They should identify individuals and groups inside and outside the school system who might help them present particular topics. People with unique and pertinent experiences should be invited into the classroom or have classes taken to them so they may share their experiences with students. Today, with great frequency, parents and others from the community serve schools in the capacity of volunteer helpers and resource persons.[4] Retired specialists, for example, can provide a valuable service when their fields are under study. They are often eager to share their knowledge and skills with young people.

Some alternative educational arrangements take students outside the school's walls into the community, calling on the voluntary services of artists, tradespeople, bankers, salespeople, writers, farmers, and scientists to supplement the traditional curriculum. Teachers customarily identify libraries, museums, and art galleries as sources of educational experiences for students, but except in the field of vocational education, teachers often overlook experiences that can be derived from stores, banks, garages, hospitals, prisons, insurance agencies, and travel agencies.

Schools in recent years have made great strides in establishing partnerships with businesses and industries in the community. Through these partnerships, a business or industry "adopts" a particular school and cooperates with it to enhance the education of its students. Supervisors will find it beneficial to develop and promote these kinds of linkages to the community. They will need to orient new teachers to community organizations and agencies that cooperate with their schools.

A supervisor might recommend that teachers who are engaged in the process of selecting resources apply a checklist (such as the one shown here) for evaluating resources and making choices.

Checklist for Selecting Resources	*Yes*	*No*
1. The resources relate directly to the objectives.	——	——
2. The resources are in keeping with the abilities of the learners.	——	——
3. The resources are in keeping with the age level of the learners.	——	——
4. The resources will be of interest to the learners.	——	——
5. The resources are varied enough to accommodate individual differences in learners.	——	——
6. The resources are accurate and up-to-date.	——	——
7. The resources are without bias, or if with bias, the bias is clearly stated and the resources are balanced to reveal different biases.	——	——
8. The resources are easily accessible to the learners.	——	——
9. The resources are without cost to the learners.	——	——

Clearly, the resources must relate to the predetermined objectives, for they are the vehicles that carry the learners to their destination. There will undoubtedly be agreement that the resources selected should match the learners' abilities, age level, and interests. Hopefully, the resources chosen will be stimulating and motivating. They should enable the teacher to provide age-appropriate learning experiences. Teachers should look beyond traditional print resources to nonprint as well, to physical objects, to artwork, to audiovisual and technological aids.

While searching for resources for the class as a whole, the teacher should also seek resources that might appeal to individuals within the group. Some materials should be relatively easy, others more difficult. Some should be concrete, others more abstract. Whatever resources are selected—whether in the form of media or in the form of resource persons—all should make available accurate and relevant knowledge.

Some teachers may take issue with the use of biased materials. Yet many of the problems facing humankind are controversial and offer no clear-cut, factual solutions. People differ on the resolution of controversial issues. You cannot study opposing ideas on controversial subjects without examining biased points of view. Whenever an individual takes a side on a controversial issue, he or she is presenting a bias. When dealing with controversial content, the teacher may offset the biases of one side by presenting the biases of other sides.

The checklist suggests that resources be readily accessible and without cost to the learners. In public schools, where learners are an immature and captive population, it is the teacher's responsibility to see that the instructional resources chosen are at the command of the learner. The teacher must also ensure that the materials to be used will be either without cost or of insignificant cost to the learners and their parents. The public school is not like a college or university, where a professor may order mature students who choose to be there to purchase books and other instructional materials or pay a variety of laboratory fees.

The alert teacher is constantly on the lookout for new instructional materials, particularly those that are free or inexpensive. Many online sources of free lesson plans are available from numerous Web sites.[5] It is a duty of the supervisor to supply teachers continuously with references to new resources that have come to his or her attention and that appear worthwhile. Furthermore, teachers can be encouraged to evaluate resources they might use by applying criteria such as those suggested in the preceding checklist.

SELECTION OF STRATEGIES

When teachers consider the problem of selecting strategies for presenting content to students, they might well paraphrase the poet: "How do I teach thee? Let me count the ways...." Many strategic avenues are open to them. Like the streets of any city, some avenues are more traveled than others, some thoroughfares receive little traffic, and some are unknown except to those in the neighborhood.

Pedagogy shares the word *strategy* with other organizations, including the armed services. We can envision, for example, the military brass mapping out a campaign and planning tactics. Some teachers might point out that there is another analogy in the use of the word *strategy*—it applies to the field of battle. We prefer not to conceptualize the classroom as a battlefield, with the teacher and students on opposing sides, but rather as a team effort, with the teacher as the leader and both teacher and students working together for a common cause.

The terms *procedures* or *strategies* appear with some of the models of instruction you saw earlier. Whichever term is used, we are talking about methods—the means of providing age-appropriate opportunities for students to encounter content. We find not only these terms in the pedagogical literature but also *tactics*, *techniques*, and *modes of instruction*.

We could, if we wished, make some subtle distinctions in these concepts. But we shall use the aforementioned terms when they apply to teaching or instruction as synonymous and interchangeable.

We do need to distinguish, however, between a teaching strategy and a learning strategy. In this text, we emphasize teaching, or instructional, strategies—those methods teachers select and use to present subject matter. We are further concerned with the supervisor's ability to help teachers select and use appropriate strategies.

Learning strategies are personalized ways by which learners internalize content, that is, learn the subject. Some learners will outline subject matter so that they can grasp the points in logical sequence. Some memorize words or sentences as keys to learning. Can any schoolchild forget the palindrome "Able was I ere I saw Elba," which has the dubious virtue of not only reminding the learner of Napoleon's first place of confinement but also being a completely reversible sentence? Same pupils put together both real words and made-up words that have meaning only to them to help them recall facts. Other pupils like to read a passage in its entirety quickly, then go back and study segments in depth. Yet other students subject themselves to silent question-and-answer sessions on content they are studying. These are all learning strategies, not teaching strategies. When we use the word *strategy* by itself in this text, we mean teaching, or instructional strategy, and equate it with procedure, method, technique, mode, or tactic.

The process of selecting strategies is part of the planning process. Not until the teacher walks into the classroom and initiates a lesson does he or she move out of the sphere of planning and into the area of implementation, or presentation.

A teaching strategy may be defined as a procedure or set of procedures for using resources and deploying the central figures in the instructional process—the teacher and the learners. With this definition in mind, we can list some of the many strategies a supervisor might suggest to teachers:

computer-assisted instruction	questioning	audio media
lecturing	discovery	video media
discussion	role playing	laboratory work
textbook exercises	tutoring	portfolios
cooperative learning	problem solving	field trips
cooperative groupings	oral reports	tests
Web-enhanced slide	written reports	homework
presentations	drill	independent study
guest presenters	distance learning	online learning

This list, though far from complete, indicates the variety of strategies teachers may use in presenting content. Variations are possible in a number of these strategies. For example, the teacher might lecture to large groups or small groups. Discussion might be conducted in small groups or even smaller seminars. Textbook exercises might be written or oral.

Students may be grouped for learning according to varying criteria; subgroupings are possible within larger groups; given a team of teachers, groupings may be arranged around team teaching or differentiated staffing patterns; collaborative and cooperative learning techniques may be employed. You can see that the range of procedures open to teachers is broader than some of them realize.

The difficult task is to select the strategy or strategies that would be most productive for the learners. By way of illustration, suppose an elementary school teacher wishes the pupils during science study to become familiar with the concept of the nitrogen cycle, the process whereby nitrogen undergoes change, nitrites and nitrates are formed for nourishment of green plants, and nitrogen returns to its original state, a process vital to the maintenance of life on earth. How can this content be placed before the learners in such a way that they will readily master the principles involved? A number of alternatives run through the teacher's mind:

1. Prepare a lecture and use only written notes.
2. Prepare a lecture and use an overhead projector to sketch the nitrogen cycle for the students.
3. Prepare a lecture and use charts that have been prepared by the teacher or former students or an instructional materials center.
4. Do a slide presentation (such as on PowerPoint) on the nitrogen cycle.
5. Use a film, tape, or disk on the nitrogen cycle.
6. Have the students conduct a search on the Internet.
7. Ask the class to open textbooks to the section on the nitrogen cycle and have students read aloud the passages in the text. The teacher could follow each reading with oral questions to determine whether students understand the concept.
8. An alternative to option 7 would be to have the students open their books and the teacher read to them—a still far-too-common procedure in many classrooms.
9. Introduce the content by raising questions such as, "What is nitrogen?" "Is there more nitrogen than oxygen in the air?" "Animals, bacteria, and green plants play a part in the nitrogen cycle—what are their roles?" The teacher may ask students to look up the nitrogen cycle in the textbook and/or reference books either as classwork or homework. Pupils report their findings to the class.
10. Lecture and ask pupils to follow up the lecture with drawings of the nitrogen cycle.
11. Use a programmed text to teach the content.
12. Appoint a committee to study the nitrogen cycle and prepare a report to be given to the class.
13. Bring in a small bag of fertilizer—for example, 6–6–6 100 percent organic. The class could discuss the difference in meaning between *organic* and *inorganic*. The teacher can show students the label on the bag that describes the contents and explain to them that 6–6–6 means 6 percent nitrate, 6 percent phosphate, and 6 percent potash. The teacher explains that growing plants need these chemicals, singles out the nitrate, and relates it to the nitrogen cycle, which the class will then study.

14. Lead the class in a study of the nitrogen cycle over a period of time, during which the class experiments with growing plants in the classroom. Several plants are given proper water and chemicals; other plants are given proper water and inadequate chemicals; some plants are given proper water and no chemicals. Students will observe that plants need sufficient food.

15. Take the class on a field trip to a farmer's pasture that is complete with cows, manure, green plants, and decaying plants. The teacher can point out the nitrogen cycle at work.

16. Organize the class into small cooperative groups with responsibilities for helping each other master the content.

How can the teacher know which of the strategies would be most effective? Surely more than one road leads to Rome; however, not all roads lead to Rome, and even among those that do, some are more circuitous than others.

The teacher can choose one strategy at random and try it. If it doesn't work, he or she can try another strategy the next time and then another until one that will work is found. To some extent, all teachers follow such a trial-and-error procedure. Intuitively, they select a strategy that at first glance seems to be effective. These teachers would verify the notion that experience is the best teacher. Over the years, after considerable trial and error they have learned which strategies have been most effective under which conditions.

But what guidance can the supervisor give new teachers to help them avoid the lengthy process of trial and error? Or what help can the supervisor give experienced teachers who want to test intuition against some criteria? How can a teacher judge in advance whether a given strategy will work? Although you can never be absolutely sure that a given procedure will work until it is put to the test in the classroom, the chance of success will be greatly increased if you help teachers develop some simple guidelines, such as the following:

1. *The strategy must be right for the learners.* The teacher must consider the age level of the students and the interests of that age level, while remaining cognizant of the learners' achievement levels. For example, in the presentation of the nitrogen cycle to elementary school pupils, a formal lecture by the teacher using written notes could be a disaster. Just minutes after the lecture has begun, the teacher may well be confronted with a classroom full of wiggling, twisting, uninterested urchins. If the teacher has a room full of poor readers, requiring them to go to reference works and encyclopedias to dig out information may be an unrewarding approach. Teachers should select strategies that look beyond the common concepts of just linguistic and mathematical intelligence to the concepts of, as Howard Gardner called them, multiple intelligences.

Rejecting the concept of global intelligence reported by a single IQ score, Gardner delineated eight intelligences: bodily-kinesthetic, interpersonal, intrapersonal, linguistic, logical-mathematical, musical, spatial,[6] and naturalist.[7] Teachers are advised to recognize and capitalize on these varying intelligences.

2. *The strategy must be right for the teacher.* Each teacher is a unique personality. Some function well in certain situations and not so well in others. Some teachers, for example, are master lecturers. Others work more effectively in small groups. Teachers who adopt a counseling point of view toward education and life are more effective in one-to-one situations than those who are more remote and detached. Some teachers, holding constructivist views of learning, see themselves as facilitators who provide authentic learning experiences so that students may create their own knowledge.[8]

Some teachers have a knack for dramatizing content, whereas others are more matter-of-fact. Some teachers are extroverted and others are introverted. Some have more background and skill in a particular subject than others. Teachers need to be aware of their strengths and limitations. In Chapter 12, we examine ways in which a supervisor may help teachers evaluate themselves. Whatever strategy teachers select must be compatible with their skills, knowledge, values, and personality.

3. *The strategy must be right for the subject matter.* This guideline is so obvious that violating it seems impossible. Yet how often do teachers teach about the content of a subject rather than the subject itself? How often do teachers accept pupils' verbalization of rules, for example, without probing to see if they understand the rules? How often do teachers accept memorization of content as mastery of content? How often do teachers structure tests in such a way that students can cram for them, regurgitate the content, then immediately let the content float off into oblivion?

How many supervisors and other visitors have walked into modern language classrooms, for example, and wondered whether the teacher was teaching a foreign language or English? When English is consistently substituted for the foreign language in the modern language classroom, the strategy does injustice to the subject matter.

Teachers violate this guideline if they use inaccurate resources. The teacher must exercise care in the selection of printed and other resources that may present as fact something that is no longer true, as in the use, for example, of out-of-date atlases and maps. The teacher must be discriminating about materials placed before the learners.

An injustice is done to the subject matter when the teacher either intentionally or unintentionally directs learners to one-sided treatments of the content. For example, if the teacher selects a research paper as a strategy for studying the racial problem in America, students should be directed to books and articles written by both black and white authors. If we are studying poverty in Latin America and looking at pictures of slums of some Latin American cities, we should at the same time study problems of the poor and homeless in urban and rural areas of our own country. Teaching controversial topics calls for careful selection of resources and strategies to bring out all dimensions of the topics.

Because their resources are often limited—sometimes to a single textbook—teachers frequently but unintentionally present a distorted picture of content. Only in recent years have social studies teachers begun to dispel some of the myths that have surrounded great personalities of history. We have begun to see famous men and women from the past as real, once living, breathing human beings, not as larger-than-life supermen and superwomen. How many of us still believe that George Washington chopped down the cherry tree and threw a silver dollar across the Potomac? How many schoolchildren were ever made aware that the nation's first president was rather tight-fisted with money, had slaves working at his splendid home at Mount Vernon, and was perhaps a bit pompous? How many children believe that when Abraham Lincoln wasn't splitting rails, he was wandering around in top hat and tails? How many children learned that Lincoln had an earthy sense of humor and enjoyed a salty joke? The teacher must select strategies that bring out the essence and preserve the integrity of the subject matter.

4. *The strategy must be right for the time available.* The amount of practice, follow-up, review, independent study, and research that will be conducted on a topic will depend on its relative importance and the time allotted for its study. Some procedures take more time and move more slowly than others. Study in depth will require more time than a superficial survey. Achievement by the learners of active mastery of the content will require more time than passive acquaintance. Time frames have already been established in every school system in terms of the number of hours in the school day and the number of days in the school year and marking periods.

Whatever the strategies selected, the teacher must make the best use of the time available. Observation in almost any school will reveal that a great deal of time is lost in the typical classroom through noninstructional activities and interruptions for one reason or another. Using a technique such as that described by Keith A. Acheson and Meredith Damien Gall, supervisors in classroom visits can observe the amount of time teachers keep the learners on task and should help teachers analyze where they went off task, how to remain on task, and how to focus on content.[9]

Teachers must consider whether they can or should permit an element of self-pacing to enter the picture. Self-pacing allows learners to take varying amounts of time to complete a particular learning task. Some students may take a shorter period of time than average; others may take longer. Time, then, becomes a variable. The traditional approach to instruction is to hold time constant and vary content. All learners work within the same time framework. Some learners master the learning task, but others never achieve the objective. When a teacher introduces the notion of self-pacing, content is held constant and time is variable, allowing all learners to achieve the objective.

Self-pacing is a feature of most competency-based approaches to instruction. Certain objectives (competencies or learning tasks) are stipulated for the learner to master. This approach acknowledges that some individuals take more time to master specific content than others. The important aim is the attainment of the objectives by all learners, even if some learners take longer than others.

A companion concept of self-pacing is criterion-referenced measurement, which is discussed further in Chapter 6. In a competency-based approach to instruction, a learner earns credit and receives a grade when the objectives have been mastered. When the criterion, the minimal level of competence, is met, the learner receives full credit. In a more traditional approach, the teacher follows a norm-referenced system of measurement and compares students to each other rather than to the criterion. The teacher considers the degree to which various learners have accomplished the task. Whether individual learners have had sufficient time to complete a learning task is not considered an important factor under a norm-referenced system. We return to these distinctions later.

Ideally, if a teacher subscribes to the concept of self-pacing, learners should be able to take all the time they need to accomplish a task. One consequence of such a procedure would be completely individualized learning. Under these conditions, the teacher's role would be much different, for he or she would work in different ways with different learners.

There is always a gap between the ideal and the practical. An instructional staff must live within certain institutional parameters. Unlimited time is simply not available to any teacher or class. Classes change, teachers change, and content changes at the beginning of new instructional periods. Therefore, if teachers wish to introduce self-pacing—certainly a defensible practice—they will have to institute a modified self-pacing plan that allows some variation in time within the larger time parameters set by the school. Instead of unlimited time to complete a task, a learner may have more than the average amount of time, up to a fixed limit established by the teacher. A teacher might give the learner several opportunities to achieve an objective, permitting the learner to attempt a task more than one time, a process some educators refer to as recycling. The teacher may permit the learner to recycle only a reasonable number of times—say, two or three—after which the press of time forces the teacher to move on. A modified self-pacing plan will permit more learners to achieve objectives than is possible when time is held constant. Some learners will still fail to attain the objectives, even if they are permitted several attempts, unless they receive remedial work and tutoring.

5. *The strategy must be right for the resources available.* A decision to use a number of reference books to explore a topic is contingent on the availability of those reference books. The finest film or disk in the world is useless without equipment to show it. Duplicated practice worksheets are possible only if the school has the supplies and equipment to reproduce them.

Earlier in this chapter, we cautioned that resources must be accessible and without cost to the learners. A teacher cannot take it for granted that resources outside the school are always available to students. A home economics teacher cannot, for example, assume that all homes are equipped with sewing machines. A language arts teacher cannot make the assumption that all homes have magazines and books. A social studies teacher cannot count on reference books and encyclopedias being available in students' homes. Teachers cannot assume the availability of such items as a typewriter, computer, VCR, DVD player, TV set, or even telephone in the home. Nor can they expect that all families, even if they have computers or television, will have Internet access or cable. Because most teachers are products of the middle class, they sometimes forget that children from many homes, particularly those of the lower socioeconomic levels, do not have the educational resources to which children of the upper socioeconomic levels are accustomed.

Nor can the teacher assume that if resources are not available in the home, students can locate them somewhere in the community. Even if the desired resources are available, many students will not be able to reach them because they lack transportation, have part-time jobs after school, or have duties at home. Lack of resources will reduce the range of strategies open to the teacher.

6. *The strategy must be right for the facilities.* Strategies calling for facilities for physical education, art, music, drama, industrial arts, science, foreign languages, computers, and other laboratory experiences, learning centers, clinics, and remedial areas imply appropriate materials, equipment, and space.

To put into practice, for example, a plan that requires large-group instruction, small-group discussion, independent study, and lab work, space problems must be resolved. Rooms of varying sizes are needed. Media facilities are required. Sliding partitions may have to be installed. Faculty may have to be deployed differently. Existing facilities must be considered when a strategy is being selected.

7. *The strategy must be right for the objectives.* Perhaps the most important guideline of all is that a direct fit must exist between the strategy chosen and the objectives the strategy is designed to achieve. If teachers have specified objectives at higher levels of the taxonomies, they must choose strategies for reaching the higher levels. A strategy to achieve the cognitive level of evaluation will differ from one to achieve the level of knowledge. A strategy to achieve the affective level of valuing will be different from one for reaching the level of responding. A procedure that would bring about attainment of the psychomotor level of adaptation would differ from one to reach the level of set. The relationship between the objectives and strategies is direct and intimate. Alone, the objectives are nothing but ideas from the teacher's mind. The strategy is the vehicle for carrying the objectives from the teacher's mind to the learner's mind and body.

By engaging in periodic analysis and discussion of these seven guidelines with teachers, the supervisor may assist teachers in selecting appropriate strategies and avoiding the uneconomical process of trial and error.

LESSON PRESENTATION

The goals are written, the objectives are stated, the tasks are analyzed and described, resources and strategies are selected, entry skills of learners are assessed, the unit plan is developed, the first lesson plan is created, and the planning process is phasing out. The implementation process is about to begin: The teacher starts the first lesson of the unit by initiating study of the unit's topic.

When the teacher steps into the classroom, the hours of prior planning should result in an effective lesson. Planning provides a sense of confidence that all systems are go. Can any experienced teacher ever forget the first time he or she soloed in front of a group of students? Can the butterflies in the stomach be compared to the actor's stage fright? Did the teacher wonder how the audience would react and how the lesson would go over?

Sometimes the teacher conducts a silent dress rehearsal the night before each lesson, running through the unit and reviewing how the lesson plan fits into the unit plan. Each part of the lesson plan must be checked to fix clearly in mind the details of each component. The teacher makes an inventory of the materials and equipment needed and tries to anticipate problems.

In practice, of course, teachers do not carry out a full-scale review of each lesson prior to presentation the following day. They do not have time for exhaustive checks, but they do make a quick check in a cursory or abbreviated fashion. They will probably spend somewhat more time readying the lesson plan for the introductory class of each unit than on succeeding plans as the unit moves along lesson by lesson.

Each day's lesson provides feedback for review and modification of the next day's lesson plan. The competent instructional supervisor who has helped the teacher plan for instruction must now help the teacher translate the plans into action.

A supervisor who visits a class in session should be able to tell with little difficulty whether the teacher has done any planning for instruction. The clues are there for any perceptive visitor to see.

- Are there any visible written plans to which the teacher refers?
- Does the teacher exhibit confidence?
- Does the teacher appear to know whether learners are understanding?
- Has the teacher communicated the objectives to the learners?

- Is there a flow to the day's activities?
- Do the learning activities recognize educational, social, intellectual, ethnic, cultural, and gender differences?
- Are there blocks of time during which nothing constructive seems to be taking place?
- Are the learners kept busy at productive tasks?
- Does the teacher rely on worthwhile learning tasks for managing the class or on threats and reprimands?
- Are the needed materials and equipment on hand and ready to use?
- Does the teacher appear to be improvising, moving from one tangent to another, prolonging activities beyond their productive time?
- Does the teacher repeat content after it is apparent that all the learners have mastered it?
- Does the teacher achieve closure, summarizing the learning by involving the learners?

The experienced supervisor can attest that adequate planning does make a difference in both teacher behavior and student behavior during the course of a lesson presentation. We can use a theatrical model to examine more closely the elements of a well-conducted lesson. For a lesson presentation to be effective, the teacher attends separately to the beginning, the middle, and the end of the lesson. A graphic presentation of the three parts of a lesson line is:

Set/Middle of the Lesson $\rightarrow$ Teaching to the Objectives (T_2O)/Closure

For each of these three parts, the teacher uses different strategies. Several of the most frequently used strategies will be examined in our analysis of lesson presentation.

Beginning the Lesson

The skilled teacher realizes that the problem of starting a lesson is a little like the problem faced by a storyteller in the initial paragraphs of a story. The writer knows that the reader's interest must be stimulated at the very beginning. The master storyteller knows how to grab the reader's attention in the first few sentences. The first two verses of the book of Genesis make us want to read on: "In the beginning God created the heaven and the earth. And the earth was without form, and void; and darkness was upon the face of the deep. And the Spirit of God moved upon the face of the waters."

An author attempts at the very beginning of a story to arouse the reader's interest and establish a particular frame of mind, or "set." The author seeks to influence the reader to respond to the message in such a way that the reader will want to learn more. An aura of mystery and suspense lures the reader on, sometimes to the point that he or she cannot put the book down until the last page is finished. Many have read a fascinating book until the wee hours of the morning! Some enduring books and movies have had such an impact on readers and viewers that people have read or seen them again and again.

On a smaller scale, we see the phenomenon of set in our daily lives as we attempt to influence others' predispositions about people, places, or things. Two girls are talking, for example, and one tells the other, "I met the most handsome boy last night. I want you to meet him." The drama critic writes in a review, "The new musical that opened last night was a smash hit." Our neighbors invite us into their home to see slides of their recent trip to Switzerland and use words such as, "If you ever go to Switzerland, you mustn't miss Lucerne." Endless TV commercials exhort us to rush out to buy the sweetest-smelling soap, the longest-lasting deodorant, and the softest toilet tissue. Daily we try to put others into a certain frame of mind, or we are recipients of others' attempts to motivate us to take certain actions.

A teacher shares a similar need to stimulate learners to put themselves in a frame of mind receptive to pursuing the content of the lesson. He or she wants to pique the learners' interest and cause them to want to learn more. The teacher wants to make the forthcoming content interesting to learners as well as to give them some notion of the relationship of the ensuing content to previous content and some idea of its relevance to them and their lives. When planning, the teacher should design some means of eliciting student interest at the start of the lesson.

Some specialists on instruction describe as *set induction* the techniques a teacher uses to put the learners in a receptive frame of mind.[10] Madeline Hunter and Douglas Russell referred to this skill as "anticipatory set."[11] Set induction is a pedagogical term used to label various techniques employed by teachers to gain students' attention, stimulate their interest, take only a short amount of time, and make them receptive to further instruction. But to bring an elephant into the classroom to introduce the color of gray to the students might prove to serve the wrong purpose!

We have all sat in classes where the teacher's opening ploy has simply killed interest. What kind of reactions may we expect from the following classic openings?

- "Open your books to page 113."
- "Okay, who's scheduled to give a report today?"
- Handing out corrected exam papers, the teacher comments, "This was a terrible set of examinations."
- "Class, today we're going to study about volcanoes." The teacher then plunges into the lesson plan.
- "Take out your workbooks and work the problems on page 30."

What kind of mind-set may be expected from the learners? Will they react with a "Ho-hum, just another day"? Will the class that did poorly on the exams react positively when they are told how bad their papers were? Will the antiquated practice of calling the roll bring them to attention and create the expectation of learning something interesting? Is the teacher's statement that the class is going to study volcanoes sufficient to motivate the learners to erupt with enthusiasm?

Teachers need to inject an element of the dramatic or semidramatic into an introduction. They should ask themselves questions like "What technique—or stunt, if you wish—will be likely to attract the students' interest?" "What do I know about my students that I can capitalize on to make them want to learn this material?"

Techniques of set induction can be quite personal. Some teachers can carry off some techniques better than others. Some teachers have an innate flare for the dramatic. Others find a modicum of just plain hamminess to be a useful tool in dealing with children and adolescents. No supervisor should expect that every lesson of every day will be a polished gem and that teachers will succeed in making students become wildly excited and eager for each day's study. But supervisors have a right to expect teachers to make more than a token gesture toward putting the learners into the proper frame of mind for studying the material. Any teacher may follow several guidelines in an effort to establish set. Even if the teacher is not able to put all learners into a receptive state of mind, at the very least he or she can point them in the right direction.

Let us assume first that we wish to establish an appropriate set for studying a topic new to the class. After examining several suggested ways of arousing interest in the new topic, we will consider ways of inducing set with continuing topics. Each lesson, whether it is the first or part of a series, should incorporate a planned introduction. What techniques can we borrow from the repertoire of experienced, skilled teachers to motivate learners to pursue the topic of a unit we have planned for them?

The teacher can bring in an article from a current magazine or recent edition of a daily newspaper pertinent to the topic and read it to the class. If the article is controversial, so much the better. Radio talk-show hosts use this technique repeatedly. Using a story reported in the press immediately shows that the topic has currency and relevance to the students' daily lives. A report on the discovery of asbestos filings in the drinking water of a Great Lakes city would stimulate interest in a study of the Great Lakes much more effectively than the teacher's announcement, "Today we're going to study the Great Lakes." Such an article could introduce not only a unit on geography of the Great Lakes region but also a unit on water or other pollution. A chart from a magazine article showing stock market cycles could be used to introduce either a unit on the stock market or a unit on graphing. The timelier the article, the better it will serve its purpose. Some students may already have read the article; this will strengthen your introductory strategy by underscoring that what they will study has importance to them. This technique can bring the past and the future as well as the present to the students' attention. A news account of the damage being done to the Colosseum by pollution from modern traffic in Rome could be used to introduce a variety of units, including the significance of the Colosseum itself and ancient Rome's contributions to the present. A unit on space could begin with a dramatic article on the Magellan probe, which revealed that Venus's atmosphere is mainly carbon dioxide and its surface temperature 900 degrees Fahrenheit, or on the Galileo probe of Jupiter and its moons, or on the dramatic clues about the birth of the universe revealed by the Hubble Space Telescope. The cooperation of American astronauts and Russian cosmonauts and those from other countries in space could introduce not only a unit on space exploration but also one on the dramatic political changes brought about by the end of the cold war.

Building on young people's fascination with computers, the teacher whose students have computers at their schools can load a pertinent Web site with appropriate graphics and links to other sites. The use of technology in teaching to the objectives of a lesson would be a more effective use of the Web.

The teacher can introduce a lesson with physical objects or pictures that may provoke a reaction. Geographical units can be initiated with samples of arts and crafts from various countries. A jade necklace, an onyx chess set, a hand-tooled leather purse, and a straw hat can arouse curiosity about the places where they originated and the people who created them. Samples of foreign currency can be used to start a unit on international money and banking. Three-dimensional geometric figures that may be taken apart and reassembled have proved helpful in beginning mathematical units.

If it is not feasible to bring certain physical objects to the classroom, photographs, slides, or filmstrips can be used effectively to induce set. Pictures of breadfruit, papaya, and passionfruit, edibles not customarily seen in most parts of the United States, can replace the fruits themselves at the start of a unit on products of the tropics. The photograph of U.S. Marines raising the American flag on Iwo Jima symbolizes the military operation in the Pacific during World War II. Pictures of the destruction of the Berlin Wall can be used to begin a unit on the unification of Germany, the restoration of democracy, or human values. Photos of firefighters hoisting the American flag at the site of the World Trade Center in New York can vividly introduce a unit on the war on terrorism, America's responses, and the heroism displayed immediately following the never-to-be-forgotten terrorist attacks of September 11, 2001.

Audio impressions can sometimes be as effective as visual impressions. Recordings of the voices of John F. Kennedy, Franklin D. and Eleanor Roosevelt, Martin Luther King Jr., and other men and women of history help learners think of these personalities of the past as real people rather than as legends. A particular atmosphere can be created in class through the judicious selection of recorded music or poetry or drama. The teacher's aim is to provide just enough stimulation to make students want to study the topic.

A simple means of creating curiosity is the technique teachers use when they write an unfamiliar word or expression on the board and let students ponder it. The word *cloning* written across the chalkboard can provoke a discussion of both the philosophical and the biological aspects of cloning when students debate whether it is possible or desirable for human beings to be able to reproduce themselves asexually. Significant words of low familiarity will serve as brain teasers. The teacher might scrawl *deoxyribonucleic acid* on the board and ask the learners to define it. Some bright student may know or guess it to be DNA, the building block of all genes and chromosomes. From there the teacher can move into a unit on heredity and genetics. The words *habeas corpus* can initiate a unit on fundamental freedoms. It is unlikely that history students will at first recognize the names Vladimir Ilyich Ulyanov or Iosif Vissarionovich Dzhugashvili, but world history would have been far different without Lenin and Stalin, respectively, the names by which they were better known. Unfamiliar but significant words and names may be found in all subject fields. The device of writing such words on the board to bring forth questions and discussion is a simple and effective way of introducing a lesson.

The teacher can stage an action that may even startle the learners. An endless variety of role-playing situations can be concocted with the aid of other teachers, parents, and students. For example, an angry parent (whose role is played by an adult friend of the teacher) barges into the classroom and accuses the teacher of using irreligious or unpatriotic textbooks. The parent storms out of the room to the bewilderment of the learners. At this point, the teacher breaks the shock effect and starts them on a study of censorship, freedom of the press, or church–state relationships. Contrived situations can bring to life the topic to be studied.

The teacher cannot, of course, fruitfully employ dramatic means of introducing every lesson. After a unit has been started, more routine methods of beginning a lesson will be in order. Yet each lesson should have some planned introduction, even if it is only an explanation of the transition to the particular lesson from the previous day's lesson. Some of the more routine but highly effective introductory procedures are:

1. *An explanation of the reasons for studying the content.* The teacher will tell the students why the content is important to them and how it can have meaning in their daily lives. Some content is easily justified on the basis that it meets both immediate and long-range needs of students. Other content is more difficult to justify but remains important; some content is not justifiable at all and would be better removed from the curriculum.

2. *A review of yesterday's lesson.* A quick review can be conducted in a number of ways. The teacher can summarize what took place the day before and how it relates to today's lesson. A student can be asked to summarize what was learned in class yesterday. The teacher can pose some questions based on the previous day's work and see how well the students comprehended the material. Sometimes only a very few minutes of review will be necessary. Other times the entire work of the preceding day may have to be repeated to ensure mastery of the content.

3. *An analysis of results of a test taken the preceding day.* If the preceding day's work included a test or quiz and the papers have been scored, the teacher should give them back immediately and go over them. The test should be used as a learning device and a review. The teacher should show students where they made their mistakes and how to correct them.

A supervisor should help the teacher devise effective procedures for initiating lessons and provide the teacher with feedback on how the students appear to receive introductory procedures. The supervisor should make the teacher aware that half the battle is won if students are interested, have developed a receptive frame of reference, understand the value of the content to be studied, comprehend the relationship of the present day's lesson to the previous day's and to future lessons, and are oriented to the direction their study will take.

Moving through the Middle of the Lesson—Teaching to the Objectives (T₂O)

When the teacher feels that the class is in the proper frame of mind, it is time to move into the heart of the lesson, teaching to the objectives (T_2O). The word *feels* is stressed here not only in connection with lesson presentation but also in relationship to the entire teaching process. Although the teaching act strives to be as scientific as possible, much of teaching still remains an art. A great deal of teaching is intuitive. We cannot say, for example, that set induction should occupy the first five minutes of each class. The teacher almost has to develop a sixth sense to judge when the learners are ready. With experience, the teacher will learn to detect the nuances and know when to start, change pace, recapitulate, and end. Teachers must learn when to switch from one technique to another, which techniques most frequently achieve the best results, and which procedures are adaptable to which types of students.

Ordinarily, many strategies are available to present any given lesson, and many combinations of those strategies are possible. As any experienced supervisor can attest, not all teachers are equally skilled in implementing all strategies. One of the big advantages of some team-teaching plans is that they capitalize on the strengths of multiple teachers. Those who are skilled at lecturing to large groups, for example, may put those skills to use when team teaching and differentiated staffing patterns are employed. When the individual teacher is alone in the self-contained classroom, however, he or she must develop at least a passable level of performance in the most frequently used strategies.

Over the years teacher educators have attempted to identify the component skills of the teaching process. These skills are generic competencies, which teachers at all levels should be able to demonstrate. Dwight Allen and Kevin Ryan identified fourteen such skills:

1. Stimulus variation
2. Set induction
3. Closure
4. Silence and nonverbal cues
5. Reinforcement of student participation
6. Fluency in asking questions
7. Probing questions
8. Higher-order questions
9. Divergent questions
10. Recognizing attending behavior
11. Illustrating and using examples
12. Lecturing
13. Planned repetition
14. Completeness of communication[12]

Madeline Hunter and Douglas Russell recommended seven steps, essentially generic teaching competencies, for more effective lessons:

1. Anticipatory set
2. Perceived objective and its purpose
3. Input (task analysis)
4. Modeling
5. Checking for understanding
6. Guided practice
7. Independent practice[13]

To this list we would add an eighth skill: closure.

Over the years, buoyed by the effective teaching research, a number of states have engaged in specifying generic teaching skills that teachers in their states should be expected to demonstrate. Some of these states have created tests and/or on-the-job assessments of these skills for purposes of certification.

In this chapter we will concern ourselves primarily with six generic teaching competencies. One of these skills has already been introduced: opening the lesson, or set induction. The chapter will terminate with a discussion of the skill of closing the lesson, or closure. To help teachers with the presentation of the central part of a lesson, teaching to the objectives (T_2O), the supervisor may assist them in developing or refining four major skills: (1) lecturing, (2) conducting a discussion, (3) questioning, and (4) providing for variation. An additional skill (or set of skills), evaluation, is discussed in Chapter 6.

Lecturing Included in the concept of lecturing are telling, explaining, describing, demonstrating, and teacher talk generally, skills that are grossly overworked. It is a fact of school life that teachers by and large talk far too much. Yet lecturing is a time-honored and highly useful technique and should not be entirely shunned by instructors. It can be an efficient means of imparting large quantities of information to a large group of students in a short period of time. However, it can also be an extremely inefficient mode of instruction and one unsuited to many learners. The strategy of lecturing can be improved if the teacher will follow a few guidelines:

1. *The learners should be mature enough to accept the mode of lecturing.* As a general rule, the younger the child, the less receptive he or she is to the technique of lecturing. Young children do not have the powers of concentration possessed by older students. Lecturing requires a self-discipline not yet developed by young children, who must be active rather than passive. Consequently, straight lecturing—that is, sustained talk—has been the stock in trade of the college professor. Whether college professors should indulge in relentless lecturing is another issue, but because college students are older, more disciplined, more motivated, and not a captive audience, the strategy of lecturing is at least passable at the college level. Some professors, of course, use other strategies, such as whole-group discussions, small-group work, and student reports.

2. *The learners should have developed adequate listening skills.* The development of listening skills is a function of both maturity and training. In recent years, the language arts have incorporated instruction in the skills of listening. There is general agreement that listening skills can be learned and improved. One needs only to attend some adult committee meetings to realize that maturity alone is no guarantee that listening skills have been perfected. Through faulty instructional procedures, teachers sometimes encourage the development of poor rather than good listening skills. The teacher must know whether the learners have sufficient skill in listening before choosing lecturing.

3. *The teacher must use language the learners understand.* The teacher must neither talk over learners' heads nor down to them—either method will lose listeners. The teacher must be careful of the vocabulary burden, making sure that all students understand the words in the lectures. If students appear puzzled after the teacher uses an unfamiliar word, the teacher should stop and define it. Teachers need to exert some caution in the use of children's slang and street language. Some teachers feel that to communicate they must use the current slang or trendy expressions. A little argot goes a long way. Children do not expect teachers to use their language; they expect teachers to play their roles as adults, and they often resent or are amused by adults' attempts to mimic them. Judicious use of selected words may help the teacher get the message across, but overworking the jargon may lose the audience. Teachers should also recognize the comprehension difficulties experienced by students with limited English-speaking ability.

4. *Every lecture should be planned.* The teacher should have prepared a written outline that sets forth the key points to be made, key questions to be raised, and relevant illustrations or real-life examples to amplify key points. Like a good lesson plan, a lecture should have an introduction, a middle, and an end. Amusing illustrations will help carry the lecture. A summary of the main points is essential.

5. *Talk alone is not sufficient.* A lecture should be supplemented whenever possible with actions (demonstration) and visual aids. Slides, charts, pictures, and transparencies help create interest. Even use of the chalkboard or white board for a "chalk talk" is superior to talk by itself.

6. *Provision should be made for feedback and follow-up.* Time should be allotted for questions from the class. The teacher should conduct some sort of evaluation to make sure that learners have mentally digested the points made in the lecture. The technique of following up a lecture to a large group with small discussion groups has much to recommend it.

In working with teachers on the strategy of lecturing, supervisors may find it helpful to apply a checklist like the one presented by Keith A. Acheson and Meredith Damien Gall, shown here as Table 4.1. The supervisor should help teachers who have a penchant for lecturing to decide whether lecturing is indeed the most effective way to teach, and if it is, what measures can be taken by teachers to gain the maximum advantage from this strategy.

Conducting a Discussion The terms *discussion* and *lecturing* are often confused. Many teachers claim to be conducting a discussion when, indeed, they are lecturing to students. Discussion implies interaction between the teacher and learners. We have used the term *discussion* somewhat loosely in referring to the narration in this text. We do so with the assumption that the instructor who adopts this text will use the narration in developing discussions with the students. An effective discussion involves not only certain individual mental and oral skills but also skills in group participation, for discussion is a group activity, not a lecture or a dialogue. The supervisor should bring the subcomponents of the generic skill of discussion, student participation and nonverbal cues, to the attention of teachers.

Student Participation The teacher should provide continuous and frequent opportunities for students to express themselves. Discussion time should give students a chance to develop skills of listening, thinking, speaking, and participating as members of a group. Maximum student participation should be sought. Teachers often have difficulty restraining themselves and giving students a chance to express their thoughts, but this is a must. In conducting a discussion, the teacher is concerned with not only illuminating the material under study but also perfecting the discussion skills themselves. So much of the world's social and business activities are transacted through discussion that these skills cannot be slighted in any course or grade.

Teachers should attempt to provide opportunities for all learners to participate and not be content with participation by only a few students. They should not let individuals dominate a discussion but should seek to develop an atmosphere in which students feel free to state their opinions and raise questions. Students should be encouraged to volunteer responses and to contribute illustrations and anecdotes from their own experiences. The teacher needs to make the students feel that class participation is an important part of the day's lesson. Students will participate more frequently when they are reassured that their opinions count for something and when they do not fear ridicule or disapproval by the teacher or their classmates.

TABLE 4.1 Checklist for Lecture-Explanation Teaching

Behaviors to Be Tallied

Meaningful Content

  1. Relates lecture content to content already familiar to students
  2. Gives example to illustrate concept
  3. Gives explanation for generalization or opinion

Student Involvement

  1. Asks students if they have questions
  2. Directs question to students
  3. Has students engage in activity

Behaviors to Be Rated	*good*				*needs improvement*
Organization					
1. Lecture has clear organization and sequence	5	4	3	2	1
2. Uses blackboard, handout, etc., to show organization of lecture	5	4	3	2	1
3. Tells students what (s)he expects students to remember from lecture	5	4	3	2	1
4. Repeats key points and summarizes them at end	5	4	3	2	1
5. Avoids digressions	5	4	3	2	1
	good				*needs improvement*
Delivery					
1. Speaks slowly and clearly	5	4	3	2	1
2. Conveys enthusiasm	5	4	3	2	1
3. Avoids reading from lecture notes	5	4	3	2	1
4. Avoids filler phrases, such as "you know"	5	4	3	2	1
5. Avoids nervous gestures	5	4	3	2	1
6. Maintains eye contact with students	5	4	3	2	1
7. Uses humor	5	4	3	2	1

Source: Keith A. Acheson and Meredith Damien Gall, *Clinical Supervision and Teacher Development: Preservice and Inservice Applications,* 5th ed. Copyright © 2003 by John Wiley & Sons, p. 216. This material is used by permission of John Wiley & Sons, Inc.

One of the teacher's tasks in conducting a discussion is to keep it under control and focused on the main topic. Students must learn to take turns talking and listen while others are speaking. The teacher generally serves as moderator but can often turn over this function to students so they can gain additional skills while he or she serves as a resource person. The teacher should help the students evaluate the significance of their own responses and questions by urging them to support their positions with facts and logical argument.

When sitting in on a discussion lesson, the supervisor should observe which students are actively participating and which ones are sitting back, which ones the teacher calls on repeatedly and which ones are never involved. The supervisor should observe whether the discussion stays on course, whether participants listen to each other, and whether they understand each other's ideas. If problems are detected in these areas, the supervisor should confer with the teacher about ways to improve the discussions.

Nonverbal Cues   Messages are often conveyed through means other than the spoken or printed word. A look, a nod, a frown, or just silence may transmit meaning to the listener. A discussion can be started, stopped, moved along, or turned in another direction by the judicious use of gestures or movement. A nod and a smile from the teacher can reinforce a student's contribution. A frown at a student who is not paying attention can bring him or her back into participation. A period of complete silence can often quiet a group and help it return to the subject at hand. The old technique of tapping on the chalkboard or overhead projector can call for increased attention to the topic under consideration.

The teacher is conveying a message to students when he or she is moving around the room and directing discussion from varying vantage points. The message may be "I want to see everybody participating" or "The noisy group in the corner must pay attention to the discussion" or "I am just as interested in the participants in the back row as in those in the front row." The teacher's movement and proximity to the learners act as stimuli for the learners to continue participating.

When the teacher adopts a puzzled expression, the student who is responding knows that the response is not clear. Teachers who are adept at charades can often draw out responses from students. Audiolingual foreign language teachers, for example, have developed a whole range of nonverbal signals for specific types of student responses.

Using silence and nonverbal cues is a little like directing an orchestra. The teacher can point to the students who are to respond, can appear to follow a student's comment with an accepting "uh huh" or nod of the head, can show bewilderment with an audible "hmm," and can show amusement with a broad smile and rolling eyes. The analogy of teaching to dramatics is again apt as we employ movement, gesture, and silence to convey certain meanings. To some individuals these are habitual traits; some may learn the cues by watching other teachers and studying their own performance. A supervisor should help teachers analyze their use of silence and nonverbal cues by watching them in action and providing them with feedback on their performances. We return to the topic of nonverbal language in Chapter 11.

Questioning   Often, what is called lecturing or discussion is in reality an oral question-and-answer session. The teacher poses questions and the students are expected to furnish the right answers. Of all classroom strategies, questioning may well be the most overworked and the most often abused.

Contrary to common practice, questioning sessions should be planned. The supervisor can readily tell when a teacher is firing questions at students off the "top of the head." The questioning session should have a specific purpose and an internal consistency, which can be achieved only through advance planning. In any question-and-answer session, the teacher should write key questions into the lesson plan to avoid forgetting essential points. Questioning is a skill that can be developed by following these rules:

1. *Because questioning is essentially a verbal, cognitive type of activity, the teacher should strive to raise the questions to the highest possible level of the cognitive domain.* This rule refers to the six levels of the Bloom taxonomy: knowledge, comprehension, application, analysis, synthesis, and evaluation.[14] In most cases, if possible, teachers should pose questions at the higher end of the classification spectrum. Too often they settle for simple recall or yes-no types of responses. Such responses neither encourage thought nor give students practice in formulating their ideas and opinions.

Although the teacher may generally seek to raise the level of questions to a higher order, certainly we would not eliminate the lower levels completely. There are times when lower-level questions are perfectly legitimate, particularly in drill sessions on material of a repetitive nature. Under some circumstances, questioning at the lower levels of the Bloom taxonomy may be more productive than higher-order questioning.[15] The important consideration, however, is that the teacher's questioning not remain at the lower levels but that the teacher consciously and deliberately move toward the higher levels. Questions at the lower level may sharpen memory, but they do little to develop more important abilities—to think and to express one's thoughts. We can illustrate this with questions at the six levels in the teaching field of English:

- *Knowledge:* Name three novels by Charles Dickens.
- *Comprehension:* Provide a summary in your own words of the first chapter of *David Copperfield*.
- *Application:* Is there a moral lesson in any of Dickens's novels you have read that applies to our society today?
- *Analysis:* What is there about *A Christmas Carol* that has made it a favorite story for more than 100 years?
- *Synthesis:* What human values run through these three novels: *David Copperfield*, *Oliver Twist*, and *Great Expectations*?
- *Evaluation:* In your judgment, which is the better novel, *David Copperfield* or *Great Expectations*? Why?

It is not always possible, depending on the content, to structure higher-order questions. Nor is it always possible to run the full gamut of questioning from lowest level to highest. The teacher's goal, as a rule, is to raise the level of questioning to the highest order possible whenever possible.

2. *The teacher should phrase questions clearly and in language the learner will understand.* The importance of using language geared to the level of the learner has already been stressed in the section on lecturing. The same principle holds true with the strategy of questioning. Not only should questions be clear, but they should also be in the teacher's own words, not those of the text materials. Questioning should be considered supplementary to text materials, an approach to content different from that used by the authors of the text materials. By the same token, students should be expected to paraphrase or respond in their own words, not by repeating the language of the text materials.

3. *The teacher should first address a question to the entire group.* A brief wait time of three to five seconds should follow while the students give some thought to the question. The teacher may then direct the question to an individual student. This practice encourages all students to listen to the questions. If the teacher calls on a student before posing a question, the others may tune out both the question and the response. On the other hand, the teacher can sometimes draw inattentive students back to the lesson by calling their names before the questions are framed. Recognize that the latter procedure is a control practice rather than an instructional one.

4. *The teacher should avoid asking more than one question at a time, before anyone has had the opportunity to respond to the first one.* Although the teacher may mean to clarify a question, multiple questions can confuse the students. Note how many times a person being interviewed on TV is confused by rapid-fire, multiple questions from the interviewer. To which question, they wonder, should they respond? Which is the most important question?

5. *Because the teacher is concerned with the development of listening skills as well as speaking and comprehending skills, he or she should not develop the habit of repeating the questions and the answers given by students.* The teacher should speak loudly and clearly enough that all students can hear. Repetition encourages students to allow their attention to wander and permits them to wait for the second go-around. Only if it is apparent that students have not understood the question should it be repeated or, preferably, rephrased. Students should be taught to develop the habit of listening the first time and to make their own responses clear and audible so that the teacher and their classmates can understand them.

6. *The teacher should distribute questions around the group to gain maximum participation.* The teacher needs to resist the temptation to confine questioning exclusively to those students whose hands are waving in the air or to those from whom the teacher is sure of getting a correct answer. The teacher should direct questions to students in the back of the room as well as in the front and to the students on the teacher's left as well as right. The teacher must guard against conscious and unconscious biases in favor of bright students, one gender over another, or one ethnic group over others.

7. *A questioning session should consume only a portion of a lesson.* Long, extended question-and-answer periods can cause the teacher to lose the audience and defeat the purpose of the questioning. One help in livening up such sessions is to cast them in the form of games. For example, by creating teams to field questions, the teacher can introduce a pleasant competitive spirit. This technique, however, is adaptable only for lower-level questions; it is too awkward for more complex and probing questions.

8. *The teacher should keep in mind the affective learning that takes place along with the cognitive.* Valuable student responses should be positively reinforced by the teacher with words or gestures of approval. When responses are not correct, the student's attempt at responding should be praised even though the content of the response itself may have to be corrected. The teacher is responsible for maintaining a classroom climate that permits students to respond, encourages all to participate, and develops a spirit of acceptance for others' ideas. Supervisors should encourage teachers to examine their questioning technique to be sure it meets these guidelines.

Providing for Variation   In literature, drama, and TV, a fast-moving story commands attention. A television producer who wants to hold an audience through the commercials knows how important it is to present the actors in varying situations, provide action, change scenery, and use appropriate audio and visual effects. The teacher can borrow some of the producer's tricks, for like the producer, the teacher must attempt to prevent boredom and lack of interest from setting in.

Unlike the producer, the teacher is up against the inexorable laws of human growth and development. Children tend to be restless and in need of movement and change. Their attention span is much shorter than that of adults—the younger the child, the shorter the attention span. Because not all young people are intrinsically motivated to encounter the material the teacher is presenting, the teacher must design age-appropriate activities and devise extrinsic means of arousing interest in the topic of study.

Variation is a key word in the task of stimulating interest. The teacher must vary the content, the pace of learning, the activities of the lesson, and even his or her own style of teaching. The supervisor may observe in the teacher's performance three components of the generic teaching skill called variation: (1) variation of the stimuli, (2) variation of learning activities for the group, and (3) variation of learning activities for the individual.

Variation of the Stimuli In every second of every class hour, countless stimuli effect certain responses in the learners and in the teacher. The human beings in the classroom, the lighting, the color of the paint on the walls and ceiling, the furniture and equipment in the room, the loudspeaker and clock, and the activity that takes place outside the doors and windows all have a bearing on the learning or lack of learning in the classroom. In the current movement of schools to require uniformity of pupil dress, under the assumption that uniformity of dress contributes positively to school environment, officials are noting the powerful effect of stimuli on learning. By far the most significant stimuli are the teacher and the learners, each of whom interacts with the other and provokes certain responses in the other.

The teacher who sits or stands motionless; makes no gestures; talks in a monotone, with no variation in pitch, tone, volume, and intonation; is unaware of the impact of nonverbal cues; and leads the class through a single, long, unchanging learning activity is violating a premise of good teaching, namely, frequent altering of the stimuli. This means, of course, that a teacher must be able to detect stimuli that affect learning in the classroom and be able to read the impact of these stimuli. When spotting signs of boredom, the teacher needs to shift gears quickly in the hope that the change will refuel the learners and bring them back to life.

An earlier section of this chapter considered the effectiveness of movement, the use of gestures to transmit meaning, and the use of silence (pausing) to secure the attention of the students. Allen and Ryan suggested that teachers master the skills of focusing, using interactional styles, and shifting sensory channels as well as the skills of movement, gestures, and pausing.[16] By focusing, these authors mean directing attention to particular objects or concepts. Typically, focusing is done with a statement such as "Keep this point in mind" or "Let's look at the table on page 25." The teacher zeroes in on an item and gives it special emphasis.

The term *interaction* has been used elsewhere in this text, and many researchers have postulated that learning is an interactive process. The soliloquist may hold an honored place in the entertainment world, but that style is decidedly out of place in the classroom, where learner achievement is the goal. Teachers should not only interact with the learners but also change the style of interaction frequently. Teachers customarily interact with groups but may also interact with individuals within a group and may direct interactions between students. All three of these interactive styles are superior to the monologue.

Shifting sensory channels as described by Allen and Ryan is a simple skill that is often overlooked. The most common sensory channel in teaching is the path from the teacher's mouth to the student's ears—spoken communication. Teachers should appeal to the visual sense as well as the aural. There may even be times when the senses of smell and touch can become the primary modes of communication.

The teacher's objective is to maintain, hold, or recapture, if necessary, the learners' attention. Manipulating and varying the stimuli can more readily gain and keep student interest.

Variation of Group Learning Activities If we identify all the learning activities that take place in class as stimuli, this second point in our discussion of providing for variation is identical to the first: Stimuli must be varied; therefore, learning activities, which are stimuli, must be varied. Supervisors can encourage teachers to use the stimulus variation of focusing, to distinguish between the specific stimuli previously mentioned and more general learning activities or strategies. The supervisor should suggest to teachers that they build into their lesson plans a variety of activities for each lesson that take into consideration the attention span of their students. Teachers should be encouraged to use many kinds of media. Setting aside the fascination students have with computers, as a general rule, a single, prolonged activity— whether lecture, panel discussion, DVD, videotape, or film—will generally not hold a group's attention and interest as well as a variety of activities. Key activities should be written into the teacher's lesson plans along with the estimated amount of time the class should devote to each activity. The object of variation of group activities is learner motivation.

Teachers must select and implement the grouping of pupils most appropriate to the learning activities. Techniques for grouping include:

1. *Subgrouping within the class.* The teacher may create special-interest groups or remedial groups. By subgrouping learners, the teacher reduces the range of achievement or interests among learners and makes instruction more individualized, though not completely personalized. Students may be grouped and regrouped for specific tasks and for special purposes. The teacher can more effectively help individuals within smaller groups realize their personal goals. Subgrouping is simpler and possibly more successful in schools where teachers are assisted by aides or where teachers are members of a teaching team.

2. *Cooperative learning.* Within the past decade, cooperative learning, also known as collaborative learning, has proved a popular variant of subgrouping. Robert E. Slavin, a leading advocate of cooperative learning, defined this technique as "a form of classroom organization in which students work in small groups to help one another learn academic material."[17] A key characteristic that distinguishes it from other forms of grouping is emphasis on the group's performance and success as well as the more traditional emphasis on individual performance within the classroom.

When organizing for cooperative learning, teachers structure small heterogeneous groups whose task is to assist each other in mastering the specified objectives. Individuals share responsibilities for instructing each other. Cooperative learning, with its emphasis on pupils' aiding each other, differs from the traditional, competitive models in which individuals vie for success in the classroom.

Varying classroom organization as circumstances dictate is a sound principle of instruction. Teachers should implement organizational plans to meet their particular objectives with particular groups at a particular time. No single pattern of classroom organization is likely to achieve all objectives. Total group instruction as opposed to subgrouping may well be the most viable and most efficient method for accomplishing certain objectives. The teacher's repertoire must encompass various ways of grouping pupils for instruction.

Variation of Individual Learning Activities Not only must activities be varied for the group as a whole, but special activities are necessary for individuals within the group. With this skill, we enter the difficult realm of individualizing instruction. The individualization of instruction is a noble teaching goal, and it has been described, analyzed, and advocated in countless books and articles. It is often made to seem like a simple task to which easy formulas can be applied. In reality, individualizing instruction is extremely difficult. The ultimate would be an individualized curriculum, individual programming, and tutorial instruction using either human or machine tutors. However, education is a mass venture quite unlike the one-to-one relationship of doctor to patient or lawyer to client. We must handle individuals within groups and as members of a larger group, the student body. Given the mass nature of education, we can still partially adapt instruction to individual differences as we attempt to move toward the ideal of individualization.

Learning is, indeed, an individual activity. No one can learn for another; one human being can help another learn, but what goes on in the mind of the individual is an intensely personal affair. The teacher, who is the primary helper during the formal education process, will use whatever skills he or she has to help differentiate instruction and make it more personal for each learner. The supervisor may point out that instruction moves toward individualization when the teacher engages in the following strategies:

1. *Allows choices.* The teacher should habitually give students opportunities to choose whenever possible. Students can be given a choice, for example, of subgroups to which they wish to belong. They can be offered choices of learning activities that have equal value, approaches they would like to take to the study of a topic, and resources they would prefer to use.

2. *Provides for independent study.* Students who are mature and interested enough to pursue a topic of study independently should be allowed to do so. The teacher may allot a portion of the student's time to independent study under supervision.

3. *Differentiates questions to individuals on the basis of their particular interests and abilities.* When conducting an oral question-and-answer session, the teacher can tailor the complexity of questions to the class's varying interests and abilities.

4. *Provides differentiated assignments.* Easier assignments may be set for slower students and more difficult assignments for faster students. The teacher may distinguish among a series of tasks those that are most difficult and assign them to the brighter students. Some extrinsic device may need to be used to motivate the faster learners to do the more difficult tasks; the practice of bonus tasks or honors assignments sometimes helps.

5. *Uses resources of varying levels of difficulty.* Learning resources should be provided beyond a single adopted textbook. Supplementary text materials should be available for varying levels of readers. There should be various types of instructional materials that present the topic being studied in different ways so that if the treatment in the textbook is not clear, students may approach the topic in another way. If computers are available, they should be used effectively.

6. *Makes use of learning resources outside the classroom.* The teacher will want to call on the services of the media center, the reading clinic (if there is one), and learning resource centers, where students may study more or less on their own. Worthwhile community resources should be used.

In individualizing instruction, the teacher should attempt to capitalize on students' particular learning styles. Some pupils learn better orally; others, visually; still others, tactilely. Some need quiet; others learn more readily with background noise or music. Some need many concrete materials; others can work with abstractions.[18]

As noted earlier, attention needs to be given to the varying types of intelligence possessed by individual students, and some effort should be made to provide learning activities that appeal to those intelligences. The supervisor should strongly reinforce the efforts of teachers who try to individualize or personalize instruction. Despite the importance and value of individualizing instruction, for some purposes it is an acceptable and sometimes better practice to hold the class together and instruct the students as a large group. In short, there is a place for large-group instruction, small-group instruction, and individualized learning activities.

The Place of Motivation[19]   Two of the generic skills discussed in this chapter—set induction and providing for variation—are aspects of the broader skill of motivating learners. The term *motivation* has two meanings. The first and primary meaning of *motivation* as related to the process of learning is the disposition or desire of the learner to learn. The second meaning, extrinsic motivation, is found in those actions teachers take to arouse the learner's desire to learn. The most effective form of motivation—perhaps the only form in its true meaning—is the desire that lives within the learner, which is referred to as *intrinsic motivation*.

One can easily observe the presence or absence of motivated learners in the classroom and school. Some students look alert, respond quickly, and show enthusiasm for what they are doing. Others appear bored, are inattentive, and are impatient for the school day to end. The highly motivated learner enjoys school and learning; the converse is true of the unmotivated learner.

More often than not, the highly motivated learner is a good reader, can handle abstractions, possesses verbal aptitude, and is intelligent. This is not to say that all intelligent pupils are highly motivated—far from it. One of the tragedies of the modern school is that some intelligent pupils are not at all motivated. They see little purpose in what they are doing. They do a minimum to get by. They may be so bright that the curriculum offers them no challenge. Creative minds are often squelched by the formal nature of education.

Learners are motivated when they conceive of themselves as capable individuals. They feel that their peers, teachers, and others in their environment recognize them as able to achieve. Students possess the desire to learn when they are dealing with materials that they understand and that are geared to their level. They are motivated when they see purpose in their activities and study.

Learners are motivated if they live in a safe, orderly, and attractive environment. They are motivated if they have opportunities to express their psychological needs for success, recognition, and approval. Students must feel that the learning experiences are for them, not for the teacher. They need to understand why the content is important, what application it may have in their lives, and why the subject matter they are studying should take precedence over other activities.

Learners are motivated when the teacher promotes a climate in which both students and teacher respect and respond positively to social and cultural differences present in the classroom. Learners are motivated when they feel a sense of pride in their backgrounds. Their self-worth is enhanced in an environment that is free of cultural, ethnic, and gender biases.

Learners are motivated when the teacher is motivated and upbeat about the subjects to be learned. Enthusiasm is contagious. The disengaged teacher cannot expect students to express interest in the subject matter, school, or learning in general.

Learners are motivated when they experience success more often than failure. The feeling of achievement that accompanies success motivates the student to want to learn more.

We would be fortunate if we could prescribe a bag of tricks that would be sure-fire means of motivation. But compelling motives differ from person to person. Consequently, the techniques that work with one individual or group may not work with others. We should be neither surprised nor discouraged if we cannot arouse enthusiasm and interest in all learners at all times. Boredom is bound to creep in from time to time. The conditions of learning may not always be optimal. The teacher may turn in a poor performance on a certain day. The students may be tired after a school event the preceding evening. Some local, state, national, or international crisis may have leaped to the forefront to shut out all attempts at school studies. The best teachers can hope for is that they may reach most of the learners most of the time.

Teachers often resort to extrinsic forms of motivation to promote the development of intrinsic motivation. The use of awards in schools is a time-honored practice. If rewards for learning are positive and kept within reasonable limits, they often succeed in encouraging students to learn. Simple rewards, such as a smiling face on a piece of work well done or praise for a student's accomplishments, can go a long way toward motivating learners.

In our evident pleasure with students who achieve in school, we as teachers should seek to distinguish between achievement that results from positive, healthy motivation and achievement that comes from negative, destructive motivation. We should be aware of the intense pressures placed by some parents on their children to achieve, perform, and succeed. The teacher needs to be understanding and not add to the negative motivation.

Closing the Lesson

Each lesson should have not only a beginning, a middle, and an end but a planned beginning, a middle, and an end. The closing of the class lesson should be controlled by the teacher and actively involve the learners; it should not be determined by the ringing of the bell or the passing of other groups or classes.

Before the class ends, the teacher will want to know whether the objectives of each lesson have been achieved. Success with the lesson may have been evident throughout the activity. However, before the group leaves for the day, the teacher should evaluate their achievement of the objectives, no matter how limited these may be. He or she can accomplish this by posing a few summary questions to learn whether the students have understood the work of the day and by encouraging questions from the group. The teacher can be misled, however, if the group has no questions. The customary teacher's remark, "Any questions?" does not always bear fruit. Students may not have understood enough of the lesson to ask intelligent questions. They may not know what they don't know and therefore cannot raise questions. Furthermore, they may be tired or ready to leave class and not want to prolong the lesson.

The teacher should allow at least a few minutes before the end of the class for a wrap-up or closure. In this time, the students will reexamine what they have achieved that day and attempt to fix the more important learnings in their minds. The teacher may achieve closure by reviewing the main points of the day's lesson or by asking the students to summarize the main points. The teacher should review with the class what they have learned—or at least what he or she expected them to learn. The teacher should not only look back over the day's work but should also show the learners the connections with previous lessons and future lessons, particularly the next day's lesson. The supervisor should look for lesson closure when visiting teachers and observing them in action. One successful strategy to illustrate an effective lesson closure is to jot down, on the chalkboard or white board, the main ideas the students remembered from the lesson for them to see. Then, use an imaginary large laundry bag to put all of those concepts in before you pull the cord and close the bag.

Toward the end of the day's lesson, teachers customarily make the assignment for the next day. In analyzing a lesson presentation with a teacher, the supervisor should not neglect the skill of assignment making. The classic mistakes in assignment making are such hurried directives from the teacher as, "Read the next chapter," "Study pages 115 to 135," and "Work the next 10 problems in your book." Such common assignments are far too simplistic for the most effective learning. The supervisor might encourage teachers to take a sampling of the assignments they have given their class during the last few days and see how they stack up against the guidelines listed here.

1. *Assignments should be clear to all students.* This means that the teacher must take enough time during the lesson to make the task understood. The directions must be in language the learners understand. Time should be allotted for student questions about the assignment.

2. *Assignments should be on work the class has already covered or the teacher is sure the learners are able to do.* If the assignment involves principles the teacher has not yet explained to the students, it is best that they not go ahead without adequate instruction. If students attempt work ahead of instruction, they may do the work incorrectly and develop wrong learnings, which are then difficult to correct.

3. *Difficulties students may have in the assignment should be anticipated, and the teacher should give suggestions on how to overcome them.* The teacher may review the points of difficulty and direct the students to resources that will be helpful.

4. *Assignments should be differentiated for varying interests and abilities.* The element of choice can often enter at this point. Though more difficult to plan than a single, blanket assignment for all, multiple assignments have the advantage of appealing to a wider number of learners.

5. *Assignments should be reasonable in terms of the amount of out-of-class work expected.* Middle and high school teachers in particular must be aware of the amount of homework they are assigning and students' total homework load.

6. Assignments *should be not only reasonable in length but also necessary.* "Busy work"—assignments for assignments' sake—should be avoided. Busy work serves only to discourage rather than promote interest. If there is no real need for an assignment, none should be made.

7. *Resources for accomplishing the assignment must be available.* The teacher cannot assume the availability of resources in the home. Consequently, the teacher must know what resources are called for and direct students to their location.

8. *It is helpful if assignments are given through more than one sensory channel.* Instead of relying exclusively on an oral direction, the teacher can supply instruction in written form as well. An oral explanation based on written instructions makes the task to be done that much clearer, for the student not only hears but also sees the assignment and, as a result, is better able to carry out the instructions.

9. *Teachers may allot a portion of the class time to allow students to begin homework assignments.* In that way the teacher may circulate among the students to help them, if necessary, and to assess whether they can perform the assignments. This technique effectively uses the concept of guided practice, where the teacher can act as a resource person to model the process, and independent practice, where the teacher circulates and observes the students while they are working.

A CHECKLIST

To provide a teacher with feedback on lesson presentation, the supervisor may wish to use an instrument such as the checklist that follows. The more items the supervisor can check in the "Yes" column when observing a teacher teaching, the better that lesson presentation may be said to be. "No" responses indicate points needing dialog between the supervisor and the teacher. The supervisor can encourage teachers to analyze their own performance by using the checklist. These self-analyses can be particularly helpful when made in conjunction with a videotape of their own teaching.

A Checklist for Lesson Presentation

On the basis of classroom observation, the supervisor will check "Yes" for those items observed in the lesson presentation and "No" for those items not observed.

Selection of Resources	*Yes*	*No*
Related to objectives	——	——
In keeping with abilities of learners	——	——
In keeping with age of learners	——	——
Of interest to learners	——	——
Varied for individual differences	——	——
Accurate and up-to-date	——	——
Without bias or balanced as to biases	——	——
Easily accessible to learners	——	——
Without cost to learners	——	——

Selection of Strategies	*Yes*	*No*
Right for learners	——	——
Right for teacher	——	——
Right for subject matter	——	——
Right for time available	——	——
Right for resources available	——	——
Right for facilities	——	——
Right for objectives	——	——

Teacher's Conduct of the Lesson
General

	Yes	No
Has written plans	——	——
Materials and equipment on hand	——	——
Exhibits confidence	——	——
Appears to know where class is going	——	——
Communicates objectives to learners	——	——
Maintains flow in the day's activities	——	——
Avoids unnecessary repetition of content	——	——
Keeps students on task	——	——
Demonstrates attention to differences among learners	——	——
Learners attentive; absence of student misbehavior	——	——

Beginning of lesson

	Yes	No
Establishes set	——	——

Middle of lesson

	Yes	No
Lectures	——	——
Ensures that learners are mature enough	——	——
Ensures that learners are developing listening skills	——	——
Ensures that learners understand language	——	——
Gives evidence of advance planning	——	——
Supplements with aids	——	——
Provides for feedback and follow-up	——	——
Secures student participation	——	——
Gives continuous opportunity for student expression	——	——
Uses silence and nonverbal cues	——	——
Uses effective questioning	——	——
Asks higher-order questions	——	——
Asks probing questions	——	——
Asks divergent questions	——	——
Avoids repeating questions and answers	——	——
Consumes only a portion of lesson	——	——
Is aware of affective learning	——	——
Provides for variation	——	——
Varies stimuli	——	——
Varies activities for the group	——	——
Varies activities for individuals	——	——

End of lesson	*Yes*	*No*
Provides for evaluation	——	——
Allows time for assignment making	——	——
Makes assignments clear	——	——
Reviews work covered, or students are able to do so	——	——
Anticipates difficult points	——	——
Differentiates for varying student interests and abilities	——	——
Makes assignments a reasonable length	——	——
Makes necessary assignments	——	——
Ensures that needed resources are available	——	——
Uses more than one sensory channel	——	——
Achieves closure	——	——

Comments/Summary

_____

_____

_____

SUMMARY

Effective teachers set clear goals, hold high expectations of students, focus on academics, maintain an orderly climate, use appropriate materials, and use time productively.

Lesson presentation involves a complex variety of skills. The supervisor can help teachers as they translate their unit and lesson plans into action. The supervisor determines whether the teacher has chosen suitable resources and selected appropriate strategies, in accordance with relevant guidelines. The supervisor helps teachers in developing generic skills of instruction, which include effective ways of beginning, carrying through, and closing a lesson.

The supervisor should encourage teachers to increase student participation and incorporate a variety of stimuli and activities in both their planning and their actual presentation. To help the supervisor work with teachers on lesson presentation, we have examined the specific skills (generic competencies) of set induction, lecturing, discussion, questioning, providing for variation, and closure. Supervisors should help teachers discover whether they are using time most productively for instructional purposes. In selecting instructional strategies, teachers need to be mindful of the problem of motivation.

In the presentation stage, the carefully laid plans come to fruition—or fail. Lesson presentation is the phase of instruction the public knows as teaching, as it is often unaware of or ignores the hours of planning, grading papers, and other miscellaneous duties required of today's teacher. The presentation phase is the most rewarding to the teacher and is what keeps most teachers in the classroom. It is during this stage that ideas leap from mind to mind, skills are mastered by those who lacked them before instruction, and knowledge is stored in the brain—primarily because of the efforts of the teacher.

QUESTIONS FOR DISCUSSION

1. Should cooperative learning replace individualized learning? If so, why and how?

2. About which should teachers be more concerned: content and skills or students' self-concepts? Why?

3. Should all students be expected to master all basic knowledge and skills? Why?

4. What is the place of direct teaching?

5. What knowledge and skills are necessary for teachers to make effective presentations?

ACTIVITIES FOR FURTHER STUDY

REFLECTIVE

1. Define these terms:

generic teaching	anticipatory set
competency	teaching strategy
probing question	higher-order question
stimulus variation	closure
set induction	divergent question
convergent question	

2. State some common errors made by teachers in presenting a lesson and describe ways in which you, as a supervisor, could help teachers overcome the errors.

3. Prepare a lecture/demonstration such as you would give to an in-service group of teachers on one of the following topics: selection of strategies, set induction, lecturing, conducting a discussion, questioning, stimulus variation, or closure.

4. Summarize two or three recent articles in professional journals on ways to individualize instruction and the (a) applicability elsewhere, (b) soundness of approach, and (c) cost of each.

5. Select a topic, choose three strategies for presenting that topic to a particular group of learners, and decide which one of the three would be most effective as an initial strategy.

6. Examine the text materials used at one grade level or in one subject and evaluate them using the criteria for resources cited in this chapter.

7. Describe or outline ways of evaluating the development of listening skills by the students.

8. Several nonverbal cues were discussed in this chapter. Make a list of other nonverbal cues you have used or seen other teachers use in their lessons.

9. Develop a list of techniques you could use to ensure you have distributed questions among the students.

10. Write a report on adapting instruction to students' individual learning styles. (See Dunn and Dunn in the chapter bibliography.)

11. Write a brief description of each of Madeline Hunter and Douglas Russell's seven steps for effective lessons (see chapter bibliography).

12. Summarize one or more reports of the effective teaching research of the past thirty years. (See Berliner; Brookover; Brophy and Evertson; Brophy and Good; Edmonds; Lezotte and Bancroft; Medley; Rosenshine in the bibliography.)

13. Write a lesson plan and indicate where you incorporate variation of learning activities for the group.

14. Critique at least two assignments given by teachers and decide whether each assignment meets the guidelines presented in this chapter.

15. Describe the eight intelligences according to Howard Gardner. (See the Checkley and Gardner references in the chapter bibliography.)

APPLICATION

1. Observe a teacher who is presenting a lesson and evaluate the presentation using the checklist near the end of this chapter. Based on your observation, decide how effective you believe the presentation was with respect to each item on the checklist.

2. Write a fifty-minute lesson plan that incorporates skills studied in this chapter.

3. Choose a topic and demonstrate set induction.

4. Prepare and demonstrate effective lecturing following the guidelines presented in this chapter.

5. Prepare and demonstrate a discussion lesson using at least four nonverbal cues.

6. Select a topic that could be taught to a particular group of learners and write two questions (which you would present to a class orally) at each level of the Bloom taxonomy of cognitive objectives.

7. Prepare and conduct a short question-and-answer session and point out how frequently you used higher-order questions.

8. Observe a teacher conducting a questioning session and evaluate the effectiveness of the questioning, applying guidelines presented in this chapter.

9. Observe a teacher presenting a lesson and decide whether he or she varied the stimuli and in what ways.

10. Demonstrate closure.

11. Place the fourteen skills identified by Allen and Ryan on the proper place of the lesson line.

NOTES

1. See Donald M. Medley, "The Effectiveness of Teachers," in *Research in Teaching: Concepts, Findings, and Implications*, ed. Penelope L. Peterson and Herbert J. Walberg (Berkeley, Calif.: McCutchan, 1979), pp. 11–27. See also Donald M. Medley, "Research in Teacher Effectiveness—Where It Is and How It Got There," *Journal of Classroom Interaction* 13 (Summer 1978): 20.

2. See Barak V. Rosenshine, "Academic Engaged Time, Content Covered, and Direct Instruction," *Journal of Education* 160 (August 1978): 38–66; and Barak V. Rosenshine, "Content, Time, and Direct Instruction," in *Research in Teaching: Concepts, Findings, and Implications*, eds. Penelope L. Peterson and Herbert L. Walberg (Berkeley, Calif.: McCutchan, 1979), p. 52.

3. See N. L. Gage, *The Scientific Basis of the Art of Teaching* (New York: Teachers College Press, 1978). See also reference in note 8.

4. George E. Pawlas, *The Administrator's Guide to School-Community Relations*, 2nd ed. (Larchmont, N.Y.: Eye on Education, 2005).

5. See, for example, Educator's Reference Desk (www.eduref.org/Virtual/Lessons), the Lesson Plans Page (www.lessonplanspage.com), and Discovery School (school.discovery.com/lessonplans). See also TeachersPayTeachers.com, an online marketplace where experienced teachers may share their lesson plans (for a fee) and new teachers may purchase plans.

6. Howard Gardner, *Multiple Intelligences: The Theory in Practice* (New York: Basic Books, 1993). See also Thomas Armstrong, *Multiple Intelligences in the Classroom*, 2nd ed. (Alexandria, Va.: Association for Supervision and Curriculum Development, 2000).

7. Kathy Checkley, "The First Seven ... and the Eighth: A Conversation with Howard Gardner," *Educational Leadership* 55 (September 1997): 8, 9.

8. For discussion of constructivist principles and practices, see Jacqueline Grennon Brooks and Martin G. Brooks, in *Search of Understanding: The Case for Constructivist Classrooms* (Alexandria, Va.: Association for Supervision and Curriculum Development, 1999).

9. See Keith A. Acheson and Meredith Damien Gall, *Clinical Supervision and Teacher Development: Preservice and Inservice Applications*, 5th ed. (Hoboken, N.J.: Wiley, 2003), pp. 172–78 for description of at-task technique.

10. See Dwight Allen and Kevin Ryan, *Microteaching* (Reading, Mass.: Addison-Wesley, 1969), pp. 18–19.

11. Madeline Hunter and Douglas Russell, "How Can I Plan More Effective Lessons?" *Instructor* 87 (September 1977): 74–75, 88.

12. Allen and Ryan, *Microteaching*, p. 15.

13. Hunter and Russell, "More Effective Lessons," pp. 74–75, 88.

14. See Chapter 3 of this text.

15. See Medley, "Effectiveness of Teachers."

16. Allen and Ryan, *Microteaching*, pp. 15–18.

17. Robert E. Slavin, "Cooperative Learning and Student Achievement," in *School and Classroom Organization*, ed. Robert E. Slavin (Hillsdale, N.J.: Lawrence Erlbaum, 1989), p. 129.

18. For discussion of students' learning styles, see Rita Dunn and Kenneth Dunn, *Teaching Students through Their Individual Learning Styles: A Practical Approach* (Reston, Va.: Reston Publishing, 1978).

19. Adapted from Peter F. Oliva, *The Secondary School Today*, 2nd ed. (New York: Harper and Row, 1972), pp. 266–73.

BIBLIOGRAPHY

ACHESON, KEITH A., and MEREDITH DAMIEN GALL. *Clinical Supervision and Teacher Development: Preservice and Inservice Applications*, 5th ed. New York: Wiley, 2003.

ALLEN, DWIGHT, and KEVIN RYAN. *Microteaching*. Reading, Mass.: Addison-Wesley, 1969.

ARMSTRONG, THOMAS. *Multiple Intelligences in the Classroom*, 2nd ed. Alexandria, Va.: Association for Supervision and Curriculum Development, 2000.

BERENSON, DAVID H., SALLY R. BERENSON, and ROBERT B. CARKHUFF. *The Skills of Teaching: Content Development Skills*. Amherst, Mass.: Human Resource Development Press, 1978.

BERENSON, SALLY R., DAVID H. BERENSON, and ROBERT R. CARKHUFF. *The Skills of Teaching: Teaching Delivery Skills*. Amherst, Mass.: Human Resource Development Press, 1979.

BERLINER, DAVID C., et al. *Phase III of the Beginning Teacher Effectiveness Study*. San Francisco: Far West Laboratory for Educational Research and Development, 1976.

BROOKOVER, WILBUR B. *A Study of Elementary School Social Systems and School Outcomes*. East Lansing: Michigan State University Center for Urban Affairs, 1977.

BROOKS, JACQUELINE GRENNON, and MARTIN G. BROOKS. *In Search of Understanding: The Case for Constructivist Classrooms*. Alexandria, Va.: Association for Supervision and Curriculum Development, 1999.

BROPHY, JERE E., and C. M. EVERTSON. *Process–Product Correlation in the Texas Teacher Effectiveness Study*. Austin: University of Texas, 1974.

BROPHY, JERE, and THOMAS L. GOOD. "Teacher Behavior and Student Achievement." In *Handbook of Research on Teaching*, 3rd ed., ed. Merlin C. Wittrock. New York: Macmillan, 1986, pp. 328–75.

CAMPBELL, LINDA, and BRUCE CAMPBELL. *Multiple Intelligences and Student Achievement: Success Stories from Six Schools*. Alexandria, Va.: Association for Supervision and Curriculum Development, 1999.

CAMPBELL, LINDA, BRUCE CAMPBELL, and DEE DICKINSON. *Teaching and Learning through Multiple Intelligences*, 3rd ed. Boston: Allyn and Bacon, 2004.

CARKHUFF, ROBERT R., DAVID H. BERENSON, and SALLY R. BERENSON. *The Skills of Teaching: Lesson Planning Skills*. Amherst, Mass.: Human Resource Development Press, 1978.

CARKHUFF, ROBERT R., DAVID H. BERENSON, RICHARD M. PIERCE, ANDREW H. GRIFFIN, and CAROLYN H. SCHOENECKER. *The Skills of Teaching: Interpersonal Skills*. Amherst, Mass.: Human Resource Development Press, 1977.

CHECKLEY, KATHY. "The First Seven ... and the Eighth: A Conversation with Howard Gardner."*Educational Leadership* 55 (September 1997): 8, 9.

"Cooperative Learning."*Educational Leadership* 47 (December 1989/January 1990): 3–66.

DAVIDSON, JACK L., and FREDA M. HOLLEY."Your Students May Be Spending Only Half the School Day Receiving Instruction."*American School Board Journal* 166 (March 1979): 40–41.

DUNN, RITA, and KENNETH DUNN. *Teaching Students through Their Individual Learning Styles: A Practical Approach*. Reston, Va.: Reston Publishing, 1978.

EDMONDS, RONALD R. *An Overview of School Improvement Programs*. East Lansing, Mich.: Institute for Research on Teaching, Michigan State University, 1983.

FLINDERS, DAVID J."Supervision as Cultural Inquiry."*Journal of Curriculum and Supervision* 6 (Winter 1991): 87–106.

GARDNER, HOWARD. *Multiple Intelligences: The Theory in Practice*. New York: Basic Books, 1993.

GARRETT, SANDRA SOKOLOVE, MYRA SADKER, and DAVID SADKER. "Interpersonal Communication Skills." In *Classroom Teaching Skills*, 4th ed., ed. James M. Cooper, pp. 185–228. Lexington, Mass.: D. C. Heath, 1990.

GOODLAD, JOHN I. *A Place Called School: Twentieth Anniversary Edition*, 2nd ed. New York: McGraw-Hill, 2004.

GOODLAD, JOHN I., KENNETH A. SIROTNIK, and BETTE C. OVERMAN."An Overview of 'A Study of Schooling.'"*Phi Delta Kappan* 61 (November 1979): 174–78.

GUNTER, MARY A., THOMAS H. ESTES, and SUSAN L. MINTZ. *Instruction: A Models Approach*, 5th ed . Boston: Allyn and Bacon, 2007.

HIATT, DIANA."Time Allocation in the Classroom: Is Instruction Being Shortchanged?"*Phi Delta Kappan* 61 (December 1979): 289–90.

HUNTER, MADELINE, and DOUGLAS RUSSELL."How Can I Plan More Effective Lessons?"*Instructor* 87 (September 1977): 74–75, 88.

JOHNSON, DAVID W., and ROGER T. JOHNSON. *Learning Together and Alone: Cooperative, Competitive, and Individualistic Learning*, 5th ed. Boston: Allyn and Bacon, 1999.

JOHNSON, DAVID W., ROGER T. JOHNSON, and EDYTHE JOHNSON HOLUBEC. *Circles of Learning: Cooperation in the Classroom*, 4th ed. Edina, Minn.: Interaction, 1993.

JOYCE, BRUCE R., MARSHA WEIL, and EMILY CALHOUN. *Models of Teaching*, 7th ed. Boston: Allyn and Bacon, 2004.

KIM, EUGENE C., and RICHARD D. KELLOUGH. *A Resource Guide for Secondary School Teaching: Planning for Competence*, 6th ed. Englewood Cliffs, N.J.: Merrill, 1995.

LEIGHTON, MARY S."Cooperative Learning." In *Classroom Teaching Skills*, 4th ed., ed. James M. Cooper, pp. 307–35. Lexington, Mass.: D. C. Heath, 1990.

LEZOTTE, LAWRENCE W., and BEVERLY A. BANCROFT."Growing Use of the Effective Schools Model for School Improvement."*Educational Leadership* 42 (March 1985): 23–27.

MCNEIL, JOHN D."A Scientific Approach to Supervision." In *Supervision of Teaching*, 1982 Yearbook, ed. Thomas J. Sergiovanni. Alexandria, Va.: Association for Supervision and Curriculum Development, 1982.

MARTORELLA, PETER H."Teaching Concepts." In *Classroom Teaching Skills*, 4th ed., ed. James M. Cooper, pp. 149–84. Lexington, Mass.: D. C. Heath, 1990.

MEDLEY, DONALD M."The Effectiveness of Teachers." In *Research in Teaching: Concepts, Findings, and Implications*, ed. Penelope L. Peterson and Herbert J. Walberg, pp. 11–27. Berkeley, Calif.: McCutchan, 1979.

PAWLAS, GEORGE E. *The Administrator's Guide to School-Community Relations*, 2nd ed. Larchmont, N.Y.: Eye on Education, 2005.

PETERSON, PENELOPE L., and HERBERT J. WALBERG, eds. *Research on Teaching: Concepts, Findings, and Implications*. Berkeley, Calif.: McCutchan, 1979.

POPHAM, W. JAMES, and EVA L. L. *Planning an Instructional Sequence*. Englewood Cliffs, N.J.: Prentice Hall, 1970.
———. *Systematic Instruction*. Englewood Cliffs, N.J.: Prentice Hall, 1970.

ROSENSHINE, BARAK V."Academic Engaged Time, Content Covered, and Direct Instruction."*Journal of Education* 160 (August 1978): 38–66.
———. "Content, Time, and Direct Instruction." In *Research on Teaching: Concepts, Findings, and Implications*, ed. Penelope L. Peterson and Herbert J. Walberg, pp. 28–56. Berkeley, Calif.: McCutchan, 1979.

SADKER, MYRA, and DAVID SADKER."Questioning Skills." In *Classroom Teaching Skills*, 4th ed., ed. James M. Cooper, pp. 111–48. Lexington, Mass.: D. C. Heath, 1990.

SHARAN, SHLOMO, ed. *Cooperative Learning: Theory and Research*. New York: Praeger, 1990.

SHOSTAK, ROBERT. "Lesson Presentation Skills." In *Classroom Teaching Skills*, 4th ed., ed. James M. Cooper, pp. 85–109. Lexington, Mass.: D. C. Heath, 1990.

SLAVIN, ROBERT E. *Cooperative Learning*. New York: Longman, 1983.

———. "Cooperative Learning." *Review of Educational Research* 50 (Summer 1980): 315–42.

———. "Cooperative Learning and Student Achievement." In *School and Classroom Organization*, ed. Robert, E. Slavin. Hillsdale, N.J.: Lawrence Erlbaum, 1989.

———. *Cooperative Learning: Theory, Research, and Practice*, 2nd ed. Boston: Allyn and Bacon, 1995.

STALLINGS, JANE A. "Using Time Effectively: A Self-Analytical Approach." In *Improving Teaching*, 1986 Yearbook, ed. Karen K. Zumwalt, pp. 15–27. Alexandria, Va.: Association for Supervision and Curriculum Development, 1987.

STRONGE, JAMES H. *Qualities of Effective Teachers*, 2nd ed. Alexandria, Va.: Association for Supervision and Curriculum Development, 2007.

WITTROCK, MERLIN C., ed. *Handbook of Research on Teaching*, 3rd ed. New York: Macmillan, 1986.

ZUMWALT, KAREN K., ed. *Improving Teaching*, 1986 Yearbook. Alexandria, Va.: Association for Supervision and Curriculum Development, 1986.

VIDEOTAPES

Educating Everybody's Children, 2001. Six tapes: *Attitudes and Beliefs*; *Capitalizing on Students' Strengths*; *Matching Instructional Methods to Students' Instructional Need*; *Increasing Interest, Motivation and Engagement*; *Creating Varied Learning Configuration*; *Making Connections for Understanding*. Association for Supervision and Curriculum Development, 1703 N. Beauregard St., Alexandria, Va. 22311?1714. (800) 933–2723. www.ascd.org.

Becoming a Multiple Intelligences School, 2000. One fifteen-minute tape. Thomas R. Hoerr conducts visit to a school following multiple intelligences theory. Book of same title. Association for Supervision and Curriculum Development, 1703 N. Beauregard St., Alexandria, Va. 22311–1714. (800) 933–2723. www.ascd.org.

WEB SITES

Association for Supervision and Curriculum Development: www.ascd.org

Education Performance Institute, University of West Florida: www.ibinder.uwf.edu

Teachers Network: www.teachernet.org

CHAPTER 5

HELPING TEACHERS WITH CLASSROOM MANAGEMENT

OBJECTIVES

After studying Chapter 5 you should be able to accomplish the following objectives:

1. Identify common sources of behavior problems.
2. Describe the characteristics of a fully functioning personality and its relationship to the problem of discipline.
3. Describe common teaching styles and their impact on discipline.
4. Describe common learning styles and their impact on discipline.
5. Describe several measures that can be taken to prevent disciplinary problems.
6. Describe several models of discipline.
7. Describe several approaches to discipline.
8. Contrast the strengths and weaknesses of behavior modification.
9. Contrast strengths and weaknesses of psychodynamic or diagnostic approaches to discipline.
10. List steps in behavior modification.
11. Analyze the methods of discipline you prefer.
12. Select appropriate corrective measures.
13. Explain the role of punishment.
14. Formulate your own views on discipline.

DISCIPLINE: A SERIOUS PROBLEM

A frazzled young elementary teacher holds her head at the end of a particularly rough day with her group of superactive children. As she fumbles for an aspirin in her handbag, it is obvious to the supervisor, who happened to drop in on this inauspicious occasion, that the children's behavior that day had been less than ideal. The supervisor empathizes with the teacher and hopes that the painkiller will relieve her headache. If only the problems of classroom management would respond to a simple formula like aspirin and then vanish overnight!

Even Socrates, one of the most famous teachers in history, must have been holding his head when he lamented, "Children now love luxury. They have bad manners, contempt for authority. They show disrespect for elders and love chatter in place of exercise. Children are now tyrants, not the servants of their households."[1]

Sometimes it seems that not much has changed since 400 B.C. Not even the venerable Socrates was able to concoct a formula that would serve as either a vaccine or a cure for misbehavior by young people. Fantasizing, harried teachers feel that student behavior problems would disappear if these conditions existed:

- If only children were mature—but they are not.
- If only children were as motivated as the teacher—but they are not.
- If only children could choose whether they wanted to come to school—but they cannot.
- If only children had no problems—but they do.

If only—teachers could go on and wistfully hope never to encounter a disciplinary problem, and proceed smoothly from planning to presentation to evaluation without stumbling on the pebbles and boulders of behavior problems. But the road is rocky and the stones are there. It is the teacher's task to clear the stones out of the way, go over them, go around them, or even push them out of the way if need be, and it is the supervisor's task to help the teachers in this arduous job.

The teacher's task in matters of discipline, control, and classroom management should not be minimized. These topics are constantly on the minds of most teachers, particularly new and inexperienced ones. The frustration of dealing with disciplinary problems has driven many teachers out of the classroom. Some have left the profession; others, ironically, have gravitated to administrative positions where they have responsibility for the disciplinary problems of an entire school instead of just the problems of their own classes. Some have taken on the mantle of the college professor, whose disciplinary problems are usually few and far between.

Discipline is a word that is easily understood by everyone but difficult to define. Perhaps the difficulty of defining the word stems from its resemblance to a Portuguese man-o'-war jellyfish: It has so many and such long tentacles. If we go back far enough—say 2,000 years—the little Roman *discipulus* was a pupil, a learner, who was subjected to *disciplina*—instruction, training, or education. Hence the use of the term *discipline* to mean an organized body of knowledge, a subject field. The *disciples* of Jesus were those who had been instructed in His teachings.

Although the word *discipline* still refers to organized fields of specialization, *discipline* in its "training" sense has come to signify order, management, conduct, deportment, and even punishment. People talk about the discipline of the school and the discipline of the class. We say the teacher maintains good discipline and disciplines the pupils. This text defines *discipline* as a state of order in the class or school environment that permits learning to proceed smoothly and productively.

Behavior is another of those words that can be understood only in context. Previous chapters discussed learning behaviors, which, in that context, signify outcomes or objectives of learning in any of the three domains of learning. To speak of behavior in the context of discipline (as opposed to a discipline) is to equate it with conduct or deportment, just as *misbehavior* means misconduct. The student who has learned to take responsibility for his or her own actions in socially acceptable ways is said to possess self-discipline, a major goal of not only discipline but also the entire process of education in our society. Those who behave in socially unacceptable ways are said to have—or, in personified form, to be—behavior problems or disciplinary problems.

A teacher not only teaches classes but also manages them, or more properly, manages the learning environment in such a way that learning can occur. The skills the teacher employs for this purpose are called collectively *classroom management*. Included within the scope of this definition are classroom routines, prevention of misbehavior, and correction of behavior problems.

Both teachers and school administrators agree that discipline is the most serious problem faced by teachers, particularly inexperienced teachers. Harvey F. Clarizio observed that "classroom management has always been one of the foremost problems for teachers. Indeed, the adequate control of a class is a prerequisite to achieving instructional objectives and to safeguarding the psychological and physical well-being of students."[2]

Since 1969, Gallup polls have surveyed the public's attitudes toward the public schools. The results are published each fall in *Phi Delta Kappan*, the journal of Phi Delta Kappa, the national society in education. Lack of discipline has consistently appeared at or near the top—until recent years, in first place—of the public's list of problems in the public schools. The public has generally ranked lack of discipline ahead of such other thorny issues as lack of proper financial support, poor curriculum/poor standards, difficulty in getting good teachers, teachers' lack of interest, and integration/busing. In the Gallup polls of the late 1980s and early 1990s, the public ranked use of drugs as the major problem in public schools. The 38th Annual Phi Delta Kappa/Gallup Poll conducted in 2006 reported that 11 percent of Americans considered lack of discipline/more control to be the third most important problem of the public schools. Lack of financial support/funding/money has remained the biggest problem identified by the respondents in the last three surveys. The remaining five important problems with the public schools, in rank order, were overcrowded schools; use of drugs/dope; pupils' lack of interest; parents' lack of support; and fighting/violence/gangs.[3]

The students, in their roles as potential misbehavers and recipients of disciplinary measures, are intimately concerned with the problem of discipline. Students expect teachers to foster a classroom environment where, regardless of whether productive learning goes on, at least their security and self-esteem are protected.

Students realize that they are a part of the American school culture. As such, they expect to encounter misbehavior from their peers, and they anticipate that they themselves may indulge in some infractions of the rules, if only to maintain their status in the culture. As a result, they expect the teacher to respond to misconduct. Earlier Gallup surveys showed that the majority of students felt the discipline of their school was about right. Only a small percentage believed the discipline was too strict, and a significant percentage considered the discipline not strict enough.[4] *Time* and CNN conducted a Teen Poll following the tragedy that occurred in 1999 at Columbine High School in Littleton, Colorado. Thirty-three percent of the 409 American teenagers responding indicated that a similar incident was likely to occur in their school. The remaining 66 percent felt that was not very likely or not likely at all.[5]

With all the stress on discipline placed by the school and community constituents, the supervisor faces a demanding challenge. Classroom management may well be the single most difficult task of public school teaching. If there is any one aspect of teaching with which beginning teachers especially need help from a supervisor, it is discipline. Fredric H. Jones observed that the problem of discipline "has gone noticed but unattended. ... Administrators want teachers to take care of it, teachers want administrators to take care of it, and the universities ignore it as though the study of it would ruin their humanistic credentials."[6]

The principal, the assistant principal for administration, and the dean of students may well ponder the issue of discipline in their school as they sit in their offices and receive a steady flow of "discipline problems" from the various classrooms. They note great variations among what teachers consider serious behavior problems—those sent to the administrators' offices. They observe that some of the teachers on the faculty have either a greater skill in handling disciplinary problems than other teachers or a greater tolerance for enduring them, for some teachers never send misbehaving pupils to an administrator's office; they prefer, as the saying goes, "to skin their own skunks." Other teachers repeatedly send children out of their classrooms because of misconduct. The administrators realize with a touch of amusement that the teachers who send them their misbehaving students expect them to handle the problems where the teachers have failed; the teachers expect them to take some drastic action in each case, whether the culprit has simply sassed the teacher or pulled a weapon.

Administrators, noticing great differences in teaching styles among the faculty, conjecture that there must be some relationship between teaching style and the presence or absence of behavior problems in the classroom. Yet no single variable can be found to be a sure predictor of skill in discipline except perhaps for the reality that a new teacher seems to have more difficulty with discipline than the experienced teacher.

Even the variable of experience, however, is not an accurate predictor of a teacher's success or failure in handling disciplinary problems. No one can say with certainty that an inexperienced teacher is always less skillful in maintaining discipline than an experienced teacher, for that is not always the case. Neither is an older teacher always better at maintaining discipline than a younger teacher. Male teachers are not always more skillful at discipline than female teachers; quite often the opposite is true. At times it seems as if some mysterious personal quality of a teacher is the secret of discipline. Among teachers in the same school, working with the same students, some teachers have few or no disciplinary problems, whereas others have constant problems. Administrators may finally conclude that those teachers who are having difficulties with discipline lack certain understandings about behavior—both the students' behavior and their own—and lack certain skills in classroom management.

What kind of program, then, can a supervisor institute to help teachers develop and improve both their understanding of behavior and their skills in classroom management? The program should include at least three components:

- Teachers should be engaged in discussions of causes of behavior problems and helped to develop basic understandings about discipline.
- Teachers should be helped to develop skills and strategies for preventing disciplinary problems.
- Teachers should be helped to choose suitable corrective measures.

CAUSES OF BEHAVIOR PROBLEMS

The disciplinary problems of schools today range from the trivial to the terrifying and from the casual to the criminal. Since the days of the Latin grammar school, teachers in America have had to contend with children who scrapped with each other, carved their initials on school furniture, scribbled on the walls, failed to pay attention, were impertinent, and disrupted learning in a variety of ingenious ways. Many of the troublemakers in American schools have gone on to become prominent and productive citizens. Only in recent times have teachers had to cope with students who bring handguns to school, use drugs, threaten others, and sometimes inflict bodily harm on both teachers and other students.

We should not make the mistake of generalizing that a large percentage of children in all schools are serious troublemakers. True, some schools do have more than their share of serious offenders, but these schools are not the norm of our educational operation. The extent of this enterprise we call public education can be seen in some recent statistics. Our children are schooled in almost 65,760 elementary public schools and 22,780 secondary public schools.[7] More than 3.5 million teachers are engaged in the education of approximately 48 million elementary and 14.6 million secondary school students.[8] According to recent projections from the National Center for Education Statistics, enrollment at public and private elementary and secondary schools will remain constant from the projected 54.5 million in 2004 to 56.6 million in 2014.[9]

Great variations in disciplinary climate exist among these 88,000-plus schools, which are located in rural and small-town America; urban settings, including the inner city; and suburbia. Some of these schools are characterized by relatively few behavior problems and only a very small number of serious problems; other schools have many behavior problems, a sizable percentage of which are serious. The serious problems— such as the use of drugs, violence, and sex offenses—tend to be highlighted and featured in the news media. Although the serious problems are numerous—more numerous than we would wish them to be—the truth is that most children and youth are law abiding and cooperative. Although the headlines of the daily press feature rising crime rates throughout the nation, the majority of our population still subscribes to the rule of law. Certainly, in those schools where serious problems are frequent, strict measures must be taken to cope with them. What plagues most teachers, however, is the continuing, repeated, frustrating behavior of students who impede not only their own learning but also that of others.

Well-disciplined schools share two characteristics: (1) the absence of disciplinary problems and (2) a total program that promotes the teaching of self-discipline. Both characteristics are goals that schools should strive to achieve even though both are difficult to realize. Self-discipline means the individual's ability to exercise self-control and to take responsibility for his or her own conduct. When self-discipline is present in a school, behavior problems disappear.

The absence of disciplinary problems per se is, however, no guarantee that self-discipline is present. Behavior problems can be held in check—at least temporarily—by strict regimentation. Stern disciplinary measures by the faculty can repress behavior problems, but at the same time they prevent the development of self-discipline by the students.

Because discipline is such a pervasive problem and teachers are eager for answers, supervisors sometimes initiate the discussion of discipline with a case study approach. Teachers share anecdotes of misbehavior with their colleagues and jointly try to recommend the best strategies for dealing with each case. Although this procedure is a useful and practical approach to the study of discipline, the case study approach is more effective after the teachers have developed some understanding of the causes of behavior problems. When they can form some hypotheses about why a child has behaved in a certain way, they can more intelligently develop solutions to the problem. In trying to understand the causes of behavior problems, teachers may realize they need to gather additional information before they can attempt to resolve a problem. The collaborative efforts of teachers and supervisors can result in clarifying the reasons children become disciplinary problems.

Some years ago in researching the subject of discipline, Oliva classified causes of behavior problems under six broad categories: causes originating with the child, with the child's group, with the teacher, with the school, with the home and community, and in the larger social order.[10] Analysis and discussion of each of these categories can contribute to the teachers' understanding of pupil behavior. The six categories of this classification scheme are in reality sources or roots of disciplinary problems. An early conclusion teachers will reach is the understanding that behavior may be manifested in class but its origins may lie somewhere else. Teachers will come to realize that problems in the classroom may very well be symptoms of some trouble rather than the trouble itself. Teachers are usually already aware that there are causes of behavior problems over which they have little or no control. For that reason our discussion of prevention and correction of behavior problems later in this chapter emphasizes those measures that are within the power of teachers to affect. As a prelude to an examination of what teachers may do about disciplinary problems, let's consider why pupils exhibit misbehavior.

Causes Originating with the Child

Personal Problems   Children experience a variety of physical, mental, social, and emotional problems that can create disciplinary difficulties in the classroom. A typical class includes children with physical disabilities, slower intellectual capacities, and social and psychological problems. Defects in hearing and vision are common handicaps, and they sometimes go undetected for years. Malnutrition is a more common problem than we sometimes realize. If there is some truth to the saying, "You are what you eat," many classroom behavior problems can be traced to faulty diets. In recent years, health issues related to allergies to the foods or drinks the children consume have been addressed. Among the items suspected of causing health problems in students are diary products, peanuts, and red food dye. Many school districts have eliminated sugary soft drinks, snacks, and candy from the schools in a mission to improve the choices students can make about what they drink and eat. The general health of the child, the presence or absence of fatigue, endocrine deficiencies, and past diseases may all be factors in the child's performance and behavior in class.

Of all the physical factors that contribute to disciplinary problems, the most common and most obvious is the child's stage of growth and development. The handling of concepts and the ability to solve problems, to sit still, to listen, to pay attention, to take turns in speaking, and to get along with others are all functions of growth and development. Biological determinants join with sociocultural determinants to make growing up in America a protracted experience for children and adolescents. Biologically, children develop in a fixed pattern—they learn to walk before they learn to talk; they learn to talk before they learn to read; they learn simple number concepts before they solve equations. Ultimately, the majority of them learn to take responsibility for their own behavior. Culturally, the American public keeps its children in school for longer periods of time than do many other societies. One reason is that the American public accepts the dictum that education opens doors for its youth. Repeated public opinion polls show doctors, lawyers, and engineers at the top of lists of preferred occupations—all jobs that call for prolonged education. (Teaching, which once ranked among the most preferred of occupations, has moved down somewhat, but despite all its problems it still enjoys considerable popularity.)

The American public keeps its children in school longer and therefore in a less than mature status to reduce competition between young people and adults for jobs. Raising the age for compulsory school attendance over the years has been a direct function of public efforts to safeguard jobs for adult breadwinners. Although growth and development are significant factors in discipline at all levels, many teachers seem to feel that the middle school and junior high years are the most difficult. Caught as they are between puberty and adolescence, preadolescents, or "tweens," as they are sometimes called, often exhibit simultaneously problems of childhood and adolescence.

An analysis of the mental abilities of children in any heterogeneous class will show a range from very slow to gifted. Children at any level—slow, average, or fast—can become behavior problems given an inappropriate learning environment. When slow learners are frustrated by their inability to cope with their studies, when average learners find nothing stimulating about their studies, and when bright students do not find their studies a challenge, they can create disciplinary problems for the teacher.

Self-Concept All human beings have common sociopsychological needs. All need love, security, recognition, approval, and success, and the lack of awareness, the frustration, and even the squelching of these needs breed countless behavior problems. William Glasser, exponent of reality therapy, identified love and self-worth as the most important needs of all humans:

> Love and self-worth are so intertwined that they may properly be related through the use of the term *identity.* Thus we may say that the single basic need that people have is the requirement for an identity: the belief that we are someone in distinction to others, and that the someone is important and worthwhile. Then *love* and *self-worth may be considered the two pathways* that mankind has discovered lead to a successful identity.[11]

Perceptual psychologists have called educators' attention to the necessity for recognizing the importance of the self-concept. Every human being has the need to become, as Carl R. Rogers termed it, "a fully functioning personality,"[12] or as A. H. Maslow called it, "a self-actualizing"[13] person, or as Arthur W. Combs labeled it, "a truly adequate person."[14]

Don E. Hamachek described how the self-concept is formed: "How we view ourselves is determined partially by how we perceive ourselves as really being, partially through how we view ourselves as ideally wanting to be, and partially through the expectations we perceive that others have for us."[15]

Combs identified four characteristics that seem to underlie the behavior of truly adequate persons: "These characteristics are: (a) a positive view of the self, (b) identification with others, (c) openness to experience and acceptance, and (d) a rich and available perceptual field."[16] Of the self-concept Combs wrote,

> The self concept, we know, is learned. People learn who they are and what they are from the ways in which they have been treated by those who surround them in the process of their growing up. ... People develop feelings that they are liked, wanted, acceptable and able from *having been* liked, wanted, accepted and from *having been*

successful. One learns that he is these things, not from being told so, but only through the experience of *being treated as though he were so*. Here is the key to what must be done to produce more adequate people. To produce a positive self, it is necessary to provide experiences that teach individuals they are positive people.[17]

Many children, however, in their association with "significant others" have learned self-doubt, low self-esteem, and fearfulness. "The self is built almost entirely, if not entirely," said Earl C. Kelley, "in relationship to others. . . . Unfortunately, many people in the world today suffer from inadequate concepts of self. . . . An inadequate concept of self, so common in our culture, is crippling to the individual."[18]

In contrasting behaviors commonly observed in students, Hamachek noted that students with high, positive self-concepts get along well with others, are friendly, and show self-confidence. Students with low, negative self-concepts generally worry, exhibit shyness, and can be overassertive.[19]

Self-Fulfilling Prophecy Many students who hold inadequate self-concepts have become victims of what is known as a *self-fulfilling prophecy*. Friends, relatives, or teachers (or possibly all) have led them to believe that they are inadequate; as a result, they have come to believe in their own inadequacy. They may have been told that they cannot read, cannot do math, cannot draw, or cannot excel in sports. If told enough times, they agree they are inadequate. This belief leads to failure, which deepens their conviction that they cannot achieve, which leads to more failure.

On the other hand, if they are told that they are adequate and that they can do the tasks asked of them, they are more often successful. With success comes the belief that they are adequate, which leads to continued success. All school personnel are in a vital position to help young people gain a sense of adequacy, which is fundamental to living and learning. Therefore, it is sound pedagogy for educators to hold learners to high expectations.

Supervisors should help teachers realize that when a child takes a seat on the first day of class, he or she has brought along certain physical, mental, social, and emotional attributes, which during the course of the year may lead to disciplinary problems.

Causes Originating with the Child's Group

Children act not only as individuals but also as members of groups. Most notably, all children are members of their classes and react with one another in their classes. To varying degrees, the behavior of each individual in a class shapes the behavior of the other individuals in that class. The learning environment, of which the teacher is the chief manipulator, can contribute to behavior problems in the group.

Children are not only members of their classes but also members of other peer groups both inside and outside school. Unless they are loners, they will have a small circle of intimate friends with whom they constantly associate. Subgroups develop within classes and can become powerful shapers of student behavior. For many, groups formed outside school permit them to achieve a sense of identity they cannot find in school.

The peer groups to which a child belongs exercise a potent influence on every group member's behavior. Peer-group pressures, particularly among adolescents, often force children into patterns of behavior that may be against their own best judgment. Long ago Allison Davis made an observation that still holds true:

> The example of the adolescent's play group and of his own kin, however, is the crucial determinant of his behavior. Even where the efforts of the parent to instill middle-class mores in the child are more than half-hearted, the power of the street culture in which the child and adolescent are trained overwhelms the parent's verbal instruction. The rewards of gang prestige, freedom of movement, and property gain all seem to be on the side of the street culture.[20]

We cannot blame youth alone for responding to group pressures. The handshaking, back slapping, gregarious, conforming Organization Man is still an ideal of our society. Neither conformity to a particular group's pressures nor nonconformity should be considered an end in itself. Conformity to the rule of law and to conventions subscribed to by society as a whole is a must—in the classroom and out. Conformity of thought, ideas, and opinions is not a goal to be sought—in the classroom or out.

Teachers are aware that there are groups, such as youth gangs, outside the class group vying for the interests of members of the class. They also need to be aware that the aims and activities of those outside groups are often more appealing to the members of their classes than is membership in the class group. They are literally in competition with other forces that demand the time, interest, and loyalty of members of their class. The textbook answer to this problem is the creation of a learning environment so appealing that children will choose academic pursuits over other interests.

The supervisor can suggest that the teacher create as favorable and positive a classroom climate for learning as possible. Some of the dimensions of this positive climate are examined later in this chapter. The supervisor can work with the teacher to try to develop a climate in which there is freedom to learn. But freedom, the supervisor hastens to add, is accompanied by restraint on the part of all members who make up the group. Without restraint, preferably self-restraint, there can be no freedom for anyone.

Causes Originating with the Teacher

A complete change of thought will be required before the majority of teachers will be willing to admit that teachers themselves can be causes of student behavior problems. Teachers who have an open, introspective personality may look within and recognize that they can be a source of student problems, and these teachers can expect positive changes to occur more readily. However, such introspection flies in the face of tradition, for it has been the custom since schools were first established to place the blame for misbehavior on the offender. It is the student, after all, who is not behaving properly. We may on occasion look beyond the child and lament, as the refrain goes, "Poor, helpless child, he's not to blame, his father's folks are just the same." From time to time we might listen instead to Cassius's words, "The fault, dear Brutus, is not in our stars, but in ourselves." Or we may recall that the comic strip character Pogo identified the enemy as us. Chapter 12 develops the theme of teacher behavior and suggests ways in which a supervisor can help teachers evaluate themselves.

A common source of disciplinary problems can be found in the teacher's methods of instruction. Objectives that are inappropriate to the learners (or inadequately specified or poorly conceptualized), poor planning, ineffective presentations, unsuitable materials, inadequate evaluation, and lack of provision for feedback—dealt with at length in previous chapters—create and magnify pupil behavior problems. It is far easier and less threatening for a teacher to admit that methods of instruction are causing disciplinary problems than it is to admit that something about his or her personality provokes problems. The supervisor should continuously work with teachers in helping them improve their methods of instruction. William B. Glasser's control theory contends that no one can make anyone do anything. He suggests that it is the job of the manager (the teacher) to manage so that it is easy for workers (the students) to see a strong connection between what they are asked to do and what they believe to be worth doing.[21] Fortunately, too, improvement in methods of teaching can be observed and measured by both the teacher and the supervisor. Improvement—translate this as *success*—spurs the teacher on to continued improvement and helps develop rapport between the teacher and supervisor.

Unfortunately, not all teacher-caused problems lie in the methods of instruction. The attitudes teachers reveal about students, learning, the school, the community, morality, democracy, and life in general can create a climate that either produces or reduces behavior problems, depending on whether these attitudes are negative or positive. Some students have learned how to upset teachers. In all too many cases, there are reports of students whose clothing does not meet the expectations of the school and school system. Cell phones and text messaging are causing new disruptions in classrooms. An increasing proportion of new teachers agree strongly that a significant number of children come to school with so many problems that it is difficult for them to be good students. According to teacher respondents to *The Metropolitan Life Survey of the American Teacher 2002*, new teachers report more challenges than experienced teachers regarding students' classroom behavior. All of the teachers reported having students who very often or often experience difficulty concentrating, daydreaming, being irritable or in bad moods, falling asleep in class, and being too hungry to concentrate.[22] In the August 2006 ASCD *Education Update*, Kathy Checkley summarized comments and suggestions made by Joy Bryan and Joyce Corbin at the annual meeting of the Association for Supervision and Curriculum Development. In "My Teacher Doesn't Like Me," they offered ways to understand and resolve student–teacher conflicts.[23] Teachers who care about their students and show it will have fewer disciplinary problems than teachers who dislike their students, their school, and their job.

Teachers' attitudes toward education and life are shaped to a great extent by their socioeconomic and cultural origins. Teachers as a group are usually middle-class people who espouse middle-class values. The culturally diverse students in our public schools manifest a range of differing values. Teachers have begun receiving additional training in teaching in a multicultural environment. Some states are requiring that this training become a more prominent part of their degree programs. Supervisors can expand on that training by arranging for in-service education on problems of teaching in multicultural settings. Teachers who participate in activities that help them understand and appreciate other cultures and have life experiences that make them reflect about other cultures often coexist better with students from other cultures.

Beyond a genuine interest in and affection for their students of all levels, teachers should all have certain personal characteristics. Both a sense of humor and a sense of confidence are essential attributes of a teacher. If these attributes are lacking in an individual, they are both exceedingly difficult to develop. Of the two traits, a sense of confidence may be developed more easily than a sense of humor. Good planning, for example, can give a teacher a sense of confidence. The teacher can develop confidence by managing instruction in such a way that students achieve their objectives. A supervisor can help a teacher develop a sense of confidence by pointing out ways to plan for instruction and present lessons effectively and can build the teacher's sense of confidence with frequent and positive reinforcement.

Whether the supervisor can help a teacher develop a sense of humor if the teacher has none is doubtful. In some cases, if the supervisor displays a sense of humor and cajoles the teacher a little, a latent seed of humor may blossom.

Much has been written in recent years about students' right to dress and groom themselves as they see fit. Certainly teachers should have a similar right to select their wardrobes and wear their hair in a manner pleasing to them. However, teachers must keep in mind that young people usually look to teachers of all ages as adults, not as their peers. The teacher's choice of dress and language should be such as to command the respect of young people. Whether or not they want the role, teachers are parent substitutes and as such have a certain culturally determined role they must play. To forsake this role is to invite disciplinary problems.

One attribute that must be mentioned is the teacher's voice. Confidence is communicated to students through what the teacher says and how it is said as well as through what the teacher does and how it is done. The teacher's voice must be strong enough to be heard—the first time—if students are to be taught listening skills. What the teacher should seek to develop is a calm, well-modulated, resonant voice and well-articulated, grammatically correct speech patterns.

The supervisor must ask teachers to look at themselves as possible sources of some of the behavior problems they encounter in their classrooms. Later in this chapter we return to the role of the teacher in preventing and correcting disciplinary problems.

Causes Originating with the School

A number of conditions beyond the boundaries of the classroom combine in the school to create disciplinary problems. Among these are the culture or ecology of the school and the curriculum. Individuals manifest characteristics that identify them as persons.

In much the same way, organizations, of which the school is a prominent example, reveal traits of their own, aside from the characteristics of the individuals and groups that work within the organization. To use an inept metaphor, we can say that organizations have their own "personalities."

Schools as organizations may be happy places or dreary institutions. They may evidence cohesiveness and high morale among faculty and students, or they may house a dispirited group of individuals. They may be on the move, or they may be apathetic and static. They may mirror a democratic society, or they may serve as examples of authoritarianism in action. They may be sharing, caring institutions, or they may be islands of disregard for people.

Each school possesses a culture of its own. Some set high standards and expect persons within the institution to live up to those standards, whether intellectual, social, or moral. Schools demonstrate what Michael Rutter, Barbara Maughan, Peter Mortimore, and Janet Ouston referred to as "overall ethos," the attitudes, values, and other behaviors exhibited by persons within the organization.[24] Others refer to this institutional phenomenon as "school climate" or "atmosphere."

The ethos of the school affects students' behavior both in school and out. Positive ethos can lead to positive attainments by students, as Rutter and others discovered in conducting research in twelve secondary schools in the inner London area.[25]

School climate impinges on student behavior in much the same way as the climate in the individual classroom affects student conduct. A perceptive visitor to a school can sense the morale of students. A visitor can tell whether students feel pride in their school and a sense of identity with it and can judge whether there exists that intangible something called school spirit. The care of the building and grounds by its inhabitants sometimes speaks louder than words. The school should be a place where students enjoy not only learning but also living. Charles E. Silberman made some harsh judgments about the schools of the 1970s when he said:

> It is not possible to spend any prolonged period visiting public school classrooms without being appalled by the mutilation everywhere—mutilation of spontaneity, of joy in learning, of pleasure in creating, of sense of self. . . . Because adults take the schools so much for granted, they fail to appreciate what grim, joyless places most American schools are, how oppressive and petty are the rules by which they are governed, how intellectually sterile and esthetically barren the atmosphere, what an appalling lack of civility obtains on the part of teachers and principals, what contempt they unconsciously display for children as children.[26]

Glasser felt that instead of stressing success, schools emphasize failure. He hit hard at the failure orientation of the schools. He pointed out that the child enters school in a successful and optimistic frame of mind: "Very few children come to school failures, none come labeled failures; *it is the school and the school alone which pins the label of failure on children.* . . . The shattering of this optimistic outlook is the most serious problem of the elementary schools."[27]

The school climate of nine secondary schools was studied by Carl Nordstrom, Edgar Z. Friedenberg, and Hilary A. Gold.[28] They found extensive presence of a negative attitude, which they called *ressentiment*. Their study of attitudes of teachers and students in these schools showed ressentiment deriving from the pressures or limitations on students' behavior and from the premium schools place on conformity. Little evidence points to real improvement in school climate since these studies were conducted. In fact, with stress on testing, budget constraints, ethnic tensions, health and nutrition problems of young people, and parental dissatisfactions, the climate of many schools is far from what we might call healthy. Theodore R. Sizer was commenting on at least one dimension of school climate when he said, "Most middle- and upper-income Americans would be both shocked and afraid of some of the places where the young citizens of the poor are now in school."[29]

Sarah Lawrence Lightfoot carried out an interesting study of six public and private high schools.[30] She selected six schools that professional and laypersons had identified as "good." Through visits to the schools, Lightfoot sought to discover the variables that accounted for the positive image portrayed by these schools. Common to all six were administrators who set a positive tone, faculties who cared for the students, rapport between teachers and students, a sense of pride in the schools' achievements, administrators' respect for their teachers, a sense of community, and a desire to improve.

Following an ecological approach, Roger G. Barker and Paul V. Gump studied the effect of size of secondary schools.[31] Taking a somewhat different tack from other studies of the school as a social culture that focused on individuals and groups, Barker and Gump sought to identify "behavioral settings" within the school that have an impact on individuals and groups. These researchers found a negative correlation between size of school and participation of students in school activities.

In advocating an ecological approach to the study of school culture, Seymour B. Sarason underscored the importance of describing the behavior settings: "Within the school culture (as well as in a lot of other places) problem behavior is wrongfully viewed as a characteristic of the individual rather than as an interaction of individual and particular setting."[32] An investigator following an ecological approach would describe the many behavior settings found in the school.

The development of a healthy school climate is everybody's business in the school, not just the responsibility of an administrator or small groups of teachers. The supervisor should engage teachers in a study of the school and classroom learning climate and in identification of areas that need correcting.

A study of the school's curriculum from the academic program to the extraclass program to the student personnel services will show that the curriculum contributes to and causes many behavior problems. When the curriculum is "out of joint," to use Shakespeare's expression, disciplinary problems can spring up like toadstools.

The curriculum can be out of joint in several ways. Though much has been said about individualized instruction, education remains a mass operation, with most instruction aimed at a hypothetical average child. The curriculum often misses the large numbers of students who fall below or above the average. Couple the curriculum—the program itself—with methods of instruction that fail to meet the needs of the slow and fast ends of the spectrum, and a breeding ground for behavior problems is created. When students cannot cope with the program, they find ways to distract themselves.

The word *relevance* has been so abused and distorted that we almost hesitate to use it. For some people, *relevance* has come to mean catering to the immediate needs of students. For us, however, a relevant curriculum is one that will help students not only in the present but also in the future. Including opportunities to use technology in learning situations would be an example of relevant curriculum. Relevant subject matter helps pupils to make decisions—to think—and to carry out life activities. B. Othanel Smith, Saul B. Cohen, and Arthur Pearl stated that relevant subject matter helps learners

- choose and follow a vocation,
- exercise the tasks of citizenship,
- engage in personal relationships,
- take part in culture-carrying activities.[33]

Glasser defined *relevance* as "the blending of one's own world with the new world of the school" and saw relevance working in two directions: The school curriculum must be relevant to the child's life, and the child's life must be relevant to the curriculum.

Thus, we have both parts of relevance:

1. Too much taught in school is not relevant to the world of the children. When it is relevant, the relevance is too often not taught, thus its value is missed when it does exist.
2. The children do not consider that what they learn in their world is relevant to the school.[34]

Glasser attacked the chronic disease of schools since time immemorial—the stress on memorization as opposed to thinking:

> Children discover that in school they must use their brains mostly for committing facts to memory rather than expressing their interests or ideas or solving problems ... beginning in the first grade ... thinking is less valuable than memorizing for success. ... Memorizing is bad enough. Worse is that most of what they are asked to memorize is irrelevant to their world; where it is relevant, the relevance is taught either poorly or not at all.[35]

The current literature advocating the development of thinking skills, which we considered in Chapter 3, is in accord with Glasser's comments, made more than three decades ago. Like the school's culture, the curriculum may be a source of behavior problems.

Causes Originating with the Home and Community

The child's family, neighborhood, and community play a profound part in shaping behavior. During preschool years and on through school to adulthood, attitudes learned from their closest associates affect children's behavior. The presence or absence of parental love is one of the most powerful determiners of children's behavior. That love is often missing, as can be seen in the number of reports of child abuse in the United States. According to a report from the Administration for Children and Families, child maltreatment for 2000 showed a small one-year increase in confirmed reports of maltreatment but indicated that instances of child abuse and neglect remained about 20 percent lower than in the peak years of 1993 and 1994. Reports of maltreatment were 11.9 per thousand children in 2004, compared to 15.3 per thousand in 1993. Consistent with previous years, 83 percent of victims were abused by one or both parents. Mothers acting alone were responsible for 39 percent of the neglect reports. Fathers acting alone were responsible for 18 percent of the abuse reports.[36] Children who are abused or rejected by their parents or other adults are much more likely to become behavior problems than children who are loved.

The parents' attitude toward education also influences children. Children who receive reassuring support from their parents are more likely to succeed in school and less likely to be behavior problems than children whose parents do not care whether they succeed. Parents err when they provide no reassurance or exert too much pressure on their children to succeed in school. Either extreme can contribute to behavior problems.

Disharmony in the home can produce student misconduct in school. A child's relationships with brothers and sisters and parental preferences for one child over the other can create difficulties. It is far too common for parents to hold up one child in the family as a model of behavior.

The neighborhood and immediate community in which a child lives make their impression on his or her behavior. Surveying some 60,000 teachers and 600,000 students in 4,000 elementary schools after passage of the Civil Rights Act of 1964, James S. Coleman and colleagues found that children's families and peers have a greater impact on children's achievement than do teachers and the material resources of the school.[37]

All children bring their problems to school. The teacher who is aware that some of a child's problems may be arising from the home environment can use this knowledge to advantage. For many children from unfavorable homes the school is, can be, or should be a warmer, more comfortable setting than their home or neighborhood.

Teachers can do little or nothing to change a child's home environment, but they can refrain from exacerbating a child's problems and from creating a classroom environment that in itself causes behavior problems.

Causes Originating in the Larger Social Order

Determining whether and how social conditions contribute to disciplinary problems is difficult. Some students cheat, for example, because they hear and read about cases of cheating by adults and conclude that cheating is the accepted way of making one's way in the world. Two additional problems teachers must deal with are bullying and cyberbullying. The illicit drug trade with its lure of quick but risky and criminal rewards is more appealing to some young people than working to acquire a socially accepted but far less lucrative job. A young person may tend to conclude that the problem in criminal behavior and antisocial behavior lies not in the conduct itself but in getting caught.

Studies of social class in America have shown that mores differ from one socioeconomic group to another. Classes differ in moral and spiritual values, permissiveness, patterns of aggression, sexual habits, and language. Our schools are middle-class institutions staffed largely by middle-class teachers, but the children in these schools are not all from middle-class environments. Children from lower socioeconomic backgrounds often have behavior patterns quite different from those of children from middle-class backgrounds; generally, children manifest the behavior patterns that allow them to survive in their environment. Changing children's behavior to conform to middle-class values of cleanliness, industriousness, refined language, and so on, however laudable, cannot be achieved overnight.

The effects of violence in everyday life on individual behavior are difficult to gauge. Violence seems to be a way of life on the contemporary American scene. Young people are bombarded with reports and stories of violence daily in the press, on TV, and in films. Children and youth are engrossed in violent video games.

Although crime rates had been falling in recent years, the Federal Bureau of Investigation reported an overall increase in violent crime offenses in 2005. Startlingly, cities with populations of 500,000 to 999,999 showed the greatest increase (8.3 percent) whereas cities of over one million inhabitants experienced a small (0.4 percent) decrease. The smallest increase (0.5 percent) was found in cities of 10,000 to 24,999, while 12.4 percent of violent crimes and 17.9 percent of property crimes involved only juveniles.[38]

Schools face an uphill battle in achieving what then-President George Herbert Walker Bush referred to as a "kinder, gentler" nation. Drug culture is pervasive throughout the country. Street gangs flourish in urban areas. Graphic violence, casual sex, and generous use of Anglo-Saxon expletives by both men and women are steady fare on TV and movie screens. More parental groups, psychologists, and government officials are becoming concerned with the large doses of sex and violence being served to children in books, recordings, TV shows, and movies. There is a growing concern that preoccupation with either sex or violence can be destructive to the individual and can result in behavior that can be destructive to society.

The Patterson and Kim survey (mentioned in Chapter 6) found that our country lacks a moral consensus and that individual Americans mostly live by their own moral codes, which often conflict both internally within themselves and externally with other people.[39] The chance that an individual teacher can make much of an impact on behavior problems that stem from the social scene is small. Teachers can and must restrain students who exhibit antisocial behavior, but they cannot make fundamental changes in society. On the other hand, suppose for a moment that every teacher, every administrator, and every supervisor in every school system of the country were aware of the impact of the larger social order on the behavior of pupils. Could not teachers' combined efforts make a dent in the antisocial behavior of students? Could not a program be designed from kindergarten up that would help resolve some of these social problems and even result in changes in society? Would not relevance of content take on new meaning?

PREVENTING BEHAVIOR PROBLEMS

The prevention of behavior problems should be foremost in the minds of teachers. When measures to prevent disciplinary problems are successful, the teacher has little worry about corrective measures. From an examination of causes of behavior problems, can the supervisor derive ways of helping teachers prevent problems? The supervisor can help and encourage teachers to take a number of actions.

Analyze Attitudes

Attitudes toward Behavior Problems Students exhibit a wide array of behaviors, from minor disorderliness to behavior that reflects deep-seated personality problems. The seriousness with which teachers view varying behaviors affects their handling of behavior problems. Not surprisingly, teachers regard those behaviors that frustrate their teaching, such as talking, inattention, impudence, disinterest, and laziness, as more serious or more relevant than personality problems, such as withdrawal, shyness, and suspiciousness.

Whereas behaviors that impede teaching may well disappear as the student matures, personality problems may cripple the individual for life. This is not to say that teachers should ignore troublesome classroom behaviors. Nor does it suggest that teachers by and large possess the skills and knowledge to treat personality disorders. But teachers should be conscious of personality problems, recognize the seriousness of such problems, and refer affected students to appropriate professionals.

Attitudes toward Children Teachers need to know what attitudes they hold about young people, and they need to assess the expectations they hold for each learner. The research of R. Rosenthal and L. Jacobson,[40] W. Burleigh Seaver,[41] J. Michael Palardy,[42] and Don E. Hamachek[43] provided evidence that teachers' expectations do make a difference in learners' achievement. An astute supervisor will notice when teachers subconsciously interact more often and more positively with some students than with others. Teachers tend to favor brighter students, those from higher socioeconomic levels, those seated near the front of the classroom, those at their favored hand (right or left)—in short, those who are nearest at hand, please the teacher, and give fewer problems of an academic or disciplinary nature. Barbara J. Weber and Les M. Omotani reported the results of two Rand Corporation studies that measured teacher efficacy—that when teachers believe they can influence student learning, they usually do. The research supported the self-fulfilling prophecy that when teachers have high expectations for students, students can be expected to live up to those expectations.[44] Manifestations of negative overt attitudes of teachers toward pupils' backgrounds, personal characteristics, and abilities stand as barriers to learning and exacerbate discipline problems. One of the generally accepted conclusions of effective teaching research in the past few decades is that teachers' high expectations benefit learners.[45] Benjamin S. Bloom and others, in advocating mastery learning, subscribed to the belief that most pupils could learn most of the subject matter teachers present to them.[46] These two attitudes—high expectations and the belief that most learners are capable of achieving—can work to promote learning and reduce behavior problems.

Attitudes toward Themselves   Teachers need to develop a feeling of their own adequacy as both teachers and people. Teachers can have a powerful influence on the development of the learner's self-concept. They need to exhibit qualities of cheerfulness, fairness, and sensitivity. They need to be not only self-actualizing people, but also effective teachers, skillful at explaining and communicating.[47] Combs concluded that good teachers feel adequate, wanted, and worthy.[48]

The supervisor should invite freewheeling discussions of teacher attitudes toward types of learners, ethnic groups, the purposes of education, satisfactions from teaching as a career, and the relative seriousness of behavior problems. Discussion is likely to show that teachers generally view problems that disrupt their classes as more serious than deep-seated personality problems.

Analyze Teaching Styles and Students' Learning Styles

The supervisor should ask teachers to look within themselves and try to decide whether their teaching styles provoke disciplinary problems. Are they autocratic martinets who repress every form of childish exuberance? Do they practice laissez-faire and let the students do as they please? Are they conscientious about planning, or do they adopt a "what-do-you-want-to-learn-today-kids?" approach to instruction? Do they project a counseling, facilitating approach to instruction as opposed to an authoritarian, dispenser-of-information approach? Do they exude confidence, or do they let students intimidate them?

Barbara Bree Fischer and Louis Fischer identified six teaching styles, described here:

- *The task-oriented.* These teachers prescribe the materials to be learned and demand specific performance on the part of the students. ...
- *The cooperative planner.* These teachers plan the means and ends of instruction with student cooperation. ...
- *The child centered.* This teacher provides a structure for students to pursue whatever they want to do or whatever interests them. ...
- *The subject centered.* These teachers focus on organized content to the near exclusion of the learner. ...
- *The learning centered.* These teachers have equal concern for the students and for the curricular objectives, the materials to be learned. ...

- *The emotionally exciting and its counterpart.* These teachers show their own intensive emotional involvement in teaching. They enter the teaching-learning process with zeal and usually produce a classroom atmosphere of excitement and high emotion. Their counterparts conduct classrooms subdued in emotional tone, where rational processes predominate, and the learning is dispassionate though just as significant and meaningful as in the classrooms of the emotionally more involved teachers.[49]

Teachers should attempt to identify the individual students' learning styles. It is quite possible that a clash between an instructor's teaching style and a student's learning style can result in disciplinary problems. The supervisor's and administrator's main task is to match, whenever and however possible, a teacher's primary teaching style with the learning styles of the students. The task is not easy for obvious reasons. Fischer and Fischer listed ten learning styles:

- *The incremental learner.* These students proceed in a step-by-step fashion, systematically adding bits and pieces together to gain larger understandings. . . .

- *The intuitive learner.* The learning style of these students does not follow traditional logic, chronology, or a step-by-step sequence. There are leaps in various directions, sudden insights, and meaningful and accurate generalizations derived from an unsystematic gathering of information and experience. . . .

- *The sensory specialist.* This student relies primarily on one sense for the meaningful formation of ideas. . . .

- *The sensory generalist.* These students use all or many of the senses in gathering information and gaining insights. . . .

- *The emotionally involved.* These are students who function best in a classroom in which the atmosphere carries a high emotional charge . . . through the teacher's use of poetry, drama, lively descriptions, and the teacher's own obvious enjoyment and involvement in the substance of learning [or] . . . in which the teacher and students carry on active, open discussions where disagreements are common.

- *The emotionally neutral.* Some students function best in a classroom where the emotional tone is low-keyed and relatively neutral.

- *Explicitly structured.* These students learn best when the teacher makes explicit a clear, unambiguous structure for learning. Limits and goals are carefully stated, guiding the intellectual tasks to be achieved as well as the behaviors that will be acceptable and unacceptable in the classroom.

- *Open-ended structure.* . . . The overall structure of the classroom is sufficiently visible, yet there is place for divergence, for exploration of relevant yet not explicitly preplanned phenomena.

- *The damaged learner.* While this category is too broad, too inclusive to be identified as a learning style, it is sufficiently important and commonplace to merit discussion. These are students who are physically normal but damaged in self-concept, social competency, aesthetic sensitivity, or intellect in such a way that they develop negative learning styles.

- *The eclectic learner.* Students who can shift learning styles and function profitably may find one or another style more beneficial, but can adapt to and benefit from others.[50]

Rita S. Dunn and Kenneth J. Dunn advocated identification of both the learner's and teacher's styles and the matching of the two.[51] Whenever possible, the teacher should use a teaching style that is compatible with the learner's style.

Analyze the Classroom Environment

Is there rapport between teacher and students and among the students themselves? Teachers will want to identify both the academic and social leaders in the class and those students who seem to be left out of classroom transactions. They will need to ask themselves whether they are encouraging a success orientation among the students as opposed to a failure orientation. They will want to develop an approach that is permissive enough to allow for pupil freedom but restrictive enough that learning can take place. They should ask themselves whether their classrooms are the "grim, joyless" places Silberman talked about.

In a healthy classroom climate, the teacher avoids using learning as a threat or a punishment. The object of instruction is to make learning as enjoyable an experience as possible, a pursuit that young people will want to continue all their lives. Teachers have been known to penalize a rambunctious class by piling on homework, by administering tests to quiet a noisy class, by threatening students with exams or low grades if they do not behave properly, and by making individuals perform meaningless academic tasks as a form of punishment.

A classroom contains telltale signs of a teacher's style. A well-organized classroom contains rules and expectations for students' behavior posted for easy reminding. Books, materials, and supplies are organized so that items that are needed often are easily accessible. How the space is used is revealed by the arrangement of the furniture and display areas. Effective teachers arrange their classrooms so that they run themselves as the students and teacher interact.

Analyze the Curriculum Continuously

Every teacher must examine the question of relevance and determine whether the curriculum can pass that test. Teachers must decide whether the particular curriculum meets the needs of the specific groups of which they have charge. Materials of instruction must be appropriate to the learners. Content that is too difficult or too simple can cause behavior problems. The supervisor has the responsibility of helping teachers with planning, implementing, and evaluating the curriculum, which we discuss in Chapters 7 and 8.

Analyze the Methods of Instruction Employed

Whenever possible, the supervisor should engage teachers in reflecting on how they organize the content, sequence it properly, present it lucidly, and evaluate its mastery fairly. They must decide whether they have set realistic objectives. They must seek feedback and check their instructional design to make sure they are employing appropriate strategies and engaging learners in appropriate content. Supervisors and teachers should analyze students' successes and failures to see whether modifications in instruction are necessary.

Teachers should stress thinking over memorization. This is both a curricular and an instructional issue. Teachers need to decide when memorization is essential and when problem-solving techniques should be employed. In previous chapters we urged teachers to aim for higher levels of cognition and move away from regurgitation of isolated facts. The noted educational philosopher John Dewey long ago recommended the adoption of the scientific method—or problem solving—as the main route to learning. Dewey's recommendation still stands as a laudable goal.

Additional research is needed on the use of repetition as an instructional technique. Teachers at all levels repeat material as a means of reinforcing learning. What we need to determine is how many times we can or should repeat subject matter before we meet with mastery or, conversely, concede negative results. Jacob S. Kounin called attention to the phenomenon of satiation—that is, the students' tiring of subject matter because of too much repetition. Kounin advised teachers who want to avoid students' satiation to give them a feeling of progress.[52]

The class should be kept moving with meaningful tasks, not with busy work. Teachers must examine each activity required of students to make sure the work has meaning and purpose. The recent focus on having students meet new academic standards clearly focuses on classroom instruction and relevant learning activities because of the need to use instructional time to its best advantage.

Successful classroom management goes hand in hand with the elements of effective instructional design: thorough planning, effective presentation, and careful evaluation. Teachers must give attention to the factor of motivation and plan for a variety of activities. Daily lesson plans should always provide for more than enough meaningful activities so time never hangs heavy, with students seeking their own direction of activity.

Problems of classroom management are eased when teachers carry out classroom routines with skill and dispatch. If materials and equipment are ready for immediate use, loss of instructional time will be minimal and behavior problems reduced or eliminated.

Gather as Much Information as Possible about Individual Learners

Information about a child's background at home and in school can sometimes help the teacher understand the child's behavior, but teachers must be very cautious about using such information. A better alternative is for teachers to find ways of helping children solely in the context of their own classrooms.

Negative judgments about a child's work and behavior in previous classes may prove harmful if a teacher does not realize that child may have changed. It is possible, too, that a personality conflict between a teacher and child resulted in negative comments in a child's record, although in recent years care has been exerted to word comments in cumulative records carefully.

Students' records are legally open to students and their parents, so teachers must be extremely judicious about their remarks in students' cumulative files. Also, teachers need to realize that hasty, negative comments about children have on too many occasions dogged them through school and into college and adulthood. These observations about the dangers of using past data are not meant to imply that we should not study the past history of a child, but that we should be wary about the data and how we use it.

Analyze the Disciplinary Models Used

We can find considerable differences in the models of discipline and approaches to discipline followed by teachers. We can also find considerable argument about which models and approaches are the most appropriate and effective. Laurel N. Tanner described five models of discipline.[53] Two of these, *training* and *behavior modification*, she labeled as established. The other three—*psychodynamic*, *group dynamics*, and *personal-social growth*—she called emergent.

With the training model, children learn habits through repetition of the desired behaviors. Through drill, students learn habitual responses, such as the proper way of arranging their chairs, sharpening pencils, and going to the restroom. Although training is, of course, necessary, this model permits little reflection, thought, or self-direction.

Behavior modification is a procedure for bringing about or extinguishing specific behaviors through the use of appropriate reinforcement. This technique can shape and control behavior.

Proponents of the psychodynamic model encourage teachers to try to understand the underlying emotional causes of behavior problems. With roots in child-centered philosophy and psychoanalysis, the psychodynamic model poses problems for teachers' use. Many teachers, lacking the necessary training, are not able to uncover causes of learners' problems. Furthermore, even if they discover the reasons for a child's misbehavior, they usually have difficulty deciding how to use that information to change the child's behavior.

The group dynamics model calls for the effective management of the class as a group. The teacher essentially orchestrates the group. Finally, the personal-social growth model encourages the development of self-discipline by providing pupils with opportunities to decide for themselves what constitutes appropriate behavior. The behavior chosen by the learner conforms to the goals established. Tanner found the group dynamics model and the personal-social growth model to be particularly helpful.

Behavior Modification   Behavior modification is a commonly used technique for coping with common classroom problems. It is based on the premise that both appropriate and inappropriate behaviors are learned. It is the teacher's task to reinforce appropriate behaviors by the use of rewards and to eliminate inappropriate behaviors by withholding rewards and/or using punishment. Wilford A. Weber spoke of the assumptions underlying behavior modification:

> The behavior-modification approach is built on two major assumptions: (1) There are four basic processes that account for learning; and (2) learning is influenced largely, if not entirely, by events in the environment. Thus, the major task of the teacher is to master and apply the four basic principles of learning that behaviorists have identified as influencing human behavior. They are: positive reinforcement, punishment, extinction, and negative reinforcement.[54]

Clarizio outlined steps for modifying behavior, which he called the four phases of positive classroom discipline:

  a. Choosing the behavior [that needs to be changed].
  b. Doing the A, B, Cs—attention is focused on the A, B, Cs—the antecedents of behavior (A), the behavior itself (B), and the consequences attached to the behavior (C).

    c. Selecting strategies ... (1) behavior formation techniques: positive reinforcement and social modeling, to restrict, reduce, or eliminate undesirable behaviors and to strengthen existent adaptive responses, to acquire new adaptive ones, and to extend desirable behaviors to other settings; (2) behavior elimination techniques: extinction, punishment, and desensitization, to weaken undesirable behaviors.

    d. Keeping track of the results.[55]

Clarizio made a strong case for the system he recommended:

Because mental health or psychoeducational specialists (psychologists, psychiatrists, social workers, and counselors) have not fully understood the teacher's role, they have offered to teachers few specific and concrete practical suggestions pertaining to the management of the child's daily behavior. ... Admonitions to be accepting, nonthreatening, and understanding of the child's needs have not helped teachers to cope with troublesome behavior. In giving advice to educators, mental health professionals seem to forget about the following aspects of the teacher's role, which make it difficult for a teacher to heed their advice:

    1. The teacher is a group worker and, therefore, cannot usually work with just one child.

    2. The teacher's primary goal is not to increase the child's personal insights but to achieve certain academic objectives.

    3. The teacher must reflect cultural values and, hence, cannot be permissively accepting.

    4. The teacher deals primarily with conscious or preconscious processes and materials.

    5. Finally, the teacher must focus on the reality of problems as they exist in the present situation.[56]

J. Michael Palardy and James E. Mudrey defined four approaches to discipline: the permissive, the authoritarian, the behavioristic, and the diagnostic.[57] They rejected the permissive and authoritarian approaches, found the behavioristic (behavior modification) wanting, and supported the diagnostic approach. Of the behavioristic approach they wrote,

Does behavior modification work? We think it does, but not to the degree or with the frequency behaviorists predict. For the approach, in our opinion, has several serious flaws. The most significant is that only the symptoms of behavior problems are dealt with, not their causes.

    Stated bluntly, but not unjustly, proponents of behavior modification argue that teachers are wasting time in trying to discover and treat underlying causes of behavior. From the point of view of advocates of behavior modification, teachers can be effective if they deal only with the behavior itself. ... As long as the cause of the child's problem is undiagnosed and untreated, he is hurting and sooner or later symptoms of that hurt will emerge.[58]

Palardy and Mudrey saw the diagnostic approach as "the most comprehensive and legitimate approach to discipline":[59]

Contrary to behavior modification, this approach assumes that there can be lasting effects on certain behavior problems only after their causes are ferreted out and treated. ... There is no quick, easy, or fail-proof formula for diagnosing the causes of pupils' behavior problems. But there is one absolutely essential step: to learn as much as possible about the pupils. ...

Most critics of this approach argue that the whole effort of diagnosis is a waste of time and energy because nothing can be done anyway... we disagree with this argument. First, because it assumes that the causes of behavior problems are never school related or school induced. Like it or not, many are.

Second, even if the diagnosis shows that the causes are not school related or school induced, much can still be done. Pupils' ego needs can be met in school, their self-respect enhanced, their enjoyment of life increased. In school, pupils can be given love and can learn to give it in return. Schools can provide food and clothing. They can make medical, dental, and psychological referrals. They can contact community action programs, welfare departments, civic organizations, churches, and even law-enforcement agencies. Schools can provide for adult education, sex education, and early education. We disagree that diagnosis is a waste of time because nothing can be done![60]

Despite its limitations, behavior modification is widely practiced in schools.

A Teacher Behavior Continuum Charles H. Wolfgang described general categories of behavior commonly demonstrated by teachers in handling disciplinary problems. He placed them on a "power continuum of teacher action, moving from the minimum power of *looking* to the maximum power of *acting* or physical intervention."[61] (See Figure 5.1.)

Following the Teacher Behavior Continuum, Wolfgang analyzed a number of disciplinary models based on three philosophies of discipline: Relationship-Listening, which "requires the use of minimum power: *looking and naming*;[62] Confronting-Contracting, which "involves *questioning*";[63] and Rules-Consequences, using the methods of "*commanding, acting,* or *modeling.*"[64]

"The continuum," said Wolfgang, "reflects the level of autonomy and control given to the student to change his own behavior or the coercive or aversive actions used by the teacher or school officials to get the desired change in student behavior and reestablish order and safety in the educational setting."[65] The supervisor and teacher may wish to examine other models in addition to those described in Wolfgang.[66]

An effective teacher seeks to control the class and shape behavior by whatever legitimate techniques he or she is adept at using. While controlling and shaping behavior, the teacher will want to gather as much information about the student as possible, uncover possible causes of misbehavior, and do whatever is within his or her means to treat the causes.

Set and Enforce Minimum Expectations of Behavior

Rules of conduct in the school and each classroom should be made known at the beginning of the year. A key factor in setting rules of conduct is pupil participation in drawing up the rules. With each succeeding year of schooling and the accompanying increase in the

↑ Looking   ↑ Naming   ↑ Questioning   ↑ Commanding   ↑ Acting/ modeling/ reinforcement

FIGURE 5.1 Teacher Behavior Continuum (TBC). *Source*: Charles H. Wolfgang, *Solving Discipline and Classroom Management Problems: Methods and Models for Today's Teachers* (Hoboken, N.J.: Wiley, 2005). Used by permission of John Wiley and Sons, Inc.

learner's maturity, a greater degree of participation in determining the rules of behavior should be extended to the students. Once the teacher's rules of conduct have been developed, they should be posted in a prominent place in each classroom. The rules also should include the school's rules of conduct. Students are much more likely to conform to standards they have helped set and in which they thereby have a degree of ownership.

We agree with Glasser that "children should have a voice in determining both the curriculum and the roles of their school. Democracy is best learned by living it."[67] Glasser recommended, wisely we believe, that once students have participated in formulating the rules, when they break the rules, the teacher should ask them to make a value judgment about their behavior, to select a better course of behavior, and to make a commitment to change.[68]

Students must be given time to practice unfamiliar behaviors. The teacher should be willing to spend sufficient time to help students develop routines and get accustomed to classroom organization and procedures. Practicing classroom routines and procedures can be an integral part of the curriculum of the grade level. Reviewing these expectations after long absences from school, such as following the winter holiday break, may be necessary.

The supervisor should assist teachers in diagnosing the learning environments they maintain to determine whether they are doing everything within their power to prevent disciplinary problems. The old expression, "An ounce of prevention is worth a pound of cure," has special relevance to the problem of discipline.

CORRECTING BEHAVIOR PROBLEMS

No matter how much the teacher may understand about causes of behavior problems, no matter how healthy and wholesome the learning climate of a class or school may be, no matter how hard the teacher may try to prevent disciplinary problems, such problems will still arise. Some teachers are masters of discipline from the first day they set foot in the classroom, whereas others develop disciplinary skills as they gain experience and confidence in controlling the behavior of young people. Sooner or later the question will come from a teacher, often in desperation, "What shall I do?" That teacher may turn to a colleague for advice or, if he or she has sufficient rapport with the principal or supervisor, may turn to one of them for help or suggestions. When a teacher has an immediate behavior problem, more than a slogan is needed. School districts adopt and enforce codes of student conduct. These codes describe the rights and responsibilities of students, parents, and schools in the areas of behavior, personal privacy, and assembly. The codes define consequences for behavior in violation of the rules, including those related to drugs, alcohol, and weapons. Some school districts define the severity of misconduct according to various levels with corresponding actions taken against the offending student.

When a behavior problem arises in the classroom, the teacher must make some response—the students expect the teacher to do so. For example, assume that an African American male student and a white male student in an eighth-grade English class suddenly leap out of their seats, call each other names, and start pummeling each other. Their teacher reacts almost instinctively, rushes up to the boys, forcefully separates them, firmly orders them to take their seats, and sets the class back to work. The immediate situation has been effectively handled. But the teacher meditates on what corrective measure or punishment, if any, should be applied to these boys so that neither they nor others will repeat the behavior. In most school systems this incident must be reported on a disciplinary form, and afterward the teacher will have to consult with the principal about what should be done as a follow-up to the incident. In some cases, the punishment may be clear-cut because fighting is considered a level II offense that results in suspension from school. With the public's support of zero tolerance regarding student misbehavior, the choices may be limited.

Many school districts require the school principal to present the guidelines for handling disciplinary disruptions in the school. By knowing those guidelines, expectations, and procedures, disruptions will be handled more expeditiously and with a greater degree of conformity. Another procedure used by many school districts requires the school-level administrators to conduct student assemblies where disciplinary procedures are presented. In some districts students are expected to have parents sign and return forms that indicate they have reviewed the established disciplinary expectations for the district and its schools. If teachers know what guidelines have faculty and administrative support at the time a behavior problem occurs, they can more readily and more intelligently decide what action they should take as a response. Any decisions regarding what type of punishment to use with a student must be centered on ensuring that all steps in due process are followed. In addition, care must be taken to meet the guidelines of a student's Individual Education Plan (IEP). The supervisor might lead teachers to agree on the following points:

1. *The corrective measure applied should fit the offense.* Showing off should be treated differently from defiance. Skipping school merits lesser punishment than pushing drugs. Stealing $20 is more serious than stealing 20 cents.

2. *The corrective measure applied should fit the offender.* The democratic practice would seem on the surface to treat all offenders equally, but mitigating circumstances are taken into consideration when imposing punishment—for example, in the case of a first offense unless the offense is of a very serious nature. The goal of correction is a change in behavior—rehabilitation. For this goal to be realized, the corrective measure must be chosen with both the offense and the offender in mind.

3. *Minor, routine types of childish misbehavior should be met with the simplest of techniques.* A glare, a stare, silence, pointing a finger at the culprit, using proximity by standing beside a misbehaving student, a terse order of "Let's be quiet" or "Knock it off," suddenly increasing the volume of the voice, changing students' seats—teachers have developed a host of personalized techniques to maintain order and to keep the class on track. There are teachers who never have to go beyond these simple techniques of control while still maintaining a productive learning environment.

The common, garden-variety misbehavior that stems from excess childish energies should be treated with a minimum of fuss. The teacher should not make a big issue of petty misbehaviors. We find teachers who insist on continuous, complete, and absolute attention and quiet—a nearly impossible goal for children and adolescents—and stamp hard on every infraction of their (the teachers') rules. From the classrooms of these teachers, children stream to the principal's office for punitive action. These teachers weaken their own image in the eyes of the children, the administrator, and the children's parents, and they may place themselves in a precarious position. When they encounter a serious problem and look for help, the administrator may conclude that they are once again "crying wolf" when there is no wolf in sight.

4. *Nonpunitive, remedial measures should be taken before resorting to punishment.* Teachers should be more concerned with helping a child change behavior than with retribution for misconduct. If they can reason with a child and obtain results in that way, they should do so. A beginning approach in cases of pupil misbehavior is an individual conference with the child during which the teacher tries to get the child to evaluate his or her behavior, see how the particular conduct has been detrimental to him- or herself and to others, and choose a better way of behaving. The conference provides the teacher with an opportunity for learning more about the child and the reasons for misbehavior. The conference also is a chance for the teacher to show a child who is a behavior problem that some adult cares enough to want to help. These conferences should be entered into in a counseling frame of mind and should not be considered occasions for laying down the law and reprimanding the perpetrator.

The conference should be conducted in private, where teacher and student can talk freely. If an individual conference with the student is not successful in changing behavior after a reasonable time, the teacher may then wish to confer with the child's parents or guardians. In many school districts this step is required before additional steps are taken. If the teacher chooses to go this route, the parent–teacher conference must be managed very carefully. Parents may be anxious to come to school to talk about their child's academic progress, but they are not so eager to visit the teacher to talk about their child's behavior problems. Many elementary school administrators expect their teachers to make contacts early in the school year. Administrators encourage teachers to relate to parents their positive comments about each student. By doing so, they can balance negative interactions with positive ones.

A polite invitation rather than a summons should be extended to the parents in the form of a letter or phone call from the teacher. The conference should be set up as a chance for the parents and teacher to communicate and to share their knowledge about the child. The goal of the conference is to find ways in which the parents and teacher can cooperate to help the child improve his or her classroom behavior. Some teachers include the student in the conference discussion because the student can add personal reasons and information about why he or she exhibited certain behaviors in the classroom. The teacher must also know what the parents' attitudes are toward discipline, as some parents may treat the child more harshly than would the school.

The teacher should call on the services of specialists and agencies both within the school and outside for help in working with behavior problems. Referrals to the guidance counselor, school psychologist, or school nurse are often first steps in the remediation process. Community agencies stand ready in most communities to provide certain kinds of help to schoolchildren—including Circles of Care, Big Brother, or Big Sister.

Teachers should not overlook the nonaggressive, docile, timid, fearful, and despondent children in the classroom. These children may not complicate the teacher's life the way aggressive children do, but in their own way they have behavior problems that are often as serious and as prolonged as the problems of overtly disruptive children.

5. *Punishment is in order if the teacher deems that there is no other way to correct an individual's behavior.* Wesley C. Becker, Siegfried Engelmann, and Don R. Thomas made a case for the use of punishment:

> Probably no area of behavioral psychology has generated more emotion, confusion, and misunderstanding than the topic of punishment. Some people believe that any use of punishment under any circumstances is immoral. . . . Teachers have been told that they should not use punishment because it doesn't work and that it produces only temporary suppression of behavior, not real change. . . . Punishment is an effective method of changing behavior.[69]

Punishment and the threat of punishment serve as deterrents to repetition of misconduct by the same offender or other offenders. It is utopian to hold that punishment will never be necessary in school. No matter how hard we strive to maintain an attractive learning environment, no matter how well disciplined the school, no matter how great an effort is made to counsel students, and no matter what preventive measures are taken, behavior problems will still arise, some of which will be serious enough to merit punishment. Becker, Engelmann, and Thomas specified two circumstances when punishment may be required:

> The first is when behavior is so *frequent* that there is little or no incompatible behavior to reinforce. . . . The second circumstance where punishment may be required is when the problem behavior is so intense that someone might get hurt, including the child himself.[70]

When punishment must be administered, it should be done in a firm, calm manner. The teacher should wait until the heat of the moment dies down before applying punitive techniques. However, punishment should be certain. The student who chooses to misbehave should know that misbehavior will result in some kind of punishment that is fair and reasonable. The supervisor should help teachers identify and use punitive measures that can be considered fair and reasonable and that are expressed in the code of conduct.

We can easily find illustrations of punitive measures that do not meet the standards of fairness, reasonableness, or soundness. Preservice and in-service education should build concepts about discipline and punishment so that teachers will employ disciplinary procedures that are both psychologically and pedagogically sound. Preservice training does not succeed in building an adequate foundation for this purpose because of the many variables involved, and in-service training under the leadership of a competent supervisor must continue the task.

Returning to the teacher's question to the principal ("What shall I do?"), what helpful guidance can be provided? The answer falls into two parts: What *do* teachers do? What *should* teachers do? The answers to these two questions are not always the same. Teachers, sometimes in collaboration with the principal, employ disciplinary measures that range from mildly punitive to rather severe: They threaten a class or an individual, scold a class or an individual, force misbehavers to apologize to the teacher or classmates, ridicule children, force children to repeat their offenses until they are weary, spank children (mostly boys), banish children from the classroom, send children to the principal's office, suspend children from school for varying periods of time, take away privileges, make children pay fines, give children demerits, subject children to personal indignities, humiliate children in front of their peers, turn children over to security guards or police, expel children from school permanently, transfer children to special schools, keep an individual or class after school, isolate misbehavers from the rest of the class, make children pay for items they have damaged, punish the whole class for an offense committed by an unidentified individual, use learning as punishment, and reduce the grades of children who misbehave. This by no means exhausts the list of punitive procedures found in the schools, for teachers can be as ingenious at inventing punitive measures as young people are at demonstrating novel forms of misbehavior.

Whether any or all of the foregoing punitive measures are either justifiable or effective in changing behavior can provoke a debate among teachers. The supervisor should encourage teachers to discuss each punitive measure and try to reach some consensus on subordinate questions, such as, What is the purpose of the measure? Is the measure more damaging than helpful to the individual? Is the measure more damaging than helpful to the group? What is the long-range effect of the measure? Will the measure serve as a deterrent? Has the measure proved effective in the past? What are the legal restrictions on the measure?

Although some teachers and administrators may disagree, we believe that a reasonable case can be made for the following punitive measures:

- Taking away school privileges.
- Requiring a student to restore, repair, or pay for damage done.
- Detaining a student after school.
- Sending a student to the office.
- Isolating a student within the class.
- Assigning a student to in-school suspension.
- Suspending a student from school or class for a period of time.
- Referring a student to security guards or police.
- Expelling a student permanently from school.
- Transferring a student to a special school.

The following types of punishment appear to us to be unreasonable:

- Subjecting students to personal indignities.
- Threatening.
- Humiliating.
- Charging fines for misbehaving.
- Using academic work as punishment.
- Lowering a child's academic mark for misconduct.

The position the authors take on punishment consists of the following elements: (1) Every behavior problem that seems to be serious enough for punitive action should be thoroughly analyzed before any action is taken; (2) the punishment should be adjusted to both the offense and the offender; (3) the punishment should be fair, reasonable, and sound; (4) the punishment should be within the law; and (5) when punishment is clearly warranted, it is the teacher's and/or principal's responsibility to administer it. The teacher's or administrator's power derives from the fact that school personnel represent the power of the adult (mature) world over the child's (immature) world; also, the school is an agency of the state, and school personnel are servants of the state and are charged with the responsibility of educating the young. Both cultural and legal factors permit school personnel to administer punishment.

In a class by itself is corporal punishment. While we personally reject corporal punishment as unsound and ineffective, a case for spanking can be made because it is acceptable to a large segment of the public and it is legally permitted in some communities. In 1977, the U.S. Supreme Court upheld the right of schools to administer corporal punishment.[71]

Ten Reasonable Punishments

Let us take a brief look at each of the ten punitive measures for which a reasonable case may be made; then let us consider the thorny problem of corporal punishment.

1. Taking Away School Privileges The loss of privileges is a natural consequence of misbehavior and is a form of punishment to which many children are accustomed at home. A child or group that creates a disruption at a school play, for example, may have the privilege of attending school assemblies taken away for a period of time. A group or child who causes turmoil at a school dance or an athletic event may be denied attendance at future events for a period of time. The child who has been granted the privilege of doing independent study and who abuses that privilege may be reassigned to more closely supervised study. Children who have been appointed by the faculty or elected by their peers to positions of leadership or responsibility and who become behavior problems may be removed from these positions. Generally speaking, the loss of privileges should be a temporary punishment. Privileges should be restored when the student has demonstrated an ability to conform and the teacher feels sure that the misconduct that provoked the loss will not recur.

2. Requiring a Student to Restore, Repair, or Pay for Damage Done When a student takes property that belongs to someone else, he or she has the obligation of bringing that property back or reimbursing the individual or individuals from whom the property was taken. When a student damages or destroys another person's property, he or she has the obligation of repairing, restoring, or paying for that property or suffering other consequences of a more serious nature. Extensive destruction of schoolrooms and buildings by vandals is a major crime and must be dealt with in other ways.

Allowing for a student's age, physical condition, financial means, and the legal restrictions, the teacher or principal should seek to have the student rectify (or at least help rectify) damage caused through misbehavior. If caught writing graffiti on the walls, for example, the student should be required to use some elbow grease and remove it. If discovered defacing a desk or table, the offender should be required to restore it as well as possible. If the offense is breaking a window, charges should be assessed for its replacement.

Because the acts of restoring and repairing materials may require the expenditure of work or money or both, the student's parents need to be consulted, give their consent, and be involved in the successful restoration or repair process. This punishment is practical only if a student has the necessary strength, skill, and knowledge to repair damage or the financial resources to pay for it. It is sometimes possible for those who do not have the funds to work off their debt at jobs in the school, by earning money in part-time jobs after school, or by repaying loans from their parents. This form of punishment has a direct bearing on the type of misconduct shown by a student and is a common measure used and accepted by society.

3. Detaining a Student after School

Detaining students after school has long been a form of punishment. It is a relatively harmless type of punishment and not always an effective one in terms of changing students' behavior. The teacher is always faced with the problem of what kind of activity the student should be engaged in while being detained. Commonly, students work on their studies during the period of detention. This practice means that academic requirements are being used as a form of punishment and can create subsequent antagonism to studies for this reason.

Punishment should follow misbehavior as soon as possible, but it is not always possible for the teacher to detain a student the same day misconduct was demonstrated. In many school districts, school board policies require teachers to notify parents of their child's misbehavior and what punishment will be administered before it is done. Transportation home, part-time jobs, after-school lessons, and after-school student activities may make immediate detention a problem. The teacher may create conflicts with parents and with other teachers who are making demands on the student's after-school time in attempting to enforce detention on the same day. Detention may have to be scheduled at a later date after the student has had a chance to readjust his or her schedule. Unfortunately, the delay diminishes the effectiveness of the punishment.

Some schools send all students who are given after-school detention to a central detention room, which teachers take turns supervising. Because detention is not a severe type of punishment, teachers tend to use it for a wide variety of relatively minor offenses. As a rule, the teacher who "sentences" a student to detention should supervise that student. This might provide an opportunity for some helpful dialogue between the teacher and offender, and if the student works on studies pertinent to that teacher's class, the teacher might give the student some aid. The requirement that the teacher supervise his or her own behavior problems means that the teacher is detained as well as the student, a procedure that may hold as little appeal for the teacher as for the student. This requirement, however, could result in reducing the number of students who are kept after school and the use of detention for trivial offenses.

Unless it can be established that every child in a class has misbehaved, the detention of an entire class after school is neither wise nor fair. Mass punishment can result in rebellion, particularly for older children who have not misbehaved and feel they are being unfairly treated. Punishment of an entire group for the offense of one or several members of a group, whether or not these offenders can be identified, is an abuse of the teacher's power. If rebellion and defiance result from an attempt to implement punishment, the teacher's status can be seriously eroded to the point that misbehavior will increase and learning will cease.

4. Sending a Student to the Office

When a child disrupts a group, it is perfectly within reason to remove the child from that group at least temporarily. The welfare of the group must take precedence over the welfare of an individual. Unfortunately, some teachers abuse this form of punishment and consistently use it for minor offenses, which in turn weakens its effectiveness. For some students a reprieve from class may be more attractive than suffering through to the end of the hour or day.

When a teacher judges it essential that a child be removed from class, the child must be sent where supervision can be provided. The most logical place for that is the administrator's office. Administrators are inclined to support a teacher who on rare occasions sends an offender to their offices. However, they tend to view the teacher who sends many students to their offices as a poor disciplinarian. The supervisor should help teachers clarify their views as to what measures they expect administrators to take with behavior problems that have arisen in their classes. Teachers must also realize that the administrator must have the full circumstances of the case before any corrective action can be taken. In some school districts, teachers are expected to complete disciplinary forms before sending a student to the principal's office. This procedure allows the principal to have necessary background information while also causing some teachers to rethink the need to remove the student because of the extra work involved. As a result, many teachers send only the most serious offenders to the office.

Some teachers paint themselves into a corner when they banish a student from class with the command not to return. Although teachers may be permitted to suspend a student temporarily from class by sending him or her to the principal's office or to a special center for behavior problems within the school, they do not have the power to suspend or expel students from school. That power rests in the school board and is administered through the principal and superintendent. An order to a student not to return is unenforceable unless the administrator agrees with the teacher that the misconduct is severe enough to merit suspension or expulsion. The teacher loses face when the student is permitted to return to class, because the teacher's order has been revealed as an empty threat.

5. Isolating a Student within the Class   Separating a misbehaving student from the other members of the class is a simple and justifiable procedure. The action demonstrates to the offender that the child's behavior is interfering with the work of the group and as such cannot be tolerated. We do not recommend standing the child in a corner or making the misbehaver sit on a stool with a dunce cap, common techniques of years ago, but the individual can be physically separated to a remote area in the room where disruptive activity will be less possible. When the offender appears to be ready to take part again in the group's activities, permission to rejoin the class should be granted. Removing a student to sit or stand in the hallway outside the classroom is ineffective and can result in the child disappearing from the area. Because a teacher is responsible for his or her students, this approach is a poor choice.

6. Assigning a Student to In-School Suspension   Some school systems employ alternatives to suspending students from school. Some elementary and secondary schools have established centers for special instruction that are, in effect, a form of in-school suspension. These centers within each school are rooms to which offenders are sent for the prescribed number of days during which they would ordinarily have been denied attendance at school. The centers are provided with a teacher as director and sometimes with the services of aides and part-time counselors. The director is expected to supervise an academic tutoring program and to conduct group counseling sessions.

Before children are assigned to the centers, their parents are advised of the action. The offenders are assigned to the centers only after other means of handling their behavior have been tried and have failed. Students may be released from the center earlier than their assigned number of days if their behavior improves, and they may be held longer if they continue to misbehave. By using this in-school technique, schools are able to reduce the number of students who would ordinarily be suspended from school. A great advantage of this technique is that with its use students are not free to roam the streets but are kept in school under supervision and are engaged in some form of learning. Some school districts have adopted the concept of "Saturday school" for middle and high school students. Misbehaving students are required to attend school to make up assignments or make up missed school days. Teachers and administrators oversee the students who attend these sessions.

7. Suspending a Student from School or Class for a Period of Time Suspension, the temporary denial of the privilege of attending school, is a corrective measure in widespread use in schools. It is a controversial measure, one of the more severe forms of punishment, and one that is limited by legal constraints. Suspension is a means that schools should not use lightly. Educators who reject suspension as a form of punishment point out that it does little good to turn offenders out on the streets, where they are denied learning and where they may get into more serious trouble. They argue that working parents are not able to supervise their children during working hours and the children are left to their own devices.

On the other hand, when a school district's code of conduct dictates or when an administrator decides an offense is serious enough to merit suspension of the offender, he or she has in mind the welfare of the group of which the student is a part and the welfare of the school generally. The administrator must resort to some measure to protect the other students from a serious offender. Suspension should be used only after remedial and less severe forms of punishment have been attempted without success.

A principal can typically suspend a student on his or her own initiative for periods of one to ten days. With the approval of the school board, the principal may be permitted to suspend a student for a longer period of time. The longer students are suspended, the further they usually fall behind in their school work and the more difficult it is for them to catch up when they return. Some provision for making up the work is necessary when they come back or else they are liable to continue as behavior problems. In many instances, school board policy requires the student to be given credit for assignments completed while he or she is suspended.

The U.S. Supreme Court has underscored the position that suspension of students should not be imposed arbitrarily. In two close (five-to-four) decisions, the Court held that a student must be granted an informal hearing by the principal before he or she can be suspended and that a school board is liable for damages if it violates a student's constitutional right by administering suspension without a hearing.[72]

8. Referring a Student to Security Guards or Police Although some educators may deplore the presence of security personnel in the schools, the security resource officer has become an established member of the staff of many of America's large, urban secondary schools. The often necessary addition of security guards to the school staff has been a result of the rather shocking increase in school crime and violence since the mid-1960s. Offenses include assaults on teachers and other students, use of alcohol and drugs, weapons, arson, vandalism, robberies, and even murder.

Both older and newer studies have shown the continuing presence of crime in the schools. The National Institute of Education's 1978 study *Violent Schools—Safe*

Schools: The Safe School Study Report to the Congress revealed serious disorders in the public schools and estimated the cost of school crime at $200 million per year.[73] *Disorder in Our Public Schools*, a 1984 memorandum of the White House Cabinet Council, cited numerous instances of violence in the schools.[74] Publications of the National School Safety Center, a joint undertaking of the U.S. Departments of Justice and Education and Pepperdine University, reveal the seriousness of school violence, assaults on students and teachers, bullying, drug use, vandalism, and carrying of weapons into school.[75] George Nicholson, director and chief counsel of the National School Safety Center, and colleagues observed that "the level of violent crime perpetrated by juveniles in our society is three times greater today [1985] than it was in 1960."[76]

The School Crime Supplement (SCS) to the National Crime Victimization Survey (NCVS) is one measure of the prevalence of criminal victimization at school and the students' perceptions of their school environment. The key findings of the *1999 School Crime Supplement: "Are America's Schools Safe? Students Speak Out"* concern the presence at school of criminal victimization, street gangs, guns and weapons, and hate-related words and hate-related graffiti; the prevalence of bullying and fear at school and while traveling to and from school; and the respondents' perceptions before and after the Columbine shootings.[77]

Various groups have made recommendations for curbing the problems of crime and violence in the schools; these range from the use of weapon detectors to establishing security departments in the schools to setting up special classes and schools for problem children to modifying teacher preparation to include more training in human relations and in working with emotionally disturbed children. An article in *Instructor* offered elementary teachers relevant suggestions for helping students live in a world with violence.[78] The goal to be achieved is a school climate free from violence.

Whereas a faculty works to create a climate in which the seeds of violence will not grow, the administrator must preserve the order and safety of all school personnel and must protect the school plant and facilities. The time to prepare for a crisis situation is not when it happens but long before, when there is time to assess, plan, and evaluate appropriate steps. Efforts that teach students how to cope appropriately with life's challenges result in positive benefits for the school, community, and individual families. Consideration should be given to provide activities in:

- Conflict resolution and anger management.
- Character education.
- Respect and tolerance of diversity.
- Peer mediation.
- Gang/drug prevention/refusal skills.
- Stress management and reduction.
- Development of self-esteem.[79]

9. Expelling a Student Permanently from School   Expulsion is an extreme measure, an ultimate action of school authorities, and bound by legal restrictions. It is used to remove students who menace the welfare of the group. Whereas suspension is a temporary denial of school attendance, expulsion is a permanent denial. Expulsion implies that the school has given up on the offender and that no further correction is possible under the school's jurisdiction. The power to expel rests in the school board. Parents must be involved, hearings must be held, and complete justification must be made for expulsion to be sanctioned.

10. Transferring a Student to a Special School   When it has been decided that a child can no longer function in a regular school and must be removed, the next question that must be raised is whether the student might make progress in another type of school. If a child is below the age of compulsory attendance and is to be removed from a school, other schooling must be arranged. Those above the age of compulsory attendance should have the option of attendance at a school that might be able to help them. Some school systems, especially large ones, operate types of social adjustment and alternative schools. These schools have been established to accommodate and educate children with behavior problems. Many of these schools are better equipped and staffed to handle a difficult teaching assignment. Special instructional programs, tutoring, and counseling are techniques used in working with children who manifest behavior problems. In some cases, if a child makes sufficient progress in a special school, transfer back to a regular school is possible.

Corporal Punishment

The debate over corporal punishment has raged ever since children were herded into institutions called schools and schoolmasters first whipped out the hickory stick. Whereas only two states prohibited corporal punishment in the early 1970s, today twenty-seven states and a considerable number of localities ban this form of punishment by state statute, state regulation, or school board action.[80] Spanking is usually a last-ditch, desperate effort before suspension, expulsion, or transferral of a child. Whether it is effective is highly questionable. Fredric Jones made his view of corporal punishment clear in this statement:

> Of all the discipline techniques in existence, corporal punishment distinguishes itself as having the fewest assets and the greatest number of liabilities. In terms of locking adult and child into a series of coercive cycles, it is the all-time champion. Those who rely on it swear by it—a testimonial to the addictive properties of quick short-term cures.[81]

The supervisor should urge teachers to study the efficacy of corporal punishment if it is permitted in their school system. They should seek answers to questions such as these: How many children received corporal punishment during a school year? What were the age, gender, and ethnic origin of the children? How severely were they spanked? Who administered the spankings? How many were spanked more than once during the year? For what offenses were they spanked? Do students view spanking as effective in changing their behavior? Do students actually fear corporal punishment? Do some students gain status in their peers' eyes as a result of being spanked? Is corporal punishment more effective in changing behavior than sending pupils to special rooms or suspending them?

The teachers must also familiarize themselves with the laws circumscribing corporal punishment. They must determine whether corporal punishment is legal in the community and state. They must learn the conditions under which spanking is permitted. For example, corporal punishment is generally administered in private and with an adult witness present. Parents usually have to be informed of the punishment. When corporal punishment is permissible, children can be spanked only on the posterior. The teachers will certainly want to learn whether any lawsuits have arisen over cases of corporal punishment, what the circumstances were, and what the courts' decisions were. If a disproportionate number of children of minority families and lower socioeconomic classes are spanked, teachers must be aware that they risk being accused of discrimination. As corporal punishment is applied almost exclusively to boys, it is surprising that school officials have not been charged more frequently with discrimination based on gender.

We believe that teachers should handle their own student behavior problems if at all possible, and this belief applies equally to corporal punishment. They must ascertain whether they are permitted to administer corporal punishment themselves or whether in their school system only an administrator may do so. When teachers are allowed to inflict corporal punishment, they must have the physical strength to do so. Incongruous situations sometimes develop when a teacher attempts to spank a student who is physically stronger than the teacher.

Corporal punishment is a severe measure; if it is used at all, it should be reserved for serious offenses. Because the intent of this punishment is to inflict pain on the offender, it should never be administered when the teacher or administrator is angry and likely to inflict serious pain or even injury. Like all forms of punishment, it should be administered in a dispassionate manner.

The supervisor should help teachers clarify their positions on the use of various punitive measures. Furthermore, because concern for students' rights and due process for the student is a growing issue, faculties must examine this concern.

In recent years, school systems, responding to the students' rights movement, have developed written codes of student conduct that are distributed to students, parents, and staff. Rules of conduct and possible remedial, corrective, and punitive measures that may be taken as a consequence of misconduct should be made known and should apply throughout the school system.[82] The supervisor should work with administrators, faculties, and students (as their maturity permits) to examine the school's disciplinary climate, analyze disciplinary measures, and be actively involved in the development or improvement of codes of conduct.

The best way of dealing with school misbehavior is by preventing it. Schools with good discipline not only correct misbehavior but also teach appropriate behavior and coping skills. Proven alternatives to corporal punishment include social skills instruction, character education programs, student recognition programs, and peer mediation.

SUMMARY

Classroom management is one of the more difficult aspects of teaching. It is an aspect that causes many teachers great concern and one with which teachers frequently need help. Preservice training programs barely scratch the surface of this complex phase of teaching; therefore, in-service training is essential to help teachers develop classroom management skills and understanding about discipline.

Parents, students, and teachers are in agreement that lack of discipline is a serious problem in schools, and they expect schools to take action to prevent, reduce, or eliminate disciplinary problems. This chapter discusses six sources of disciplinary problems: the child, the child's group, the teacher, the school, the home and community, and the larger social order.

A number of models and approaches to discipline are in use in the schools. Among models that have been recommended by various authorities are the training, behavior modification, psychodynamics, group dynamics, personal-social growth, and diagnostic models. Varying approaches to discipline have been identified, including relationship-listening, confronting-contracting, and rules/rewards-punishment.

The school's culture and curriculum can contribute to students' behavior problems. Faculty members should seek to order the class and school environment in such a way that disciplinary problems will be minimized. When behavior problems do arise, remedial, nonpunitive measures should be tried to correct those problems before punitive measures are taken.

The following corrective measures are suggested as reasonable: taking away school privileges; requiring a student to restore, repair, or pay for damage done; detaining a student after school; sending a student to the principal's office; isolating a student within the class; assigning a student to in-school suspension; suspending a student from school or class for a period of time; referring a student to security guards or police; transferring a student to a special school; and expelling a student from school permanently.

Corporal punishment is a corrective measure acceptable to some educators and rejected by others. A school system must decide, laws permitting, whether to use corporal punishment. Within that context the faculties of individual schools of a district need to decide whether they wish to resort to corporal punishment.

The supervisor may profitably invite faculty study of four facets of the problem of discipline: causes of behavior problems, models and approaches to discipline, preventive measures, and corrective measures. The supervisor should keep before the teachers the understanding that the object of all discipline is to help the learner develop self-discipline.

QUESTIONS FOR DISCUSSION

1. What are some of the reasons that teachers have problems with student discipline and classroom management that you have experienced?
2. How can teachers improve the self-concepts of their students?
3. What can a supervisor do to help teachers improve the culture of a school?
4. How can a teacher create a classroom environment in which every student comes to believe, "I count, I care, and I can"?
5. What did Alfie Kohn (see bibliography), researcher and author, mean when he said, "It is remarkable how often educators use the word *motivation* when what they mean is *compliance*"?

ACTIVITIES FOR FURTHER STUDY

REFLECTIVE

1. Describe the primary causes of student misbehavior that you have experienced.
2. Write a paper on the culture of the school and its impact on student behavior.
3. Identify several behavioral settings in a school and show how they affect teachers, students, or both.
4. Make a classification of what you consider reasonable and unreasonable forms of punishment.

5. Prepare a report on the relationship between pupil behavior and one of the following: (a) the teacher's attitudes on discipline, (b) instructional design, (c) grading practices, (d) peer-group relationships, (e) parental attitudes toward education, and (f) the curriculum.

6. Identify six behavior problems of students and how you would correct two of the most important ones.

7. Write a paper on students' rights, explaining the meaning of due process and citing pertinent court cases. In your paper, show your position on student rights.

8. Write a paper suggesting ways in which learners may be taught self-discipline.

9. Write a research paper on a number of court decisions (state and federal) on suspension and expulsion.

10. Discover and report three examples (on three different grade levels) of self-discipline being taught.

11. Write a paper on corporal punishment, citing state and federal court cases and stating your position.

12. Specify possible steps to be considered by a teacher who is having the following student behavior problems: (a) truancy, (b) excessive tardiness, (c) aggressive behavior in the classroom, and (d) withdrawing behavior in the classroom.

13. Obtain copies of your local school board's policy manual and state school code and prepare a report on disciplinary measures permitted.

14. Gather and report data on assaults on teachers and students in schools of your community for the past two years.

15. Gather data on the cost of school crime in your community for the past two years.

16. Write a paper showing whether you believe that Charles E. Silberman's assertion that schools are "grim, joyless places" still holds true and state your reasons. If you agree with Silberman (see bibliography), recommend ways to make schools more joyful places.

17. Write a review of Arthur W. Combs's book, *The Professional Education of Teachers* (see Note 26).

18. Report on the five models of discipline discussed by Laurel N. Tanner (see bibliography).

19. Prepare a position paper on behavior modification.

20. Describe the neo-Skinnerian model of discipline discussed in C. M. Charles (see bibliography).

21. If your local school system has a written student code of conduct, obtain a copy and critique it. If your school system does not have a written code of conduct, sketch an outline of topics that should be covered in it. (This can be a group project.)

22. Determine what Jacob S. Kounin (see bibliography) meant by "withitness" and "overlapping."

23. Review *Teaching Students through Their Individual Learning Styles: A Practical Approach* by Rita S. Dunn and Kenneth J. Dunn (see bibliography) and draw implications for discipline.

24. Prepare a talk that you as a supervisor would give to a group of teachers on prevention of disciplinary problems.

APPLICATION

1. Create an instrument for evaluating disciplinary climate and practices in the classroom.

2. Visit four teachers in their classrooms, analyze the group climate in those classrooms, make a brief summary of each situation, and suggest ways in which you feel the group climate might be improved.

3. Talk with six teachers; compile statements of their beliefs on what they feel are the most serious behavior problems in their school and what they feel can be done about them. Drawing on these talks, summarize some teacher attitudes that a supervisor may be expected to contend with and suggest ways you would go about dealing with these attitudes.

4. Visit one or more schools and report on ressentiment practices you discover. Report how a supervisor might help teachers correct the practices. (For reference on ressentiment, consult Nordstrom, Friedenberg, and Gold in the bibliography.)

5. Make an audiotape recording of an interview with a group of students on their feelings about their school. Write a report showing how a supervisor would go about using student input like this for making changes.

6. Identify and report on schools that maintain special classes for children with behavior problems and special schools in the community for this purpose.

7. Conduct a limited survey of parental attitudes on discipline.

8. Interview a sample of students and security guards in schools that have security personnel and report on the relationship between students and guards.

9. Observe several experienced teachers and several inexperienced teachers and formulate a judgment about whether experienced teachers have fewer disciplinary problems than inexperienced teachers.

10. Sit in the assistant principal's (or principal's) office for several hours or a day and observe and keep a log of types of disciplinary problems sent to the assistant principal (or principal).

11. Analyze a school's records of behavior problems for one school year and tabulate the number of problems by age, intelligence test scores, gender, ethnic origin, social class, and status of the home.

12. Role-play with a peer a parent–teacher conference on a case in which the son has been caught smoking marijuana in the boys' restroom.

13. Role-play with a peer a conference between a teacher and a sixth-grade girl who has stolen a dollar from one of her classmates.

NOTES

1. *Education Digest* 19 (January 1954): 20.
2. Harvey F. Clarizio, *Toward Positive Classroom Discipline*, 3rd ed. (New York: Wiley, 1980), p. 1.
3. Lowell C. Rose and Alec M. Gallup, "The 38th Annual Phi Delta Kappa/Gallup Poll of the Public's Attitudes Toward the Public Schools," *Phi Delta Kappan* 88, no. 1 (September 2006): 45.
4. Stanley Elam, ed., *The Gallup Poll of Attitudes toward Education 1969–1973* (Bloomington, Ind.: Phi Delta Kappa, 1973), pp. 57, 66–67.
5. Eric Pooley, "Portrait of a Deadly Bond," *Time* 153 (May 10, 1999): 26–35.
6. Fredric H. Jones, *Positive Classroom Discipline* (New York: McGraw-Hill, 1987), p. 9.
7. U.S. Department of Commerce, Office of Educational Research and Improvement, National Center for Education Statistics, *Digest of Education Statistics, 2005* (Washington, D.C.: U.S. Government Printing Office, 2006), p. 107.
8. Ibid., p. 16.
9. U.S. Department of Education, Office of Educational Research and Improvement, *Projections of Education Statistics to 2014,* 33rd ed., 2005 (Washington, D.C.: U.S. Government Printing Office, 2002), p. 11.
10. Peter F. Oliva, "High School Discipline in American Society," *National Association of Secondary School Principals Bulletin* 40 (January 1956): 1–103.
11. William Glasser, *Schools without Failure* (New York: Harper and Row, 1969), pp. 13–14. Emphasis in original.

12. Carl R. Rogers, "Toward Becoming a Fully Functioning Person," in *Perceiving, Behaving, Becoming*, 1962 Yearbook, ed. Arthur W. Combs (Alexandria, Va.: Association for Supervision and Curriculum Development, 1962), pp. 21–33.

13. A. H. Maslow, "Some Basic Propositions of a Growth and Self-Actualization Psychology," in *Perceiving, Behaving, Becoming*, ed. Arthur W. Combs, pp. 34–49.

14. Arthur W. Combs, "A Perceptual View of the Adequate Personality," in *Perceiving, Behaving, Becoming*, ed. Arthur W. Combs, pp. 50–64.

15. Don E. Hamachek, *Encounters with the Self*, 2nd ed. (New York: Holt, Rinehart and Winston, 1978), p. 33.

16. Combs, "A Perceptual View of the Adequate Personality," p. 51.

17. Ibid., p. 53. Emphasis in original.

18. Earl C. Kelley, "The Fully Functioning Self," in *Perceiving, Behaving, Becoming*, ed. Arthur W. Combs, pp. 9–20.

19. Hamachek, *Encounters with the Self*, p. 222.

20. Allison Davis, "Socialization and Adolescent Personality," *Adolescence*, 43rd Yearbook, Part I (Chicago: National Society for the Study of Education, 1944), p. 210.

21. William B. Glasser, "The Quality School," *Phi Delta Kappan* 6 (February 1990): 425–35.

22. Dana Markow and Marc Scheer, *The Metropolitan Life Survey of the American Teacher 2002* (New York: Harris Interactive, 2002).

23. Kathy Checkley, "My Teacher Doesn't Like Me," in *Education Update* (Alexandria, Va.: Association for Supervision and Curriculum Development, 2006), pp. 1–2, 6.

24. Michael Rutter et al., *Fifteen Thousand Hours: Secondary Schools and Their Effects on Children* (London: Open Books, 1979), p. 56.

25. Ibid., pp. 145–62.

26. Charles E. Silberman, *Crisis in the Classroom* (New York: Random House, 1970), p. 10.

27. Glasser, *Schools without Failure*, p. 26. Emphasis in original.

28. Carl Nordstrom, Edgar Z. Friedenberg, and Hilary A. Gold, *Society's Children: A Study of Ressentiment in the Secondary School* (New York: Random House, 1967).

29. Theodore R. Sizer, *Horace's Compromise: The Dilemma of the American High School* (Boston: Houghton Mifflin, 1984), p. 179.

30. Sarah Lawrence Lightfoot, *The Good High School* (New York: Basic Books, 1983).

31. Roger G. Barker and Paul V. Gump, *Big School, Small School: High School Size and Student Behavior* (Palo Alto, Calif.: Stanford University Press, 1964).

32. Seymour B. Sarason, *The Culture of the School and the Problem of Change* (Boston: Allyn and Bacon, 1971), p. 93.

33. B. Othanel Smith, Saul B. Cohen, and Arthur Pearl, *Teachers for the Real World* (Washington, D.C.: American Association of Colleges for Teachers Education, 1969), p. 130.

34. Glasser, *Schools without Failure*, pp. 52–53.

35. Ibid., pp. 29–30.

36. Data from U.S. Department of Health and Human Services, National Center on Child Abuse and Neglect, National Child Abuse and Neglect Data System, available online at www.acf.hhs.gov/news.

37. James S. Coleman et al., *Equality of Educational Opportunity* (Washington, D.C.: U.S. Office of Education, 1966). This study is often referred to as the Coleman Report.

38. Press release, Federal Bureau of Investigation, June 12, 2006, Web site, http://www.fbi.gov/pressrel/pressrel06/prelim2005061206.htm, retrieved September 30, 2006.

39. James Patterson and Peter Kim, *The Day America Told the Truth: What People Really Believe about Everything That Really Matters* (New York: Prentice Hall Press, 1991). See Chapter 6 of this text for more.

40. See R. Rosenthal and L. Jacobson, *Pygmalion in the Classroom* (New York: Holt, Rinehart and Winston, 1968).

41. See W. Burleigh Seaver, "Effects of Naturally Induced Teacher Expectancies," *Journal of Personality and Social Psychology* 28 (December 1973): 333–42.

42. See J. Michael Palardy, "What Teachers Believe, What Children Achieve," *Elementary School Journal* 69 (April 1969): 370–74.

43. See Hamachek, *Encounters with the Self*, pp. 225–31.

44. Barbara J. Weber and Les M. Omotani, "The Power of Believing," *Executive Educator* 16 (September 1994): 35–38.

45. See, for example, endnotes of John H. Ralph and James Fennessey, "Science or Reform: Some Questions about the Effective Schools Model," *Phi Delta Kappan* 64 (June 1983): 689–94.

46. Benjamin S. Bloom, J. Thomas Hastings, and George F. Madaus, *Handbook of Formative and Summative Evaluation of Student Learning* (New York: McGraw-Hill, 1971), p. 46.

47. See Arthur T. Jersild and Frances B. Holmes, "Characteristics of Teachers Who Are Liked Best and Disliked Most," *Journal of Experimental Education* 9 (December 1940): 139–51. See also Paul Witty, "An Analysis of the Personality Traits of the Effective Teacher," *Journal of Educational Research* 40 (May 1947): 662–72.

48. Arthur W. Combs, *The Professional Education of Teachers: A Perceptual View of Teacher Preparation* (Boston: Allyn and Bacon, 1965), p. 71.

49. Barbara Bree Fischer and Louis Fischer, "Styles in Teaching and Learning," *Educational Leadership* 36 (January 1979): 251.

50. Ibid., pp. 246–50.

51. Rita S. Dunn and Kenneth J. Dunn, *Teaching Students through Their Individual Learning Styles: A Practical Approach* (Reston, Va.: Reston Publishing, 1978).

52. Jacob S. Kounin, *Discipline and Group Management in Classrooms* (Huntington, N.Y.: R. E. Krieger, 1977).

53. Laurel N. Tanner, *Classroom Discipline for Effective Teaching and Learning* (New York: Holt, Rinehart and Winston, 1978), pp. 5–18.

54. Wilford A. Weber, "Classroom Management," in *Classroom Teaching Skills*, 4th ed., ed. James M. Cooper (Lexington, Mass.: D. C. Heath, 1990), p. 257.

55. Clarizio, *Toward Positive Classroom Discipline*, pp. 8–16.

56. Ibid., p. 4.

57. J. Michael Palardy and James E. Mudrey, "Discipline: Four Approaches," in *Teaching Today: Tasks and Challenges*, ed. J. Michael Palardy (New York: Macmillan, 1975), pp. 315–24.

58. Ibid., pp. 318–19.

59. Ibid., p. 319.

60. Ibid., pp. 319, 323, 324.

61. Charles H. Wolfgang, *Solving Discipline and Classroom Management Problems: Methods and Models for Today's Teachers*, 6th ed. (Hoboken, N.J.: Wiley, 2005), p. 2.

61. Thomas Gordon, and Noel Burch, *T.E.T.: Teacher Effectiveness Training* (New York: David McKay, 1978).

62. Ibid., p. 2.

63. Ibid.

64. Ibid.

65. Ibid., pp. 2–3.

66. See C. M. Charles, *Building Classroom Discipline: From Models to Practice*, 2nd ed. (White Plains, N.Y.: Longman, 1985).

67. Glasser, *Schools without Failure*, p. 37.

68. Ibid., pp. 22–23.

69. Wesley C. Becker, Siegfried Engelmann, and Don R. Thomas, *Teaching 1: Classroom Management* (Chicago: Science Research Associates, 1975), pp. 255–61.

70. Ibid., p. 260.

71. *Ingraham v. Wright*, 430 US 651 (1977).

72. *Goss v. Lopez*, 419 US 565 (1975); *Wood v. Strickland*, 420 US 308 (1975).

73. National Institute of Education, *Violent Schools—Safe Schools: The Safe School Study Report to the Congress* (Washington, D.C.: National Institute of Education, 1978).

74. Gary L. Bauer, *Disorder in Our Public Schools* (Washington, D.C.: White House Cabinet Council, 1984).

75. See, for example, Stuart Greenbaum and Brenda Turner, eds., *Safe Schools Overview*, National School Safety Center Resource Paper (Malibu, Calif.: National School Safety Center, Pepperdine University, November 1990).

76. George Nicholson, Ronald Stephens, Rory Elder, and Vicky Leavitt, "Safe Schools: You Can't Do It Alone," *Phi Delta Kappan* 66 (March 1985): 496.

77. Lynn A. Addington, Sally Ruddy, Amanda Miller, and Jill DeVoe, *Are America's Schools Safe? Students Speak Out: 1999 School Crime Supplement* (Washington, D.C.: National Center for Education Statistics, U.S. Department of Education, 2002.

78. "How to Teach Children about Living in a World with Violence," *Instructor* 1 (July/August 1995): 64–79.

79. See Karen H. Kleinz, "Never Say Never: Violence and Tragedy Can Strike Anywhere," *School Violence: An NAESP/NSPRA Special Resource* (Fall 1998): 1–4.

80. The Center for Effective Discipline, available at www.stophitting.org.

81. Jones, *Positive Classroom Discipline*, p. 344.

82. For a plan in which rules may vary from class to class, see Roland S. Barth, "Discipline: If You Do That Again—," *Phi Delta Kappan* 61 (February 1980): 398–400.

BIBLIOGRAPHY

AXELROD, SAUL. *Behavior Modification for the Classroom Teacher*, 2nd ed. New York: McGraw-Hill, 1983.

BANKS, JAMES A., and CHERYL A. McGeeBANKS, eds. *Handbook of Research on Multicultural Education*, 2nd ed. San Francisco: Jossey-Bass, 2004.

BARTH, ROLAND S. *Improving Schools from Within: Teachers, Parents, and Principals Can Make the Difference*, 2nd ed. San Francisco: Jossey-Bass, 1990.

BECKER, WESLEY C., SIEGFRIED ENGELMANN, and DON R. THOMAS. *Teaching*. Chicago: Science Research Associates, 1977.

BERRY, R. LADSON, and ROBERT E. GLENN. "Values Worth Teaching." *Teaching for Excellence Special Report*. Spartanburg, S.C.: Teaching for Excellence, 1999.

BLOOM, BENJAMIN S., J. THOMAS HASTINGS, and GEORGE F. MADAUS. *Handbook of Formative and Summative Evaluation of Student Learning*. New York: McGraw-Hill, 1971.

CANTER, LEE, and MARLENE CANTER. *Assertive Discipline: A Take-Charge Approach for Today's Educator*. Seal Beach, Calif.: Canter and Associates, 1976.

CHARLES, C. M. *Building Classroom Discipline: From Models to Practice*, 2nd ed. New York: Longman, 1985.

CLARIZIO, HARVEY F. *Toward Positive Classroom Discipline*, 3rd ed. New York: Wiley, 1980.

COLEMAN, JAMES S., et al. *Equality of Educational Opportunity*, reprinted ed. Salem, N.H.: Ayer, 1988.

COMBS, ARTHUR W. "A Perceptual View of the Adequate Personality." In *Perceiving, Behaving, Becoming*, 1962 Yearbook, ed. Arthur W. Combs. Alexandria, Va.: Association for Supervision and Curriculum Development, 1962.

———. *The Professional Education of Teachers: A Perceptual View of Teacher Preparation*. Boston: Allyn and Bacon, 1965.

COMBS, ARTHUR W., and DONALD SNYGG. *Individual Behavior: A Perceptual Approach to Behavior*, rev. ed. New York: Harper, 1959.

Crime in the United States: Uniform Crime Reports. Washington, D.C.: U.S. Department of Justice, Federal Bureau of Investigation, annually.

CURWIN, RICHARD L., and ALLEN N. MENDLER. *Discipline with Dignity*. Alexandria, Va.: Association for Supervision and Curriculum Development, 1999.

DANIELSON, CHARLOTTE. *Enhancing Student Achievement: A Framework for School Improvement*. Alexandria, Va.: Association for Supervision and Curriculum Development, 2002.

DAVIS, ALLISON. "Socialization and Adolescent Personality." *Adolescence*, 43rd Yearbook, Part I. Chicago: National Society for the Study of Education, 1944.

DOBSON, JAMES C. *Dare to Discipline*. Wheaton, Ill.: Tyndale House Publishers, 1970.

DREIKURS, RUDOLF, PEARL CASSEL, and DAVID KEHOE. *Discipline without Tears*, 2nd ed. New York: Hawthorne Books, 1974.

DUNN, RITA S., and KENNETH J. DUNN. "Learning Styles/Teaching Styles: Should They... Can They... Be Matched?" *Educational Leadership* 36 (January 1979): 238–44.

———. *Teaching Students through Their Individual Learning Styles: A Practical Approach*. Reston, Va.: Reston Publishing, 1978.

EMMER, EDMUND T., CAROLYN M. EVERTSON, and MURRAY E. WORSHAM. *Classroom Management for Middle and High School Teachers*, 7th ed. Boston: Allyn and Bacon, 2006.

ENGELMANN, SIEGFRIED. *Preventing Failure in the Primary Grades*. New York: Simon and Schuster, 1969.

EVERTSON, CAROLYN M., EDMUND T. EMMER, and MURRAY E. WORSHAM. *Classroom Management for Elementary Teachers*, 7th ed. Boston: Allyn and Bacon, 2006.

FISCHER, BARBARA BREE, and LOUIS FISCHER. "Styles in Teaching and Learning," *Educational Leadership* 36 (January 1979): 251.

FREEMAN, NANCY K., and GLORIA S. BOUTTE. "Eliminating Gender Bias in the Classroom." *Kappa Delta Pi Record* 33 (Fall 1996): 24–27.

FROSCHL, MERLE, and NANCY GROPPER. "Fostering Friendships, Curbing Bullying." *Educational Leadership* 56 (May 1999): 72–75.

GETZELS, JACOB W., and EGON C. GUBA. "Social Behavior and the Administrative Process." *School Review* 65 (Winter 1957): 423–41.

GLASSER, WILLIAM. "The Quality School." *Phi Delta Kappan* 6 (February 1990): 424–35.

———. *Reality Therapy: A New Approach to Psychiatry.* New York: Harper and Row, 1975.

———. *Schools without Failure.* New York: Harper and Row, 1969.

GORDON, THOMAS, and NOEL BURCH. *T.E.T.: Teacher Effectiveness Training.* New York: David McKay, 1978.

HAMACHEK, DON E. *Encounters with the Self*, 4th ed. Fort Worth, Tex.: Harcourt Brace Jovanovich College, 1992.

HARRIS, THOMAS A. *I'm OK—You're OK: A Practical Guide to Transactional Analysis.* New York: BBS, 1999.

HENDERSON, JAMES G., and ROSEMARY GORNIK. *Transformative Curriculum Leadership*, 3rd ed. Upper Saddle River, N.J.: Prentice Hall, 2007.

HERNDON, JAMES. *How to Survive in Your Native Land.* Portsmouth, N.H.: Boynton/Cook, 1997.

———. *The Way It Spozed to Be.* New York: Simon and Schuster, 1968.

"How to Teach Children about Living in a World with Violence." *Instructor* 1 (July/August 1995): 64–79.

"Humanizing America's High Schools." *American School Board Journal*, Theme Issue, 186 (September 1999): 20–44.

JERSILD, ARTHUR T., and FRANCES B. HOLMES. "Characteristics of Teachers Who Are Liked Best and Disliked Most." *Journal of Experimental Education* 9 (December 1940): 139–51.

JOHNSON, DAVID W., and ROGER T. JOHNSON. *Reducing School Violence through Conflict Resolution.* Alexandria, Va.: Association for Supervision and Curriculum Development, 1995.

JONES, FREDRIC H. *Positive Classroom Discipline.* New York: McGraw-Hill, 1987.

KELLEY, EARL C. "The Fully Functioning Self." In *Perceiving, Behaving, Becoming*, 1962 Yearbook, ed. Arthur W. Combs. Alexandria, Va.: Association for Supervision and Curriculum Development, 1962.

KOHN, ALFIE. *Beyond Discipline: From Compliance to Community*, 10th anniversary ed. Alexandria, Va.: Association for Supervision and Curriculum Development, 2006.

KOUNIN, JACOB S. *Discipline and Group Management in Classrooms.* Huntington, N.Y.: R. E. Krieger, 1977.

LEMLECH, JOHANNA KASIN. *Classroom Management: Methods and Techniques for Elementary and Secondary Teachers*, 3rd ed. Prospect Heights, Ill.: Waveland Press, 1999.

LIGHTFOOT, SARAH LAWRENCE. *The Good High School: Portraits of Character and Culture.* New York: Basic Books, 1983.

MADSEN, CLIFFORD K., and CHARLES H. MADSEN Jr., *Teaching/Discipline: A Positive Approach for Educational Development*, 4th ed. Raleigh, N.C.: Contemporary, 1998.

MASLOW, ABRAHAM H. *Motivation and Personality*, 3rd ed. New York: Harper and Row, 1987.

———. "Some Basic Propositions of a Growth and Self-Actualization Psychology." In *Perceiving, Behaving, Becoming*, 1962 Yearbook, ed. Arthur W. Combs. Alexandria, Va.: Association for Supervision and Curriculum Development, 1962.

———. *Toward a Psychology of Being*, 3rd ed. New York: Wiley, 1999.

MCEWAN, ELAINE K. *How to Survive and Thrive in the First Three Weeks of School.* Thousand Oaks, Calif.: Corwin Press, 2006.

MERCURE, CHRISTINE M. "Alternatives to Corporal Punishment." In *Here's How.* Alexandria, Va.: National Association of Elementary School Principals, 1994.

NISSMAN, BLOSSOM S. *Teacher-Tested Classroom Management Strategies*, 2nd ed. Upper Saddle River, N.J.: Pearson/Prentice Hall, 2006.

NORDSTROM, CARL, EDGAR Z. FRIEDENBERG, and HILARY A. GOLD. *Society's Children: A Study of Ressentiment in the Secondary School.* New York: Random House, 1967.

OAKES, JEANNIE. *Keeping Track: How Schools Structure Inequality.* New Haven, Conn.: Yale University Press, 1985.

PATTERSON, JAMES, and PETER KIM. *The Day America Told the Truth: What People Really Believe about Everything That Really Matters.* New York: Prentice Hall Press, 1991.

POOLEY, ERIC. "Portrait of a Deadly Bond." *Time* 153 (May 10, 1999): 26–35.

RAILSBACH, CHARLES E. "Promoting Good Classroom Management." In *Here's How.* Alexandria, Va.: National Association of Elementary School Principals, 1992.

RAJPAL, PURAN J. "What Behavior Problems Do Teachers Regard as Serious?" *Phi Delta Kappan* 53 (May 1972): 591–92.

RATHS, LOUIS E., MERRILL HARMIN, and SIDNEY B. SIMON. *Values and Teaching: Working with Values in the Classroom*, 2nd ed. Columbus, Ohio: Merrill, 1978.

ROGERS, CARL R. "Toward Becoming a Fully Functioning Person." In *Perceiving, Behaving, Becoming*, 1962 Yearbook, ed. Arthur W. Combs. Alexandria, Va.: Association for Supervision and Curriculum Development, 1962.

ROSE, LOWELL C., and ALEC M. GALLUP. "The 38th Annual Phi Delta Kappa/Gallup Poll of the Public's Attitudes Toward the Public Schools." *Phi Delta Kappan* 88, no. 1 (September 2006): 41–56.

RUTTER, MICHAEL, BARBARA MAUGHAN, PETER MORTIMORE, and JANET OUSTON. *Fifteen Thousand Hours: Secondary Schools and Their Effects on Children*. London: P. Chapman, 1994.

SANFORD, JULIE P., and EDMUND T. EMMER. *Understanding Classroom Management: An Observation Guide*. Englewood Cliffs, N.J.: Prentice Hall, 1988.

SARASON, SEYMOUR B. *The Culture of the School and the Problem of Change*, 2nd ed. Boston: Allyn and Bacon, 1982.

SEAVER, W. BURLEIGH. "Effects of Naturally Induced Teacher Expectancies." *Journal of Personality and Social Psychology* 28 (December 1973): 333–42.

SHORT, PAULA M., RICK JAY SHORT, and CHARLIE BLANTON. *Rethinking Student Discipline: Alternatives That Work*. Thousand Oaks, Calif.: Corwin Press, 1994.

SIMON, SIDNEY B., LELAND W. HOWE, and HOWARD KIRSCHENBAUM. *Values Clarification*, new rev. ed. New York: Warner Books, 1995.

SIZER, THEODORE R. *Horace's Compromise: The Dilemma of the American High School*. Boston: Houghton Mifflin, 2004.

STEPHENS, RONALD D. *Safe Schools: A Handbook for Violence Prevention*. Bloomington, Ind.: National Education Service, 1995.

STRONGE, JAMES H. *Qualities of Effective Teachers*, 2nd ed. Alexandria, Va.: Association for Supervision and Curriculum Development, 2007.

TANNER, LAUREL N. *Classroom Discipline for Effective Teaching and Learning*. New York: Holt, Rinehart and Winston, 1978.

VATALARO, MARGHERITA. "Enhancing Learning and Interpersonal Relationships." *Kappa Delta Pi Record* 35 (Spring 1999): 115–17.

WALKER, DEAN. "Preventing Violence in Schools." *Research Roundup*. Alexandria, Va.: National Association of Elementary School Principals, 1994/95.

WEBB, L. DEAN. *School Violence Planning*. Reston, Va.: National Association of Secondary School Principals, 2000.

WEBB, L. DEAN, and CHARLES D. BAKER. *Responding to School Violence*. Reston, Va.: National Association of secondary School Principals, 2000.

WEBER, WILFORD A. "Classroom Management." In *Classroom Teaching Skills*, 4th ed., ed. James M. Cooper, pp. 229–306. Lexington, Mass.: D. C. Heath, 1990.

WICKMAN, E. K. *Children's Behavior and Teachers' Attitudes*. New York: Commonwealth Fund, 1928.

WILLIAMS, PATRICIA A., ROBERT D. ALLEY, and KENNETH T. HENSON. *Managing Secondary Classrooms: Principles and Strategies for Effective Management and Instruction*. Boston: Allyn and Bacon, 1999.

WILSON, ERTHA, JUNE ALEXANDER, and BARBARA SPANN. "How Do You Rate as a Classroom Manager?" *Instructor* 103 (July/August 1993): 30–37.

WOLFGANG, CHARLES H. *Solving Discipline Problems: Methods and Models for Today's Teachers*, 6th ed. Hoboken, N.J.: Wiley, 2005.

NEWS JOURNAL

School Journal, published three times a year by the National School Safety Center, Pepperdine University, 24255 Pacific Coast Highway, Malibu, Calif. 90263.

PROFESSIONAL INQUIRY KIT

Classroom Management. 1998. Robert Hanson, presenter. Eight activity folders and a videotape. Association for Supervision and Curriculum Development, 1703 North Beauregard Street, Alexandria, Va. 22311-1714. (800) 933–2723. www.ascd.org.

DVD

Classroom Management That Works. 2004. Three programs on DVD and a Facilitator's Guide. Also available as a videotape series. Association for Supervision and Curriculum Development, 1703 North Beauregard Street, Alexandria, Va. 22311-1714. (800) 933–2723. www.ascd.org.

VIDEOTAPES

Classroom Management That Works Tape 1: Sharing Rules and Procedures. 2004. One thirty-minute videotape and a Facilitator's Guide. Association for Supervision and Curriculum Development, 1703 North Beauregard Street, Alexandria, Va. 22311-1714. (800) 933–2723. www.ascd.org.

Classroom Management That Works Tape 2: Developing Relationships. 2004. One thirty-minute videotape and a Facilitator's Guide. Association for Supervision and Curriculum Development, 1703 North Beauregard Street, Alexandria, Va. 22311-1714. (800) 933–2723. www.ascd.org,

Classroom Management That Works Tape 3: Fostering Student Self-Management. 2004. One thirty-minute videotape and a Facilitator's Guide. Association for Supervision and Curriculum Development, 1703 North Beauregard Street, Alexandria, Va. 22311-1714. (800) 933–2723. www.ascd.org.

CHAPTER 6

HELPING TEACHERS EVALUATE INSTRUCTION

OBJECTIVES

After studying Chapter 6 you should be able to accomplish the following objectives:

1. Explain the differences between evaluation, measurement, and testing.
2. Contrast norm-referenced and criterion-referenced measurement.
3. Define formative and summative evaluation and explain when to use each.
4. Describe purposes and techniques of preassessment.
5. Write and identify well-constructed essay-test items and explain the purposes for which they should be used.
6. Write and identify well-constructed objective-test items and explain the purposes for which they should be used.
7. Develop and lead faculties to adopt and apply guidelines for a sound marking system.
8. Develop and lead faculties to adopt and apply guidelines for a sound reporting system.
9. Formulate your philosophical position about evaluating student achievement.

EVALUATION: AN ESSENTIAL PHASE

From the day of birth until the day of death, human beings are subjected to continuous evaluation by fellow human beings. In fact, a person's deeds may continue to be evaluated long after he or she is gone from the scene. The infant is told by parents, with appropriate gestures and tone of voice, "That was very naughty." The teenage girl views her boyfriend as a combination of Hercules and Apollo. The wife lets her husband know of her displeasure with the appraisal "You never help me around the house." The boss produces a feeling of elation in an employee by saying, "That was brilliant work. I'm going to give you a raise." The teacher is happy when the supervisor gives praise for a job well done: "That was a great class you had today." The student, who is at the low end of the educational totem pole, knows that no day will go by without some kind of evaluation and hopes today will be the day to hear, "You answered every question on the test correctly."

The evaluation of instruction requires a complex set of skills on the part of the teacher. It is an essential phase of the instructional process but a phase that can lead to inaccuracies and even abuse if not performed skillfully. This chapter examines some fundamental concepts of evaluation and suggests evaluation techniques that the supervisor should encourage.

PREASSESSMENT

Recall the boxes that represent the five-part model of instruction shown in Chapter 3 (Figure 3.2). The third box has the label "preassessment" and the fifth box "evaluation." The model shows the feedback lines from evaluation to each of the other blocks: formulation of goals, formulation of objectives, preassessment, and implementation of instruction.

Terms other than *preassessment* and *evaluation* might be used, such as *preevaluation* and *evaluation*, or *pretesting* and *posttesting*. Whatever the terms used, both the third and fifth blocks of the five-part model of instruction are evaluation components. They are similar in that the teacher may use some of the same techniques to conduct a preassessment and an evaluation. They are different with respect to both timing and purpose.

Preassessment takes place before instruction. The purpose of preassessing is twofold. First, the teacher wants to learn whether the students have already mastered the skills and knowledge planned for presentation so that they do not have to study what they already know. The scope and sequence of a curriculum should prevent this; however, students may well have mastered the content to be studied in other grades, at other times, and even outside the school.

Second, the teacher wants to know whether the students possess the requisite skills and knowledge to begin study of the material. The literature on instruction talks of entry skills or entry behavior. The lack of student entry skills is often apparent in programs that are part of a sequence. Students may enter higher levels of the sequence (for example, fourth-grade language arts, sixth-grade arithmetic, second-year algebra, third-year Spanish) without sufficient mastery of skills and knowledge from preceding levels.

What do the results of preassessment say to the teacher? First, if students do not know the content of the material to be studied, the teacher should permit them to encounter the material. Second, if students have the requisite entry skills, the teacher can confidently introduce them to the content to be studied. If they do not possess the necessary entry skills, remediation must be provided.

The supervisor should encourage teachers to conduct a preassessment at the beginning of each unit. Preassessments can be conducted through the use of evaluation techniques, such as teacher-made tests, standardized tests, or student essays; they can also be done with less formal means, such as oral questioning and discussions. The supervisor should encourage teachers to go beyond the traditional forms of preassessment: prerequisite courses, grades in other courses, and other teachers' comments about the performance of students in their classes. The information from these sources may prove helpful, but there are no substitutes for teachers' own preassessment of learners' entry skills.

A favorite and commendable technique of teachers who conduct preassessments is the pretest–posttest. The terminal evaluation (posttest) is created at the beginning of the unit. Another version of the posttest is given to students as a pretest. Students take the pretest at the beginning of instruction and the posttest at the end of instruction. The teacher compares the results to see how much gain has been made during the period of instruction. If students have shown gain on the posttest, the teacher cannot always be sure that the gain has resulted from classroom instruction alone. The students may have picked up some of the skills and knowledge elsewhere, but unless the teacher is attempting to determine whether the instruction has alone made the difference, where students obtained the skills and knowledge is not paramount. The important fact is that they have performed at a satisfactory level of mastery on the posttest, whereas they had performed less well on the pretest.

A pretest on the content to be studied may not reveal with certainty which entry skills students lack. Consequently, further probing or testing may be necessary to pinpoint which entry skills must be learned before instruction begins on the new material.

The format of a unit described in Chapter 3 recommended that the teacher incorporate into the plan a statement of the entry skills necessary to begin study of the unit. This exercise forces the teacher to identify those skills and knowledge that the learners must have if they are to be successful with the ensuing content.

CONTINUING ASSESSMENT

When asked why they assess or evaluate, teachers offer a variety of answers. Some teachers say they evaluate so they can inform students of their progress in the subject. Others say they evaluate to provide a basis for assigning marks. Still others say they evaluate so they can send report cards home to parents and inform them about their children's work.

If asked what it is that they evaluate, they again give multiple answers. Some teachers say they evaluate the students' performance in class; others, that they evaluate students in relation to each other in the class. A few teachers state that they evaluate the instruction, the instructional procedures, or themselves.

The process of evaluation may be viewed as assessing achievement of the objectives of instruction by each of the learners who make up a class. There should be a direct line from the objectives originally set forth at the beginning of a unit or course to the evaluation techniques used before, during, and at the end of instruction. Evaluation seeks to determine whether students have mastered the objectives. The results of evaluation are also used to make necessary modifications in the instructional design. Whether or not the students achieve says something to the teacher about the effectiveness of the design itself and the effectiveness of the instructional procedures. When students fail to achieve the objectives of instruction, several hypotheses about the reasons for this failure may be explored. It could well be that the students have failed through lack of effort, study, or motivation, or through combinations of these factors, but some reasons may be tied to the instruction:

- The objectives were not related to the task.
- The objectives were not clear to the learners.
- The objectives were not behaviorally stated and therefore not subject to accurate evaluation.
- Preassessment was poorly conducted.
- The teacher did not provide remediation before proceeding with the content.
- Resources were inappropriate or unavailable.
- Strategies were not appropriately selected.
- Content did not relate directly to the objectives.

- Continuing assessment was neglected.
- Terminal evaluation did not relate directly to the objectives.
- The teacher was ineffective in managing the group, keeping the members focused on the instruction, and presenting the content.
- Sufficient review of the material was lacking.

Evaluation should be thought of as an integral part of instruction, not as an activity separate from instruction. For this reason, evaluation should always be present. The teacher wants to know not only how well students will perform at the end of a unit or course but also how well they have mastered each day's work. The supervisor can help teachers master a variety of formal and informal evaluation techniques that they can call on as the need arises.

Evaluation at the end of the lesson or day may consist of nothing more than several oral questions posed by the teacher, or it may be only silent observation of the way students tackle the work of the day. Calling for students to summarize the day's lesson can be an evaluation technique. Daily reflections by the teacher about the instruction and learning that took place also can be very informative. Periodic progress checks during the course of the unit should be conducted to show whether the learners are staying with the teacher and what needs to be reviewed and perfected.

When evaluation is mentioned in a school setting, testing—largely of the paper-and-pencil variety—most frequently comes to mind. This is only natural, for schools have traditionally administered paper-and-pencil tests, schooling is to a great extent cognitive in nature, and assessment is most easily served by paper-and-pencil tests. Teachers devote a good deal of time to the construction and administration of paper-and-pencil tests; therefore, this chapter will devote some space to principles of testing that the supervisor may wish to incorporate into an in-service training program. However, the supervisor should help teachers use other evaluation techniques as well:

- Oral questioning.
- Observation of students at work.
- Portfolios.
- Oral and written reports.
- Evaluation of group work.
- Surveys and questionnaires.
- Attitude inventories.
- Evaluation conferences.
- Actual performance of skills.
- Self-evaluation.
- Anecdotal reports.
- Autobiographies.
- Projective techniques.
- Evaluation of class participation.
- Summaries and résumés.

NORM-REFERENCED AND CRITERION-REFERENCED MEASUREMENT

Before proceeding further, we need to agree on the language of evaluation. As most teacher trainees are aware, many colleges and universities offer courses in tests and measurement or in measurement and evaluation.

Although all three terms are related, *testing* is different from *measurement* and *measurement* is different from *evaluation* or *assessment*. In this text, the global concept is *evaluation* and is synonymous with *assessment*. *Evaluation* or *assessment* as it relates to instruction means the process of making judgments about specific aspects of a learner's behavior; it consists of a set of skills by which an instructor determines whether the learner has mastered the established objectives.

Measurement is a phase of evaluation during which the instructor quantifies instances of the learner's behavior; the quantitative data provide the teacher with a basis for assigning marks or grades—at least in the cognitive and psychomotor domains. A test is an instrument for measuring, for ascertaining the degree of mastery of expected behaviors. *Testing* is the process of administering the test instrument.

The distinctions among *evaluation*, *measurement*, and *testing* are more than just semantic, and the supervisor will do well to explore these differences with teachers. The behavior of a learner can be evaluated without measuring; however, behavior cannot be measured without testing. In Chapter 3, we noted that it is not always possible to observe and measure the achievement of objectives in the affective domain. We can measure mastery of cognitive objectives—at least, learner achievement of these objectives can be sampled— and the presence of psychomotor skills can be measured; but in dealing with attitudes, feelings, interests, and emotions—the affect—it may or may not be possible to observe the attainment of these objectives. Less possible is measuring or quantifying the degree of mastery of affective outcomes.

Measuring and quantifying the attainment of affective objectives can be done through personality tests and interest tests. More accurately, these instruments are called personality inventories and interest inventories. Standardized inventories of personality and interest provide behavioral norms for the groups that took the inventories. But these norms or standards should not be thought of as accurate measurements of individual behavior in the same way that reading skills can be measured and physical fitness demonstrated. With affective instruments, we encounter difficulty in attempting to label answers "right" or "wrong." The affective behaviors of an individual might be compared with socially stated norms. Those who do not agree with socially stated norms might be labeled "wrong," and those who do agree with them as "right." Failure to live up to middle-class norms, neurosis, interest in illegal activities, and racism might all be called wrong. The point is that these outcomes cannot be measured with any degree of certainty. There is no certainty that the socially stated norms are really the norms practiced by many—possibly even the majority— of the population, as Alfred Kinsey and later sex researchers discovered. In a 1991 study of behaviors and values held by Americans, Jim Patterson and Peter Kim discovered lack of consensus on values and respondents' admission of behaviors that depart from more traditional values often voiced in our society.[1]

What is possible in the affective domain is for the instructor to specify as well as possible objectives that he or she hopes to be able to observe in the classroom. Some of these objectives will not be visible during the time the learner spends with the teacher but may blossom in later years. Attitudes and feelings can be surveyed with various types of inventories that ask for agreement or disagreement or for gradations thereof. For outcomes that are observable, instructors may evaluate their presence or absence with "yes, the outcome is present," or "no, the outcome is not present." They cannot use this crude measurement, however, to form a basis for marking students on the affect in the same way they rate them on the achievement of cognitive and psychomotor skills.

This discussion of evaluation of affective skills is preliminary to observing that most of the measurement that takes place during schooling is assessment of achievement in the cognitive and psychomotor domains. We will return to the problems of evaluating and reporting the attainment of affective objectives, but the major part of this chapter is devoted to the measurement of cognitive and psychomotor behaviors and to those aftermaths of measurement—marking and reporting pupil progress and achievement.

Norm-Referenced Measurement

In practice, schools use two different approaches to measurement: norm-referenced measurement and criterion-referenced measurement. Norm-referenced measurement is the historic approach to measurement in the schools. Both approaches to measurement weigh the student's achievement against some standard or norm. When following a norm-referenced approach, the instructor compares a learner's achievement with the norm of some group that was subjected to the same measuring instrument. That group may be (and most frequently is) the learner's own class. The teacher may first of all create a test, administer it, and score it, making judgments about individual performance relative to the performance of all members of the group. Using some mathematically acceptable statistical concept (see Chapter 8), the teacher determines an average around which the majority of scores cluster. Some students will achieve above that average and some below. The average group has, in effect, set the standard against which each individual's performance is compared. What the scores on a test may mean in terms of mastery of the objectives is not always clear.

If teachers administer the same test or equivalent forms of a test to successive groups of learners, over the years they may build up a set of standards or norms that show the performance of these previous groups. Teachers may then choose, as a second option, to measure an individual's achievement against these standards, called *local norms*. As a third alternative, teachers may choose to administer a standardized test, prepared and available from a commercial publisher. In this case, teachers compare the performance of their students on the test against the norms of the group(s) to which the test maker administered the test. These groups may be (and commonly are) groups far distant from the local scene, and they may or may not be representative of the teacher's own current group of students. The standards achieved by these groups are reported as norms in the test manuals that accompany the test, and students' performance is compared against these standards.

As a fourth procedure, teachers may accumulate local norms on the standardized test and compare performance of learners in their current classes against the performance of previous learners on that same standardized test or equivalent form. Thus, teachers who follow a norm-referenced approach to measurement have four options as bases for comparison of student achievement:

1. The performance of all other individuals in the class on the basis of a teacher-made test.
2. The performance of previous groups in past years to whom the teacher has administered the same teacher-made test or equivalent form thereof.
3. The performance of groups to whom the standardized-test maker has administered the test.
4. The performance of previous groups in the same subject in the same school on the same standardized test or equivalent form thereof.

The key qualifiers of a norm-referenced system of measurement are *comparative*, *relative*, and *competitive*. Norm-referenced measuring compares learners with each other; its standards are relative rather than absolute; it recognizes degrees of mastery; and it encourages competition among learners. Our schools largely have employed and championed the norm-referenced approach to measurement. This competitive approach to measurement has been espoused by the majority of the teaching profession, by the public at large, and perhaps (though this is less certain) by the majority of students. The letter-grade system, A–F, discussed later in this chapter, is an integral part of the norm-referenced system. The C grade represents a mystical (perhaps mythical) average.

The roots of the norm-referenced system lie in the statistical concept of the normal curve, which assumes that certain attributes (such as intelligence) are distributed among the population as a whole and the possession of these attributes can be depicted in the form of a bell-shaped curve. When a test of intelligence, for example, is administered to a large, random sample of the population, a mean score (the sum of all scores divided by the number of scores) may be determined. This mean score coincides with the median score (middle score), and the majority of those who took the test cluster around this mean/median score. Thus, it may be said, somewhat loosely and unscientifically, that a quotient of 100 determined as a result of dividing the mental age of a student shown on a test of intelligence by the chronological age of the student and multiplying by 100 represents average intelligence.

Of the four options that serve as bases for comparison of student achievement, the prevailing option has been the first one—comparison of an individual's achievement against the performance of all other individuals in the class on the basis of a teacher-made test. Because the performance of a particular group sets the standard, that standard may vary from section to section of the same subject and from year to year. The standard for a group that as a whole performed poorly may be lower than the standard for a group that performed well on the test.

The norm-referenced system can show how well students perform in relation to their peers and can provide data for assigning marks. Because the nature of norm-referenced measurement is comparative and competitive, the norm-referenced approach must be used when individual screening and selection are required.

Criterion-Referenced Measurement

Under a criterion-referenced system of measurement, an individual student's performance is compared not against the achievement of other learners but against the attainment of the objectives of instruction. Following this approach, the teacher determines whether each student has mastered the objectives specified in the planning stage of instruction. The student has either mastered the objectives or has not. Once the student has mastered the objectives, the content is considered to have been passed, and the next objectives are presented. If the student does not demonstrate mastery of the objectives, additional time for study and practice are needed.

The application of criterion-referenced measurement is seen most readily perhaps in the psychomotor domain. An elementary school student can demonstrate skill in tying shoes, writing letters of the alphabet, skipping or hopping, and using a crayon or marker. The secondary school student can show the ability to construct an angle of sixty degrees by using a pencil, paper, ruler, and protractor; type forty words a minute accurately on a word processor or an electric typewriter; remove, clean, and properly gap an auto's spark plugs and replace them; and chin on a horizontal bar ten times without stopping.

The application of criterion-referenced measurement in the cognitive domain is a little less apparent. On any test of cognitive outcomes, the teacher must set some level of mastery. For example, an objective in fifth-grade social studies might read: "Given a paper-and-pencil test on this unit, the student will achieve 80 percent mastery" (or will answer correctly eight of the ten questions). The 80 percent level of mastery is an arbitrary one set by the teacher after due reflection and consideration of what the group is likely to do. It may be based on the teacher's experience with previous classes. The literature of evaluation often overlooks the fact that levels of mastery on criterion-referenced tests are to a large extent determined by norm-referenced means. A level of mastery set on the basis of the teacher's experience with other groups at other times brings norm-referenced principles into play. Mastery in the cognitive domain is revealed by an arbitrary percentage and therefore is somewhat different from mastery in the psychomotor domain. Mastery in the psychomotor domain represents the presence or absence of the particular skill. In the cognitive domain, whatever percentage is set, even 100, represents only an approximation of mastery of the subject matter, for any cognitive test is only a sampling of the whole content. A score of 80 percent, for example, signifies that the learner has achieved a level of 80 percent on the test items that the teacher has chosen to put on the test.

As already noted, caution must accompany use of the term *measurement* in respect to affective objectives. We believe that the attainment of affective outcomes may and should be evaluated, but these outcomes should not be subjected to statistical treatment, scoring, or marking with the traditional symbols of a grading system. The problem of reporting attainment of affective outcomes is discussed in this chapter's section on marking and reporting.

Criterion-referenced measurement has become an attractive alternative to norm-referenced measurement in recent years. The behavioral objectives movement, which started in the late 1960s, has given impetus to criterion-referenced measurement. Underlying concepts of this movement are a competency-based approach to instruction, self-pacing, and learning for mastery.

In discussing learning for mastery, Benjamin S. Bloom, J. Thomas Hastings, and George F. Madaus clearly pictured the conflicting philosophical positions on measurement:

> Each teacher begins a new term or course with the expectation that about a third of his students will adequately learn what he has to teach. He expects about a third to fail or to just "get by." Finally, he expects another third to learn a good deal of what he has to teach, but not enough to be regarded as "good students." This set of expectations, supported by school policies and practices in grading, is transmitted to the students through the grading procedures and through the methods and materials of instruction. This system creates a self-fulfilling prophecy. . . .
>
> This set of expectations, which fixes the academic goals of teachers and students, is the most wasteful and destructive aspect of the present educational system. . . .
>
> Most students (perhaps more than 90 percent) can master what we have to teach them, and it is the task of instruction to find the means which will enable them to master the subject under consideration. A basic task is to determine what we mean by "mastery of the subject" and to search for the methods and materials which will enable the largest proportion of our students to attain such mastery.[*]

If teachers are teaching for mastery and students are learning for mastery, a measurement system must test for mastery. This situation implies a criterion-referenced approach whereby student achievement is compared to some standard of mastery of the content set by the teacher and not by group norms. In recent years, state and local school district assessment programs have moved heavily into criterion-referenced measurement. Whether a student passes to the next grade level or is awarded a high school diploma is based in some states and localities on criterion-referenced tests. Some states and districts employ a combination of criterion-referenced and standardized norm-referenced tests.

RELATION OF EVALUATION TO OBJECTIVES

Evaluation begins with the statement of the objectives of instruction. Sometimes the objectives, which are stated in the form of learning tasks, are the test items themselves, as shown in the following examples:

- Define the words *cognitive*, *affective*, and *psychomotor*.
- Sight-read a musical passage.
- Balance a series of chemical equations.
- Compare the weekly cost of food for a family of four in different parts of the country and account for variations.
- Produce a documented research paper on the causes and effects of inflation.
- After studying several conflicting proposals for solving the country's drug problem, choose the proposal that seems to be the best solution to the problem, and state the reasons for your choice.

---

[*] Excerpts from Benjamin S. Bloom, J. Thomas Hastings, and George F. Madaus, *Handbook on Formative and Summative Evaluation of Student Learning* (New York: McGraw-Hill, 1971). Reproduced with permission of the McGraw-Hill Companies.

These six cognitive illustrations proceeded from the lowest to the highest levels of the Bloom taxonomy. Each objective is, in effect, a test itself, although the complexity of each objective as a test is increasingly more involved as we go from the lowest order of knowledge to the highest order of evaluation.

In the psychomotor domain, the following objectives may also serve as test items:

- Recognize a broken water pump in the automobile by the noise it makes.
- Demonstrate the proper way to hold a clarinet.
- Imitate the instructor's karate movement.
- Plant tomato seeds in a suitable container.
- Correctly operate a data-processing software package.
- Use traditional hula dance movements to express a story.
- Design and create a ceramic jar.

These psychomotor objectives are actually performance tests rather than verbal tests. The teacher can evaluate these kinds of performances by observing the learner in the act of demonstrating the perceptual-motor skills.

In the case of both the cognitive and the psychomotor illustrations given here, mastery of the objective can be measured. The teacher can establish an acceptable level of mastery for each of the objectives. We cannot establish a level of mastery of affective objectives, however, for items such as these:

- Develop a sensitivity to the problems of the elderly.
- Enjoy reading historical novels.
- Express a positive school spirit.
- Judge persons of different ethnic groups as individuals rather than as members of groups.
- Develop the habit of collecting facts before making a decision.

Although some objectives in the cognitive domain may also serve as tests of performance, this is not always the case. The objective "Given a paper-and-pencil test on this unit, the pupil will correctly answer eight out of ten questions" is not a test in itself. The teacher must carry this objective one step further and write the actual test items. The teacher may also have to refine the criteria for measuring accomplishment of some objectives. For example, the objective that calls for students to produce a research paper requires a statement of the bases for grading the paper. The teacher may choose as criteria a minimum length, correct English usage, proper documentation, and proper form for bibliography.

Many teachers—perhaps a majority—tend to write cognitive tests at the end of instruction. They wait to see what they have covered and then sample the content of that material. Experts in evaluation and instruction recommend the opposite—that teachers write cognitive tests at the beginning of instruction or early in the course. Some recommend that the terminal evaluation for a unit or course be written right after the objectives are written. The teacher then would have two tasks right after writing the objectives: preparing the preassessment instrument and preparing a preliminary terminal assessment instrument.

Michael Scriven recommended the construction of a pool of test items in the early phase of instruction:

> Even though the project is only at the stage of finishing the first unit of a projected ten-unit curriculum, it is entirely appropriate to be formulating questions of the kind that it is proposed to include in the final examination on the final unit or, for that matter, in a follow-up quiz a year later.[2]

By designing the test items before instruction starts or in the early phase of instruction, the teacher can more readily achieve consistency between the objectives and the test items. When the teacher waits until instruction is finished, some of the objectives specified at the beginning may be overlooked. The teacher may choose to administer a final examination covering only the final unit; but if the choice is made to administer a final exam covering the whole course, the pool of test items should be initiated at the very beginning of the course. In a similar manner, if the teacher administers a final test on a unit of a program, construction of the test items should begin when the unit is introduced.

By starting the evaluation process at the beginning stage of instruction, the teacher can more readily conduct what Scriven called a "consistency analysis."[3] Scriven urged that there be consistency among the goals (i.e., objectives) of a course, the content of the course, and the pool of test items.

FORMATIVE AND SUMMATIVE EVALUATION

The literature on evaluation and research is rich with technical terms, some of which are discussed in this text; others are left to the specialists in measurement and evaluation. The focus of this text is on the needs of classroom teachers and the supervisor who works with them in carrying out evaluation for the improvement of instruction.

Two terms, *formative evaluation* and *summative evaluation*, have gained great currency in recent years and are concepts with which the supervisor should help teachers develop familiarity. *Formative evaluation* as applied to instruction makes up those assessment procedures the teacher uses during the course of instruction, and *summative evaluation* refers to those evaluation techniques the teacher uses at the end of instruction. In the cognitive domain, formative evaluation may be equated with progress tests and summative evaluation with final examinations. The reaction of many teachers to these terms may be, "I've been doing that for years." What the teachers may not have been doing is refining the formative and summative processes to achieve maximum effectiveness.

An evaluation process is effective when the teacher can determine whether the learner has achieved mastery of the subject. The evaluation is less likely to show learners' mastery of the subject in the following situations:

- The teacher does not prespecify the instructional objectives.
- The teacher does not relate test items directly to the objectives.
- The teacher waits until the end of instruction to create the test items.
- The teacher fails to capitalize on the results of formative evaluation and to modify instruction.
- The teacher writes tests that poorly sample the content and contain poorly written items.

Bloom, Hastings, and Madaus encouraged teachers to "break a course or subject into smaller units of learning" and to administer at the end of each unit "brief diagnostic progress tests," which they referred to as *formative evaluation.*[4] Although many teachers follow this practice, they often stop at this point and simply use the results of these progress tests to form part of the student's grade at the end of a marking period. Bloom, Hastings, and Madaus recommended frequent progress tests and saw their use as helping "ensure that each set of learning tasks has been thoroughly mastered before subsequent tasks are started."[5] They described the purposes of these frequent tests: "For the student who has thoroughly mastered the unit, the formative tests should reinforce the learning and assure him that his present mode of learning and approach to study are adequate. For the student who lacks mastery of the unit, the formative test should reveal the particular points of difficulty—that is, the specific questions he answered incorrectly and the ideas, skills, and processes he still needs to work on."[6]

Bloom, Hastings, and Madaus stressed the importance of using the formative tests for diagnosing learning difficulties and for prescribing what the student needs to do to overcome these difficulties. The authors took a position with which many teachers may not agree:

> We are of the opinion that formative tests should not be assigned grades or quality points. The tests are marked to show *mastery* and *nonmastery*. The nonmastery evaluation is accompanied by a detailed diagnosis and prescription of what has still to be done before mastery is complete. It is likely that the use of grades on repeated progress tests prepares students for the acceptance of less than mastery.[7]

They admit that there is limited evidence on this point, and certainly teachers who do use progress tests for the dual purpose of diagnosing and grading would not be remiss.

A major purpose of both formative and summative evaluation is to furnish feedback for redesigning the instructional model. Formative evaluation provides feedback for ongoing revision of objectives and instructional procedures, whereas summative evaluation provides feedback for later revision. Summative evaluation in the form of a final examination serves not only to provide a score that will be used in grading the learner's achievement but also to indicate changes that should be made in instruction with subsequent groups. Bloom, Hastings, and Madaus saw summative evaluation as less threatening to students if they have undergone frequent progress tests: "The student who consistently demonstrates mastery on the recurring tests should be able to reduce his anxiety about his course achievement."[8]

TESTING

Although the teacher may describe tests as opportunities for students to demonstrate mastery of the content, to students tests are usually distasteful hurdles, something to be tolerated as part of their education. Most students take testing in stride. A small percentage of students even welcome tests as an opportunity to show what they know, but others regard each test as a traumatic experience. Certainly, most students learn the power of tests in the early years of schooling and come to know full well the implications of performance on tests. Tests are the instruments that determine marks, scholastic status, promotions, graduation, entrance into higher levels of education, and employment.

The impact of tests is readily apparent in any class. Having observed in countless classrooms of in-service and student teachers from the 1950s up to the time of writing this text, we can confirm that tests remain the prime motivator of instruction at all levels. We have heard the teacher say, "This will be on the state tests you will take later this year" or "Let's review for your test on Friday." It sometimes seems that pupils are in a constant state of preparation, with the test as be-all and end-all.

The supervisor, on some appropriate occasion with a group of teachers, might raise the question, "Why do we test?" After the initial teacher reaction that this is an absurd question, the supervisor might start to get answers such as these:

- To learn what students know.
- To discover who are the best students in the class.
- To discover who are the poorest students in the class.
- To accumulate data for calculating marks and/or to share with parents.

After some discussion, it develops that teachers test:

- To provide incentive for study.
- To help students develop practice in the skill of taking tests.
- To serve as a punitive device for controlling unruly classes.

It may take some probing before the supervisor draws out responses like these:

- To meet the state's expectations and requirement to test all students at specific grade levels.
- To learn whether students have attained the objectives.
- To diagnose learning difficulties.
- To appraise the effectiveness of instruction.
- To judge the effectiveness of the teacher.

The last response raises the specter of a concept in education today that is not too popular with teachers—namely, accountability. Historically, when students fail to achieve in school, the fault has been assigned to the students themselves. It is said that they do not study, they are lazy, they are unmotivated, they don't have the proper background—any number of both legitimate reasons and rationalizations for learners' lack of achievement. Teachers in the past have been accountable for their teaching performance to their superintendent, principal, and school board and, in a rather indirect and vague way, to parents and the public at large.

Today, the public has grasped the notion that learners' achievement is in direct relationship to the effectiveness of teachers as instructors and that some judgment should be made of the teachers' effectiveness. This has been an appealing concept to politicians at the local, state, and national levels and to taxpayers. Accountability implies that teachers are instrumental in the success or failure of students, and when students fail, teachers are as responsible as the learners or even more so. Teachers' groups have resisted the accountability movement because they claim with some justification that they are unable to control all the variables that affect learners' achievements. They cite forces outside the school and sometimes years of educational neglect that are beyond the capacities of even the best instructors to overcome.

The concept of accountability cannot be completely eliminated, however. Most supervisors can attest that there are unsuccessful teachers as well as unsuccessful students. The supervisor's primary task is to try to help ineffective teachers become effective ones.

One product of the accountability movement has been to make teachers more conscious of their responsibilities in respect to learners' achievement. Consequently, they strive harder so that their students will score well on both standardized achievement tests and their own teacher-made tests. The norm-referenced approach to measurement in one way obstructs accountability, for by varying standards of performance some learners will always do poorly in relation to other learners. The concepts of criterion-referenced measurement and learning for mastery of content are compatible with accountability. If the objectives of instruction are clear and realistic, if content and methods directly relate to achieving the objectives, and if tests are designed to measure learners' attainment of the objectives, fewer students will be assessed as doing poor work. Bloom, Hastings, and Madaus reiterated the generalization that most students can master what we have to teach them:

> Thus, we are expressing the view that, given sufficient time and appropriate types of help, 95 percent of students ... can learn a subject with a high degree of mastery. To say it another way, we are convinced that the grade of A as an index of mastery of a subject can, under appropriate conditions, be achieved by up to 95 percent of the students in a class.[9]

Success on tests, particularly standardized tests of achievement, has become more critical. Central to state reforms, efforts have been made to provide assessment of student performance at various grade levels. Along with statewide testing programs, some local school systems have set student achievement on criterion-referenced tests as one factor in evaluating the performance of both teachers and principals. Some school districts have responded to public accountability by publishing test results on a school-by-school basis, allowing the public to make judgments about the relative success of their children's schools.

The pressure for school reform, brought about mainly by students' poor academic performance, created a demand for parental choice of public or private school, with governmental help to parents in the form of tax credits or vouchers for use at schools of their selection. Promoted by then-President George Herbert Walker Bush and the National Governors' Association (and reaffirmed by Presidents Bill Clinton and George W. Bush), voluntary national examinations in English, mathematics, science, history, and geography at the fourth-, eighth-, and twelfth-grade levels constitute one of six national goals supposed to have been achieved between the date of their proclamation in 1990 and 2000.[10]

On January 8, 2002, President George W. Bush signed into law the No Child Left Behind Act (NCLB). The law represented his education plan and contains the most sweeping changes in the Elementary and Secondary Education Act (ESEA) since it was enacted in 1965. The main purpose of the act was to strength the federal government's role in K–12 education. One of the president's four basic education principles—stronger accountability for results—focuses on the standards that a child should meet for all grades. The NCLB Act maintained the 1994 ESEA requirements for assessments in reading and math at three grade spans (3–5, 6–9, and 10–12) through the 2004–2005 school year. Annual assessments were required in reading and math for grades 3–8 beginning in 2005–2006, with science assessments in 2007–2008 (but only in the same three grade spans of the 1994 ESEA law).[11]

State Assessments

Local, state, and national dissatisfaction with the achievement of students in public schools has thrust us into a period of strong emphasis on assessment.

Charged by NCLB, states have had to spell out their content standards with subsequent development of tests that assess achievement of those standards. California, for example, specifies what students must achieve in particular subjects by the end of each grade. California's mathematics content standards for grade 3 includes the following standards that we show as illustrations:

Number Sense

1.0 Students understand the place value of whole numbers.

Algebra and Functions

1.2 Solve problems involving numeric equations or inequalities.

Measurement and Geometry

2.5 Identify, describe, and classify common three-dimensional geometric objects (e.g., cube, rectangular solid, sphere, prism, pyramid, cone, cylinder).

Statistics, Data Analysis, and Probability

1.0 Students conduct single probability experiments by determining the number of possible outcomes and make simple predictions.

Mathematical Reasoning

3.0 Students move beyond a particular problem by generalizing to other situations.

Each standard is followed by specific objectives that some educators would refer to as enablers. For example, Number Sense 1.0 is followed by five objectives, one of which (1.4) asks students to "Round off numbers to 10,000 to the nearest ten, hundred, and thousand."[12]

What we find in schools at the early part of the twenty-first century and presumably well into it are state exams at various grade levels capped by an exit examination that determines whether or not students receive a high school diploma.

National Assessments

A fairly wide variety of standardized tests and inventories is available for use by school personnel. We can find standardized instruments to measure achievement in various subjects and others to assess intelligence or to inventory interest, aptitude, and personality. Each of the tests comes with a manual of norms reporting the performance of the groups on which the tests were standardized.

Schools may make use of some or all of these types of tests for general background information about the learners. If the teacher administers a standardized test, it will most likely be a test of achievement in a discipline. Other types of tests and inventories, such as intelligence, interest, and aptitude, are normally administered by specialized school personnel, and the results are made available to teachers to help them plan instruction.

We deal with standardized tests only briefly in this text, for we believe they are inappropriate instruments for measuring instructional objectives in particular classrooms and for serving as a basis for marks or promotion. Standardized tests of achievement do serve a very valid purpose, however, in permitting comparison of the local group's achievement with the achievement of the norm groups. Finding out how well the students have done in comparison to groups elsewhere, is helpful to the teacher, and the data do give the teacher some guidance in terms of what content should be included in the program.

As far as classroom teachers are concerned with regard to standardized tests, they should know how to (1) select an appropriate standardized achievement test, (2) administer and score the test, and (3) interpret results. The supervisor should help teachers develop these skills and can direct them to catalogs of test publishers and to such standard references as *The Mental Measurements Yearbook*,[13] which contains reviews of various kinds of standardized tests and provides information on the reliability and validity of the tests as well as the adequacy of the norms reported and the costs. Manuals that accompany the tests describe procedures for administering and scoring them and for interpreting the results. Chapter 8 discusses some of the common statistical concepts the supervisor will wish teachers to be familiar with so that they may interpret test results.

Teacher-Made Tests

Each time a teacher feels it is appropriate to give a test, he or she must make a number of decisions. The teacher must decide whether to give a paper-and-pencil test or to require the students to demonstrate actual physical performance of an objective; whether to administer a written test or an oral test; whether to administer the test to the group all at once or to students individually. If the teacher decides on written tests, he or she must decide whether to give an objective test, an essay test, or a combination of the two. If a test is defined as a student's effort to demonstrate achievement of specific objectives, oral and written reports or written papers may be substituted for objective- and essay-type examinations.

The tests must be an accurate reflection of what the teacher sets out to achieve with the learners and what has been covered in the course. Tests that accompany the textbook and other materials used in the instructional program should be used with caution. These published tests reflect the objectives of the author(s) of the book and not the classroom teacher. A test must reflect the objectives that have been taught by the teacher, not printed in the book. This caution extends to the use of computer banks as well, as illustrated by a chemistry teacher in a central Florida high school who had a computer generate a twenty-five item, multiple-choice test on a unit by selecting random items. The proposed test did not contain a single item on the major topics that the class had studied.

Both the actual demonstration of skills and tangible products of instruction must be evaluated in phases of the fine arts, business education, industrial arts, and career and technical education. No written report or paper-and-pencil examination can substitute for actual performance when the teacher wishes to know whether a student can create an attractive piece of pottery, transcribe dictation, put paneling on the walls of a room, or swim the length of a pool.

When tests of actual performance or authentic assessment are to be used, teachers must inform the students in advance what criteria constitute a level of mastery of the particular skills. The time it takes to complete a job and the number of errors that will be permitted may be appropriate criteria. Qualitative judgments of a finished product are also necessary. A piece of pottery, for example, may be judged on such characteristics as originality, symmetry, size, finish, and color. The evaluation of tangible end products and psychomotor skills is more difficult than the scoring of paper-and-pencil objective tests. In some ways it is analogous to scoring essay tests. The task of evaluating both actual performance and essay tests is made easier and more reliable if teachers specify in advance the criteria they will apply and communicate these criteria to the learners.

In all fields of study, at times tests of actual performance may be more appropriate than paper-and-pencil tests and oral examinations may be more pertinent than written ones. Generally, the typical classroom teacher will most frequently use the paper-and-pencil group test, although many teachers are utilizing the electronic versions of tests that are part of the curriculum they teach. Given the exigencies of mass education and the cognitive nature of most instruction, the paper-and-pencil group test is the most economical and practical way of testing cognitive achievement. Individual tests, though highly desirable, are impractical except for certain diagnostic and remedial purposes. Lengthy written reports place too much of a demand on teacher time to represent a routine solution to the problem of assessing achievement. Nor is there sufficient time for either individual or group oral reports from all members of a class on all the content of a program or grade level. Consequently, teachers must resort to administering group written tests as indications of performance in the cognitive domain.

Essay Tests   Two major types of paper-and-pencil tests are in wide use in the schools—the essay test (or subjective test) and the objective test. However, essay tests are not completely subjective, nor are objective tests completely objective: Subjectivity comes into play in constructing both types of tests. Regarding scoring these types of tests, objective tests reduce the element of judgment on the part of the scorer and for that reason may be labeled objective.

When the supervisor discusses the use of essay and objective tests with teachers, teachers disclose attitudes ranging from antipathy toward essay tests to almost exclusive use of this type of test, and from complete rejection of objective tests to their exclusive use. Discussions of this nature sometimes omit the recognition that the two types of tests serve different purposes. Although both types are designed to measure students' mastery of content, they do not have the same functions.

An essay test may measure a limited amount of content but in addition may evaluate a student's ability to write coherently, to organize thoughts, to describe situations, to make comparisons, to use English properly, to make applications of content, to demonstrate writing style, to summarize content, to cite research, and to elaborate reasons for positions taken. Essay tests sample a limited portion of the content, whereas objective tests sample a much wider range of content. An essay test may consist of only one or a few test items; an objective test may consist of many items. A balance needs to be struck between essay testing and objective testing. On one hand, consistent use of objective tests from elementary school through secondary school can leave the learner deficient in sustained writing. Consistent essay testing would, on the other hand, leave instructors uncertain of the learners' breadth of mastery of content.

Essay tests are more difficult to construct than many teachers believe, and they are certainly difficult to score. In the press for time, some teachers tend to dash off both essay and objective test items. Such a practice is much more harmful in the case of essay tests than in the case of objective tests. An objective test allows learners many opportunities to reveal knowledge of the subject, whereas an essay test limits the number of items and therefore the learners' chances of demonstrating achievement.

Essay-test items should communicate to learners exactly what they have to do and what degree of mastery is considered an acceptable performance. A common and unsatisfactory essay-test item is seen in the example, "Discuss current relationships between the United States and Russia." The supervisor might ask a group of teachers what is wrong with such an item. Those teachers who have had training in measurement and evaluation may respond that the question is not specific enough. It does not indicate to the students what they must do to give a complete answer and to achieve maximum credit. So, a supervisor's calling for analysis of test questions has some value, if only to serve as a reminder to teachers that it is possible to improve test items.

One exercise that a supervisor may conduct with a group of teachers is to administer an essay item such as the previous example to the teachers and then ask teachers to score each other's answers. This is often an illuminating activity to many teachers, for if their experiences run parallel to those of other groups, the scores they assign to each other's answers will range from failing to outstanding, from F to A, and probably all grades in between. If the teachers are short on time, the supervisor may duplicate the response made by a student to an essay item and ask teachers to grade that response. We have occasionally used an editorial written by a school principal for the school paper for this purpose, and without any identification, the unnamed principal has consistently been graded from failing to superior.

This little exercise shows the unreliability of many essay tests. A test should yield the same score, or close to the same score, regardless of who scores it or when it is scored. The unreliability of essay-test items can also be demonstrated when the same scorer grades the items at different times. A particular mood at a particular time can affect the grade the scorer gives a learner. If an essay item is subject to such variation in its scoring, we cannot say that that item measures mastery of content. It measures only those aspects of content and learner behavior the teachers subjectively determine it to measure at the time they are scoring the item.

The example given could be sharpened and thereby made more reliable by expanding it and specifying what the teacher desires for a full answer. An improvement in the item can be made as follows:

> Discuss current relations between the United States and Russia. In your answer, state two points of agreement and two points of disagreement between the two countries. State what has been reported in the sources you have read to be the position of each of the following on the points of disagreement: (1) the president of the United States, (2) the president of the Russian Federation, and (3) the U.S. Congress. Finally, state your own position on each of the four points of agreement and disagreement and the reasons for your position.

This revised version will help increase the reliability of scoring of the item. However, it will still not eliminate the problem, for some teachers will still score other behaviors in addition to the content called for. Some will grade spelling, grammar, style of writing, length of response, and even handwriting. The teacher's prerogative to grade these additional behaviors is not in dispute; but if these behaviors are being graded, that information must be communicated to the learner as well as the relative weights to be assigned to each behavior.

One of the teacher's tasks preliminary to any scoring is the construction of a key that outlines the points the learners should touch on in their answers. Constructing a key is a step many teachers skip, and the absence of a key contributes to the unreliability of the grading. Without a key against which to compare a student's response, the teacher is liable to forget significant points that he or she is supposed to be looking for; without a key, the teacher can also be unduly swayed and sidetracked by students who write well or at length but who fail to include significant points of content. The supervisor could ask the teachers once again to score an answer to an essay question and this time supply a key to each member of the group to learn whether using it decreases the range of scores.

A student's chances of demonstrating mastery of content are improved when the teacher increases the number of test items on any given essay test. As a general rule, it is unwise to give an essay test consisting of only one test item. The more test items there are on a given test, the wider is the sampling of the content. A student may "bomb out" on a particular test item, but additional test items can give the student an opportunity to demonstrate at least some degree of mastery. The single-item test can induce unnecessary anxiety in the learner, who wonders whether he or she will be lucky enough to be able to respond to the item the teacher selects.

More test items will require shorter answers, which is not necessarily a bad feature. If a teacher wishes to test for sustained writing, an occasional or term paper that students write outside class may serve this purpose much better than an essay test. Let us illustrate a few variations of essay-test items, following the classification in Bloom's taxonomy of the cognitive domain. Essay-test items may be constructed for each of the six major categories of the taxonomy as the following examples show:

1. *Knowledge:* State the steps by which a federal bill becomes a law.

2. *Comprehension:* Explain in fifty words or fewer what message John Donne was conveying when he wrote, "Never send to know for whom the bell tolls, it tolls for thee."

3. *Application:* Briefly describe what is meant by the economic law of supply and demand and give three examples of the operation of this law in the American marketplace in the last five years.

4. *Analysis:* Contrast the characteristics of a developed nation and an underdeveloped nation by citing four ways in which a developed nation differs from an under-developed nation. Following your statement of differences, tell whether you would classify each of the following as an underdeveloped nation or a developed nation: (1) the United States, (2) El Salvador, (3) Thailand, (4) Israel, (5) the United Kingdom, (6) Ethiopia. Select one additional nation of your own choice that meets the character-istics of an underdeveloped nation and describe efforts it is making to become a developed nation.

5. *Synthesis:* If you were the chief of police of this community, describe what actions you would recommend to reduce the number of automobile accidents in the community. In your answer, show that you are familiar with primary causes of accidents and data on fatalities, injuries, and property damage from automobile accidents in the community.

6. *Evaluation:* A legislator of our state, which has no state income tax, proposed that an income tax of 2.5 percent on taxable income above $10,000 be levied. Evaluate this proposal as to (1) the need for such a tax, (2) possible uses to which the tax revenues might be put, (3) effects of the tax on various socioeconomic classes in the state, and (4) the likelihood of its acceptance by the people. Compare the benefits and disadvantages of the proposed income tax with the benefits and disadvantages of increasing the state sales tax from 5 to 6 percent.

The supervisor should encourage teachers to write full and clear essay-test items and to avoid the common, inadequate "Discuss." Generally, some elaboration is necessary beyond the simple command to discuss. Essay-test items can be given a particular twist by substituting other words for *discuss,* including *describe, compare, contrast, outline, analyze, apply, summarize, evaluate, state the reasons,* and *show the relationships.*

One final suggestion might be offered to teachers on scoring essay tests. When a test consists of more than one item, many teachers prefer to rate each item for all the students before going on to the next item. In that way, they avoid skipping around from item to item and are able to keep in mind the specific points they are looking for in each response. Essay tests have a definite place in the instructional process, but they must be carefully constructed and used for the purposes they serve best.

Objective Tests   Whereas essay tests sample limited content in depth, objective tests can sample breadth but not depth of content. The length of answers to essay-test items sometimes deludes the teacher into thinking that breadth of content is being tested. If a teacher wishes to test for knowledge of a subject, the supervisor should recommend an objective test as a far better instrument for this purpose than an essay test. The objective test can cover much more ground and can sample a field of study in a much shorter time.

A test is said to be objective if it eliminates the need for judgment on the part of the scorer. Any person should be able to take the key of an objective test and arrive at the same score as any other person. Consequently, objective tests are much more reliable than essay tests. Subjectivity does enter into objective testing, however, in two ways. At the beginning, the teacher must make subjective decisions on which items to include on a test. The first step is to refer to the objectives and then analyze the content. Because each test represents a sampling of content, the teacher will incorporate only the more important items of content in a test. Subjectivity can also enter into the process of scoring objective tests. There are times, for example, when a student will give a correct response to an item that is different from the response the teacher expected. The wording or construction of a test item sometimes leaves the item open for judgment by the student and fails to elicit the response indicated by the teacher.

In their own way, good objective-test items are just as difficult to write as good essay-test items are. It is difficult but not at all impossible to write objective-test items that measure cognitive behavior above the lowest levels of the Bloom taxonomy. A useful exercise for the supervisor to carry out with a group of teachers is to ask them to bring in for analysis and discussion an assortment of objective-test items that have appeared on their tests. The discussion and analysis should be carried on in a friendly, positive manner so that the teachers will not feel threatened by the exercise. Through this exercise, the teachers will ordinarily come to realize that many of the items confine themselves to low-level cognition, many items are worded ambiguously, some do not relate to the unit or course objectives, and some call for obvious answers.

A collection of teachers' objective-test items will usually consist of at least five major types of items: (1) recall, (2) multiple choice, (3) alternative response, (4) matching, and (5) rearrangement. We will describe and illustrate each of these types of items and then apply the Bloom taxonomy of the cognitive domain to objective testing.

Recall A recall item offers no choice of responses for the test-taker and requires a direct answer that must be retrieved from the learner's memory. In its varied forms it is probably the most common type of objective item used, one of the easiest to construct, and the one that is most subject to original answers if the teacher has not carefully structured the item. The types used most often are direct questions, commands, and statements to be filled in, which are also called completion items. The student's life is filled with both oral and written recall items in the form of direct questions that require short answers.

- Where did the Mayan Indians live?
- What is the sum of 12 plus 9?
- When did Columbus first reach the New World?

To be an objective item, the question must yield a single or separate short answer. The direct question "Why did we fight in Vietnam?" would lead to an essay answer and would not be appropriate as an objective item.

Recall items may be structured as commands:

- Name the present U.S. secretary of state.
- List three sources of protein in the diet.
- Mention four contributions of ancient Rome.

Each of these commands can be responded to in brief form. No elaboration is necessary or wanted. The student must draw on his or her own fund of information to supply the correct answers.

Recall items may also be written as statements to be completed:

- The result obtained when we divide 12 by 1/2 is _____.
- The chemical formula for table salt is _____.
- "The Gift of the Magi" was written by _____.
- The fiftieth state admitted to the United States is _____.

Questions, commands, and completion are three styles of recall items. Note that all the examples call for low-level cognition—specific factual data—and reduce the need for guessing by the student. Naturally, students can guess at the whole answer, but they do not have alternative responses presented that may suggest answers. An active command of the knowledge is necessary to answer recall items.

Subjectivity can enter into the scoring of recall items when more than one correct response is possible. For example, one of the preceding illustrations asks students to mention four contributions of ancient Rome. Let us suppose the teacher expected the responses *laws*, *roads*, *aqueducts*, and *military weapons*. A student might respond *architecture*, *military tactics*, *language*, and *literature* as well as a number of other possible acceptable answers. In each case the teacher must judge whether the unexpected answer is correct and, if it is, give the student credit for it. If a teacher gets correct responses to an item that are different from the responses expected, the fault lies with the test item and not with the students.

Students' answers can sometimes contain surprises for the teacher if the test items are poorly constructed. The following example is an ambiguous item: "George Washington was born in __." The teacher might be looking for the answer 1732 but might receive the answer Virginia, an equally creditable response. Would it help, assuming that a date is the expected answer, to write, "George Washington was born on __"? Probably not, for the student could answer Pope's Creek Farm or February 22 or February 22, 1732. A real sharpie might answer February 11 or February 11, 1732, which was the actual date according to the calendar in use at that time. To avoid ambiguity, completion items sometimes must be cued, as "George Washington was born in __ (year)," or written more fully, "George Washington was born in the year __." The recall item must be directed to the specific response or responses that the teacher desires the students to make. A student who gives a correct answer regardless of where that answer has been learned should be given full credit for the answer.

The supervisor should help teachers detect ambiguity in test items and suggest ways to avoid this problem by pointing out that the function of the test item is to determine whether the students know that particular item of content. Teachers sometimes inadvertently provide clues to the correct responses by varying the length of the blanks in completion items and by using "a" or "an" unwisely. All blanks on a completion test should be of uniform length to prevent students from guessing. Similarly, the correct answer might be suggested by the article a or an in an item such as "A house made of blocks of ice and inhabited by Eskimos is called an __." If the student is conscious of language, he or she knows the correct answer must start with a vowel. An improved version of this item would be "Houses built of blocks of ice and inhabited by Eskimos are called __." A single blank should always be used rather than a number of blanks equal to the number of words in the correct response.

Some measurement specialists recommend that the blank come at the end of the item. Although that format is desirable and perhaps most common, the teacher may sometimes wish to vary it.

Although even objective tests should strive to measure higher levels of cognition, it is often necessary to test for lower-level cognition. Recall items perform that function admirably.

Multiple Choice A multiple-choice test item provides students with a statement or question and a number of responses from which the student selects one or more according to the directions. Most teachers and professional test makers favor this type of item for its versatility and ability to sample content in a limited time. The multiple-choice item is subject to guessing to a much greater degree than is a recall item. However, compared to some types of objective items discussed later in this section, the multiple-choice test item reduces the student's ability to guess the correct response. When there are four responses, for example, from which a student must select one, the chance of guessing correctly is one in four.

Multiple-choice items can be used in any cognitive field and may range from very simple to very complex. They may be used to test for low-level cognition and for higher levels, as you will see later in this section. They come in a number of varieties, such as "Select the right answer," "Select the incorrect answer," and "Select the best answer." They may call for one response or many responses and they may require considerable thought, as anyone who has wrestled with responses such as "all of the above," "none of the above," and "a, c, and d but not b" can attest. Let's examine a few of these items from a number of subjects:

$12 + 4 = 3 +$
   a. 12
   b. 13
   c. 14
   d. 15

Day:Night $=$ _____ : Black
   a. Blue
   b. White
   c. Green
   d. Red

Mark Twain is author of all these novels except
   a. *Huckleberry Finn*
   b. *Tom Sawyer*
   c. *Pudd'nhead Wilson*
   d. *Henry Esmond*

If $x = 2$ and $y = 4$, $2x + 2y =$
   a. 6
   b. 12
   c. 4
   d. 10

The formula for water is
   a. H_2SO_4
   b. H_2O
   c. H_2O_2
   d. HCl

The proper response a driver should make when his or her auto begins to skid on ice is

    a. jam on the brakes and slide through

    b. throw the shift into neutral and coast

    c. hold the wheel tight and keep steady

    d. turn the wheel in the direction of the skid

    e. turn the wheel in the opposite direction of the skid

    f. step hard on the accelerator

A person with *savoir-faire* is

    a. reticent

    b. knowledgeable

    c. impressionable

    d. contagious

Note that for readability, each choice starts on a different line. We want to assess what a student knows or understands and do not want to confuse the person with choices that run together. For this reason, the ACT, SAT, and other tests use separate lines. Teacher-made tests should do the same.

More than likely, as the supervisor and teachers examine sample test items, they will find some common errors of construction. Analysis of these errors will suggest some guidelines, such as those below, that the supervisor may propose to teachers to help them write multiple-choice items.

1. *As a rule of thumb, it is a good idea to provide at least four responses for each item.* The more responses there are, the less chance that the student will guess correctly. There comes, of course, a point of diminishing returns in terms of time for pupils to read items and respond to them and in terms of actual space required to present the items. A general practice is the use of four or five responses per item; the same number of responses should be offered for each test item.

2. *The answers to a multiple-choice test consisting of many items should not follow a consistent pattern that the student can guess.* Although it expedites scoring if the answers to eight consecutive questions are a, b, c, d, a, b, c, d, for example, many students will decipher the pattern and respond accordingly.

3. *Responses should all be the same length or almost the same length and consistent in form.* For example, let's take the preceding Mark Twain item. Suppose it read this way:

Mark Twain is author of all these novels except

    a. *Huckleberry Finn*

    b. *Innocents Abroad*

    c. *Pudd'nhead Wilson*

    d. *Call of the Wild*

Which response would you have made if you did not know the title of the novel Twain did not write? Chances are you would select *Call of the Wild*, which is different in form—four words instead of two, as in all the others. The test-taker's tendency is to select a response that is different in length or form from the other responses. If the different form is the correct response, the student may guess it and be rewarded for the guess. Dostoyevsky sticks out like a sore thumb in the item below:

Crime and Punishment was written by

    a. Capote

    b. Dostoyevsky

    c. Lewis

    d. Doyle

The student who did not know would likely guess Dostoyevsky and would be right. On the other hand, the teacher may play the game with the student a bit and make one of the incorrect responses different, as shown here:

All were famous generals of ancient times except

    a. Caesar

    b. Hannibal

    c. Cicero

    d. Scipio Africanus

If the student chooses Scipio Africanus because it is different in form from the others, the choice would be incorrect, as Cicero is the correct answer in this case. The purpose of writing an item like this is not to trick a student deliberately; there is no trick, as these were all personages of history and Scipio Africanus was indeed a general. The teacher wants to reward knowledge and not the ability to guess.

The supervisor should encourage teachers to build up a pool of test items so that they can mix them on subsequent testing. They should strive to create items with increasing complexity and those that test more than low-level cognition. Teachers who work within the same field of study can help each other critique test items and can even share items.

Alternative Response   Alternative-response items, as the name implies, give the test-taker two choices, from which they must select one. The most common form of this type is the true-false item, a much overworked kind of objective item. A major advantage of alternative-response items is their ability to sample an extensive amount of content in a short space and short time. Their major disadvantage is that students have a 50 percent chance of guessing correctly. Typical of a multitude of true-false items are the following, to which students would respond by circling the T for true or F for false:

T F   Thomas Jefferson was the third president of the United States.

T F $6 \times 9 = 54$

T F   The seasons in the Northern Hemisphere are the reverse of the seasons in the Southern Hemisphere.

T F   Leap year comes every other year.

True-false items can be made more difficult and therefore less objective if the student is required to state the reason for any false answer. Asking a student to state why an answer is false is a perfectly acceptable testing procedure, but the teacher will soon realize that this slows down the scoring process and might require making judgments about the stated reason.

Alternative-response items may appear in forms other than true-false. Language concepts, for example, can be tested in the following ways:

(Its, It's) time to go.

The student may circle or underline the correct response or strike out the incorrect response. The teacher may simplify scoring by placing blanks after each item in a column and asking students to write the correct responses on the blanks.

A language arts teacher might ask students to tell whether the italicized words are prepositions.

	YES	NO
After he left, I found the note.	____	____
I saw *her* come in.	____	____
The man spoke *to* his dog.	____	____
I couldn't hear, *for* he had turned his head.	____	____

The pupil checks "Yes" if the italicized word is a preposition, "No" if it is not.

One of the vowel sounds of the English language is tested in this example of an alternative-response item.

Mark the sounds of *a* in each of the following words if the word is the same or different as in the word *cat*:

	SAME	DIFFERENT
hat	____	____
hate	____	____
jar	____	____
had	____	____

Alternative-response items hover around the low levels of cognitive learning, particularly with true-false items. The language arts illustrations at least move up to the level of application. True-false items seem especially easy to create, and as a result, the teacher stumbles into pitfalls—or the learner may stumble into pitfalls dug by the teacher.

A supervisor might collect or write examples of true-false items such as those that follow and ask teachers what the problem is in their construction:

T	F	It is always cold in Alaska.
T	F	It never snows in Florida.
T	F	It is sometimes permissible in the United States to make a right turn on a red light.
T	F	Every country of South America has Spanish as its official language.
T	F	No country of South America has two official languages.

Discussion will reveal that all these statements have qualifiers that make it easy for a learner to guess the answer. This same deficiency can be found in the construction of other types of objective-test items. Words like *always*, *never*, *sometimes*, *every*, *all*, and *no* should be avoided. If the question cannot be restructured, it should not be placed on a test. The student already has a 50 percent chance of guessing correctly, and the teacher does not want to give away the items.

Another common error is illustrated in these examples:

T F   Agriculture is the most important business of California.
T F   Watergate was the worst political scandal in U.S. history.
T F   It is warm in Hawaii all year round.

Each of these items calls for some judgment on the part of the test-taker. Qualifiers like *important* or *most important* should be avoided unless they are clearly spelled out: Agriculture is most important in what way? in terms of dollars generated? number of persons employed? number of people affected? Possibly, historians will judge the Watergate scandal to be the worst political scandal, but we did have the Teapot Dome Scandal and the Iran-Contra affair, not to mention President Clinton's near-impeachment. By whose criteria is Watergate the worst or not the worst scandal? The example "It is warm in Hawaii all year round" may be designed to test knowledge of Hawaii's tropical climate, but warm is a relative term. Warm compared to what? How many degrees is warm? If anyone has been in Hawaii when the thermometer occasionally hits sixty degrees in February, he or she might wish for a touch of heat in the house.

Alternative-response items, like all objective items, must be clear. The double negative does not lend clarity to an item, as "It is not uncommon to find snow in Yellowstone National Park in the summer." The teacher should avoid involved, obtuse, and convoluted statements. Items should be direct, clear, and precise and yield only one correct answer.

Because of the problem of guessing, alternative-response tests should not be used consistently or exclusively. When they are used, it is advisable to construct a test with a fairly sizable number of items. One additional guideline should be mentioned: By no means should the teacher copy statements verbatim from the textbook for tests. Students who are familiar with the text may remember the passages from the book and receive unwarranted help from this familiarity.

Matching and Rearrangement Items   Matching and rearrangement items are two varieties of objective items that provide a little stimulation and challenge on the order of puzzles and make for good variation. Both are somewhat difficult to construct and require more time to score than any of the three other types of items, with the possible exception of recall items. The matching-test item seeks to show whether students can recognize and pair up a specific stimulus with a specific response. A single theme runs through the pairs of stimuli and responses, as in the case of writers and their novels:

1. Swift   ____   *The Vicar of Wakefield*
2. Scott   ____   *Gulliver's Travels*
3. Carroll   ____   *The Forsyte Saga*
4. Goldsmith   ____   *Ivanhoe*
5. Galsworthy   ____   *Alice in Wonderland*
                  ____   *Little Women*

In this matching item, students write the numbers they find to the left of the authors' names in the appropriate blank to the left of the titles. To reduce guessing by the process of elimination the teacher should provide at least one more response than there are stimuli. Otherwise, if a student knows all the responses except one, the last response would be a "freebie."

In the next example, students are required to solve each math problem before pairing the stimuli and responses.

	____	$2 \div 1/2$
1. 54	____	$21 \div 1/7$
2. 9	____	$24 \div 2/3$
3. 4	____	$12 \div 3/4$
4. 32	____	$18 \div 1/3$
5. 16	____	$8 \div 1/4$
	____	$6 \div 2/3$

In constructing matching items, the teacher should take care that members of the pair are not opposite each other and that the correct answers do not form a pattern, as 1, 2, 3, 4, 5 in succession.

Rearrangement items test for knowledge of a particular sequence. If order is an important feature to the teacher, the rearrangement item fulfills this requirement. The teacher provides a statement or command and a set of responses out of sequence. The student must put the items into their proper sequence by writing 1 beside the first item in the sequence, 2 next, and so on, as in the next two examples:

Rank the states from 1 to 7 according to the latest U.S. Census population figures:

( ) Ohio

( ) Pennsylvania

( ) Florida

( ) California

( ) New York

( ) Texas

( ) Illinois

In listing a book that has a single author in a bibliography, there is a standard order in which items are written. Mark from 1 to 6 the order in which the items should appear.

( ) city of publisher

( ) number of pages

( ) name of author

( ) name of publisher

( ) title of work

( ) date of publication

Recall, multiple-choice, alternative-response, matching, and rearrangement questions all have their place on objective tests. They each have distinct advantages and disadvantages. Students should be exposed to all types of items if for no other reason than for stimulus variation, which heightens student interest.

The Bloom Taxonomy and Objective-Test Items   The question may be raised concerning whether objective-test items can measure achievement in the highest levels of cognitive learning. Let's take a look at some illustrations of objective-test items for each of the major categories of the Bloom taxonomy.

Knowledge
A synonym for *lethargic* is

    a. cool

    b. taut

    c. slow

    d. long

Of the planets listed below, the one that is closest to our sun is

    a. Jupiter

    b. Venus

    c. Saturn

    d. Mars

Comprehension
The question "Do you mean American time or Latin time?" implies

    a. North Americans have the custom of arriving late for appointments.

    b. Latin Americans have the custom of arriving late for appointments.

    c. North America lies in time zones different from South America.

    d. Time zones in South America are the reverse of those in North America.

The moral of Daphne Du Maurier's short story "The Birds" is

    a. People can triumph over anything.

    b. Nature can get out of balance.

    c. Birds are vital to humankind's existence.

    d. Birds are rapidly becoming extinct.

    e. People should help their feathered friends.

Application
If a man loads 50 kegs of nails on a truck in 1 hour, to find out how many cases he could load in 8 hours you would

    a. subtract 8 from 50

    b. divide 50 by 8

c. add 8 to 50

d. multiply 50 by 8

Underline all the Spanish nouns that follow the regular rule for identifying feminine nouns.

a. casa

b. mano

c. cosa

d. mesa

e. pelo

f. pozo

Analysis

The following sentence contains an error:

My friend Jimmy Lane don't know how to read.

The error is

a. absence of commas

b. use of the apostrophe

c. agreement of the verb

d. spelling of *friend*

The snake in the picture shown by the teacher has all the characteristics of a

a. king snake

b. chicken snake

c. coral snake

d. milk snake

Synthesis

Add the fifth step in the sequence of steps for multiplication on the pocket calculator that we used in class.

a. Press the "clear" button

b. Enter the number to be multiplied

c. Press the (multiplication) button

d. Press the number of the multiplier

e. _____

f. Read the product in the window.

A boy went into a store with 25 cents. He wanted to buy lollipops, which cost 3 cents each, and pieces of bubble gum, which cost 2 cents each. He decided to buy six lollipops and spend the remainder on as many pieces of bubble gum as he could buy. To find out how much change he would receive, you would need to follow certain steps. Mark from 1 to 5 the steps you would take to solve this problem in the order in which you would take them.

( ) Multiply 3 × 2.

( ) Subtract 18 from 25.

( ) Multiply 6 × 3.

( ) Subtract 6 from 7.

( ) Divide 7 by 2.

Evaluation

Of the four test items that follow, select the one that meets the characteristics of a well-constructed T–F item as described in this text:

a. T F It is not uncommon to find mountain streams that are polluted.

b. T F Apples are the most important product of the state of Washington.

c. T F Milk is the best beverage.

d. T F Washington, D.C., is the capital of the United States.

The students will preview three films made for children. On the basis of criteria studied in class, the students will assign each film a rating of 1, 2, 3, or 4 stars (four is the highest rating). The rating for the first film is

a. one star

b. two stars

c. three stars

d. four stars

Although it is common and acceptable practice for both teacher-made and standardized tests to consist of a single type of objective-test item, such as multiple choice, we would recommend as a general rule that teacher-made tests include a variety of types of objective-test items. Testing should be considered an instructional strategy. To use tests effectively as instructional techniques, the teacher should score them and convey the results to the students as rapidly as possible.

Some teachers have students use Scantron® or other optically scanned answer sheets to record their responses to multiple-choice or matching-test items. The Scantron® forms are similar to those used for standardized tests that require students to use a pencil and confine their responses to neatly filled-in circles, ovals, rectangles, or squares.

A special machine is needed to scan, mark, and summarize responses given by each student. After the form containing the answer key is sent through the machine, the students' forms can be graded in a matter of minutes. In addition to learning how each student did on the exam, a teacher can have a composite made of all students' scores along with an item analysis of right/wrong responses.

EVALUATING AFFECTIVE OBJECTIVES

Earlier in this chapter, we observed that cognitive objectives may be measured by essay and objective tests and psychomotor skills by tests of actual performance. Standards of mastery may be set and observed for learning in these two domains. Judgments must be made for cognitive essay tests and for performance of psychomotor skills. In both these cases, the standards against which the cognitive and psychomotor performance will be weighed should be established beforehand, written down, and communicated to the test-takers.

You will find it difficult or impossible to observe mastery of many affective objectives, and for that reason it is preferable to think of assessment of affective objectives as evaluation rather than measurement. Although we may administer instruments to assess attainment of affective objectives and even subject the results to statistical treatment, the assessment of affective objectives should be used for purposes other than marking and reporting in the traditional sense of marking and reporting.

The affective domain, which comprises feelings, emotions, and attitudes, may be assessed in a variety of ways. Among these techniques are the following:

1. *Observation.* Observation is the most common technique for evaluating performance in any domain. The experienced teacher develops skills in observing the performance of individuals and groups both in and out of class. Affective behavior is shown through comments students make in class, their behavior in school and out, the enthusiasm they show, and questions they raise. The teacher may elicit certain kinds of behavior by placing students in particular situations, asking them to role-play, and posing controversial issues.

2. *Essays.* Students may be asked to write compositions that will reveal their feelings and positions on issues. The teacher may suggest personalized topics, such as "My Favorite Subject in School," "The Worst Experience of My Life," and "What It Means to Be Cooperative." The teacher might also suggest topics that are more cognitive in nature but still designed to bring out attitudes of the learner, such as "The Role of Welfare in Our Society," "Equal Rights for Women," and "Opportunities for Service in the Community."

3. *Opinionnaires.* Attitudes of students may be surveyed with alternative-response items:

> Circle the letter A if you agree with the statement and D if you disagree.

> A D Handguns should be outlawed.

Some teachers and professional inventories provide for a continuum of responses from "strongly agree" to "strongly disagree."

> Circle SA if you strongly agree, A if you agree, U if you are undecided, D if you disagree, and SD if you strongly disagree with the statement.

> SA A U D SD The personal use of marijuana should be a criminal offense.

Attitude inventories may yield scores, but these scores should be considered simply compilations of responses that give a picture of the positions taken by individuals and the group, and not considered correct and incorrect responses. In some cases the choice U is not offered as an option, which forces the respondent to make a choice in agreement or disagreement with the statement.

To construct items and exercises for evaluating affective objectives, the teacher goes back to the objectives in the same way as for assessing objectives in the cognitive and psychomotor domains and tries to design assessment items that come as close as possible to showing whether the learner has met the affective objectives.

The supervisor should engage teachers in discussion of ways to evaluate affective objectives and should raise such questions as, "Which affective objectives should we seek?" "In what ways can accomplishment of these objectives be observed?" "Which affective objectives should be stressed over others?" "What shall we do with the results of evaluation of affective objectives?" and "Are there any affective objectives that we should insist on for every student or do all of them pertain only to the individual? For example, if a student believes that dishonesty is the only way to get along in life, should this attitude be of any concern to the teacher?" Evaluation of objectives in the affective domain presents problems very different from evaluation of objectives in the cognitive and psychomotor domains.

OTHER EVALUATION TECHNIQUES

The major portion of this chapter concerns testing. Yet evaluation through means other than testing occupies a far greater portion of a teacher's time.

Observation of Class Participation

Although tests are not and should not be given every day, observation of student achievement, usually the most common evaluation technique, occurs daily. Most observation is informal and unstructured. Teachers gain impressions about the work of students in their classes and make judgments about their achievement by carefully examining how students go about their work, the depth of their understanding of the content, and the quality of their questions and responses.

The teacher is concerned not only with the students' achievement but also with their participation—how they interact with each other and with the teacher. Some other student behaviors the teacher looks for are attentiveness and interest shown, frequency with which students participate, and responsiveness. If active participation by all class members is a goal, the teacher can devise a systematic way of observing and evaluating class participation. The rating instrument shown in Figure 6.1 is one means for the teacher to provide subjective individual feedback to the student on class participation as judged by the teacher.

Oral Reports

Oral reports by individuals, committees, panels, and so on provide the teacher with another way to assess student performance. The teacher should provide students who are to present oral reports with the criteria against which they will be rated. Common standards include clarity of presentation, correct language usage, supporting data, enunciation, and evidence of preparation. Both individual and group oral reports can be rated by using instruments such as those shown in Figures 6.2 and 6.3. Whenever evaluation instruments are used, the teacher should make the results known to the students so they may improve their future presentations.

EVALUATION OF CLASS PARTICIPATION

Student:_____   Date:_____

CHARACTERISTIC	A Excellent	B Good	C Fair	D Poor	F Failing
Attentiveness and interest shown					
Frequency of participation					
Merit (quality) of answers and questions raised					
Extent of volunteering					
Contributions of significant anecdotes, illustrations, and facts to assist in topics under discussion					

Comments:

Composite Grade: _____

FIGURE 6.1   Evaluation of Class Participation. *Source:* Adapted from Peter F. Oliva, *The Secondary School Today,* 2nd ed. (New York: Harper and Row, 1972), p. 528.

INDIVIDUAL ORAL PRESENTATION OR REPORT

Student: _____   Date: _____

CHARACTERISTIC	Low 1	2	3	4	High 5
The speaker was prepared.					
The speaker's presentation was clear to the listeners.					
The speaker's voice was audible.					
The speaker's voice was not monotonous.					
The speaker's language usage was correct.					
The speaker was animated and enthusiastic.					

Comments:

Composite Grade: _____

FIGURE 6.2   Individual Oral Presentation or Report. *Source:* Adapted from Peter F. Oliva, *The Secondary School Today,* 2nd ed. (New York: Harper and Row, 1972), p. 533.

CHARACTERISTIC	Low 1	2	3	4	High 5
There was evidence of preparation in respect to content.					
There was evidence of preparation in respect to organization and presentation of the material.					
All the students in the reporting group had the opportunity to participate in the report					
All the students spoke audibly.					
All the students used language correctly.					

GROUP ORAL PRESENTATION OR REPORT

Group Members: _____

_____

Comments to the group:

Composite Grade: _____

FIGURE 6.3 Group Oral Presentation or Report. *Source:* Adapted from Peter F. Oliva, *The Secondary School Today,* 2nd ed. (New York: Harper and Row, 1972), p. 534.

Written Assignments

As common as oral reports are written assignments of varying types, from a set of problems to be worked or questions to be answered to brief compositions to research papers. In each case, the teacher should provide the learners in advance with a set of standards by which the work will be judged. For routine written homework, that standard may simply be completion of the assignment because it is impossible for teachers to grade all written assignments. On the other hand, the teacher must take the time to grade major written assignments and report the results to the learners.

Portfolio Assessment

Portfolio assessment calls for a collection of student work samples that demonstrate achievement of objectives. Portfolios have been used by art teachers for some time. Teachers in other areas now collect samples of student work. Examining samples of work the students have assembled in portfolio form helps the teacher determine whether students have achieved planned objectives. The teacher may wish to place value on the work samples, based on announced criteria, and may calculate their value along with tests in the assignment of a grade.

In some instances the items placed in a student's portfolio have been prescribed by the state or local school district. Teachers often have opportunities to suggest which items would reflect an accurate portrayal of student achievement. In some cases, where some latitude and encouragement exist, teachers allow students to select items to be included in their portfolios.

One important asset of a portfolio is self-evaluation. Portfolio assessment offers students a way to take charge of their learning; it also encourages ownership, pride, and high self-esteem. Portfolios further provide an opportunity for parents to view samples of their children's work. We have worked with elementary education interns who assembled a class portfolio that was a composite of works reflecting the students' achievements of the district's goals. Such a composite portfolio contains information that can be used for program assessment.

Creative Assignments

Creative assignments, such as scrapbooks and artwork, give evidence of certain types of learning. Many areas of the curriculum offer opportunities for students to create some tangible products that demonstrate various skills and knowledge. Whether each of the creative assignments is to be graded, students must know in advance the criteria on which they will be judged.

Group Work

When students work on assignments in groups, the teacher and the members of the group should strive to evaluate their work as a group. Evidence should be obtained concerning how effectively each member of the group carried out individual responsibilities. From time to time, it is possible and desirable for the class to participate in evaluating the work of individuals and groups in the class. This technique requires the teacher to lay certain ground rules for students' evaluation of the performance of other students. They must be taught to do so in a positive, constructive way. Figure 6.4 illustrates an instrument that permits students to evaluate their own work as members of a committee or group.

This particular instrument uses the letter grading system. Should the teacher not wish to couple the evaluation with letter grades, a numerical scale or categories such as excellent, very good, good, fair, and poor can be used.

Self-Evaluation and Joint Evaluation

A total evaluation plan should include opportunities for pupils to develop the skill of evaluating their own performance. Students can benefit from sharing their own perceptions of their work with the teacher. The students' self-evaluations do not substitute for the teacher's evaluation of their work nor ultimately determine a mark; rather, the self-appraisals provide the teacher with a type of information that is often otherwise missed and with clues for assisting individual students. Students—particularly those at the secondary school level—might be asked to rate themselves on such criteria as their performance on tests, quality and regularity of homework, participation in class discussions, participation in a small group, effort expended, cooperation with teacher and fellow pupils, ability to listen, and conduct in class. It can be helpful to discover how realistic students' perceptions are of their own work and how much their appraisals and those of the teacher diverge.

SELF-EVALUATION FOR COMMITTEE MEMBER

Please rate yourself on each of the following phases of your committee's work by encircling the appropriate letter.

PLANNING   (Extent of your participation in planning sessions)

A   B   C   D   F

Rationale for this rating:

PREPARATION   (Library research, search for materials, committee work outside of planning and class sessions)

A   B   C   D   F

Rationale for this rating:

TEACHING   (Performance during class periods devoted to your topic)

A   B   C   D   F

Rationale for this rating:

Composite Grade: _____
Write A, B, C, D, or F

Student: _____   Date: _____

FIGURE 6.4   Self-Evaluation for Committee Member. *Source*: Adapted from Peter F. Oliva, *The Secondary School Today*, 2nd ed. (New York: Harper and Row, 1972), p. 537.

A self-appraisal instrument can be designed that reflects the various criteria the teacher deems important. It can be made into a joint evaluation process, which would necessitate appraisal conferences with each pupil. The form can be completed independently by the student and teacher, shared at a conference, and a composite evaluation jointly determined. Such an instrument is shown in Figure 6.5.

A key characteristic of cooperative learning models is performance of the group as a whole. Teachers can provide some mechanism for group members to assess their performance as a group. Figure 6.6 enables the teacher and group members, each rating separately, to assess the group's performance. The ratings can be a simple Yes or No; letter or numerical symbols; or words such as excellent, good, and so on. In all cases, as you will see in the next section on marking, when symbols are used, they must be defined. Items on any evaluation form for student use must be tailored to the maturity level of the students.

JOINT EVALUATION OF STUDENT ACHIEVEMENT

Student: _____   Date: _____

Teacher: _____   Subject: _____   Period: _____

Place an A, B, C, D, or F in each blank.

	Student's Appraisal	Teacher's Appraisal	Weight
Achievement (tests)	_____	_____	2/6
Quality of written assignments (homework, class work, research papers, term reports, book reports)	_____	_____	1/6
Preparation for class	_____	_____	1/6
Assigned readings (completed, understood)	_____	_____	1/6
Participation in class discussions (value of contributions, frequency, attentiveness)	_____	_____	1/6

Comments:

Composite Grade: _____

FIGURE 6.5   Joint Evaluation of Student Achievement. *Source*: Adapted from Peter F. Oliva, *The Secondary School Today,* 2nd ed. (New York: Harper and Row, 1972), p. 537.

INDIVIDUAL EVALUATION OF GROUP'S PERFORMANCE

Group Members: _____

Title: _____   Date: _____

	YES	NO
1. Group members mastered the specified objectives.	_____	_____
2. The group remained on task.	_____	_____
3. The group used time eficiently.	_____	_____
4. The group met established deadlines.	_____	_____
5. The group organized its work eficiently and fairly.	_____	_____
6. Group members made positive contributions.	_____	_____
7. Group members fulfilled their responsibilities.	_____	_____
8. Group members helped each other.	_____	_____
9. Group members presented a quality finished product.	_____	_____

Comments:

FIGURE 6.6   Individual Evaluation of Group's Performance. *Source*: Adapted from Peter F. Oliva and George E. Pawlas, *Supervision for Today's Schools,* 7th ed. (New York: Wiley, 2004), p. 245. Reprinted with permission.

The teacher may elect to ask students to sign the evaluation, which provides some insights into the evaluator's attitudes and skills as well as the group's performance. The teacher may wish to make a composite summary of the members' evaluations attitudes and share that summary as well as his or her own with the group. Whether or not students sign the evaluations, individual evaluations should not be shared with the group.

Theoretically, teachers can devise an instrument by which members of a group can rate each other's performance. We do not advocate such a process because negative results from one's peers—some young people can be harsh critics—can be too destructive of the ego and serve to discourage rather than motivate learners. Peer evaluations, even if used with adults, must be structured, conducted, and controlled with great caution.

Although testing may occupy a prominent place in the instructional program, the teacher should not rely exclusively on testing as a means of evaluation. Some of the outcomes of education cannot be assessed by ordinary testing. The teacher's evaluation skills should include more than expertise in the construction and administration of essay and objective tests and should include a variety of techniques other than testing. When the supervisor discovers that teachers need to develop their evaluation skills, some in-service training is in order.

Pop quizzes, book reports, and countless other devices can be part of a total formal assessment program. It is wise to remember that frequent and multiple assessment opportunities enhance the learning process.

MARKING STUDENT ACHIEVEMENT

At the end of each marking period, every teacher engages in a pseudoscientific activity known as *marking. Marking*, or *grading*, as it is also called—a concept that conjures up visions of a steamroller leveling a road—has all the appearance of a science. Teachers administer tests, collect data, subject the data to statistical treatment, and finally come up with a symbol—the letter grade. They place that grade on some sort of reporting form and give it to the student and parents. The school divides its years into a number of marking periods, and teachers repeat the grading process at the end of each marking period and wrap up student achievement in one symbol that represents performance for the year. The most common system of grades, particularly at the secondary school level, is a five-letter system: A, B, C, D, and F. We know that the student who receives an A will be much happier than the student who receives an F. If a student or parents ask a teacher what a given symbol means— say, a B—some teachers will give answers akin to Humpty Dumpty's line in *Through the Looking Glass*: "It means just what I choose it to mean."

Assume for a moment the role of the mathematics department head in a secondary school that has no consistent policy on marking—that is, on grading practices—and leaves such decisions entirely in the hands of each individual teacher. This department head is concerned about the grading practices among the teachers of the department. At the end of the current marking period, she made the rounds of the six teachers' classrooms and discovered a variety of practices, including these:

- A teacher adding up all numerical scores compiled by each student during the marking period, dividing by the number of scores, determining the mean or average score, then converting the scores to letter grades based on an arbitrary scale: A = 95–100; B = 85–94; C = 75–84; D = 65–74; F = scores below 65.

- A second teacher fitting grades to a modified normal curve with a few A's, a few F's, a larger number of D's, and the majority of grades B's and C's.
- Third, a teacher who gave only A's and B's.
- A fourth teacher who gave F's to two-thirds of the class.
- Another teacher who gave every student an A.
- The sixth and last teacher, who based grades exclusively on written tests.

The inconsistencies in grading practices among teachers in the same department leads the department head to open a discussion with the teachers during one of their joint planning periods. The department head asks the teachers to consider two questions: What are the purposes of grading? On what guidelines can we as a group agree?

A group of elementary school teachers would be in agreement with this group of high school teachers if the high school group saw the reasons listed here as the purposes of a grading system:

- Reporting to students how well they have done during the marking period and at the end of the year.
- Reporting to parents how well their children have done in the subject.
- Deciding on students' promotions to the next grade level.
- Motivating students.
- Deciding which students' names will be placed on the honor roll.

A group of high school teachers might also state the purposes of marking as

- Reporting to employers and colleges. (This purpose is often paramount with high school teachers.)
- Deciding on graduation and awards at graduation.

Grading is a serious business for both teachers and students. Learners are conditioned from the day they set foot in the school to know that grades, regardless of the symbols used—pass–fail, satisfactory–unsatisfactory, 0–100 percent, or A–F—are important. Both teachers and parents have pushed students to bring home grades as high as possible. Far too commonly, marks produce conflict between parents and their children, particularly when parents lack patience and understanding of their children's difficulties. Teachers, students, and parents alike see tangible and intangible rewards stemming from high grades. Marks do serve as motivators for many children; conversely, they serve as sources of frustration and despair for others.

The responsibility for grading is a real form of power that teachers exert over learners. Conscientious teachers spend many anguished moments during their teaching careers over the grades they assign to students. Recognizing the pressure that marks put on students, they use every means possible to make each grade a fair and just approximation of achievement. But no matter how scientific the process of grading may appear, grades are at best only approximations of achievement. Every mark given by a teacher calls for a judgment, which is sometimes based on very limited evidence. Unfortunately, given the premium on marks, for many students the symbols themselves have become more important than the achievement the marks supposedly represent.

All marking systems have certain inherent problems, some of which are seeds for controversy among teachers and between teachers and the public. It would be a most rewarding in-service activity if the supervisor could lead teachers to consensus on certain practices they will follow in implementing the marking system of their school. Resolution and agreement are needed on such issues as these:

- Shall grades be based on mastery of content (criterion-referenced) or on comparative achievement of learners (norm-referenced)?
- How much evidence is needed for determining a grade?
- What factors should be considered in arriving at a grade in subject matter achievement?
- Should grading practices in homogeneous classes differ from grading practices in heterogeneous classes?
- Should achievement in the affective domain be evaluated and reported? If so, how?
- What do letter grades mean?
- What score constitutes passing a test? a marking period? a course? a grade level?
- Should a student's ability be considered in assigning a mark?
- Should a student's effort be considered in assigning a grade?
- Should a student's deportment be considered in assigning a grade?

Any of these questions can easily start a heated argument. Teachers customarily base their practices not only on empirical data but also on philosophical premises they hold concerning the learner, the learning process, and society. By sharing their beliefs, teachers may ultimately modify their views and reach some common understandings. The supervisor should strive to obtain consensus among teachers on a few basic principles of marking:

1. *Marks should reflect as nearly as possible mastery of content.* As Bloom, Hastings, and Madaus pointed out, most learners in school can learn most of the content if they are properly placed in school to begin with and if instruction is skillfully implemented.[14]

2. *A multitude of evidence is necessary for determining a grade.* Success at any level or in any program should not rest on a single examination or a couple of tests. A variety of evaluation techniques should be employed, and repeated opportunities should be provided for the learners to demonstrate achievement.

3. *The meaning of each letter symbol should be defined in behavioral terms, and those meanings should be communicated to students and parents.* Whatever factors teachers consider in assigning grades should be made known, and any factors that are not communicated should not be considered.

4. *Marks in a discipline should reflect subject matter achievement. Extraneous behaviors in class or out should be recognized by means other than marks in the subject.* A frequent and often subliminal abuse of this principle is found in situations in which teachers consider a student's conduct in class and penalize him or her for misbehaving by reducing the mark in subject matter achievement. Sometimes teachers engage in the dubious practice of offering extra credit for good deeds, such as contributing food to a charitable organization or even attendance at school functions.

5. *In schools that have set up a competency-based education program, the faculty must decide what letter grade represents satisfactory attainment of minimal competencies at each grade level and in each course.* Whether students are grouped heterogeneously or, with decreasing frequency, homogeneously for learning, the minimal grade for satisfactory achievement of the prescribed minimal competencies should be, in our estimation, equivalent to a B. We are really dealing here with two conflicting systems when competency-based education is superimposed on an A–F letter-grade system. Competency-based education is really binary in nature. Either you master the competencies or you don't. Thus, we are dealing with a situation that begets satisfactory–unsatisfactory, pass–fail, or A–B. Because many students, teachers, and parents regard a C grade, supposedly average, as unsatisfactory work, C will not suffice as the grade for achieving the minimal competencies. If B is the grade for acceptable performance on minimal competencies, there is still room for brighter or more industrious or more motivated students to perform at a higher level and attain A grades.

6. *Symbols for marking and reporting conduct, attitudes, personal habits, and other affective outcomes should be different from the symbols for reporting achievement in the cognitive and psychomotor domains.* We make no brief for any particular set of symbols. In practice, secondary schools have tended to stick with the A–F system for marking cognitive and psychomotor achievement, whereas elementary schools have frequently used two- or three-point systems such as satisfactory (S) and unsatisfactory (U), or S, U, and N (needs improvement). If affective objectives are evaluated and reported—and we believe some of them should be—other letters or numbers should be used for this purpose. A three-point scale such as 1, 2, 3 or H (high), M (moderate), L (low) is a feasible alternative.

7. *Whatever measures teachers can take to reduce or remove the threatening nature of marks should be taken.* They can reduce the stress placed on tests and marks and report cards and help learners adjust to them more easily. Teachers sometimes contribute to students' low marks by the manner in which they emphasize tests. A little positive set induction when administering a test can reduce students' anxiety and help them develop a sense of confidence.

Marking practices can serve the purposes for which they were intended if a careful set of guidelines is developed and put into practice. Improper marking practices can serve as a continuing source of conflict between students and teachers and between parents and teachers. Supervisors need to assist faculties in developing sound marking systems.

REPORTING STUDENT ACHIEVEMENT

Sooner or later the inevitable happens. Each student receives a piece of paper with the symbols that announce how well or how poorly he or she has done in school for that particular marking period. In theory, the report card is meant to communicate to parents the progress and achievement made by the learners. In practice, a report card by itself tells parents very little. It tells nothing about the process by which the teacher decided on the grade. If a student brings home low grades, the report card may not reveal why the grades are low or what the student must do to bring the grades up.

Over the years, schools have experimented with a variety of report cards and varying procedures for handling them. Some schools mail cards directly to the home instead of sending them with the pupils. Some secondary schools use single cards for reporting all subjects, whereas other schools use individual report forms for each subject. Some reporting forms consist of only a single card; others are made of multiple copies. Some are handwritten by the teacher, and others are machine processed. Some provide space for teachers' comments, and others add space for parents' comments. Some cards must be returned to the school, and other report forms are kept at home. If report cards have any common characteristic, it is the inadequacy of the information supplied and the interpretation of the symbols used. True, there are often words or phrases that seek to interpret the grades, such as "A means excellent work," "C is average work," and so on. But these words tell little more than the letter grade itself.

Unfortunately, teachers are locked into the reporting system, and it requires lengthy and concerted faculty action in conjunction with the community to make a change. There are, however, ways to make the reporting system more meaningful and informative: First, teachers might supplement the limited information on the report card with a narrative report of student progress. In the narrative the teacher can point out areas in which the student does well and areas in which the student needs improvement. The narrative form of reporting has been popular with elementary school teachers and has in fact supplanted other types of reporting in some elementary schools. With the large number of students taught by secondary school teachers, a narrative for every student, though ideal, would be impractical. The secondary school teacher might reserve the narrative for those students who have done something exceptionally well and for those who are having particular difficulty. The secondary school teacher may take advantage of space on those reporting forms that provide for teacher's comments. Elementary, middle, and secondary school teachers should be willing, and in many instances are required, to supplement the reporting system with parent conferences.

Second, the school might, as many have done, adopt the practice of sending home interim or progress reports during the marking period instead of waiting until the end of the period to report to parents. If parents know in enough time that their children are doing poor work in school, they may be able to work with them and help them improve. If the numbers of students preclude progress reports for each one, interim reports could be sent out only when students are having difficulty, their grade in the course has dropped, or they appear in danger of failing the course or grade.

Third, the teacher should regularly counsel students on their work, make suggestions for improving, and listen to those who are having difficulties.

These supplements to the report card can go a long way toward enabling both students and parents to understand what the symbols on the cards mean, where the learners are having problems, and what the students must do to achieve mastery of the content. Supervisors need to help faculties analyze and improve their reporting systems.

SUMMARY

Evaluation is conceived as an integral part of the instructional system. The main purpose of evaluation is to determine whether students have met the prespecified objectives.

The process of evaluation begins with preassessment of entry skills students must exhibit to pursue the subject successfully. Formative evaluation should be conducted to check learners' progress during a unit, and summative evaluation should assess terminal behaviors.

Testing is one of the tools for assessing cognitive and psychomotor objectives. The teacher customarily makes use of two types of tests: essay and objective. Care must be exercised in the construction of test items so that they accurately measure attainment of the objectives.

In addition to testing, teachers may employ observation, oral and written reports, creative assignments, group evaluation, and self-evaluation. The accomplishment of affective objectives may be evaluated through techniques other than testing, such as observation, surveys, inventories, essays, opinionnaires, and self-evaluations.

Marks or grades should accurately reflect the degree to which students have met the objectives of instruction. Efforts should be made to define marks and make them as meaningful as possible. In the case of affective objectives, the symbols used should be different from those used for reporting achievement of cognitive and psychomotor objectives.

Reporting systems are designed to let students, parents, and others know how well the learner is performing in school. The reporting system can be improved through the use of narrative reports, progress reports, and evaluation conferences.

The supervisor is urged to develop a number of in-service activities to help teachers with the improvement of skills of evaluation, measurement, testing, marking, and reporting.

QUESTIONS FOR DISCUSSION

1. What issues would you discuss with teachers concerning norm-referenced and criterion-referenced measurement? Why would you select those issues?

2. How would you explain these terms and their purposes/functions to teachers?

    a. formative evaluation

    b. summative evaluation

3. Which is the better way to assess students' progress: through the use of essay tests or objective tests? Why?

4. Should passing a state exit exam be a requirement for high-school graduation? Why or why not?

5. What ways and methods would a supervisor employ to help teachers improve their observation techniques?

ACTIVITIES FOR FURTHER STUDY

REFLECTIVE

1. Define the following:

    evaluation

    assessment

    measurement

    testing

    formative evaluation

    summative evaluation

    criterion-referenced measurement

    norm-referenced measurement

2. Select a topic for a unit in a subject you know well and specify the entry skills necessary for initiating study of that unit. Specify the means you would use to assess those skills.

3. Select a unit you have prepared in the past and describe in written form the total evaluation plan for that unit, including formal and informal evaluations and continuing and terminal evaluations.

4. Describe how you would calculate marks for a student at the end of the year and how you would determine whether a student passes the course or level.

5. *For those who are currently teaching:* Examine a unit test you have given to a group of students and on which they have not done well. Describe in what way results of the test have a bearing on the objectives of the unit, preassessment, and instructional procedures. *For those who are not currently teaching:* Secure a unit and test data from a teacher you know and make a similar analysis.

6. Suggest entry skills students should possess to begin study of
   a. First grade
   b. Word processing I
   c. World history
   d. Algebra I

7. State the ways you believe the attainment of affective objectives should be evaluated and reported.

8. Write a position paper on the Bloom, Hastings, and Madaus thesis (see Chapter bibliography) that more than 90 percent of students could learn most of what we have to teach them.

9. Compare the Bloom taxonomy as revised in Lorin W. Anderson and David Krathwohl, eds. (see chapter bibliography) with the original Bloom taxonomy.

10. Be prepared to compare Anita J. Harrow's taxonomy of the psychomotor domain with the Elizabeth J. Simpson taxonomy in (a) categories and (b) use. (See Chapter bibliography.)

11. Compare Robert J. Marzano's taxonomy of Educational Objectives (see chapter bibliography) with the Bloom taxonomy.

12. Find out the passing grade in the high school you attended as a student. Compare passing grades of your high school with those of other high schools and account for the differences, if any.

13. State your position on the following: A grade of 70 should be considered passing in every subject in every school of your state. Give the reasons for your position.

14. Describe how to use portfolios in assessing student achievement.

APPLICATION

1. Prepare an instrument or a set of criteria for evaluating a group oral report and administer it either to your own or another teacher's students when a group oral report is being given.

2. Confer with at least two teachers and discover whether they are using a norm-referenced or a criterion-referenced approach to measurement, and (tactfully) whether they know the distinctions between the two approaches.

3. Specify a usable set of criteria for evaluating
   a. A four-legged wooden stool made in ninth-grade industrial arts
   b. A fifth-grader's oral report on the Grand Canyon
   c. A sixth-grade committee report (oral) on "History of the American Flag"
   d. A pair of earrings made of black coral (eighth-grade arts and crafts)
   e. A senior's term paper on "The Uses of Computers"

4. State whether each of the following test items is well or poorly constructed. If you decide an item is poorly constructed, state your reason(s) and tell how the item can be improved.

T F Television is the most important source of news today.

T F Popes have always had their residence at the Vatican.

A Native American tribe that inhabited the continental United States was
a. The Aztecs
b. The Mayans
c. The Sioux

A Communist country is
a. Peru
b. China
c. Mali
d. Iraq

List four products France exports for sale.

The American Revolution ended in ____.

Discuss the Federal Reserve System.

5. Confer with at least two teachers and determine whether they have made any attempt to preassess entry skills for the units they are presently teaching. Summarize your findings.

6. Create an instrument for evaluating students' participation in class.

7. Attend a teacher's class for thirty minutes and, using the instrument you designed for activity 6, evaluate the class participation of the students.

8. Create an instrument by which a teacher and/or the members of a group may evaluate the group's performance.

9. Obtain a report card of a friend's or relative's child and, with permission, bring it to class and try to interpret to the class the meaning of the grades.

10. Create test items that you consider to be well constructed. Develop two essay-test items and two each of the following types of objective-test items: recall, multiple choice, alternative response, matching, and rearrangement.

11. Confer with at least two teachers and gather their reactions to the use of essay and objective tests.

12. Interview at least two teachers to find out how they determined the marks they gave to their students at the end of the last marking period. Summarize your findings in a written report.

13. Obtain a teacher-made objective test (it can be your own) and classify the test items on it according to the six major categories of the Bloom taxonomy of the cognitive domain. Decide at which level most of the test items fall.

14. Create two sample multiple-choice items to measure achievement at the following levels of cognition: application, analysis, synthesis, and evaluation.

15. Obtain an essay test (it can be your own) and evaluate it on the basis of the criteria in the following checklist:

Checklist for Evaluating Essay Tests

General	Yes	No
a. The questions relate to the objectives.	____	____
b. The purpose of the test items is clear.	____	____
c. The wording of the items is unambiguous.	____	____
d. There is more than one essay item.	____	____
e. The questions are focused so students know what will constitute a complete answer.	____	____
f. Students are told what factors will be evaluated in scoring.	____	____
g. Students are told weights assigned to each question.	____	____
h. A scoring key has been prepared, showing key points students must cover to receive full credit for each answer.	____	____
i. There is sufficient time for students to respond fully.	____	____
j. English usage is correct.	____	____

16. Obtain an objective test (it can be your own) and evaluate it on the basis of the criteria in the following checklist:

Checklist for Evaluating Objective Tests

General	Yes	No
a. The test items relate to the objectives.	____	____
b. The test includes a variety of types of test items.	____	____
c. The items adequately sample the content.	____	____
d. The items are clearly written.	____	____
e. The items avoid clues that give away the answers.	____	____
f. The items avoid the language of the text materials.	____	____
g. A key has been prepared.	____	____
h. The items can be scored objectively.	____	____
i. English usage is correct.	____	____

In addition to the general criteria, the following specific criteria apply to the various types of objective test items:

Completion Items	Yes	No
a. The items allow for only one correct answer.	____	____
b. Each item when completed will make a sentence.	____	____
c. Each item has only one blank to be filled in.	____	____
d. All blanks to be filled in are of equal length.	____	____

Multiple-Choice Items	Yes	No
a. There are at least four responses for each item.	___	___
b. The test avoids a consistent pattern of response.	___	___
c. The responses to each item are plausible.	___	___
d. The responses to each item are of approximately the same length.	___	___
e. Unless the directions specify otherwise, the items call for only one answer.	___	___

Alternative-Response Items

	Yes	No
a. The items avoid qualifiers that give away the answers.	___	___
b. The items avoid double negatives.	___	___
c. Cognitive items avoid opinions and judgments.	___	___
d. The test avoids a consistent pattern of response.	___	___

Rearrangement Items

	Yes	No
a. The responses are approximately the same length, where possible.	___	___
b. The responses for each item are scrambled so that correct responses do not follow each other.	___	___
c. The test avoids patterns of response.	___	___

Matching Items

	Yes	No
a. For each item there is at least one more response than stimuli.	___	___
b. Stimuli and matching responses are on different lines.	___	___
c. Each item is complete on one page.	___	___
d. The test avoids patterns of response.	___	___

NOTES

1. Jim Patterson and Peter Kim, *The Day America Told the Truth: What People Really Think about Everything That Really Matters* (New York: Prentice Hall, 1991).
2. Michael Scriven, "The Methodology of Evaluation," *AERA Monograph Series on Evaluation: Perspectives of Curriculum Evaluation*, no. 1 (Chicago: Rand McNally, 1967), pp. 56–57. Made available from Xerox University Microfilms, 300 North Zeeb Road, Ann Arbor, Mich. 48106.
3. Ibid., p. 57.
4. Benjamin S. Bloom, J. Thomas Hastings, and George F. Madaus, *Handbook on Formative and Summative Evaluation of Student Learning* (New York: McGraw-Hill, 1971), p. 53.
5. Ibid., p. 54.
6. Ibid.
7. Ibid.
8. Ibid.
9. Ibid., p. 46.
10. See "The National Goals—Putting Education Back on the Road," *Phi Delta Kappan* 72, no. 4 (December 1990): 259–314.
11. No Child Left Behind. Available online at www.ed.gov or www.nclb.gov.
12. California State Board of Education, *Content Standards, Mathematics, Grade Three* (Sacramento, Calif.: California Department of Education, 2006). See Web site http://www.cde.ca.gov/be/st/ss/mthgrade3.asp, retrieved September 25, 2006.

13. Robert A. Spies, Barbara S. Plake, and Linda L. Murphy, eds., *Mental Measurement Yearbook*, Vol. 16 (Lincoln, Neb.: Buros Institute of Mental Measurements, University of Nebraska–Lincoln, 2005).
14. Bloom, Hastings, and Madaus, *Handbook*, p. 46.

BIBLIOGRAPHY

ANDERSON, LORIN W., and DAVID R. KRATHWOHL, eds. *A Taxonomy for Learning, Teaching, and Assessing: A Revision of Bloom's Educational Objectives.* New York: Longman, 2001.

ARMSTRONG, THOMAS. *Multiple Intelligences in the Classroom*, 2nd ed. Alexandria, Va.: Association for Supervision and Curriculum Development, 2000.

BARON, MARK A., and FLOYD BOSCHEE. *Authentic Assessment.* Arlington, Va.: American Association of School Administrators, 1997.

BECKER, WESLEY C., SIEGFRIED ENGELMANN, and DON R. THOMAS. *Teaching 3: Evaluation.* Chicago: Science Research Associates, 1975.

BLOOM, BENJAMIN S., J. THOMAS HASTINGS, and GEORGE F. MADAUS. *Handbook on Formative and Summative Evaluation of Student Learning.* New York: McGraw-Hill, 1971.

BLOOM, BENJAMIN S., GEORGE F. MADAUS, and J. THOMAS HASTINGS. *Evaluation to Improve Learning.* New York: McGraw-Hill, 1981.

BUSHWELLER, KEVIN. "Teaching to the Test." *American School Board Journal* 184 (September 1997): 20–25.

California State Board of Education. *Content Standards, Mathematics, Grade Three.* Sacramento, Calif.: California Department of Education, 2006. Retrieved September 25, 2006, from http://www.cde.ca.gov/be/st/ss/mthgrade3.asp.

CAWELTI, GORDON, ed. *Handbook of Research on Improving Student Achievement*, 2nd ed. Arlington, Va.: Educational Research Service, 1999.

CHASE, ELAINE, DAVID W. MUTTER, and W. RANDOLPH NICHOLS. *Program Evaluation* 186 (August 1999): 26–28.

GAY, L. R., GEOFFREY E. MILLS, and PETER AIRASIAN. *Educational Research: Competencies for Analysis and Applications*, 8th ed. Upper Saddle River, N.J.: Prentice Hall, 2006.

GRONLUND, NORMAN E. *Constructing Achievement Tests*, 3rd ed. Englewood Cliffs, N.J.: Prentice Hall, 1982.
——— *Preparing Criterion-Referenced Tests for Classroom Instruction.* New York: Macmillan, 1973.

GRONLUND, NORMAN E., and ROBERT L. LINN. *Measurement and Evaluation in Teaching*, 6th ed. New York: Macmillan, 1990.

HARROW, A. J. *A Taxonomy of the Psychomotor Domain: A Guide for Developing Behavioral Objectives.* White Plains, N. Y.: Longman, 1972.

JACOBS, HEIDI HAYES. *Mapping the Big Picture: Integrating Curriculum and Assessment, K–12.* Alexandria, Va.: Association for Supervision and Curriculum Development, 1997.

LINN, ROBERT L., and NORMAN E. GRONLUND. *Measurement and Assessment in Teaching*, 9th ed. Upper Saddle River, N.J.: Prentice Hall, 2005.

MARZANO, ROBERT J. *Designing a New Taxonomy of Educational Objectives.* Thousand Oaks, Calif.: Corwin Press, 2001.

MILLS, RICHARD. "Portfolios: An Exciting Angle on Student Performance." *School Administrator* 46 (December 1989): 8–11.

POPHAM, W. JAMES, and EVA L. BAKER. *Systematic Instruction.* Englewood Cliffs, N.J.: Prentice Hall, 1970.

"Reporting What Students Are Learning." *Educational Leadership* 52 (October 1994): 4–58.

SCRIVEN, MICHAEL. "The Methodology of Evaluation." *AERA Monograph Series on Evaluation: Perspectives of Curriculum Evaluation*, no. 1. Chicago: Rand McNally, 1967.

SIMON, SIDNEY B., and JAMES A. BELLANCA, eds. *Degrading the Grading Myths: A Primer of Alternatives to Grades and Marks.* Washington, D.C.: Association for Supervision and Curriculum Development, 1976.

SIMPSON, ELIZABETH J. "The Classification of Educational Objectives in the Psychomotor Domain." in *The Psychomotor Domain* 3, 43–56. Washington, D.C.: Gryphon House, 1972.

SPIES, ROBERT A., BARBARA S. PLAKE, and LINDA L. MURPHY, eds. *Mental Measurement Yearbook*, Vol. 16. Lincoln, Neb.: Buros Institute of Mental Measurements, University of Nebraska-Lincoln, 2005.

TENBRINK, TERRY. "Evaluation." In *Classroom Teaching Skills: A Handbook*, 4th ed. , ed. JAMES COOPER, pp. 337–76. Lexington, Mass.: D. C. Heath, 1990.

TOMBARI, MARTIN L., and GARY D. BORICH. *Authentic Assessment in the Classroom: Applications and Practice.* Upper Saddle River, N.J.: Merrill, 1999.

TYLER, RALPH W., ROBERT M. GAGNÉ, and MICHAEL SCRIVEN. "Perspectives of Curriculum Evaluation." *AERA Monograph Series on Curriculum Evaluation,* no. 1. Chicago: Rand McNally, 1967.

"Using Performance Assessment. Using Portfolios." *Educational Leadership* 49 (May 1992): 8–78.

VIDEOTAPES

Developing Performance Assessments. 1996. Sixty-minute videotape and a Facilitator's Guide focus on the development and use of creative performance tasks teachers are using. Viewers will learn how to design measurable performance tasks. Association for Supervision and Curriculum Development, 1703 North Beauregard Street, Alexandria, Va. 22311-1714. (800) 933-2723. www.ascd.org.

Good Morning Miss Toliver. 1993. One twenty-seven-minute videotape that looks at how Kay Toliver combines math and communication arts skills to inspire and her students. FASE Productions, 4801 Wiltshire Boulevard, Suite 215, Los Angeles, Calif. 90010. (800) 404–3273. www.fasenet.org.

Using Classroom Assessment to Guide Instruction. 2002. Three thirty-minute videotapes and a Facilitator's Guide. Association for Supervision and Curriculum Development, 1703 North Beauregard Street, Alexandria, Va. 22311-1714. (800) 933-2723. www.ascd.org.

LEADERSHIP IN CURRICULUM DEVELOPMENT

Elizabeth Crews/Stock, Boston

CHAPTER 7

HELPING TEACHERS PLAN AND IMPLEMENT CURRICULA

OBJECTIVES

After studying Chapter 7 you should be able to accomplish the following objectives:

1. Draw or describe your preferred model for curriculum development.
2. Draft a statement of philosophy and aims suitable for submission to a faculty committee for its consideration and revision.
3. Distinguish among aims, curriculum goals, and curriculum objectives.
4. Write curriculum goals and curriculum objectives.
5. Describe and apply the Tyler Rationale.
6. Distinguish between a comprehensive approach to curriculum development and a problem-centered approach.
7. Construct an outline for a curriculum guide.
8. Construct an outline for a course of study.
9. Construct an outline for a resource unit.
10. Explain what is meant by scope of the curriculum and how scope is determined.
11. Explain what is meant by sequence of the curriculum and how sequence is determined.
12. Explain what is meant by balance in the curriculum and how balance is achieved.
13. Distinguish between curriculum goals and objectives and instructional goals and objectives.
14. Describe how to organize a school and/or school system for curriculum development.

A MODEL FOR CURRICULUM DEVELOPMENT

The first chapter of this book described the three fold responsibilities of the supervisor: *instructional development*, *curriculum development*, and *staff development*. Chapters 7 and 8 explore the responsibilities of the supervisor in assisting teachers with the complex undertaking called curriculum development.[1] Part of the complexity is semantic: The word *curriculum* has different meanings to different people. To some, the curriculum consists of all the experiences children undergo wherever they may be: in school, at home, or on the street. To others, the curriculum is a set of subjects that children "take." To compound the semantic problem further, some educators call a written curriculum plan a curriculum. When they write curriculum guides, they say they are "writing a curriculum."

Part of the complexity of curriculum development is also substantive: Although we can read and design curriculum plans and guides, what we see are in reality manifestations of the curriculum, not the curriculum itself. The curriculum itself is a concept—a planned concept—and observing a curriculum in action, as opposed to examining a curriculum plan that is to be put into action, reveals not curriculum but instruction.

Instruction—whether in the classroom or in extra-class activity, whether in the guidance office or in the media center—is the means of putting the curriculum into action. Furthermore, attempting to observe a curriculum reveals only parts of the whole—those parts within a particular classroom or department or subject or level—not the grand design. Curriculum goes beyond immediate space and time, making it a difficult concept with which to work.

Working with the curriculum is difficult also because it usually involves more than one person. A successful curriculum requires an interdependent working relationship among all school personnel and cooperative planning for that relationship.

The word *development* tacked onto *curriculum* compounds the pedagogical problem. What is curriculum development? How do you develop a curriculum? Who develops a curriculum? What does a curriculum look like after it is developed? When is a curriculum fully developed? Is there such a thing as an underdeveloped curriculum? Although these questions are pertinent, they are not easy to answer if we wish to go beyond superficiality. The answers to these questions in the literature may offer semantic difficulties, which stand as barriers to clear communication. Specialists in the field of curriculum talk and write about *curriculum development*, *curriculum planning*, *curriculum improvement*, *curriculum construction*, *curriculum reform*, *curriculum change*, and *curriculum evaluation*. All these terms are, of course, interrelated but not necessarily synonymous.

Although it is apparent that the authors of this text believe that curriculum development is vital in today's schools, we might note parenthetically that some curriculum theorists have taken the position that the age of "curriculum development" is over.[2]

Before examining the theme of curriculum development and the respective roles of supervisor and teachers in the task of curriculum development, let us define the terms *curriculum* and *curriculum development* to provide a frame of reference for subsequent discussion. By *curriculum* we mean those experiences of children that come under the supervision of the school. Included in the concept of curriculum as described in this textbook are (1) all in-school experiences, including classroom learning experiences; student activities; use of the media center, laboratories, learning resource centers, physical education facilities assemblies, cafeteria; and social functions; and (2) out-of-school learning experiences directed by the school, including homework, field trips, and use of community resources.

Curriculum development, as perceived in this text, is a joint endeavor involving all school personnel, parents, other lay citizens, students, and indeed members of the local, state, and national political structures, but with primary responsibilities resting on curriculum specialists/supervisors and teachers. In the literature, *curriculum development* and *curriculum improvement* are used synonymously, and they are used virtually interchangeably in this book as well. If we were to make a slight distinction between the two, development might be conceptualized as planning at the initial stages; then, once a curricular plan is instituted, continuous development is curriculum improvement.

In definitions of *curriculum development*, the manner in which portions of the curriculum will be taught is not typically included. The question of how takes us into curriculum's companion field—instruction. Of course, curriculum and instruction cannot really be separated in practice. This text gives separate attention to curriculum and instruction, but this can be done for purposes of analysis only. Without a curriculum, there can be no instruction; without instruction, a curriculum is lifeless. The intimate relationship between curriculum and instruction underscores the need for the supervisor to work in both the instructional development and curriculum development domains. Neither curriculum nor instruction is subordinate to the other. Both are equally important, and the supervisor has a responsibility to help teachers with improvement of both.

Curriculum development involves an almost continuous process of decision making. Teachers are engaged in this process when they attempt to answer questions such as these:

- What training should we offer in the use of technological aids?
- At what grade level should we start a program in use of computers?
- When do we introduce fractions?
- Which exploratory experiences should we provide in the middle school?
- Is vocational agriculture needed in this community?
- Should geometry precede intermediate algebra?
- Where should we begin study of foreign languages?
- How much time should we devote to study of the American Revolution?
- How many years of science should we require for graduation from our high school?
- What experiences essential to young people are omitted from our curriculum?
- Should our curriculum be subject-centered or child-centered?
- Are we providing experiences for the development of self-discipline on the part of the learner?
- Shall we add sexuality education to the curriculum?
- Shall we add drug education (e.g., DARE) to the curriculum?
- Are there enough carryover sports in the physical education program?
- For what jobs in the community should our vocational program prepare young people?
- What program should we offer for children whose native language is other than English?
- Does our curriculum incorporate multicultural education?
- Should boys take a course in homemaking?
- Do elementary school students need the services of a guidance counselor?
- Do we have a balance between general education and specialized education in the curriculum?
- Should elementary school students develop skills in word processing?
- Are we identifying and responding to the health needs of our students?
- Should we separate exceptional children and put them into special classes?
- Should we adopt a continuous progress or nongraded plan?
- What kinds of musical experiences are appropriate for elementary school children?
- Are we providing opportunities for creative expression by students?

The foregoing questions exemplify the hundred kinds of issues a school system must address if its curriculum is not to remain dormant. Some of the questions must be asked repeatedly, for curriculum development is a continuous, unending process. You will note that arguments can develop over almost any of these questions. Controversy can become heated when the public and the public's political representatives weigh in on issues such as prayer in the schools and the use of books to which some individuals or groups object. The answer to a curriculum question at one time may not suffice at another time. Circumstances change, and the curriculum must change to reflect the new circumstances.

Most of the foregoing illustrative questions involve decision making by groups of teachers, sometimes the total faculty of a school, and often the faculties of all schools in a particular school system. Many of the questions are interdisciplinary in nature and call for input from many grades and fields of study.

These kinds of questions require prolonged study before decisions can be reached. Whereas instructional methods can be altered on short notice, curriculum changes take time—to examine, to make decisions, to implement, and to evaluate. Consequently, curriculum development is oriented toward the future. Improvements desired for next year or the year after should be studied this year. Some of the curriculum problems that schools encounter arise because faculties may rush into curriculum change before adequately studying all its ramifications.

Curriculum development is normally a group undertaking. This does not mean that the individual teacher does not become involved in curriculum improvement within his or her own grade level or subject. The individual teacher must make many curriculum decisions. He or she must decide what limitations will be placed on the content chosen and in what order to present units. He or she must make sure that the content not only is relevant but also interrelates with previous study and future study by the students.

When curriculum decisions cross discipline lines, as they often do, a group of teachers under the leadership of a supervisor must conduct a study of the curriculum problems and make recommendations to the faculty and administration for changes they deem desirable. Teachers group and regroup depending on the nature of the curriculum problem under study. The problem of choosing an elementary school reading program will certainly involve all elementary school teachers in a particular school and will probably involve all elementary school teachers in the entire school system. The formation of a group that represents all teachers concerned with a problem is usually the means by which curriculum development is initiated.

Depending on the nature of the problem and the extent of its effect, curriculum development may be carried on by a building supervisor or a central-office supervisor with the faculty or segments of the faculty of a particular school, or by a central-office supervisor with the faculties of all schools of a particular level or levels throughout a school district. If a problem is localized in one particular school, curriculum development may be confined to that school. If, however, a problem and its solution will affect teachers and students in more than one school, curriculum development must proceed on a districtwide rather than a schoolwide basis. In practice, teachers and supervisors frequently and continuously engage in schoolwide and districtwide curriculum development.

For example, the questions of what language arts experiences should be taught in a secondary school language arts program and the sequence in which the experiences should be programmed are appropriately the domain of the language arts faculty of that school and other schools in the district. Decisions on these matters may be made in consultation with the appropriate supervisors, such as the team leader, grade coordinator, department head, assistant principal for curriculum, supervisor of language arts, director of instruction, assistant superintendent for curriculum and instruction, and appropriate administrators. A decision on whether to require an additional year of mathematics for graduation from high school is appropriately the concern of the total secondary school faculty of a school system. Any addition of a course to the curriculum or a course deletion has an effect on all teachers.

The supervisor has several responsibilities in the process of curriculum development. He or she may initiate a broad study of the curriculum by enlisting teachers in the preparation or revision of the school's philosophy. The supervisor may stimulate teachers to identify curriculum problems of concern to them or may even suggest problems that might be of interest. He or she helps set up the groups and subgroups needed for study of a problem. It is the supervisor's responsibility to provide time, facilities, and resources that teachers must have to perform curriculum development. Unless these ingredients are made available to teachers, curriculum development is doomed to failure. The lack of these resources is a major reason the curriculum of many schools remains static. Teachers must be granted school time to work on curriculum revision. They should not be expected to tackle the strategic problems of curriculum improvement on their own time or without compensation.

Curriculum development will cost a school system a certain amount for released time for teachers, provision of substitutes as needed, and purchase of materials that are essential for adequate study. School administrators must make a value judgment concerning whether a school system can afford the consequences of not continuously revitalizing its curriculum and as a result delivering an outmoded, irrelevant curriculum to its learners.

THE SUPERVISOR IN CURRICULUM DEVELOPMENT

Some supervisors concentrate too much of their energy on curriculum development, to the exclusion of leadership in the other two domains, instructional development and staff development. They overemphasize locating and disseminating curriculum materials, writing curriculum guides, and the like.

Some of these supervisors may simply feel more comfortable in the curriculum domain, where much of the work takes place outside the classroom. By concentrating on curricula, they feel, they can effect changes more readily than by working with individual teachers in improving their methods of instruction. As a result, they may enter the domain of curriculum development and rarely exit. Unless a supervisory staff is large enough to differentiate leadership responsibilities in each of the three domains, a perpetual sojourn in the territory of curriculum development is as inappropriate as a detour past the domain, as if it were the Slough of Despond from *The Pilgrim's Progress*.

It is often said that the supervisor acts as a catalyst, or change agent. In the job of curriculum development, the supervisor helps teachers identify curriculum problems and facilitates the search for solutions. Supervisors stimulate teachers to look at the curriculum and come up with recommendations for improvements. The supervisor is the leader who sparks dissatisfaction with the status quo and makes teachers want to change. The supervisor is also a curriculum worker, one participant among many in a cooperative process—a respected participant, one hopes. The supervisor's authority and claim to respect should result not just from status but also from the credibility that he or she enjoys with fellow workers. The supervisor is not the sole developer and should not behave as one. It takes two or more people to develop a curriculum.

To achieve credibility, the supervisor must have specialized skills. He or she must be grounded in curriculum theory, know what solutions have been tried in the past and how they have fared, and be cognizant of current developments in curriculum, nationally and internationally. Supervisors should be aware of, for example, the results of the *National Assessment of Educational Progress* (NAEP).[3] The curriculum supervisor who is unaware of developments in foreign schools and the math supervisor who is not familiar with international studies of achievement in mathematics[4] are lacking valuable knowledge that they should be able to share with teachers.

The supervisor must possess research skills and be able to help teachers develop curriculum proposals, analyze research, spot biases in research, and interpret findings to teachers. The supervisor's role in curriculum development calls for knowledge of learning theory and sensitivity to problems of society. Among the supervisor's necessary skills is the ability to manage work groups and facilitate their endeavors.

APPROACHES TO CURRICULUM DEVELOPMENT

Planning

Where does a supervisor begin this task of curriculum development? Two approaches may be followed, both of which can be effective. The first, the comprehensive approach, permits a total view of the curriculum. The second, the problem-centered approach, is confined to study of specific curriculum problems identified by teachers. Each approach has its own purposes. The comprehensive approach requires a global look at the curriculum and uncovers previously unidentified problems, whereas the problem-centered approach is a response to problems already identified by faculty members. A supervisor will take both approaches, often concurrently, conducting a problem-centered study while a comprehensive study is going on. The supervisor may plan for and initiate a comprehensive study while simultaneously responding to the need for study of particular problems.

The Comprehensive Approach

The comprehensive approach to curriculum development may be conceptualized in the form of the simplified model in Figure 7.1.[5] You will note that this model with its three

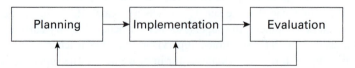

FIGURE 7.1 A Simplified Model for Curriculum Development.

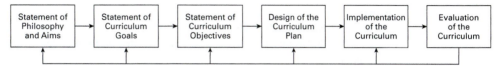

FIGURE 7.2 Expanded Model for Curriculum Development. [For a more detailed, expanded model, which integrates an instructional model with a curriculum model, see Peter F. Oliva, *Developing the Curriculum*, 6th ed. (Boston: Allyn and Bacon, 2005), chap. 5.]

components is the same as the simplest model of instruction discussed in Chapter 3, except that the word *implementation* is used instead of *presentation*. Whereas the simplified model of instruction advises us to plan, present, and evaluate instruction, the simplified model of curriculum improvement guides us to plan, implement, and evaluate *curriculum*. In both cases, we are following the same process, but in each case we are working with a different entity. We could readily follow the simplified model for curriculum development, but the expanded model in Figure 7.2 offers greater insights into the process.

Both the models of instruction found in Chapter 3 and the two models of curriculum development discussed in this chapter follow a systematic approach. Using the expanded, six-part model for curriculum development, we begin by specifying where we are going and what we wish to achieve (philosophy and aims, goals, and objectives); we design a curriculum plan; we put a plan into operation to attempt to achieve the objectives (implementation); we evaluate the success of the plan; and we provide feedback so we can revise the components of the model. The process is cyclical and unending.

Evaluation of the curriculum is shown as the last stage of the model. In effect, however, evaluation proceeds concurrently with planning and implementing. During these earlier stages, curriculum workers design and faculty review the evaluation plans. Ultimately, data are collected and analyzed for the purpose of affirming, modifying, or rejecting the curriculum plans and practices.

Faculties embarking on curriculum development ordinarily work on one of three levels: class, grade, or subject level; schoolwide level; or systemwide level. When the supervisor engages teachers in a comprehensive approach to the total curriculum, study groups are formed that are representative of the entire school or the entire school system. The supervisor must take responsibility for setting up the machinery for the curriculum study and help identify the groupings of teachers necessary for pursuing the study. Study committees must be established that are representative of the total faculty or faculties concerned, but at each stage of curriculum study the total faculty or faculties must be informed, consider committee reports, and react to proposals for curriculum change before they are put into operation.

To look comprehensively at the total curriculum, groups of teachers must be formed across grade levels and across disciplines. The initial formation of these groups is exceedingly important, for they should be representative of the broad spectrum of interests of teachers. The supervisor is seeking commitment from teachers; to achieve that commitment, teachers must feel that they are adequately represented on groups working in their name.

The model for curriculum development implies a fixed sequence of tasks. A study of the curriculum begins with writing a statement of the philosophy and aims espoused by the school or school system, which is followed by stating curricular goals and then by specifying curricular objectives. Each of the statements—philosophy and aims, goals, and objectives, which may be drawn up by a representative committee or committees—should meet with faculty approval.

Following approval of the objectives, curriculum proposals are developed by the representative committees and considered by the faculty; those that are endorsed by the faculty are then implemented. In the last stage of the model, evaluation plans are designed, reviewed by the faculty, and then carried out.

One committee that represents the faculty may provide the leadership for all phases of the study, or two or three committees may divide the responsibilities. Because there is a logical flow from philosophy and aims to goals to objectives, it is desirable to establish a Committee on Philosophy and Aims, Goals, and Objectives, which would be the task force for the first three components of the model. In addition to teachers, who would constitute the majority, representatives of the nonprofessional staff, the community, and the student body (given appropriate maturity level) should serve on this committee, so views of constituencies other than teachers can be made known. When this committee finishes its task, the same or other groups will draft specific curricular plans and will design and conduct the evaluation of those plans.

The first five components of the model for curriculum development—philosophy and aims, curriculum goals, curriculum objectives, design of the plan, and implementation—are considered in this chapter. Evaluation of the curriculum is examined in the next chapter. To establish a frame of reference for the discussion in this chapter, we look at the preparation of statements of philosophy and aims, curriculum goals, and curriculum objectives that are schoolwide or systemwide and not specific to a particular grade or discipline.

Statements of philosophy and aims for an individual school should evolve as sets of beliefs and purposes espoused by the entire school faculty, regardless of discipline or grade level. Sets of schoolwide curriculum goals and objectives should be adopted by the faculty before a committee begins writing curriculum goals and objectives for a particular discipline or grade level. Committees within the discipline or grade level should be established at a later time for writing curriculum goals and objectives that are in keeping with the broader goals and objectives agreed on by the total faculty. Leadership in the development of the curriculum of the particular teaching fields is a function of a specialist supervisor, whereas leadership in the development of overall curriculum rests with a generalist supervisor. The extent and degree of involvement of faculties as a whole in the process of curriculum development is a function of size. The larger the school or school system, the greater will be the responsibilities placed on representatives of the faculty or faculties.

Writing a School's Philosophy and Aims

Statement of Philosophy   Writing a school philosophy is primarily an affective exercise. Teachers who develop a statement of philosophy must verbalize their beliefs and express their feelings about education. Whether or not teachers realize it, the way they behave in the classroom is a direct reflection of beliefs they hold about the learners, education, and society. Teachers who believe that learning should be a pleasant experience behave differently from teachers who believe that learning must be a distasteful experience—like taking medicine—for it to do the learner any good. Teachers also order their curriculum and methods according to their beliefs. If they believe in the worth of each individual, they construct a curriculum and employ methods that attend to diversity and aim to foster individual development. When teachers write a philosophy, they are forced to look within themselves and clarify, perhaps for the first time, what they truly believe about education.

Frankly, the exercise of writing a statement of philosophical beliefs is not terribly popular with teachers. One reason for this is cultural. The United States is known not as a nation of philosophers but as a country of pragmatists; our people tend to express a penchant for action, not thought, and for practice, not theory. This penchant causes students in teacher education institutions to express impatience with courses that they label "theory." The most popular courses in teacher education are the "nuts and bolts" courses and the practice courses, such as student teaching. Teacher educators have long been considered impractical idealists, too immersed in theory and too remote from the firing line. The professional educator has his or her work cut out to convince the teacher trainee that foundations such as philosophy of education indeed have a place in both preservice and in-service education. The professional educator must do what he or she advocates that the teacher do with students—demonstrate that a field such as philosophy is relevant. The goal of demonstrating the relevance of philosophy can be achieved in two ways. First, the preservice trainees or the in-service teachers should at some point approach philosophy from their own personal perspectives and clarify what they believe. Second, they should analyze the ways their philosophies are applied in the classroom and ways the teaching practices they use devolve from their philosophical beliefs.

Teachers often balk at writing statements of philosophy, not only because they are impatient for practical solutions to problems, as opposed to theoretical statements, but also because doing so is an introspective exercise. The pragmatic, even materialistic outlook on life precludes time for searching minds and hearts. Nor is it just a question of the time it takes for thinking through one's beliefs. People would much rather expose their actions than their thoughts.

Teachers express impatience with writing philosophical statements because they realize that philosophical beliefs cannot be labeled right or wrong in the same way factual statements can. They know that teachers will hold differing views about the rightness or wrongness of a philosophical statement and that such differences will produce time-consuming arguments, which they would just as soon avoid. Yet such arguing is the most significant part of the exercise of writing a philosophy. Discussion of profound ideas helps individuals shape their own beliefs. But placing their beliefs in the crucible of public opinion is a test many teachers would prefer to skip.

Teachers sometimes object to writing a statement of philosophy because they feel the end result will be a set of clichés devoid of meaning and impossible to translate into practice. When they begin the task of writing a philosophy with this attitude, the outcome is predictable—a philosophical statement that is empty and dead.

Most commonly, teachers are confronted with the necessity of producing a statement of philosophy in connection with regional accreditation of their school, a process discussed in the next chapter. Because accreditation acts as a pressure on teachers to develop a philosophical statement, there is danger that the task will become an academic exercise done as part of the accreditation process and not for its own intrinsic value. The supervisor should not wait until some pressure such as an accreditation process pushes a group of teachers to set down in writing their philosophical beliefs. Nor should a supervisor or principal ever make writing a philosophy more academic and more empty by rushing into the void and writing the philosophy him- or herself. Although teachers may resist writing a philosophy, they are likely to literally deride a school philosophy that has been written by a supervisor or an administrator and rightfully reject it as an expression of a faculty philosophy.

Teacher resistance to the task of writing a philosophy should not be magnified because the resistance is usually gentle. Teachers can and do intellectualize the need for some sort of philosophical statement. The job of the supervisor is to get teachers to internalize the task, see a real need for the exercise, and give them hope that the effort to produce the statement will be rewarded by visible results in practice.

We do not imply that all or even most schools lack a statement of philosophy and that these statements must always be developed from scratch. Where a statement of philosophy exists, the task of the Committee on Philosophy and Aims, Goals, and Objectives is to review the existing statement, reaffirm it, modify it, or toss it out and begin anew, as they deem most appropriate.

Assume for purposes of illustration that a committee is charged with the task of drafting a statement of philosophy for a school that has never engaged in this exercise before. What should be included in such a statement? Several ideas immediately come to mind. The statement of philosophy should include the group's beliefs about these four elements:

- Purposes of education
- Nature of learning
- Nature of the learner
- Nature of society

The National Study of School Evaluation recommended some time ago a still useful set of twelve items that elementary school faculties should consider for possible inclusion in a statement of philosophy.[6] These items serve as guiding principles for faculties drafting a philosophical statement:

1. Relevance of the statement of philosophy to the larger purposes of the American democratic commitment.
2. Attention to intellectual, democratic, moral, and social values basic to satisfying the needs of the individual and his culture.
3. Recognition of individual differences.
4. The special characteristics and unique needs of elementary school students.
5. Concern for the nature of knowledge and for the nature of the learning process as they apply to learners and their total development.
6. Consistency of philosophy with actual practice.

7. Identification of the roles and relationships expected of the community, the student, the teacher, and the administration in the educational process of the school.

8. The role of the elementary school program of the school district and the importance of articulation with the other elements of the overall educational program.

9. The responsibility for making a determination as to a desirable balance among activities designed to develop the cognitive, affective, and psychomotor domains.

10. The relationship of the school to all other educational learning centers.

11. The responsibility of the school toward social and economic change.

12. The accountability of the school to the community it serves.

After the statement is drafted, it should be ratified by the whole school faculty, and it then becomes the statement of principles from which the goals and objectives of the school are derived and a set of principles against which practice must be tested. Following is an illustration of a statement of philosophy, developed by the faculty of the Carbondale, Illinois, Community High School.[7]

CARBONDALE COMMUNITY HIGH SCHOOL, DISTRICT 165, CARBONDALE, ILLINOIS

A Philosophy of Education

We believe it is the responsibility of School District 165 to provide:

An educational program which will aid the children of this community to grow physically, intellectually, morally, and emotionally, that they may live happily as children and that they may become adult citizens of a democracy, realizing the most complete life possible within the limits of their individual needs, interests, and abilities. Complete citizenship embodies the dignity of the individual and his/her responsibility to the group, both of which can be nurtured best through democratic living in a democratic situation.

As a basis for building this educational program:

We believe education is a growth process by which people learn to think and act more effectively.

We believe in the individual's worth and dignity as a person.

We believe the individual's welfare is dependent upon the welfare of others and all must have an understanding of the mutual rights and problems of all people.

We believe that a respect for and an understanding of the policies of democratic government must be held by all.

We believe that the privileges of the democratic way of life enjoyed by the individual imply a responsibility to help maintain this democracy.

We believe that complete citizenship can be realized only through the development of a personality, characterized by intellectual, emotional, and social maturity.

We believe that we must provide ways and means for the individual to discover and develop his/her ability and personality, in the classroom and in extracurricular activities.

We believe that in our democratic society, an opportunity for the development and mastery of fundamental attitudes, habits and skills must be offered to all the people according to their abilities.

We believe each person should acquire an understanding of and a respect for the traditions, customs and heritages of this country which have contributed to its development and which will affect its future progress.

We believe the home, the church, the community and the school must cooperate to assist young people in developing spiritually and morally.

We believe in providing for a wise use of leisure time that there may be increased pleasure in living, as well as increased efficiency.

The inevitable question raised concerning statements of philosophy is: What if the philosophical beliefs of a school faculty are divergent, as is often the case? For example, what if some teachers subscribe to essentialistic doctrines and believe that subject matter should take precedence over the learner, whereas others adhere to a pragmatic stance that places the needs of the learner before subject matter? What if some teachers endorse the role of the school as a passive transmitter of knowledge and cultural heritage, whereas other teachers champion the role of the school as a leader in reconstructing society?

The heart of the exercise of writing a statement of philosophy causes teachers to reveal their beliefs, and differences in beliefs can make the task exciting. The process of resolving differences of philosophy is the same as the process of resolving any issue where viewpoints collide: it entails a search for consensus. The supervisor should strive to help teachers reach consensus. Because human beings differ, 100 percent consensus may be an impossible goal, but the supervisor should try to bring about as wide an agreement as possible. Only those items on which there is consensus of at least a majority of the faculty should be incorporated into the finished statement. Those items on which consensus is lacking should be subjects for continuing study and discussion; they may come up for consideration when the statement of philosophy is reviewed in the future. Once consensus is achieved, however, and a statement of philosophy is accepted by the faculty as a whole, each teacher is bound by that philosophy and should behave in accordance with it. There is nothing unusual in expecting teachers to act in accordance with a group-adopted philosophical statement; that is the essence of the democratic process. Although every person is ensured input in the formative stages, once adopted, the statement is binding on all the participants. Neither a nation nor a school could function if every individual were at complete liberty to go his or her own way and reject consensus that has been democratically achieved. Those who disagree with majority consensus may still work within the context of the democratic process to bring about changes more to their liking.

Statement of Aims   A statement of aims can be considered an extension of the statement of philosophy. Faculties often produce documents entitled "Philosophy and Aims." The philosophy itself is cast into statements of belief. An accompanying statement of aims, derived from the philosophy, is a set of broad purposes of education. Curriculum goals and objectives refine the aims. The aims themselves are value-laden and therefore reveal philosophical positions.

Typically, school philosophies begin with a statement of beliefs and then draw the aims of education from those beliefs. Instead of or in addition to writing its own aims, a faculty may wish to borrow well-known statements of aims, such as the oft-cited Seven Cardinal Principles. The Commission on the Reorganization of Secondary Education proposed, among other principles, the following aims for secondary education: "health, command of the fundamental processes, worthy home membership, vocation, citizenship, worthy use of leisure, ethical character."[8]

Curriculum workers, in fact, should be aware of significant state and national proclamations of aims and goals for schools. They should be familiar with statements of the past that may still have relevance for schools, such as the principles of the Commission on the Reorganization of Secondary Education just mentioned, various statements of the

Educational Policies Commission,[9] and *A Nation at Risk*.[10] They should also be conversant with more recent pronouncements, such as *America 2000*, in which former President George H. W. Bush and the National Governors' Association in 1989 set forth six national goals for achievement by the year 2000:

- All children will start school ready to learn.
- The high school graduation rate will increase to at least 90 percent.
- Students in the fourth, eighth, and twelfth grades will demonstrate proficiency in English, mathematics, science, history, and geography.
- American students will rank first in math and science.
- Every adult American will be literate.
- Every school will be free of drugs and violence.[11]

Under President Bill Clinton's administration, two more goals were added:

- Teachers will have access to training programs to improve their skills.
- Every school will strive to increase parental involvement and participation in their children's education.[12]

That the lofty goals set at the turn of the twenty-first century are far from being achieved is attested by the No Child Left Behind (NCLB) Act of 2001, passed by the 107th Congress and signed by President George W. Bush on January 8, 2002. This sweeping revision of the 1965 Elementary and Secondary Education Act demonstrates full well the impact of federal legislation on school curricula—for example, setting the goal for every student to be able to read at grade level or above not later than the end of grade three.

The NCLB Act required more accountability of the states and local school systems, allowed flexibility in the use of federal funds, and increased parental choice in the form of school transfers, supplementary educational services such as tutoring, and charter schools. The act stressed reading, supporting the Reading First and Early Reading First initiatives. Central to the legislation was the goal of improving the academic achievement of the economically and educationally disadvantaged, migrant children, minorities, and homeless children. The act further called for the employment of qualified teachers in all classrooms.

Statements of aims and general goals are meant to be universal, applying to all schools within a state in the case of statewide proclamations and to all schools in the country in the case of nationwide pronouncements. Certainly, statements of aims and goals on the local level should, as a rule, be compatible with state and national goals. In making statements of aims or general goals, local school faculties are saying that they believe schools in general should foster these purposes, that the broad aims they subscribe to for their schools and their communities are desirable for schools and communities throughout the country. Curriculum goals and objectives turn the general aims and goals of education into school-specific purposes.

Writing Curriculum Goals   After the faculty has established the philosophical principles and aims to which it claims allegiance, it should turn its attention to a statement of curriculum goals. In some cases, faculties may specify curriculum goals by taking statements of aims and making them applicable to the local school.

The same confusion exists between goals and objectives that pertain to the curriculum as exists between goals and objectives with respect to instruction. The direction of curriculum development is sharpened if goals are distinguished from objectives. Both goals and objectives should be stated in terms of expectations of the learner rather than expectations of the school. Curriculum *goals* are expectations of the learners as they encounter the curriculum and are stated in rather general, nonbehavioral terms. Curriculum *objectives* are expectations of the learners as they encounter the curriculum and are stated in more limited, measurable, and behavioral terms.

The Educational Policies Commission, a body of the National Education Association, years ago developed a classic statement spelling out what it considered to be the needs of youths in secondary schools.[13] This statement of needs, which are in reality goals for secondary education, is widely known as the "Ten Imperative Needs of Youth" and consists of the following declarations:

1. All youth need to develop salable skills.

2. All youth need to develop and maintain good health and physical fitness.

3. All youth need to understand the rights and duties of the citizen of a democratic society.

4. All youth need to understand the significance of the family.

5. All youth need to know how to purchase and use goods and services intelligently.

6. All youth need to understand the methods of science.

7. All youth need opportunities to develop their capacities to appreciate beauty in literature, art, music, and nature.

8. All youth need to be able to use their leisure time well.

9. All youth need to develop respect for other persons, to grow in their insight into ethical values and principles, and to be able to live and work cooperatively with others.

10. All youth need to grow in their ability to think rationally, to express their thoughts clearly, and to read and listen with understanding.

If a secondary school faculty substituted *our* for *all*, it would have a statement of curricular goals—not that it is recommended that a statement of philosophy, aims, goals, or objectives be taken bodily from some source external to the school's faculty. The process of developing these statements is as important as—and may even be more important than—the products themselves.

The statement of the curricular goals is the first step in applying the school's statement of philosophy and aims. A number of years ago, the Dade County (Florida) Public Schools developed a rather detailed statement of goals they referred to as Goals for Student Development. This statement, incorporated into the school board's policies, dovetailed with the educational goals of the state of Florida. Consisting of seven Goal Areas, each of which was delineated with subgoals, this statement spelled out the curriculum goals of that school system. Reproduced below are the seven Goal Areas.[14]

GOALS FOR STUDENT DEVELOPMENT

Goal Area I:

Communication and Learning Skills Students shall acquire, to the extent of their individual physical, mental, and emotional capacities, a mastery of the basic skills required in obtaining and expressing ideas through the effective use of words, numerals and other symbols.

Goal Area II:

Citizenship Education Students shall acquire and continually improve the habits and attitudes necessary for responsible citizenship.

Goal Area III:

Career and Occupational Education Students shall acquire a knowledge and understanding of the opportunities open to them for preparing for a productive life, and shall develop those skills and abilities which will enable them to take full advantage of those opportunities—including a positive attitude toward work and respect for the dignity of all honorable occupations.

Goal Area IV:

Mental and Physical Health Students shall acquire good health habits and an understanding of the conditions necessary for the maintenance of physical, emotional, and social well-being.

Goal Area V:

Home and Family Relationships. Students shall develop an appreciation of the family as a social institution.

Goal Area VI:

Aesthetic and Cultural Appreciations Students shall develop understanding and appreciation of human achievement in the natural sciences, the humanities and the arts.

Goal Area VII

Human Relations Students shall develop a concern for moral, ethical and spiritual values and for the application of such values to life situations.

Writing Curriculum Objectives After the first two phases of the curriculum development process have been completed—after the faculty has thrashed out its statement of philosophy and aims and has adopted a statement of curriculum goals—the supervisor then takes them into the task of specifying curriculum objectives. Statements of curriculum objectives must ultimately be drafted and accepted on two levels: first, schoolwide (or systemwide), cutting across disciplines and grade levels, and second, within a particular discipline or grade level. The Committee on Philosophy and Aims, Goals, and Objectives may be charged with the task of developing the set of schoolwide objectives, and special committees from the disciplines or grade levels may undertake the job of specifying curriculum objectives peculiar to their special fields.

The progression from the statement of philosophy and aims to the statement of goals and finally to the statement of objectives is increasingly more specific. Like the statement of goals, the statement of objectives should focus on what the learner does as opposed to what the school does. Well-defined curriculum objectives meet the same standards that well-defined instructional objectives do. They state what learners are expected to achieve, under what conditions they must demonstrate the behavior, and what level of performance they must attain.

As a general rule, it seems best when writing both goals and objectives in whatever area—instruction, curriculum, administration, supervision, or other—to focus on the person or persons who must perform the desired behavior. This is particularly important in the case of objectives. The subsequent process of evaluation is simplified when the evaluator knows who is expected to do what under what conditions and to what degree of mastery. If the objectives do not show these elements, the evaluator first needs to revise the objectives so that these elements are clearly shown.

Some faculties write their curriculum goals and objectives in terms of what the school—and by inference the school's program or curriculum—will do rather than what the learners will do. Let's contrast the two ways of writing statements of goals and objectives by hypothesizing a junior–senior high school, grades seven to twelve, composed predominantly of a white, English-speaking student body, whose faculty believes the students should have some exposure to another language and culture. The faculty might write a curriculum goal statement—typical of many that can be found—that emphasizes the school's role: "The school should promote an understanding of another culture through the medium of foreign language study." Contrast that statement with the following statement, which starts off by mentioning the learners: "Students should gain an understanding of another culture through the medium of foreign language study." Admittedly, there is not a great deal of difference between these two goal statements, and the differences are not crucial in goal statements, for in practice we do not measure achievement of goals; we measure achievement of objectives.

Let us assume this same faculty attempts to write an objective for achieving the aforementioned goal. It might state: "The school will extend the study of Spanish downward from the high school to include grades seven and eight, making a six-year sequence." This statement omits mention of the learners, does specify the action ("extend the study . . . sequence"), does not mention conditions under which the action will take place, and offers no level of performance that would be helpful in subsequent curriculum evaluation.

The supervisor might suggest a revised version of the objective, such as, "In keeping with a three-year developmental plan, by the end of next year every student in the ninth grade will have the opportunity to elect Spanish, and one-third of the ninth-graders will have enrolled in Spanish; by the end of the second year every student in the eighth grade will have the opportunity to elect Spanish, and one-third of the eighth-graders will have enrolled in the study of Spanish; by the end of the third year every student in the seventh grade will have completed a one-semester exploratory course in Spanish."

Does this example of a curriculum objective meet the criteria for a well-defined objective? Yes, it does. First, it focuses on the students. Second, it specifies the action (the students will have the opportunity and will enroll, enrolling actually being the action). Third, it spells out the conditions under which the action takes place (in keeping with a three-year development plan, by the end of the next year, by the end of the second year, by the end of the third year, and a one-semester exploratory course). Finally, it establishes a level of performance (every student in the ninth grade, one-third of the ninth graders; every student in the eighth grade, one-third of the eighth graders; and every student in the seventh grade). These levels of performance illustrate the distinction made earlier between level of performance in the case of curriculum objectives and level of performance in respect to instructional objectives. The level of performance in the case of a curriculum objective is measured in reference to the achievement of groups of learners, whereas the level of performance in the case of an instructional objective is measured for each individual.

Curriculum goals address the needs of groups of students. Curriculum objectives state what the students as a group will accomplish, specify or imply conditions under which the performance will be carried out, and indicate a general or specific level of group performance.

Periodically, the faculty of a school should subject its curriculum to comprehensive study. This provides an opportunity to look at the curriculum in toto and to avoid the common error in curriculum development of taking a patchwork approach that consists of adding and dropping courses and units.

If there are specialist supervisors available in a school system that is conducting a curriculum study, these supervisors may enter into the process when the comprehensive study has been completed and initiate the development of goals and objectives pertinent to the particular specialties or grade levels. The goals and objectives of the special fields or grade levels must be compatible with the general goals and objectives of the school.

Writing Curriculum Guides   The specialist can help teachers take a comprehensive look at an entire discipline, field, or grade level. For example, the supervisor may work with the social studies teachers of a secondary school with the object of improving the entire social studies program. Writing a curriculum guide that covers the entire sequence of a field—in this case, social studies—is a common way that teachers become involved in systematic study of a particular field or across fields.

A curriculum guide is a general plan for a particular sequence of courses within a discipline, a particular sequence of grade levels, or interdisciplinary programs. A curriculum guide may also be written for a particular grade level or course within a discipline. Curriculum guides are created in a number of formats, one of which includes these elements:

1. Introduction, which should include (a) some reference to the school's statement of philosophy and aims; (b) some reference to schoolwide curriculum goals and objectives that pertain to the field, for example, citizenship; and (c) curriculum goals and objectives for all students in the particular field or grade levels.

2. Instructional goals.

3. Instructional objectives.

4. Learning activities.

5. Evaluation techniques.

6. Resources, both human and material.

We find guides, for example, on Language Arts K–4, Career Education in the Senior High School, and Mathematics Grades 4–6. Teachers develop a variety of curriculum materials or products. When a curriculum product is limited, as it may be, to a detailed plan for an individual course, as, for example, twelfth-grade American history, it becomes a course of study (see below). When a curriculum product is limited, as it may be, to a general plan for teaching a particular topic, it becomes a resource unit (see below).

One advantage of curriculum projects exemplified by the creation of curriculum guides, courses of study, and resource units lies in the fact that teachers not only go through the process—a valuable outcome in and of itself—but also come out with a useful product.

The task of writing curriculum materials clearly demonstrates again the inseparability of curriculum and instruction. When we include instructional goals and objectives, activities, resources, and evaluation techniques in the materials, we are moving from programmatic concerns (curriculum) into methods (instruction). In practice, when teachers write curriculum guides, courses of study, and resource units, they go beyond the curriculum questions of *what? when? where?* and *by whom?* and into the instructional question of *how?*

As curriculum development narrows from study of the entire curriculum of the school to study of the curriculum of an entire sequence within the total curriculum to study of the curriculum of a course or grade level to study of a particular topic, curriculum goals and objectives evolve into instructional goals and objectives. The emphasis shifts from levels of performance of groups of students, which would serve as an indicator of the success of the curriculum, to levels of mastery expected of individuals, which would serve as an indicator of the success of instruction.

The Problem-Centered Approach

Although teachers do not always see the advantage or necessity of carrying out a complete and comprehensive review of the curriculum, they can become highly motivated to pursue the study of curriculum problems they themselves have identified. One or more teachers may wish, for example, to study ways of improving the reading program of the elementary school. A group of teachers might desire to find better ways of caring for the needs of the exceptional children in the school. Several teachers on an elementary school team may aim at initiating elements of computer-assisted instruction. A number of teachers might be interested in developing a multicultural education program. The high school science teachers might express dissatisfaction with the school biology program and wish to overhaul it. The teachers of the primary grades might like to experiment with a whole-language approach in their grades. The mathematics teachers in a middle school, as a result of studying the achievement of their students in mathematics, might raise the question of whether their program is suitable for their students. A middle school teacher of social studies might want to implement cooperative programs in her classroom. The problems that teachers identify and the revisions of programs or other innovations they suggest may be within a particular field or grade level or may cut across fields or grade levels. In either case, the problems or programs are specific pieces of the curriculum and not the total curriculum of the school, nor even the total sequence of a particular field. For that reason, we refer here to the study of specific problems and programs as the *problem-centered approach*.

Following the problem-centered approach, the supervisor responds to needs identified by the teachers. This does not mean that the supervisor must act only as a responder to teachers' needs; rather, the supervisor should also serve as a galvanizer, an idea person who assists teachers in identifying curriculum problems and developing innovative programs. In this capacity, the supervisor suggests ideas to teachers and attempts to stimulate their interest by raising questions such as the following: "What would you think of . . .?" "Have you thought about this kind of program?" "Do you think such a plan would work in our school?" and "I just came across a report of a successful program at a school in New Mexico. Would you care to read about it?" The supervisor and the teachers jointly share the responsibility for uncovering problems and working toward their solutions.

Psychologically, the problem-centered approach has a great deal of merit, for teachers view it as an approach that will help them solve problems and improve programs with which they are intimately involved. As an alternative to identifying a special problem or a particular program, the supervisor might suggest that the teachers work with him or her on the development of a year's course of study or syllabus for a particular subject or grade or on the construction of a resource unit on a particular topic to be presented during the year.

Courses of Study   A course of study is a curriculum document that covers only one subject or one year's work. Some people refer to a course of study as a *syllabus*. Typically, however, a syllabus is an outline of the topics of a course, whereas a course of study includes several features in addition to the topics. Below is a minimal list of elements that should be included in a course of study:

1. Instructional goals
2. Instructional objectives
3. Entry skills necessary for successful pursuit of the subject
4. Sequence of topics or units
5. Suggested learning activities
6. Suggested evaluation techniques
7. Suggested resources

Some courses of study include all text materials and tests in addition to the preceding elements, making the course of study highly prescriptive.

Resource Units   The creation of a resource unit is a still narrower curriculum planning exercise in which a group of teachers prepares a curriculum document that focuses on a particular topic. For example, a group of elementary school teachers might develop a resource unit on Our National Parks. A group of secondary school teachers of history might construct a resource unit on Understanding and Combatting Terrorism. The resource unit provides suggestions that teachers can use in developing unit plans for study of the topic in their own courses or grades. Minimal components of a resource unit are these:

1. Instructional goals
2. Instructional objectives
3. Suggested learning activities
4. Suggested evaluation techniques
5. Suggested resources

Thus, we can trace the production of curriculum documents or products from curriculum guide to course of study, to resource unit, to teaching/learning unit, to, finally, the daily lesson plan.

The process by which teachers study the curriculum and create materials is part of curriculum development, whereas the process by which teachers carry out the curriculum is instruction.

The problem-centered approach should be followed in addition to but not in place of the comprehensive approach. The problem-centered approach permits teachers to take a close look at the trees, but without the comprehensive approach they may not see the forest. Both the comprehensive approach and the problem-centered approach have the same point of departure: specification of goals and objectives. Teachers should define where they are leading the learners before they jump into their vehicles and take off.

Design of the Plan

Between the completion of the statement of objectives and the implementation stage, curriculum plans must be drawn up. A curriculum plan that impacts more than one classroom will ordinarily be written by a committee of teachers. It should be presented in the form of a proposal to the entire faculty of which the committee is representative. When the curriculum change to be recommended is small, requiring no new resources and involving no great changes in staffing patterns or assignments, the plan may be very simple. When teachers decide to recommend a major innovative program, which will involve new distributions of resources and staff, a detailed proposal is necessary. A good deal of study, research, and thought must go into the development of a proposed plan. A full-blown proposal consists of the following parts:

1. Description of the proposed plan, including a schedule for its implementation.
2. Rationale and justification for the plan or program.
3. Summary of the research related to the plan or program, with information on the success or failure of similar plans or programs elsewhere, if any.
4. Human and material resources needed, including facilities necessary.
5. Estimated costs of the plan or program.
6. Plan for evaluating the success of the innovation.

The development of a curriculum proposal is not a job that can be entered into lightly. It requires serious study and intelligent consideration of the many factors involved. It is all well and good for a group of middle school teachers, for example, to propose a program of computer literacy. But what are the implications of such a proposal? What would be the goals and objectives of the program? What would be the justification for offering such a program? What resources would be needed? How many new staff would be required? Where would staff be obtained? What equipment and materials would be required? Where would classes be held? What might have to be removed from the curriculum to find time for the new study proposed? What would the new program cost the school district? How will the success of the program be determined? The supervisor plays a vital role in helping teachers find answers to such questions so that a reasonable and feasible proposal can be drafted.

A school or school system must establish the machinery for review and ratification of curriculum proposals, for an active faculty can generate numerous proposals, and obviously not all proposals can be endorsed and implemented. A common route for curriculum proposals is from a group of teachers to the principal. If the change proposed is within the jurisdiction of the school alone and the school has the resources necessary, the principal can, if he or she wishes, endorse the proposal and it can be implemented. If aspects of the proposal go beyond the school and particularly if they necessitate new funds and staffing, the principal will have to refer the proposal to the superintendent, and the superintendent may then need to seek support from the school board. This route, however, bypasses a good many teachers who might have an interest in the proposed program or who might be affected directly or indirectly. When the reallocation of resources becomes a factor, every teacher is concerned. Consequently, some systematic procedure should be set up for faculty review, evaluation, and endorsement of curriculum proposals.

Each school should create a Curriculum Committee to which proposals emanating from faculty members should be directed. The Curriculum Committee acts as the faculty's gatekeeper, screening proposals, studying the implications of each, ensuring a level of quality, and ultimately referring recommended proposals to the faculty as a whole. This process is slower than the route from a group of teachers directly to the administrator, but it subjects proposals to a thorough and public analysis, prevents rash action, and ensures a broader basis of support from the faculty. Certainly, if empowerment of teachers means anything at all, it means teacher participation and responsibility in shaping the curriculum. A vehicle like a Curriculum Committee is a means of involving teachers in the fundamental professional activity of curriculum development.

One of the major responsibilities of a Curriculum Committee (and subsequently the entire faculty) as it evaluates curriculum proposals is consideration of how specific proposals fit into the grand scheme of the curriculum. All the bits and pieces of the curriculum should fit together and relate to each other. Reference should be made to the school's or school system's statements of philosophy and aims, goals, and objectives when action is being taken on specific proposals.

Involvement of Others

Up to this point, the roles of teachers, supervisors, and administrators in the process of curriculum development have been stressed, but not to be omitted is input from students, the public, and other school personnel. Although the faculty may carry most of the responsibility for curriculum development, efforts must be made from the stage of writing the philosophy through endorsing the curriculum proposal to obtaining input from students, the nonprofessional staff, and the public. One way of achieving this input is by empowering these groups through participation on school committees, such as the Committee on Philosophy and Aims, Goals, and Objectives and the Curriculum Committee.

The concept of empowerment extends not only to professionals but also to laypeople and students. Reflecting the demand to involve patrons of the school and, to some extent, students, schools often look to advisory councils, some of which have been established by state mandate, for help in making decisions about the operation of the school, including the basic question of what shall be taught, how it will be translated into action, and how it will be evaluated.

Schools have met with varying success at involving students and the public on professional committees. The maturity of the students and the availability of laypersons are factors that must be weighed when school committees are established. Nevertheless, input from groups other than the faculty is vital.

CONTINUING PROBLEMS OF CURRICULUM DEVELOPMENT

As teachers involve themselves in curriculum development, they will encounter four recurrent major problems: scope, sequence, balance, and organization. Each of these four problems must be resolved during the planning stage, requiring some very difficult decisions on the part of the faculty.

Scope of the Curriculum

The *scope* of the curriculum consists of the experiences or subject matter or content to which the learners are exposed. The content of every field of learning is so vast and is expanding at such a rate that covering any field in its entirety is impossible, although many teachers strive to do so. Some hard decisions must be made concerning what content should be selected for inclusion in the curriculum and what limitations will be placed on that content. Delineating the scope of the curriculum entails a search for answers to two basic questions: "Who should make the decisions about what content should be included in the curriculum?" and "What content should be included?"

Who Should Decide on Content?   The question "Who should decide on content?" is simpler to answer than "What content should be included in the curriculum?" The professional faculty should make the decisions on the scope of the curriculum—and on sequence, balance, and organization as well—after obtaining as much input as possible from as many sources as possible, including students and the public.

A faculty—working as a total faculty, as a portion of the faculty, or as individual teachers—must decide what experiences, courses, and topics will become a part of the curriculum. Whether the entire faculty, a portion of the faculty, or individual teachers make the decisions on content depends on the aspect of the curriculum under consideration. The scope of the content would appear in a curriculum proposal and in a curriculum guide. As indicated earlier in this chapter, major decisions on curriculum that affect more than one teacher and involve the allocation of resources and staff should be put through the approval process with review by the Curriculum Committee and the entire faculty. Curriculum decisions involving minor changes within fields or subjects and not involving questions of resource allocation and staffing are appropriately the prerogative of the particular teachers involved and need not go through the entire review process. The supervisor should help teachers determine whether a curricular revision should be taken to the Curriculum Committee and/or the entire faculty. It would not be necessary, for example, for a group of Algebra I teachers to submit a revised course of study in Algebra I to the Curriculum Committee and then to the faculty as a whole. On the other hand, if the algebra teachers wished to lengthen the study of algebra from two years to three years, that decision would be the province of the Curriculum Committee and the entire faculty. It is not necessary to involve the Curriculum Committee or the faculty in a review of resource units that fit into the scope of a particular grade or course or field unless a proposed unit embodies content of a controversial nature that might reflect on the entire faculty. Teachers in health or science, for example, who wish to offer a unit or course or sequenced program on sexuality education would be well advised to seek faculty approval, as a great deal of controversy surrounds this area of study.

Broad decisions on content fall within the jurisdiction of the entire faculty of the school or, in many cases, the faculties of the school system as a whole. For example, if a group of elementary school teachers proposes that the elementary school adopt a new reading program, its proposal must be considered by all teachers. On the other hand, if a group of modern language teachers decides to shift the program from a grammar-translation method to an audio-lingual method, the modern language teachers need not clear this proposal through the total approval process. In the latter case, the total faculty has made its input through endorsement of modern language study and need not concern itself with the specifics of content and the methods to be employed. A group of English teachers who draft a resource unit on contemporary British novelists need not take their resource unit to the Curriculum Committee and entire faculty but may make the decisions on this content themselves. The individual teacher also has freedom to choose content, for example, within the resource unit. The teacher may choose to have students read a novel by William Golding instead of a novel by Alec Waugh, which was suggested in the resource unit, or may substitute Golding's *Lord of the Flies* for *The Spire*. In short, teachers make decisions on content, sometimes in large groups, sometimes in small groups, and sometimes individually.

Teachers are compelled to make curriculum decisions within certain restrictions. Some decisions on content have already been made for the teacher. Decisions that have been made for the teacher tend to be broader in scope than those that individual teachers or groups of teachers will make. Some decisions are of long standing. The curriculum of a school was fleshed out by a group of planners before that school even opened its doors. The existing curriculum of a school is one limit on the individual teacher's freedom to select content. A fifth-grade teacher, for example, whose elementary school offers a program in Spanish, cannot elect to toss out Spanish and substitute German on the personal belief that German is a more important language. If the teacher believes strongly that German should be taught instead of Spanish, other teachers must be involved in consideration of the idea and must present a plan through the established channels for faculty approval.

The locality (through the school board) and the state (through its board of education, department of education, and legislature) place some restrictions on teachers' freedom to choose content. The tendency is for the locality and state to mandate certain offerings. A locality may stipulate, for example, that it will exceed the state's minimum requirements in certain subjects. Where a state might demand a minimum of three years of social studies for graduation, a locality might require four years. Where a state might require a specific number minutes of instruction in reading per day in the elementary school, the locality might require more. The local school board, elected by the people of the district and serving as agents of the state, has the power to make these kinds of decisions for the schools it administers.

The state board of education, acting for the state in educational matters, makes curriculum decisions affecting all schools of the state. It sets minimum standards that all schools must meet. It often puts forth a statement of goals of education in the state, which must be considered by local faculties in the curriculum planning process. The state department of education administers policies set by the state board and establishes regulations that all school systems in the state must follow.

The state legislature occasionally makes a foray into the curriculum arena. When state legislators translate their curricular beliefs into law, their decisions are binding on the schools. Thus, found in the curriculum are legislatively mandated courses on the effects of alcohol, tobacco, and drugs on the human body; on the election process; and on the U.S. Constitution.

Throughout the 1980s, intent on reforming their educational systems, states became more prescriptive in what they required of local school systems. Not only did they stipulate instructional objectives to be achieved by students in various disciplines, but they also mandated the processes for assessing students' mastery of the objectives. For a while, the movement toward state mandating diminished to some extent, while at the same time movements to empower teachers and parents at individual schools grew in strength, enabling both administrative and curricular decisions to be made at the local school level. However, teachers throughout the country must now cope with renewed strong state and federally mandated assessment, which, of course, impacts the curriculum.

One other impingement on the teacher's power to select content is the textbook. The textbooks used within a school act not only as a resource but also as a limitation on the teacher's choice of content. The teacher who is new to a school will find that textbooks have already been chosen. Teachers who are already on the scene may have had some input into the process of selecting textbooks. The process normally calls for faculty recommendations, but textbooks are usually purchased in quantities and must be used for several years, as a result of either local or state requirements. Frequently, certain series of textbooks are adopted, and these must be used at various grade levels. Consequently, the individual teacher is bound by the final choices, which have been made as a consequence of group deliberations. The individual teacher may or may not be pleased by the choices made but must live with them for the school life of those textbooks. In some states, multiple adoptions of textbooks are made, and the teacher may select from a number of options, a procedure that expands his or her freedom to choose content.

The textbook is less of an infringement on the teacher's freedom to choose content if supplementary materials and access to the Internet are available. Some schools and communities are richer in this respect than others. Supplementary materials and computers permit the teacher to go beyond the textbook for additional information and other points of view. It should be added, however, that in some cases where these resources are available, some teachers elect not to go beyond the adopted textbook. They find that reliance on a single textbook is an easier path to follow. The search for suitable supplementary and Internet-based materials and their incorporation into teaching plans require more time and more decisions by the teacher. The supervisor has the continuing responsibility of helping in the search for useful resources and making them known to teachers.

These limitations on the process of selecting content—by the locality, state, or adopted textbook—do place some restrictions on teachers. The locality or state may require a particular field of study and may even supply a curriculum guide—usually developed by a group of teachers—that specifies minimal competencies to be achieved by students. Yet many decisions on content remain to be made by the teacher. Within each discipline, the teacher must select topics that go beyond the minimal competencies and must choose the methods for presenting the subject matter.

What Content Should Be Included?   More difficult to answer than "Who should decide on content?" is the question "What content should be included?" Once the curriculum decision has been made that the school will offer a particular program, whether that decision has been made by the existing curriculum, the school's faculty, faculties of the school district, the school board, or the state, the teacher who is designated to present that content has a multitude of decisions to make.

Every field covers an enormous territory of facts, skills, and attitudes from which selection has to be made. Not all knowledge is of equal worth,[15] but school curricula often seem structured in such a way as to imply that all knowledge is equally valuable. The most conspicuous example of this is the traditional high school, which allocates the same amount of time for every course in the curriculum, following the concept of the Carnegie unit, which goes back to the first decade of the twentieth century. In attempting to decide on the scope of the curriculum, teachers must keep in mind one overriding criterion: They should include in the curriculum that knowledge, those skills, and those affective learnings that will be of most worth to students throughout their lives.

The teacher (or teachers working together) is the final judge concerning which cognitive, affective, and psychomotor learnings will be taught to the students. Then, after having made the difficult decisions, the teacher must organize the content into coherent form and follow that organization when presenting the content to the students.

The teacher may choose simply to follow the selected learnings, the organization, and the methods of the adopted textbook. He or she may take the number of chapters or topics in the textbook, divide it by the number of weeks in the school year, and thereby calculate the number of weeks to be spent on each chapter or topic. Or the teacher may adhere strictly to a suggested or mandated curriculum guide and not go beyond it. These mechanical approaches to content selection lead the teacher to defer all content decisions to the authors of the textbook or curriculum guide.

Teachers should inject themselves into the selection process and not be passive agents. They must make the decisions concerning which content is of most worth and not permit decisions over which they have jurisdiction to be made by others. Because not all knowledge is of equal value, teachers must set priorities on content. The supervisor must assist teachers in developing the skills needed in choosing or rejecting content and establishing criteria for priority of content.

This text discusses selection of content in a broad context, meaning the selection of subject matter, courses, or topics, which must subsequently be broken down into instructional goals and objectives from which content within a field may be said to derive.

One way to make curriculum decisions, derived from the work of Ralph W. Tyler, is known as the Tyler Rationale, which has proved to be a popular means of thinking about the curriculum and selecting content.[16]

The Tyler Rationale proposes that the curriculum worker consider three sources of content (student, society, and subject) and two screens (philosophy of education and psychology of learning). From the three sources are derived tentative general objectives (which might be either curriculum goals or instructional goals). These goals (or general objectives) are passed through the two screens to yield precise instructional objectives.

Content is derived from the three sources: student, society, and subject. The rationale implies that each of the sources is important and has a bearing on the curriculum decisions being made. Content being considered for inclusion in the curriculum should be weighed against the three sources, and answers should be found to these questions: Does the content meet the needs of students? Does the content satisfy a societal need? Does the content fit into the internal logic of the subject matter, and is it recommended by persons who are regarded as specialists in the field?

If the content meets these tests, teachers can formulate some tentative general objectives. The teachers would then decide whether the content is compatible with their stated philosophy and psychologically feasible. If the content meets these last two tests, it may be considered for inclusion in the curriculum.

Using Tyler's terminology, we can illustrate the application of the rationale with a situation in which a group of physical education teachers wishes to introduce a unit on volleyball into the curriculum. First, we relate the unit on volleyball to the three sources.

- SOURCE: STUDENT. Does the unit meet the needs of students? Yes, it does. Students have a need for active sports. Volleyball develops a team spirit and provides an outlet for group competition. It is a sport that students themselves have requested. It is also a sport they can carry over into adult life.
- SOURCE: SOCIETY. Does the unit meet any societal need? Yes, it does. Adults have the need for wholesome recreation, and volleyball is one way of satisfying this need. People of all ages can play volleyball and gain enjoyment from it.
- SOURCE: SUBJECT. Is volleyball an integral part of the field of physical education? Yes, it is. It is a sport recommended by many experts in the field of physical education as an excellent form of physical exercise and as a source of pleasure.

Because volleyball has met these three tests, we can draw up some tentative general objectives—for example, "Students should develop skills in carryover sports like volleyball," "Students should demonstrate physical fitness," "All students should learn to participate in team sports, such as volleyball."

After determining the tentative general objectives, the teachers should ask themselves whether the unit on volleyball is compatible with their philosophical beliefs. They should decide whether this unit makes operational any philosophical statement on which the faculty has agreed. It should not be difficult to establish the position that volleyball is one way of appealing to individual differences and interests. As faculties are usually in agreement that the school should contribute to the student's physical as well as mental and intellectual development, volleyball would be compatible with the philosophy of education espoused by our hypothetical group of teachers.

The tentative general objectives must also be passed through the psychology of learning screen. The skills of volleyball are within the range of the learners at their stage of growth and development. Learners would be positively motivated to play volleyball, and this activity would help them satisfy the basic psychological needs of success, approval, and movement.

The unit on volleyball has been successfully derived from all three sources and has successfully passed through the two screens. It is now the teacher's task to specify what W. James Popham and Eva L. Baker referred to as the precise instructional objectives.[17] We might offer as examples, "The student will demonstrate the proper way of serving" and "On a paper-and-pencil test on the rules of the game of volleyball the student will achieve a score of 90 percent."

Daniel Tanner and Laurel N. Tanner spoke to some of the problems of the Tyler Rationale.[18] In spite of its problems, the Tyler Rationale provides a challenging way of thinking about curriculum development and has proved a useful tool in this process.

Sequence of the Curriculum

The *scope* of the curriculum tells what subject matter will be presented, and the sequence of the curriculum tells in what order the subject matter will be presented. Faculties must sequence experiences, courses, series of courses (sequences of a discipline), and topics within courses. By custom, students may not study fourth-grade mathematics until they have mastered third-grade mathematics. But what characterizes the content of fourth-grade mathematics? Some teachers never raise this kind of question. They take for granted grade placement of content—and placement of content within a grade level—and assume that the placement has been arrived at by deliberate thought; in fact, however, placement of content has often been arbitrary. A common rationale for grade placement of content is tradition: We have always done it this way. Surely, there must be a better reason why the content of fourth-grade mathematics follows the content of third-grade mathematics. Ostensibly, fourth-grade mathematics follows third-grade mathematics because the content of the two levels is sequential—success in fourth-grade mathematics depends on success in third-grade mathematics.

There must be a good reason why teachers in elementary school present addition first, then subtraction, follow with multiplication, and end with division. There must be a reason algebra follows arithmetic and does not precede it. There must be a reason calculus is delayed until the last year of high school or until college.

How do we account for the fact that World History precedes twelfth-grade Problems of Democracy in many high schools? Why are the civilizations of 2,000 years ago studied before those of the twentieth century? What makes the history of the school's home state a seventh-grade subject rather than a tenth-grade subject? Why does geometry precede second-year algebra in some secondary schools? Why do students read Shakespeare's *Julius Caesar* before they read *Hamlet*?

These questions reflect problems of sequencing. Jerome S. Bruner raised issues of sequencing when he hypothesized that "any subject can be taught effectively in some intellectually honest form to any child at any stage of development."[19] One implication of this hypothesis is that children are capable of more than they have generally been given credit for. Must first-year algebra, for example, be reserved for eighth or ninth grade, or can algebra be taught "in some intellectually honest form" to children as young as kindergartners? This type of question suggests that two inquiries must be made when sequencing content. One is empirical: *Can* content be placed at a particular grade level or at a particular point within a grade level? The other is philosophical: *Should* content be placed at a particular grade level or at a particular point within a grade level? Because algebra *can* be taught to kindergartners, *should* it be taught to kindergartners? Over the years, we have witnessed the shift of subject matter downward from college to the secondary school and from the secondary school to the middle and elementary school. Has the shift been made after due consideration of the purposes for such a move, or has it been made because of ill-defined reasons like "it seems the best thing to do"?

On what bases, then, may we determine the sequence of content? First, and rather obviously, simple content should precede complex content. Each step in complexity requires certain prerequisite knowledge and skills. This principle implies an analysis of the structure of the discipline and examination of the internal logic of the subject matter. We teach the building blocks of language, the sounds, before we teach words. Mastery of the sounds helps the learner in developing word-attack skills. We teach nouns before we teach pronouns—words that substitute for nouns. We teach concepts before we teach principles, because we must master concepts before we can use them in rules.

Second, instruction must be developmentally appropriate. Content must match the maturation level of the learners. Kindergartners, as a rule, are not ready for cursive writing, and this content must be delayed until children have developed enough coordination to write in cursive form. Content requiring a long attention span must be placed appropriately, for we know that the attention span of learners increases with age and acculturation. Work involving the use of hazardous tools and materials must be delayed until children are old enough to observe fundamental safety precautions.

Third, content that satisfies the immediate needs of learners usually precedes content aimed at long-term needs. The social studies curriculum of the elementary school is often organized according to this principle. Children study the world closest to them—their school, home, neighborhood, community—before they look beyond to the state, then the nation, and finally the world at large. They learn to write personal letters before they learn to write essays, which meets not only the third principle (satisfaction of immediate needs of learners) but also the first (simple content precedes complex).

Fourth, sequences are often determined from the faculty's statements of philosophy and aims, goals, and objectives. Although these statements are guides more to scope than to sequence, they may also provide direction for sequence. For example, the sequence of modern language instruction today is derived from the philosophy, aims, goals, and objectives of the faculty. The goals of modern language instruction are, in order of priority, (1) understanding the language, (2) speaking the language, (3) reading the language, and (4) writing the language. Years ago, reading and writing were the major goals, with little emphasis on understanding the spoken tongue and speaking it. As the goals changed, the content changed and the sequence of that content was altered.

Fifth, chronological order serves as a guide to sequencing some content. History is normally taught in chronological order, as is the literature of certain epochs. This principle allows for a very logical sequence, but unfortunately it is not always the most motivating to the learner psychologically. Why, for example, couldn't the order of the history curriculum be reversed, starting with the most recent events—which would meet the criterion of immediate needs of learners—and working backward? Or why is a more complicated pattern not possible: the study of a recent historical event coupled with the search for its antecedents in the past? What is there about nineteenth-century literature that necessitates its study before twentieth-century literature?

Sequences must be established, and sometimes these sequences will be arbitrary. When two units of content are of equal complexity and when the study of one is not dependent on the prior study of the other, the teacher must make an arbitrary judgment about which unit will come first. When a series of units is progressively more complex and involves a hierarchy of knowledge and skills, the units must be placed in proper order.

The task of sequencing content recalls the necessity of specifying and testing for entry skills. If there is a hierarchy of skills in a particular sequence and if success at each succeeding level is dependent on success at a previous level, the teacher must preassess the prerequisite skills.

When working with a group of teachers on the problem of sequencing content, the supervisor should keep before the group the necessity of their answering this question: On what basis has the content been placed where it is?

Balance in the Curriculum

When teachers work together to outline the scope of the curriculum, they must give attention not only to what content will be included in the curriculum but also to the relationship between the various segments of the curriculum. They must strive to implement the principle of *balance*. Balance implies that no portion of the curriculum will overwhelm another portion.

A school's curriculum is out of balance when the school is known only for its razzle-dazzle marching band or its powerhouse football team. The curriculum is out of balance when children are made to study outmoded content that will be obsolete by the time they graduate from high school. The curriculum is out of balance when it revolves completely around content of the learners' choice.

Although some of the decisions on balance are internal to a particular subject or discipline, many of the decisions are interdisciplinary in nature and must be resolved by the whole faculty. Vested interests play a part in making decisions on balance, and it takes a larger group beyond the vested interests to ensure a balanced curriculum. Among the aspects of a curriculum that require balancing are these:

1. *There must be a balance between general education and specialized education.* Because general education is a main function of the elementary school, imbalance between general education—courses or experiences required of all students—and specialized education is more common to the secondary school. General education equips the student to cope with problems of daily living, develop certain basic knowledge and skills, become familiar with our culture, and develop the attitudes and competencies of good citizenship. Specialized education seeks to develop knowledge and skills within a discipline and is often preparatory to advanced study of the discipline or specific careers.

When there is imbalance, we find specialized education stressed over general education or vice versa. Most teachers have a strong commitment to their own teaching fields, and they naturally become strong partisans for study of their disciplines, which can lead to a tug-of-war for the loyalties and interests of the students. Both general education and specialized education are important, but one should not eclipse the other.

2. *There must be a balance between the academic and the vocational aspects of the curriculum.* The college prep sequence of a comprehensive high school should not consume all the attention and resources of the school. In vocational schools, a sizable portion of the curriculum should be allocated to general education.

3. *There must be a balance between content aimed at the immediate and the long-range needs of learners.* Although it is advisable to begin with studies that satisfy the immediate needs of learners, a faculty is negligent if it builds its curriculum exclusively on children's immediate needs. Children are not mature enough to recognize some of the needs they will have later in life. Teachers must help them recognize the value of content required to satisfy future needs. On the other hand, the appeal to future needs cannot justify an overwhelming emphasis on studies in which children have little interest. Education is both preparation for the future and training in the here and now. The content of the curriculum should reflect balance between satisfaction of present and future needs.

4. *There must be a balance between the child-centered approach and the subject-centered approach to curriculum.* These two approaches have historically locked horns, the subject-centered curriculum coming out on top at most times, with the possible exception of the heyday of progressive education in the 1930s. A rapprochement took place after World War II. The subject-centered curriculum had a brief and intense revival in the late 1950s as a reaction to the Soviet Union's progress in science and technology and has once again surged to the forefront with the renewed emphasis on basic skills and on academics. We need to balance the best features of the child-centered curriculum with the best features of the subject-centered curriculum, and supervisors need to help teachers realize that one cannot divorce the learner from what is being learned.

The concept of balance requires study and decisions by teachers in all disciplines and at all grade levels. The principle of balance must also be applied within disciplines and within courses. A common imbalance in the English curriculum, for example, at the secondary school level and almost universally on the college level, is a heavy concentration on the study of literature to the detriment of the study of the language. The curriculum of a discipline is out of balance when students encounter the content exclusively through rote memorization as opposed to problem solving. The curriculum is out of balance when teachers spend an inordinate amount of time on their own special interests and ignore other vital content. The supervisor should continuously examine the curriculum for imbalance and should lead teachers in finding ways to correct it.

Organization of the Curriculum

During the planning stage, decisions must be made about the organization of the curriculum. We must decide how the curriculum will be set up and delivered. Shall we change existing patterns for engaging the learners in the planned curricular experiences?

Ostensibly, curriculum planners begin with certain organizational parameters: a fixed number of days in the school year and a predetermined schedule—products of decisions made in prior years. What planners must decide is whether to make changes in the present organizational structure.

Some organizational practices will in all likelihood remain constant and probably should remain constant—for example, the use of interdisciplinary teams at the middle school level. Some practices will in all likelihood remain constant when they should be changed—for example, overreliance on the Carnegie unit at the high school level.

That changes in the delivery system can be made and are being made is seen in the examination, experimentation, and incorporation of a variety of innovations throughout the country. School systems in the past decade have, for example, increased the number of credits required for high school graduation. Some of the innovations under consideration are relatively new, such as single-track and multitrack year-round schools. More frequently than in the past, plans for extending the school year from the traditional 180 days to as many as 210, emulating countries like Japan, are under study in some school systems.

Some of the newer organizational practices look to the past for direction, such as the use of double periods or block schedules at the high school level, the use of rotating schedules at the middle and senior high levels, the renewed interest in integrating curriculum content at all levels, and the advocacy of performance-based education.

In some cases, instead of creating new organizational practices, curriculum planners decide to abandon existing organizational structures in keeping with the results of past implementation, such as the move away from open-space learning areas in the elementary school. More dramatically, with the advent of the computer and its capabilities for research via the Internet and online instruction, delivery of the curriculum outside the confines of the school building has become a reality.

When schools are considering organizational change, supervisors have the heavy responsibility of reviewing the success or failure of similar changes in other school systems throughout the country. They need to restrain teachers from hyping innovations until there is reliable evidence that the innovative practices lead to greater student achievement than previous practices. The inclination to jump on the bandwagon of the latest innovation should be resisted. "With-it-ness," though a virtue in maintaining classroom control, is not necessarily a virtue in organizing the curriculum. Some innovations may be incompatible with the school's culture, the community, the philosophy of the school, and the students' needs.

Supervisors charged with examining the school's structure for curriculum delivery should avoid both extremes of accepting the status quo as perfection and seizing each new practice that comes along. Supervisors should lead teachers in deliberate and cautious change.

Curricular Reform

Supervisors need to stay current with curricular developments. Changes in curriculum content and organization are evolving as educators grasp for solutions to the problem of underachieving public schools. Reform and restructuring, buzzwords of the 1980s and 1990s, remain current.

As noted earlier, during the 1980s, reform of the public schools took the path of state mandates that prescribed instructional objectives and assessment of student achievement. Despite all the efforts of the many states engaged in massive reform movements, the decade of the 1980s saw little improvement in student achievement.

Showcased in the 1990s and on into the 2000s are plans to permit parental choice of school, public or private, with some form of governmental aid—subsidies or tax credits or vouchers. Proponents of government support reason that deficient schools will be forced to improve to meet competition from other public and private schools. On the scene also are home schools, charter schools, and public schools operated by contracting private organizations.

Efforts at reform in the 2000s combine previous movements at curriculum reform while empowering teachers, students, and patrons of the school, along with a pronounced emphasis on assessment of academic standards, particularly in reading and mathematics, as evidenced by the No Child Left Behind Act.

Controversial Problems

During the planning stage the supervisor should engage teachers in examining some of the controversial curriculum issues of the day. Among the problems that many schools encounter are these:

- Providing for children with exceptionalities—providing the least restrictive environment, writing Individual Education Plans, and including children with exceptionalities in the regular classroom.

- Confronting the necessity for providing health education to combat use of alcohol, drugs, and tobacco; the appropriate form of sexuality education, including AIDS education; and the highly controversial establishment of health clinics in the secondary schools, which may distribute information about both contraception and condoms.

- Achieving racial and ethnic integration, a problem still unresolved in some localities despite *Brown v. Board of Education of Topeka, Kansas* and subsequent court rulings.[20]
- Creating a curriculum to reflect cultural diversity.
- Deciding on the place of bilingual education in the curriculum of schools hosting native speakers of languages other than English.
- Balancing diversity of values as represented by various ethnic and national groups with generalized, overarching American values.
- Determining the role of religion in the schools.
- Dealing with the problem of censorship of books, materials, and content.
- Eliminating gender inequity.

The supervisor should involve teachers in pursuing solutions to controversies that are apparent in their school systems, in formulating their own positions on the issues, in devising professional means of coping with the issues, and, most important, in demonstrating enough vision and initiative to prevent curriculum controversies from arising.[21]

Implementation and Evaluation

When all the endorsements to a curriculum proposal have been obtained and the administrator and school board have given the green light, the plan can be implemented. The proposal has indicated who would carry out the program and under what conditions. A schedule has been established, showing when the program will begin, at what points it will be evaluated, and when a decision will be made on whether to continue it.

The plan spells out what will be covered in the program and the curriculum organization necessary for carrying out the plan. Furthermore, the plan details costs and means of providing funds for its successful operation.

At this stage, detailed instructional goals and objectives must be set forth by the teachers delivering the content and appropriate strategies and resources selected. From this point on, the success of the curriculum plan is in the hands of the instructors. The supervisor continues to assist teachers through the implementation stage. He or she works with them to put into effect the evaluation plan that is outlined in the curriculum proposal and helps them with both formative evaluation during the course of the program and summative evaluation at the end.

Nothing in the group process for curriculum development, however, should impede the initiative of a teacher or teachers who wish to try out new approaches and techniques in their own classrooms—provided that those approaches and techniques are not detrimental to the students and do not impinge on other members of the faculty and their classes. An elementary school teacher who wishes to experiment with cooperative learning, for example, should feel free to do so. Pragmatic experimentation of both a curricular and instructional nature in the individual classrooms, sometimes referred to as *action research*, should be encouraged.

Plans for curriculum development should incorporate an evaluation plan. Once the plan is implemented, efforts must be made to evaluate its progress and results, a topic we discuss in the following chapter.

SUMMARY

Curriculum is conceived as all the experiences the learner engages in under the supervision of the school. Curriculum development or improvement is a continuous process carried out by faculties under the leadership of the curriculum specialist/supervisor.

Curriculum development begins with a statement of philosophy and aims agreed on by consensus of the faculty. The school's statement of philosophy and aims is translated first into broad curriculum goals, then into specific curricular objectives. The curriculum goals and objectives have a direct bearing on the instructional goals and objectives in each course or grade level.

Two approaches to curriculum development are suggested: the comprehensive approach, which provides for an overall study of the curriculum, and the problem-centered approach, which focuses on problems identified by teachers and on segments of the curriculum.

A six-part model for curriculum development consists of the following components: statement of philosophy and aims, statement of curriculum goals, statement of curriculum objectives, design of the plan, implementation of the curriculum, and evaluation of the curriculum. Both the comprehensive approach and the problem-centered approach have a place in curriculum study and are sometimes carried on concurrently.

Four continuing problems of curriculum development demand the attention of the supervisor and teachers: scope, sequence, balance, and organization. Guidelines for coping with these problems are suggested.

Curriculum development requires supervisors to be familiar with efforts to change, reform, and restructure the schools. Curriculum leaders work with faculties in finding ways to solve controversial curriculum issues and prevent controversies from arising.

The supervisor plays an instrumental role in promoting curriculum development. Nonprofessional school personnel, laypersons, and students should be brought into the process.

QUESTIONS FOR DISCUSSION

1. What knowledge is of most worth?
2. What effect does the movement toward empowerment of teachers and parents have on the curriculum?
3. What do you see as the major goals of the curriculum?
4. What effect should the presence of diverse ethnic groups have on the curriculum?
5. How should teachers deal with controversial content?

ACTIVITIES FOR FURTHER STUDY

REFLECTIVE

1. Write a paper describing the supervisor's role in curriculum development.
2. Outline basic philosophical beliefs you hold about education.
3. Give your own definition of curriculum.
4. Explain the differences between a comprehensive approach to curriculum development and a problem-centered approach.

5. Locate a curriculum guide and evaluate it on the basis of criteria discussed in this chapter.

6. Locate a course of study and evaluate it on the basis of criteria discussed in this chapter.

7. Describe the components of the Tyler Rationale.

8. *Those who are teaching:* List several curriculum problems you believe are in need of study in your school. *Those who are not teaching:* Interview a teacher in a school and report curricular problems identified by that teacher.

9. *Those who are teaching:* Explain the process by which curriculum proposals are adopted in your school. *Those who are not teaching:* Explain your belief on how curriculum proposals should be adopted.

10. Examine a curriculum sequence in operation in any elementary, middle, or secondary school and report the bases on which the sequencing decisions were made.

11. Search the literature and report on any continuing problems of curriculum development other than scope, sequence, balance, and organization. (Suggested reference: Peter F. Oliva, *Developing the Curriculum*, 6th ed., chap. 13.)

12. Suggest curriculum elements that need balancing in addition to those described in this chapter. (Suggested reference: Peter F. Oliva, *Developing the Curriculum*, 6th ed., chap. 13.)

13. Analyze a curriculum guide or course of study in your field or grade level and conjecture on how decisions on scope were made.

14. State your position on the following controversial issues that impact the curriculum:

    a. Parents should be free to choose their children's schools, including home schooling, if they wish.

    b. Secondary school health clinics should distribute condoms to their students.

    c. Intelligent design should be a part of the curriculum.

    d. Schools should promote the melting pot concept of values.

15. Identify a controversial issue in a school system you know well. Describe what, if anything, has been done about the issue and your views on solving the problem.

APPLICATION

1. Select an elementary school subject at one grade level or a middle or secondary school subject, break a year's work into units, and place the units in sequence. Justify your sequence.

2. Locate a statement of philosophy and aims of a school you know well, examine it, and report practices in the school that are in keeping with the stated philosophy and aims and those that are not furthering the philosophy and aims.

3. Repeat Application 2 with the school's statement of curriculum goals.

4. Repeat Application 2 with the school's statement of curriculum objectives.

5. Find evidence of imbalance in a school's curriculum and suggest ways to correct the imbalance.

6. Write an illustration of a curriculum goal and two curriculum objectives derived from the goal.

7. Illustrate the difference between a curriculum goal and an instructional goal by writing an example of each.

8. Illustrate the difference between an instructional goal and an instructional objective by writing an example of each.

9. Check on the process of curriculum development in any school of your choosing and report whether students and laypersons are involved in the process and, if so, how.

10. Research and outline a staff development workshop that you as a supervisor could conduct on any one of the following instructional and curricular developments/practices:

   a. Computer-assisted instruction

   b. Constructivist psychology

   c. Cooperative learning

   d. Core knowledge (cultural literacy)

   e. Sexuality education

   f. Whole language

11. Outline a staff development workshop that you as a supervisor could conduct on multicultural diversity or on gender discrimination in the curriculum.

NOTES

1. For a full treatment of curriculum development, see Peter F. Oliva, *Developing the Curriculum*, 6th ed. (Boston: Allyn and Bacon, 2005).

2. See, for example, William F. Pinar, William M. Reynolds, Patrick Slattery, and Peter M. Taubman, *Understanding Curriculum* (New York: Peter Lang, 1996), pp. 5–6.

3. *National Assessment of Educational Progress*, Educational Testing Service Periodic Reports, Princeton, N.J. See also Chapter 8 of this book.

4. See Ina V. S. Mullis et al., *Trends in International Mathematics and Science Study* (TIMSS 1999 and TIMSS 2003). From the International Association for the Evaluation of Educational Achievement (IEA) in association with the TIMSS and PIRLS International Study Center, Lynch School of Education, Boston College, Chestnut Hill, Mass. 2007 study in progress.

5. For discussion of models for curriculum development, see Oliva, *Developing the Curriculum*, chap. 5.

6. National Study of School Evaluation, *Elementary School Evaluative Criteria*, 2nd ed. (Falls Church, Va.: National Study of School Evaluation, 1981), p. 39. These materials are no longer available. For current paper and Web-based surveys see National Study of School Evaluation, Schaumburg, Ill.

7. Carbondale Community High School District 165, Carbondale, Ill. Reprinted by permission.

8. Commission on the Reorganization of Secondary Education, *Cardinal Principles of Secondary Education*, Bulletin no. 35 (Washington, D.C.: U.S. Office of Education, 1918).

9. Educational Policies Commission, *The Purposes of Education in American Democracy*, 1938; *Education for All American Youth*, 1944; *The Central Purpose of American Education*, 1961 (Washington, D.C.: National Education Association).

10. National Commission on Excellence in Education, *A Nation at Risk: The Imperative for Educational Reform* (Washington, D.C.: U.S. Government Printing Office, 1983).

11. National Governors' Association, *America 2000* (Washington, D.C.: National Governors' Association, 1990). The governors began discussion of national education goals at their meeting with President Bush in Charlottesville, Virginia, in September 1989. See also Lamar Alexander, *Time for Results: The Governors' 1991 Report on Education* (Washington, D.C.: National Governors' Association, 1991).

12. *Goals 2000 Educate America Act*, March 31, 1994.

13. Educational Policies Commission, *Education for All American Youth*, p. 216.

14. Dade County Public Schools, "Goals for Student Development," *District Comprehensive Educational Plan, Fiscal Years 1974–79* (Miami, Fla.: Dade County Public Schools, 1974), pp. 8–11.

15. See Arno Bellack, "What Knowledge Is of Most Worth?" *High School Journal* 48 (February 1965): 318–32. See also Herbert Spencer, "What Knowledge Is of Most Worth?" in *Education: Intellectual, Moral, and Spiritual* (New York: John B. Alden, 1885), p. 32. Reprinted in 1963 by Littlefield, Adams, Paterson, N.J.

16. Ralph W. Tyler, *Basic Principles of Curriculum and Instruction* (Chicago: University of Chicago Press, 1949).

17. W. James Popham and Eva L. Baker, *Establishing Instructional Goals* (Englewood Cliffs, N.J.: Prentice Hall, 1970).

18. Daniel Tanner and Laurel N. Tanner, *Curriculum Development: Theory into Practice*, 4th ed. (Upper Saddle River, N.J.: Merrill/Prentice Hall, 2007), p. 139.

19. Jerome S. Bruner, *The Process of Education* (Cambridge, Mass.: Harvard University Press, 1960), p. 33.

20. *Brown v. Board of Education of Topeka, Kansas*, 347 U.S. 483, 74 Sup. Ct. 686 (1954).

21. For fuller treatment of reform, restructuring, continuing and controversial curriculum problems, see Oliva, *Developing the Curriculum*, chaps. 9 and 15.

BIBLIOGRAPHY

Balance in the Curriculum, 1961 Yearbook. Alexandria, Va.: Association for Supervision and Curriculum Development, 1961.

BELLACK, ARNO. "What Knowledge Is of Most Worth?" *High School Journal* 48 (February 1965): 318–32.

BRACEY, GERALD W. "The 16th Bracey Report on the Condition of Public Education." *Phi Delta Kappan* 88 (October 2006): 151–66.

———. "TIMSS: The Message and the Myths." *Principal* 77 (June 1998): 18–22

BRUNER, JEROME S. *The Process of Education*. Cambridge, Mass.: Harvard University Press, 1960; rev. 1977.

Commission on the Reorganization of Secondary Education. *Cardinal Principles of Secondary Education*. Bulletin no. 35. Washington, D.C.: U.S. Office of Education, 1918.

Dade County Public Schools. "Goals for Student Development." *District Comprehensive Educational Plan, Fiscal Years 1974–79*. Miami, Fla.: Dade County Public Schools, 1974.

DOLL, RONALD C. *Curriculum Improvement: Decision Making and Process*, 9th ed. Boston: Allyn and Bacon, 1996.

Educational Policies Commission. *The Central Purpose of American Education*. Washington, D.C.: National Education Association, 1961.

———. *Education for All American Youth*. Washington, D.C.: National Education Association, 1944.

———. *The Purposes of Education in American Democracy*. Washington, D.C.: National Education Association, 1938.

GLATTHORN, ALLAN A., FLOYD BOSCHEE, and BRUCE M. WHITEHEAD. *Curriculum Leadership: Development and Implementation*. Thousand Oaks, Calif.: Sage Publications, 2006.

HARRINGTON-LUEKER, DONNA. "Charter Schools." *American School Board Journal* 181 (September 1994): 22–26.

HENSON, KENNETH T. *Curriculum Planning: Integrating Multiculturalism, Constructivism, and Education Reform*, 3rd ed. Long Grove, Ill.: Waveland Press, 2006.

HUSÉN, T., ed. *International Study of Achievement in Mathematics*, 2 vols. New York: Wiley, 1967.

JACKSON, PHILIP W., ed. *Handbook of Research on Curriculum: A Project of the American Educational Research Association*. New York: Macmillan, 1992.

LAPOINTE, ARCHIE E., NANCY A. MEAD, and GARY W. PHILLIPS. *A World of Differences: An International Assessment of Mathematics and Science*. Princeton, N.J.: Center for the Assessment of Educational Progress, Educational Testing Service, 1989.

MCKNIGHT, CURTIS C., et al. *The Underachieving Curriculum: Assessing U.S. School Mathematics from an International Point of View*. Champaign, Ill.: Stipes Publishing, 1987.

MCNEIL, JOHN D. *Curriculum: A Comprehensive Introduction*, 5th ed. New York: Longman, 1996.

MULLIS, INA V. S., et al. *Trends in International Mathematics and Science Study*. Chestnut Hill, Mass.: Boston College, 1999.

———. *Trends in International Mathematics and Science Study*. Chestnut Hill, Mass.: Boston College, 2003.

National Commission on Excellence. *A Nation at Risk: The Imperative for Educational Reform*. Washington, D.C.: U.S. Government Printing Office, 1983.

"The National Goals—Putting Education Back on the Road." *Phi Delta Kappan* 72 (December 1990): 259–314.

National Governors' Association. *America 2000*. Washington, D.C.: National Governors' Association, 1990.

National Study of School Evaluation. *Breakthrough School Improvement: An Action Guide to Greater and Faster Results*. Schaumburg, Ill.: National Study of School Evaluation, 2005.

———. *School Improvement: Focusing on Student Performance*. Schaumburg, Ill.: National Study of School Evaluation, 1997.

NOLL, JAMES W. *Taking Sides: Clashing Views on Controversial Educational Issues*, 12th ed. Guilford, Conn.: Dushkin/McGraw-Hill, 2003.

OLIVA, PETER F. *Developing the Curriculum*, 6th ed. Boston: Allyn and Bacon, 2005.

PINAR, WILLIAM F., WILLIAM M. REYNOLDS, PATRICK SLATTERY, and PETER M. TAUBMAN. *Understanding Curriculum*. New York: Peter Lang, 1996.

POPHAM, W. JAMES, and EVA L. BAKER. *Establishing Instructional Goals*. Englewood Cliffs, N.J.: Prentice Hall, 1970.

SAYLOR, J. GALEN, WILLIAM M. ALEXANDER, and ARTHUR J. LEWIS. *Curriculum Planning for Better Teaching and Learning*, 4th ed. New York: Holt, Rinehart and Winston, 1981.

SPENCER, HERBERT. "What Knowledge Is of Most Worth?" In *Education: Intellectual, Moral, and Spiritual*. New York: John B. Alden, 1995. Reprinted, Paterson, N.J.: Littlefield, Adams, 1963.

TABA, HILDA. *Curriculum Development: Theory and Practice*. New York: Harcourt Brace Jovanovich, 1962.

TAKAHIRA, SAYURI, PATRICK GONZALEZ, MARY FRASE, and LAURA HERSH SALGANIK. *Pursuing Excellence: A Study of U.S. Twelfth-Grade Mathematics and Study: Initial Findings from the Third International Mathematics and Science Study*. Washington, D.C.: U.S. Department of Education, National Center for Education Statistics, 1998.

TANNER, DANIEL, and LAUREL N. TANNER. *Curriculum Development: Theory into Practice*, 4th ed. Upper Saddle River, N.J.: Merrill/Prentice Hall, 2007.

TYLER, RALPH W. *Basic Principles of Curriculum and Instruction*. Chicago: University of Chicago Press, 1949.

WILES, JON, and JOSEPH C. BONDI. *Curriculum Development: A Guide to Practice*, 7th ed. Upper Saddle River, N.J.: Prentice Hall, 2007.

ASCD ACTION TOOL

Wiggins, Grant, John L. Brown, and Ken O'Connor. *Guide for Instructional Leaders, Guide 2*. Alexandria, Va.: Association for Supervision and Curriculum Development, 2003.

ELECTRONIC NEWSLETTER

ASCD SmartBrief. Monday–Friday. ascd@smartbrief.com.

MULTIMEDIA

Cummings, Carol. *Curriculum Integration*. 1998. This multimedia kit includes eight folders that offer group activities, research articles, and learning tasks that explain the principles and practices of integrated curricula. A videotape is also included. Association for Supervision and Curriculum Development, 1703 North Beauregard Street, Alexandria, Va. 22311–1714. (800) 933–2723. www.ascd.org.

WEB SITES

Association for Supervision and Curriculum Development: www.ascd.org

National Association of Elementary School Principals: www.nassp.org

National Association of Secondary School Principals: www.nassp.org

National Study of School Evaluation: www.nsse.org

No Child Left Behind (Elementary and Seciondary Education Act):
    www.ed.gov/nclb/landing.jhtml
    www.ed.gov/policy/elsec/leg/esea02/index.html

Phi Delta Kappa: www.pdkintl.org

Trends in International Mathematics and Social Study (TIMSS):
    timss.bc.edu/timss1999.html
    timss.bc.edu/timss2003.html

CHAPTER 8

HELPING TEACHERS EVALUATE CURRICULA

OBJECTIVES

After studying Chapter 8 you should be able to accomplish the following objectives:

1. Describe a model of curriculum evaluation.
2. Choose and defend your preferred model of curriculum evaluation.
3. Describe the supervisor's role in curriculum evaluation.
4. Explain the ten basic research concepts presented in this chapter.
5. Describe the four types of research presented in this chapter.
6. Explain what is meant by context, input, process, and product evaluation.
7. Outline a plan for a curriculum needs assessment.
8. Explain the nature and purposes of evaluative criteria.
9. Explain what is meant by curriculum mapping and state its uses.
10. Cite several general references useful in researching a topic.
11. Identify the National Assessment of Educational Progress.

CURRICULUM EVALUATION: ESSENTIAL AND DIFFICULT

A distraught teacher sat across from the supervisor and began to tell her story: "Last night after our evaluation workshop, I went home exhausted and flopped on the bed. I fell into a restless sleep and had a terrible nightmare." In her best nondirective manner the supervisor said, "Tell me about your nightmare."

The teacher, reinforced by the supervisor's interest, continued: "I dreamed that I was picked up by a tornado and set down in the middle of a conference of educational researchers. They were speaking a language I was convinced was not of this world, and for some strange reason I wanted to associate it with ancient astronauts. Their discussions were animated and from what I could gather there were differences of opinion among the conference participants. I tuned in as attentively as I could, which wasn't difficult, for the voices were rather loud, and I heard in rapid-fire succession:

input	formative	validity
product	summative	reliability
CIPP	context	model
process	t-test	inferential
CSE	Q-sort	noninferential
norm		

"When someone yelled 'null hypothesis,' I suddenly woke up and sat bolt upright in bed, sweating." The teacher looked at the supervisor and asked plaintively, "What does this dream mean? Is there something the matter with me?"

The supervisor smiled, reassured her that nothing was wrong, and then, departing from her nondirective manner, said, "I see four possible interpretations of your dream," hesitating to use the word *hypotheses*. "First, we might have served stale doughnuts at the evaluation workshop last night. Second, we threw too much at the group at one time. Third, you have a guilt feeling—you'd like to be doing more research, but for some reason or another you don't do it. Fourth, the researchers are not communicating to you, the teacher. Since I picked up the doughnuts myself, fresh from the bakery, we can discount the first interpretation. I suspect we can attribute your nightmare a little bit to each of the other three possibilities. In fact, your nightmare brings home to me the necessity for the supervisor to clarify the role of the teacher in evaluation and research. This is a task to which I must give priority."

This fictitious exchange between a teacher and supervisor expresses a feeling some teachers have when confronted with the tasks of evaluation and research. We have seen that evaluation is an integral component of models of both instruction and curriculum development. Of all components, evaluation is the one that is most frequently neglected or conducted poorly. Evaluation is such an essential phase of both instructional and curricular design that the profession cannot afford to slight it or ignore it. Chapter 6 introduced concepts of evaluation as they applied to the instructional process. This chapter extends some of the basic evaluation concepts and applies them to the process of curriculum development. It is concerned primarily with evaluation of the curriculum in whole or in part rather than with evaluation of instructional techniques per se. Making a rigid distinction between instruction and curriculum is inadvisable, however, because the two are inseparable.

When we speak of curriculum evaluation, the first thing that occurs to some educators is testing students' achievement in specific areas of the curriculum, such as reading, mathematics, and so on. In fact, we need to evaluate much more than just the success of the learners. We need to account for the learners' success or failure. We need to know whether and how a program is working; if it's not working, we need to know why. We need to evaluate the following in addition to the subject matter achievement of students in each discipline and grade:

- Curriculum goals and objectives.
- Instructional goals and objectives.
- Specific programs, both in the formative stage and at the end of a trial period.
- Teachers' reactions to the curriculum.
- Parents' and other laypersons' reactions to the curriculum.

- General effectiveness of the school's program.
- Quality and effectiveness of curriculum materials.
- Organization of the curriculum.
- Process for curriculum development and its effectiveness.
- Projections for the future.
- The evaluation program itself.

Evaluation seeks to provide answers on which decisions can be based for change and future action. Teachers employ evaluation techniques when they attempt to answer such questions as these:

- Is homogeneous grouping more effective than heterogeneous grouping?
- Does an open-space program yield better results than a self-contained classroom?
- Is online instruction in mathematics as effective as in-class instruction?
- Do poorly behaved students improve if they are sent to centers for special instruction?
- Does a community service program make any difference in students' knowledge of the world of work?
- Does geometry teach students to think?
- Does participation in a physical education program contribute to improved student health habits?
- Does a career education program succeed in retaining in high school those students who otherwise would have dropped out?
- Is the scholastic achievement of students affected by the extra-class activity program, and if so, in what way is it affected?
- Does homemaking develop skills of worthy home membership?

Many of the answers given to curriculum questions such as these have been based on judgment without hard evidence. Teachers and others have assumed, for example, that the more years a learner is exposed to a discipline, the higher will be his or her level of attainment in that discipline. Another belief is that certain courses in the curriculum develop students' ability to think better than other courses. These assumptions are based on very flimsy evidence. James A. Beane offers a definition of a curriculum that all schools should strive to offer: "That curriculum is a 'coherent' curriculum—one that holds together, that makes sense as a whole; and its parts, whatever they are, are unified and connected by that sense of the whole."[1]

Each of the curriculum questions raised suggests additional questions. When we ask, "Is homogeneous grouping more effective than heterogeneous grouping?" we must also ask, "What do you mean by *homogeneous grouping*?" "What kind of homogeneous grouping are we talking about?" "What do you mean by more effective—more effective in what respects?" The ramifications of questions about a curriculum show the complexity of evaluation, which may account for one of the reasons evaluation is often omitted or handled poorly.

Curriculum, like education, of which it is a part, is a complex system made up of people, places, and things. Because of this complexity, it is very difficult for a teacher to know that a particular program, a particular unit of content, or a particular teaching strategy has made a difference in the end result. For this reason, educational research often reaches such conclusions as "There was no significant difference in the two approaches" or "The results were inconclusive" or "An experimental approach achieved a result as good as the original approach." Although such conclusions may actually be significant in themselves, their indecisiveness has created impatience among teachers with educational research in general.

Preservice teacher education generally devotes little time to training in evaluation and research, an omission that must be addressed by graduate or in-service education. The supervisor must determine how great the need is and what particular training is called for.

One reason for the difficulty teachers have with evaluation and research is the esoteric language of evaluation, which requires special training to understand. Experts in evaluation have the same problem in communicating evaluation concepts to teachers that teachers have in communicating pedagogical concepts to the public. Making evaluation even more difficult to understand are the conflicting opinions of experts in the field on how evaluation and research should be conducted.

A beneficial first step toward improved communication could be a summit conference of experts in evaluation at which they would standardize the language of evaluation and research. The classroom teacher might then know whether formative evaluation is process research, whether process research is the same as process evaluation, and whether terminal evaluation is summative evaluation. Unlike the profession of writing, which requires a wide vocabulary and many synonyms, the specializations of evaluation and research demand a limited, precise vocabulary. Mathematics is sometimes called the "queen of the sciences" because its terminology is precise and its concepts are clear. A hypotenuse cannot be called a diagonal or a slant-line. In deference to Gertrude Stein, a hypotenuse is a hypotenuse is a hypotenuse. It is one of the anomalies of the profession that the fields of evaluation and research, which draw heavily on mathematics and statistics, permit on occasion a looseness of language. This looseness makes it difficult for the teacher, who is expected to be an applier and consumer, to put sound evaluation principles into operation in the school.

A major reason that the evaluation component of curriculum design is slighted in school systems is the lack of qualified people to assume responsibility for leadership in this field. In fact, although it may seem at times that schools employ an army of supervisors, even supervisory assistance is lacking or limited in many school systems, let alone the assistance of trained evaluators.

THE SUPERVISOR'S ROLE IN EVALUATION

Evaluation of both the curriculum and instruction has taken on an increasing importance in the past few years. The impetus has come from two related movements: (1) empowering parents to choose the schools their children will attend and (2) granting families governmental financial aid of one type or another to make that choice possible. The new state and national examinations will certainly reflect on the success of schools in affecting student achievement. Increasingly more common throughout the country, parental choice and such devices as vouchers and tax credits have proved popular with the public, if not with all public school educators.

The desirability of allowing parents to select schools gained national support in spring 1991 with then-President George Bush's education proposals, labeled *America 2000*. The proposals were presented by Lamar Alexander, at that time Secretary of Education, whose education agenda as former governor of Tennessee had gained favorable attention nationwide. These federal proposals not only called for parental choice of school but also for 535 model demonstration schools; awards to high-achieving students; and national examinations in English, mathematics, science, history, and geography at the fourth-, eighth-, and twelfth-grade levels.

The No Child Left Behind Act of 2001 contained President George W. Bush's four basic principles. One of those principles, increased flexibility and local control, gives parents options in helping their children if they are enrolled in schools chronically identified as in need of improvement. Starting with the 2002–2003 school year, parents with a child enrolled in a school identified as in need of improvement could transfer that child to a better-performing public school or public charter school.

Competition, then, has been injected into the picture, forcing schools to examine and in many cases improve the curriculum and instruction to attract and hold a clientele driven by parental choice. As never before, schools must demonstrate their effectiveness. Evaluation is the means of such demonstration.

In the absence of fully qualified specialists in evaluation, the supervisor must provide the necessary leadership in curriculum evaluation and research. Supervisors must possess or achieve a level of competence in the skills of evaluation and research at a much more sophisticated level than that of most teachers. For research to be conducted, the supervisor must have the teachers' cooperation and support. He or she can help teachers design proposals and collect and interpret data and can serve as the resource person to whom teachers turn for specialized help. Later in this chapter we examine ways the supervisor can help teachers with evaluation.

As a rule, teachers are generally participants rather than researchers in the evaluation process. The terms *applier, consumer,* and *interpreter* of research are often used in describing the evaluative role of teachers. The teacher should be able to analyze completed research to discover implications for his or her school. With the help of a specialist, the teacher should be able to design simple proposals and conduct what we describe later as "action research." But for the most part, the teacher should not be expected to be a researcher.

Considering the necessity of evaluation for keeping the curriculum alive and given the shortage of specialized assistance in evaluation, the supervisor must fulfill the role of leader in curriculum evaluation. In this capacity, the supervisor should be able to help teachers in a number of ways.

Research Orientation

The supervisor should help teachers develop an inquiring point of view—a research orientation. A supervisor should raise questions with teachers and encourage them to raise questions about the curriculum, such as "How do I know if a program works or is successful?" "What kinds of data do I need to determine the effectiveness of a program?" "Is this program better than other programs?" "What effect does an innovation have on students?" "Aside from being new, does an innovation have any other merits?" "How can I improve a program?" "What do test results mean?" and "What are the objectives of a program, and how can I assess the attainment of those objectives?"

The supervisor should, if possible, encourage teachers to try new instructional strategies and new programs and learn whether these are more effective than the old approaches and programs. The supervisor should encourage teachers to develop an evaluation mentality and not remain content with the curriculum as it is. Unfortunately, many state accountability mandates and performance standards have dictated the curriculum that must be taught in many subject areas and grade levels. No school has reached utopia in curriculum development, nor will do so, for the curriculum must change to reflect the new needs of learners and society. Continuous evaluation is at the heart of change. Although schools can and do make changes in their curricula without evaluation through a trial-and-error process, systematic evaluation can show the direction of changes that need to be made and reduce the time spent on wasteful trials.

BASIC RESEARCH CONCEPTS

The supervisor should tactfully verify the teacher's understanding of basic research concepts. If the supervisor finds a teacher's understanding of the concepts to be inadequate, he or she should consider some in-service training to correct this deficiency. With more decisions about a school's instructional program being made at the local school level, teachers may look to school administrators who have competency in educational research to help them in their training. For advanced research concepts, they may call on the services of the research or supervisor specialist from the district or university.

Although experts in measurement may disagree, most teachers can function at a minimal level of research competency with an understanding of only ten basic concepts. This text cannot serve as a course in research methods, but it can describe these ten concepts.

1. *The normal curve.* The normal, or bell-shaped, curve is a statistical representation of the distribution of a trait such as intelligence, which is presumed to be distributed "normally" throughout the human population. Built into the concept of the normal curve is the understanding that the population it represents is a reasonably large group chosen at random. This attribute is extremely important when test scores are being interpreted. With a large random sample of the population, the test maker can assume that the performance of the population that took the test approximates the performance of the population in general in respect to the trait measured by the test.

Figure 8.1 is a graphic representation of a normal curve. The tallest line represents the mean of whatever is being measured. Fifty percent of the scores fall to the right of the mean and 50 percent to the left. By convention, the scores to the right are higher than the mean score, and the scores to the left are lower than the mean score. In a normal distribution of scores, the mean score (arithmetic average) and the median score (mid-score) coincide.

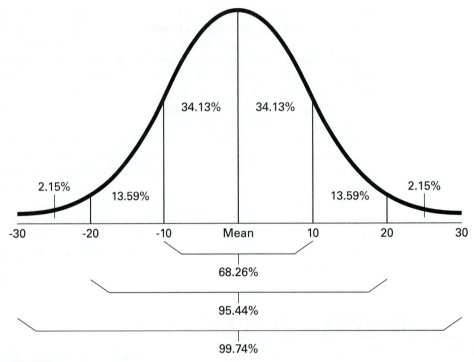

FIGURE 8.1 The Normal Curve.

The vertical lines to the right and left of the mean, which indicate standard deviations from the mean and are represented by the symbol Σ (sigma), show the percentages of scores that are likely to fall within one, two, or three standard deviations from the mean. (*Standard deviation* is the seventh of the ten concepts teachers need; it is discussed below.) Thus, we can say that 68.26 percent of the scores will fall within one standard deviation on either side of the mean; 95.44 percent will fall within two standard deviations from the mean; and 99.74 percent will come within three standard deviations from the mean.

The normal curve is a useful concept in interpreting scores made on standardized tests that have been normed on large, random samples of the population. It can help teachers see how their students compare with a "normal" population of students on the same test. The normal curve concept should never be used to calculate the distribution of marks given to students in classes. It is a misuse of the concept for teachers to decide that 2 percent of their students must earn A's and F's, 14 percent B's and D's, and 68 percent C's. The supervisor should help teachers detect abuses of the concept of the normal curve.

2. *Mean.* The mean is one of the measures of central tendency. It is the arithmetic average of a group of scores: the sum of the scores divided by the number of scores. The layperson ordinarily refers to this concept as the "average."

3. *Median.* The median, another measure of central tendency, is the midpoint in a set of scores. In other terminology it is known as the *fiftieth percentile*. Fifty percent of the scores in a given distribution fall at or below the median, and 50 percent fall at or above the median. Because the median is the middle score, it is less affected by extreme scores than the mean. Of the two measures of central tendency, the mean and the median, the mean is much more widely used, for it serves as a basis for other statistical calculations.

4. *Reliability.* The term *reliability* is equated with the term *consistency*, an essential characteristic of a test. A reliable test should consistently yield similar results under repeated administrations. Chapter 6 pointed out that essay tests tend to have low reliability. A test is unreliable not only when it yields different results on subsequent testings but also when it yields different results if scored by different scorers. As previously noted, the scoring of essay tests can be made more reliable by creating a key in advance of the scoring.

No test is 100 percent reliable in the sense that identical results can be ensured on repeated administrations. When teachers select a standardized test, they want to know whether that test is reliable. To learn this, they consult the test maker's manual, which reports reliability in terms of a coefficient of correlation. The closer the coefficient of correlation, which is expressed in hundredths, comes to +1.00, the higher is the reliability of a test. Thus, for example, a coefficient of .90 would indicate that the test is reliable.

5. *Validity.* Besides being consistent or reliable, a test should be valid; that is, it should measure what it is supposed to measure. Reliability and validity are both essential characteristics of testing instruments. At best, however, no test is a perfect instrument; no test is 100 percent valid. Like the reliability coefficient, the validity coefficient is reported in the test manual that accompanies a standardized test. The validity coefficient is likewise expressed in hundredths, and the closer the coefficient comes to +1.00, the more valid is the test. A validity coefficient of .55, for example, would indicate that the test had only moderate validity.

6. *Coefficient of correlation.* The concept of the correlation coefficient was introduced in the definitions of the terms *reliability* and *validity*. A coefficient of correlation is a mathematical measure for showing relationships between two variables—for example, between two different types of tests, between two administrations of the same test, and between scores made on a test and some external criterion.

Coefficients are expressed from +1.00, which is indicative of a perfect positive correlation between two variables, to –1.00, which is indicative of a perfect negative correlation between two variables. The midpoint of this range, .00, implies that there is no relationship between the two variables. Coefficients of correlation are expressed by the mathematical symbol r.

Generally speaking, a negative coefficient of correlation can be as useful to the statistician as a positive coefficient of correlation. It is helpful to know, for example, that one test correlates negatively with another test. In the cases of reliability and validity, however, an inconsistent or invalid test is of little use to a prospective test purchaser, and the test maker is not likely to market tests that produce a negative coefficient of reliability or of validity.

7. *Standard deviation.* The standard deviation is a measure of variability that indicates the spread of a set of scores. The teacher will have occasion to use the standard deviation in interpreting scores made by students on a standardized test. What the teacher needs to know is that the higher the value of the standard deviation, the wider the spread of the scores. The value of the standard deviation will be found in the test manual. As already noted, 68.26 percent, or approximately two-thirds, of the scores in a normal distribution are found within one standard deviation of the mean. Thus, for a test whose mean is 100 and whose standard deviation is 10, 68.26 percent of the scores may be expected to fall between 90 and 110. By the same token, 95.44 percent of the scores will range from 80 to 120, and 99.74 percent will come between 70 and 130.

8. *Standard scores.* A standard score, known as the *sigma score* and designated with the symbol *z*, results when a raw score is converted to a figure that represents a value in terms of the standard deviation. Use of standard scores allows comparisons to be made of a student's scores on different tests for which the total number of points is not the same. If raw scores are used to calculate means, a distorted picture may emerge and make it difficult to compare scores. For example, what inferences could be drawn in comparing two scores made by a student on two different tests whose means are 50 and 46? The means are affected by extremes, and the comparison is difficult. But suppose we could start from a common mean, say 0, as we do with standard scores; we could then decide whether a student has done better on one test than on another.

Take the case of a student who has scored 60 on a standardized test of business English and 40 on a standardized test of business arithmetic. The mean on the test of business English is 50 and the standard deviation is 5. The mean of the business arithmetic test is 46 and the standard deviation is 6. The statistician employs a simple formula to convert the raw score to a standard score:

$$z(\text{standard score}) = \frac{X(\text{raw score}) - m(\text{mean})}{S(\text{standard deviation})}$$

Applying the formula to the test of business English ([60 − 50]/5) gives us a standard score of +2. The business arithmetic test gives (40 − 46)/6 = −1. In the case of the student's score of 60 on the business English test, the sigma score +2 indicates that the score of 60 is two standard deviations above the mean. The score of 46 on the business arithmetic test shows up as a sigma score of −1, which is one standard deviation below the mean. A quick reference to Figure 8.1 shows us that with a score in business English that is two standard deviations above the mean, the student has scored better than 97 percent of the students in the sample that set the norms. In business arithmetic, however, the student scored lower than 84 percent of the norming sample. This information is much more meaningful than the raw scores of 50 and 46. The sigma score is a procedure for weighting scores equally so that more accurate comparisons can be made than with raw scores.

9. *Norms.* Norms are scores made by the group or groups on which a test was standardized; as such, these scores become standards against which individual test scores are compared, hence the terms *standardized test* and *norm-referenced measurement*. Test makers report the norms of tests in their manuals. The norms reported are based on test scores made by a large, random sample of the population and are generally interpreted as having national significance.

Test makers report norms most frequently in terms of (1) age norms, (2) grade norms, and (3) percentile rank. Age norms are expressed in years and months—for example, 10–5, which indicates a level of achievement in the trait measured by the test at an age level of ten years, five months. This level of achievement must be compared with the student's actual chronological age. For example, a child of eight years, five months chronological age who achieves a score on a standardized arithmetic test that puts the child at an age norm of ten years, five months is two whole years advanced for his or her chronological age.

The grade norm fulfills a function similar to the age norm, but its point of reference is the year and month of school. A grade norm of 7.8 represents the eighth month of the seventh grade. Grade norms are written with decimals and are based on a ten-month school year. By way of illustration, a child in the fourth month of the eighth grade (8.4) who achieves a score on a standardized reading test that places him or her at the eighth month of the seventh grade (7.8) is reading below grade level.

The percentile rank is another means of expressing the relative position of scores made by those who take a standardized test. The middle, or median, score is said to be at the fiftieth percentile. Fifty percent of the scores fall at or above the fiftieth percentile, and 50 percent fall at or below it. The student who achieves the middle score is considered to be equal to or surpassed by 50 percent of the student population and to have equaled or surpassed 50 percent. The student who ranks at the ninety-eighth percentile has done very well on the particular trait measured by that test. That student has equaled or surpassed 98 percent of the population and is equaled or surpassed by only 2 percent.

The norm data give the interpreter of results of a standardized test some indication of how students to whom they may administer a test fare in relation to those persons who were in the sample of the population on whom the test was standardized.

10. *Mode.* The mode is the measurement or value that occurs most frequently in a set of data. The mode is of primary value in describing large data sets. Because it emphasizes data concentration, the mode has applications in such fields as marketing as well as in the description of large data sets collected by state and federal agencies. In calculating the mode for the following ten quiz grades — 7, 8, 6, 9, 10, 8, 8, 9, 5, 7 — because 8 occurs most often, the mode is 8.

A mastery of these ten concepts should enable teachers to fulfill their roles as interpreters of research at a minimal level of competency. These concepts can provide a beginning point for in-service training under the guidance of the supervisor.

TYPES OF RESEARCH

The supervisor should help teachers distinguish among different types of research, with a view toward identifying types in which teachers may be customarily engaged and kinds that are more likely to be the responsibility of research teams. There are essentially four types of research:

1. *Basic research.* Otherwise known as *fundamental* or *pure research*, basic research is normally carried on in the laboratory or in laboratory-like situations with animals or human subjects for the purpose of testing theoretical principles of behavior and with no particular application in mind. Studies of the ways in which animals and human beings learn are basic research. As a rule, the classroom teacher does not conduct basic research studies.

2. *Applied research.* Much of the research in education is applied research, the study of the applicability of instructional principles and learning theory in the classroom. Teachers are frequently involved in applied research studies under the direction of a supervisor or research specialist. Applied research follows generally accepted principles of research methodology, and its purpose is to find the means of improving the curriculum and the instructional process.

3. *Action research.* Many teachers are engaged in this form of research and should be encouraged to pursue it by their supervisors. Action research consists of less controlled studies of specific applications of learning theory and methodology in a particular classroom. The teacher who tries out a new method of instruction and attempts to compare the success of that method with the success of previous methods is engaging in action research. We may think of action research as a type of applied research and as a study of the applicability of a principle or method in a specific situation. Action research is one means of fostering the research orientation of teachers. This type of research has been popular with curriculum workers but has not always been acceptable to specialists in measurement and research. The specialist in evaluation prefers to obtain results from research studies that can be generalized beyond the immediate classroom. He or she also likes to be assured that the variables in a study are more stringently controlled than they are in much action research.

Although action research cannot replace more controlled research, it is a valuable tool for teachers who wish to improve the curriculum and their "instructional techniques."[2]

4. *Descriptive research.* Descriptive research is an accurate accounting of general or selected aspects of a given situation. This particular category of research includes a variety of types of studies in which teachers participate. What is commonly referred to as a *status study*—for example, a study of the extent to which schools in a state have remedial reading laboratories—is a form of descriptive research. Surveys of current practices and of opinions of groups conducted as a part of a needs assessment are descriptive research. A descriptive report of what goes on at a particular time in a classroom is a type of descriptive research that some evaluators call *process research.* Unfortunately, the term *process research* is also used to mean formative evaluation, the testing of a prototype model, and the periodic checking of the progress of a program, as well as a noninferential type of study of classroom activities.

Basic, applied, and action research are types of *experimental research.* Teachers frequently engage in *action* and *descriptive research* with minimal supervision, and they occasionally participate in *applied research* with closer supervision.

TEACHER PARTICIPATION IN RESEARCH

The supervisor should help teachers develop curriculum proposals and participate in research studies. The nature of proposals and the degree of teacher participation will depend on the magnitude of the studies. If a proposed study is to be a rigorous piece of applied research, it will ordinarily be drafted by the supervisor or a research specialist and will conform to a detailed set of guidelines, such as those required by the U.S. Department of Education for proposals submitted to it for funding. If it is a modest piece of applied research affecting a large portion of the faculty or the entire faculty of a school, a proposal may be developed along the lines suggested for plan design in the previous chapter. If one or two teachers wish to carry out a piece of action research that will affect only their own classes, a streamlined, simplified proposal may be all that is needed, consisting of a statement of the proposal, hypotheses to be tested, and procedures to be followed, including means of evaluating. This is the type of research most teachers will conduct.

Proposals for action research usually originate with the teachers themselves—for instance, research aimed at an examination of a school's language arts program. Such questions as "Is there a correct balance among the components of reading, writing, speaking, and listening?" "How does the language arts program align with state and national standards?" and "Are assessments accurately measuring what was taught?" should be asked. Proposals for more sophisticated research may originate with teachers but more likely will come from supervisors or research specialists. Wherever they originate, if teachers will be participants, the proposals should be discussed with them before writing begins. The cooperation of the teachers must be ensured, and their continuous participation must be a certainty. The teachers will need to feel committed to the study. They may be called on to assist in formulating hypotheses, validating the objectives and the instruments, carrying out procedures, collecting and analyzing data, and making decisions based on data analysis.

Even with action research, teachers should seek to validate the goals and objectives of the proposed program and the instruments they will use. The instruments can be validated by subjecting them to review by other specialists in the field in which the research study falls. The goals and objectives may be validated by this same review process by experts or by reference to published findings of others who have studied the problem.

The supervisor should be as concerned with teachers' development of the skills of creating curriculum proposals as with the end product—the curriculum proposal itself. Writing curriculum proposals is one method of promoting a research orientation among teachers.

TYPES OF EVALUATION

The supervisor should help teachers distinguish between different types of evaluation and select and use an evaluation model. For purposes of analysis, types of evaluation are distinguished from types of research. This is a somewhat arbitrary classification, as evaluation and research are closely related. The terms that describe evaluation and research are sometimes used in the literature interchangeably. *Formative evaluation*, for example, may be referred to as *process research*, but process research is not just formative evaluation. We will briefly discuss some of the more frequently encountered terms. The terms and the models of evaluation discussed are worth exploring at length through in-service programs.

First, we will review two terms introduced in the chapter on the evaluation of instruction: *formative evaluation* and *summative evaluation*. Formative evaluation is essentially an analysis of a program at its early stages, the testing of a prototype program so that changes can be made during the course of the program before it has gone too far. Summative evaluation is terminal evaluation; it is conducted at the end of the program and allows the teacher or evaluator to decide whether the program has been successful and whether the objectives have been reached.

Evaluation Models

Evaluation models can serve not only to extend the teacher's understanding of evaluation concepts but also as guides for carrying out a curriculum study. We have selected two well-known models to examine. The CIPP (Context, Input, Process, and Product)

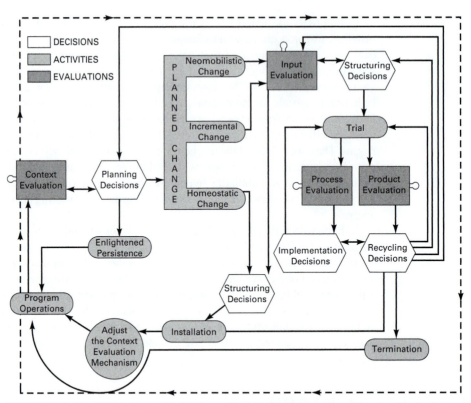

FIGURE 8.2 The CIPP Evaluation Model. *Source:* Daniel L. Stufflebeam et al., *Educational Evaluation and Decision Making* (Itasca, Ill.: F. E. Peacock, 1971), p. 236. Reprinted with permission of Phi Delta Kappa.

Evaluation Model, shown in Figure 8.2, contains four evaluation components: context evaluation, input evaluation, process evaluation, and product evaluation (see rectangles in Figure 8.2).[3] The CSE (Center for the Study of Evaluation) Evaluation Model, shown in Figure 8.3, comprises five evaluation phases: needs assessment, program planning, implementation evaluation, progress evaluation, and outcome evaluation.[4] Let's briefly review the evaluation components of each of these two evaluation models. First, the terminology of the CIPP Evaluation Model:

1. *Context evaluation.* Context evaluation is the first component of the CIPP Evaluation Model. According to this model, the evaluation process begins with an analysis of the context, or environment, in which a curriculum study is to be conducted. It continues with a description of the environmental conditions, both actual and hoped for. It includes an assessment of the needs of the system and a determination of the unmet needs of the system. It also accounts for the reasons that needs are not being met.

2. *Input evaluation.* This second phase of the CIPP Evaluation Model consists of making decisions on procedures that will be followed in pursuit of the objectives. The evaluators at this stage must choose from alternative routes to the realization of the objectives. In making these decisions, the evaluators must keep in mind the limitations of resources, such as available time and funds.

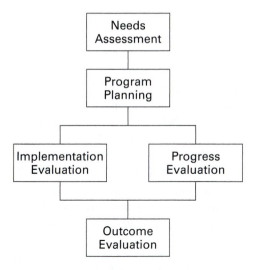

FIGURE 8.3 The CSE Evaluation Model.
Source: Center for the Study of Evaluation,
Evaluation Workshop I: An Orientation, Participants'
Notebook (Del Monte Research Park, Monterey,
Calif.: CTB/McGraw-Hill, 1971), p. A-2. Reprinted
with permission from McGraw-Hill, Inc.

3. *Process evaluation.* The third element of the CIPP Evaluation Model, process evaluation, is monitoring of the curriculum plan as it unfolds. The evaluators look for deficiencies in the system and attempt to correct them. They maintain a continuing record of what is happening during the implementation process.

4. *Product evaluation.* The fourth and final component of the CIPP Evaluation Model is product evaluation. This evaluation is both formative and summative, as it seeks to measure both during the curriculum study and at the end of the study whether the objectives have been reached.

Now compare the terminology of the CSE Evaluation Model:

1. *Needs assessment.* The CSE Evaluation Model begins with needs assessment as its first component. Generally, a needs assessment is the process of identifying unmet needs of a school system by comparing the achievement levels of that school system with its stated objectives. The discrepancies between achievement levels and objectives are needs that are not being met by that school system. Meeting these unmet needs requires the development of new objectives. Note that the CIPP Evaluation Model includes needs assessment as part of the context evaluation phase.

2. *Program planning.* The CSE Evaluation Model has program planning as its second stage. At this stage, performance objectives are specified and a program is selected and prepared. Also at this stage, input evaluation, as in the CIPP Evaluation Model, comes into play with an analysis of various strategies for accomplishing the objectives and of the resources that can be made available.

3. *Implementation evaluation.* The third component of the CSE Evaluation Model, implementation evaluation, is a check of the various parts of the program design to determine whether the design has been implemented properly. This stage of evaluation is an effort to spot difficulties; learn whether the personnel involved, the materials and equipment needs, and the facilities to be used are all in order; and discover whether the program is meeting its time and budgetary commitments. Implementation evaluation is related to process evaluation in the CIPP Evaluation Model.

4. *Progress evaluation.* During the course of a program, the evaluator arranges to obtain continuous feedback on whether the program objectives are being met so that adjustments can be made in the program. Progress evaluation, formative in nature, is the fourth element of the CSE Evaluation Model.

5. *Outcome evaluation.* The fifth and final stage of the CSE Evaluation Model is outcome evaluation, or a terminal assessment of the program's accomplishments. At this stage, decisions are reached concerning whether the objectives have been realized and whether the program should continue. Outcome evaluation is essentially the same as product evaluation in the CIPP Evaluation Model, when conducted at the end of the program. In more general terms, outcome evaluation is equivalent to summative evaluation.

The terms used in these two models are some of the most frequently encountered evaluation terms, but they are by no means an exhaustive listing of the concepts in this complex field. The models and descriptions have been selected to give the prospective supervisor a flavor of the thinking that goes on in the field of evaluation. The supervisor should explore more specialized sources for help in working with teachers in evaluating the curriculum. Together, they may select from the models described here or from other models as guides to the process of evaluation.[5]

At some point, teachers and supervisors should examine the evaluation plan itself. They should ask such questions as, "Are we following a model for curriculum evaluation?" "Do we have a comprehensive evaluation plan?" "Have we collected both formative and summative data?" "Have we used proper means of gathering data?" "Have we involved the right people?" "Do we need to use outside evaluators?" and "Have we validated the curriculum goals and objectives?"

When fulfilling the role of curriculum evaluators, supervisors and teachers would be well advised to familiarize themselves with the standards developed by the Joint Committee on Standards for Educational Evaluation.[6] This committee proposed thirty standards centered around four concerns: the utility, feasibility, propriety, and accuracy of an evaluation. The utility standards address such questions as the identification of the audience, credibility of the evaluators, and clarity and timeliness of the evaluation report. The feasibility standards include consideration of the practicality and cost-effectiveness of the evaluation procedures. Propriety standards relate to such concerns as conflicts of interest, the public's right to know, and the rights of human participants. The accuracy standards direct evaluators' attention to such items as the validity and reliability of measurement, the analysis of quantitative and qualitative information, and the objectivity of reporting. The supervisor should exercise leadership in curriculum evaluation by helping those charged with evaluation of a program apply the thirty standards.

CONDUCTING A CURRICULUM NEEDS ASSESSMENT

The supervisor should assist a faculty in planning, conducting, and analyzing an assessment of curriculum needs. As the name implies, a curriculum needs assessment is an evaluation of program needs. It is a process for deciding whether the objectives of the school are being reached and whether there are needs of learners that are not being met. A needs assessment conducted by a faculty is significant not only for the data it generates but also for the excellent in-service training it provides teachers in one aspect of evaluation.

A needs assessment should not be viewed as a specific evaluation program with a fixed set of procedures that can be applied anywhere but rather as a general procedure that varies from school to school and from school system to school system. Although the general process is similar from locality to locality, the choice of instruments for collecting data, the steps followed, and the detailed procedures will differ considerably.

A needs assessment has two basic purposes: (1) determining whether stated objectives have been accomplished and (2) identifying needs that have not been met and for which objectives have not been stated. A faculty may approach a needs assessment on a broad scale, studying the academic, physical health, mental health, and social needs of learners.

Before it can begin a needs assessment, a faculty must go back to its statement of curriculum objectives. If it has not developed a statement of objectives, this task must be the first item of business. The objectives serve as the takeoff point for the assessment. Although a faculty will specify many curricular objectives, it may wish to assess needs only in respect to those objectives it believes to be most important or urgent. To accomplish this task, the faculty will rank the curricular objectives in order of relative importance and will assess those at the top of its ranking. Although the high-priority objectives will be assessed first, it should be understood that a faculty will ultimately survey all objectives.

Once the curriculum objectives have been specified, the faculty must then plan ways by which achievement of the objectives is being or will be measured. Many data are already available in the school (e.g., in teachers' records, principal's office, guidance office, and school nurse's files). Additional data will need to be collected to supplement existing data. The faculty must decide on the means it will employ to collect the necessary data. Normally, it will use standardized test data, teacher-test data, questionnaires, health records, rating scales, and checklists.

Because the faculty is taking a broad look at the school's program, an adequate needs assessment attempts to gather data from the widest possible number of sources. Students, teachers, administrators, other school personnel, and the lay public should all provide input into a needs assessment.

The faculty should indicate specifically what evaluative data it will need to decide whether each of the stated objectives is being met. Once it has gathered the evaluative data, it must then decide, on the basis of those data, whether the learners are reaching the objectives. For each objective being realized, the faculty can congratulate itself. For each objective not being accomplished, the faculty must answer these questions: (1) Is the objective that is not being met still valid and worth pursuing? (2) What should be done about this situation? If the objective is deemed no longer valid, it can be dropped from the school's statement of objectives. However, if the objective is judged still worthwhile and is not being reached, some strategy for reaching it must be devised—this unattained objective is an unmet need.

But a needs assessment should go further than determining whether the currently stated objectives are being met. The assessment should serve as a means of validating the goals and objectives themselves. Unstated objectives that teachers, administrators, other school personnel, students, and patrons of the school identify may also be unmet needs if enough persons believe they are. A common technique for getting at the question of unstated objectives (or, conversely, stated objectives that many people feel are not needed) is the questionnaire, or opinion survey. The opinions of students and former students (graduates and dropouts), all school personnel, and a representative sample of the community should be sought. In sampling lay opinion, we do not hold with the technique employed by some schools—sampling only the community leaders or the power structure of the community. Nor do we recommend that sampling be confined to parents of children in the schools. Education in a community is everybody's business and not simply the domain of an elite or parents of school-age children. One of the subsets of the community that is easiest to ignore is the disadvantaged or poor segment; special effort should be taken to make sure faculties have gathered data from this source as well.

On questionnaires of this type, the recipients are asked to identify goals and objectives of the school, problems they believe exist in the school, subject matter they feel to be lacking, programs they would like to see incorporated into the school's program, instructional approaches they would like to see attempted, student services they would like to see added, ways in which they feel school funds should be expended, and qualifications they believe teachers should possess. The advent of parental choice of school makes the survey of public opinion more crucial than ever.

The final step in a needs assessment is the ranking of unmet needs. From this point, the faculty begins to devise strategies and programs for meeting the unmet needs.

Objections have been raised to the needs assessment process. Some maintain it is too time-consuming. They feel that teachers already know what the school needs. They claim that needs assessments focus on lacks instead of strengths and that the results of needs are always the same.

On the other hand, the proponents of needs assessments, including us, see the process as an opportunity to involve all the constituencies of the school—teachers, students, and laypersons—and make them feel that their opinions are important. Moreover, needs assessments offer a systematic process for identifying gaps in the curriculum.

When a school system opts to conduct a needs assessment, the supervisor in charge should first gather descriptions of needs assessments carried out elsewhere. For example, a number of years ago, the Research and Development Utilization Project of the Georgia Department of Education developed a needs assessment process that included a checklist of six steps:[7]

Step 1 Initiate the needs assessment process.

Step 2 Conduct perceived needs assessment.

Step 3 Verify perceived needs by objective means.

Step 4 Determine systemwide need priorities.

Step 5 Choose need to be addressed by improvement efforts.

Step 6 Conduct a causal analysis of the need to be improved.

A needs assessment is an effective evaluation process that reveals to curriculum planners where the curriculum is not meeting the needs of the learners. The process causes the planners to set priorities and develop plans for meeting student needs. As has been noted, procedures for a needs assessment vary from community to community depending on the desires of those charged with the task.

The Delphi Technique

Like business and industry, school systems can no longer afford to focus only on the here and now. They must anticipate the future needs of students. A promising procedure for predicting future educational needs, the Delphi Technique, has enjoyed popularity in the social sciences and education.[8] When a researcher—for example, a supervisor—wishes to employ the Delphi Technique, he or she prepares a set of statements that is sent out in written form to respondents who are considered experts in the field.

The statements, which may be developed by the supervisor in collaboration with teachers and others, consist of possible goals, values, and programs. The respondents to the instrument that contains the statements independently predict dates, in the fashion of the Delphic oracle, by which they believe the goals, values, or programs will be realized. A number of experts in education, for example, might be polled for the dates (years) by which they believe certain programs will become reality, such as universal parental choice of school or open enrollments in public schools, provision of computers for every student, and proficiency of all students in reading and mathematics.

The Delphi Technique involves repeated administration and refinement of the instrument and permits revision of their answers by individual respondents, who do not collaborate or consult with each other. The technique should not be thought of as a controlled research study or identification of specific unmet needs of a particular school. One strength of the Delphi Technique is that it encourages future-oriented thinking and identifies the beginnings of possible trends. Another strength is that it can bring about consensus among experts without direct collaboration.

The purpose of the Delphi Technique is to attempt to forecast trends by relying on informed guesses by experts. The best judgments of experts are gathered, their predictions are summarized, and the results are made known to those who may be concerned. The results of a Delphi study in education may cause school personnel to focus on modifications of aspects of education. For example, if a number of educators believe that mastery of the basic number facts by all children will not become reality until twenty years from now (if ever), curriculum planners should stop and ponder the significance of that prediction. By finding the consensus of experts, curriculum planners can shed light on needs for program planning and curriculum development. If the goal is worth seeking (which respondents may indicate) and if the accomplishment of the goal will require many years, the Delphi study says that, in effect, we had better get moving now on plans to reach that goal.

A Delphi study can also reinforce or contradict beliefs held by the supervisor and other school personnel. If the experts who respond to a study believe that cooperative learning will be common practice within the next ten years, they may be identifying the beginning of a trend. School systems that have already planned for and put into operation cooperative learning plans would judge that they are at least in keeping with a developing trend. They may even assume that the trend is occurring as a response to certain needs. On the other hand, if the experts feel that cooperative learning will not become common for another twenty-five years, school systems that do not adopt this practice would need to decide whether they should do so or whether approaches other than cooperative learning should take higher priority.

The supervisor who wishes to try the Delphi Technique might assemble a group of interested teachers and other school personnel and brainstorm with them about possible goals, values, and programs that could be included on an instrument to be sent out to a number of experts. When the items for the instrument have been selected, the supervisor duplicates the instrument and sends it out to the experts—for example, college professors of education, administrators, other supervisors, or state department of education specialists.

When the respondents return their instruments, the supervisor tabulates them and sends a revised instrument back to them along with a summary of the results, including the range of predicted dates by which they anticipate items will be realized. The respondents are encouraged to refine their predictions and/or state reasons if their predictions fall at extremes of the range of responses. The supervisor then repeats the process, again furnishing a summary of the results to the respondents and reporting the reasons given by respondents for extreme answers. The supervisor may repeat the process as many times as it appears fruitful and the respondents are willing to participate. As a general rule, after three or four times the responses tend to converge into consensus. This process may take several months or longer to complete. For that reason, the Delphi Technique should not be used if immediate information is needed.

The supervisor summarizes the final results of the study and distributes them to respondents and others, including teachers. Following distribution of the results, the supervisor meets with groups of teachers to discuss the implications of the findings and to set strategies for tackling some of the problems revealed by the study.

EVALUATIVE CRITERIA

Supervisors may be involved in working with teachers and other school personnel in the school improvement process. For years, the process involved the use of a national set of standards for secondary schools called *Evaluative Criteria*.[9] These criteria were developed by educators under the direction of the National Study of School Evaluation. Standards were eventually established to evaluate the three levels of schooling: elementary, middle school/junior high, and high school. The secondary school standards appeared in 1940 and were revised every ten years. In 1963, standards were adopted for middle schools and junior high schools. The first standards for elementary schools appeared in 1973.

These criteria grew out of efforts of the six regional accrediting associations to specify standards that secondary schools would have to meet to be accredited, that is, to earn the stamp of approval of the accrediting association. The purpose of the criteria was to ensure fulfillment of a set of minimum standards and provide a systematic procedure for studying and improving all phases of a school's program.

The standards contained in the respective sets of criteria were used most often in conjunction with a school's efforts to achieve accreditation by its regional association. Regardless of whether the criteria were used as a part of the accreditation process, they offered a valuable set of standards for any faculty and they set forth an effective self-study procedure, which faculties might consider following.

When using the criteria, the total faculty subjected its program to continuing study over a period of time, ordinarily a year. To conduct a self-study, the building supervisor (the principal or someone designated by the principal) provided for the following steps:

1. Appoint or elect a steering committee of the faculty to spearhead the study.

2. Assign each member of the faculty to one or more subcommittees.

3. Provide time for reports of the subcommittees to the entire faculty, with subsequent discussion of each report.

4. Modify the school's program as the study moves along.

5. Arrange for a visit by a visiting committee of the regional accrediting association, if the study is tied into the accreditation process. (This step would be omitted if the school is not seeking new or continuing accreditation.)

6. Follow up and modify the school's program during and at the conclusion of the study. If the study was conducted as part of the accreditation process, the visiting committee will have made recommendations for the school's consideration, and these recommendations will have been studied for possible implementation.

The National Study of School Evaluation (NSSE) and the six regional school accreditation commissions in the late 1990s published a set of guidelines, *School Improvement: Focusing on Student Performance*, to provide schools with a research-based framework to help them develop and sustain meaningful school improvement.[10] Their guide presents the six parts of the continuous planning process:

Part 1: Developing the Profile, which focuses on the process of developing a comprehensive profile of the students and community the school serves.

Part 2: Defining Beliefs and Mission, which defines the purpose and direction of the school through its adopted mission statement.

Part 3: Defining Desired Results for Student Learning, which matches identified goals and expectations for student learning with the school's mission and beliefs.

Part 4: Analyzing Instructional and Organizational Effectiveness, which involves the school's personnel in the evaluation of their instructional and organizational practices with regard to the students' learning.

Part 5: Developing the Action Plan, which focuses on a school's identification and targeting a school's goals and the research-based and data-driven initiatives to reach the goals. Timelines, strategies, and personnel responsibilities become part of the action plan.

Part 6: Implementing the Plan and Documenting Results, which means putting the school improvement plan into action. During this part of the improvement process, schools are expected to monitor the implementation of the school improvement plan and gather evidence of achieving goals for improvement, while maintaining the commitment toward continuous improvement.

Although the process is presented in linear fashion here, it is circular in nature—a continuous process that can and should be revisited as new conditions require.

Schools today commonly engage in some form of self-study. By so doing in addition to assessing their mission, defining clear goals, and effecting change, school administrators and staff learn to work cooperatively with students, parents, other community members, and each other.

CURRICULUM MAPPING

A number of educators have advocated a useful evaluation technique known as *curriculum mapping*. In essence, a curriculum map is an analysis of what a teacher has actually taught and the amount of time spent on the tasks. As Fenwick W. English explained,

> Curriculum mapping is a content analysis of the classroom curriculum as the teacher teaches it. It is an analysis of the *real* curriculum.[11]

English pointed out that unlike a lesson plan that is designed for future presentation, "a curriculum map is in the past tense, i.e., what was taught, last week, last semester, last year, and a representation of time on task of the teacher involved."[12]

Noting the elements of the curriculum that have been presented to the students and the amount of time devoted to each phase of the curriculum, Heidi Hayes Jacobs defined curriculum mapping in the following manner:

> Curriculum mapping is a procedure for collecting data about the operational curriculum in a school or district referenced directly to the calendar.[13]

English also described the characteristics of curriculum maps:

> While mapping formats may vary, most maps have at least two constants: content taught and time spent. Content may include not only conventional subject matter but anything children are expected to learn: processes, activities, or methods. The intent is to portray time devoted to each major learning task within each classroom or other functional unit.[14]

The comparison of curriculum maps of teachers of all sections of the same grade level or subject can reveal great variations in topics taught and the amount of time spent on each. When school districts administer a systemwide test to students in all sections of a grade or subject, these variations in content and time can create problems for the learners. This can also be experienced when students from several elementary schools matriculate to a middle school or junior high, and again when those students enter high school. The supervisor can help teachers examine what they have actually taught through the technique of curriculum mapping.

The values of curriculum mapping were summed up by English when he observed,

> Curriculum mapping reveals to a staff, principal, or supervisor what is actually being taught, how long it is being taught, and the match between what is being taught and the district's testing program. The curriculum developer can use the results to gradually make the written curriculum and the real curriculum more congruent with one another.[15]

EVALUATION OF MATERIALS AND STUDIES

The supervisor should assist teachers in evaluating both curriculum materials and research studies and contemporary articles written by classroom teachers who have developed and used successful strategies that may be useful to other teachers. A major responsibility of the supervisor is to be on the lookout for new curriculum materials and channel them to teachers who might use them. The supervisor should help teachers decide whether the new materials would be useful in their situation. Together with the teachers, the supervisor should examine the purposes of the materials, the uses to which they could be put, the limitations of the materials, and the costs.

The supervisor also has the responsibility of alerting teachers to reports of research studies that may be significant to them. It is usually much easier for the supervisor to fulfill the task of locating and disseminating curriculum materials than it is to search out and distribute reports of research. Supervisors receive unsolicited curriculum materials and announcements from various manufacturers and publishers. Those who attend regional, state, or national meetings often are given curriculum items for possible use.

Supervisors do not, as a rule, have too much difficulty bringing new curricular materials to the attention of teachers. This is one task of supervision in which some supervisors overcompensate for their lack of effort in locating and disseminating research that may help teachers in their school system. It is also difficult to decide whether a research study, once located, is important enough to be made available to teachers. The identification of research studies has become easier with the accessibility of ERIC documents and other research sources through computer networks.

Fortunately, helpful tools are available to assist the supervisor in finding research studies. In some cases, these tools may already be available in the school system somewhere. In other cases, the school system can purchase certain resources for the specific purpose of helping school personnel keep up with research.

Where can the supervisor turn to locate research studies? The sources are many and are usually available in most college and university libraries, in some large public libraries, and sometimes in the professional libraries of school systems. A few of the more significant sources are listed here:

1. *U.S. Department of Education.* The department maintains an updated list of research reports and related publications on its Web site (www.ed.gov/index.jhtml).

2. *Reader's Guide to Periodical Literature* (New York: H. W. Wilson Company). This standard reference fulfills the same function as the *Education Index* except that it indexes articles from journals of general interest. The guide is published monthly. Most libraries bind all the issues for one year into a single volume. (See www.hwwilson.com/ Databases/Readersg.htm for more information; full electronic access to the texts is a paid service.)

3. *ERIC materials.* Established in 1964 by the former U.S. Office of Education, ERIC (Educational Resources Information Center) is a comprehensive source of educational information (www.eric.ed.gov). ERIC indexes journals in education (www.eric.ed.gov/ ERICWebPortal/Home.portal?_nfpb=true&_pageLabel=JournalPage&logoutLink=false) and provides a thesaurus of descriptors (www.eric.ed.gov/ERICWebPortal/Home. portal?_nfpb=true&_pageLabel=Thesaurus&nfls=false).

4. *Dissertation Abstracts International* (Ann Arbor, Mich.: University Microfilms). This monthly publication contains abstracts of doctoral dissertations written in the United States and Canada. The user of this publication can order a copy of a dissertation on microfilm from University Microfilms. Dissertation abstracts may be accessed online from ProQuest Digital Dissertations, Ann Arbor, Michigan, by connecting through a subscription institution.

5. *Publications of the American Educational Research Association* (Washington, D.C.). These publications contain reviews and reports of research studies on a wide variety of topics. Among the AERA publications are *American Educational Research Journal* (quarterly), *Educational Researcher* (monthly), *Monograph Series on Evaluation: Perspectives of Curriculum Evaluation* (six monographs), *Review of Educational Research* (quarterly), and *Review of Research in Education* (annually). (www.aera.net)

6. *The National Assessment of Educational Progress.* Supervisors, particularly specialist supervisors in selected fields, should keep themselves and their teachers abreast of findings of the National Assessment of Educational Progress (NAEP), funded by the Office for Educational Research and Improvement of the U.S. Department of Education and one of the most extensive testing projects undertaken in the United States. Originally based in Denver under the aegis of the Education Commission of the States, NAEP began collecting data on the achievement of four age groups throughout the country in ten subject areas and their attitudes toward the subjects.

The NAEP program dates from the efforts of Ralph Tyler and the Committee on Assessing the Progress of Education, which, under the instigation of the Carnegie Corporation in 1964, began development of a nationwide program to assess the educational progress of learners. At the onset of NAEP, the program came under heavy attack from professional educators, who feared this assessment could lead to a national standardized curriculum, a step that has been anathema to most educators but quite appealing to a sizable segment of the public. The educators were concerned that comparisons of schools and even individuals might be made from the data, which might destroy the images of schools that showed up poorly and might cause harm to individuals. Despite these objections, the NAEP moved ahead by identifying objectives in ten subject areas: science, writing, citizenship, reading, literature, social studies, music, mathematics, career and occupational development, and art. Following specification of the objectives, criterion-referenced assessment instruments were developed.

Assessment began in 1969–1970, and the first results were reported in 1970. In the 1980s, NAEP engaged in the assessment of student achievement in computer competence, geography, and history. NAEP has conducted periodic assessments and reassessments. At present, NAEP assesses achievement in eleven subject areas: the Arts, Civics, Economics, Foreign Language, Geography, Mathematics, Reading, Science, U.S. History, World History, and Writing.

NAEP has been able to allay the fears of professional educators by its refusal to establish norms on the various tests or to make individual scores known. The program collects data and reports them for the nation by participating states and for students' gender; race/ethnicity; eligibility for free/reduced-price lunch; and grades 4, 8, and 12.

NAEP leaves the interpretation of the results to the local communities. The results give supervisors and teachers a useful set of data for comparative purposes and may aid in curriculum development. One advantage of the national assessment program is that results in certain areas may throw out clues to school districts for conducting their own local assessments. The national assessment program has also established a model that states are using in their own assessment programs.

The Education Commission of the States administered NAEP during its first fourteen years. On July 1, 1983, administration of NAEP was transferred to the Educational Testing Service in Princeton, New Jersey. Supervisors seeking information on the NAEP may obtain assessment reports and a newsletter from the NAEP, Educational Testing Service, Princeton, New Jersey. (nces.ed.gov/nationsreportcard)

7. *International assessments.* Assessments of achievement in subject areas by learners in various countries are difficult to come by, but where they do exist and are available, they may have at least an academic interest for supervisors and teachers and may have implications for curriculum planning. The problems of testing across cultures and making comparisons of performance are large indeed. Educational philosophies, goals, and objectives vary from country to country and affect both the curriculum and instructional methods. Student populations and socioeconomic factors as well as teacher training are variables that make comparisons tricky. Nevertheless, any supervisor who is on top of what is happening in curriculum evaluation should at least be familiar with significant studies that have been widely disseminated. Mention was made in the previous chapter of international studies of achievement in mathematics. Over the years studies have been conducted that assessed and compared student achievement in a number of countries. Notable are the studies in mathematics and science carried out by the International Association for the Evaluation of Educational Achievement (IEA) in the 1960s, 1970s, and 1980s[16]; the First International Assessment of Educational Progress (IAEP) in 1988[17]; and repeated testings of Trends in International Mathematics and Science Study (TIMSS) surveyed by IEA in association with Boston College.[18]

Although we may have some reservations about these studies, we all wish that American students had performed better in the comparisons than they did. In 1991, then-President George H. W. Bush expressed this desire by presenting the *America 2000* education package. Together, he and the nation's governors, in a move reaffirmed by Congress and later President Clinton, proposed to the country a lofty and formidable goal: to raise the ranking of American students, in mathematics and science achievement, to first in the world by 2000.[19] As noted earlier, Two additional goals—expectations for professional development for educators and increased parental involvement in learning—were added to the national program under the Clinton administration, when it was also renamed Goals 2000.[20]

More demanding are the provisions of the No Child Left Behind Act of 2001 (NCLB) that require schools to show adequate yearly progress and all students to perform at the proficient level on state tests by 2013–2014.[21]

STATE ASSESSMENT PROGRAMS

The supervisor should assume responsibility for directing teachers in state assessment programs and in evaluation of the school's program for purposes of state accreditation. Pressured by NCLB, states have moved heavily into statewide assessment of student achievement, especially in reading and mathematics. Some of the states are capitalizing on the NAEP model, using their own criterion-referenced tests. Other states have called for both criterion-referenced and norm-referenced testing at various levels of the educational ladder. Results obtained from state assessments have particular significance for communities within the state. The supervisor should discuss with teachers the results of state assessments; together they should interpret the data and plan for curriculum changes that seem warranted.

State departments of education are charged with the responsibility of evaluating and/ or accrediting schools within their states. States vary in the procedures they use to evaluate individual schools and to decide whether they meet state standards. The purpose of state evaluation and accreditation is the maintenance of minimal standards by the schools of the state, not only in respect to the curriculum but in all aspects of the schools' operations. States ordinarily carry out periodic assessments of schools for purposes of state accreditation, sometimes in conjunction with regional accrediting association visits.

Florida furnishes an example of a state's development of a set of standards. In 1996, the Florida State Board of Education approved the Sunshine State Standards to provide expectations for student achievement in the state. The standards were written in seven subject areas, each divided into four separate grade clusters: pre-K–2, 3–5, 6–8, and 9–12. This format was chosen to provide flexibility to school districts in designing curricula based on local needs. The Sunshine State Standards are a collection of concepts students are expected to know and understand as they pass through school. The standards do not tell teachers how or what to teach, and they are not lesson plans. They were developed in consultation with teachers, administrators, and parents and are intended to serve as guidelines that tell teachers and parents what students are expected to know. Since the adoption of the standards, they have been expanded to include Grade Level Expectations. These Grade Level Expectations provide the basis for state assessments at each grade 3–10. In addition to the Grade Level Expectations, course-specific information for students in grades 6–12 can be found in the Florida Course Descriptions.

LOCAL ASSESSMENT PROGRAMS

The supervisor will work with teachers to plan and carry out local assessments of student achievement in various subject areas. Whether or not the state requires participation in its assessment program, local school districts will find it helpful to develop their own assessment programs. Local assessment programs may supplement state and national assessments, fill in the gaps not tested by the state and national programs, and provide experiences that prepare students for state and national assessments. Local school systems may use input from state, national, and even international studies in developing their own assessment programs. Such programs are a part of the needs assessment referred to earlier. As well as identifying unmet needs, local assessment programs facilitate comparisons among schools within the school district. The selection or creation of appropriate testing instruments will be a major problem in local assessment, and for this problem the supervisor may need to seek assistance from research specialists either inside or outside the school system. The supervisor will be called on to display a wide repertoire of knowledge and skills in working with teachers on the critical task of curriculum evaluation.

SUMMARY

Evaluation is a fundamental part of the curriculum development process. Through evaluation, teachers learn whether stated objectives have been reached. Only through evaluation can intelligent curriculum decisions be made.

The supervisor plays a major role as leader and resource person in the evaluation phase of curriculum development. Although a research director or evaluation specialist might possess a higher degree of skill in evaluation and research than the supervisor, these positions may be rare in the school systems, and the supervisor must fulfill the role of leader in evaluation.

In carrying out this role, the supervisor should seek to help teachers develop an evaluative frame of mind, an inquiring attitude, and a research orientation. The supervisor should help teachers state curricular objectives in performance terms in order to simplify the task of evaluation.

The understanding of ten basic research concepts will help teachers in their role as consumers and appliers of research. Knowledge of these concepts will enable teachers to utilize standardized test data more effectively and interpret research studies that have been conducted inside and outside the school system.

The supervisor should acquaint teachers with various types of evaluation and research. The purpose of acquainting teachers with the kinds of studies that are conducted is to show them the range of possibilities and to indicate types of studies in which they are most likely to be involved. Generally, teachers engage in descriptive research, action research, and some applied research.

The supervisor should help teachers develop skill in conducting needs assessments to discover unmet needs. Thorough needs assessments obtain input from students, teachers, administrators, other school personnel, and the community. A special caution is suggested—those conducting needs assessments should be concerned that data are sought from all segments of the community and not just from selected segments.

Teachers should be instructed in the use of evaluation materials developed for both state and regional accreditation. Although regional accreditation is voluntary, state evaluation and accreditation are required. A self-study by a faculty utilizing a set of national criteria is a comprehensive way of evaluating a total school program.

The supervisor should keep teachers informed of information on state, national, and international assessments of achievement of learners. Regardless of whether a school district participates in a state, national, or international assessment program, it should develop its own local assessment program under the leadership of the supervisor. The purposes of local assessment are (1) to identify unmet needs, (2) to compare schools within a district, and (3) to make decisions about the curriculum.

The supervisor in the role of an evaluative resource person should be knowledgeable about sources of research information and should program time in such a way that he or she can review recent research and disseminate research information to the teachers being supervised.

QUESTIONS FOR DISCUSSION

1. How could a supervisor help a teacher determine whether the curriculum being followed meets the needs of all the students?
2. How could a supervisor help a teacher do an action research project?
3. Why should a needs assessment be the first step in curriculum development?
4. Why should a supervisor have teachers use curriculum mapping?
5. What outside influences/forces make it necessary to evaluate the curriculum on a continuous basis?

ACTIVITIES FOR FURTHER STUDY

REFLECTIVE

1. Search the literature and report on a model of curriculum evaluation other than those described in this chapter.
2. Find a report of a curriculum study carried on in a school outside your own district and prepare a critique of the study concerning research design, validation of the goals and objectives,

validation of the instruments, procedures used, treatment of the data, conclusions, and applicability to your school district.

3. Define *mean, median, reliability, validity, norm, percentile, correlation coefficient, standard score, standard deviation*, and *mode*.

4. Examine and write a brief report on the nature and use of the *Thesaurus of ERIC Descriptors*.

5. Examine the regional accreditation report of a school that has obtained accreditation by its regional accrediting association and decide which recommendations of the visiting committee have been implemented since the report was issued and which have not been implemented. If a recommendation has not been implemented, formulate hypotheses about why the recommendation has not been put into practice.

6. Write a paper using selected references accounting for objections researchers make to action research and propose some ways to overcome these objections.

7. List at least three curriculum problems or instructional problems in a field of specialization you know well that would be suitable for action research.

8. List at least three curriculum problems in a field of specialization you know well that call for rigorous applied research studies.

9. Choose a field of your interest or expertise in which assessments have been made by the National Assessment of Educational Progress and report findings and implications of the results.

10. Conduct a brief study employing the Delphi Technique.

11. Write a paper describing the roles of each of the following in curriculum evaluation:
    a. Principal
    b. Supervisor
    c. Teacher
    d. Students
    e. Public

12. Report on how schools in your state define adequate yearly progress.

13. Locate and report on the standards required of all public schools in your state.

14. If your state has an accreditation process, compare the criteria required for state accreditation with criteria required for regional accreditation.

APPLICATION

1. Draft a plan for an introductory in-service program on curriculum evaluation.

2. Design an instrument to assess student academic needs. Administer this instrument to a random sample of twenty to twenty-five students and summarize your findings.

3. Design an instrument to assess public attitudes toward the school's curriculum. Administer this instrument to a random sample of twenty to twenty-five laypersons and summarize your findings.

4. Choose a curriculum problem and design a plan to study that problem.

5. Construct and analyze a curriculum map for your choice of grade or subject for a period of one semester.

6. Choose a curriculum topic and conduct a search for information about it in ERIC.

7. Choose a curriculum topic and locate abstracts on it in *Resources in Education*.

8. Choose a curriculum topic and locate studies on it in the *Current Index to Journals in Education*.

9. Sample and report opinions of at least five teachers concerning the forces they believe have the greatest impact on curriculum change. Ask them to identify any curriculum change that has come about as a result of local research.

10. Interview at least six teachers to learn whether they have participated in any type of evaluative study of the curriculum in the past five years. If they have, report the type of study and determine whether the study was required (as, for example, a study in connection with state or regional accreditation).

11. Talk with the principal of a school and ascertain his or her views on the necessity of curriculum evaluation and what he or she believes is going on in the school in the way of curriculum evaluation. Raise the same question with (a) the assistant principal for curriculum, if there is one; (b) a generalist supervisor; and (c) a specialist supervisor (the specialist could be a grade coordinator, team leader, or department head) at the same school.

12. Identify in your school system a curriculum innovation that in its initial proposal contained a plan for evaluating its success. List criteria on which to analyze the evaluation plan and critique the plan on the basis of these criteria.

13. *Those who are teaching* will design and carry out a piece of action research and report either progress or final results. *Those who are not teaching* will interview a teacher who is conducting a piece of action research and report on its design, procedures, and results.

NOTES

1. James A. Beane, ed., *Toward a Coherent Curriculum—1995 Yearbook of the Association for Supervision and Curriculum Development* (Alexandria, Va.: Association for Supervision and Curriculum Development, 1995), p. 3.

2. For further treatment of action research, see Craig A. Mertler, *Action Research: Teachers as Researchers in the Classroom* (Thousand Oaks, Calif.: Sage Publications, 2006) and Geoffrey E. Mills, *Action Research: A Guide for the Teacher Researcher* (Upper Saddle River, N.J.: Merrill/Prentice Hall, 2007).

3. Daniel L. Stufflebeam et al., *Educational Evaluation and Decision Making* (Itasca, Ill.: F. E. Peacock, 1971).

4. The Center for the Study of Evaluation, *Evaluation Workshop I: An Orientation* (Del Monte Research Park, Monterey, Calif.: CTB/McGraw-Hill, 1971). See also Stephen Klein, Gary Fenstermacher, and Marvin C. Alkin, "The Center's Changing Evaluation Model," *Evaluation Comment* 4 (1971): 9–12.

5. For other models of curriculum evaluation, see J. Galen Saylor, William M. Alexander, and Arthur J. Lewis, *Curriculum Planning for Better Teaching and Learning*, 4th ed. (New York: Holt, Rinehart and Winston, 1981), chap. 7; and Peter F. Oliva, *Developing the Curriculum*, 6th ed. (Boston: Allyn and Bacon, 2005), chap. 13.

6. The Joint Committee on Standards for Educational Evaluation, *The Program Standards: How to Assess Evaluations of Educational Programs*, 2nd ed. (Thousand Oaks, Calif.: Sage, 1994).

7. Willard Crouthamel and Stephen M. Preston, *Needs Assessment: User's Manual*; *Needs Assessment: Resource Guide*; *Needs Assessment: Checklist of Steps* (Atlanta: Research and Development Utilization Project, Georgia Department of Education, 1979).

8. See Olaf Helmer, "Analysis of the Future: The Delphi Method," in *Technological Forecasting for Industry and Government Methods and Applications*, ed. James R. Bright (Englewood Cliffs, N.J.: Prentice Hall, 1968), pp. 116–22; Olaf Helmer, "The Delphi Method—An Illustration," in *Technological Forecasting for Industry and Government Methods and Applications*, ed. Bright, pp. 123–33; T. J. Gordon, "New Approaches to Delphi," in *Technological Forecasting for Industry and Government Methods and Applications*, ed. Bright, pp. 134–43. See also W. Timothy Weaver, "The Delphi Forecasting Method," *Phi Delta Kappan* 52 (January 1971): 267–71; Frederick R. Cyphert and Walter L. Gant, "The Delphi Technique: A Case Study," *Phi Delta Kappan* 52 (January 1971): 267–71.

9. National Study of School Evaluation, *Evaluative Criteria*, 6th ed., 1987 (secondary); *Middle School/Junior High School Evaluative Criteria*, rev. ed., 1979; *Elementary School Evaluative Criteria*, 2nd ed., 1981; *Secondary School*

Evaluation Criteria: Narrative Edition, 1975; *Evaluative Criteria for Middle Level Schools*, 1990 (Falls Church, Va.: National Study of School Evaluation). (These materials are no longer available.)

10. National Study of School Evaluation, *School Improvement Focusing on Student Performance* (Schaumburg, Ill.: National Study of School Education, 1997). See also National Study of School Evaluation, *Breakthrough School Improvement: An Action Guide for Greater and Faster Results* (Schaumburg, Ill.: National Study of School Evaluation, 2005).

11. Fenwick W. English, "Curriculum Mapping," *Professional Educator* 3 (Spring 1980): 11–12.

12. Ibid., p. 11.

13. Heidi Hayes Jacobs, ed., *Getting Results with Curriculum Mapping* (Alexandria, Va.: Association for Supervision and Curriculum Development, 2004), p. 1.

14. Fenwick W. English, "Curriculum Mapping," *Educational Leadership* 37 (April 1980): 559.

15. Ibid.

16. T. Husén, ed., *International Study of Achievement in Mathematics*, 2 vols. (New York: Wiley, 1967). See also Joseph Featherstone, "Measuring What Schools Achieve: Learning and Testing," *New Republic* 169 (December 15, 1973): 19–21; and T. Neville Posthlethwaite, "International Educational Surveys," *Contemporary Education* 42 (November 1970): 61–68, and Second International Mathematics Study, *The Underachieving Curriculum: Assessing U.S. School Mathematics from an International Point of View* (Champaign, Ill.: Stipes, 1987).

17. See Archie E. Lapointe, Nancy A. Mead, and Gary W. Phillips, *A World of Differences: An International Assessment of Mathematics and Science* (Princeton, N.J.: Educational Testing Service, Center for Assessment of Educational Progress, 1989).

18. See endnote 4, Chapter 1.

19. *National Goals for Education* (Washington, D.C.: U.S. Department of Education, July 1990).

20. *Goals 2000 Educate America Act* (Washington, D.C.: U.S. Department of Education, 1994).

21. *Public Law 107–110*, the No Child Left Behind Act of 2001, reauthorized the Elementary and Secondary Education Act of 1965.

BIBLIOGRAPHY

ALKIN, MARVIN C., ed. *The Encyclopedia of Educational Research*, 6th ed. New York: Macmillan, 1992.

American Educational Research Association. *American Educational Research Journal*. Washington, D.C.: American Educational Research Association, quarterly.

———. *Educational Researcher*. Washington, D.C.: American Educational Research Association, monthly.

———. *Monograph Series on Evaluation: Perspectives of Curriculum Evaluation 1–6*. Ann Arbor, Mich.: Xerox University Microfilms.

———. *Review of Educational Research*. Washington, D.C.: American Educational Research Association, quarterly.

———. *Review of Research in Education*. Itasca, Ill.: F. E. Peacock, annually.

BEANE, JAMES A. *Toward a Coherent Curriculum—1995 Yearbook of the Association for Supervision and Curriculum Development*. Alexandria, Va.: Association for Supervision and Curriculum Development.

BRIGHT, JAMES R., ed. *Technological Forecasting for Industry and Government Methods and Applications*. Englewood Cliffs, N.J.: Prentice Hall, 1968.

CALHOUN, EMILY. *How to Use Action Research in the Self-Renewing School*. Alexandria, Va.: Association for Supervision and Curriculum Development, 1994.

The Center for the Study of Evaluation. *Evaluation Workshop I: An Orientation*. Monterey, Calif.: CTB/McGraw-Hill, 1971. Participant's Notebook and Leadership Manual.

CROUTHAMEL, WILLARD, and STEPHEN M. PRESTON. *Needs Assessment: Checklist of Steps; Needs Assessment: Resource Guide; Needs Assessment: User's Manual*. Atlanta: Research and Development Utilization Project, Georgia Department of Education, 1979.

CYPHERT, FREDERICK R. ed., and WALTER L. GANT. "The Delphi Technique: A Case Study." In *Technological Forecasting for Industry and Government Methods and Applications*, ed. James R. Bright. Englewood Cliffs, N.J.: Prentice Hall, 1968.

DRAKE, SUSAN M, and REBECCA C. BURNS. *Meeting Standards Through Integrated Curriculum*. Alexandria, Va.: Association for Supervision and Curriculum Development, 2004.

EARLEY, MARGARET J., and KENNETH J. REHAGE, eds. *Issues in Curriculum: A Selection of Chapters from Past NSSE Yearbooks*. Chicago: National Society for the Study of Education, 1999.

EICHELBERGER, R. TONY. *Disciplined Inquiry: Understanding and Doing Educational Research*. New York: Longman, 1989.

ENGLISH, FENWICK W. "Curriculum Mapping." *Educational Leadership* 37 (April 1980): 558–59.

―――. "Curriculum Mapping." *Professional Educator* 3 (Spring 1980): 8–12.

GALL, MEREDITH D, JOYCE P. GALL, and WALTER R. BORG. *Educational Research: An Introduction*, 8th ed. Boston: Allyn and Bacon, 2007.

GAY, L. R., and PETER W. AIRASIAN. *Educational Research: Competencies for Analysis and Application*, 6th ed. Upper Saddle River, N.J.: Merrill, 2000.

Goals 2000 Education America Act. Washington, D.C.: U.S. Department of Education, 1994.

GORDON, T. J. "New Approaches to Delphi." In *Technological Forecasting for Industry and Government Methods and Applications*, ed. James R. Bright. Englewood Cliffs, N.J.: Prentice Hall, 1968.

HARRIS, SUE. "The Third International Mathematics and Science Study (TIMSS)," *Mathematics in School* 23 (November 1994): 34–35.

HELMER, OLAF. "Analysis of the Future: The Delphi Method." In *Technological Forecasting for Industry and Government Methods and Applications*, ed. James R. Bright. Englewood Cliffs, N.J.: Prentice Hall, 1968.

―――. "The Delphi Method—An Illustration." In *Technological Forecasting for Industry and Government Methods and Applications*, ed. James R. Bright. Englewood Cliffs, N.J.: Prentice Hall, 1968.

HERMAN, JOAN L., and LYNN WINTERS. *Tracking Your School's Success: A Guide to Sensible Evaluation*. Newbury Park, Calif.: Corwin Press, 1992.

HINES, VYNCE A., and WILLIAM M. ALEXANDER. *High School Self-Evaluation and Curriculum Change*. Final Report, Project 3120, Contract No. OE 6–10–154, Bureau of Research, Office of Education. Washington, D.C.: U. S. Department of Health, Education, and Welfare, 1967.

HUSÉN, TORSTEN, ed. *International Study of Achievement in Mathematics, 2 vols*. New York: Wiley, 1967.

JACOBS, HEIDI HAYES, ed. *Getting Results with Curriculum Mapping*. Alexandria, Va.: Association for Supervision and Curriculum Development, 2004.

JOHNSON, MAURITZ, Jr. *Intentionality in Education: A Conceptual Model of Curricular and Instructional Planning and Evaluation*. New York: Center for Curriculum Research and Services, 1977.

Joint Committee on Standards for Educational Evaluation. *The Program Evaluation Standards: How to Assess Evaluations of Educational Programs*, 2nd ed. Thousand Oaks, Calif.: Sage, 1994.

KAUFMAN, ROGER A. *Needs Assessment: A Focus for Curriculum Development*. Alexandria, Va.: Association for Supervision and Curriculum Development, 1975.

LAPOINTE, ARCHIE E., NANCY A. MEAD, and GARY W. PHILLIPS. *A World of Differences: An International Assessment of Mathematics and Science*. Princeton, N.J.: Educational Testing Service, Center for Assessment of Educational Progress, 1989.

LEEDY, PAUL D. *Practical Research: Planning and Design*. Columbus, Ohio: Merrill, Prentice Hall, 1997.

LINN, ROBERT L., and NORMAN E. GRONLUND. *Measurement and Assessment in Teaching*, 7th ed. Upper Saddle River, N.J.: Merrill, 2000.

MARZANO, ROBERT J., DEBRA PICKERING, and JAY MCTIGHE. *Assessing Student Outcomes: Performance Assessment Using the Dimensions of Learning Model*. Alexandria, Va.: Association for Supervision and Curriculum Development, 1993.

MCKNIGHT, CURTIS C., et al. *The Underachieving Curriculum: Assessing U.S. School Mathematics from an International Point of View*. Champaign, Ill.: Stipes, 1987.

MERTLER, CRAIG A. *Action Research: Teachers as Researchers in the Classroom*. Thousand Oaks, Calif.: Sage Publications, 2006.

MILLS, GEOFFREY E. *Action Research: A Guide for the Teacher Researcher*. Upper Saddle River, N.J.: Merrill/Prentice Hall, 2007.

MULLIS, INA V. S. *Trends in International Mathematics and Science Study*. Chestnut Hill, Mass.: Boston College, 2003.

National Study of School Evaluation. *Breakthrough School Improvement: An Action Guide to Greater and Faster Results*. Schaumburg, Ill.: National Study of School Evaluation, 2005.

―――. *School Improvement: Focusing on Student Performance*. Schaumburg, Ill.: National Study of School Evaluation, 1998.

―――. *School Improvement Planning Software*. Schaumburg, Ill.: National Study of School Evaluation, 1998.

OLIVA, PETER F. *Developing the Curriculum*, 6th ed. Boston: Allyn and Bacon, 2005.

POPHAM, W. JAMES. *Assessment for Educational Leaders*. Boston: Allyn and Bacon, 2006.

POSTHLETHWAITE, T. NEVILLE. "International Educational Surveys." *Contemporary Education* 42 (November 1970): 61–68.

SAGOR, RICHARD. *How to Conduct Collaborative Action Research*. Alexandria, Va.: Association for Supervision and Curriculum Development, 1993.

SAYLOR, J. GALEN, WILLIAM M. ALEXANDER, and ARTHUR J. LEWIS. *Curriculum Planning for Better Teaching and Learning*, 4th ed. New York: Holt, Rinehart and Winston, 1981.

SCRIVEN, MICHAEL. "The Methodology of Evaluation." *Perspectives of Curriculum Evaluation*, AERA Monograph Series on Curriculum Evaluation, no. 1. Chicago: Rand McNally, 1967.

Second International Mathematics Study. *The Underachieving Curriculum: Assessing U.S. School Mathematics from an International Point of View*. Champaign, Ill.: Stipes, 1987.

SOWELL, EVELYN J. *Curriculum: An Integrative Introduction*, 3rd ed. Upper Saddle River, N.J.: Merrill/Prentice Hall, 2005.

STUFFLEBEAM, DANIEL L., WALTER J. FOLEY, WILLIAM J. GEPHART, EGON G. GUBA, ROBERT J. HAMMOND, HOWARD O. MERRIMAN, and MALCOLM M. PROVUS. *Educational Evaluation and Decision Making*. Itasca, Ill.: F. E. Peacock, 1971.

TYLER, RALPH W. *Basic Principles of Curriculum and Instruction*. Chicago: University of Chicago Press, 1949.

———, ed. *Educational Evaluation: New Roles, New Means*. 68th Yearbook of the National Society for the Study of Education. Chicago: University of Chicago Press, 1969.

TYLER, RALPH W., ROBERT M. GAGNÉ, and MICHAEL SCRIVEN. *Perspectives of Curriculum Evaluation*. AERA Monograph Series on Curriculum Evaluation, no. 1. Chicago: Rand McNally, 1967.

WEAVER, W. TIMOTHY. "The Delphi Forecasting Method." *Phi Delta Kappan* 52 (January 1971): 267–71.

WEB SITES

American Association of School Administrators: www.aasa.org

Association for Supervision and Curriculum Development: www.ascd.orgx

Dissertation Abstracts International: il.proquest.com/brand/umi.shtml

Educational Research Service: www.ers.org

Educational Resources Information Center (ERIC): www.eric.ed.gov

Educational Testing Service: www.ets.org

Florida Sunshine State Standards: www.firn.edu/doe

National Assessment of Educational Progress: nces.ed.gov/nationsreportcard

National Center for Education Statistics: nces.ed.gov

No Child Left Behind Act of 2001: www.ed.gov/nclb

National Staff Development Council: www.nsdc.org

National Study of School Evaluation: www.nsse.org

Phi Delta Kappa International: www.pdkintl.org

ProQuest Digital Dissertations: www.lib.umi.com/dissertations

Reader's Guide to Periodical Literature: www.hwwilson.com/Databases/Readersg.htm

Trends in Mathematics and Science Study: timss.bc.edu/isc/publications.html

PART IV

LEADERSHIP IN STAFF DEVELOPMENT

Bill Aron/PhotoEdit

CHAPTER 9

HELPING TEACHERS THROUGH IN-SERVICE PROGRAMS

OBJECTIVES

After studying Chapter 9 you should be able to accomplish the following objectives:

1. Define staff development and in-service education.
2. State characteristics of an effective in-service program.
3. Describe your preferred model of in-service education.
4. Conduct an in-service needs assessment.
5. Describe features of a school district master plan for staff development.
6. Describe features of an individual school plan for staff development.
7. Propose an outline for writing in-service training components.
8. Suggest several types of in-service activities.
9. Suggest defensible incentives for teacher participation in in-service activities.
10. Explain whether and when outside consultants should be used.
11. Conduct an evaluation of an in-service activity.
12. Propose criteria for evaluating a master plan for staff development.

SUPERVISION AND STAFF DEVELOPMENT

Our travels into the world of supervision bring us now to the domain of staff development. It would be a rare specialist in supervision who would advise us not to work in this domain. Where specialists differ, as we have seen in Chapter 2, is on the following questions:

- Is supervision only staff development?
- Is staff development the same as in-service education?
- Do we provide in-service education for groups or individuals or both?

Let's recall the model of supervision presented in Chapter 1. This model depicts three domains, side by side, with no barriers to block off interaction among them. Following this model, we saw distinctions among the domains of instructional development, curriculum development, and staff development as matters of emphasis rather than discreteness. We pointed out that supervision flows from one domain to the other, and supervisors may work in two or more domains simultaneously. Nevertheless, the model depicts three domains, not one.

Some specialists in supervision would limit the task of supervision to a single domain. Others may choose to focus on the improvement of *instruction* or of *curriculum* rather than on the improvement of *staff members*. Staff development connotes the idea of *training*, the goal of which is improvement of the persons who make up the organization and thus improvement of the organization itself.

The term *human-resource development* appears in some teacher and administrator preparation programs. For example, reacting to requests from school districts, the Florida Council on Educational Management (FCEM) updated and revised its Human Resource Management Development program. That system included recruitment, screening, selection, appointment, development, and performance appraisal.[1] The basic premise of the Florida program was that one characteristic of a good school is a commitment to excellence and student achievement that is shared by students, parents, school staff, and administrators. Strong support was given to decentralized school systems that promoted the freedom to design and implement programs that met the needs of individual schools. Along with this freedom came the responsibility of all of the school's stakeholders to become active partners in accepting and acting on this responsibility. Thus, the knowledge and skills of supervisors were expected to play a key role in the development of human resources at all schools.

The foundation for human-resource development developed by FCEM served the state of Florida for many years. Now every state has to comply with the requirements of the No Child Left Behind (NCLB) Act of 2001. Among the seven main requirements of the act are two that focus on highly qualified teachers and professional development for teachers. Each state's NCLB proposal had to contain annual measurable objectives for the implementation of the highly qualified teacher and high-quality professional development requirements of the act.[2]

Teachers may undergo staff development within the instructional and curriculum domains as they do when they perfect skills in instructional and curriculum development, by learning new pedagogical skills and becoming familiar with new programs. They may also undergo training that does not fall within the realms of instructional development and curriculum development—for example, developing pride in their organization, enhancing their self-concepts, developing leadership skills, participating in quality circles for solving management problems, and coping with stress. Many teachers who achieved National Board Certification reported that the year-long process had been the most thorough and rewarding staff development they had ever experienced.

Not every activity engaged in by teachers includes training. Some focus on carrying out instructional and curriculum tasks, solving instructional and curriculum problems, and creating materials. Professional teachers reject the notion that every activity is a training experience. In some sense every professional experience is developmental, but we do not limit our conception of supervision to staff development alone.

Purposes of Staff Development

Most specialists in supervision agree that staff development is a function of supervision. Most also agree that in-service education is a function of supervision. There is considerable disagreement, however, about whether staff development is the same as in-service education. We have used the terms *staff development* and *in-service education* synonymously in this text, as did Lloyd W. Dull,[3] as this is how these terms are often used in present practice.

Not all specialists in supervision, however, would agree with that usage. Some would maintain that *staff development* is the broader term because it includes working with individuals and groups in both formal and informal situations, whereas *in-service education* is limited to working with groups in formal training programs.

Others view in-service education as training that helps teachers do their present jobs better, whereas staff development is training for the purpose of developing new knowledge and skills beyond teachers' current assignments. Still others hold that staff development is an organized program to help teachers feel better about themselves and their jobs and develop personal skills, whereas in-service education is training for new curricula and the improvement of pedagogical skills.

Ben M. Harris conceptualized in-service education as part of staff development.[4] He divided staff development into two categories: staffing and training. Included in the concept of staffing were selecting, assigning, evaluating, retiring, and dismissing staff. The training aspect included in-service education and advanced preparation, which were defined in Chapter 2.

Thomas J. Sergiovanni and Robert J. Starratt saw the term *in-service education* as implying a deficiency that the teacher must overcome, whereas *professional development* and *renewal* are terms focusing on teacher growth.[5] Donald C. Orlich, like Harris, identified *staff development* as broader than *in-service education*, with the former including the latter. In this case, in-service education satisfies immediate training needs, whereas staff development is more comprehensive, including personal development.[6] Bruce Joyce and Beverly Showers offer the proposition that staff development is a service organization within the educational system.[7]

We could make further semantic distinctions by injecting the terms *professional development* and *personal development* into our discussion. In its purest sense, professional development encompasses training activities aimed at improving the teacher's skills in his or her present position or at developing the teacher for service within the profession outside classroom teaching. Personal development embraces activities directed toward enhancing the teacher's general knowledge, attitudes, interpersonal skills, values, and so on.

In this chapter, we use the term *staff development* as we defined it in Chapter 2, where we equated it to in-service education: "a program of organized activities for both groups and individuals planned and carried out to promote the personal and professional growth of staff members, in this case, teachers." Staff development is in-service education, or put another way, the staff is developed through in-service education. In-service education may be either remedial or developmental, corrective or enriching. Furthermore, *staff development* as used in this text subsumes *professional development* and *personal development*, which are particular types of staff development or in-service education. No matter which term is preferred, the major emphasis should remain the same: the utilization of activities that help teachers improve instruction.

To learn why staff development is necessary, let's examine what happens in our profession. Every spring, on the campuses of hundreds of colleges and universities, several thousand young people receive the long-awaited degree that certifies they have completed their teacher-training program. With degree and state credentials in hand, they join the search for teaching jobs. In four years of training—the most common period throughout the country—they have accumulated enough course credits to graduate, have completed forty to fifty courses in a wide range of fields, and may have achieved a minimum level in a certain number of professional competencies.

Because approximately one-half of a college program consists of general education—a necessary and desirable feature—only about half of a college education for teachers consists of work in the teaching field and pedagogy. The preservice trainees' program usually culminates in a brief student-teaching experience of eight to fifteen weeks, and the amount of actual hands-on experience during that time differs from school to school and from supervising teacher to supervising teacher. Given all the knowledge and skills necessary for successful teaching, the college training program is only a beginning, and the need for a continuing in-service program is apparent.

Programs for teachers in the field provide the instructional staff with opportunities to refresh their knowledge and improve skills that have been developed in a rudimentary fashion in the college training program and to achieve new knowledge and develop new skills called for in their teaching assignments. In-service education combats complacency and satisfaction with the status quo, which can set in as new teachers adjust to the routines of their positions.

The Supervisor's Role in In-Service Education

It is the supervisor's job to stimulate teachers to want to find new and better ways of accomplishing their instructional duties and improving the curriculum. The supervisor has the responsibility for identifying all teachers' in-service needs through surveys, requests from teachers, and observation. The supervisor plans, sets into operation, and evaluates in-service programs. In conjunction with teachers, the supervisor directs the development of the master plan for staff development, makes its components known, facilitates its use, and monitors which teachers participate in which activities.

The supervisor's role is made more difficult by lack of agreement and uncertainties about the scope and nature of in-service education. Pendred Noyce contends that a new standard should be in place for decision makers to use as staff development activities are planned. She contends that the first and most important acknowledgment, among others, for doing professional development is so that students will learn more.[8] Some issues related to in-service education, previously discussed in Chapter 2, follow.

1. *There is no agreement that in-service education is really necessary.* One school of thought holds that teachers are trained, professional people; once they are employed, they have little need for continuing education. This group believes that teachers will learn as they teach and that they can take care of what little updating they need by self-study. For the next era of public education, Stephanie Hirsh and Dennis Sparks developed eleven staff development resolutions for the future. They based these resolutions on the premise that professional learning, through various models, is at the core of the teacher's workday, and the dual focus on teacher and student ensures that both have opportunities to learn and perform at high levels.[9] Accountability has arrived.

2. *There is no agreement on whether in-service education is effective.* A number of years ago, summarizing several research studies John T. Lovell commented:

> It was ... found that teachers do not perceive that they are getting the services they need and often perceive supervisors as spending much of their time in the central offices working on administrative tasks not directly related to the needs of teachers. There was also evidence that the direct services that teachers were receiving were ineffective according to certain criteria of effectiveness.[10]

Fred H. Wood and Steven R. Thompson maintained that "most staff development programs are irrelevant and ineffective, a waste of time and money."[11] The effectiveness of in-service education is extremely difficult to verify, especially in terms of its ultimate purpose: the improvement of student achievement. Much of the research focuses on teachers' perceptions of the effectiveness or ineffectiveness of in-service programs. Harris mentioned several studies, some of which supported and some of which were critical of in-service education.[12]

David W. Champagne attributed students' improvement in basic skills, increases in SAT scores, improved student attitudes toward school, improved school attendance, and decreases in vandalism and teacher absenteeism (in a Pennsylvania study in the mid-1970s) to a staff-development program that instructed teachers on how to offer high-interest projects in their classes.[13] Champagne pointed to the success of the Newington (Connecticut) Public Schools in turning around teacher attitudes toward supervision from highly negative to highly positive through a well-planned staff-development program.[14] Roland Barth maintains that by strengthening the relationships among the educators in a school, a culture of collegiality will develop.[15]

3. *There is disagreement on what kinds of in-service education are best.* Some specialists advocate group study; others propose clinical approaches; some want peer supervision; still others recommend self-study by the teacher. These differing opinions make it difficult for practitioners to decide where to focus their efforts.

4. *There is uncertainty about the thrust of in-service education.* Should we, for example, spend time correcting deficiencies or providing enriching, developmental activities? Should in-service education be reactive to such factors as increased knowledge in all fields, increased use of technology, changes in students served, and changes in public opinion about what schools should emphasize? Or should we be proactive and develop in-service programs that anticipate such changes and take teachers to the forefront of new developments? Should supervisors wait and watch, or should they move out and expand?

5. *There is disagreement on the role of theory in in-service education.* Teachers tend to want practical help with the day-to-day problems of instruction. They see little value in theory, which they believe—often erroneously—does not aid them in the classroom. Lovell confirmed that most research studies "indicated that teachers and supervisors desired service directly related to the improvement of classroom instruction."[16]

Teachers, by and large, express the same negative attitudes toward theory that they express toward theory's companion, philosophy. They do not agree with John Dewey that

> theory is in the end, as has been well said, the most practical of all things, because this widening of the range of attention beyond nearby purpose and desire eventually results in the creation of wider and farther-reaching purposes and enables us to use a much wider and deeper range of conditions and means than were expressed in the observation of primitive practical purposes.[17]

Supervisors must take care how they introduce theory into in-service education.

6. *There are uncertainties about which teachers in-service education should assist.* Should supervisors provide programs for beginning teachers, experienced ones, or both? Should they serve effective teachers, ineffective ones, or both? Are the beginning teachers the most ineffective, the most in need of help? There are those who believe that supervisors should not waste time on the poorest teachers, as they cannot be salvaged anyway. On the other hand, both moral and legal considerations require that teachers must be helped and supported before they can be terminated.

7. *There is uncertainty about the proper focus of in-service education.* How should in-service education seek to develop teachers?

- As instructors? If so, in-service programs must concentrate on methods.
- As curriculum developers? If so, teachers must be trained to plan, implement, and evaluate programs.
- As people? If so, this focus calls for training in human-relations skills.
- As subject matter specialists? If so, content of the discipline is the name of the game.
- As experts in the ecology of the classroom? If so, supervisors need to assist teachers in becoming more sensitive to linguistic nuances, nonverbal communication, and social and cultural differences.
- As educated citizens? If so, supervisors would plan programs in liberal studies that enhance the teachers' general knowledge or cultural literacy. In-service education usually concentrates on professional development of the teacher rather than personal development, with the exception of training in group dynamics.

8. *There is uncertainty about whether it is best to respond to teachers' needs through a comprehensive, long-range plan or through separate, discrete plans that are designed to satisfy particular needs.* Programs more often respond to specific needs and are thus reactive in nature, rather than anticipating needs and thus being proactive. Single training sessions commonly require no follow-up sessions during which teachers may demonstrate mastery of the skills and knowledge presented in the sessions. Roy A. Edelfelt commented,

> In most cases needs have been translated into programs piecemeal. Programs are often oneshot sessions on a single topic (e.g., discipline techniques, management of stress and conflict, economic education) or courses that address a particular need (e.g., personal writing, conversational French, or learning activities for the gifted and talented).[18]

9. *There is the question of whether staff-development activities should be planned and coordinated at the individual school level or at the school district level.* Decisions must be made about the amount of time and funding allotted for staff development on a school-by-school basis versus systemwide. Etta R. Hollins reported on the impact of the Urban Literacy Institute's activities on helping teachers address their own professional development while also improving literacy instruction for low-income urban students. Teachers met at their local schools for an hour a week, kept a weekly journal, and worked to improve their ability to teach literacy.[19]

10. *There is uncertainty about how to motivate teachers to participate in in-service education.* It would be the best of all possible worlds if teachers were intrinsically motivated to demand training for self-improvement. To a certain extent, teachers will seek training to resolve immediate needs. Their participation in all types of in-service sessions usually will increase if they have helped decide on topics and can be involved in the presentation of the sessions.

With the influx of technology into schools, added emphasis has been placed on the need to provide appropriate staff-development opportunities for classroom teachers. For example, the Concord, North Carolina, school district, located twenty minutes northeast of Charlotte, has developed an extensive staff-development program that includes ninety-five courses offered on a district level. Technology specialists (teachers who have been trained in the use of technology and who hold a state license) work in nearly all of the district's twenty schools. The school system spends a significant portion of the district's technology budget on staff development.[20]

We can conclude without a doubt that *after-school, required* in-service programs are both deadening and certain to arouse teacher hostility. Teaching is exhausting work, and burnout may lead to many teachers leaving the profession. Supervisors often work with teachers who experience burnout. This recognition often takes the form of in-service seminars on stress and burnout. Yet these seminars usually focus on what the *teacher* can do to minimize stress and avoid burnout. What may be needed are more in-service programs for administrators and supervisors on what *they* might do to reduce or eliminate both the teachers' and their own stress and burnout. If in-service education is to be successful, we must look to extrinsic motivation and provide incentives. Some of these incentives are examined later in this chapter.

11. *There is disagreement on who should control in-service education.* Should the chief administrator or the director of staff development make the decisions on what will be offered through in-service education and how? Should the teachers themselves control their in-service education, either through their associations and unions or through teacher education centers? Teachers are increasingly insisting on being involved in the planning of in-service education. For example, 93 percent of 646 teachers in a Tennessee survey of attitudes toward in-service education responded positively to the notion of teacher involvement in planning.[21]

Toni Sharma, a fourth-grade teacher, in an amusing but pointed article, satirized in-service education by likening it to the plight of Flossie, the cow, which Grandpop penned in a stanchion and Zeke, the inseminator, artificially inseminated:

> Too often, those in charge of inservice training make decisions for teachers just like the ones Zeke and Grandpop made for Flossie. They decide when to bring us together. They assume that injections of information they select will be helpful to all teachers, regardless of their individual needs. They assume that teachers have too narrow a perspective and that teachers' opinions are not valid. And finally, they assume that a direct and measurable outcome must result from inservice training.
>
> Unfortunately, it's all too easy to subscribe to those assumptions. ... I have allowed my head to be penned in the stanchion.
>
> Now I want to take charge. ... I want to determine my own needs, set my own goals, decide when and how and with whom I'll work toward those goals. I am going to control my own learning.[22]

Similar results could well be found in like studies if conducted today.

As the movement toward empowerment of teachers continues to gain in strength and intensity, teachers are having more say over their professional destinies. The results of the 1990 survey of some 21,000 elementary and secondary school teachers conducted by the

TABLE 9.1 Teacher Involvement In Decision Making

Area	Percentage of Teachers Who Stated Only Slightly Involved or Not at All in 1990	Percentage of Teachers Who Stated Only Slightly Involved or Not at All in 1987
Shaping the Curriculum	35	37
Designing Staff Development/ In-Service Programs	57	57
Deciding on How the School Budget Is Spent	80	81
Selecting New Teachers	90	93
Evaluating Teacher Performance	92	90

Source: Adapted from Carnegie Foundation for the Advancement of Teaching, *The Condition of Teaching*, 1990 (Princeton, N.J.: Carnegie Foundation for the Advancement of Teaching, 1990), pp. 55–56. © 2003. The Carnegie Foundation for the Advancement of Teaching. Reprinted with permission.

Carnegie Foundation for the Advancement of Teaching heralded the beginning stages of teacher empowerment. In response to a question on the extent of involvement of teachers in various tasks and in comparing the involvement in 1990 with results from a similar study in 1987, the Carnegie Foundation discovered a sizable percentage of teachers only slightly or not at all involved in areas where teachers should be involved if the concept of empowerment is to mean anything, as shown in Table 9.1.[23]

The No Child Left Behind (NCLB) Act of 2001 changed the requirements for most paraprofessionals working in federally funded schools that serve special needs students. Currently, teacher aides and those who help in the media center and with computers must have a high school education. Now, newly hired paraprofessionals must have an associate's degree or sixty credits from an accredited institution. Those aides who are currently working in schools must have the associate's degree or sixty credits earned by 2005. The NCLB Act allows a third option of passing a standardized examination.

The professional development needs of paraprofessionals provide supervisors with new opportunities to improve the skills of possibly millions of paraprofessionals.[24]

ASSUMPTIONS ABOUT IN-SERVICE EDUCATION

Whatever model of in-service education a school or school system follows, it is based on certain assumptions. Fred H. Wood, Steven R. Thompson, and Sister Frances Russell outlined a model of in-service education based on a set of assumptions that we believe hold true for any model:

1. All personnel in schools, to stay current and effective, need and should be involved in in-service throughout their careers. . . .
2. Significant improvement in educational practice takes considerable time and is the result of systematic, long-range staff development. . . .

3. In-service education should have an impact on the quality of the school program and focus on helping staff improve their abilities to perform their professional responsibilities. . . .

4. Adult learners are motivated to risk learning new behaviors when they believe they have control over the learning situation and are free from threat of failure. . . .

5. Educators vary widely in their professional competencies, readiness, and approaches to learning. . . .

6. Professional growth requires personal and group commitment to new performance norms. . . .

7. Organizational health including factors such as social climate, trust, open communication, and peer support for change in practice influences the success of professional development programs. . . .

8. The school is the primary unit of change; not the district or the individual. . . .

9. School districts have the primary responsibility for providing the resources and training necessary for a school staff to implement new programs and improve instruction. . . .

10. The school principal is the gatekeeper for adoption and continued use of new practices and programs in a school. . . .

11. Effective in-service programs must be based upon research, theory, and the best education practice.[25]

As a case in point, the following eight key elements developed for technology staff-development activities by the advisory boards of *Electronic Learning, Instructor,* and *Middle Years,* in conjunction with industry experts in technology staff development, apply to *all* staff-development activities:

1. Even if outside consultants are used for workshops, local staff is available for follow-up.

2. Following workshops, teachers have easy access to the same technology they were trained on.

3. Teachers are the primary trainers of teachers.

4. Training is tied directly to classroom/curriculum/school reform objectives.

5. A minimum of 25 percent of the technology budget is set aside for staff development.

6. Learning to use technology is required, not voluntary.

7. Principals, superintendents, and other administrators take technology staff development courses along with their teachers.

8. Time for technology staff development is integrated into teachers' work schedules.[26]

Three themes come through repeatedly, loudly, and clearly in discussions of in-service education: In-service programs should be a continuing operation, they should be comprehensive, and they should be cooperatively planned and developed.

CHARACTERISTICS OF EFFECTIVE IN-SERVICE PROGRAMS

School systems vary widely in respect to both the quantity and quality of their in-service programs. Some in-service programs operate on a casual, informal, troubleshooting basis, whereas others offer highly structured, planned programs in addition to the informal, unstructured type. Factors that appear to make a difference in the quantity and quality of in-service opportunities are (1) the motivational level of the teachers, (2) leadership from administrators and supervisors, and (3) financial resources.

Where teachers accept the need and desirability of continuing their professional education, in-service programs thrive. Where administrators and supervisors take an active role in promoting and planning in-service opportunities, and where funds are available, teacher participation in in-service training is high.

Citing studies by Patricia Kells et al. and Patricia J. Jamison, Leonard C. Burrello and Tim Orbaugh listed the following six major observations about what constitutes effective in-service education:[27]

1. In-service education should be designed so that programs are integrated into and supported by the organization within which they function. A comprehensive plan for in-service education in the school and/or district should be drawn up and funding should be made available.

2. In-service education programs should be designed to result in collaborative programs. The plan should include ways to involve all the constituencies of the school: teachers, administrators, supervisors, nonteaching staff, students, and laypersons.

3. In-service education programs should be grounded in the needs of the participants. The plan should be developed from an assessment of the needs and interests of the persons to be served.

4. In-service education programs should be responsive to changing needs. The plan should allow for changes as conditions change and as research brings forth new knowledge.

5. In-service education programs should be accessible. The location, physical facilities, and timing are all important factors to be considered in an in-service education plan.

6. In-service education activities should be evaluated over time and be compatible with the underlying philosophy and approach of the district. Evaluative data are needed to carry out future planning and implementation.

In-service programs are designed to bring about improvements, innovation, and change. Researchers at the University of Texas, among others, observed that the personal dimension was a key factor in instituting innovations. To facilitate the process of effecting innovations, the University of Texas Research and Development Center developed the Concerns-Based Adoption Model (CBAM), by which staff-development leaders can determine stages of concerns of each teacher about an innovation and levels of their use of innovations. Gene E. Hall et al. categorized teacher concerns in six stages of development—from simple awareness to refocusing of their thinking toward adaptation that may improve the innovation. Hall and co-workers outlined eight levels of use teachers make of an innovation—from nonuse to renewal during which the teacher strives to improve on the innovation.[28]

The supervisor of staff development should lead both school and nonschool personnel in examining the assumptions and principles on which in-service education will be designed. A profitable activity would be to measure stages of development of teachers' concerns about an innovation and their levels of using an innovation. Supervisors can be more effective in bringing about innovations when they can identify stages of teachers' concerns, stages of personal development, and their level of use of an innovative practice or program.

A MODEL FOR IN-SERVICE EDUCATION

To learn the steps the supervisor should take in establishing an in-service education program, we can turn to the general utility model, which you have seen twice before— once as a simple model of instruction and once as a basic model of curriculum development. We have added two components and converted the general model into a sequence of steps for managing an in-service education program (see Figure 9.1).

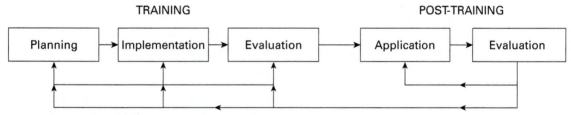

FIGURE 9.1 A Model for In-Service Education.

This figure shows that the training phases of in-service education consist of planning the training, carrying it out (implementation), and evaluating it. Because the purpose of training is to bring about changes in the classroom and/or in the person, we must look beyond the training phases. In the after-training period, we get the training program into operation in the classroom (or in our personal behavior) and evaluate our success in the classroom or in our personal lives (these phases of the post-training period have been labeled *Application* and *Evaluation*). Thus, we have a model with two submodels: *Training* and *Post-Training*. The feedback lines cycle within the training model, within the post-training model, and between the two submodels. Let's examine each of the five phases of the model. First, we'll consider the three components of the training submodel: Planning, Implementation, and Evaluation. Then we'll look at the two components of the post-training submodel: Application and Evaluation.

Planning

Most of the literature on in-service education recommends a survey, or needs assessment, of the in-service needs of the clientele to be served, as a first step in the process.

Peter A. Williamson and Julia A. Elfman stated the steps of the in-service needs assessment succinctly as follows:

- The first step is the creation of a staff-development committee for the building. ...
- Next, the committee should identify the needs of the school. ...
- Third, rank the needs. ...
- Then, design a plan of action.[29]

The professional staff should have the opportunity to identify training needs. The most critical and most pervasive should be placed at the top of the list for in-service training. Teachers sometimes disagree with administrators and supervisors over which needs are most pressing in a school system. Unless a program is mandated by the state or by the local school board, administrators or supervisors would be well advised to defer to the judgment of the teachers when there are differing opinions over training programs for teachers. Unless teachers see the value of a training program, no lasting results may be expected from it.

State Assessments One approach to identifying needs of teachers is through a statewide survey. A survey conducted in the mid-1970s by Jay Lutz and Garrett Foster highlighted differences between perceived needs of beginning teachers and those of experienced teachers.[30] Were we to conduct a similar study in any state today, we would undoubtedly find the same needs. This type of survey is not used as much in recent years because many states are allowing school districts and individual schools to make decisions about in-service opportunities.

District Assessments A yearly survey conducted in one large Florida school district, Brevard County, furnishes an illustration of a district needs assessment and planning guide. Each school principal and site in-service representative is responsible for early completion of a three-page Inservice Planning Guide describing details of training planned by the school for the two Building Inservice Days, any other major training initiatives during in-service days, and a prioritized list of school training needs requested by the School Advisory Council. This school district, the forty-seventh largest in the United States, is divided into regional areas. The more than eight thousand instructional personnel in the school district may select from activities at their school or at another site in the school district.[31]

Local School Assessments More educators are coming to believe that the most effective instructional, curricular, and staff-development plans are those based at the individual school. The concept of school-based management, generally construed as applying to budgeting, is being extended to all areas of leadership, not just the managerial aspects of school operation. John I. Goodlad spoke to this point when he said, "The optimal unit for educational change is the single school with its pupils, teachers, principal—those who live there every day—as primary participants."[32] Several years later he reaffirmed this position.[33]

School principals are expected to exercise leadership in assessing the in-service needs of teachers in their schools, analyzing data that may reflect in-service needs, and preparing a staff-development plan for that school. Supervisors can serve as resource persons to the principals and teachers as they work to provide the best instruction possible.

Of needs assessments in general, Linda L. Jones and Andrew E. Hayes cautioned,

> The literature on inservice education almost always recommends a thorough assessment of teacher needs before staff development efforts. The need for doing this has been well established, but planners of staff development programs and persons conducting research on staff development may wrongly assume that statements of needs made by teachers are their needs rather than symptoms of needs that must be diagnosed more completely.[34]

These authors are pointing to the problem inherent in any survey of felt or perceived needs. The respondents must know what they know and what they do not know. They may perceive themselves to have knowledge or skills that they do not actually possess or may even ask for repetition of topics of which they can already demonstrate mastery. Jones and Hayes commented, "Needs perceptions are an inadequate indicator of staff development needs."[35]

Yet we would not want to eliminate surveys of perceived needs. Teachers want, even demand, involvement in planning and opportunities to select the programs in which they will participate. Like curriculum needs assessments, in-service needs assessments should be verified by additional means, such as data on student achievement, parental feedback, and supervisors' observations of classroom performance. In the event of discrepancy between perceived needs and actual needs, unless teachers can be persuaded otherwise, we believe we must take the path counseled by the perceptual psychologists and deal with perceptions before we can deal with *reality*.

By whatever means, supervisors and those who work with them must obtain from the prospective participants their preferences for in-service activities. Once the teachers' choices are made known, these must be ranked in order of preference. From that point, a plan must be drawn up that will indicate which of the top needs will be addressed, how, and at what cost.

Master Plans   Supervisors of staff development typically draw up master plans for their school districts. These plans are based on feedback obtained from surveys of in-service needs. Most school systems prepare new plans annually. Some develop plans to cover a longer period, sometimes up to five years, with annual updating. Master plans describe each course, workshop, and other activity, which are referred to as *components*; master plans often read like a college catalog.

Components are made available to the teachers. Some components are delivered in the form of group study; some may be completed either in a group or independently; others are individualized components by their very nature—for example, educational travel and supervision of student teachers.

Components are written and delivered by teachers, supervisors, and college instructors. Components are designed to develop basic teaching skills, to update the teachers' knowledge and skills, and/or to provide exploratory experiences. Some states require their school systems to submit comprehensive master plans for approval. The aforementioned school district, Brevard County, Florida, offers a wide variety of staff-development courses.[36] An example is shown in Figure 9.2.

School systems usually keep meticulous records of approvals of courses, completion of courses by individuals, types of offerings, statistics, and evaluations of programs and instructors. Some states allow teachers to use their attendance at in-service sessions as a way to accrue points required for recertification.

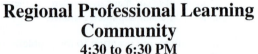

Regional Professional Learning Community
4:30 to 6:30 PM
OCEAN BREEZE ELEMENTARY

GOAL: TO HELP TEACHERS IMPROVE STUDENT ACHIEVEMENT THROUGH RESEARCH BASED INFORMATION AND COACHING

Thursday, August 17, 2006	Thursday, September 7, 2006
Thursday, October 5, 2006	Thursday, November 2, 2006
Thursday, December 7, 2006	Thursday, January 11, 2007
Thursday, February 1, 2007	Thursday, March 1, 2007
Thursday, April 12, 2007	Thursday, May 3, 2007

❑ **FOCUS:**
  - **Academic Improvement Plan (AIP Strategies)**
  - **Parent Conference Techniques**
  - **Harry Wong's Tapes on Classroom Management**

All classroom teachers are invited to come and participate in this great professional development opportunity.
For more information, contact:
Ruth Howell   Peggy Yelverton
howellr@brevard.k12.fl.us   yelvertonp@brevard.k12.fl.us

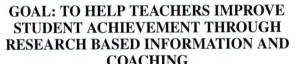

FIGURE 9.2 Professional Development Workshop Announcement. *Source:.* Ocean Breeze Elementary School, Indian Harbour Beach, Florida. Reprinted with permission of the School Board of Brevard County, Florida.

Individual School Plans   Staff-development plans of the individual school and the district supplement each other. The district's master plan reaches beyond the needs of the teachers of the individual school. Studies of in-service needs of teachers in the individual school must be followed up with some kind of plan. A typical school's staff-development plan for a year would include:

- Dates on which activities take place
- Hours devoted to each activity
- Activities
- Resource persons
- Participants' tasks
- Completion dates

Writing Components   At some point, supervisors, teachers, or outside consultants face the task of writing training programs. Although formats may differ, an outline that has proved satisfactory for writing in-service components is the following:

- Title page
- General description
- Objectives
- Pretest
- Training activities
- Training materials
- Post-test

When teachers are asked to write components for a district master plan or individual school plan, they should be given released time and/or extra pay for this additional service, which is over and above their normal assigned teaching duties. Furthermore, a cost accounting must be made for each in-service activity to ensure that the school and district stay within their staff-development budgets.

Implementation

The in-service activities should be varied in respect to both type of activity and time devoted to each. As discussed below, a number of possibilities for providing a varied in-service program are open to the supervisor:

1. *Formal college or university courses.* A common type of in-service activity, and sometimes the only organized activity, is the college or university course, which may be taught on the campus of a nearby college or university or off campus in the local schools. Those courses can be taught on a campus in the evening, on weekends, in intensive periods of time, and by taking the courses to teachers in the school district. Continued communications between a school district's person in charge of staff development and a college of education representative should result in meaningful activities for all teachers.

2. Locally developed or sponsored staff-development courses or modules. Many school systems have set supervisors and teachers to work, with or without the aid of outside consultants, at writing in-service programs, which are then made available to other teachers wishing to improve their knowledge and skills in certain areas. Teachers and supervisors often participate in developing components (sometimes called "teacher-training modules") such as these:

- Using data to improve student achievement
- Lesson planning
- Nonverbal behavior
- Conducting a class discussion
- Using the resources of the Internet in the classroom
- Classroom management
- Conflict resolution and peer mediation
- Cooperating with parents
- Inclusive classrooms
- Questioning techniques
- Developing a culturally diverse classroom
- Behavior modification
- Alternative assessment techniques
- Writing classroom tests
- Updates on specific curriculum areas

The development of teacher-training components is valuable not only in terms of product—the completed component, which may be used for in-service education—but also in terms of process—the professional growth of the teachers who do the writing.

3. Workshops and institutes. It is often difficult or impossible to distinguish a workshop from an institute. Generally speaking, workshops provide participants with opportunities to work together to find solutions to problems they have identified. Institutes bring information and suggested solutions to problems to participants and may or may not offer opportunities for the participants to work together. Workshops typically focus on hands-on activities with much teacher participation. Most workshops and institutes run from one to three days, though some, like more formal "courses," may last a couple of weeks or longer.

Workshops and institutes may be staffed by local personnel or by outside consultants and may or may not be tied in with a college or university for awarding academic credit. In organizing workshops or institutes the supervisor has the responsibility for making sure that the participants understand the objectives, for working out logistical arrangements, and for conducting an evaluation to help plan for future needs.

4. Conferences. The conference is a group meeting in which a variety of developmental activities, such as lectures, panels, symposia, and so on, take place. It is a technique for imparting information and ideas to a large group of people in the shortest possible time. A supervisor may find it expedient to call a conference of teachers to hear a specialist on a particular topic or to clarify certain issues or problems. Whenever possible, conference presentations should be followed by small-group discussions. Participants at most conferences play a passive role; this makes conferences a more limited in-service strategy than workshops, institutes, or courses.

Locally sponsored conferences take precedence over distant conferences as in-service activities. Attendance of teachers at state, regional, and national conferences and conventions of professional associations is a worthy developmental activity, but most school systems find it too costly to send many teachers to out-of-town conferences. As a result, attendance at distant meetings, if permitted at all, is ordinarily limited to the few teachers who serve as officers of the associations (whose expenses are often paid by the associations), who have some important role on the program of the association's convention, or who are willing to cover their own travel and convention costs.

Very few schools have fully tapped the potential of state, regional, and national conferences and conventions for use in in-service education. School systems could further such use of conferences by encouraging professional leave days for attendance at conferences. Also, those whose expenses are paid by the school system should be expected to prepare written (or oral) reports of what they learned from the conference and to share the reports with their peers.

5. *Supervision of student teachers and interns.* Directing a student teacher can be a valuable learning experience for both the student teacher and the supervisor. Some teachers see the supervision of a student teacher as a chore to be tolerated rather than as an in-service educational experience. Student teachers, if properly involved, can be a tremendous help to a teacher, for they bring with them not only a pair of willing hands but also some of the latest ideas, strategies, and techniques from which the observant supervising teacher can profit. Some teachers are reluctant to accept student teachers because of the expectations placed on teachers to have their students meet state test requirements.

The supervisor of staff development should present having a student teacher as a privilege and a help rather than a burden. In cooperation with the teacher education institution from which the student teacher comes, the supervisor should help identify those teachers who will make effective student-teacher supervisors. In addition, some states now require teachers to have been trained in the supervision of student teachers.

Although student teaching is ordinarily the culmination of the preservice training program for the student teacher, it should be considered a two-way street. Several states now have year-long internships, including those for individuals who have not gone through a teacher education program.

6. *Visiting days.* Some school systems release a teacher for a day to go to another class or school to observe other teachers and/or to discuss mutual teaching problems. By visiting other teachers, the individual is able to broaden his or her horizons, may find solutions to troubling problems, may learn new approaches and techniques, and may discover new materials that could prove helpful in their classes.

7. *Approved travel.* Some school systems permit teachers to engage in educational travel, which can be directly helpful in their classrooms. To gain supervisory approval for travel as an in-service activity, teachers frequently must submit a plan with a rationale and must report on their travel after they return.

The foregoing techniques are seven of the most common forms of organized in-service education programs. Dynamic school systems do not limit themselves to one or two types of programs but engage in many. Supervisors of in-service education would do well to keep in mind guidelines for effective staff-development programs proposed by Wood and Thompson:

- Include more participant control over the "what" and "how" of learning;
- Focus on job related tasks that the participants consider real and important;
- Provide choices and alternatives that accommodate the differences among participants;
- Include opportunities for participants in inservice training to practice what they are to learn in simulated and real work settings as part of their training;
- Encourage the learners to work in small groups and to learn from each other; and
- Reduce the use and threat of external judgments from one's superior by allowing peer-participants to give each other feedback concerning performance and areas of needed improvement.[37]

Incentives for Participation   The school system must establish incentives for teachers to participate in organized in-service activities. Personal satisfaction and professional improvement are not sufficient incentives by themselves. Today's school systems are encountering increasing resistance from organized teachers to demands on their time without compensation. In-service programs will cost a school system money, and funds for training programs must be incorporated into the total budget. School systems offer several types of incentives to teachers to secure their participation in in-service programs:

1. *Released time.* Typically, teachers may be expected to remain after school for short periods of time and attend faculty meetings. Contractual arrangements between a school board and an organized group of teachers often specify the exact number of hours and number of meetings that are considered part of the teachers' obligations. Although the periods of time may sometimes be used for in-service training, they are often too short and too few for any sustained group study. Beyond the stipulated obligations of teachers, released time during the school day (and/or other incentives acceptable to the teachers) must be provided if any meaningful in-service programs are to be conducted. Some school systems use the mechanism of teacher workdays, certain days during the year when teachers are on duty but children are not in attendance. Some systems allot a concentrated period of days at the end of the school year or before school opens in the late summer or fall during which teachers are paid and in-service activities may take place. Other systems release teachers for in-service projects and hire substitutes to take their places while they are participating. Jones High School in Orlando, Florida, seeks to meet some of its staff-development needs through voluntary weekly (Tuesday) forums. Teachers attend during their planning periods. The activity is repeated every period throughout the day. Although repetition may be burdensome to the presenters, this format gives priority to the teachers' schedules. It does not require them to come early or stay late.

We can gain some idea of how staff development is actually being conducted by reviewing the results of a national survey. The first national survey of technology staff development conducted by an independent research company, Willard and Shullman, for *Electronic Learning*, *Instructor*, and *Middle Years*, indicated that 37 percent of the respondents participated in staff-development activities during the school day. Thirty-one percent participated after school, 14 percent on official district release days, 6 percent during the summer, and 3 percent over a weekend.[38]

Activities requiring extended blocks of time and considerable hands-on practice must follow other scheduling formats. A fundamental principle for in-service activities sponsored by the local school system is the provision of time for the teachers to participate on their own time. For these activities to succeed, there will need to be incentives from the school system for teachers to participate.

2. *In-service credits for salary increments.* Some school systems with well-organized in-service programs allot credit for participation in each activity. Credits are known variously as staff-development units (SDUs), continuing education units (CEUs), master plan points (MPPs), and professional incentive points (PIPs). In cases where the district's plan for staff development is approved by the state department of education, these types of credits may be applied, like college credits, to extending or renewing a certificate; this is an attractive inducement to many teachers. Certain school systems, on their own, require teachers to undertake some in-service work to renew their tenure.

Teachers earn credits on a formula basis. Five SDUs, for example, commonly require fifty hours of class time (or the equivalent in self-study), which make them roughly comparable to five quarter hours of college academic credit. With these incentives, teachers may be expected to participate on their own time.

3. *Financial support for college study.* To encourage them to take courses at nearby colleges and universities, some school systems pay teachers for a given number of college credits earned during the year. Ordinarily, these credits must be directly related to the teacher's field of specialization.

Reimbursement for college study makes formal study appealing to many teachers. Because school systems pay higher salaries to teachers with advanced degrees, academic credit from a college or university is often a sufficient incentive in itself. However, after the teacher has achieved that degree (or a given number of college credits beyond the bachelor's degree), some device, such as reimbursement for college study, is desirable to encourage the teacher to continue self-improvement.

Supervisors should work with colleges and universities in the area to secure, if possible, favorable tuition rates for school personnel. They frequently negotiate with colleges and universities for tuition certificates for teachers who serve the higher education institutions as supervisors of student teachers or interns.

Various states are considering strategies to keep the best, most effective teachers in classrooms. In addition, some states, including Florida, are considering a new structure that would classify teachers into four categories. The top two categories, Senior Teacher and Mentor Teacher, include teachers who would lead other teachers in professional development and school improvement activities and would mentor other teachers.[39]

Funding Successful in-service education cannot be provided without an investment of time and money. Staff-development programs are funded from a variety of sources: the local district, the state, and teachers themselves. With continuing emphasis on achieving high-quality education, staff-development needs should be given priority in funding. Local school systems often build staff-development monies into their budgets. As states are mandating evaluations of teacher performance, a natural concomitant is state funding for staff development for both remedial and developmental purposes.

To supplement their resources, some school systems charge a small fee to those who participate in in-service activities. A laudable goal would be to provide all staff-development activities without cost to the participants. The availability of in-service components without fee would be one further incentive for teachers to participate. In-service education should be perceived as a major responsibility to be supported by local and state funds. Education might well emulate the business world, where companies commit a significant portion of their budgets to continuing development of their employees.

Use of Consultants Staff-development plans rely heavily on persons within the school system to serve as instructors. Faculty members who have demonstrated proficiency in knowledge of curriculum or in the use of effective strategies may serve as consultants to their colleagues. On the other hand, the services of consultants from outside the school system are often sought for workshops, institutes, and conferences. The use of outside consultants is a stock method of providing in-service training, and though the employment of outside consultants is often necessary and may result in changes in teacher behavior through exposure to the consultant's views, care must be exercised in the employment of consultants and the uses made of their services.

In an early study entitled *High School Self-Evaluation and Curriculum Change*, Vynce A. Hines and William M. Alexander found that teachers consider the use of consultants from outside the school system to be one of the least important factors in curriculum change.[40] According to this study, the factors teachers rated as more influential in curriculum change were the administrative staff of their own school, the administrative staff of the school system, the regional accrediting association, the faculty of the school, and the state department of education. A similar study today would almost certainly reaffirm these findings.

When planning for the use of outside consultants, the supervisor may gain the maximum productivity from their visits by following a few simple rules:

1. The supervisor should seek faculty input in the selection of consultants.

2. The consultants chosen should be qualified beyond question for the roles asked of them. The supervisor should do some advance checking, preferably with school systems that have called on the consultants' services in the past, to be sure that the consultants chosen are the best-qualified persons available.

3. The consultants should be oriented well in advance to the task expected of them. Far too much valuable consultant time is lost when a consultant orients him- or herself to the task after arriving on the scene.

4. The consultants should be available for questions and discussion following their presentations. The consultant who hurries in, makes a presentation, and quickly exits often leaves a group at the very point when the participants could benefit from interaction with him or her. Some consultants have important things to say, and some share research they have conducted or new techniques they have found helpful.

For workshops and institutes, however, where teachers settle down to find specific answers to immediate problems or learn new techniques for accomplishing their instructional duties, the services of experts should be sought. They will lead the teachers through the study they are undertaking and remain with them long enough (*at the very least* for an extended and unhurried question-and-answer session) to permit them to begin discovering answers to their many questions and problems.

Evaluation

To assess the effectiveness of in-service education and to strengthen subsequent programs, continuing evaluation is essential. The achievement of participants, each in-service activity, and school and master plans for staff development should be evaluated.

The evaluation of participants' achievement in in-service programs conducted by school systems tends to be less formal than assessment in college courses. More often than not, in-service activities do not lend themselves to terminal examinations. Evaluation of in-service programs can consist of the supervisor's observation of the participants' performance during the activity and afterward, of oral and written reports during the in-service program, and of short quizzes—for example, pretests and posttests.

Each in-service activity must be evaluated as to the content, the delivery system, and the instructor (or consultant). It has become standard operating procedure for the staff-development coordinator or the in-service activity instructor to distribute an end-of-activity evaluation form, which participants fill out anonymously. Two illustrations will give us an idea of the types of information gathered from in-service education participants.

For several years, the Association for Supervision and Curriculum Development has administered evaluation forms at the conclusion of sessions at its professional development programs and annual conferences. These brief evaluation forms are seen in Figures 9.3 and 9.4. Members of the Human Resources Division of the School District of Brevard County, Florida, request participants to complete the form shown in Figure 9.5.

Post-Training Application and Evaluation

Perhaps even more important than end-of-activity evaluations is follow-up evaluation of participants' performance after the activity. The ultimate test of an in-service activity is translation of the knowledge and skills learned into the participant's personal and/or professional behavior. What a school system really needs to know is whether the activity made any difference in teacher performance, that is, whether the teachers applied in the classroom the knowledge and skills they learned in training. Consequently, some plan needs to be developed to evaluate attainment of an activity's objectives over a period of time.

The success or failure of in-service programs rests heavily on the shoulders of those supervisors charged by the administrators with the direction of staff-development activities. Success of staff-development programs correlates directly with the leadership skills of the supervisor. The more input that person receives from those who will be involved, the better the chance of those activities being successful.

Professional Development Program Evaluation Form

Program Title:

We would appreciate knowing how you rate this program in comparison to similar professional development sessions you have attended. For each of the items below, please provide a 1 to 5 rating by filling in the SCANTRON form in pencil or ink pen.

Example:

CORRECT

INCORRECT

1=strongly disagree   2=disagree   3=undecided   4=agree   5=strongly agree

Overall Program

1. The total program was of high quality.

   Comments:_____

2. The objectives of the program were met:

   A.

   B.

3. The program content will be useful to me.

   Comments:_____

Presenter: _____

4. The speaker's overall effectiveness was high.

5. The content of the speaker's presentation was useful.

6. The speaker used effective instructional techniques.

7. The speaker used high quality materials.

   Comments:_____

Presenter: _____

8. The speaker's overall effectiveness was high.

9. The content of the speaker's presentation was useful.

10. The speaker used effective instructional techniques.

11. The speaker used high quality materials.

    Comments:_____

FIGURE 9.3 Professional Development Program Evaluation Form. *Source:* Association for Supervision and Curriculum Development (Alexandria, Va.: Association for Supervision and Curriculum Development). Reprinted with permission of the Association for Supervision and Curriculum Development.

Presenter: _____

	👎				👍

12. The speaker's overall effectiveness was high.   ⊏1⊐ ⊏2⊐ ⊏3⊐ ⊏4⊐ ⊏5⊐

13. The content of the speaker's presentation was useful.   ⊏1⊐ ⊏2⊐ ⊏3⊐ ⊏4⊐ ⊏5⊐

14. The speaker used effective instructional techniques.   ⊏1⊐ ⊏2⊐ ⊏3⊐ ⊏4⊐ ⊏5⊐

15. The speaker used high quality materials.   ⊏1⊐ ⊏2⊐ ⊏3⊐ ⊏4⊐ ⊏5⊐

Comments: _____

_____

_____

Meeting Facilities

16. The accommodations were of high quality (i.e., guest rooms, restaurants, public areas, etc.)   ⊏1⊐ ⊏2⊐ ⊏3⊐ ⊏4⊐ ⊏5⊐

17. The hotel guest services were of high quality (i.e., check-in, restaurants, room service, cleanliness, etc.)   ⊏1⊐ ⊏2⊐ ⊏3⊐ ⊏4⊐ ⊏5⊐

18. I liked the hotel location.   ⊏1⊐ ⊏2⊐ ⊏3⊐ ⊏4⊐ ⊏5⊐

Comments: _____

_____

_____

ASCD's Registration Process: (Optional)

19. Responses to requests for information are courteous and timely.   ⊏1⊐ ⊏2⊐ ⊏3⊐ ⊏4⊐ ⊏5⊐

20. ASCD's registration process is well organized and efficient.   ⊏1⊐ ⊏2⊐ ⊏3⊐ ⊏4⊐ ⊏5⊐

Comments: _____

_____

I would recommend this program to a colleague.   YES ☐   NO ☐

My job title is: _____   Please fill in if ASCD member ☐
Please fill in if HRDP member ☐

Please list other topics, issues and speakers which you would like to see offered as future ASCD Professional Development programs:

_____

_____

Comments:

_____

_____

_____

FIGURE 9.3 (*continued*)

ANNUAL CONFERENCE EVALUATION FORM ASCD CH

TOPIC

1. Applicability to my work
2. Quality of information
3. Quality of handouts/materials shared
4. Presentation accurately described in Program book

PROCESS

1. Overall use of effective teaching strategies
2. Opportunity for interaction and discussion
3. I met colleagues with whom I will be able to network
4. Because of attending this session, I am interested in learning more about the topic presented

OVERALL RATING OF ACTIVITY PRESENTER(S)

NAME:
1. Organized/Prepared
2. Overall rating as presenter

NAME:
1. Organized/Prepared
2. Overall rating as presenter

NAME:
1. Organized/Prepared
2. Overall rating as presenter

NAME:
1. Organized/Prepared
2. Overall rating as presenter

(Rating columns: EXCELLENT, GOOD, FAIR, POOR, NOT APPLICABLE)

- MAKE HEAVY **DARK** MARKS THAT COMPLETELY FILL EACH BLOCK
- **EXAMPLE:** ▬ BLOCK IS FILLED **COMPLETELY**
- ERASE **COMPLETELY** TO CHANGE
- DO NOT USE A RED PEN

★ ★

PLEASE MAKE FURTHER COMMENTS HERE:

_____
_____
_____
_____
_____
_____
_____

★ ★

ABOUT ME My job title is:

☐ Principal – Elementary	☐ Teacher – Elementary	☐ Superintendent	☐ Curriculum Specialist
☐ Principal – Middle/Jr. High	☐ Teacher – Middle/Jr. High	☐ Central Office	☐ Supervisor
☐ Principal – High School	☐ Teacher – High School	☐ Professor	

☐ Other_____

★ ★

PLEASE CONTINUE THE EVALUATION ON THE BACK OF THIS FORM. THANK YOU.   **ASCD COPY**

FIGURE 9.4 ASCD Session Evaluation Form. *Source:* Association for Supervision and Curriculum Development, *Annual Conference Evaluation Form* (Alexandria, Va.: Association for Supervision and Curriculum Development). Reprinted with permission of the Association for Supervision and Curriculum Development.

OPINION SURVEY

(This Opinion Survey can be used for ANY inservices/workshop.)

Name _____ School _____

Course/Workshop_____ Dates _____

Please circle the answer that best represents your experience in this activity:

Your input will be used to reinforce effective techniques and improve weaker components of the training. Thank you for your time and thoughtful reflection.

1.   The content of this inservice was relevant to my needs as a teacher.

   All of it   **Most of it**   **Little of it**   **None of it**

   Additional Comments:

2.   The instructor(s) modeled the same skills, techniques, and strategies that I should use in the classroom.

   Whole workshop   **Much of the time**   **Little of the time**   **Never**

   Additional Comments:

3.   I was able to practice, during the workshop, the skills I am learning.

   Yes; sufficient practice   **Yes; not enough practice**   **No**

   Additional Comments:

4.   The instructor provided feedback to me on my performance during the training session.

   Yes; sufficient feedback   **Yes; not enough feedback**   **No**

   Additional Comments:

   Additional Overall Comments:

FIGURE 9.5 Workshop Opinion Survey. *Source:* School Board of Brevard County, Florida. Reprinted with permission of the School Board of Brevard County, Florida.

CONTROL OF IN-SERVICE EDUCATION

The locus of control of in-service education is a subject of controversy. Disagreements center on such questions as, "Who shall make the policies pertaining to in-service education?" "How shall decisions be made about in-service offerings?" and "How shall in-service budgets be expended?" The school board, the superintendent, and the director of staff development are too simplistic as answers to the first question. True, the school board sets all school policies, the top executive administers them, and the administrator's aides carry out responsibilities delegated to them. But within the larger context of school management are varying opinions and practices related to the provision of in-service education.

Administration of in-service education in the public schools rests with four offices: (1) the principal of the individual school, (2) the central-office director of staff development, (3) the intermediate unit, and (4) the teacher education center. The first two offices come within the jurisdiction of the local school superintendent. The third falls beyond the purview of the local superintendent. The fourth center may or may not lie within the authority of the superintendent.

Historically, in-service education has been the responsibility of the normal schools and colleges of education. From the mid-twentieth century, school districts have assumed a large role in establishing and operating in-service programs. Increasingly, school district administrators are delegating responsibilities for staff-development programs to the principals of the individual schools within the system. Of this trend, Dull said, "During the past decade the focus of control over staff development has moved rapidly from institutions of higher education to local school districts, and even from the school district to the local school where principals are providing more and more leadership in staff development."[41]

Some states have established intermediate units known as regional or cooperative educational service agencies. These agencies, headed by a superintendent or director, serve a number of school districts. In some areas of the country, particularly the sparsely settled rural regions, regional educational service agencies offer the lion's share of staff-development activities. Some of the urban areas have chosen to participate in the support of the regional educational service agencies and use the services of the supervisors on the agencies' staffs. Other urban districts have not worked with the regional educational service agencies and manage their own staff-development programs. Still others call on the regional educational service agencies as needed while at the same time conducting their own staff-development programs.

Teacher Education Centers

The rise of teacher education centers in the 1970s had a significant impact on the administration and operation of staff-development programs. The teacher education center in America can be traced to the teacher centers that started to spring up in Great Britain in the mid-1960s. We should, however, at the outset, distinguish between the *teacher center* and the *teacher education center*. Although both types of center have a bearing on staff development, they are not identical.

Teacher centers were physical plants that housed all kinds of instructional, curriculum, and professional materials for teachers' use. They served as meeting places for workshops, conferences, and the like. They were sites where teachers came together professionally and socially. In some respects, they were staffed curriculum laboratories or curriculum materials centers. Illustrative of this type of center were not only the British teacher centers but also the Centres Régionaux de Documentation Pédagogique, which have been in existence in France for many years. Some school districts in the United States established British and French types of teacher centers. These centers belonged to the school district and were entirely under the authority of the super-intendent and school board.

Patterns of organization of teacher education centers throughout the United States differed considerably. Teacher education centers variously possessed a single building, several buildings, or no building at all. They may or may not have provided the helpful facilities and resources to be found in a teacher center. In other words, the teacher education center may or may not have incorporated a teacher center within its plan.

The teacher education center was a concept based on certain assumptions, among which were the following:

- Greater control over staff-development programs should be placed in the hands of those most directly affected—the teachers.

- To an ever-increasing extent, in-service programs offered by schools of education should be taken off campus and placed in the real world of the teacher.

- Teachers, administrators, and college professors, sometimes in collaboration with students and laypersons, should cooperatively plan and carry out in-service activities.

With ten teacher education centers created through state funding under the Teacher Education Center Act of 1973, the state of Florida became an early leader in the teacher education center movement. In 1991, all sixty-seven of the county districts were affiliated, as a result of state mandate, with one of the state's forty-eight teacher education centers. Florida defined a teacher education center as

> an organized arrangement to promote collaboration in teacher education, both preservice and in-service. It involves teachers, school districts, and teacher education institutions. A teacher education center draws resources from existing teacher education programs. It does not replace these institutions. It is especially concerned with those aspects of teacher education requiring mutual involvement of concerned institutions.[42]

Where teacher education centers were operational, more of the in-service education heretofore conducted on the campuses of teacher education institutions moved off the campuses and into the regions served by the centers. The centers provided experiences in real schools with real children. Teacher education centers injected realism into the preparation of prospective teachers and into in-service training programs.

SUMMARY

Staff development and *in-service education* are used interchangeably in this chapter and text. Supervisors spend considerable time in planning, implementing, and evaluating staff-development programs. In fact, no task looms larger on the supervisor's agenda than helping develop the school district's human resources through staff-development activities.

In-service education programs should be planned and carried out in cooperation with those for whom the programs are designed. Several issues and assumptions were examined and a model of in-service education was presented, consisting of three training components and two post-training components.

Planning for in-service education begins with an assessment of needs as perceived by the teachers. After needs are surveyed, they are ranked and top needs are filled.

Active school systems make available to teachers a wide variety of opportunities for improving themselves both personally and professionally. The goal of in-service education is the continuous professional development of the teachers, which in turn will enhance the achievement of the learners. Among the types of organized in-service programs are college and university courses, workshops and institutes, conferences, supervision of student teachers and interns, visiting days, and approved travel.

Directors of staff development are often charged with the task of preparing a comprehensive master plan for their school districts. Principals are frequently assigned the job of creating a staff-development plan for their schools.

To gain teachers' participation in organized in-service training, some incentives are essential. Among the incentives found to be successful in school systems are released time, salary increments based on the accumulation of in-service credits, financial support for college and university study, reduced tuition rates for teachers attending colleges and universities, certificates for supervisors of student teachers and interns entitling them to register for college or university courses, pay differentials for advanced degrees or accumulated college and university credits, and in-service activities without cost to teachers.

Supervisors should plan for the evaluation of in-service activities. Participants should evaluate the contributions of the staff, the instruction, the facilities, and their own accomplishments. They should be given the opportunity to express their satisfaction or dissatisfaction with the activities, materials, procedures, and personnel. An evaluation form tailored to the particular in-service activity should be developed by the supervisor and staff of the in-service activity and distributed to the participants to fill out at the end of the program. Supervisors should conduct follow-up evaluations to learn whether teachers are using what they learned in in-service programs.

Control of in-service education is an issue. Staff-development activities are sponsored by individual schools, the central office, intermediate units, schools and departments of education, and teacher education centers.

Some school districts have established teacher centers, which house resources for teachers and serve as meeting places. Some school systems alone or in cooperation with other systems have created teacher education centers, which assume a major role in planning and administering in-service education. Providing various options for in-service education can lead to a staff better prepared to face the challenges of teaching. Effective presentations, cost-effective delivery systems, and a staff willing to participate make for more effective instruction. The true measures of success of professional development programs are improvement in student achievement and enhancement of teacher effectiveness, motivation, and satisfaction.

QUESTIONS FOR DISCUSSION

1. Why do some people refer to the supervisor as the ultimate team leader?
2. Why does the nature of the relationships among the adults who inhabit a school have more to do with the school's quality and character and with the accomplishments of its pupils than any other factor?

3. What is the importance of each of the five components of an in-service education model: planning, implementation, evaluation, application, and reevaluation?

4. What should be included in a staff-development course announcement for your level or subject of teaching?

5. What would you include in a needs assessment focused on in-service needs of teachers?

ACTIVITIES FOR FURTHER STUDY

REFLECTIVE

1. Define staff development, in-service education, and professional development.

2. Distinguish between a workshop, institute, seminar, and course as applied to in-service education.

3. Analyze a master plan for staff development; using a set of criteria that you have located or developed, point out its strengths and weaknesses.

4. Analyze a staff-development plan for an individual school; using a set of criteria you have located or developed, point out its strengths and weaknesses.

5. Summarize the in-service education model proposed by Fred H. Wood, Steven R. Thompson, and Sister Frances Russell (see bibliography at the end of the chapter).

6. Write a report on the development and status of teacher education centers in the United States.

7. List characteristics of an effective in-service activity.

8. Report on follow-up evaluation of any in-service activity conducted in your school or school district within the last five years.

9. Prepare a report on the Concerns-Based Adoption Model (CBAM) for determining stages of teacher concerns about an innovation and their levels of use of the innovation. (See Note 28 for references by Gene E. Hall and Susan Loucks and Gene E. Hall, Susan F. Loucks, William L. Rutherford, and Beaulah W. Newlove.)

APPLICATION

1. Poll a group of teachers and summarize their views on the following:
   a. What types of in-service activities do they prefer?
   b. Do they feel they have input into the organization of in-service training programs?
   c. What incentives do they believe are needed to secure teacher participation in in-service programs?
   d. Are they aware of in-service opportunities in their school system?
   e. Do they feel satisfied with the range and type of in-service opportunities?

2. Consult with administrators and supervisors in a school system and/or search the literature for types of organized in-service education opportunities not mentioned in this chapter.

3. Find out and report the annual cost of in-service activities of a school system you know well. Tell what percentage of funding comes from state sources, what percentage from local sources, and what percentage (if any) from federal sources. Calculate the cost of in-service education per pupil. Decide whether the total expenditure for in-service education is too much, too little, or about right.

4. Develop an instrument for evaluating a specific workshop, institute, conference, or other in-service activity; attend that activity; apply the instrument you have developed; summarize the data; and draw conclusions.

5. Develop a set of guidelines to help teachers achieve the maximum benefits from supervising student teachers or interns.

6. Gather and report data from several school systems elsewhere in the state or nation on prevailing practices concerning incentives provided for teachers to secure their participation in in-service training.

7. If there is a teacher education center in the area, obtain information about the center by interviewing center officials or by examining literature of the center about its in-service programs. Describe the composition of the teacher education center advisory council or committee and tell to whom the center director reports. Prepare a report that summarizes the in-service programs, shows the roles of the center and the teacher education institutions with which the center works, and contrasts in-service programs as conducted by the center with in-service programs as they exist without a center. Determine whether there is any change in the role of supervisors of a school system when a teacher education center exists in the system.

8. Conduct an in-service needs assessment in your school. Verify teachers' perceived needs against empirical data.

9. Survey the attitudes of teachers in a school about in-service education. If you discover negative attitudes, account for the negativism and suggest ways to overcome it.

10. Learn whether an intermediate unit (regional educational service agency) serves your school district. If so, find what services it provides and how many consultants it has and in what areas they specialize.

11. Draft a plan for a workshop or an institute on a topic you believe is needed by a school system you know well. Include in your plan objectives, activities, materials, personnel, and means of evaluation.

12. Draft a plan for a conference on a topic you believe is needed by a school system you know well. Include in your plan objectives, activities, materials, personnel, and means of evaluation.

NOTES

1. Florida Association of District School Superintendents, *Human Resources Management and Development, 1990–2000*, 3rd ed. (Tallahassee, Fla.: Florida Association of District School Superintendents).
2. The New Florida Department of Education Web site, http://fldoe.org.
3. Lloyd W. Dull, *Supervision: School Leadership Handbook* (Columbus, Ohio: Merrill, 1981), p. 110.
4. Ben M. Harris, *In-Service Education for Staff Development* (Boston: Allyn and Bacon, 1989), pp. 18–21.
5. Thomas J. Sergiovanni and Robert J. Starratt, *Supervision: A Redefinition*, 8th ed. (Boston: McGraw-Hill, 2007), pp. 215–16.
6. Donald C. Orlich, *Staff Development: Enhancing Human Potential* (Boston: Allyn and Bacon, 1989), pp. 4–6.
7. Bruce Joyce and Beverly Showers, *Student Achievement through Staff Development* (White Plains, N.Y.: Longman, 1995), p. 25.
8. Pendred Noyce, "Professional Development: How Do We Know If It Works?" *Education Week* 3 (September 13, 2006), pp. 44+, 36–37.
9. Stephanie Hirsh and Dennis Sparks, "Staff Development Resolutions for the Next Millennium," *High School Magazine* 7 (October 1999): 20–24.
10. John T. Lovell, "Instructional Supervision: Emerging Perspective," in *The Role and Responsibilities of Instructional Supervisors, Report of the ASCD Working Group on the Roles and Responsibilities of Supervisors*, A. W.

Sturges, chairman (Alexandria, Va.: Association for Supervision and Curriculum Development, October 1, 1978), p. 43.

11. Fred H. Wood and Steven R. Thompson, "Guidelines for Better Staff Development," *Educational Leadership* 37 (February 1980): 374.

12. Ben M. Harris, *Improving Staff Performance through In-Service Education* (Boston: Allyn and Bacon, 1980), pp. 33–37.

13. David W. Champagne, "Does Staff Development Do Any Good?" *Educational Leadership* 37 (February 1980): 401–2. See "An Exercise in Freedom: A Place Where Test Scores Appear to Be Rising," in *The Test Score Decline*, ed. L. Lipsitz (Englewood Cliffs, N.J.: Educational Technology, 1977).

14. Champagne, "Does Staff Development Do Any Good?" pp. 402–3. See ERIC report by William P. Ward, ED 119 387 EA 008 045.

15. Roland Barth, "Improving Relationships within the Schoolhouse," *Educational Leadership* 63 (March 2006), pp. 8–13.

16. Lovell, "Instructional Supervision," p. 35.

17. John Dewey, *The Sources of a Science of Education* (New York: Liveright, 1929), p. 17.

18. Roy A. Edelfelt, "Critical Issues in Developing Teacher Centers," *Phi Delta Kappan* 63 (February 1982): 390.

19. Etta R. Hollins, "Transforming Practice in Urban Schools," *Educational Leadership* 63 (March 2006), pp. 48–52.

20. Jessica Siegel, "The State of Teacher Training," *Electronic Learning* 14 (May/June 1995): 51.

21. Harris, *Improving Staff Performance*, p. 37.

22. Toni Sharma, "Inservicing the Teachers," *Phi Delta Kappan* 63 (February 1982): 403.

23. Carnegie Foundation for the Advancement of Teaching, *The Condition of Teaching*, 1990 (Princeton, N.J.: Carnegie Foundation for the Advancement of Teaching, 1990), pp. 55–56.

24. Linda Jump, "Extra Education Requirements a Hardship for Teacher Aides," *Florida Today*, February 8, 2003, pp. 1B, 7B.

25. Fred H. Wood, Steven R. Thompson, and Sister Frances Russell, "Designing Effective Staff Development Programs," in *Staff Development/Organization Development*, 1981 Yearbook (Alexandria, Va.: Association for Supervision and Curriculum Development, 1981), pp. 61–63. See also the slightly revised version in Fred H. Wood, Frank O. McQuarrie Jr., and Steven R. Thompson, "Practitioners and Professors Agree on Effective Staff Development Practices," *Educational Leadership* 40 (October 1982): 28–29.

26. Siegel, "The State of Teacher Training," p. 50.

27. Leonard C. Burrello and Tim Orbaugh, "Reducing the Discrepancy between the Known and the Unknown in Inservice Education," *Phi Delta Kappan* 63 (February 1982): 385–86. See Patricia P. Kells et al., *Quality Practice Task Force Final Report* (Bloomington, Ind.: National Inservice Network, 1980); and Patricia J. Jamison, "The Development and Validation of a Conceptual Model and Quality Practices Designed to Guide the Planning, Implementation, and Evaluation of Inservice Education Programs," doctoral dissertation, College Park, University of Maryland, 1981.

28. See Gene E. Hall and Susan Loucks, "Teacher Concerns as a Basis for Facilitating and Personalizing Staff Development," *Teachers College Record* 80 (September 1978): 36–53. See also Gene E. Hall, Susan F. Loucks, William L. Rutherford, and Beaulah W. Newlove, "Levels of Use of the Innovation: A Framework for Analyzing Innovation Adoption," *Journal of Teacher Education* 26 (Spring 1975): 52–56; and John P. Miller and Wayne Seller, *Curriculum: Perspectives and Practice* (White Plains, N.Y.: Longman, 1985), pp. 249–63.

29. Peter A. Williamson and Julia A. Elfman, "A Commonsense Approach to Teacher Inservice Training," *Phi Delta Kappan* 63 (February 1982): 401.

30. Jay Lutz and Garrett Foster, "Greater Involvement Urged," *Florida Schools* 37 (February 1975): 20–21.

31. Brevard County Office of Human Resources, *School Inservice Planning Guide 2002–2003* (Melbourne, Fla.: Brevard County Office of Human Resources, April 2002).

32. John I. Goodlad, *The Dynamics of Educational Change: Toward Responsive Schools* (New York: McGraw-Hill, 1975), p. 175.

33. John I. Goodlad, *A Place Called School: Prospects for the Future* (New York: McGraw-Hill, 1984), pp. 318–19.

34. Linda L. Jones and Andrew E. Hayes, "How Valid Are Surveys of Teacher Needs?" *Educational Leadership* 37 (February 1980): 390.

35. Ibid., p. 391.

36. Brevard County Public Schools, *District Inservice Day*, October 18, 2002.

37. Wood and Thompson, "Guidelines for Better Staff Development," p. 377.

38. Siegel, "The State of Teacher Training," p. 48.

39. "State's Best Teachers Could Make $100,000," Associated Press, *Florida Today*, February 7, 2003, p. 1B.
40. Vynce A. Hines and William M. Alexander, *High School Self-Evaluation and Curriculum Change*, Final Report, Project 3120, Contract no. OE 6-10-54, Bureau of Research, Office of Education (Washington, D.C.: U.S. Department of Health, Education, and Welfare, August 1967), p. 64.
41. Dull, *Supervision*, p. 111.
42. Florida Department of Education, *State Council for Teacher Education Centers Annual Report* (Tallahassee: Florida Department of Education, 1975), p. 2.

BIBLIOGRAPHY

BARTH, ROLAND. "Improving Relationships within the Schoolhouse." *Educational Leadership* 63 (March 2006): 8–13.

BRANDT, RON, BETTY DILLON-PETERSON, BRUCE JOYCE, EMILY CALHOUN, FRED WOOD, THOMAS R. GUSKEY, MICHAEL FULLAN, RICHARD SCHMUCK, and SUSAN LOUCKS-HORSLEY. "Reflection on 25 Years of Staff Development." *Journal of Staff Development* (Fall 1994): 2–8.

Brevard County Office of Human Resources. *Brevard County Master Inservice Plan 2006–2007*. Viera, Fla.: Brevard County Office of Human Resources, www.brevard.k12.fl.us.

CALDWELL, SARAH J. *Staff Development: A Handbook of Effective Practices*. Oxford, Ohio: National Staff Development Council, 1989.

Carnegie Foundation for the Advancement of Teaching. *The Condition of Teaching, 1990*. Princeton, N.J.: Carnegie Foundation for the Advancement of Teaching, 1990.

Center on Evaluation, Development, and Research. *Staff Development*. Bloomington, Ind.: Center on Evaluation, Development, and Research, Phi Delta Kappa, 1985/86.

CHAMPAGNE, DAVID W. "Does Staff Development Do Any Good?" *Educational Leadership* 37 (February 1980): 400–403.

DALE, E. LAWRENCE. "What Is Staff Development?" *Educational Leadership* 40 (October 1982): 31.

DEWEY, JOHN. *The Sources of a Science of Education*. New York: Liveright, 1929.

DILLON-PETERSON, BETTY, ed. *Staff Development/Organization Development*, 1981 Yearbook. Alexandria, Va.: Association for Supervision and Curriculum Development, 1981.

DOLL, RONALD C. *Supervision for Staff Development: Ideas and Application*. Boston: Allyn and Bacon, 1983.

DUKE, DANIEL L. "How a Staff Development Plan Can Rescue At-Risk Students." *Educational Leadership* 50 (December 1992/January 1993): 28–33.

DULL, LLOYD W. *Supervision—School Leadership Handbook*. Columbus, Ohio: Merrill, 1981.

EDELFELT, ROY A. "Critical Issues in Developing Teacher Centers." *Phi Delta Kappan* 63 (February 1982): 390–93.

ELLIS, SUSAN S. "Principals as Staff Developers—We Better Know What We're Asking Teachers to Do: An Interview with Larry Dixon." *Journal of Staff Development* 16 (Spring 1995): 56–58.

GUSKEY, THOMAS R. *Evaluating Professional Development*. Thousand Oaks, Calif.: Corwin Press, 2000.

———. "Results-Oriented Professional Development: In Search of an Optimal Mix of Effective Practices." *Journal of Staff Development* 15 (Fall 1994): 42–50.

GUSKEY, THOMAS R., and DENNIS SPARKS. "What to Consider When Evaluating Staff Development." *Educational Leadership* 49 (November 1991): 73–76.

HALL, GENE E., and SUSAN LOUCKS. "Teacher Concerns as a Basis for Facilitating and Personalizing Staff Development." *Teachers College Record* 80 (September 1978): 36–53.

HARRIS, BEN M. *Improving Staff Performance through In-Service Education*. Boston: Allyn and Bacon, 1980.

———. *In-Service Education for Staff Development*. Boston: Allyn and Bacon, 1989.

———. *Supervisory Behavior in Education*, 3rd ed. Englewood Cliffs, N.J.: Prentice Hall, 1985.

HIRSH, STEPHANIE. "Developing Teachers' Instructional Skills." *High School Magazine* 7 (September 1999): 4–8.

HIRSH, STEPHANIE, and DENNIS SPARKS. "Staff Development Resolutions for the Next Millennium." *High School Magazine* 7 (October 1999): 20–24.

HOLLINS, ETTA R. "Transforming Practice in Urban Schools." *Educational Leadership* 63 (March 2006): 48–52..

JOYCE, BRUCE, ed. *Changing School Culture through Staff Development*. 1990 Yearbook. Alexandria, Va.: Association for Supervision and Curriculum Development, 1990.

Joyce, Bruce, and Beverly Showers. *Student Achievement through Staff Development*, 3rd ed. Alexandria, Va.: Association for Supervision and Curriculum Development, 2002.

Knoll, Marcia K. *Supervision for Better Instruction: Practical Techniques for Improving Staff Performance.* Englewood Cliffs, N.J.: Prentice Hall, 1987.

Loucks-Horsley, Susan, Catherine K. Harding, Margaret A. Arbuckle, Lynn B. Murray, Cynthia Dubea, and Martha K. Williams. *Continuing to Learn: A Guidebook for Teacher Development.* Oxford, Ohio: National Staff Development Council, 1987.

Loucks-Horsley, Susan, Nancy Love, Katherine E. Stiles, Susan E. Mundry, and Peter W. Hewson. *Designing Professional Development for Teachers of Science and Mathematics*, 2nd ed. Thousand Oaks, Calif.: Corwin Press, 2003.

Lovell, John T. "Instructional Supervision: Emerging Perspective." In *The Role and Responsibilities of Instructional Supervisors. Report of the ASCD Working Group on the Roles and Responsibilities of Supervisors.* Chairman, A. W. Sturges. Alexandria, Va.: Association for Supervision and Curriculum Development October 1, 1978.

Lutz, Jay, and Garrett Foster. "Greater Involvement Urged." *Florida Schools* 37 (February 1975): 20–21.

Novelli, Joan. "A New Look at Teacher Centers." *Instructor* 100 (November 1990): 28, 33–35.

Noyce, Pendred. "Professional Development: How Do We Know if It Works?" *Education Week* 26 (September 13, 2006): 44+, 36–37.

Orlich, Donald C. *Staff Development: Enhancing Human Potential.* Boston: Allyn and Bacon, 1989.

Petzko, Vicki Nord. "Preventing Legal Headaches through Staff Development: Considerations and Recommendations." *NASSP Bulletin* 82 (December 1998): 35–42.

Readings from Educational Leadership: Coaching and Staff Development. Alexandria, Va.: Association for Supervision and Curriculum Development, 1989.

Schurr, Sandra. *How to Improve Discussion and Questioning Practices: Tools and Techniques.* Reston, Va.: National Association of Secondary School Principals, 2000.

Schurr, Sandra, and John Lounsbury. *Revitalizing Teaming to Improve Student Learning.* Reston, Va.: National Association of Secondary School Principals, 2001.

Sergiovanni, Thomas J., and Robert J. Starratt. *Supervision: A Redefinition*, 8th ed. Boston: McGraw-Hill, 2007.

Sharma, Toni. "Inservicing the Teachers." *Phi Delta Kappan* 63 (February 1982): 403.

Showers, Beverly, Bruce Joyce, and Barrie Bennett. "Synthesis of Research on Staff Development: A Framework for Future Study and a State-of-the-Art Analysis." *Educational Leadership* 45 (November 1987): 77–87.

Siegel, Jessica. "The State of Teacher Training." *Electronic Learning* 14 (May/June 1995): 43–53.

Sparks, Dennis C. "A Paradigm Shift in Staff Development." *Journal of Staff Development* 15 (Winter 1994): 26–29.

Sparks, Dennis, and Stephanie Hirsh. *A New Vision for Staff Development.* Alexandria, Va.: Association for Supervision and Curriculum Development, 1997.

Sparks, Dennis, and Susan Loucks-Horsley. *Five Models of Staff Development for Teachers.* Oxford, Ohio: National Staff Development Council, 1990.

Sparks, Georgea Mohlman. "Synthesis of Research on Staff Development for Effective Teaching." *Educational Leadership* 41 (November 1983): 65–72.

"Staff Development: An Important Part of Leadership." *NASSP Bulletin* (September 1991).

Stone, Fulton, Geraline Heard, Ann L. Ishler, Sandee Crowther, Kathy Boyer, Sue Schiff, and Joan Solomon. "Staff Development Policy Making in the States." *Journal of Staff Development* 16 (Spring 1995): 8–15.

Todnem, Guy R., and Michael P. Warner. "Assessment While Initiating a SIP Process." *Journal of Staff Development* 16 (Winter 1995): 54–56.

———. "Demonstrating the Benefits of Staff Development: Using Assessment Data in SIP Decision-Making." *Journal of Staff Development* 16 (Spring 1995): 62–64.

Wiles, Jon W., and Joseph C. Bondi. *Supervision: A Guide to Practice*, 6th ed. Upper Saddle River, N.J.: Prentice Hall, 2004.

Williamson, Peter A., and Julia A. Elfman. "A Commonsense Approach to Teacher Inservice Training." *Phi Delta Kappan* 63 (February 1982): 401.

Wood, Fred H., Frank O. McQuarrie, and Steven R. Thompson. "Practitioners and Professors Agree on Effective Staff Development Practices." *Educational Leadership* 40 (October 1982): 28–31.

WOOD, FRED H., and STEVEN R. THOMPSON. "Guidelines for Better Staff Development." *Educational Leadership* 37 (February 1980): 374–78.

WOOD, FRED H., STEVEN R. THOMPSON, and Sister FRANCES RUSSELL. "Designing Effective Staff Development Programs." In *Staff Development/Organization Development*. 1981 Yearbook, ed. Betty Dillon-Peterson, pp. 59–91. Alexandria, Va.: Association for Supervision and Curriculum Development, 1981.

YARGER, SAM J. "The Legacy of the Teacher Center." In *Changing School Culture through Staff Development*. 1990 Yearbook, ed. Bruce Joyce, pp. 104–16. Alexandria, Va: Association for Supervision and Curriculum Development, 1990.

JOURNALS AND OTHER PERIODICALS

Journal of Staff Development (quarterly), *Results* (eight per year), and *Tools for Schools* (monthly). All are available as part of membership in the National Staff Development Council, P.O. Box 240, Oxford, OH 45056. (800) 727-7288. www.nsdc.org.

VIDEOTAPES

ASCD Professional Development Planners. A total solution to professional development planning for various curriculum areas and instructional strategies. Association for Supervision and Curriculum Development, 1703 North Beauregard Street, Alexandria, VA 22311-1714. (800) 933-2723. www.ascd.org.

ASCD NETWORK

Staff Development. For the name of the current facilitator of the staff development network, contact Douglas J. Soffer, Assistant Executive Director, Constituent Relations, ASCD, 1703 North Beauregard Street, Alexandria, VA 22311-1714. (800) 933-2723. www.ascd.org.

CHAPTER 10

HELPING TEACHERS ON A ONE-TO-ONE BASIS

OBJECTIVES

After studying Chapter 10 you should be able to accomplish the following objectives:

1. Define formative evaluation as it applies to teacher performance.
2. Distinguish between clinical supervision and general supervision.
3. Describe one or more models of clinical supervision.
4. Describe skills needed by the supervisor for clinical supervision.
5. Select or create and apply appropriate classroom observation instruments.
6. Demonstrate selected techniques of classroom observation.
7. Assess your own readiness to render clinical supervision.
8. Plan for the use of teacher colleagues in supervision.

FORMATIVE EVALUATION

Recall for a moment two of the three components of a teacher evaluation system: formative evaluation and summative evaluation. Formative evaluation, discussed in this chapter, is assessment of teacher performance by an instructional supervisor during the year for the purpose of improving instruction. Summative evaluation, the topic of Chapter 13, is assessment of teacher performance by an administrator for the purpose of making decisions about such matters as tenure, retention, career ladder, and merit pay.

If the school system is large enough, an instructional supervisor will probably be the formative evaluator and the administrator will be the summative evaluator. Formative evaluators may be central-office or individual school personnel. From the central office come curriculum coordinators or consultants and other instructional supervisors. In the elementary schools, there are lead teachers, curriculum resource teachers, team leaders, grade coordinators, and peers. In secondary schools, in addition to peers, department heads may serve as formative evaluators. In the middle schools, we may encounter formative evaluators in positions similar to those in both elementary and secondary schools. However, the summative evaluator may also be the formative evaluator, as in the case of a principal in more schools that have no other supervisory personnel. The principal's summative evaluations will be based on formative evaluations. The formative evaluations fulfill a dual purpose in this case: They provide information that can be used for improving instruction and for making personnel decisions.

If a school system is large enough, it should have two kinds of formative evaluation: one by the instructional supervisor with no summative evaluation and one by the administrator, culminating in a summative evaluation.

When two different formative evaluations are possible, the evaluation done by the instructional supervisor should not be reported to the administrator unless the teacher requests it or agrees to it. In this chapter, our focus is on the formative evaluation carried out by the instructional supervisor. We especially examine the structured approach to formative evaluation known as clinical supervision.

CLINICAL SUPERVISION

In Chapter 2, we considered whether supervisors should work primarily with groups or with individuals. Many specialists in supervision believe that supervisors should concentrate their energies on individual teachers in their classrooms. These specialists recommend that supervisors take what is called a clinical approach.

The term *clinical supervision* came into vogue in 1961, when Morris L. Cogan used it in a proposal he made at Harvard University titled *Case Studies and Research in Clinical Supervision*. As Cogan himself pointed out, the term met with a great deal of resistance.[1] The words evoke images of doctors and laboratory technicians analyzing and diagnosing a patient's ailments. No one looks forward with delight to a trip to the clinic.

Yet the concepts of analysis, diagnosis, and remediation can apply as well in professional education as in medicine or dentistry or athletics. When Cogan spoke of supervision, he meant clinical supervision unless he specified otherwise. He defined clinical supervision in the following way:

> Clinical supervision may therefore be defined as the rationale and practice designed to improve the teacher's classroom performance. It takes its principal data from the events of the classroom. The analysis of these data and the relationship between teacher and supervisor form the basis of the program, procedures, and strategies designed to improve the students' learning by improving the teacher's classroom behavior.[2]

Cogan offered a simple test for distinguishing between general and clinical supervision. Clearly, he felt that clinical supervision should be stressed over general supervision:

> *general supervision* subsumes supervisory operations that take place principally outside the classroom. ... *General supervision*, therefore, denotes activities like the writing and revision of curriculums, the preparation of units and materials of instruction, the development of processes and instruments for reporting to parents, and such broad concerns as the evaluation of the total educational program.[3]

Although clinical supervision as a concept appears to be a rather recent development, in the early history of this field we can find a type—though a quite different type—of clinical supervision. The earliest supervisors served as inspectors. They visited classrooms, observed teachers' performance, and checked on classroom conditions. They did analyze; they did diagnose; and if they proposed remediation, it was more in line with the concept of a medical prescription. Supervision in the individual teacher's classroom preceded organized in-service education of groups of teachers. The supervising principal, headmaster, or superintendent felt it was his or her obligation to discover what was happening in the various classrooms. The intent was more to ensure that the teacher was carrying out approved policies, procedures, and programs than to provide assistance to the teacher for the improvement of instruction. Under an aura of investigation, early "snoopervisors" were decidedly clinical in the purest sense of the word: detached, aloof, critical, and judgmental. They wanted to see that rooms were kept clean, bulletin boards neat, property protected, shades properly drawn, children well disciplined, and lessons heard and repeated by the learners.

The purposes and practices of clinical supervision today differ radically from historical approaches to supervision of individual teachers. One factor, however, remains constant. Clinical supervision is primarily an individualized approach.

Robert H. Anderson and Robert J. Krajewski, in revising the work of Robert Goldhammer, defined *clinical supervision* as

> that aspect of supervision which draws upon data from first-hand observation of actual teaching, or other professional events, and involves face-to-face and other associated interactions between the observer(s) and person(s) observed in the course of analyzing the observed professional behaviors and activities and seeking to define and/or develop next steps toward improved performance.[4]

They attributed the following nine characteristics to clinical supervision:

1. It is a technology for improving instruction.
2. It is a deliberate intervention into the instructional process.
3. It is goal-oriented, combining school needs with the personal growth needs of those who work within the school.
4. It assumes a working relationship between teacher(s) and supervisor(s).
5. It requires a high degree of mutual trust, as reflected in understanding, support, and commitment for growth.
6. It is systematic, although it requires a flexible and continuously changing methodology.
7. It creates productive (i.e., healthy) tension for bridging the gap between the real and the ideal.
8. It assumes that the supervisor knows a great deal about the analysis of instruction and learning and also about productive human interaction.
9. It requires both preservice training, especially in observation techniques, and continuous in-service reflection on effective approaches.[5]

Clinical supervision should be perceived as a concept, not a single, fixed set of procedures. Practices may vary—though as we see when we examine models of clinical supervision, they do not vary as widely as might be supposed. As Goldhammer said, however, "a face-to-face relationship between supervisors and teachers" is fundamental to clinical supervision.[6] In this chapter, we explore the basic model of clinical supervision—the one-to-one relationship between supervisor and teacher.

Goldhammer took note of "variations of the basic model that include group supervision, that is, supervision of individual teachers by groups of supervisors, groups of teachers by groups of supervisors, and groups of teachers by an individual supervisor."[7] Although supervision of a teacher's classroom performance by a group of supervisors may be possible, we feel the group variations of the model have limited usefulness, feasibility, and practicality. A one-to-one basis appears to us to be the most effective approach to clinical supervision. One possible exception may occur with well-knit teaching teams in which peers collaborate to provide guidance to their own members. Another viable group approach to supervision is use of intensive assistance teams whose purpose is to help marginal teachers (see Chapter 13).

Edward Pajak viewed the emergence of clinical supervision as

> an evolutionary adaptation that helped preserve the traditional values of supervision—e.g., decentralized, rational, cooperative problem solving—within the environment of sweeping educational change that prevailed during the 1960s. Clinical supervision deemphasized issues of large-scale curriculum implementation and schoolwide change, and refocused supervision's legacy of democracy, cooperative planning, problem solving, and action research on classroom events and processes.[8]

THE SUPERVISOR'S ROLE IN CLINICAL SUPERVISION

Whether supervision is evaluation is one of the perennial issues of this field. Some experts reject the term *evaluation* when applied to instructional supervision. They prefer terms such as *facilitating, collaborating, consulting, helping, coaching*, or *mentoring*. Our position is that any time a person makes a judgment about another person, place, or thing, that person is engaging in *evaluation* or, if you prefer, *assessment*. The heart of the evaluation issue is what we do with the evaluation data. Evaluation can be positive and helpful. It does not have to be negative and destructive.

Referring to the possible "sting" of evaluation, Keith A. Acheson and Meredith Damien Gall identified evaluation as "the most controversial function of clinical supervision."[9] They observed:

> Although the primary purpose of clinical supervision is to help teachers develop and improve through cooperative planning, observation, and feedback, it is often part of a larger process that has as its purpose decisions about tenure, promotion, retention, and dismissal.[10]

Acheson and Gall would lessen the sting of evaluation with "the observations of the evaluator-supervisor of preservice and inservice teachers augmented by those of peers (other teachers whose data will not be used for judgmental, threatening purposes)."[11]

When the same person is charged with responsibility for both formative and summative evaluation, the dilemma may be minimized if the supervisor has a high degree of competence and strong interpersonal skills. Teachers will accept evaluation of the rating type (summative) and evaluation of the helping variety (formative) from the same person if they have confidence in that person. The dilemma, of course, is eliminated when formative evaluation is carried out by a staff supervisor and summative by a line administrator-supervisor.

Ralph L. Mosher and David E. Purpel called for clinical supervisors skilled not only in analyzing teaching but also in curriculum development. They further stated:

> Clinical supervision is one means by which teachers can confront and modify both the content and the practice of teaching. Indeed, it is virtually inseparable from curriculum development activity, both in its theoretical principles and as a strategy for involving teachers in analysis of their instruction. The most productive way to get teachers to analyze and change how they teach, in the writer's experience, is to involve them in analysis of what they teach.[12]

Noreen Garman saw the role of the supervisor in clinical supervision as being friend, confidante, and respected colleague.[13] She described clinical supervision as embracing four concepts:

- Collegiality: an internal state embodying a spirit of "connectedness," that is, identification with another person for whom one holds respect and affection.
- Collaboration: teacher and supervisor sharing a common language so that they may share each other's perceptions.
- Skilled service: the supervisor's special competence based on training and experience from which teachers can benefit.
- Ethical conduct: exercising judgment and maintaining trust.[14]

There is considerable disagreement among specialists in supervision over the question of whether the supervisor-teacher relationship should be a superior-subordinate relationship or a relationship between equals. Some experts feel that the superior-subordinate relationship is necessary to nudge teachers to make changes. These people believe that because the superior-subordinate relationship does exist, we should make the best of it. Others feel that, although the superior-subordinate relationship exists, the inequality of the partners should be deemphasized or ignored. Still others feel that a superior-subordinate relationship has no place in the modern-day supervision of professionals and can be dispensed with, at least in the case of staff supervisors who do not possess line authority.

Robert J. Alfonso and Lee Goldsberry made clear the existence of the supervisor's authority:

> Supervision is a formal organizational act; moreover, supervision always implies a superordinate-subordinate relationship. The terms "peer supervision" and "colleague supervision" may be contradictions, for one cannot be both a peer/colleague and a supervisor at the same time. Clearly, teachers can and should help each other in a variety of ways, but a supervisor is vested with organizational authority for decision making about others.[15]

In another context Alfonso with co-authors Gerald R. Firth and Richard F. Neville examined the dimensions of leadership and concluded that leaders should maintain some psychological distance from subordinates. They developed this point in the following passage:

> Supervisors are likely to be more effective if they do not become an integral part of the teacher group. While obviously joined to them and responsible for them, a sense of psychological distance is necessary. This is not to suggest that supervisors need to

be aloof, undemocratic, or "company people," but rather that their relationships to teachers must permit psychological freedom and objectivity. While writing on supervision has often suggested a close relationship, research indicates that maintaining some degree of psychological distance enhances a supervisor's ability to make discriminations between teachers and to assess their ability and effectiveness more clearly and objectively. Supervisors need to maintain the delicate balance that enables one to operate freely as a member of a group while still retaining a recognized degree of psychological detachment.[16]

On the other hand, Garman advocated a close relationship when she said, "A heightened sense of collegiality is possible when I can imagine myself as a member of an organic unit, when the distinction between supervisor and teacher is less discernible and I can transcend my conventional role status."[17]

Differing interpretations of the supervisor's role highlight once again the problem of the dual roles of many supervisors: helper and evaluator. The helper has little or no need of psychological distance, whereas the evaluator finds maintaining distance useful and perhaps necessary. The clinical supervisor, who works in a helping, face-to-face relationship with teachers, has less need to maintain a superior-subordinate relationship than the administrative supervisor, who must make hard decisions about retention and dismissal.

The supervisor enters the process of clinical supervision as a knowledgeable helper. He or she brings to the process skills in pedagogy and personal relations. He or she knows how to analyze teaching, diagnose difficulties, confer with teachers, and make recommendations to teachers for improvement. The supervisor knows sources of information and materials, is able to help with assessment of student performance, and can assist in interpreting applicable research. In addition, the supervisor possesses skills to help teachers with curriculum development.

Clinical supervision "depends upon direct, trained observation of classroom behaviors," noted Jon Wiles and Joseph Bondi. "As a process," they continued, "clinical supervision helps the teacher identify and clarify problems, receive data from the supervisor, and develop solutions to problems with the help of the supervisor."[18]

MODELS OF CLINICAL SUPERVISION

The literature offers us a number of models of clinical supervision that recommend certain steps or stages to be followed. As early as 1930, George C. Kyte proposed such a model. Although he did not use the label "clinical," he suggested a pattern that anticipated the clinical approach thirty years later. Referring to supervisory observation—the heart of clinical supervision—Kyte outlined a three-phase process:

1. Planning for the observation of teaching.
2. Getting the most out of the observation period.
3. Analyzing the teaching observed.[19]

In discussing the first phase, Kyte emphasized the plans the supervisor would make for the forthcoming observation as well as for preobservation conferencing, a key feature of clinical supervision models. He noted the desirability of conferences with the teacher both before and after observing and described the two kinds of conferences:

> Two kinds of individual conferences are conducted in supervision. The less common one in practice, though markedly important, is that which is preparatory to work projected. The series of first conferences with a new teacher, the consultations planned in response to a teacher's request for help on a new undertaking, and the interviews for the purpose of planning classroom experimentation frequently are of this nature. The more common type of conference, however, is that which occurs after a supervisory visit has been made to the classroom, or the products of pupils' efforts have been submitted to a supervisory officer.[20]

By putting these elements together, we create the following four-stage model:

1. Preobservation conference and planning for the observation

2. Observation

3. Analysis of the data

4. Postobservation conference

Some of Kyte's recommendations are remarkably contemporary, as shown here.

1. *Regarding planning and preparation for observation:*

Purposeful planning includes (a) the selection of sound objectives, (b) the analysis of teacher personnel, (c) the survey of learning conditions, (d) the diagnosis of teaching difficulties, (e) the determination of teacher needs, and (f) the choice of supervisory aid.[21] When the supervisor has made adequate preparation for the visit to a classroom, he will enter the room with a clear understanding of what he expects to stress in his observation, why he should so place his emphasis, and how he will make use of the results to aid the teacher.[22]

2. *Regarding observation:*

[The author] has observed teaching, taking personal notes, and using a trained secretary to obtain stenographic notes. . . . The reaction of the teachers to their first experience of this nature was somewhat unfavorable. . . . When copies of the notes were given to them and they were told that the stenographic records would be used as the basis of the conference, they frankly admitted that the notes proved helpful to them before they came to the conference, and very helpful as a basis for getting help through the conference. . . . After the third experience, they were unanimous in their recommendation that detailed records be made during the supervisory observation, because of the greater aid resulting.[23] . . . Frequently the supervisors utilize published forms, or ones that they have improvised for their own use in recording their observations.[24]

3. *Regarding analysis of the observation data:*

Just as soon after the observation as possible, the supervisor should set aside time to go over his notes in order to add items which may recur to him while the observed lesson is still freshly impressed upon him. He should give careful thought to the lesson as a whole, and to the points which he noted with a view to preparing for the conference. . . . A careful analysis of the lesson should be made by the supervisor before conferring with the teacher. If the supervisor is to be a super-teacher, he must make the same sort of preparation for his

TABLE 10.1 Distribution of Items Regarding the Techniques of Teaching Listed Frequently in Twenty-Five Teacher-Rating Devices

	Rating Devices	
Nature of Items Listed	Number	Percent
Making the assignment	19	76
Discipline of the pupils	19	76
Training pupils to study	17	68
Attention to individuals' needs	17	68
Participation of pupils	16	64
Skill in questioning	16	64
Care of hygienic conditions	16	64
Skill in stimulating thought	15	60
Selection of subject matter	15	60
Organization of subject matter	15	60
Definiteness of instructions	14	56
Skill in motivating work	13	52
Skill in habit formation	13	52
Securing and holding interest	12	48
Definite and clear aims	12	48
Careful preparation of teacher	12	48
Care of routine	12	48
Economic use of school time	11	44
Use of instructional materials	10	40
Neatness of room	10	40
Orderliness of room	10	40
Evidence of growth of pupils	10	40

Source: George C. Kyte, *How to Supervise: A Guide to Educational Principles and Progressive Practice of Educational Supervision* (Boston: Houghton Mifflin, 1930), p. 151, Reprinted with permission of Houghton Mifflin, Inc.

"recitation" with the teacher, the conference, as the teacher is expected to make for his classroom recitation.[25]

Kyte found twenty-five "teacher-rating devices," which we would now call observation instruments, published between 1920 and 1930. He summarized the items assessed by these devices, as shown in Table 10.1. Note that many of the items are skills that present-day observation systems seek to assess.

Kyte suggested ways of recording classroom observations in the following passage:

In addition to long-hand and stenographic accounts of observations, other means of attempting to gather objective data are used. Many printed forms exist which suggest various ways of collecting the desired information. Check-lists, word- or phrase-responses, and complete sentences are typical methods of recording the supervisor's reactions. Still another and a more recent type is exemplified by the chart of the classroom used, with a legend for recording child-participation.[26]

Kyte dealt with the continuing questions of whether to make announced or unannounced visits (both have their place)[27] and how long a visit to make (elementary: thirty minutes; secondary: one period).[28] Kyte's work was very much in line with present clinical supervision practice.

Understanding the concept of clinical supervision is easier if we, like Cogan, perceive it as a cycle with a number of recurring stages or phases.[29] Several authorities have suggested models to guide the practice of teachers and supervisors as they engage in the cycle of supervision. Among models of clinical supervision that can be found in the literature are those of Goldhammer,[30] Mosher and Purpel,[31] Cogan,[32] Acheson and Gall,[33] and Jerry J. Bellon and Elner C. Bellon.[34]

Although models differ in number of stages or phases, they all possess three essential ingredients: (1) There is some kind of contact or communication with the teacher prior to an observation; (2) there is some type of classroom observation; and (3) there is some kind of follow-up of the observation. For some of the proponents of clinical supervision, the process involves two—and only two—players: one supervisor and one teacher. To others, a teacher-peer may substitute for the supervisor. In still more complex versions of the process, a number of peers—as in the case of teaching teams—may substitute for the supervisor. We examine the concept and use of colleagues in the supervisory process later in this chapter when we discuss peer supervision, coaching, and mentoring.

Whether the helper's role in clinical supervision is performed by a supervisor from the central office or from the individual school or by a teacher's peer(s), three phases appear to be essential to the process: (1) preobservation conference, (2) observation, and (3) postobservation conference.

Preobservation Conference

The word *conference* as used in the cycle of clinical supervision is, we believe, almost too formal a term. It implies an atmosphere, a structure, and a length that can arouse a teacher's negative feelings. Add the term *clinical* and we have a potential for setting up an avoidance behavior on the part of the teacher. Teachers might be more accepting and solicitous of help if in their presence we used words such as *chat, talk*, or *dialogue* instead of *conference*, and *individualized, personal*, or *classroom* instead of *clinical*. Among supervisors, however, we can continue to use the technical language that has already been invented.

A preobservation conference is a face-to-face talk between teacher and supervisor prior to the supervisor's visit to the teacher's classroom. The purpose of the preobservation conference is to settle on necessary preliminaries. The two participants in the conference have already agreed or assumed that the supervisor will visit the teacher and observe the teacher's performance. Ideally, the teacher is as desirous of having the supervisor visit as the supervisor is of making the visit. Whether the teacher looks forward to help of this nature from the supervisor will depend on whether a feeling of mutual respect has been developed between the two. Conceivably, clinical supervision can be carried on without the existence of mutual respect, but in that event the cycle is perfunctory, resented by the teacher, and doomed to failure. Although we would limit the concept of peer supervision to assistance given by one teacher to another, the clinical supervisor should be a peer in the best sense of the term.

Sometimes it seems as if clinical supervision—or any type of supervision—is the supervisor's show. In all stages of the cycle of clinical supervision, the teacher and supervisor should perceive each other as working together for the ultimate benefit of the learners.

At the preobservation conference, the teacher and supervisor together should decide which class the supervisor will visit and when. Thus, the supervisor's schedule is set in advance. The evaluator of teacher performance may feel the need for unannounced visits, but these are not necessary for the clinical supervisor. The clinical supervisor is not seeking to check on teachers, to keep them "on the ball," or to assess their competence or professionalism for administrative purposes. The clinical supervisor is coming to visit, observe, and help as a trained, skilled colleague who can provide another pair of eyes and ears for what is said and heard in a classroom.

Once the teacher and supervisor have decided on a specific class, the teacher will provide background to help the supervisor understand the composition of the group. The teacher will inform the supervisor about the background of the learners and will discuss difficulties he or she is encountering with the group.

In the preobservation conference the teacher will identify special teaching problems he or she is encountering and with which he or she would like some help. Thus, the two participants focus on specific teacher and student behaviors that the supervisor will observe. The teacher may feel the need for someone to observe and provide feedback about such specific behaviors as these:

- Verbal interaction between students and teacher.
- The teacher's use of oral questioning.
- The teacher's methods of subgrouping.
- Students' verbal and nonverbal interaction with one another.
- The teacher's presentation of a particular item of content.
- The teacher's use of simple control techniques.
- The teacher's voice patterns.
- The teacher's nonverbal behavior.
- The teacher's use of classroom management techniques.
- The teacher's individualized help to learners.
- The teacher's awareness of what's happening in the classroom.
- The teacher's use of media in presenting a lesson.
- The clarity with which the teacher gives directions.
- The teacher's use of language—correct grammar and spelling.
- The teacher's sensitivity to cultural diversity in the classroom.
- The teacher's awareness of equity and equality when dealing with students of each gender.
- The teacher's ability to deal with students who have special needs.

The teacher will acquaint the supervisor with the unit and lesson plans that will be taught when the supervisor visits. The teacher will explain the objectives of the lesson, the methods of presentation, and the techniques of evaluating student performance. The teacher and supervisor will agree on the supervisor's role during the visit. Although some educators think it is permissible for the supervisor to play an active role during the visit—for example, to talk with students—most consider the appropriate role of the supervisor to be that of unobtrusive observer. Also, if the supervisor is to make an accurate record of what is taking place during an observation, he or she cannot be distracted from this task, nor should he or she distract the teacher with interjections into the proceedings. We agree with Goldhammer, who said, "As a rule, Supervisor should not intervene in the teaching in any manner during Observation. . . . Supervisor should only intervene by explicit prior agreement with Teacher, and in a manner seeming mutually agreeable and appropriate to both except, of course, in physical emergencies."[35]

The supervisor and teacher should agree on procedures the supervisor will follow to record data. Thus, the teacher will not be upset when the supervisor makes marks on an observation instrument or sits busily writing a verbatim account of the events.

The teacher and supervisor should decide whether the use of audio- or videotaping is desirable and, if so, must work out details of their use. The participants need to agree on how long the supervisor will remain in the classroom and where the supervisor will be seated.

Regarding the time needed, Acheson and Gall advised, "Planning conferences need not be long. Twenty to thirty minutes is usually sufficient for the first planning conference unless the teacher has a particularly difficult problem to discuss or unless the teacher and supervisor are strangers to each other. Later planning conferences might require only five to ten minutes."[36]

The supervisor should seek to calm any anxieties the teacher may have about the visit. Assuring the teacher of the confidentiality of the data will help. Specialists suggest that conferences be conducted either in the teacher's classroom or office or at another mutually agreed-on location—not in the supervisor's office. Holding the follow-up conference in the teacher's classroom allows for easy access to the setting in which the teaching occurred. References then can be made to the teacher's location, student access to materials, chalkboard, and group activities. Conferencing in the supervisor's office perpetuates the notion of a superordinate-subordinate relationship, which the supervisor should attempt to deemphasize. The supervisor should let the teacher know when he or she will be able to provide feedback about the observation. The supervisor will explain to the teacher that he or she will need some time after the conference to analyze the data and prepare for a postobservation conference. In the preobservation conference, the groundwork is laid for the observation.

Although we are in agreement with supervision specialists who see merit in conducting preobservation conferences, we would be remiss if we did not advise the reader that, as with so many educational practices, we do not have unanimous agreement about the value of preobservation conferencing. Madeline Hunter, for example, let her objections be known, advocating elimination of the preobservation conference. Hunter cited time constraints and other reasons.[37]

Observation

If we were to draw up a list of supervisory tasks that require specialized skills, classroom observation would head the list. On the surface, observation would seem simple. The supervisor enters the classroom, preferably at the start of a lesson, sits down at the back of the room, watches for a half-hour to an hour, makes notes, gets up, and leaves. Yet classroom observation demands a high level of technical and analytical skills. The supervisor must know what to look for, how to look for it, and how to collect, analyze, and interpret the data.

Every observation is a new situation; classroom transactions are never the same. The supervisor must draw on all his or her training and experience to turn in a credible performance at observing the teacher and students in action.

What to Observe   Two basic approaches to observation are possible; the choice is dependent on the purpose of the supervisor's visit. For want of better terms, we call the two approaches global and specific. Some examples of global are the artistic approach and the interpretative and ecological approaches.

Global Approach   The global approach to teacher observation is aimed at a generalized assessment of teacher performance on a wide variety of teaching skills, usually generic in nature. The global approach appears to be the more common approach of both staff and line supervisors. The supervisor often uses an instrument of some type to guide the observation of teacher performance, although he or she may record the classroom events without resorting to an instrument. Whatever instrument or system is to be used, the teacher must be made familiar with it.

A global approach is a useful technique for the staff supervisor when the teacher and supervisor wish to make a general appraisal of the teacher's performance. As the global approach is essentially oriented toward an assessment of the teacher's total performance, it is particularly suitable for use by line supervisors—that is, administrator-supervisors—as a basis for summative evaluation. The administrator-supervisor, by observing a teacher several times and assessing the teacher's overall performance, can compile sufficient data to make an annual, summative appraisal of performance.

As mentioned in the previous chapter, efforts have been made over the past two decades to identify the generic skills or competencies that make up the teaching act. The profession has moved closer to the concept of teaching as a science. Thus, supervisors have adopted what we might call a scientific approach, diagnosing teacher performance in respect to specific, identifiable behaviors.

Artistic Approach   Some experts would have us look more closely at teaching as an art rather than a science and, thus, supervision as an art rather than a science. Elliot W. Eisner listed several of the fallacies he saw in scientific supervision, as follows:

- *the fallacy of additivity* which is committed by attempting to study or supervise teaching using a procedure that implies or assumes that the incidence of particular teaching behaviors—structuring, giving examples, positive and negative reinforcement, and so forth—all have equal pedagogical weight and can be added together to secure an index of the quality of teaching. . . .
- *the fallacy of composition,* that the whole is equal to the sum of its parts. This is committed when the quality of teaching is determined by counting the incidence of teacher behaviors in a variable or category and then adding to this sum the scores produced in other variables. . . .
- *the fallacy of concreteness.* This fallacy is an offshoot of behaviorism which holds that the exclusive referent for observation is the manifest behavior of the student. . . . When we observe pupils or teachers we do not merely look at the behavior they display, but also at its meaning and the quality of their experience. . . .

- *the fallacy of the act* ... the tendency to neglect the process of educational life as it unfolds in classrooms and schools. ...
- *the fallacy of method:* neglecting those aspects of teaching that are immune to the criteria and instruments that the researcher employs.[38]

Eisner advocated an artistic approach to supervision, by which he meant

> an approach to supervision that relies on the sensitivity, perceptivity, and knowledge of the supervisor as a way of appreciating the significant subtleties occurring in the classroom, and that exploits the expressive, poetic, and often metaphorical potential of language to convey to teachers or to others whose decisions affect what goes on in schools, what has been observed.[39]

Instead of focusing on just the readily observable specific teaching skills, Eisner would have the supervisor attempt "to improve the quality of educational life in the school."[40] Eisner believed that the supervisor must "hear the music" as well as observe the action; he or she must judge the character and quality of the teacher's performance, not just the quantitative aspects:

> Teachers, too, are differentiated by their style and by their particular strengths. Artistically oriented supervision would recognize this style and try to help the teacher exploit it by strengthening the positive directions already taken. ... The connoisseur of teaching, like the connoisseur of the violin or cello, would appreciate these characteristic traits of the performer in addition to the general overall quality of the performance. In other words, both the general level of teaching competence and the unique characteristics of the performance would be perceived and appraised.[41]

Eisner did not believe that artistic supervision could be accomplished with rating instruments. The artistic supervisor, he maintained, must possess the ability to appreciate what is happening in the classroom, which he labeled "educational connoisseurship," and to interpret the quality of performance to the teacher, which he called "educational criticism."[42]

Practically, such artistic supervision would require a virtuoso performance that may be beyond the range of many persons who hold supervisory positions. The preparation of specialists who can tune into the varied nuances of teaching also poses a problem.

Interpretive and Ecological Approaches Like an artistic approach, other current approaches reject or deemphasize some of the present processes and practices in analyzing teacher competencies. Proponents of these approaches would abandon or minimize the scientific approach to supervision, which seeks to collect objective data on the teacher's demonstration of generic competencies. In its place they advocate interpretive or hermeneutic and ecological approaches to classroom supervision.

Proponents of an interpretive approach would replace the scientific approach, which draws on the methodology of the natural sciences, with an approach from the social sciences. The interpretive school holds that supervisors must go beyond the collection and analysis of generic teaching skills and raise questions with the teacher about why teachers and students performed as they did in a given class. They maintain that teaching is context-specific and differs from teacher to teacher and from class to class.

Neither usual preobservation conferencing nor customary data collection nor typical postobservation conferencing is essential to the interpretive or ecological approaches. Some feel that the preobservation conference should be primarily an occasion for gathering information about the teacher's intentions. Some perceive the postobservation conference—a widely advocated and practiced procedure—as often ritualistic, focusing on the diagnosis of teacher behaviors.[43]

The ecological approach features analysis of the linguistic and cultural patterns of the classroom, an awareness of the metaphors in the teaching and supervisory process, and a sensitivity to the use of both verbal and nonverbal language. The ecological agenda comprises not a clinical diagnosis of generic teaching skills but an analysis of the social and cultural implications of the teacher's and students' language and actions in the classroom. According to C. A. Bowers and David J. Flinders, "It is the ability to recognize the classroom as a language/culture medium that most clearly shapes and defines the appropriate role of the supervisor."[44] They recommended that supervisors look for the structure of the lesson; the presence or absence of cultural and gender biases in language, actions, and content; culturally appropriate participation patterns; assumptions on which language used by the teacher is based; nonverbal communication; and student involvement.[45]

Generally, the thrust of instructional supervision at the present time continues to emphasize the diagnosis of specific, observable teaching behaviors and the collection of objective data that can be discussed with the teacher. Although some people maintain—and rightly so—that data can never be completely objective and that most data are just an approximation of what is happening in the classroom, supervisors who are aware of their own biases and values can seek to be as objective as possible. Probably no observation, regardless of the approach followed by the supervisor, can ever be completely objective. Yet the effort to strive for objectivity has long been sanctioned by administrators, supervisors, and teachers themselves, who have often decried the lack of objectivity on the part of persons evaluating their performance.

The artistic, interpretive, and ecological approaches to supervision would replace or decrease emphasis on generic teaching behaviors, structured evaluation instruments, and supervisor-teacher distance with collegial interpretation of the classroom environment and events that took place in the classroom during observation. Present practices and training programs remain somewhat more geared to the scientific approach to supervision.

How to Record   Depending on what the teacher and supervisor have agreed should be observed, they have the choice of recording classroom events by electronic means, written means, or a combination of the two. If they elect to use the first, a decision must be made, assuming the necessary equipment is available, between audio- and videorecording. An audiotape is a helpful supplement to the supervisor's observation and provides a verbatim oral record of what has occurred. An audio record is deficient in that it does not reveal movement and nonverbal behavior of both teachers and students. For this reason, the supervisor's presence is necessary even if an audiotape is made of the lesson.

Videorecording holds much promise as a supervisory tool. If the group is small, the recording can reveal most or all of the class transaction. With videorecording, analysis of classroom events can be made by the teacher alone as well as by the teacher in consultation with the supervisor. Attempts have been made to apply this technique to the supervision of student teachers. Videorecording can augment the supervisor's help by providing additional data beyond what the supervisor has garnered from classroom visits.

Regardless of the means of recording, the teacher and supervisor must agree on their use. The presence of electronic equipment can cause teachers and students to be distracted; however, a practice run or two will take the edge off the novelty. After recording loses its newness, the teacher and students shed their self-consciousness at being before the camera.

For the supervisor to concentrate on the lesson, a technician should be available for the actual recording. This could be done by a trained cadre of older students if media technicians are not available. Because cameras and camcorders are so prevalent today, it is surprising that more supervisors and teachers do not make greater use of these technological aids in the improvement of instruction.

Even if electronic equipment is used in observing, the supervisor must become proficient in recording classroom events by written means. Among the available techniques are (1) verbatim recording, (2) note taking, (3) selective verbatim, (4) anecdotal records, and (5) charting.

Verbatim Recording   Goldhammer strongly recommended that the supervisor make verbatim records of the classroom events.[46] He argued logically that verbatim records provide an accurate account of what has taken place and permit the supervisor to recall with the teacher exactly what occurred. Verbatim records are the written counterpart of electronic records. The supervisor has taken down what has been said word for word, creating an exact transcript of the lesson.

To record a lesson verbatim, the supervisor must be adept at recording either by longhand or shorthand. The authors of this text are not advocates of verbatim recording. We feel this technique keeps supervisors so busy that they do not have time to discern the nuances of what is happening in the classroom. Unless the supervisor is isolated at the back of the room, the recording of the lesson word for word can in itself be distracting to the teacher and students.

Note Taking   The supervisor may discreetly take notes on everything and anything observed. Remember that the majority of observations conducted by clinical supervisors will focus on specific behaviors. It does not seem necessary to record behaviors beyond those that the supervisor has agreed to observe, as would be necessary in verbatim recording. A verbatim record is not necessary if the lesson is captured by either audio or video means. Making notes is less conspicuous and therefore less distracting than verbatim recording. Judicious notes made by a keen observer can provide an adequate recording of the classroom activities. The supervisor may find it helpful to record the time (hour and minutes) at which each note was written.

Acheson and Gall suggested a type of note taking that they called an *anecdotal record*—a technique that can be used when the teacher and supervisor have not identified specific behaviors to observe.[47] The anecdotal record, consisting of "short," "objective," and "nonevaluative" handwritten sentences, provides a description of classroom events.[48] Acheson and Gall recommended that the handwritten notes be typed so they may be more easily studied by the teacher.[49]

Selective Verbatim   Somewhat less than a complete verbatim transcript and somewhat more than simple notes is *selective verbatim,* a word-for-word recording of *selected* rather than *total* verbal events. Perhaps a fair analogy to the selective verbatim technique is the recording of "sound bites."

The supervisor may selectively sample a variety of verbal events during the observation period, may choose to record specific behaviors that he or she feels are significant, or may limit recording to specific behaviors previously agreed on by the supervisor and teacher. The supervisor may wish to use a combination of verbatim recording and note taking. Recording of observation data can be a very personal undertaking and, like handwriting, may not be decipherable from one supervisor to the other.

Specific Approach   When verbatim recording, note taking, and selective verbatim recording address behaviors specified in advance by the teacher and supervisor, the supervisor is following what we can term a *specific approach.* Acheson and Gall included prior selection of verbal events in their definition of selective verbatim:

> Selective verbatim requires the supervisor to make a written record of exactly what is said, that is, a verbatim transcript. Not all verbal communication is recorded, however. The supervisor and teacher select beforehand the particular types of verbal events to be transcribed; it is in this sense that the verbatim record is "selective."[50]

The teacher and supervisor in the preobservation conference may decide on the specific behaviors of teachers and students that the supervisor will observe. The supervisor then concentrates on evidence of the presence or absence of the specific behaviors. Thus, if the teacher and supervisor have agreed, for example, that the supervisor will diagnose the teacher's skill in providing reinforcement to the learner, the supervisor will confine the observation and analysis to that particular skill.

Mosher and Purpel listed the following noteworthy factors in teaching:

- The teacher's ability to communicate.
- The logic of the teaching strategy or method employed.
- The teacher's performance of "instrumental tasks."
- The motivational effect of the teaching.
- The quality of the personal relationship established between the teacher and his students.
- Content.[51]

A number of specific, observable behaviors are subsumed under each factor. Some teachers may wish supervisors to look at one or more steps in the Madeline Hunter model (mentioned in Chapter 4) or with the supervisor may identify other skills to be observed.

In the preobservation conference, the teacher and supervisor specify the particular behaviors to be included in the observation to follow. The analysis of these behaviors is what the teacher and supervisor discuss in the postobservation conference. In the event the supervisor observed something that occurred during the classroom observation but was not supposed to be recorded, mentioning it in the postobservation conference could be a major issue. One of the authors of the text recorded those incidents in selective verbatim notes of the classroom visits. Mentioning those incidents was left until the end of the conference and when the teacher would ask, "Did you observe anything else?" At that point, the teacher's request became the go-ahead to share the details of the incidents.

Instruments   Many supervisors prefer to use an instrument of some kind to guide their observations. Which instrument they use will depend on the decision made by the teacher and supervisor about whether the supervisor will make a comprehensive—that is, the global approach—analysis of the teacher's performance or whether he or she will limit the observation to specific behaviors. Let's examine two types of instruments: one to make a comprehensive or global assessment and one to evaluate specific behaviors.

Global   We do not have to look far to find examples of instruments designed to survey teaching behaviors rather broadly. The movement toward the specification of generic competencies stimulated school systems to create instruments for assessing those competencies. The checklist shown at the end of Chapter 4 illustrates an instrument that could be—and has been—used to assess the generic competencies discussed in the early chapters of this book.[52]

If you examine instruments from various school systems over a period of time, you will note the tendency to reduce the number of competencies and to make provision for comments. Comprehensive observation instruments are widely used by both staff supervisors and line administrators.

Specific   With regard to the use of instruments for evaluating specific behaviors, the range of possibilities is both expanded and narrowed. It is expanded because the specific behaviors are so varied; it is narrowed because the number of instruments for evaluating particular behaviors is so small. For some specific behaviors there are no existing instruments, in which case the supervisor will either have to create one or use another means for gathering the data.

The supervisor may be fortunate enough to find a ready-made instrument. The Flanders Interaction Analysis Categories instrument discussed in Chapter 12 is an example of an instrument created to evaluate one specific set of behaviors: verbal interaction.[53] Charles M. Galloway designed a system for evaluating nonverbal behavior, primarily the teacher's.[54] Jacob S. Kounin developed a system for evaluating classroom management and discipline.[55] A search of the literature will reveal a number of instruments that may be useful to the supervisor. As a starting point, you may wish to see the examples and to consult the bibliographies at the end of this chapter and Chapter 13.

If the supervisor is unable to find or create an instrument to evaluate specific behaviors agreed on by the teacher and supervisor, selective verbatim recording or making notes of classroom events may be the solution. If using an instrument, recording selective verbatim responses, or taking notes does not appear feasible, charting specific behaviors may be a way to record observation of certain classroom behaviors. In addressing the practice of coaching (discussed later in this chapter), Karolyn J. Snyder predicted a move from the global to the specific when she commented, "The focus of coaching is likely to shift in the future away from predictable teaching behaviors for all situations, toward situational patterns with variable student populations and contexts."[56]

Techniques Other Than Instrumentation   Supervisors may employ techniques other than use of instruments when observing a teacher. They may record events globally through verbatim and selective verbatim techniques. They may collect data on many behaviors by using what Acheson and Gall have labeled a "wide-lens" approach: anecdotal records, audiotaping, and videotaping.[57]

Charting   Supervisors may record specific behaviors through charting techniques. Starting with a class seating chart and a devised key, the supervisor can record a wide variety of data, determining which pupils are on task and which off task, observing and recording the flow of communication between teacher and pupils and among students, and sketching the movement of the teacher and students about the room.[58]

By the careful use of symbols of his or her own choosing, the supervisor can record on a class seating chart a great deal of information about what is taking place. Observation is the stage in clinical supervision during which data are collected. The supervisor must master skills of observing and recording classroom events.

Postobservation Conference

Soon after the observation, the teacher and supervisor meet once again at a mutually satisfactory location for the phase most specialists believe to be the most difficult and most important in the entire cycle: the postobservation or follow-up conference. The major purpose of the postobservation conference is to offer feedback to the teacher about the teacher's performance. Certainly, perceptive teachers can think through and make an analysis of their own performance. With a videorecording of their performance, experienced teachers should be able to diagnose their teaching almost as well as the supervisor can. But feedback from an interested helper enables teachers to see their performance as others see it.

The discussion at the follow-up conference should focus on the data collected by the supervisor, not on the supervisor's experiences, biases, and feelings. The supervisor must take every precaution to keep the conference from being a threatening situation to the teacher. Therefore, the proper subject of the conference is the teaching observed by the supervisor, not the teacher.

Experts generally agree that a short period of time should elapse before the supervisor and teacher get together to discuss the data. This allows the supervisor time to organize and analyze the data and to prepare for the conference. Thus, at the preobservation conference, the supervisor will have advised the teacher that he or she will need a day or more to transcribe notes; listen to or view recordings; search for evidence of the behaviors that were to be observed; organize notes in some coherent form; and decide what approach to take in the conference. The supervisor may make some nonjudgmental comments at the end of the observation, assuring the teacher that he or she will be back in touch in a day or two to set a time for the conference. At this point, they might tentatively select a day and time convenient to both.

Madeline Hunter identified six types of supervisory conferences: five instructional (i.e., postobservation) and one evaluative ("the summation of what has occurred in and resulted from a series of instructional conferences").[59] Hunter set forth purposes and objectives for each of the five types of instructional conferences, as follows:

1. Type A Instructional Conference—*Purpose:* To identify, label, and explain the teacher's effective instructional behaviors giving research-based reasons for their effectiveness so the teacher knows what he or she has done and why it worked, and in the future can do it on purpose. *Objective:* At the end of the conference (not in some nebulous future) the teacher will identify teaching decisions and behaviors that promoted learning and state why they were effective. . . .

2. Type B Instructional Conference—*Purpose:* To stimulate the development of a repertoire of effective teaching responses so the teacher is not limited to those most frequently used. *Objective:* Teacher and observer will generate alternatives to behaviors which were effective in the observed lesson in case they should be less effective in a different situation. . . .

3. Type C Instructional Conference—*Purpose:* To encourage teachers to identify those parts of a teaching episode with which they were not satisfied so that, in collaboration with the observer, strategies for reducing or eliminating future unsatisfactory outcomes will be developed. *Objective:* The teacher will identify solutions with potential for changing unsatisfying aspects of the lesson. . . .

4. Type D Instructional Conference—*Purpose:* To identify and label those less effective aspects of teaching that were not evident to the teacher and to develop alternative procedures that have potential for effectiveness. *Objective:* The teacher will select alternative behaviors he or she might substitute for behaviors perceived by the observer (and hopefully by the teacher) as not so effective. . . .

5. Type E Instructional Conference—*Purpose:* To promote continuing growth of excellent teachers. *Objective:* The teacher will select next steps in expanding his or her own professional growth.[60]

Participants should not perceive the postobservation conference as an assessment of the teacher's performance comparable to the principal's summative evaluation, but as an opportunity for the supervisor to provide valuable feedback for the teacher's consideration. To conduct an effective conference, the supervisor must know how to give helpful, and sometimes negative, feedback without injuring the teacher's ego or arousing defensive behaviors. Kyte suggested a three-point outline for the conference that remains good procedure:

1. Strong points of the lesson
2. Weak points in the lesson
3. Doubtful points not clearly understood[61]

Mosher and Purpel recommended that the supervisor avoid making two types of analysis with the teacher: a simple inventory of events and a recounting of critical incidents that took place during the observation. Instead, they advised that the supervisor help the teacher discern "*recurring patterns* in content, teaching or student behavior and of their *possible interrelations*."[62]

The supervisor's manner and attitudes are as important as the technical analysis made for the teacher. In Chapter 2 you read of contrasts between directive and nondirective behavior. A nondirective posture can put the teacher at ease. For example, a few processing-type comments at the beginning of the conference can go a long way toward establishing rapport. A question to the teacher such as "How did you feel about the lesson?" can be useful in breaking the ice. Surely, the supervisor should not come to the conference with a rigid analysis on the basis of which he or she proceeds to lecture the teacher. The supervisor needs to avoid sermonizing and conveying a loftier-than-thou superiority. Supervisors should remember that it is far easier to tell a person, especially after the fact, how to do something than to do it themselves.

Supervisors should remember that teachers want specific help, specific suggestions. They want supervisors to talk to specific points that can help them improve. The supervisor needs to appear friendly but professional.

A nondirective approach that probes for the teacher's feelings and an analysis of his or her own performance is generally appropriate, but directive behavior at times may be necessary. For example, the supervisor may need to focus on a point with an expression such as "Here's the way I see it. I believe it would have been more effective if . . ." The degree of directiveness and nondirectiveness needs to be tailored to the individual teacher and to the relationship between the teacher and the supervisor. When nondirective measures fail with an uncommunicative or inarticulate teacher, the supervisor may need to resort to more directive means.

The supervisor must detect which dominant behavior will be most effective with a particular teacher and adjust his or her style accordingly. Thus, the supervisor's behavior is not a monolithic, unchanging, machinelike process with a single orientation that will be unfailingly successful in all situations; rather, it is a flexible, changing, human process. Much as teachers must take students from where they are, supervisors must adjust their approach to the individual teachers with whom they work.

The postobservation conference has maximum chance for success if both the teacher and the supervisor manifest a sense of confidence in their own roles. A successful conference cannot occur without a feeling of rapport, which the supervisor should have established with the teacher long before initiating the cycle of clinical supervision.

PROBLEMS IN CLINICAL SUPERVISION

Clinical supervision is not without its critics, who raise the following questions:

- Who will do the supervising?
- Do we have the necessary resources?
- For whom should clinical supervision be provided?
- Are there other models for assisting teachers that are as effective as or more effective than clinical supervision?

Each of these issues is examined in the next sections.

Who Will Do the Supervising?

Two of the issues explored in Chapter 2 pose the questions of whether the administrator can be the supervisor and whether supervision is evaluation. Much of the literature on instructional supervision, including this textbook, urges consultative, developmental supervision to distance itself as much as possible from administration. Other experts express an opposing view, holding that it is the building administrator's responsibility to supervise teachers both clinically and otherwise. They feel that the evaluative aspects of supervision cannot be divorced from the clinical. Given the constraints on the typical school administrator's time, it is difficult to see how he or she can devote significant amounts of time to helping teachers improve instruction. Barbara Nelson Pavan pointed to research studies that corroborated teachers' dissatisfaction with the help provided by their principals.[63]

In a discussion of the principal serving as instructional leader, Goldhammer, Anderson, and Krajewski noted, "Unfortunately, principals are often as beleaguered and time-pressed as their central office colleagues; and while it is increasingly fashionable to talk about the instructional-leadership role of the principal, often that person is hard pressed to do the job well."[64] It is worth reiterating that in some schools where the principal serves as both administrator and instructional supervisor, help in supervising is often available but unused in the form of department heads, grade coordinators, team leaders, and school-based resource people.

Another question, considered in Chapter 2, is raised in reference to supervision in general: Should the clinical supervisor be a generalist or a specialist? Both prevailing practice and present-day preservice and in-service training programs appear to be slanted toward the use of generalists who can appraise generic teaching skills. Much of the literature, including this textbook, aims at the development of skills in supervising across disciplines and levels.

Mosher and Purpel, on the other hand, stressed the importance of the supervisor's specialization in the teaching field:

> The supervisor is, first, a content specialist, because it is not considered feasible to analyze teaching effectiveness independently of the content of what is being taught. This may appear to labor the obvious. Nonetheless, the question of whether people can supervise across subject-matter areas is very much an issue in supervision.[65]

Given the choice, we would be inclined to use the services of instructional supervisors who are trained and experienced in their fields of specialization as well as in general methods of instruction. But as Voltaire made us realize, the quest for the best of all possible worlds can be both ludicrous and not very productive. Wealthier school systems can probably afford to deploy a cadre of specialists who are at the same time generalists. The less-well-to-do school districts may have to work with one or more generalists who are not familiar with specialties outside their own field(s) of specialization. In any case, whether a school system uses generalists or specialists as supervisors, effective supervision is still possible with appropriate in-service training.

Collegiality in Supervision

Dissatisfaction with supervisory help (or the lack of it), an absence of designated supervisors, lack of time in the care of supervisors who are designated to serve all teachers, and a natural inclination to look to one's immediate colleagues for assistance have resulted in variations on the typical designated supervisor-teacher clinical model. More frequently, teachers are assuming responsibilities for helping each other in the improvement of instruction. Goldhammer, Anderson, and Krajewski espoused the concept of collegiality, stating that "now, more than ever, we stress the dimension of *collegiality*, and urge that CS [clinical supervision] be seen as a tool for use in not only the usual superordinate-subordinate relationship but also peer relationships as well."[66] Three variations of a collegial approach to supervision are *peer supervision, coaching*, and *mentoring*.

Peer Supervision   The principle of peer or collegial supervision is introduced when classroom teachers call on their department heads, grade coordinators, team leaders, lead teachers, and other classroom teachers for assistance. That help may be rendered on a casual, informal basis or, increasingly, on a planned, structured basis. The practice of peer supervision is growing even though some educators feel that the concept itself is an anomaly—as the very word *supervision* implies a superordinate-subordinate relationship.

In her study of 240 beginning teachers in Florida and Georgia, Joyce Bowman Coleman found that peer teachers provided more supervisory assistance to first-year teachers than did administrators or designated supervisors and that beginning teachers valued and preferred supervisory help from peers to help from administrators or other supervisors.[67] Alfonso and Goldsberry found that "teachers report other colleagues to be their first source of professional help, even when supervisory assistance is available."[68] Training peers in observation and conferencing techniques, as well as providing time for them to carry out their supervisory tasks, is essential to an effective, structured program of peer supervision. Where mutual respect and trust exist, peer or collegial supervision can be an effective process.

Coaching   Schools may institute coaching models in which teachers help each other develop new teaching strategies and resolve instructional problems. Bruce Joyce and Beverly Showers pioneered the application of the sports term *coaching* to the development of classroom instructional strategies.[69] Snyder viewed coaching as "a data-based technique that enables staff members to learn new skills, to modify practices, to solve problems together, and to develop basic skills."[70] As a structured adaptation of collegial supervision, coaching provides a means for teacher teams of two or more to work together and help each other. Florida principals whose schools have been labeled with grades of D or F, for example, are required to hire reading and math coaches to help classroom teachers learn new teaching methods, develop lessons, decipher data, and prepare exams. In addition, the coaches provide demonstration lessons, co-teach, and work with small groups of students.

Robert J. Garmston described three coaching models: technical, collegial, and challenge.[71] With technical coaching, two teachers or consultants with teachers are paired to practice a specific skill taught in a staff-development program. Collegial coaching offers a model in which pairs of teachers observe and critique each other on strategies designated by the teacher to be observed. Conducted in small groups rather than in pairs, challenge coaching begins with identification of an instructional problem and proceeds through group deliberation to attempt to solve the problem.

Mentoring   Mentoring of novice teachers or protégés is now part of teacher induction programs in many school districts across the country.[72] Susan Villani reminded us that the word *mentor* comes from Mentor, the teacher of Telemachus, son of Odysseus.[73] As a broad concept, mentoring implies assistance given by a knowledgeable, experienced person to a less knowledgeable, less experienced person. School systems look to mentoring not only to help new teachers in their transition into the profession but also to help retain teachers by reducing teacher turnover and burnout.

Schools look to teachers with the requisite personal and professional skills to serve as mentors. Mentors are often motivated to serve because of their identification and recognition as superior or master teachers and by a desire to help newcomers in the profession. Provision of released time and a stipend serve as additional incentives.

Portner saw mentors as fulfilling the functions of relating, assessing, coaching, and guiding, with the end result that those teachers for whom mentoring has been provided will become proficient at making their own informed instructional decisions.[74] Villani noted four ways in which mentors may accomplish their mission:

- Provide emotional support and encouragement.
- Provide information about the daily workings of the school and the cultural norms of the school community.
- Promote cultural proficiency regarding students and their families.
- Cognitive coaching.[75]

Although mentoring can lead to growth on the part of both the new teacher and the mentor, Lois J. Zachary, employing the metaphor of mentoring as a journey, offered the following caveat to mentors:

> In order to lay a solid foundation for building an effective learning relationship, mentors must have a clear understanding of their own personal journey. Mentors who fail to differentiate between self and other in a mentoring relationship run the risk of mentor cloning, that is, projecting their own lived experience onto the mentee.[76]

Collegial supervision and its variants—peer supervision, coaching, and mentoring—extend supervisory resources by enlisting teachers themselves in the process. Extensions of the more common supervisory-teacher model of clinical supervision may very well result in drastic changes in the role of the supervisor. For example, Garman discussed the formation of an "organic team" of six teaching colleagues who directed their own activities.[77] A supervisor who works with a group of this nature would serve as a facilitator and resource person.

Collegiality in supervision can supplement or conceivably even replace more customary modes of instructional supervision. Recognizing the need for instructional supervision and the shortage of instructional supervisors, Alfonso and Goldsberry suggested

> a new role for supervisors. They might become "orchestrators" of instructional supervision, persons who serve a broker role in the school system, identifying needs and then selecting and recruiting from throughout the school or school system those persons who can contribute to specific tasks of instructional improvement.[78]

These authors recommended that instructional supervisors take on the responsibility for developing colleagueship in supervision.

Teacher colleagues—peer coaches, mentors, master teachers, and lead teachers—often accept responsibilities other than helping teachers on a one-to-one basis. Recognition and incentives are customarily provided for these collegial supervisors in the form of differentiated staffing, career ladder, and merit pay plans, a topic to which we return in Chapter 14.

Do We Have the Necessary Resources?

Time, money, and personnel—all interrelated—pose problems when a school system is deciding whether to launch a program of clinical supervision. We can calculate a large amount of time per teacher if we tally the hours for each phase of clinical supervision. A bare minimum of time to be spent for each teacher is shown here:

Preobservation conference	20 minutes
Observation	30 minutes
Analysis of data	30 minutes
Postobservation conference	30 minutes
	110 minutes

Thus, the supervisor needs at the very least approximately two hours per teacher per cycle of clinical supervision; this figure is somewhat unrealistically on the low side. You can see the enormity of the time problem if you multiply this estimate by the number of times the teacher and supervisor repeat the cycle, allow time for the supervisor to make a record of the preobservation and postobservation conferences, allocate time for word-processing transcripts or notes of observation, increase the time of observation from thirty minutes to fifty, and set aside time for what Goldhammer called a "postmortem" or "postconference analysis."[79] The time factor is further enlarged if arrangements must be made for electronic media; time is doubled if the supervisor is to review an audio- or videorecording of the lesson. If teachers are to become an integral part of the supervisory process as in peer supervision, time and money must be found for releasing them from some classroom duties and for their training. Funds must also be provided, as in the case of mentors, for stipends.

For Whom Should Clinical Supervision Be Provided?

Ideally, clinical supervision should be available to all teachers—experienced, inexperienced, effective, ineffective, pedestrian, and talented. Given the paucity of resources and the demands of the job, it is doubtful that an adequate program of clinical supervision can be made available to every teacher. Consequently, those teachers who are having problems are more likely to need and call for assistance of this nature.

Some supervisors feel it best to ignore those teachers who are doing high-quality work. Hunter, however, argued against neglecting excellent teachers. She commented, "We have learned to challenge gifted students to encourage continuing growth, but often our gifted teachers are left to provide their own stimulation or to become bored and atrophied."[80] Excellent teachers are just like excellent athletes or others who are at the top of their profession and regularly receive feedback on their performance. As someone once said, "Feedback is the breakfast of champions."

If adequate material and human resources are indeed available, clinical supervision should be provided for all teachers who wish to secure this type of aid. The instructional supervisor, as contrasted with the administrative supervisor, cannot and should not thrust himself or herself on the teacher. Thus, a number of teachers may opt out of the opportunity to receive help from the supervisory consultant. To some degree, supervisors can judge their own success by the demand of teachers for their services.

If a school system is not able to cater to the supervisory needs of all teachers, it must do what school systems have always done—set priorities and/or put out fires. Those who are most in need must be assured of help if for no other reason than the well-being of their students. A better solution, of course, would be sufficient funding for our schools so that adequate supervision can be made available to all who need and want it.

Are There Models Other Than the Clinical?

Allan A. Glatthorn proposed what he termed "differentiated supervision." Glatthorn explained, "Differentiated supervision includes three developmental options" (*intensive development, cooperative development*, and *self-directed development*) "and two evaluative options" (*intensive evaluation* and *standard evaluation*).[81] Viewing teachers as professionals, Glatthorn would allow them, within limits, to choose the types of supervision in which they would participate.

The clinical model calling for diagnosis of teaching behaviors and recommendations for improvement has taken root. It is reinforced by the practice of specifying teacher competencies. It offers a system that has had a lengthy period of development.

We can argue about process and procedures, but logic supports a one-to-one, face-to-face relationship between a teacher and an able supervisor as an unequaled means of helping the teacher grow. In fact, it is a way of helping both the teacher and supervisor grow. When personal and professional growth takes place, the entire school system and its clientele benefit. Clinical supervision provides a setting for such growth to occur. We concur with Saundra J. Tracy and Robert H. MacNaughton, who said, "Perhaps the greatest legacy of clinical supervision reflected in current supervisory practice is its emphasis on working directly with teachers to improve instruction."[82]

SUMMARY

Clinical supervision is the provision of supervisory help to individual teachers. It is formative in nature, designed to assist the teacher to improve instruction. The typical clinical model calls for a one-to-one, face-to-face relationship between the teacher and supervisor. Clinical supervision focuses on the events that take place in the classroom.

Models of clinical supervision posit a cycle that consists of a number of stages or phases. Minimally, a model would encompass three stages: preobservation conference, observation, and postobservation conference.

In the preobservation conference, the teacher and supervisor make plans for the supervisor's forthcoming visit to the classroom. They decide on specific behaviors or events to be observed. During the observation, the supervisor looks for evidence of the behaviors or events and makes a record of what occurred.

Two types of observations can be made: global and specific. In global observation, the supervisor records all teacher behaviors; in specific observation, he or she notes selected behaviors that have usually been agreed on in advance. Among the means for recording classroom events are anecdotal records, verbatim and selective verbatim transcripts, note taking, audio/multimedia, instruments, and charting.

A postobservation conference should take place after the supervisor has had time to analyze and organize the data. Both pre- and postobservation conferences should occur in a mutually acceptable location. In the cycle of clinical supervision, the supervisor plays the role of knowledgeable, trained, and experienced peer of the teacher. He or she should demonstrate skill in following nondirective, collaborative, and directive approaches and know when to use each.

Clinical supervision requires the supervisor to possess skills in observing, diagnosing, prescribing, and conferencing. In addition, the supervisor must manifest attitudes of a helping relationship and interest in the teacher.

The aim of clinical supervision is improvement of instruction and thereby improvement in student achievement. It is not designed for evaluating teachers for administrative purposes.

Peer supervision, coaching, and mentoring offer viable models for delivering clinical supervision. The provision of adequate time, personnel, equipment, and materials poses a problem for school systems that want to conduct a program of clinical supervision.

Alternatives to the clinical model have been suggested, such as differentiated supervision. Although more research is needed, there is some indication that clinical supervision can be effective.

QUESTIONS FOR DISCUSSION

1. How should supervisors determine what to look for when observing teachers?
2. Should supervisors use observation instruments when observing teachers? If so, what type would you suggest?
3. Under what circumstances would peer supervision be most feasible?
4. When could mentors replace other designated supervisors?
5. What are the reasons adequate clinical supervision is/is not possible?

ACTIVITIES FOR FURTHER STUDY

REFLECTIVE

1. Describe each of the following:
   a. Clinical supervision
   b. Peer supervision
   c. Developmental supervision
   d. Differentiated supervision
2. Prepare a report on one or more of the following models of clinical supervision (see bibliography at end of chapter):
   a. Acheson and Gall
   b. Bellon and Bellon
   c. Cogan

    d. Goldhammer, Anderson, and Krajewski

    e. Mosher and Purpel

3. Prepare a report on Goldhammer's model of clinical supervision (see chapter bibliography).

4. Contrast the first edition of Goldhammer's book with the third edition, revised by Anderson and Krajewski (see chapter bibliography).

5. Report on any existing programs of clinical supervision that you can locate.

6. Report on the kinds of data that can be recorded by means of a class seating chart.

7. Prepare a review of Elliot W. Eisner's views on artistic supervision (see chapter bibliography).

8. Review the literature on interpretive or hermeneutic and ecological approaches to supervision. Describe their assumptions and recommended practices. (See references by Noreen B. Garman and C. A. Bowers and David J. Flinders, for example.)

9. Critique Allan A. Glatthorn's proposals for differentiated supervision (see chapter bibliography).

10. Prepare a report on Carl D. Glickman's descriptions of nondirective, collaborative, and directive supervisory behaviors (see chapter bibliography).

11. Respond to this question: Under what conditions should clinical supervisors conduct global assessments of the teacher's performance?

12. Defend or challenge the concept of peer supervision, stating reasons.

13. In the literature or in practice, locate models of clinical supervision that are not on a one-teacher-to-one-supervisor basis. Discuss the pros and cons of group models.

14. Prepare a report on any programs of peer supervision, coaching, or mentoring found in the literature or in a school with which you are personally familiar.

15. Critique the article by Thomas J. Sergiovanni (see chapter bibliography) in which he distinguishes science from scientism.

16. Describe the basic tenets of the following approaches to supervision and identify one or more advocates of each approach:

    a. Scientific

    b. Artistic

    c. Interpretive (hermeneutic)

    d. Ecological

17. Describe the three models of assisting and assessing educational personnel discussed by Saundra J. Tracy and Robert H. MacNaughton (see chapter bibliography):

    a. Means-oriented model

    b. Ends-oriented model

    c. Teacher concern-oriented model

APPLICATION

1. Role-play a preobservation conference.

2. Observe a class in action and make a written verbatim record of the events for twenty minutes.

3. Observe a class in action and record the events by using selective verbatim recording for thirty minutes.

4. Observe a class in action and record the events by means of notes for thirty minutes.

5. Using the book by Keith A. Acheson and Meredith Damien Gall as a guide, select a seating chart exercise, try it out on a class, and report on your experience in using the technique (see chapter bibliography).

6. Videorecord a class and analyze the recording. If the teacher of the class wishes, conduct a second analysis with him or her.

7. Collect and analyze samples of classroom observation instruments.

8. Select one of the following specific behaviors and choose or create an instrument by which you would assess it. If you use an existing instrument, cite the specific instrument and source:

   a. Verbal interaction

   b. Nonverbal behavior

   c. Providing feedback to the students

   d. Stimulus variation

   e. Individualization of instruction

9. Design, conduct, and report on a simple study to determine the following:

   a. Whether principals feel they can be effective as instructional supervisors.

   b. Whether teachers feel the principal can be effective as an instructional supervisor.

10. Design, conduct, and report on a simple study to determine the following:

    a. Whether supervisors feel they can assist teachers effectively in a field of specialization for which they have not been trained.

    b. Whether teachers feel supervisors can assist them effectively in a field of specialization for which the supervisors have not been trained.

11. Design your own classroom observation instrument for global evaluation of teacher performance.

12. Apply the observation instruments you created for activities 8 and 11 in a live situation or with a videotape of an actual classroom situation and interpret the data.

13. Select or create and apply in a live situation an observation instrument designed to assess overall performance of a teacher on specific rather than generic teaching skills in a particular subject area, such as the evaluation of teaching third-grade reading, the teaching of sixth-grade science, the teaching of beginning algebra, and the teaching of tenth-grade physical education.

NOTES

1. Morris L. Cogan, *Clinical Supervision* (Boston: Houghton Mifflin, 1973), p. 8.
2. Ibid., p. 9.
3. Ibid.
4. Robert Goldhammer, Robert H. Anderson, and Robert J. Krajewski, *Clinical Supervision: Special Methods for the Supervision of Teachers*, 3rd ed. (Fort Worth, Tex.: Harcourt Brace Jovanovich, 1993), p. 34.
5. Ibid., pp. 52–53.
6. Robert Goldhammer, *Clinical Supervision: Special Methods for the Supervision of Teachers* (New York: Holt, Rinehart and Winston, 1969), p. 54.
7. Ibid.
8. Edward Pajak, *Approaches to Clinical Supervision: Alternatives for Improving Instruction*, 2nd ed. (Norwood, Mass.: Christopher-Gordon Publishers, 2000), p. 4.

9. Keith A. Acheson and Meredith Damien Gall, *Clinical Supervision and Teacher Development: Preservice and Inservice Applications*, 5th ed. (Hoboken, N.J.: Wiley, 2003), p. 12.

10. Ibid., p. 85.

11. Ibid., p. 84.

12. Ralph L. Mosher and David E. Purpel, *Supervision: The Reluctant Profession* (Boston: Houghton Mifflin, 1972), pp. 110–11.

13. Noreen Garman, "The Clinical Approach to Supervision," in *Supervision of Teaching*, 1982 Yearbook, ed. Thomas J. Sergiovanni (Alexandria, Va.: Association for Supervision and Curriculum Development, 1982), pp. 35–52.

14. Ibid., p. 38.

15. Robert J. Alfonso and Lee Goldsberry, "Colleagueship in Supervision," in *Supervision of Teaching*, 1982 Yearbook, ed. T. Sergiovanni, (Alexandria, Va.: Association for Supervision and Curriculum Development, 1982), p. 94.

16. Robert J. Alfonso, Gerald R. Firth, and Richard F. Neville, *Instructional Supervision: A Behavior System*, 2nd ed. (Boston: Allyn and Bacon, 1981), p. 121.

17. Garman, "Clinical Approach to Supervision," p. 42.

18. Jon Wiles and Joseph Bondi, *Supervision: A Guide to Practice*, 6th ed. (Upper Saddle River, N.J.: Merrill/Prentice Hall, 2004), p. 266.

19. George C. Kyte, *How to Supervise: A Guide to Educational Principles and Progressive Practice of Educational Supervision* (Boston: Houghton Mifflin, 1930), p. 138.

20. Ibid., p. 171.

21. Ibid., p. 142.

22. Ibid., p. 147.

23. Ibid., pp. 149–50.

24. Ibid., p. 150.

25. Ibid., pp. 156–57.

26. Ibid., p. 160.

27. Ibid., p. 139.

28. Ibid., p. 158.

29. Cogan, *Clinical Supervision*, p. 10.

30. Goldhammer, *Clinical Supervision*, pp. 56–72; Goldhammer, Anderson, and Krajewski, *Clinical Supervision*, chap. 3.

31. Mosher and Purpel, *Supervision*, p. 81.

32. Cogan, *Clinical Supervision*, pp. 10–13.

33. Acheson and Gall, *Clinical Supervision and Teacher Development*, pp. 8–11.

34. Jerry J. Bellon and Elner C. Bellon, *Classroom Supervision and Instructional Improvement: A Synergetic Process*, 2nd ed. (Dubuque, Iowa: Kendall/Hunt Publishing, 1982), chaps. 4, 5, and 6.

35. Goldhammer, *Clinical Supervision*, p. 89.

36. Acheson and Gall, *Clinical Supervision and Teacher Development*, p. 124.

37. See Madeline Hunter, "Let's Eliminate the Preobservation Conference," *Educational Leadership* 43, no. 6 (March 1986): 69–70.

38. Elliot W. Eisner, "An Artistic Approach to Supervision," in *Supervision of Teaching*, 1982 Yearbook, ed. T. Sergiovanni, (Alexandria, Va.: Association for Supervision and Curriculum Development, 1982), pp. 55–57.

39. Ibid., p. 59.

40. Ibid., p. 60.

41. Ibid., pp. 60–61.

42. Ibid., p. 62.

43. Noreen Garman, "Theories Embedded in the Events of Clinical Supervision," *Journal of Curriculum and Supervision* 5 (Spring 1990): 211.

44. C. A. Bowers and David J. Flinders, *Culturally Responsive Teaching and Supervision: A Handbook for Staff Development* (New York: Teachers College Press, 1991), p. 5.

45. Ibid., pp. 30–51.

46. Goldhammer, *Clinical Supervision*, pp. 88–89.

47. Acheson and Gall, *Clinical Supervision and Teacher Development*, p. 190.

48. Ibid., pp. 190–91.

49. Ibid., p. 192.

50. Ibid., p. 148.

51. Mosher and Purpel, *Supervision*, pp. 92–95.

52. This checklist has been used in a form slightly modified at the suggestion of Dr. Sarah W. J. Pell of Florida International University. The modified form omits the sections on selection of resources and selection of strategies; provides a space for comments to the right of the Yes and No columns; and adds at the bottom places for data on duration of time in minutes, names of teacher and school, grade, and date.

53. Ned A. Flanders, *Analyzing Teaching Behavior* (Reading, Mass.: Addison-Wesley, 1970).

54. Charles M. Galloway, "An Exploratory Study of Observational Procedures for Determining Teacher Nonverbal Communication," doctoral dissertation, University of Florida, 1962. *Dissertation Abstracts International*, 1962, p. 2310.

55. Jacob S. Kounin, *Discipline and Group Management in Classrooms* (New York: Holt, Rinehart and Winston, 1970).

56. Karolyn J. Snyder, "School Transformation: The Context for Professional Coaching and Problem Solving," in *Clinical Supervision: Coaching for Higher Performance*, eds. Robert H. Anderson and Karolyn J. Snyder (Lancaster, Pa.: Technomic, 1993), p. 33.

57. Acheson and Gall, *Clinical Supervision and Teacher Development*, chap. 11.

58. See ibid., chap. 10, for helpful discussion of techniques of this type.

59. Madeline Hunter, "Six Types of Supervisory Conferences," *Educational Leadership* 37 (February 1980): 412.

60. Ibid., 409–12.

61. Kyte, *How to Supervise*, pp. 187–88.

62. Mosher and Purpel, *Supervision*, pp. 97–98.

63. Barbara Nelson Pavan, "Examining Clinical Supervisory Practice," in *Clinical Supervision: Coaching for Higher Performance*, eds. Robert H. Anderson and Karolyn J. Snyder, eds. (Lancaster, Pa.: Technomic Publishing, 1993), p. 152.

64. Goldhammer, Anderson, and Krajewski, *Clinical Supervision*, p. 33.

65. Mosher and Purpel, *Supervision*, p. 83.

66. Goldhammer, Anderson, and Krajewski, *Clinical Supervision*, p. 34.

67. Joyce Bowman Coleman, "The Perceived Quantities and Qualities of Supervisory Assistance Provided to Beginning Teachers in Florida and Georgia," doctoral dissertation, Athens, University of Georgia, 1986.

68. Alfonso and Goldsberry, "Colleagueship in Supervision," p. 91.

69. See Bruce Joyce and Beverly Showers, "The Coaching of Teaching," *Educational Leadership* 44 (October 1982): 4–10.

70. Snyder, "School Transformation," p. 32.

71. Robert J. Garmston, "How Administrators Support Peer Coaching," *Educational Leadership* 44 (February 1987): 18–26.

72. Hal Portner, *Mentoring New Teachers* (Thousand Oaks, Calif.: Corwin Press, 1998), pp. 3–4. See also Betty Achinstein and Steven Z. Athanases, eds., *Mentors in the Making: Developing New Leaders for New Teachers* (New York: Teachers College Press, 2006), and Debra Eckerman Pitton, *Mentoring Novice Teachers: Fostering a Dialogue Process*, 2nd ed. (Thousand Oaks, Calif.: Corwin Press, 2006).

73. Susan Villani, *Mentoring Programs for New Teachers: Models of Induction and Support* (Thousand Oaks, Calif.: Corwin Press, 2002), p. 7.

74. Portner, *Mentoring New Teachers*, pp. 7–8.

75. Villani, *Mentoring Programs for New Teachers*, pp. 9–12.

76. Lois J. Zachary, *The Mentor's Guide: Facilitating Effective Learning Relationships* (San Francisco: Jossey-Bass, 2000), p. 7.

77. Garman, "Clinical Approach to Supervision," pp. 48–49.

78. Alfonso and Goldsberry, "Colleagueship in Supervision," p. 107.

79. Goldhammer, *Clinical Supervision*, p. 273.

80. Hunter, "Supervisory Conference," p. 412.

81. Allan A. Glatthorn, *Differentiated Supervision*, 2nd ed. (Alexandria, Va.: Association for Supervision and Curriculum Development, 1997), pp. 6–8.

82. Saundra J. Tracy and Robert H. MacNaughton, *Assisting and Assessing Educational Personnel: The Impact of Clinical Supervision* (Boston: Allyn and Bacon, 1993), p. 323.

BIBLIOGRAPHY

ACHESON, KEITH A., and MEREDITH DAMIEN GALL. *Clinical Supervision and Teacher Development: Preservice and Inservice Applications*, 5th ed. New York: Wiley, 2003.

ACHINSTEIN, BETTY, and STEVEN Z. ATHANASES, eds. *Mentors in the Making: Developing New Leaders for New Teachers*. New York: Teachers College Press, 2006.

ALFONSO, ROBERT J., GERALD R. FIRTH, and RICHARD F. NEVILLE. *Instructional Supervision: A Behavior System*, 2nd ed. Boston: Allyn and Bacon, 1981.

ALFONSO, ROBERT J., and LEE GOLDSBERRY. "Colleagueship in Supervision." In *Supervision of Teaching*, 1982 Yearbook, ed. Thomas J. Sergiovanni. Alexandria, Va.: Association for Supervision and Curriculum Development, 1982.

ANDERSON, ROBERT H., and KAROLYN J. SNYDER, eds. *Clinical Supervision: Coaching for Higher Performance*. Lancaster, Pa.: Technomic, 1993.

BELLON, JERRY J., and ELNER C. BELLON. *Classroom Supervision and Instructional Improvement: A Synergetic Process*, 2nd ed. Dubuque, Iowa: Kendall/Hunt Publishing, 1982.

BERRY, BARNETT, and RICK GINSBERG. "Creating Lead Teachers: From Policy to Implementation." *Phi Delta Kappan* 71 (April 1990): 616–21.

BEY, THERESA M., and C. THOMAS HOLMES, eds. *Mentoring, Developing Successful New Teachers*. Reston, Va.: Association of Teacher Educators, 1990. ERIC Document ED 322 118 SP 032 484.

BORICH, GARY D. *Observation Skills for Effective Teaching*, 5th ed. Upper Saddle River, N.J.: Prentice Hall, 2007.

BOWERS, C. A., and DAVID J. FLINDERS. *Culturally Responsive Teaching and Supervision: A Handbook for Staff Development*. New York: Teachers College Press, 1991.

———. *Responsive Teaching: An Ecological Approach to Classroom Patterns of Language, Culture, and Thought*. New York: Teachers College Press, 1990.

CHAMPAGNE, DAVID W., and R. CRAIG HOGEN. *Consultant Supervision: Theory and Skill Development*. Wheaton, Ill.: CH Publications, 1981.

"The Coaching of Teaching." *Educational Leadership* 40 (October 1982): 3–59.

COGAN, MORRIS L. *Clinical Supervision*. Boston: Houghton Mifflin, 1973.

COLEMAN, JOYCE BOWMAN. "The Perceived Quantities and Qualities of Supervisory Assistance Provided to Beginning Teachers in Florida and Georgia." Doctoral dissertation, Athens, University of Georgia, 1986.

COSTA, ARTHUR L., and ROBERT J. GARMSTON. *Cognitive Coaching: A Foundation for Renaissance Schools*, 2nd ed. Norwood, Mass.: Christopher-Gordon Publishers, 2002.

DARESH, JOHN C., and MARSHA A. PLAYKO. *Supervision as Proactive Leadership*, 4th ed. Prospect Heights, Ill.: Waveland Press, 2007.

DOLL, RONALD C. *Supervision for Staff Development: Ideas and Application*. Boston: Allyn and Bacon, 1983.

DUKE, DANIEL L., and RICHARD J. STIGGINS. *Teacher Evaluation: Five Keys to Growth*. Washington, D.C.: National Education Association, 1986.

EISNER, ELLIOT W. "An Artistic Approach to Supervision." In *Supervision of Teaching*, 1982 Yearbook, ed. Thomas J. Sergiovanni. Alexandria, Va.: Association for Supervision and Curriculum Development, 1982.

FLANDERS, NED. A. *Analyzing Teaching Behavior*. Reading, Mass.: Addison-Wesley, 1970.

———. "Interaction Analysis and Clinical Supervision." *Journal of Research and Development in Education* 9 (Winter 1976): 47–57.

FLINDERS, DAVID J. "Supervision as Cultural Inquiry." *Journal of Curriculum and Supervision* 6 (Winter 1991): 87–106.

GALLOWAY, CHARLES M. *Silent Language in the Classroom*. Bloomington, Ind.: Phi Delta Kappa Educational Foundation, 1976.

GARMAN, NOREEN B. "The Clinical Approach to Supervision." In *Supervision of Teaching*, 1982 Yearbook, ed. Thomas J. Sergiovanni. Alexandria, Va.: Association for Supervision and Curriculum Development, 1982.

————. "Clinical Supervision: Quackery or Remedy for Professional Development?" *Journal of Curriculum and Supervision* 1 (Winter 1986): 148–57.

————. "Theories Embedded in the Events of Clinical Supervision: A Hermeneutic Approach." *Journal of Curriculum and Supervision* 5 (Spring 1990): 201–13.

GARMAN, NOREEN B., CARL D. GLICKMAN, MADELINE HUNTER, and NELSON L. HAGGERSON. "Conflicting Conceptions of Clinical Supervision and the Enhancement of Professional Growth and Renewal: Point and Counterpoint." *Journal of Curriculum and Supervision* 2 (Winter 1987): 152–77.

GARMSTON, ROBERT J. "How Administrators Support Peer Coaching." *Educational Leadership* 44 (February 1987): 18–26.

GARUBO, RAYMOND C., and STANLEY WILLIAM ROTHSTEIN. *Supportive Supervision in Schools.* Westport, Conn.: Greenwood Press, 1998.

GLATTHORN, ALLAN A. *Differentiated Supervision*, 2nd ed. Alexandria, Va.: Association for Supervision and Curriculum Development, 1997.

————. *Supervisory Leadership: Introduction to Instructional Supervision.* Glenview, Ill.: Scott, Foresman/Little, Brown, 1990.

GLICKMAN, CARL D. *Developmental Supervision: Alternative Practices for Helping Teachers Improve Instruction.* Alexandria, Va.: Association for Supervision and Curriculum Development, 1981.

————. *Leadership for Learning: How to Help Teachers Succeed.* Alexandria, Va.: Association for Supervision and Curriculum Development, 2002.

————, ed. *Supervision in Transition*, 1992 Yearbook. Alexandria, Va.: Association for Supervision and Curriculum Development, 1992.

GLICKMAN, CARL D., STEPHEN P. GORDON, and JOVITA M. ROSS-GORDON. *SuperVision and Instructional Leadership: A Developmental Approach*, 7th ed. Boston: Pearson/Allyn and Bacon, 2007.

GOLDHAMMER, ROBERT. *Clinical Supervision: Special Methods for the Supervision of Teachers.* New York: Holt, Rinehart and Winston, 1969.

GOLDHAMMER, ROBERT, ROBERT H. ANDERSON, and ROBERT J. KRAJEWSKI. *Clinical Supervision: Special Methods for the Supervision of Teachers*, 3rd ed. Fort Worth, Tex.: Harcourt Brace Jovanovich, 1993.

GOTTESMAN, BARBARA L. *Peer Coaching for Educators*, 2nd ed. Lanham, Md.: Scarecrow Press, 2000.

GRAHAM, PEG, ed. *Teacher/Mentor: A Dialogue for Collaborative Learning.* New York: Teachers College Press, 1999.

GRAY, WILLIAM A., and MARILYNEE M. GRAY. "Synthesis of Research on Mentoring Beginning Teachers." *Educational Leadership* 43 (November 1985): 37–45.

HUNTER, MADELINE. "Let's Eliminate the Preobservation Conference." *Educational Leadership* 43 (March 1986): 69–70.

————. "Six Types of Supervisory Conferences." *Educational Leadership* 37 (February 1980): 408–12.

HYMAN, RONALD T. "Peer Coaching: Premises, Problems, Potential." *Education Digest* 56 (September 1990): 52–56.

————. *School Administrator's Faculty Supervision Handbook.* Englewood Cliffs, N.J.: Prentice Hall, 1986.

JONSON, KATHERINE FEENEY. *Being an Effective Mentor: How to Help Beginning Teachers Succeed.* Thousand Oaks, Calif.: Corwin Press, 2002.

JOYCE, BRUCE, and BEVERLY SHOWERS. "The Coaching of Teaching." *Educational Leadership* 44 (October 1982): 4–10.

KYTE, GEORGE C. *How to Supervise: A Guide to Educational Principles and Progressive Practice of Educational Supervision.* Boston: Houghton Mifflin, 1930.

LITTLE, JUDITH WARREN, and LINDA NELSON, eds. *Mentor Teacher: A Leader's Guide to Mentor Training.* San Francisco, Calif.: Far West Laboratory for Educational Research and Development, 1990. ERIC Document ED 328 940 EA 021 515.

MAXWELL, C. R. *The Observation of Teaching.* Boston: Houghton Mifflin, 1917.

McGREAL, THOMAS L. *Successful Teacher Evaluation.* Alexandria, Va.: Association for Supervision and Curriculum Development, 1983.

MOSHER, RALPH L., and DAVID E. PURPEL. *Supervision: The Reluctant Profession.* Boston: Houghton Mifflin, 1972.

ODELL, SANDRA J. *Mentor Teacher Programs.* Washington, D.C.: National Education Association, 1990.

OLSEN, KAREN D. *The Mentor Teacher Role: Owner's Manual*, 5th ed. Oak Creek, Ariz.: Books for Educators, 1989. ERIC Document ED 319 722 SP 032 356.

PAJAK, EDWARD. *Approaches to Clinical Supervision: Alternatives for Improving Instruction.* 2nd ed. Norwood, Mass.: Christopher-Gordon Publishers, 2000.

PAVAN, BARBARA NELSON. "Examining Clinical Supervisory Practice." In *Clinical Supervision: Coaching for Higher Performance*, eds. Robert H. Anderson and Karolyn J. Snyder. Lancaster, Pa.: Technomic, 1993.

———. "Clinical Supervision: Some Signs of Progress." *Texas Tech Journal of Education* 7 (Fall 1980): 241–51.

PITTON, DEBRA ECKERMAN. *Mentoring Novice Teachers: Fostering a Dialogue Process*, 2nd ed. Thousand Oaks, Calif.: Corwin Press, 2006.

PORTNER, HAL. *Mentoring New Teachers*, updated ed. Thousand Oaks, Calif.: Corwin Press, 2003.

REIMAN, ALAN J., and LOIS THIES-SPRINTHALL. *Mentoring and Supervision for Teacher Development.* New York: Longman, 1998.

ROBBINS, PAM. *How to Plan and Implement a Peer Coaching Program.* Alexandria, Va.: Association for Supervision and Curriculum Development, 1991.

SCHERER, MARGE, ed. *A Better Beginning: Supporting and Mentoring New Teachers.* Alexandria, Va.: Association for Supervision and Curriculum Development, 1999.

———. "Improving Professional Practice." *Educational Leadership* 63, no. 6 (March 2006): 8–92.

SERGIOVANNI, THOMAS J. "The Metaphorical Use of Theory and Models in Supervision." *Journal of Curriculum and Supervision* 2 (Spring 1987): 221–32.

———. "Science and Scientism in Supervision and Teaching." *Journal of Curriculum and Supervision* 4 (Winter 1989): 93–105.

———. "Toward a Theory of Clinical Supervision." *Journal of Research and Development in Education* 9 (Winter 1976): 3–19.

———, ed. *Supervision of Teaching*, 1982 Yearbook. Alexandria, Va.: Association for Supervision and Curriculum Development, 1982.

SHOWERS, BEVERLY. "Teachers Coaching Teachers." *Educational Leadership* 42 (April 1985): 43–48.

SNYDER, KAROLYN J. "School Transformation: The Context for Professional Coaching and Problem Solving." In *Clinical Supervision: Coaching for Higher Performance*, eds. Robert H. Anderson and Karolyn J. Snyder. Lancaster, Pa.: Technomic, 1993.

"Staff Development through Coaching." *Educational Leadership* 44 (February 1987): 3–36.

STRONGE, JAMES H. *Qualities of Effective Teachers*, 2nd ed. Alexandria, Va.: Association for Supervision and Curriculum Development, 2007.

TANNER, DANIEL, and LAUREL TANNER. *Supervision in Education: Problems and Practices.* New York: Macmillan, 1987.

Tennessee Education Association. *Bridges to Strength: Establishing a Mentoring Program for Beginning Teachers: An Administrator's Guide.* Charleston, W.Va.: Appalachia Educational Laboratory, 1988.

TRACY, SAUNDRA J., and ROBERT H. MACNAUGHTON. *Assisting and Assessing Educational Personnel: The Impact of Clinical Supervision.* Boston: Allyn and Bacon, 1993.

U.S. Department of Education. *One on One: A Guide for Establishing Mentor Programs.* Washington, D.C.: U.S. Department of Education, 1990.

VILLANI, SUSAN. *Mentoring Programs for New Teachers: Models of Induction and Support.* Thousand Oaks, Calif.: Corwin Press, 2002.

WAGNER, LAURA A. "Ambiguities and Possibilities in California's Mentor Teacher Program." *Educational Leadership* 43 (November 1985): 23–29.

WILES, JON, and JOSEPH BONDI. *Supervision: A Guide to Practice*, 6th ed. Upper Saddle River, N.J.: Merrill/Prentice Hall, 2004.

ZACHARY, LOIS J. *The Mentor's Guide: Facilitating Effective Learning Relationships.* San Francisco: Jossey-Bass, 2000.

ZUMWALT, KAREN K., ed. *Improving Teaching*, 1986 Yearbook. Alexandria, Va.: Association for Supervision and Curriculum Development, 1986.

VIDEOTAPES

Improving Instruction Through Observation and Feedback. 2002. Three twenty-five- to thirty-minute videotapes with Facilitator's Guide. Tape 1: *Different Models of Providing Classroom-Based Assistance.* Tape 2: *Observation Techniques.* Tape 3: *Approaches to Working Closely with Teachers.* Association for Supervision and Curriculum Development, 1703 N. Beauregard St., Alexandria, Va. 22311–1714. (800) 933-2723. www.ascd.org.

The Teacher Series. 2001. Six twenty-five- to thirty-minute videotapes with two comprehensive Facilitator's Guides. See especially Tape 4: *Teacher as Peer Coach.* Association for Supervision and Curriculum Development, 1703 N. Beauregard St., Alexandria, Va. 22311–1714. (800) 933-2723. www.ascd.org.

WEB SITES

Association for Supervision and Curriculum Development: www.ascd.org
National Staff Development Council: www.nsdc.org

CHAPTER 11

HELPING TEACHERS WORK TOGETHER

OBJECTIVES

After studying Chapter 11 you should be able to accomplish the following objectives:

1. Describe leadership skills needed by the supervisor.
2. Describe types of leadership styles and decide which style you prefer to follow.
3. Explain the supervisor's role as change agent.
4. Explain key concepts in group/organizational development and tell how they apply to the role of the supervisor.
5. Identify problems and suggest improvements in the use of oral, written, and nonverbal language.
6. Describe impediments to successful group work and the supervisor's role in reducing them.
7. Design a training program in group interaction.

LIVING IN GROUPS

Unless you live in the middle of the Gobi Desert, much of your life from the cradle to the grave will be spent in groups of some kind or other. Almost every person is a member of a primary group—a family—and goes to school in groups and plays in groups. As giant urban concentrations, or megalopolises, continue to sprawl up, down, and across North America, and as the beehive high-rise condo complex becomes more and more common, individuals will be thrown closer together. The era of the rugged individualist has just about disappeared (if indeed it has not already), and group living has become not only a way of life but also a way of survival. Even in the Gobi Desert, patterns of group behavior arise when the camel trains stop at the caravansary; and when two or more camel herders meet, a group is born. If the inhabitants of the Gobi do not discover each other, sooner or later a group of touring American educators will discover them, and by their example of group organization, reveal to them the group process in action.

The phenomenon of group endeavor is not new in the United States. As early as the nineteenth century, Frenchman Alexis de Tocqueville observed:

> Americans of all ages, all conditions, and all dispositions constantly form
> associations. They have not only commercial and manufacturing companies, in
> which all take part, but associations of a thousand other kinds, religious, moral,

serious, futile, general or restricted, enormous or diminutive. The Americans make associations to give entertainments, to found seminaries, to build inns, to construct churches, to diffuse books, to send missionaries to the antipodes; in this manner they found hospitals, prisons, and schools. If it is proposed to inculcate some truth or to foster some feeling by the encouragement of a great example, they form a society. Wherever at the head of some new undertaking you see the government in France, or a man of rank in England, in the United States, you will be sure to find an association.[1]

Most of the nation's work is conducted through group interaction. This is also true of the school; most of the work of the school is carried out through the interaction of the school personnel. Although the teacher in the self-contained elementary, middle, or high school classroom may face students alone (and with them form a separate teacher-student grouping), much of the planning, policy making, curriculum development, and decision making that affect the individual teacher take place in group situations.

A teacher today can no longer work completely independently of other teachers, as the teacher may have done in the days of the little red schoolhouse. Every decision a teacher makes has the potential of affecting other teachers in the school. There is need for some degree of consistency among faculty in their interpretations of policies and procedures, which they should have had a hand in drafting. A faculty must function as a group, and the success of a school is in large measure determined by the success with which teachers are able to work together. A corollary to this statement is the proposition that the success of a supervisor is to a considerable degree determined by his or her success in helping teachers work together.

To some teachers, it seems as if their lives are one grouping and regrouping after another, with each group requiring a new set of relationships. Teachers may be members of a host of school committees and groups—the faculty as a whole, ad hoc committees, standing committees, departments, teaching teams, in-service study groups, school advisory councils, curriculum councils, parent-teacher associations, teacher-student organizations, school district committees, professional organizations, associations of special fields, state committees, and national groups.

Presumably, all the groups to which a teacher belongs have certain objectives. Whether a group's objectives are realized depends on a number of variables: the quality of leadership in the group, the quality of followership in the group, and the skills of interaction among all members of the group. Groups fail to achieve their objectives when any one of these variables is deficient.

Suppose an anthropologist is studying a group of teachers at their national convention. He spends the three days of the conference dropping in on various meetings and group sessions and takes copious notes. After observing the work sessions—and incidentally participating in the social agenda—he studies his notations, among which are the following:

- General assembly—keynote address on "Teaching: Its Joys and Tribulations"—the first persons to arrive fill up the last two rows in the auditorium. They are asked to move forward.

- Panel discussion on cooperative learning—last half-hour is dialogue between two of the panelists.

- Seminar on computer-assisted instruction—"resource person" doesn't show, calls in his regrets.

- Seminar on alternative schools—guest speaker—continuous coming and going of the audience.
- Discussion group on parental choice of school—discussion digresses to disciplinary problems in the schools.
- Seminar on reading problems—one participant cuts off others in the group, dominates the discussion.
- Seminar on lengthening the school day—group becomes polarized, half pro, half con.
- Panel discussion on restructuring schools—two hours allotted, half an hour for each of four discussants; first speaker talks fifty minutes; last speaker winds up with ten minutes.
- Roundtable on whole language—everyone attempts to talk at the same time.

Our anthropologist wonders what the participants in these groups brought away from the conference. Admittedly, these were pro tempore groups composed of people who were relative strangers to each other. Nevertheless, he wonders if the groups should not have been more productive. As he compares them with groups that gave evidence of productivity, he tries to sort out some of the threads. He detects in the groups that had problems a lack of interest among the participants, a lack of commitment to the group's activity, a lack of organization and planning, a lack of sensitivity among the group participants for the concerns of others, a lack of ability or willingness to listen to each other, a lack of communication skills, a lack of a feeling of achievement as a result of group deliberation, and often, perhaps most serious of all, a lack of purpose.

It might be conjectured that groups at a conference do not give a true picture of groups in action. Teachers are away from home; the groups are transient and temporary; most of the participants have little control over the organization, content, and conduct of the deliberations. Our anthropologist would like to test the premise that when teachers know each other intimately and work side by side daily, their group sessions are more productive. He learns of a senior high school that has just begun a self-study in preparation for a year-end visit by a committee from the regional accrediting association. He is given carte blanche to attend any of the sessions of faculty and committees he wishes, and he takes full advantage of the invitation. He is not surprised when he finds the following situations:

- The Committee on Philosophy, Aims, Goals, and Objectives is about evenly divided among those who might be labeled "child-centered" and those who might be called "subject-centered." They seem unable to resolve their differences. One member of the child-centered faction by default writes the committee's "report," which they will submit to the total faculty.
- The Committee on School and Community has a difficult time apportioning the work. Data have to be collected and put into tabular and graphic form. Several teachers say they lack time to do this job. Because few volunteer for specific tasks, the chairperson has to assign responsibilities arbitrarily.
- When the Committee on Philosophy, Aims, Goals, and Objectives reports to the total faculty, several teachers sit in the back of the room talking, another is reading a newspaper, several arrive late, and two have scheduled other appointments. Time runs out before the faculty can reach consensus.

- The language arts group spends an entire session airing their concerns about students' deficiencies in reading and writing.
- The mathematics group whips through its set of standards without thought or discussion in forty-five minutes.
- The foreign language teachers engage in a prolonged, heated discussion of who should take foreign languages—should foreign languages be required of everybody or restricted to the academically talented?
- The Guidance Committee wanders into the subject of the administrator's failings.

Are these groups productive? Some would say yes; others would say no, depending on their orientation to the group process itself. Each of these groups appears to have problems.

Supervisors, and especially if they are also school administrators, will spend a great part of their professional lives meeting with groups of teachers—total faculties, departments, teams, task forces, study groups, and committees. They will work with groups of teachers from single schools and with groups representing many or all schools of a district. They will have many meetings that are unproductive. On the other hand, there will be times when the supervisors will feel that a group's effort could not have been more productive, and they will feel gratified at having participated in situations such as the following:

1. An early childhood teaching team becomes aware of problems in handling children of minorities in its classes, proposes analysis of the problem, studies the problem thoroughly, works diligently to formulate proposals for better meeting the needs of these children, and energetically attempts to implement its proposals.

2. A committee of elementary school teachers becomes concerned with the school's grading system, looks at alternate ways of grading, and drafts a proposal to take to the faculty for its consideration.

3. A middle school faculty, which feels its preadolescents as a group are lacking in motivation and are uninterested in school, engages in a free-wheeling discussion of why the students act as they do and ends its discussion with a motion to analyze the relevance of the curriculum. A task force is created under the leadership of the supervisor to examine the curriculum and report back to the faculty with recommendations for making the curriculum more relevant.

4. The English department in a high school undertakes an analysis of the reading achievement level of the students in its school. Finding many students with reading deficiencies, the teachers agree on a proposal that instead of blaming the elementary and middle school faculties for the students' deficiencies outlines ways for the total faculty to implement remedial and developmental programs and to institute techniques of teaching reading in the content areas.

In each of these four situations, the teachers have felt an obligation and responsibility to participate fully and to give of their energies and ideas. Not only has each teacher taken responsibility for participating, but everyone has sensed that his or her ideas and concerns were valued by both the group leader and other group members and that all members have had the opportunity to express their ideas and concerns. The members of these groups felt that their missions were worthwhile.

THE SUPERVISOR AS GROUP LEADER

Instructional supervisors fill a leadership role in helping the groups with which they work develop a sense of cohesiveness in an atmosphere of mutual trust and support. The goal of group development in today's schools is the creation of a sense of community in which teachers, administrators, supervisors, pupils, parents, and other laypeople work cooperatively to foster student growth and development. These constituencies join forces in an effort to make of the school a learning community.

Achieving the status of learning community requires continuous interaction among the school's constituencies. Linda Lambert and colleagues observed that "learning communities are difficult to create," that "members of school communities are individuals—often individualists—with diverse philosophies, experiences, expertise, and personalities."[2] Given this diversity, no single plan exists for the creation of a learning community. General principles, however, include identification of goals, collaboration, sharing, respect for one another, mutual trust, and recognition of the persons involved as a team rather than as a collection of isolated individuals.

To succeed in furthering the sense of community, the supervisor must be both a student of and a practitioner in human relations, interpersonal skills, and group dynamics.

Definition of Leadership

The successful supervisor must demonstrate the capacity to lead others. The effective instructional supervisor must not only possess leadership skills but also be able to nurture leadership in others. Carl D. Glickman, Stephen P. Gordon, and Jovita M. Ross-Gordon noted that "learning the skills of working with groups to solve instructional problems is a critical task of supervision."[3]

Many studies have sought to discover the nature of leaders and leadership.[4] Unfortunately, because leadership is a human quality, like most human qualities it defies precise description, quantification, generalization, and predictability. We can find almost as many definitions of leadership as there are of supervision. Several of them are given here:

> The leader is the individual in the group given the task of directing and coordinating task-relevant group activities.[5]
>
> Leadership may be considered as the process (act) of influencing the activities of an organized group in its efforts toward goal setting and goal achievement.[6]
>
> We define leadership as that behavior of an individual which initiates a new structure in interaction within a social system; it initiates change in the goals, objectives, configurations, procedures, inputs, processes, and ultimately the outputs of social systems.[7]

Although most administrators feel they are leaders and bristle when it is suggested otherwise, James M. Lipham distinguished between an administrator and a leader:

> The leader is concerned with initiating changes in established structures, procedures, or goals; he is disruptive of the existing state of affairs. The administrator . . . may be identified as the individual who utilizes existing structures or procedures to achieve an organizational goal or objectives . . . the administrator is concerned primarily with maintaining, rather than changing established structures, procedures, or goals. Thus, the administrator may be viewed as a stabilizing force.[8]

Unfortunately, some school systems do not want their administrators and supervisors to be leaders. The school boards and the communities in these cases are happy with things just as they are. They want administrators and supervisors who will conserve, not disrupt, maintain rather than change. They lack dynamism and are satisfied with the status quo. Unfortunately, those administrators and supervisors who enter systems of this kind imbued with a zeal to exert leadership and effect change soon discover that if they wish to remain in the system, they must conform to local expectations.

W. H. Cowley (1928) and Robert L. De Bruyn (1976) defined leader and leadership in simple terms. Cowley saw a leader as "an individual who is moving in a particular direction and inducing others to follow after him."[9] De Bruyn's definition of leadership was "causing others to want what you are doing to accomplish the work of the school."[10] Leadership can be conceptualized as the ability to cause people to make improvements in the institution.

Traits of Leaders

Society and all its institutions would benefit greatly if someone could draw up a foolproof list of traits that leaders should possess. On everyone's list would probably be

- Initiative
- Forcefulness
- Decisiveness
- Expertise
- Enthusiasm

Yet studies of leadership have shown no consistent pattern of traits that all leaders possess.[11] The studies have revealed that compared to their followers, leaders generally are

- More self-confident
- Slightly more intelligent
- More motivated to succeed
- More mature emotionally
- More gregarious
- More goal-oriented
- Taller

Some would add that leaders are more disposed than others to take risks and to accept the consequences of their actions. Many leaders demonstrate they dare to be different from others. Others would say that a leader must be assertive or aggressive. If we may assume that there are more leaders among administrators than among other school personnel, then it also pays to be male, white, Anglo Saxon, and Protestant (WASP), for more administrators in the United States possess these characteristics than do not. With the exception of gender, we might write off these characteristics as the effect of sheer numbers. Because there are more WASPs in the country, it appears logical that a higher percentage of administrators would fall into that category. The phenomenon of male dominance of school leadership positions may be explained by cultural conditioning and plain old chauvinism. But how do we explain that the majority of superintendents and principals of secondary schools are social studies and physical education majors? Art, foreign language, and music majors in top positions of leadership are less common. Is it a matter of numbers again? Social studies and physical education are popular fields, and in some parts of the country a surplus of these degree holders is evident. Then why is the English major not at the top in leadership positions? English is also a heavily populated field. Do those who have leadership skills gravitate instinctively to social studies and physical education? Is it because these disciplines are people-oriented whereas other fields are more subject-oriented? Or do the disciplines make the leader?

Ralph M. Stogdill conducted an extensive review of leadership studies and concluded, on the basis of ten or fifteen of these studies, that the average leader exceeds the average member of a group in a number of respects, including intelligence, dependability, sociability, initiative, and verbal facility. Several traits—originality, judgment, aggressiveness, and humor—showed the highest correlation with leadership. Other factors—age, height, and weight—evidenced low positive correlation.[12]

Even if a supervisor possesses every desirable trait on everyone's shopping list, there is still no certainty that once in the position, he or she will evidence successful leadership skills. Successful leadership is as much a matter of the situation as of the personal skills and characteristics of the person designated to lead. Persons who may fail in one setting may very well succeed in another. Paul Hersey and Kenneth H. Blanchard described a model of Situational Leadership consisting of four leadership styles differing in the degree to which they combine relationship (supportive) and task (guiding) behavior in the managerial setting.[13]

One trait that has not shown up as common to all leaders but that is worthy of further research is the elusive characteristic of charisma, the personal magnetism of a leader. Experts in administration have given surprisingly little attention to the phenomenon of charisma. Should we therefore deduce that charisma is unimportant to the success of leaders?

Certainly, we can recall charismatic leaders out of the past. Moses and Jesus must have possessed charisma. Exhibiting both charisma and visions, Joan of Arc rallied French soldiers to follow her in battle against the English. John F. Kennedy is almost always mentioned as an American president who had charisma. Generals George S. Patton and Douglas MacArthur of World War II fame were generals with charisma. Charismatic and famed for his speeches was the abolitionist Frederick Douglass. Most professional entertainers demonstrate charisma. We could speculate whether Adolf Hitler would have risen to a position of power if he had not been so charismatic.

Charisma is a power that enables leaders to attract people to follow them, sometimes to the ends of the earth. Some indefinable something in the individual's personality, whether a product of the genes or the environment or both, enables the charismatic individual to assemble a following. What little literature there is on this subject suggests that leaders who possess charisma are fortunate, for it adds a dimension to their leadership that noncharismatic individuals do not possess. At the same time, charisma is not an essential characteristic of leadership, which is fortunate, as charismatic leaders are in short supply.

Much of the literature on supervision treats leadership behavior as if it were generic, applicable to both administration and supervision. That is, the literature assumes that principles and skills of leadership are common to both administrators and supervisors. Generally, this is true. However, distinctions should be drawn in degree if not in substance between the skills needed by instructional supervisors and those needed by administrators. With that differentiation in mind, we can consider skills of leadership that logically and empirically appear to apply to both supervisors, who are leaders in staff positions, and administrators, who are leaders in line positions.

Styles of Leadership

A more profitable avenue of study than examining traits of leaders is examining styles or approaches to leadership. Two of these—three, if we include the more common mix of the basic two—have been described. Table 11.1 shows the terminology that four often-cited sources have applied to the two styles.[14] Although the terminologies differ, style 1 incorporates principles of directive behavior, focus on the needs of the institution, and concern for status. Style 2 emphasizes nondirective behavior, focus on the person, and openness of the system. The supervisor who embraces style 1 is directive (ordering, prescribing, telling) in behavior, task-oriented rather than people-oriented, and concerned about administrative efficiency. The supervisor who employs style 2 is nondirective (helping, facilitating, counseling), conscious of interpersonal relations, and concerned about the human dimension of supervision. In practice, supervisors must learn to adapt both styles to their situations. As there is a time to reap and a time to sow, there is a time to exhibit authoritarian behavior and a time to stress human-relations skills.

The instructional supervisor who occupies a staff or advisory rather than a line or power position should be an exemplar of style 2, using style 1 only in rare instances in which teacher behavior runs counter to the best interests of the students and the institution. In truth, staff personnel cannot follow style 1 in their own right because they are not armed with line authority and must either be recipients of authority delegated by the administrator or refer troublesome problems to the administrator. Human relations must be the strong suit of the supervisory leader.

Human-relations-oriented supervisors work in a cooperative mode with the teacher. They offer assistance; they serve as resource persons and advisers. They are concerned with building rapport and mutual trust. They create a nonthreatening climate where teachers' weaknesses can be revealed without punishment and where remediation can be undertaken without embarrassment. They are colleagues and friends whose purpose is helping the teachers improve instruction so that together they may enhance student learning.

TABLE 11.1 Two Basic Styles of Leadership

	Lewin, Lippitt, and White	McGregor	Fiedler	Morphet, Johns, and Reller
Style 1	Authoritarian	Theory X	Task-oriented	Traditional, monocratic, bureaucratic
Style 2	Democratic	Theory Y	Relations-oriented	Emerging, pluralistic, collegial

Thomas J. Sergiovanni and Robert J. Starratt would have supervisors move beyond a human-relations approach to what they called *human-resources supervision*.[15] The human-relations supervisor, like the task-oriented supervisor, has an increase in school effectiveness as the goal, with teacher satisfaction as a means to the goal. The human-resources supervisor has teacher satisfaction as the goal, with increased school effectiveness as the means to that goal.

The human-resources supervisor pays close attention to teachers' satisfaction with their jobs, their commitment and loyalty to the organization, the presence or absence of mutual trust among members of the organization, the mechanisms for teachers' input into the system's operation, and the frequency and quality of communication among members of the organization.

Sergiovanni drew a thoughtful distinction between "value dimensions" and "value-added dimensions" of leadership. He viewed the more traditional aspects of leadership as value dimensions designed to ensure functioning of the schools, such as directive managerial behavior and use of extrinsic motivators. Advocating a move toward "value-added leadership," he included among value-added dimensions collegiality and use of intrinsic motivators. Sergiovanni contrasted "calculated leadership" (a value dimension) with "leadership by outrage" (a value-added dimension). Calm and detached administrative behavior is characteristic of "calculated leadership"; passion, personal involvement, deep commitment, and risk taking are characteristics of "leadership by outrage." Sergiovanni observed that principles of value-added leadership are just now making their appearance in the business and educational literature.[16]

Although consensus is lacking on which skills are essential to the group leader, authorities on leadership seem to agree that in addition to the human orientation, supervisors should be skilled in (1) decision making, (2) effecting change, (3) organizational development, (4) communicating, and (5) group process. Some of the salient points of each of these interrelated skills as they relate to the role of the supervisor are discussed in more detail.

Decision Making

President Harry Truman summed up the heart of the administrative process in the famous slogan he kept on his desk in the Oval Office: "The buck stops here." Ultimately, the administrator must make and be responsible for decisions. Although school administrators and supervisors will not be called on to make earth-shattering decisions like Truman's decision to drop the atomic bomb on Japan, nevertheless the ability to make decisions is the most important single ingredient of administrative and supervisory behavior. Numerous authorities have emphasized the importance of decision-making skills for the successful administrator or manager.[17]

Some would certainly add decisiveness to a list of traits that administrators and supervisors should possess. Unfortunately, teachers and others often interpret decisiveness as the ability to make on-the-spot judgments and decisions. Administrators and supervisors must be able to sense when they can fulfill the desires of their followers for immediate decisions and when they should suspend judgment until more facts are available. Discretion is not only the better part of valor; it is also the better part of decision making. Administrators and supervisors who render snap judgments and call them correctly will certainly gain status. On the other hand, once they start to make bad decisions and suffer unpleasant consequences, they can plummet in the eyes of their followers. Administrators and supervisors need to develop a companion skill known as tolerance for ambiguity. Not all decisions can, must, or should be made on the spot. Sometimes no decision is the wiser decision. The astute administrator or supervisor knows when to make a snap judgment, when to delay for further facts and then come to a decision, and when to make no decision, allowing time for the situation to correct itself.

Administrators and supervisors are called on daily to render many small or large decisions. They must make decisions about planning, implementing, evaluating, and recycling. Supervisors' decisions fall within the three domains discussed in Chapter 1: instructional, curriculum, and staff development.

In Chapter 8, on curriculum evaluation, you became familiar with the CIPP model, which is a systematic process for making educational decisions. The model shows clearly the pervasiveness of the task of decision making. It shows the kinds of changes that may take place, the kinds of evaluations that are carried out, and the types of decisions that must be made. This model features planning, structuring, implementing, and recycling decisions as tasks of educational evaluation. Though focusing on educational evaluation, the model serves as an overview of decision making generally. Evaluation is the rendering of judgments, and in that respect evaluation is decision making. Every time an administrator or supervisor makes a decision, he or she evaluates the situation prior to rendering a judgment; then the judgment itself must be evaluated and sometimes revised.

Decision making is so habitual to competent administrators and supervisors that they do not perceive themselves as going through a process. Yet each time we make a decision we go through a series of steps or stages. In many instances, the human brain runs through the stages so rapidly that we are not aware we are analyzing the problem before making a decision. What we are doing is actually problem solving.

A number of models of the decision-making process consist of steps to be taken by the administrator or supervisor.[18] For guidance in decision making, we might fall back on the old reliable generic model for problem solving, referred to as the *scientific method*. In conducting research, we follow certain steps of an orderly process:

- Identify the problem.
- Formulate a hypothesis.
- Collect data.
- Analyze data.
- Draw conclusions.
- Verify, reject, or modify the hypothesis.

In one sense, decision making is research. To reach some decisions, we must conduct thorough research. Everyday, routine decisions do not require a great deal in the way of bona fide research, but the elements of data collection, analysis, and so on are there, perhaps only in embryonic form. We can adapt the research model and make it more operational in nature, as shown here:

- Identify the problem.
- Select the solution from alternatives.
- Put the solution into operation.

- Evaluate the solution.
- Recycle the decision, if needed.

We should not confuse immediate decisions with off-the-top-of-the-head decisions. Administrators and supervisors must often make immediate decisions. Even then, however, they should base them on the best data, which administrators and supervisors often have at their fingertips. Off-the-top-of-the-head decisions are usually intuitive, hasty, ill-considered decisions that ignore data. In choosing a solution to a problem, it is essential to use all available data, to avoid spontaneous, off-the-top-of-the-head judgments. Only in crises or emergencies, when there is no time to gather data—the data must come out of the administrator's or supervisor's experience—can spontaneous decisions be justified.

Robert J. Alfonso, Gerald R. Firth, and Richard F. Neville have drawn twenty-three implications for decision theory for *instructional supervisory* behavior.[19] Among these are the following four propositions:

> Proposition 1: Conscious decision making provides the opportunity for organizational growth and refinement.
>
> Proposition 13: Decision making can be made more responsive and effective when it is recognized that decisions are seldom optimal, but are typically the selection of the best choice among those available.
>
> Proposition 14: Decision making is swayed by the dynamic interaction between internal and external environments, and by the psychological makeup of the decision maker.
>
> Proposition 16: Although executive decisions are important in establishing goals, decisions made at the operational level are still more important, since they directly affect personal commitment and, thereby, production and effectiveness.[20]

Supervisors make decisions both unilaterally and in cooperation with others in the course of their daily work. The supervisor alone may have to decide, for example, which competing demands to meet and which needs to fill. "To which classroom will I go today?" is a supervisory decision. Of course, the decision should not be purely arbitrary but should be based on the best available data.

Supervisors should, however, seek to expand the scope of cooperative decision making. The supervisor should not, for example, decide unilaterally to initiate a curricular innovation, to select a certain series of textbooks, to devise a system of classroom observation, or to institute a staff-development program. These are matters for cooperative decision making, which not only helps solve problems but also helps develop a sense of community.

Supervisors should not only be concerned with their own decision making but should also seek to help teachers make decisions. Teachers want assistance with such problems as these: What is the best way to handle certain types of students? Did I handle a particular student correctly? Should I introduce more inquiry learning? Supervisors' success is gauged at least in part on how successfully they make decisions and how effective they are at helping others reach decisions.

Effecting Change

In the span of years since the end of World War II, American schools have experimented with team teaching, nongraded schools, programmed instruction, instructional television, open-space education, individualized guided education, computer-assisted instruction, mainstreaming, inclusion, and a host of other innovations. Some of these innovations have remained; others have disappeared. Change, however, continues to be the order of the day.

Behavioral scientists tell us that institutions must change if they are to grow and develop. Can you imagine the Latin Grammar School (with its heavy emphasis on Latin and Greek and its absence of modern foreign languages, industrial arts, business education, interscholastic athletics, marching band, and guidance) as the model secondary institution of the twenty-first century? Can you imagine public education restricted to males, as in the days of the Latin Grammar School and early academies or as it still is in some other countries?

Change has been exceedingly rapid in contemporary society, toppling old mores and values. Whereas change used to come slowly, modern technology, communication, and transportation catapult us into change often before we are emotionally ready.

What school systems need is planned change—not haphazard or impulsive change. Nor can a school system afford to maintain the status quo, no matter where the system is located. The students who are the products of the system suffer as much from no change as from unplanned change. Were students to spend their whole lives in a single community and in one career, the school might have a ready excuse for maintaining the status quo. Perhaps what was good enough for our grandparents would, under those conditions, be good enough for our grandchildren. But our country is large; our people are mobile; our industries are far-flung. Technology has the bad habit of making careers obsolete so that more training and retraining become necessary throughout life.

The school system that is "on the cutting edge" will not only plan and effect change but also anticipate change. It will use such procedures as the Delphi Technique, which was mentioned in Chapter 8, consulting the experts who are willing to gaze into their crystal balls and predict where schools are going five, ten, fifteen, twenty-five years hence. The omnipresence of computers and other forms of technology, the diminishing reserves of fossil fuels, the high cost of housing, the decrease in farming population, urban sprawl—all have their role in producing changes in our society, which in turn impact schools, learning, and education.

The instructional supervisor is in the forefront of the change process in education. The supervisor is in a strategic position to influence the largest professional group, teachers, to make changes in the system. In this process the supervisor is often referred to as a change agent. In the language of the behavioral scientist, a change agent helps a client system bring about change. The change agent works with individuals and groups to effect improvements. In the case of the instructional supervisor, changes are sought in instruction, in the curriculum, and in the staff. A change agent is concerned with changes in the behavior of the people who belong to the organization, the goals of the organization, the structure of the organization itself, and the technical processes the organization employs.

The change agent recognizes that if an institution is to maintain its vitality, it must grow and develop, just as individuals grow and develop. The change agent strives to plan for change, to control and eliminate unplanned change. The change agent would be the first to reject the notion of change for the sake of change. Change must be purposeful. It must come about because it produces better results than what preceded it.

Change may mean instituting a completely new practice. It may also mean replacing a practice already in operation. Thus, the change agent has entrenched attitudes to overcome if teachers feel commitment to the old practice. The status quo is far more comfortable and certainly requires less work than moving in new directions. The change agent must take teachers with him or her each step in the process, helping them determine whether the new practice is superior to the old. Demonstrations of effectiveness elsewhere can help secure teacher acceptance. Piloting and gradual phasing in of an innovation can be helpful techniques for ensuring commitment.

We encounter disagreement over the question of whether a change agent should come from inside or from outside the system. Although there are cogent arguments for the employment of change agents from the outside, there are practical arguments for choosing change agents from within the system. School systems may not be able to afford the services of people from the outside. They already have employees in supervisory roles who can serve as agents of change. Capable supervisors have already established a sense of trust with other school personnel; trust is an essential ingredient in the change process.

Behavioral scientists call the procedures they use to effect change *intervention techniques or strategies*. Change-agent supervisors work with teachers to improve their teaching skills by providing in-service education opportunities. They seek solutions to system problems through the group process, which necessitates the formation of committees, task forces, and councils. A change to a new reading program in the elementary school, for example, will require study and commitment among those who will be expected to plan, execute, and evaluate it.

Change agents work with teachers to improve the curriculum. Cooperatively, teachers and supervisors conduct needs assessments and decide on ways to fill gaps in the curriculum. A change from separate disciplines to an integrated curriculum or from a traditional to a magnet school, for example, will require deliberation and approval by all the constituencies of the school.

Change agents work with teachers and administrators to revise school policies and procedures that have become outmoded or nonfunctional. They help teachers perfect interpersonal skills through self-instruction and training sessions.

Some changes are minor; others are major. Some changes affect only a single teacher; others touch all school personnel and the community as well. The goal of many changes is adoption throughout the system. In fact, farsighted change agents hope that an innovation tested and found successful in their schools will be adopted by school systems throughout the country. The behavioral objectives movement, for example, which began to develop in the late 1950s with the work of such educators as Ralph W. Tyler at the University of Chicago, has been widely accepted across the nation. This change was not perceived as a modification of instructional practice for a particular school but rather a change that had universal relevance.

On a systemwide level, a central-office supervisor or administrator can act as a change agent. In the individual school, the principal, fulfilling his or her role as instructional leader, can and should be the primary change agent. Shirley M. Hord and others saw leadership in change often brought about not by one leader—a principal, for example—but by a facilitating team composed of principal, central-office supervisor or administrator, and teachers from whom peers sought help.[21]

The change process is essentially an exercise in human-relations skills. A curriculum change, for example, can result only when people are changed. An administrator can command change and can even bring about surface conformity. What an administrator cannot command is a commitment to a mandated change. People accept change when they feel they have a personal stake in it and when they believe change will improve the lives of those affected by it.

Supervisors must be open individuals who are receptive to change themselves. Because the impetus for change must often come from the leader, a closed personality who sees little value in change ("if it works, don't fix it") can block a school's progress. Schools need self-starting, energetic, future-looking persons in supervisory positions.

Alfonso, Firth, and Neville set forth thirty-seven propositions about *change theory* that are of importance to instructional supervisors.[22] From this list, we note the following, which seem of particular significance:

> Proposition 1: Planning and initiating change will be more effective when the objectives and policies of the organization are clear, realistic, and understood. . . .
>
> Proposition 11: The effectiveness of a change effort will be increased when one sees the nature of the change as enhancing one's own personal relationships and status in the organization. . . .
>
> Proposition 19: Change will be more effective if it does not appear to disturb the existing organizational structure of status, relationship, and recognition. . . .
>
> Proposition 29: Change agents will be more effective when the change agent, as perceived by other group members, has prestige and acceptance within the group.[23]

The supervisor is a key change agent. Effecting change is what the supervisor's job is all about. Whether as group leader or as individual counselor, the supervisor helps the people in the system and the system itself be better than they would have been without his or her intervention.

Although modern theories of administration and supervision advocate participation of subordinates in the management of institutions, we would err if we implied that change always occurs through the extensive involvement of the persons affected by it. State mandates, for example, have produced significant changes in curriculum and management of school systems, with varying degrees of involvement of school persons at the local level and varying degrees of commitment to the changes. Even states, however, ordinarily involve representatives of school systems when planning for change. Legislators, state board of education members, and employees of the state department of education can often be influenced before putting a change into place.

On the local level, where all school persons are readily accessible and under supervision of a central administrator, we see little need for locally mandated innovations without meaningful involvement of teachers and others from the time the idea is suggested through planning, implementing, and evaluating the change.

Organizational Development

Leaders help not only people but also their organizations to grow and develop. In one sense, organizational development is a type of change process. Key terms in organizational development are

- Interaction of groups
- Team building
- Conflict resolution
- In-service education
- Systems planning
- Communication
- Collaboration
- Change agents

- Role clarification
- Leadership behavior

Wendell L. French and Cecil H. Bell Jr. wove together some of the basic concepts of organizational development in the following definition:

> A long-range effort to improve an organization's problem-solving and renewal processes, particularly through a more effective and collaborative management of organization culture—with special emphasis on the culture of formal work teams— with the assistance of a change agent, or catalyst, and the use of the theory and technology of applied behavioral science, including action research.[24]

The administrator or supervisor who seeks to develop the organization would help a group gather data about its current situation, analyze the data, detect places where improvements in its functioning could be made, and recommend ways to improve. Central to the process are the group's endeavors to understand itself, become more cohesive, and cooperatively find solutions to its problems.

Group difficulties may stem from (1) poor interpersonal relationships among groups and individuals and (2) poor management (leadership). Interpersonal relationships may be improved through group deliberation/group process and through group encounter techniques like sensitivity training (T-groups). Particularly important in the development of healthy interpersonal relationships is the reduction or elimination of conflict.

Fred Luthans identified four types of conflict that develop in organizations:

> (1) hierarchical conflict (between the various levels of the organization. . .); (2) functional conflict (between the various functional departments of the organization. . .); (3) line-staff conflict (between line personnel and staff personnel. . .); and (4) formal-informal conflict (between the formal and informal organizations. . .).[25]

A widely cited model of educational administration developed by Jacob W. Getzels and Egon Guba depicted the interrelationships of institutional roles and individual needs in creating the particular behavior of the social institution. Their model, which appears in Figure 11.1, posited a nomothetic (institutional, sociological) dimension and an idiographic (personal, psychological) dimension.

Nomothetic Dimension

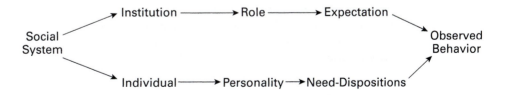

Idiographic Dimension

FIGURE 11.1 Getzels-Guba model of Educational Administration as a Social Process. *Source*: Jacob W. Getzels, "Administration as a Social Process," in *Administration Theory in Education*, ed. Andrew W. Halpin (New York: Macmillan, 1958), pp. 152–53. Reprinted with permission of Jacob W. Getzels.

Getzels and Herbert A. Thelen developed an even more complex model by adding anthropological (cultural), group, and biological dimensions, which further affect the observed behavior of the institution.[26]

From the Getzels-Guba model, we can deduce that

1. The school is a social system.

2. Social systems evidence two classes of phenomena (dimensions): the nomothetic, by which an institution prescribes certain roles for its employees with certain expectations for each role, and the idiographic, by which individuals with their own peculiar personalities try to satisfy their own needs-dispositions.

3. The behavior of people within the system and the particular characteristics of the system are functions of the interaction of both dimensions.

4. Leaders of a social system may be any one of three types: they may lean to the nomothetic or normative dimension, emphasizing the goals of the institution; they may lean to the idiographic or human dimension, emphasizing the goals of the individuals who make up the system; or they may shift from one dimension to the other as required by the needs of the institution and the persons employed by the institution. (In the last case such leadership has been referred to as transactional.)

5. Three types of conflicts may arise in a social system: intrarole, intrapersonality, and role personality. Intrarole conflicts occur under three different circumstances: (1) The person who holds a particular role is subjected to disagreement among groups about the expectations of the role. Teachers, for example, may view the principal's role somewhat differently from the way students or parents view the role. (2) The person who holds the role is subjected to disagreement from within a given group about the expectations of the role. Different teachers, for example, may view the principal's role differently. (3) The person who holds a role is called on to fill more than one role at the same time. Administrators, for example, may have to perform at the same time as instructional supervisors.

Intrapersonality conflicts come about when the holder of a role has conflicting personality needs. A principal, for example, may be torn between a desire to please teachers and a desire to please the superintendent. Because the superintendent is "the boss," the decision is often easy to make.

Role-personality conflicts result when the expectations assigned to a role differ from the needs-dispositions of the holder of the role. For example, the job description for a principal might specify that he or she has to be a strong disciplinarian, but at the same time the principal may not believe in corporal punishment.

Conflicts are resolved and managed in a variety of ways, some of which are more effective and longer lasting than others. For example:

- *Administrative order.* This solution is far from satisfactory. It may result in temporary conformity, but it leaves the conflict to fester and erupt again.

- *Consensus.* Achieving agreement from most or, if possible, all participants in a conflict is the ideal way to resolve conflicts.

- *Compromise.* Some people feel that compromise is unsatisfactory as each side has to give up something. On the other hand, compromise takes place every day in our society and is especially apparent in the governmental structures of our republic.

- *Changing the structure of the organization to eliminate sources of conflict.* Persons can be moved around, down, up, or even out. Procedures can be changed so that the organization may function more smoothly.

- *Policy formulation.* Conflicts arise in the absence of policies to guide action. They can be reduced by the group's creation of policies to which all can subscribe.

- *New solutions.* Creative solutions may be found; these may be a departure from the existing practices that provoked conflict.

A fruitful activity early in the role of the supervisor as group leader is the engagement of teachers in clarifying their views on education, schooling, learners, and teaching, which some writers refer to as "platform."[27] Such an activity enables teachers not only to clarify their views for themselves but also to share those views with others.

Mutual understanding, harmony, and team spirit are paramount goals in organizational development.

The organization may be developed through improved management techniques. Management training, therefore, is an important feature of organizational development. Key concerns of managers interested in developing the organization are (1) involvement of personnel, (2) planning, (3) time, and (4) stress.

Involvement of Personnel   The best way to ensure positive change in an organization is to involve the personnel of the organization in its operation. Subordinates need to feel that they have some stake in the organization. They want a chance to express their ideas. Japanese industry provides such channels through their *quality-control circles*, often called simply *quality circles*. In this approach, which William G. Ouchi has labeled *Theory Z*,[28] Japanese employees meet regularly with their supervisors in groups whose mission is to identify problems of the organization and recommend solutions. Through involvement in running the organization, workers develop loyalty and commitment to its goals.

Observers of the industrial scene credit organizational principles referred to as *total quality management* (TQM), advocated by W. Edwards Deming, an American, with helping the Japanese revitalize their economy after World War II. Deming proposed that workers and managers share responsibilities for managing the enterprise and jointly seek solutions to their organization's problems.[29] It is interesting that principles of shared management originated in the United States, migrated to Japan where they were adopted, and only relatively recently have been put into practice in some American corporations. Although the Japanese economy, for a variety of reasons, has experienced some faltering in recent years, the principle of workers sharing in management remains solid. Teacher empowerment, quality circles, and site-based management are successfully practiced in many American schools.

Planning A planning technique that has grown in popularity is known as MBO or MBO/R, management by objectives/results. Those who manage or supervise by objectives follow an orderly process, which includes the following steps:

1. Specify the goals of the institution.
2. Specify the objectives of the institution and standards of performance of the target group(s).
3. Select strategies to accomplish the objectives.
4. Identify resources needed: human and material.
5. Establish timelines for achieving objectives.
6. Implement the strategies.
7. Evaluate success in accomplishing objectives.
8. Recycle.

Some supervisors project objectives and timelines over a five-year period, for example, and then prepare full and detailed plans annually. Management or supervision by objectives for results is a logical and systematic way of planning, implementing, and evaluating the work of the organization.

Time and Stress If organizations are to thrive, the human beings who make the systems go must remain physically and emotionally healthy. For the human beings to maintain vitality, they must learn to manage the bothersome companion elements of time and stress.

For many administrators and supervisors, there is never enough time to get it all done. Work, as we know, is infinitely expandable. Compulsive, perfectionist individuals find themselves running hard just to keep up. The relentless computers and other forms of technology and their human programmers keep adding to the workload, so that sometimes the harder we run, the farther behind we seem to get. At some point, someone—a thoughtful administrator, a perceptive supervisor, or a facilitator from the outside—needs to blow the whistle and ask individuals to analyze what they are doing, how they are doing it, what is really necessary, how time is being utilized, and what factors are provoking stress.

Time can be managed from two perspectives. First, we can all examine whether the organizational tasks that we now feel to be necessary are really essential. Do we need all the committee meetings, for example? Are we, perhaps, closet meeting-lovers (which is almost as bad as being overt meeting-haters)? Does every administrator have to grind out requests for reports from subordinates to satisfy his or her own administrative needs and justify his or her own position? Why, for example, must different "shops" within the same system demand the same factual data from subordinates, each in a slightly different format?

We need "human engineers" in our social systems who are empowered to confront each generator of paperwork and require that person to justify the existence of each item. Why must the standard response to even the simplest requests for action be "write me a memo" when a phone call or face-to-face dialogue or e-mail would be sufficient? In most cases, without a doubt, in spite of the increasing use of e-mail, much of an organization's paperwork could still be eliminated without causing the organization any harm. Imagine the savings in time and money from such a reduction!

Second, employees must make decisions on how to set priorities for demands on their time. All of us are prone sometimes to spend time on trivial matters and to neglect the significant ones. All of us sometimes let others control our time instead of seizing the moment ourselves. Many years ago, Gilbert R. Weldy suggested sixteen guidelines for managing time wisely:

1. Analyze how time is used and misused.
2. Establish priorities.
3. Budget time by appointing a time.
4. Delegate with discretion.
5. Set a deadline.
6. Develop enthusiasm.
7. Concentrate totally.
8. Be courteous.
9. Control "other imposed" time.
10. Recognize and respond to fatigue.
11. Save time in meetings.
12. Read with discrimination.
13. Help your memory.
14. Use clerical services judiciously.
15. Plan work to save time.
16. Use time to improve skills.[30]

Stress arises from a number of pressures, some of which are self-imposed and some of which come from the outside. We may not be able to prevent pressures from without, but we can learn to respond to them. We can certainly (at least to some degree) control self-imposed stress. If we manage our time wisely, for example, we can cut down on occasions for stress. If we take ourselves a bit less seriously, we can reduce stress. If we try to get our priorities straight, we can decrease stress. If we learn to say no on occasion, we can both reduce stress and save time. If we are a highly stressed type to begin with, we should not gravitate to stressful positions. It is amazing to see how many teachers who have difficulty managing stress in the classroom aspire to positions as administrators and supervisors! Each prospective administrator and supervisor must ask him- or herself these questions: Do I have the personality to assume a leadership position? Do I work well under pressure? Do I have a tolerance for ambiguity?

Michael C. Giammatteo and Dolores M. Giammatteo offered several suggestions for managing stress.[31] They proposed that executives develop an awareness of their own reaction to stressful conditions, a tolerance level, and techniques for reducing stress. Executives should determine whether they are Type A individuals, who are prone to stress

TABLE 11.2 Type A Behavior: Awareness Exercise

Are you a Type A? Do you characteristically exhibit Type A behavior? Quickly fill out the following questionnaire to see.

Yes	No	Don't Know	
—	—	—	1. I'm frequently in a hurry.
—	—	—	2. I'm typically doing several projects at the same time.
—	—	—	3. I'm always pushed by deadlines.
—	—	—	4. I usually take on as many (or a few more) projects as I can handle.
—	—	—	5. I really seek recognition from my boss and/or peers.
—	—	—	6. I believe it's important for a person to push herself or himself for success, and I seek out opportunities for promotions and advancements.
—	—	—	7. I enjoy competition in all areas.
—	—	—	8. I really enjoy winning, and hate to lose.
—	—	—	9. My job is the most important thing in my life.
—	—	—	10. I sometimes feel I neglect my family by putting my job first.
—	—	—	11. I'm usually too busy with my job to have time for many hobbies or outside activities.
—	—	—	12. When I'm given a job I really feel personally responsible for its success—i.e., even though others may be involved, I feel that it just won't come out as well unless I'm personally involved from start to finish.
—	—	—	13. I have trouble trusting people easily.
—	—	—	14. I tend to talk fast.
—	—	—	15. When speaking I believe in giving special emphasis to my meaning with strong vocal inflection and gestures.
—	—	—	16. I feel some impatience in most meetings and conversations—I just wish they would speed up and get on with it.
—	—	—	17. I tend to get irritable and lose my cool easily when obviously simple things don't go right.
—	—	—	18. I make a list of things I must get done each day.
—	—	—	19. I generally have strong opinions on most things.
—	—	—	20. I don't seem to get much time to keep up with my reading.

If you answered yes to 15 of these questions, you may be falling into the "Type A" behavior pattern.

Source: Michael C. Giammatteo and Dolores M. Giammatteo, *Executive Well Being: Stress and Administrators* (Reston, Va.: National Association of Secondary School Principals, 1980), pp. 20–21. Reprinted with permission of the National Association of Secondary School Principals.

and even heart attack. Giammatteo and Giammatteo provided a checklist (see Table 11.2) for executives (equally applicable, in our opinion, to leaders of all types, including instructional supervisors) to determine whether they are Type A personalities.

Those whose answers are predominantly yes (15 or more "yes" answers) are Type A personalities: hard-driving movers and shakers; those whose answers are predominantly no are Type B personalities: relaxed, easygoing, laid back, and less subject to stress. Obviously, what is needed is an administrator or a supervisor who is a combination of the two types, an A/B type, who knows when to work hard and when to relax.

Executives should develop an ability to anticipate and avoid stressful conditions. They need to ignore minor stressful events, and they need to be more trusting that their subordinates will perform as they should. Executives should learn to allocate time for personal and family interests, delegate responsibilities, and even on occasion reduce standards or expectations. We all need to remind ourselves now and then that the world can run very well without us.

Stress is a major, perhaps the major factor in teacher, administrator, and supervisor burnout. Countless studies reveal the damaging effects of stress on individual health. Not only must supervisors recognize and manage their own stress, they must also be aware of teachers' stress and help them handle their jobs, which in recent years have become much more stressful than in days past. Supervisors as change agents need to help both teachers and themselves to use time wisely and to reduce stress.

Communication

Supervisors must be able to communicate effectively with both groups and individuals. The ability to project and understand messages is a fundamental skill of administrators and supervisors. Supervisors must give attention to (1) oral language, (2) written language, (3) nonverbal language, and (4) silent language.

Oral Language To some people, professionals and laypersons alike, effectiveness in communication is equated with the ability to be articulate, to express oneself orally, to deliver ripostes on the spot, and to answer questions lucidly or at least with verbal dexterity. Articulateness is a skill much prized by the public, who often settle for glibness over substance, for style over content.

Former U.S. president Jimmy Carter put his finger on this problem when he commented on his own difficulty in communicating:

> I am not a great speaker and am sometimes not at ease with large groups. I acknowledge those characteristics freely. They have been pointed out to me often enough to convince me. I can think on my feet. A poll of oldtime White House correspondents ranked me first in handling press conferences. It is hard to express effectively all sides of a complicated issue, and I tend to do that. It is much easier to take one simplistic side of an issue and express it clearly.[32]

Whether or not a politician says anything of substance, the public is impressed by the William Jennings Bryan types who bestir them not to "crucify mankind on a cross of gold." Like charisma, articulateness is a trait much to be desired. It puts its possessor one rung up on the status ladder. The ability to speak and respond clearly is essential. That ability, however, should be accompanied by forthrightness, candor, and substance.

Supervisors must know how to communicate with people at various levels. They do not address adults as they do children. They do not fire a rapid barrage of idiomatic English at members of minority groups who barely speak the language. They do not use the "refined" language of "high society" with the less educated. They do not use "ten-dollar" words where "half-dollar" words are needed to cement communication. They don't use football language in addressing the ladies' sewing circle. They do not use barroom language at a church wedding. They do not use education jargon in talking to the parents' advisory committee. They do not talk to teachers as if they were untrustworthy, lazy, disloyal, or uncooperative. They do not name-drop, throw in obscure or incomplete references, or relate in-house jokes—not if they hope to communicate.

Supervisors who are aware of the power of language not only choose their words carefully but also watch their tone. Tone often speaks louder than the words and sometimes reveals meaning that is just the opposite of the words. Although the lyrics may say one thing, the melody may put forth a different motif.

In our society, quite contrary to some societies, speakers are expected to be animated and cheerful. They are expected to maintain eye contact with the recipient of their messages. Americans tend to go to the heart of the problem, whereas some other cultures are less direct, indulging in small talk and social pleasantries like having tea or coffee before getting down to serious communication. It must have been an American who invented the business lunch, a custom designed to use every working moment and relegate the joys of eating to a secondary role.

Sometime in their preparation, supervisors should take linguistics and speech courses and, if necessary, speech therapy. They should also study basic principles of communication. Alfonso, Firth, and Neville listed twenty-eight propositions pertaining to *communication skills.*[33] Among these are the following:

> Proposition 10: Communication will be more effective when the views of the sender and the receiver(s) are in harmony. . . .
>
> Proposition 14: Communication will be more effective in influencing group behavior and attitudes when it utilizes discussion and decision making.
>
> Proposition 15: Communication will be more effective when the sender and receiver are dealing with situations in which both have obtained previous experience. . . .
>
> Proposition 18: Communication will be more effective if the style and techniques selected by the sender are consistent with the expectations of the receivers.
>
> Proposition 19: Communication will be more effective if senders take into account social and educational similarities and differences between themselves and receivers, as well as those among receivers.
>
> Proposition 20: Communication will be more effective if senders take into account their own personality characteristics and those of receivers.[34]

The ability to communicate orally with one's clientele is not only the stock of the salesperson but also the primary tool of the supervisor.

Written Language Only slightly behind oral communication in importance is the ability of supervisors to express themselves in written form. In their daily work they write letters, memos, curriculum guides, evaluations of materials and teachers, newsletters, research reports, and other documents. Recipients of written materials make judgments about the source and the materials on the basis of their style, accuracy, clarity, necessity, and proper use of English. As with oral communication, tone is also important. We have all been recipients of imperious memoranda, and you know how we reacted.

Administrators and supervisors get themselves in trouble with correspondence in which a careless phrase or word creates animosity on the part of the receiver. Senders should not write messages when they are angry or at a low ebb. Messages should always be reread for accuracy, tone, and language usage before they are sent to others.

The sender should consider the purpose of each message. If the sender must write a negative communication, it is wise to hold the message for a day or two while he or she reconsiders the problem. Writing may well be the wrong way to deliver negative messages, especially if we are talking about messages destined for people in the system; oral communication may be much fairer, more effective, and even courageous. Too many people in status positions hide behind memos, fearing to confront a person in a face-to-face situation in which the recipient can respond.

Many times it is effective practice to accompany oral communication with written; the two reinforce each other. They attend to the difference in people's learning styles. Some people learn more effectively through their ears; others through their eyes. As Alfonso, Firth, and Neville posited, "Proposition 5: Communication will be more effective in promoting change if the sender utilizes many communication channels rather than a few."[35]

One final caution is in order: The supervisor should decide whether a written message, be it paper or e-mail, is absolutely necessary. Time is required to write it, and the receiver has to take time to read it and may be required or desire to respond, which can make the cycle start all over. If the message is on paper, office supplies are consumed and someone has to deliver it. Supervisors who often complain about being swamped with memos must ask themselves whether they are contributors to the paper or e-mail trail.

Nonverbal Language More attention should be given to the study of nonverbal language. Teachers are expected to be animated and to convey enthusiasm. They do so as much through gestures, eye movements, interjections, smiles, frowns, posture, meaningful sounds, and laughter as through words. In fact, nonverbal language can say more than words. A guilty look on a person's face can shout that he or she is lying. We recognize the look and are convinced that the person is lying despite any verbal protestations to the contrary.

C. A. Bowers and David J. Flinders identified three channels of nonverbal communication and pointed out that these channels may have cultural implications: proxemics, or the way the teacher uses classroom space; kinesics, or body language; and prosody, or patterns of the teacher's voice.[36] Charles Galloway observed that nonverbal behaviors are better than words for expressing emotion.[37]

Human beings send messages through body movements and gestures. Describing body language, Julius Fast said:

> We all, in one way or another, send our little messages out to the world. We say, "Help me, I'm lonely. Take me, I'm available. Leave me alone, I'm depressed." And rarely do we send our messages consciously. We act out our state of being with nonverbal body language. We lift one eyebrow for disbelief. We rub our noses for puzzlement. We clasp our arms to isolate ourselves or to protect ourselves. We shrug our shoulders for indifference, wink one eye for intimacy, tap our fingers for impatience, slap our forehead for forgetfulness.[38]

Fast reinforced the theme of his book on body language with a delightful dedication: "This book is gratefully dedicated to all the passengers of the second car in the Independent Subway's F train, eastbound from Fifth Avenue at 5:22 P.M."[39]

Desmond Morris and his colleagues traced the origins and distribution of common gestures used in many parts of the world. Complete with illustrations, their book interprets the meaning of numerous gestures, including some of the most insulting, used by a sizable portion of the human race.[40]

The supervisor needs to study the meaning of gestures in our society and in other cultures. The United States is, after all, a multicultural nation. Our schools today reflect this diversity, creating the need for multicultural awareness and education. We have only to walk down the streets of San Francisco's Chinatown, New York's Little Italy, Miami's Little Havana, or Seattle's Little Saigon to become aware of subcultures on the American scene. The adults of the subculture (and the children to a lesser extent) perpetuate the spoken and written languages, traditions, rituals, and customs of the old country.

Different cultures communicate by using different gestures. In some cultures, it is not insulting to point a finger at a person; in others, it is. In some cultures, you can touch a person when you speak; in others, you must not. Some cultures believe in eye contact; others believe eye contact is rude. Some say no by raising their chins and giving a little click of the tongue; others shake the head from side to side. An acceptable gesture in one culture can even be an obscenity in another.

Supervisors need to develop a sensitivity to the nonverbal language of the persons with whom they work. They should help teachers read the nonverbal language of pupils. Regarding nonverbal communication, Alfonso, Firth, and Neville advised: "Proposition 21: Communication will be more effective if verbal messages and nonverbal cues from the sender reinforce each other."[41] Supervisors should be skillful in using and reading nonverbal language and must help teachers use and understand it as well.

Silent Language   Edward T. Hall wrote a well-known little book called *The Silent Language*, in which he explained the pitfalls people of one culture stumble into when they find themselves in another culture without an understanding of existing but silent cultural characteristics.[42] Although Hall included elements of nonverbal language, his concept of the silent language goes beyond nonverbal language. He listed ten kinds of human activities that vary from culture to culture and that he called the Primary Message Systems:

1. *Interaction*: ways we interact with our environment, as through speech and writing. This is the only Primary Message System that involves language.

2. *Association*: ways in which human beings associate with each other, including rank and status.

3. *Subsistence*: ways in which cultures feed themselves and go about earning subsistence; attitudes toward manual labor; characteristic economy.

4. *Bisexuality*: behavior of the sexes toward each other and toward the opposite sex; behavior expected or permitted of each sex by the culture.

5. *Territoriality*: ways human beings defend their turf.

6. *Temporality*: differing conceptions of time, including punctuality or the lack of it.

7. *Learning*: differences in ways of learning to learn.

8. *Play*: recreation and leisure.

9. *Defense*: ways in which cultures protect themselves from enemies, potential and real, and from adversities of nature.

10. *Exploitation* (use of materials): ways of exploiting the environment, as through technology, for example.[43]

Hall's target audience was Americans going abroad. He believed that by understanding the Primary Message Systems of other cultures, travelers could avoid cultural dissonance and conflict. His concept of a silent language, however, is useful to supervisors who are in school systems with an ever-increasing multicultural population. The Primary Message Systems, though perhaps muted by the North American culture, can still be operant and may be more pronounced in some school personnel and students than in others. We would single out attitudes about feminine and masculine behavior, protectiveness of one's vested interests and space, attitudes toward time and its use, and attitudes toward curricula and methods as having special significance to the supervisor in our pluralistic society.

If a supervisor is to be an effective group leader, he or she must demonstrate skills in communication. The supervisor must be both a practitioner and a student of language. The supervisor needs to be able to help teachers understand and cope with cultural diversity.

Group Process

For our analysis, let's discuss the process supervisors follow when they accept the role of group leader. Of course, the supervisor will not always serve as leader of a group; teachers may and should fill leadership positions as the situations demand. In fact, leadership from the group should be encouraged by the supervisor, and he or she should continuously provide opportunities for developing leadership. It is unfortunate, perhaps, that discussing group process involves the terms *leaders* and *followers*, for the term *follower* implies an unthinking docility that is undesirable here. The leader-follower terminology also plants the idea that the leader is never a follower and that followers are never leaders. In professional groups, such as teacher committees, teams, and faculties, that is not the case at all, for leadership and followership are roles that are constantly rotated as the occasion demands and as certain kinds of expertise are called for. Some teachers who consistently play the role of follower and never seek to exert leadership may do so because status leaders may have conditioned them to believe that followership is their only role, and therefore, they have never tested their own leadership skills.

The development of leadership skills from within the group should be a goal the supervisor places high on the agenda, making the supervisor, in effect, the leader of leaders. The term *follower* as used here connotes no demeaning status but simply means a person who is not serving as a leader at that time. Let's look at how the supervisor's skills in group process can help teachers work together. The following guidelines are applicable to the deliberations of a task-oriented work group:

1. A good deal of what is called processing can take place at the initial meeting of a faculty group. It is then that members of the group are introduced to one another and housekeeping chores are dispensed with. Coffee and donuts—or, in this health-conscious age, fruit and other nonfattening foods—are served at this time, a commendable way to loosen up a group and establish a pleasant working atmosphere. In the introductory remarks, the supervisor will help the group feel that their task is important and that they are the ideal ones to carry it out. Relevance of their task is just as important to a group as relevance of content is to a learner. If the task is trivial and unimportant, professional people should not be asked to waste their time on it.

2. The goals and objectives of the group's work should be set at the initial or next meeting. Commonly, the goal has already been determined prior to the group's formation.

Indeed, it is the reason the group was established. The goal may come in the form of a charge from the administrator or from the faculty. The group's task is to refine the goal and from it derive the specific objectives of its work. It must decide not only on its objectives but also on how to pursue them—who will do what, on what kind of time schedule it will operate, and how it will evaluate its work. The time schedule is an important feature some groups overlook; consequently, they put off a significant portion of their work until the last minute. A task force would do well to specify completion dates for segments of its work. This procedure not only helps keep the work on schedule but also reassures the group periodically that it is making progress. Feedback showing continuous progress is a strong motivator to keep a group working on a task.

3. The supervisor has the responsibility for keeping the group on task, which is often no easy job. The word *taskmaster* is too strong as it implies a despotism that is not advocated; but it is the supervisor's duty to try to prevent groups from digressing and to remind them of the topic at hand when they do go off on tangents.

Some supervisors make the mistake of interpreting their leadership role as one that is nondirective or laissez-faire. With such an approach, however, groups can flounder, procrastinate, and fail to achieve their objectives. Someone must serve as the "gatekeeper," the work conscience of the group, and the supervisor is in a strategic position to fulfill that role.

The role of group leader requires more than merely presiding at group meetings; it necessitates planning and continuous facilitation. The leader must make sure ahead of time that those who are scheduled to present data for the group's deliberation will be ready and present. He or she must be certain that all resources will be available to the group at the time the group needs access to them. Equipment, materials, and resource people must be arranged for well in advance of a meeting and be ready for use if the group is to be kept on task. Once the group is in session, the leader continues to serve as a facilitator who attempts to secure the maximum participation of all members of the group.

4. The supervisor must demonstrate skill in the group process. It is up to the supervisor to recognize what types of group member behaviors impede the group's progress and to know when individuals are performing what some call self-serving functions. For example, he or she should be able to detect individuals who exhibit aggressive behavior, dominate the discussion and cut off their colleagues, make a play for attention, thwart the group's efforts, and have their own special axes to grind. At the same time, the supervisor should be perceptive enough to realize that some members have withdrawn from participation, some appear uninterested, and some are fearful of expressing themselves.

As a responsible chairperson, a supervisor can reduce some of the problems that may occur because the members are not themselves skilled in the group process. Although parliamentary procedure with all its refinements is neither necessary nor desirable in most work groups, reliance on some of its basics may prove helpful to the group leader. As a parliamentary leader, the supervisor can insist that people speak one at a time. He or she can fail to recognize the attention getter and the individual who wishes to monopolize the discussion.

Ideally, the supervisor should try to obtain the participation of every member of the group. Every member should be made to feel that his or her contributions are significant enough to be considered and discussed. In almost every group, however, we find people who are quick starters, those who are more verbal and more vocal than others and are always ready to voice their opinions. The quick starter can be a boon to the group leader by helping get discussion under way with minimal prodding. At the same time, the quick starters should not be permitted to run away with the discussion. Frequently, a few vocal participants in a group carry on a discussion as if they were the only ones present. The group leader can neither permit nor afford to permit a few verbal individuals to usurp the discussion. The leader must seek input from the slow starters, ask for their opinions, turn to them for reactions, and pose questions to them. For both the quick starters and slow starters, the development of discussion skills may be a by-product of a task-oriented group process.

The supervisor involves group members not only in the discussion phases of the group's work but also in carrying out specific responsibilities designed to accomplish their mission. When the task is complex, subtasks must be assigned and distributed among the entire group so that as many members as possible will feel a close identity with the group's work. The easiest solution to the division of labor is to leave it to volunteers, but that is not always best for the growth of both the individuals and the group. A volunteer may not be the most qualified person in the group to perform a particular task. Besides, others who participate not vocally but silently should be drawn into the task. The supervisor resolves this problem by requesting those who are most qualified to accept specific subtasks regardless of their verbal skills and by encouraging distribution of assignments as broadly as possible among the members.

5. At the end of each session, the supervisor should summarize what the group has agreed on, and decisions should be made about what steps will be taken next. Each person's assignments and responsibilities should be clearly understood before the group adjourns. Whenever possible, the group should reach closure on issues under discussion and not leave them hanging. The supervisor has to take care not to force closure prematurely or to prevent closure by dragging out a discussion.

6. Periodically, the group should take stock of its progress, evaluate its accomplishments, and determine whether it is on schedule. Every member of the group should know exactly where the group is at any time. If there are subgroups working, they should keep the parent group continuously advised of their progress. The supervisor helps pace the group's progress by calling attention to when phases of the task have been completed, what remains to be done, and when the objectives have been realized.

7. The group must be made to feel that its efforts have been worthwhile. When a group is working on a particular problem for which it offers a solution, the ultimate hope is that the group's recommendations will be put into practice. Nothing is more motivating to a group than to see its recommendations carried out. Teachers know that not every recommendation of every group can be put into operation. Barring actual adoption of a group's recommendations, however, its proposals should be granted a full hearing, and if the recommendations cannot be accepted, the group should be told why. Far too many times service on a committee has left teachers with the hopeless feeling that nothing will come of all the time and effort they put into the committee's work. It is understandable that teachers are often reluctant to commit to some committee projects when their past experience tells them the effort will have no result.

The group leader is a key factor in a group's success or failure in achieving its purposes. The leader sets the stage for the group's deliberations and oversees the operation. But the success of a group does not depend on the leader's skills alone. Each member must possess sufficient skills in interaction to further the interests of all. When a group is involved in a task-oriented situation, it may learn interaction skills incidentally as by-products of its work. In an ongoing task-oriented situation, the supervisor should be aware that the members of the group are functioning at two levels. They are or should be working to accomplish the objectives of the group as well as to develop their own interaction skills. Although training in skills is tangential to the endeavor of a task-oriented group, special training in the functioning of groups and group interaction is a worthwhile in-service project.

Task versus Process   Groups are made up of two kinds of participants: those who are task-oriented and those who are process-oriented. Task-oriented people want to have the objectives clearly defined. They want to proceed with the job, get it done, and feel a sense of achievement. They are conscious of time pressure and impatient with digressions that prevent the group from realizing its goals.

Process-oriented individuals believe that the goals of the group are of secondary importance. In their minds, the interaction among people is what really counts. As a result of interaction, the goals themselves may change. The interaction is the true goal, not the task imposed by a superior or by the group itself. Process-oriented people believe that everyone should have the opportunity to express him- or herself to the fullest, not only about cognitive matters but also about how he or she feels toward the topic under discussion.

It is a rare faculty group that does not have members of both persuasions. Surely a task orientation without process can lead to sterile and perfunctory decisions, but process without task orientation can lead to group frustration and stagnation. As a group leader, the supervisor must achieve a healthy balance between the two orientations, enough that the task-oriented will feel the job is being accomplished and the process-oriented will feel they have had sufficient opportunity to express their views.

If you have attended group sessions, you probably have seen that when group deliberations fail, they do so more often because of a lack of task orientation than because of a lack of process orientation. An overemphasis on process has caused many groups to give up on their tasks. Given their workloads and the many demands on their time and energies, teachers simply cannot tolerate unlimited processing.

A certain amount of processing must occur before a group can get deeply into its task, but the leader must help the group complete its processing so it can move toward achievement of its goals. The Summer 2006 issue of *Leadership Compass* focused on "Creating High-Functioning Teacher Teams" and contained valuable suggestions for supervisors and educators with whom they are working.[44]

GROUP PROCESS VERSUS GROUP COUNSELING

There is a world of difference between the type of group processing—verbal interaction—that is related to a group's pursuit of a goal and the type of group processing that is a goal in itself. In the profession there is a saying that educational change results from a change in people. Although this position is praiseworthy, you can take issue with some of the efforts made to implement the saying. Some supervisors foster a type of group process that is designed not to accomplish a specific task but to help teachers solve their personal problems—in effect, group counseling. When helping teachers with personal problems is the focus of group activity, the group process is the task rather than the vehicle for accomplishing the task.

We do not discount the necessity for helping some teachers with personal problems, but we do not see this as a substitute for educational decision making. It should not be bootlegged in under the guise of decision making, presented as a compulsory or near-compulsory type of activity, or conducted by the typical supervisor. A therapy program should be attempted only by those who are fully qualified to provide that type of help. Far too many supervisors have dabbled in group counseling without sufficient training. Attendance as a participant or trainee at a group therapy institute or workshop does not qualify supervisors to engage in group counseling, which is an effort to help teachers solve their personal problems. Perhaps this is an example of the "physician heal thyself" syndrome, in which some supervisors attempt to solve their own personal problems by trying to help others solve theirs.

Group process as interaction among members of a group trying to accomplish a particular task should be distinguished from group process with the goal of solving the members' personal problems. Ideally, the supervisor, in the role of group leader, guides a group toward accomplishment of its task but also helps the group develop its interaction skills. In-service training concerning how groups operate, problems in group deliberation, and roles of leaders and followers is decidedly in order. As a matter of fact, personality modification—the goal of group counseling—may come about through training in group interaction skills. For example, those experienced with groups know that hostility in a member can impede the work of a group. For the group to advance, the hostility roadblock must be overcome. To begin, the group may first attempt to examine the process of group deliberation. By referring to some of the many studies of human groups, the members of the group learn about barriers to group endeavors, including the phenomenon of hostility. This is an intellectualized, conceptual approach. The aim is not to identify the hostility with a particular member of the group; the hope is that the person will recognize the problem and change his or her behavior. The supervisor as leader is not concerned with the roots of the member's hostility—whether the member hates his or her father or mother or this school, or whether he or she feels unfulfilled or is in the throes of a divorce or is short of money or any of the other countless sources of this type of behavior. The reasons for a person's hostility are external to the group's concerns.

Although a member's hostility is important to that individual, the endeavors of the group take precedence over his or her personal problems. If the supervisor is to retain the other members of the group, who are experiencing frustration as a result of interaction with the hostile member, the supervisor must, as leader, move the work of the group forward. In a group-counseling situation, members of the group would have every opportunity to release their aggressions, frustrations, and hostilities, but the typical faculty work group is not a counseling situation; it is a task-oriented workforce with limited time and energy. Because the supervisor works with faculty groups on problems of curriculum and instruction, their time and energy must be dedicated to the solution of those problems. If the supervisor attempts to keep the group on target, the hostile member may be able to intellectualize the problem to the point of being able to shelve his or her hostility and permit the group to achieve its mission. This does not mean that all hostility disappears, nor does it indicate that the member is even one step closer to solving a personal problem. It does mean that the individual has learned to subordinate a personal problem at least long enough for the group to complete its task.

Nothing in these comments should be interpreted as implying that counseling of whatever persuasion—individual or group—is not important. Indeed, it is. A teacher's personality has a tremendous impact on his or her students. An enlightened school system will provide opportunities for teachers to obtain individual or group counseling, led by persons trained in leading the activities, if they wish to do so. But group counseling led by persons trained in leading the activities in whatever form—T-groups, encounter groups, therapy groups, sensitivity groups—should not be mixed with a task-oriented group process, nor should it be a required part of an in-service training program, a point elaborated toward the end of this chapter.

In this light, the supervisor who is concerned about helping teachers work together should consider a three-part plan consisting of the following elements:

1. The supervisor's development of his or her own leadership skills in conducting task-oriented group sessions.

2. Provision of an in-service program on the development of group interaction, human relations, and communications skills—a voluntary, elective program, preferably with tangible incentives for participation.

3. Provision of group-therapy-type sessions on a completely voluntary basis and under the direction of trained counselors.

TRAINING IN GROUP INTERACTION

When the supervisor discovers that groups he or she is working with are experiencing difficulty and that members of the groups are unable to communicate with each other, it may be expeditious to set up a program designed to help teachers develop interaction skills. Training in interaction skills has application not only for teachers' relationships with each other but also for their relationships with students, other school personnel, and parents. Because training in interpersonal and human-relations skills skirts the fringes of awareness and sensitivity training, this type of training ought to be elective. In fact, participation in any type of training that is primarily for personal development should be voluntary. To make participation appealing to teachers, however, some sort of incentive system should be in operation, as noted in the preceding chapter.

Unless supervisors have had the necessary training—very commonly they have not—they will need to ask specialists in communication skills or human-relations skills to conduct the training. Consultant monies are often available for staff-development programs, and supervisors might well consider bringing in consultants for this purpose.

In-service education for the development of interaction skills may take a variety of forms. Two promising routes, which may be viewed as companion techniques rather than separate procedures, are (1) formal study and discussion of some of the literature on the sociology and social psychology of human groups and (2) practice in demonstrating interpersonal skills in a group setting. Although either of these techniques can be implemented without the other, the training program is much stronger if it includes both components. Consultants for the formal study may be found among university specialists in sociology, psychology, education, or management. Consultants for the practice or laboratory training may come from universities' and other agencies' specialists in human-relations skills, social psychology, and communications.

In the first phase of an in-service program on group interaction, the consultant may take the group through some of the classic literature on group formation and functioning. The participants might read and discuss, for example, George C. Homans's *The Human Group*, which provides an excellent introduction to this topic.[45] The consultant might have the participants read and discuss some of the literature on the famed Western Electric research, which provided evidence that when workers are involved in planning, research, and profit sharing their productivity rises.[46] These researchers speak also to the well-known Hawthorne Effect—a rise in productivity as a result of workers' feelings of involvement rather than from a change of technique. Teachers might be made familiar with material such as Stuart Chase's popular book, *Roads to Agreement*, which interprets the purpose and functioning of groups in lay language and suggests ways to resolve group conflicts.[47]

No study of group behavior can omit the research of Kurt Lewin, Ronald Lippitt, and Ralph K. White on experimentally created social climates.[48] In studying the effects of three types of adult leadership—authoritarian, democratic, and laissez-faire—on four groups of eleven-year-old children, Lewin, Lippitt, and White made these discoveries:

> Under the authoritarian leadership, the children were more dependent upon the leader, more discontent, made more demands for attention, were less friendly, produced less work-minded conversation than under the democratic leadership. There was no group initiative in the authoritarian group climate.
>
> The laissez-faire atmosphere produced more dependence on the leader, more discontent, less friendliness, fewer group-minded suggestions, less work-minded conversation than under the democratic climate. In the absence of the laissez-faire leader, work was unproductive. The laissez-faire group was extremely dependent upon the leader for information. Relationships among the individuals in the democratic leadership atmosphere were friendlier. Those under the democratic leadership sought more attention and approval from fellow club members. They depended upon each other for recognition as opposed to recognition by the leader under the authoritarian and laissez-faire systems . . . in the absence of the leader the democratic groups proceeded at their work in productive fashion.[49]

The Lewin, Lippitt, and White studies have implications for the types of group climate leaders foster, and they suggest that leaders should examine the social climate of the groups with which they work.

Consultants frequently engage trainees in a study of roles played by individuals in group settings, such as "information giver," "harmonizer," "gatekeeper," and "blocker," terms of great currency in studies of a group's inner workings. Kenneth D. Benne and Paul Sheats have used these terms and others for their classification of roles played by members of a group.[50] By studying a set of descriptive terms such as the well-known Benne-Sheats classification scheme, teachers who are investigating the functioning of groups may begin to become aware of some of the maintenance tasks required of groups and some of the positive and negative roles played by group members. In the case of negative roles, a teacher may begin to recognize some of the impediments to the group process, may attempt to learn whether any of the negative descriptors could apply to him or her, and may change behavior if it appears that a negative descriptor does indeed fit.

PRACTICE IN INTERACTION SKILLS

Following the more formal study of group behavior and the functioning of individuals in group settings, laboratory experiences can be created that provide participants with opportunities to demonstrate interaction skills. Training in interaction, communication, and human-relations skills can supplement training in generic instructional skills and study of subject matter. Because training in interaction or interpersonal skills runs the risk of some psychological discomfort for some participants, only those trained in the use of group interaction laboratory techniques should attempt to conduct this type of training.

Although training in group interaction comes close to group counseling and awareness training, it stops short of in-depth counseling on personal problems. Its aim is to improve the dynamics of the group, not to provide therapy for individuals' personal problems. Although leaders of training programs in interaction skills must possess special training, they need not necessarily be trained psychologists.

Record of Behavior of Individuals in Groups

A fruitful approach to training in interaction skills is an adaptation and application of the Benne-Sheats classification system just mentioned. The roles played by individuals in groups are shown in Table 11.3. An instrument can be created, such as the record of behavior of individuals in groups (Figure 11.2), which can be used to analyze the roles played by members of a group as they work together. The record of behavior converts the Benne-Sheats classification into an instrument by which an observer can record the number of times each individual plays a particular role.[51] The record of behavior lists at the left the task, maintenance, and individual roles played by members of a group. Spaces are provided so that an impartial observer can tally instances of specific role performances by individual members of the group. The purpose of such a procedure is to make members of a group more aware of the roles they play.

Using the record of how individuals behave in groups, faculties can devise procedures for studying their own behavior. By digesting the feedback that comes out of each study, they can improve their group's functioning.

PROVISION OF GROUP THERAPY-TYPE SESSIONS

An observer of the schools does not need much time to conclude that some teachers need help. The critics of education have pointed out enough horrifying examples to underscore the need of some teachers for help with their personal problems. However, because some teachers need help does not mean that all teachers do; those who do may not profit from the "help" that may be given them.

Undoubtedly, as a part of a school system's program for the personal and professional development of teachers, opportunities should be made available for therapy, awareness, or sensitivity training in one or more of its many varieties. Under no circumstances, however, should this type of training be required.

TABLE 11.3 Roles of Individuals in Groups

Group task roles

a. Initiator-contributor: Suggests ideas, ways of solving problems, or procedures.

b. Information seeker: Seeks facts.

c. Opinion seeker: Asks for opinions about the values of suggestions made by members of the group.

d. Information giver: Supplies facts or facts as he/she sees them.

e. Opinion giver: Presents his/her own opinions about the subject under discussion.

f. Elaborator: States implications of suggestions and describes how suggestions might work out if adopted.

g. Coordinator: Tries to synthesize suggestions.

h. Orienter: Lets group know when it is off task.

i. Evaluator-critic: Evaluates suggestions made by group members as to criteria which he/she feels important.

j. Energizer: Spurs the group to activity.

k. Procedural technician: Performs the routine tasks that have to be done such as distributing materials.

l. Recorder: Keeps the group's record.

Group building and maintenance roles

a. Encourager: Praises people for their suggestions.

b. Harmonizer: Settles disagreements among members.

c. Compromiser: Modifies his/her position in the interests of group progress.

d. Gatekeeper: Tries to assure that everybody has a chance to contribute to the discussion.

e. Standard setter or ego ideal: Urges the group to live up to high standards.

f. Group observer and commentator: Records and reports on the functioning of the group.

g. Follower: Accepts suggestions of others.

Individual roles

a. Aggressor: Attacks others or their ideas.

b. Blocker: Opposes suggestions and group decisions.

c. Recognition seeker: Seeks personal attention.

d. Self-confessor: Expresses personal feelings not applicable to the group's efforts.

e. Playboy: Refrains from getting involved in the group's work, with sometimes disturbing behavior.

f. Dominator: Interrupts others and tries to assert own superiority.

g. Help seeker: Tries to elicit sympathy for himself/herself.

h. Special interest pleader: Reinforces his/her position by claiming to speak for others not represented in the group.

Source: From Kenneth D. Benne and Paul Sheats, "Functional Roles of Group Members," *Journal of Social Issues* 4, no. 2 (Spring 1948): 43–46. Reprinted with permission of Blackwell Publishing.

Although school systems may provide incentives for participation in group-counseling sessions, teachers should clearly understand the nature of the training program they are getting into and should have the right to refuse to participate. Sometimes sensitivity training is brought surreptitiously into task-oriented groups without the advance knowledge and consent of the participants. Other unacceptable techniques

	Members								
	A	B	C	D	E	F	G	H	I
Task roles									
Initiator–contributor									
Information seeker									
Opinion seeker									
Information giver									
Opinion giver									
Elaborator									
Coordinator									
Orienter									
Evaluator–critic									
Energizer									
Procedural technician									
Recorder									
Building/maintenance roles									
Encourager									
Harmonizer									
Compromiser									
Gatekeeper									
Standard setter									
Group observer									
Follower									
Individual roles									
Aggressor									
Blocker									
Recognition seeker									
Self-confessor									
Playboy									
Dominator									
Help seeker									
Special interest pleader									

FIGURE 11.2   Record of Behavior of Individuals in Groups. *Source*: Kenneth D. Benne and Paul Sheats, "Functional Roles of Group Members," *Journal of Social Issues* 4, no. 2 (Spring 1948): 43–46. Reprinted with permission of Blackwell Publishing.

for garnering attendance at awareness sessions are the use of peer pressure and, worst of all, administrative fiat.

Sensitivity sessions can be recommended for those participants who volunteer for the program and who recognize a need for the training. Without the individual's willing participation, results will be minimal or even harmful. If teachers are coerced or pressured to participate in awareness sessions, they start the program with a level of hostility, can actively sabotage the sessions, or can shrewdly play games with the trainer and other members of the group.

The supervisor's role in sensitivity training is to help organize voluntary sessions, preferably systemwide (or on a broader scale yet) rather than limited to the faculty of one school who must face each other day in, day out. The supervisor should help make arrangements for the sessions, help secure thoroughly trained staff, notify faculty of the sessions, and then step out of the trainer's way. The supervisor should not serve either as a member of the trainer's staff or as a participant in the program. The presence of a person who in any way is viewed by the trainees as a superior and in a position to penalize them for "opening up" will only impede the group and may in fact destroy its effectiveness.

These recommendations on sensitivity training are meant to be a middle ground between extravagant claims by some advocates of sensitivity training and unreasonable objections of some opponents of all forms of awareness training. The extreme advocates see sensitivity training as the greatest tonic since cod liver oil and the extreme naysayers view awareness training as a witch's brew. Sensitivity training is one way some teachers can learn to work together.

National Staff Development Council

Supervisors will find the National Staff Development Council a valuable source of help and support. Founded in 1969, the council promotes staff-development practices and programs, sponsors workshops, and holds annual national conferences on staff development. The association disseminates information and shares ideas through its publications: *Results, Tools for Schools, The Learning Principal, The Learning System, Teachers Teaching Teachers*, and the *Journal of Staff Development*.[52] Unlike the much larger and much older Association for Supervision and Curriculum Development, whose interests encompass curriculum, instruction, and supervision at all levels of the educational ladder, the National Staff Development Council focuses on the needs of local school district supervisors in their roles as staff developers.

SUMMARY

Supervisors spend a considerable portion of their time with teachers in groups of varying size and composition. To accomplish much of the school's work, teachers must learn to function together in groups, and one of the goals of supervision is the enhancement of teachers' skills in working cooperatively. Groups are composed of both task-oriented and process-oriented people. The task-oriented seek to get the job done, and the process-oriented are concerned with individual expression and self-fulfillment. Although a certain amount of processing is necessary in any group endeavor, most faculty groups should be task-oriented.

Supervisors must possess leadership skills. They should generally follow a democratic, human-relations-oriented approach but must know when to use an authoritarian, task-oriented approach. To be effective leaders, supervisors must be skilled in decision making, effecting change, organizational development, communication, and group process.

Decision making is at the heart of administrative and supervisory behavior. The supervisor can expect to be called on to serve as a change agent, contributing to the development of both staff members and the organization.

Organizations possess both an institutional and a personal dimension. The behavior of the members of the institution and the uniqueness of the institution itself result from the interaction of the two dimensions.

Supervisors must be able to manage their own time, stress, and conflicts and simultaneously help staff members do likewise. Supervisors must be skillful in the use of oral, written, and nonverbal language. They should help staff members develop awareness of the importance of their own oral, written, and nonverbal communication skills. Supervisors must also help teachers understand the cultural phenomenon of silent language.

A supervisor should exert democratic group leadership and should help teachers develop skills in the group process. Goals and objectives should be established at the beginning of the group's work, and after the group has begun its work it should try to keep on task. Groups should evaluate their progress and should be assured that their efforts will be recognized. The most effective type of recognition is full consideration or adoption of group decisions.

The supervisor works to develop skills in group interaction in two ways: (1) by example and direction in the performance of a task and (2) by instituting special voluntary training in group interaction skills. Training in interaction skills should include study of group behavior and functioning and provision of opportunities for individuals to demonstrate interaction skills.

Sensitivity training should be made available to teachers on a voluntary basis and should be under the direction of specialists trained in group therapy.

QUESTIONS FOR DISCUSSION

1. How do qualifications needed by supervisors differ from those of administrators?
2. How can you handle teachers who disrupt the work of a task force of which they are members?
3. How can the school's internal politics be detrimental to the school's goals?
4. How would you go about building a team-focused school?
5. How would you nurture leadership among the faculty?

ACTIVITIES FOR FURTHER STUDY

REFLECTIVE

1. Distinguish among leader, administrator, and manager.
2. Describe the characteristics of Theory X and Theory Y leaders (see Douglas M. McGregor in chapter bibliography).
3. Identify three styles of leadership and tell which style you prefer and why.
4. Write a paper contrasting human-relations supervision and human-resources supervision.
5. Contrast value-added dimensions with value dimensions of leadership as perceived by Thomas J. Sergiovanni (see chapter bibliography).

6. Make a list of your own propositions regarding (a) decision making, (b) change theory, and (c) communication skills. Also, consult Robert J. Alfonso, Gerald R. Firth, and Richard F. Neville (see chapter bibliography) for additional propositions.

7. Tell how the supervisor works in the capacity of change agent.

8. Define the term *organizational development* and explain how this term differs from *staff development*.

9. List several sources of conflict in an organization and tell what the supervisor can do to reduce each.

10. Explain the terms *nomothetic* and *idiographic* and their significance.

11. Describe Theory Z and draw implications for school supervisors (see William G. Ouchi in chapter bibliography).

12. Prepare a report on American companies that use a quality-circles-style approach to group participation in management.

13. Suggest ways to improve the management of your time.

14. Identify several sources of stress and tell how you would manage these.

15. Study the literature on management by objectives/results and write a critique of the process.

16. Suggest several ways of improving communications between (a) supervisor and administrator, (b) supervisor and teachers, (c) among teachers.

17. Read and write a report on Charles Galloway's *Silent Language in the Classroom* (see chapter bibliography). Draw implications for the supervisor and teacher.

18. Read and write a report on Julius Fast's *Body Language* (see chapter bibliography). Draw implications for the supervisor and teacher.

19. Read and write a report on Desmond Morris et al., *Gestures: Their Origins and Distribution* (see chapter bibliography). Draw implications for the supervisor and teacher.

20. Read and write a report on Edward T. Hall's *The Silent Language* (see chapter bibliography). Draw implications for the supervisor and teacher.

21. Explain and give examples of (a) nonverbal language, (b) body language, and (c) silent language.

22. Describe the three channels of nonverbal communication—proxemics, kinesics, and prosody—as used by C. A. Bowers and David J. Flinders (see chapter bibliography) and draw implications for the supervisor and teacher.

23. Describe skills needed to lead (a) a faculty meeting, (b) a faculty study committee, and (c) an encounter group.

24. Distinguish between task-oriented and process-oriented groups. Draw implications for the instructional supervisor.

25. Explain the place of group therapy or sensitivity sessions in in-service education.

26. Describe the Getzels-Guba model of educational administration as a social process and draw implications for the supervisor (see chapter bibliography).

27. Describe the Getzels-Thelen model of the classroom group as a social system and draw implications for the supervisor (see chapter bibliography).

28. Write a position paper on one of these topics: (a) Supervision Must Be Primarily Task-Oriented, or (b) Supervision Must Be Primarily Process-Oriented. Support your position with quotations from at least two references not mentioned in this chapter.

29. Report the specified goals and objectives of any faculty work group of which you are now a member or of which you have recently been a member. Comment on the adequacy of the statement of goals and objectives of this group.

30. Compile a bibliography of at least six references you would recommend to teachers on group behavior. (Omit references cited in this chapter.)

31. List a set of interaction, human-relations, and communications skills that you believe are essential to the teacher as classroom group leader.

32. Write a paper using selected references on the topic Techniques for Developing Human-Relations Skills of Teachers.

33. Prepare a report on the contributions of W. Edwards Deming to the field of management.

34. Summarize, citing several text and/or periodical references, principles of Total Quality Management.

35. Search the literature and report on recommendations for making the school a learning community.

APPLICATION

1. Plan a series of study sessions on group behavior to include types of consultants needed, resources to be used, and media to be employed.

2. Plan an in-service program for training in interpersonal skills.

3. Serve as a member of a task-oriented faculty group and write a report diagnosing problems in the group process. (Individuals should not be named in the report.)

4. Serve as a leader of a task-oriented faculty group and write a self-evaluation of your performance as the group's leader.

5. Observe (with permission) a faculty group in action and apply an instrument such as one based on the Benne-Sheats classification of roles; provide the group with feedback from your observation.

6. Observe chairpersons of at least two faculty groups in action and, without identifying the chairpersons, classify their leadership as democratic, authoritarian, or laissez-faire.

7. Examine the curriculum development program of a school you know well and list opportunities teachers have had to work together on that program in the past five months. (Do not list routine administrative faculty meetings.)

8. Poll several teachers and ask the following questions: In your experience, are most faculty committees productive or not productive? If you believe they are productive, give evidence. If you believe they are not productive, what are the reasons for their lack of productivity? Summarize the teachers' comments in a short paper.

9. Discover and report to class what opportunities for group leadership have been made available to teachers in a school you know well in the past six months.

10. Determine and report to class the attitudes of at least two teachers toward a program of sensitivity training for teachers.

11. Ask at least two teachers to suggest ways in which a supervisor can help teachers work together. Summarize the teachers' suggestions and report them to your class.

NOTES

1. Alexis de Tocqueville, *Democracy in America, Part the Second: The Social Influence of Democracy*, trans. Henry Reeve (New York: J. and H. G. Langley, 1840), rev. Francis Bowen (New York: Knopf, 1945), p. 106.
2. Linda Lambert, Michelle Collay, Mary E. Dietz, Karen Kent, and Anna Ershler Richert, *Who Will Save Our Schools?: Teachers as Constructivist Leaders* (Thousand Oaks, Calif.: Corwin Press, 1997), p. 68.

3. Carl D. Glickman, Stephen P. Gordon, and Jovita M. Ross-Gordon, *SuperVision and Instructional Leadership: A Developmental Approach*, 7th ed. (Boston: Allyn and Bacon, 2007), p. 322.

4. See John K. Hemphill and Alvin E. Coons, *Leader Behavior Description* (Columbus: Personnel Research Board, Ohio State University, 1950). See also Ralph M. Stogdill, *Handbook of Leadership: A Survey of Theory and Research* (New York: Free Press, 1974); and Rensis Likert, *The Human Organization: Its Management and Value* (New York: McGraw-Hill, 1967).

5. Fred E. Fiedler, *A Theory of Leadership Effectiveness* (New York: McGraw-Hill, 1967), p. 8.

6. Ralph M. Stogdill, "Leadership, Membership, and Organization," *Psychological Bulletin* 47 (January 1950): 4. See also Stogdill, *Handbook of Leadership*, p. 10.

7. James M. Lipham and James A. Hoeh Jr., *The Principalship: Foundations and Functions* (New York: Harper and Row, 1974), p. 182.

8. James M. Lipham, "Leadership and Administration," *Behavioral Science and Educational Administration*, 63rd Yearbook, Part II, ed. Daniel E. Griffiths (Chicago: National Society for the Study of Education, 1964), p. 122.

9. W. H. Cowley, "Three Distinctions in the Study of Leaders," *Journal of Abnormal and Social Psychology* 23 (July–September 1928): 145.

10. Robert L. De Bruyn, *Causing Others to Want Your Leadership* (Manhattan, Kan.: R. L. De Bruyn & Associates, 1976), p. 14.

11. See Ralph M. Stogdill, "Personal Factors Associated with Leadership: A Study of the Literature," *Journal of Psychology* 25 (January 1948): 35–71. Reprinted in Stogdill, *Handbook of Leadership*, chap. 5. See also Ralph B. Kimbrough and Michael Y. Nunnery, *Educational Administration: An Introduction*, 3rd ed. (New York: Macmillan, 1988), pp. 346–48.

12. Stogdill, *Handbook of Leadership*, pp. 62–63.

13. Paul Hersey and Kenneth H. Blanchard, *Management of Organizational Behavior: Utilizing Human Resources*, 5th ed. (Englewood Cliffs, N.J.: Prentice Hall, 1988), pp. 169–201.

14. Kurt Lewin, Ronald Lippitt, and Ralph K. White, "Patterns of Aggressive Behavior in Experimentally Created 'Social Climates,'" *Journal of Social Psychology* 10 (May 1939): 271–99; Douglas M. McGregor, *The Human Side of Enterprise* (New York: McGraw-Hill, 1960); Fred E. Fiedler, *A Theory of Leadership Effectiveness*; Edgar L. Morphet, Roe L. Johns, and Theodore L. Reller, *Educational Organization and Administration: Concepts, Practices, and Issues*, 4th ed. (Englewood Cliffs, N.J.: Prentice Hall, 1982).

15. Thomas J. Sergiovanni and Robert J. Starratt, *Supervision: A Redefinition*, 8th ed. (Boston: McGraw-Hill, 2007), pp. 17–20. See also Raymond Miles, "Human Relations or Human Resources?" *Harvard Business Review* 43 (July–August 1965): 148–63; Mason Haire, Edwin Ghiselli, and Lyman Porter, *Management Thinking: An International Study* (New York: Wiley, 1966).

16. Thomas J. Sergiovanni, *Value-Added Leadership: How to Get Extraordinary Performance in Schools* (Orlando, Fla.: Harcourt Brace Jovanovich, 1990).

17. See Chester I. Barnard, *The Functions of the Executive* (Cambridge, Mass.: Harvard University Press, 1938); Daniel E. Griffiths, *Administrative Theory* (New York: Appleton-Century-Crofts, 1959); Herbert A. Simon, *The New Science of Management Decision* (New York: Harper and Row, 1960).

18. See Griffiths, *Administrative Theory*, pp. 92–113. See also Alvar Elbing, *Behavior Decisions in Organizations*, 2nd ed. (Glenview, Ill.: Scott, Foresman, 1978).

19. Robert J. Alfonso, Gerald R. Firth, and Richard F. Neville, *Instructional Supervision: A Behavior System*, 2nd ed. (Boston: Allyn and Bacon, 1981), chap. 7.

20. Ibid., pp. 228, 233, 234, 235.

21. Shirley M. Hord, William L. Rutherford, Leslie Huling-Austin, and Gene E. Hall, *Taking Charge of Change* (Alexandria, Va.: Association for Supervision and Curriculum Development, 1987), pp. 84–85.

22. Alfonso, Firth, and Neville, *Instructional Supervision*, chap. 8.

23. Ibid., pp. 273, 276, 278, 282.

24. Wendell L. French and Cecil H. Bell Jr., *Organization Development* (Englewood Cliffs, N.J.: Prentice Hall, 1973), p. 15.

25. Fred Luthans, *Organizational Behavior*, 6th ed. (New York: McGraw-Hill, 1992), p. 391.

26. See Jacob W. Getzels and Herbert A. Thelen, "The Classroom Group as a Unique Social System," in *The Dynamics of Instructional Groups: Sociological Aspects of Teaching and Learning*, 59th Yearbook, Part II, ed. Nelson B. Henry (Chicago: National Society for the Study of Education, 1960), p. 80.

27. See Sergiovanni and Starratt, *Supervision: A Redefinition*, pp. 70–84.

28. See William G. Ouchi, *Theory Z: How American Business Can Meet the Japanese Challenge* (Reading, Mass.: Addison-Wesley, 1981). See also Joel Kotkin and Yoriko Kishimoto, "Theory F," *Inc.* 8 (April 1986): 53–60. The F in Theory F stands for fear.

29. W. Edwards Deming, *Out of the Crisis: Productivity and Competitive Position* (Cambridge: Massachusetts Institute of Technology, 1986).

30. Gilbert R. Weldy, *Time: A Resource for the School Administrator* (Reston, Va.: National Association of Secondary School Principals, 1974).

31. Michael C. Giammatteo and Dolores M. Giammatteo, *Executive Well-Being: Stress and Administrators* (Reston, Va.: National Association of Secondary School Principals, 1980).

32. "The Man from Plains Sums It Up," *Time* (October 11, 1982): 63.

33. Alfonso, Firth, and Neville, *Instructional Supervision*, pp. 174–86.

34. Ibid., pp. 178–82.

35. Ibid., p. 176.

36. C. A. Bowers and David J. Flinders, *Culturally Responsive Teaching and Supervision: A Handbook for Staff Development* (New York: Teachers College Press, 1991), pp. 16–18, 44–48. See also David J. Flinders, "Supervision as Cultural Inquiry," *Journal of Curriculum and Supervision* 6 (Winter 1991): 87–106.

37. Charles Galloway, *Silent Language in the Classroom* (Bloomington, Ind.: Phi Delta Kappa Educational Foundation, 1976), p. 10.

38. Julius Fast, *Body Language* (New York: M. Evans, 1970), pp. 15–16.

39. Ibid., p. 4.

40. Desmond Morris et al., *Gestures: Their Origins and Distribution* (New York: Stein and Day, 1979).

41. Alfonso, Firth, and Neville, *Instructional Supervision*, p. 182.

42. Edward T. Hall, *The Silent Language* (New York: Doubleday, 1959).

43. Ibid., pp. 45–46.

44. National Association of Elementary School Principals (NAESP), "Creating High-Functioning Teacher Teams," *Leadership Compass* 3 (Summer 2006), pp. 1–8.

45. George C. Homans, *The Human Group* (New York: Harcourt Brace Jovanovich, 1950).

46. F. J. Roethlisberger and William J. Dickson, *Management and the Worker* (Cambridge, Mass.: Harvard University Press, 1939). For a critical view of the Western Electric researches see Berkeley Rice, "The Hawthorne Defect: Persistence of a Flawed Theory," *Psychology Today* 16 (February 1982): 70–74.

47. Stuart Chase, *Roads to Agreement* (New York: Harper and Row, 1951).

48. Lewin, Lippitt, and White, "Patterns of Aggressive Behavior."

49. Lewin, Lippitt, and White research as summarized by Peter F. Oliva, "High School Discipline in American Society," *National Association of Secondary School Principals Bulletin* 40 (January 1956): 7–8.

50. Kenneth D. Benne and Paul Sheats, "Functional Roles of Group Members," *Journal of Social Issues* 4 (Spring 1948): 43–46, a discussion of roles as developed by the First National Training Laboratory in Group Development, 1947.

51. See Thomas J. Sergiovanni and Robert J. Starratt, *Emerging Patterns of Supervision: Human Perspectives* (New York: McGraw-Hill, 1971), p. 199, for Sample Observation Sheet based on roles described by Benne and Sheats.

52. National Staff Development Council, P.O. Box 240, Oxford, Ohio 45056.

BIBLIOGRAPHY

Alfonso, Robert J., Gerald R. Firth, and Richard F. Neville. *Instructional Supervision: A Behavior System.* Boston: Allyn and Bacon, 1981.

Barnard, Chester I. *The Functions of the Executive*, 30th anniversary ed. Cambridge, Mass.: Harvard University Press, 1968.

Barth, Roland S. *Improving Schools from Within: Teachers, Parents, and Principals Can Make the Difference.* San Francisco: Jossey-Bass, 1990.

———. *Learning by Heart.* San Francisco:: Jossey-Bass, 2001.

———. *Lessons Learned: Shaping Relationships and the Culture of the Workplace.* Thousand Oaks, Calif.: Corwin Press, 2003.

Benne, Kenneth D., and Paul Sheats. "Functional Roles of Group Members." *Journal of Social Issues* 4 (Spring 1948): 41–49.

BENNIS, WARREN G., KENNETH D. BENNE, and ROBERT CHIN, eds. *The Planning of Change*, 4th ed. Orlando, Fla.: Holt, Rinehart, and Winston, 1985.

BOWERS, C. A., and DAVID J. FLINDERS. *Culturally Responsive Teaching and Supervision: A Handbook for Staff Development*. New York: Teachers College Press, 1991.

———. *Responsive Teaching: An Ecological Approach to Classroom Patterns of Language, Culture, and Thought*. New York: Teachers College Press, 1990.

CHASE, STUART. *Roads to Agreement: Successful Methods in the Science of Human Relations*. Westport, Conn.: Greenwood Press, 1970.

COWLEY, W. H. "Three Distinctions in the Study of Leaders." *Journal of Abnormal and Social Psychology* 23 (July–September 1928).

DARESH, JOHN C. *Supervision as Leadership*, 4th ed. Prospect Heights, Ill.: Waveland Press, 2007.

DEAL, TERRANCE E., and KENT D. PETERSON. *Shaping School Culture: The Heart of Leadership*. San Francisco: Jossey-Bass, 1999.

DE BRUYN, ROBERT L. *Causing Others to Want Your Leadership*. Manhattan, Kan.: R. L. De Bruyn & Associates, 1976.

DEMING, W. EDWARDS. *Out of the Crisis*, 1st MIT Press ed. Cambridge, Mass.: MIT Press, 2000.

DILLON-PETERSON, BETTY, ed. *Staff Development/Organization Development*. 1981 Yearbook. Alexandria, Va.: Association for Supervision and Curriculum Development, 1981.

DRUCKER, PETER F. *Management: Tasks, Responsibilities, Practices*. New Brunswick, N.J.: Transaction, 2006.

ELBING, ALVAR. *Behavior Decisions in Organizations*, 2nd ed. Glenview, Ill.: Scott, Foresman, 1978.

FAST, JULIUS. *Body Language*. New York: M. Evans, 1970.

———. *The Body Language of Sex, Power, and Aggression*. New York: M. Evans, 1977.

FIEDLER, FRED E. *A Theory of Leadership Effectiveness*. New York: McGraw-Hill, 1967.

FLINDERS, DAVID J. "Supervision as Cultural Inquiry." *Journal of Curriculum and Supervision* 6 (Winter 1991): 87–106.

FRENCH, WENDELL L., and CECIL H. BELL Jr. *Organization Development*. Englewood Cliffs, N.J.: Prentice Hall, 1973.

GALLOWAY, CHARLES. "The Nonverbal Realities of Classroom Life." In *Observational Methods in the Classroom*. Charles Beegle and Richard H. Brandt, eds. Alexandria, Va.: Association for Supervision and Curriculum Development, 1973.

———. *Silent Language in the Classroom*. Bloomington, Ind.: Phi Delta Kappa Educational Foundation, 1976.

GETZELS, JACOB W. "Administration as a Social Process." In *Administrative Theory in Education*. Andrew W. Halpin, ed. New York: Macmillan, 1958.

GETZELS, JACOB W., and HERBERT A. THELEN. "The Classroom Group as a Unique Social System." In *The Dynamics of Instructional Groups: Sociological Aspects of Teaching and Learning*, 59th Yearbook, Part II. Nelson B. Henry, ed. Chicago: National Society for the Study of Education, 1960.

GIAMMATTEO, MICHAEL C., and DOLORES M. GIAMMATTEO. *Executive Well-Being: Stress and Administrators*. Reston, Va.: National Association of Secondary School Principals, 1980.

GLICKMAN, CARL D., STEPHEN P. GORDON, and JOVITA M. ROSS-GORDON. *SuperVision and Instructional Leadership: A Developmental Approach*, 7th ed. Boston: Allyn and Bacon, 2007.

GRIFFITHS, DANIEL E. *Administrative Theory*. New York: Appleton-Century-Crofts, 1959.

HALL, EDWARD T. *The Silent Language*. New York: Anchor, 1990.

HEMPHILL, JOHN K., and ALVIN E. COONS. *Leader Behavior Description*. Columbus: Ohio State University, 1950.

HERSEY, PAUL, KENNETH H. BLANCHARD, and DEWEY E. JOHNSON. *Management of Organizational Behavior: Utilizing Human Resources*, 8th ed. Upper Saddle River, N.J.: Prentice Hall, 2001.

HOMANS, GEORGE C. *The Human Group*. New Brunswick, N.J.: Transaction, 1992.

HORD, SHIRLEY M., WILLIAM L. RUTHERFORD, LESLIE HULING-AUSTIN, and GENE E. HALL. *Taking Charge of Change*. Alexandria, Va.: Association for Supervision and Curriculum Development, 1987.

KOTKIN, JOEL, and YORIKO KISHIMOTO. "Theory F." *Inc.* 8 (April 1986): 53–60.

LAMBERT, LINDA, MICHELLE COLLAY, MARY E. DIETZ, KAREN KENT, and ANNA ERSHLER RICHERT. *Who Will Save Our Schools?: Teachers as Constructivist Leaders*. Thousand Oaks, Calif.: Corwin Press, 1997.

LANDSBERGER, HENRY A. *Hawthorne Revisited. Management and the Worker: Its Critics, and Developments in Human Relations in Industry*. Ithaca, N.Y.: Cornell University, 1958.

———. "Creating High-Functioning Teacher Teams." *Leadership Compass* 3 (Summer 2006): 1–3.

LEWIN, KURT, RONALD LIPPITT, and RALPH K. WHITE. "Patterns of Aggressive Behavior in Experimentally Created 'Social Climates.'" *Journal of Social Psychology* 10 (May 1939): 271–99.

LIKERT, RENSIS. *The Human Organization: Its Management and Value.* New York: McGraw-Hill, 1967.

LIPHAM, JAMES M. "Leadership and Administration." In *Behavioral Science and Educational Administration*, 63rd Yearbook, Part II, Daniel E. Griffiths ed., Chicago: National Society for the Study of Education, 1964.

LIPHAM, JAMES M., and JAMES A. HOEH, Jr. *The Principalship: Foundations and Functions.* New York: Harper and Row, 1974.

LUTHANS, FRED. *Organizational Behavior*, 11th ed. Boston: McGraw-Hill/Irwin, 2006.

McGREGOR, DOUGLAS. *The Human Side of Enterprise*, annotated ed. New York: McGraw-Hill, 2006.

MILES, RAYMOND. "Human Relations or Human Resources?" *Harvard Business Review* 43 (July–August 1965): 148–63.

MORPHET, EDGAR L., ROE L. JOHNS, and THEODORE L. RELLER. *Educational Organization and Administration: Concepts, Practices, and Issues*, 4th ed. Englewood Cliffs, N.J.: Prentice Hall, 1982.

MORRIS, DESMOND, PETER COLLETT, PETER MARSH, and MARIE O'SHAUGHNESSEY. *Gestures, Their Origins and Distribution.* New York: Stein and Day, 1979.

OUCHI, WILLIAM G. *Theory Z: How American Business Can Meet the Japanese Challenge.* Reading, Mass.: Addison-Wesley, 1981.

OWENS, ROBERT G., and THOMAS C. VALESKY. *Organizational Behavior in Education: Adaptive Leadership and School Reform*, 9th ed. Boston: Pearson/Allyn and Bacon, 2007.

RICE, BERKELEY. "The Hawthorne Defect: Persistence of a Flawed Theory." *Psychology Today* 16 (February 1982): 70–74.

ROETHLISBERGER, F. J., and WILLIAM J. DICKSON. *Management and the Worker: An Account of a Research Program Conducted by the Western Electric Company, Hawthorne Works, Chicago.* Cambridge, Mass.: Harvard University Press, 1939.

SERGIOVANNI, THOMAS J. *Building Community in Schools.* San Francisco: Jossey-Bass, 1994.

———. *Moral Leadership: Getting to the Heart of School Improvement.* San Francisco: Jossey-Bass, 1992.

———. *Value-Added Leadership: How to Get Extraordinary Performance in Schools.* San Diego: Harcourt Brace Jovanovich, 1990.

SERGIOVANNI, THOMAS J., and ROBERT J. STARRATT. *Emerging Patterns of Supervision: Human Perspectives.* New York: McGraw-Hill, 1971.

———. *Supervision: A Redefinition*, 8th ed. Boston: McGraw-Hill, 2007.

SIMON, HERBERT A. *The New Science of Management Decision*, revised ed. Englewood Cliffs, N.J.: Prentice Hall, 1977.

STOGDILL, RALPH M. *Handbook of Leadership: A Survey of Theory and Research.* New York: Free Press, 1974.

———. "Leadership, Membership, and Organization." *Psychological Bulletin* 47 (January 1950): 1–14.

———. "Personal Factors Associated with Leadership: A Study of the Literature." *Journal of Psychology* 25 (January 1948): 35–71.

TOCQUEVILLE, ALEXIS DE. *Democracy in America, Part the Second: The Social Influence of Democracy.* Translated by Henry Reeve. New York: J. and H. G. Langley, 1840. Reprint New York: Knopf, 1945.

WELDY, GILBERT R. *Time: A Resource for the School Administrator.* Reston, Va.: National Association of Secondary School Principals, 1974.

WELLER, RICHARD H. *Verbal Communication in Instructional Supervision: An Observational System for and Research Study of Clinical Supervision in Groups.* New York: Teachers College Press, 1971.

WILES, JON, and JOSEPH C. BONDI. *Curriculum Development: A Guide to Practice*, 5th ed. Upper Saddle River, N.J.: Merrill, 2000.

ZUMWALT, KAREN K. *Improving Teaching*, 1986 Yearbook. Alexandria, Va.: Association for Supervision and Curriculum Development, 1986.

PUBLICATIONS

Results, Tools for Schools, Journal of Staff Development, The Learning Principal, The Learning System, and Teachers Teaching Teachers, National Staff Development Council, P.O. Box 240, Oxford, Ohio 45056. (513) 523-6029. www.nsdc.org.

CHAPTER 12

HELPING TEACHERS EVALUATE THEIR OWN PERFORMANCE

OBJECTIVES

After studying Chapter 12 you should be able to accomplish the following objectives:

1. Identify and describe three components of teacher evaluation systems.
2. Develop and use a teacher self-appraisal instrument.
3. Explain the meaning of external and internal analysis as applied to teacher performance.
4. Describe several models of teaching.
5. Analyze your own model of teaching.
6. Produce and classify protocol materials.
7. Use teacher-training packages in helping teachers improve instruction.
8. Develop and use an instrument for student evaluation of teacher performance.
9. Develop and use an instrument for parent evaluation of teacher performance.

THREE FACES OF EVALUATION OF TEACHER PERFORMANCE

Teachers sometimes feel that they are the most scrutinized professionals in the world. They live in the public eye. They are subject to more restrictions on their behavior than most other professionals, excluding the clergy. Their performance in class and their behavior out of class are evaluated by the public, students, other teachers, and administrators.

Preservice teachers should be advised to expect continuous evaluation of their performance as a way of life. The profession has come to admit that there are wide variations in knowledge, energy, dedication, and skill among the more than two million teachers throughout the United States. The profession has also acknowledged that developments in all subject fields and in pedagogy have been and continue to be rapid, necessitating continual assessment of and in-service study by school personnel.

At the same time, teachers, administrators, and supervisors are aware that the evaluation of human performance in any field is a difficult, sensitive matter subject to gross mistakes and misjudgments. No aspect of teaching can be more threatening to teachers than evaluation of their performance. No aspect of administration can be more agonizing for a conscientious administrator than evaluation of teachers. The administrator who asserts that evaluation of teacher performance is easy, nonthreatening, and routine seriously underestimates its complexities and effects. Administrators with this attitude probably have forgotten their own reactions to evaluation as teachers and have not been subjected to systematic, formal evaluation as administrators.

Although teachers need to be receptive to evaluation as a means of improving themselves and the profession, school systems need to devise ways to evaluate teachers that are feasible, fair, humane, and as objective as possible. Potentially, more than 15,000 systems of teacher evaluation could exist, one for each of the more than 15,000 school districts that make up the enterprise of American public education. Some states require a specific, uniform assessment program for certain purposes—for example, state certification—but even in those cases, many school districts within the state may follow their own systems of evaluation for their own purposes in addition to the state-required program.

In this chapter and the next, we examine the complex issue of observing and evaluating teacher performance. As we discuss teacher evaluation, we talk about both evaluation of instruction (and, to some extent, evaluation of the course or subject) and evaluation of the instructor. These two aspects are, of course, interrelated. By *evaluation of instruction* we mean appraisal of the effectiveness of the instructional skills and strategies chosen by the teacher. By *evaluation of the instructor* we mean assessment of the teacher's classroom performance (behavior), his or her effectiveness in employing the skills and strategies selected, and certain personal and professional attributes. In these two chapters we use the words *evaluation, assessment*, and *appraisal* interchangeably.

A fully developed program of teacher evaluation consists of three components: *self-evaluation, formative evaluation*, and *summative evaluation*. The last term, *summative evaluation*, refers to the annual assessment done by the administrator, not only for the purpose of improving instruction but also and primarily for assessing personnel. The latter purpose involves making decisions about whether to offer a teacher another teaching contract and eventually a long-term teaching contract with tenure; advancement to a leadership position; and, in those situations that have it, merit pay and/or advancement on the career ladder. (Summative evaluation is discussed in Chapter 13.)

The second term, *formative evaluation*, refers to ongoing assessment of teacher performance. Administrators and supervisors visit teachers periodically, observe their classes, and confer with the teachers to help them improve their instruction. (We looked at this component in Chapter 10.)

Thus, the focus of this chapter is on self-evaluation—the ways teachers may appraise their own performance and the means by which supervisors can help them do so. All school systems have a method of summative evaluation of teacher performance, and most have implemented a formative evaluation system as well. Fewer school systems, however, have developed a systematic process for reflection on the teaching act, which leads to teacher self-appraisal. We believe that a systematic, structured way of encouraging teachers to reflect on what they did to ensure that students learned and to evaluate themselves is essential and should be an integral part of the evaluation process.

Some school districts are encouraging teachers to complete preobservation planning forms to share with the person who will observe the lesson. The forms used for this purpose from the Littleton, Colorado Public Schools is shown in Figure 12.1, while a similar form

PRE-OBSERVATION PLANNING FORM

Staff Member: _____ Date/Time of Observation: _____
Content Area: _____ Observer: _____

<u>Learner objective:</u> (One item that you want your students to be able to do as a result of this lesson):

<u>Assessment:</u> (What assessment data or evidence was used to determine this teaching point was needed by your student?)

<u>Diagnosis/analysis:</u> (How did you evaluate/analyze the data/assessment and track the strengths/needs of students as well as the growth?)

<u>Planning:</u> (What approach will be used? ... resources needed? How will students be grouped?)

<u>Teaching:</u> (How will you model/demonstrate this teaching point? What strategies will you use? How will you help students make connections with previous learning? What type of feedback will students receive?)

<u>Learning:</u> (What evidence will you be looking for that indicates that studing learning has occurred? How will you know that students have met your objective? Bring examples to the post conference.)

Are there any unique characteristicis of this class?

FIGURE 12.1 Pre-observation Planning Form. *Source*: Littleton Public Schools, Littleton, Colorado. Reprinted with permission of the Littleton Public Schools.

used in the Webster Groves, Missouri, Public Schools is shown in Figure 12.2. Although the forms are different in their presentation, both serve the purpose of getting teachers focused on the planning, presentations, and assessments that are part of the lesson.

Each of the school districts utilizes postobservation forms to be completed by the teachers and prior to the postobservation conference. The form used in Littleton is Figure 12.3, while the Webster Groves form is Figure 12.4.

PRE-OBSERVATION FORM
WEBSTER GROVES SCHOOL DISTRICT
(To be completed by teacher, prior to observation)

Teacher	School	
Grade/Subject/Course	**Date**	
Administrator/Supervisor		
District curriculum objective (s)		
1. What content and instruction practices/methods will be used?		
2. Describe the students in the class.		
3. What is the lesson objective?		
4. What resources were used in planning?		
5. Describe the plan of instruction.		
6. How will student learning be assessed?		
7. Describe any special circumstances of which the observer should be aware.		
8. Is there anything in particular you want observed?		

Teacher's signature   Date   Administrator's/Supervisor's signature   Date

Signature(s) indicates the above has been reviewed and discussed. Copies to teacher and administrator / supervisor.

FIGURE 12.2 Pre-observation Planning Form. *Source:* Webster Groves School District, Webster Groves, Missouri. Reprinted with permission of the Webster Groves School District.

These lines from Robert Burns may run through the mind of the supervisor pondering the task of helping teachers evaluate themselves:

Oh wad some power the giftie gie us
To see oursels as ithers see us!
It wad frae monie a blunder free us
An' foolish notion.

Postobservation Reflective Questions for Teachers

---

1. Did this lesson plan fit as well as I thought it would when I designed this unit? Why or why not?

2. What evidence do I have that students learned what I intended? Were my instructional goals met? How many students met the objective(s)?

3. What changes in the lesson plan did I make as the lesson progressed? What changes will I make before I do it again?

4. What questions do I want to ask my observer?

FIGURE 12.3 Postobservation Reflective Questions for Teachers Form. *Source*: Littleton Public Schools, Littleton, Colorado. Reprinted with permission of the Littleton Public Schools.

The thoughtful supervisor knows that to help improve the curriculum and instruction, he or she must possess the ability to help teachers see themselves "as ithers see us." The supervisor must possess the ability or skills necessary to encourage teachers to look at their own behavior with a view to improving themselves. Moreover, the supervisor should be able to look at his or her own supervisory behavior, a topic discussed in Chapter 14.

LESSON REFLECTION FORM
WEBSTER GROVES SCHOOL DISTRICT

Teacher	School	
Grade/Subject/Course		Date
Administrator/Supervisor		
1. Did my students learn what I intended? Were my lesson goals met? How do I know?		
2. Were my questioning and discussion techniques effective? What improvements could I make?		
3. Were my students engaged in learning? How could I tell?		
4. What feedback did I provide to my students?		
5. Was there a part of the lesson where I needed to be flexible or make adaptations? Explain.		
6. As I reflect on the lesson, would I teach the lesson the same way again?		
7. Other comments:		

Teacher's signature   Date   Administrator's/Supervisor's signature   Date

Signature(s) indicates the above has been reviewed and discussed. Copies to teacher and administrator / supervisor.

FIGURE 12.4 Lesson Reflection Form. *Source:* Webster Groves School District, Webster Groves, Missouri. Reprinted with permission of the Webster Groves School District.

The skill of introspection is difficult to develop. When trying to help teachers evaluate themselves, the supervisor may encounter some formidable resistance. Among the notions teachers hold about evaluation of their behaviors are these:

- It is the student alone who should be evaluated; the teacher occupies a position beyond evaluation.

- Apart from the teacher, no one is capable of making an evaluation of that teacher's behavior.

- Every teacher has reached such a high state of professional competence that evaluation is not necessary.

- Teachers already know how to teach twice as well as they have the time or energy to teach or are permitted to teach.

- No other profession makes the assumption that a professional person must be regularly evaluated.

- Teaching is such a highly personalized and individualized art that emphasis on evaluating generic teaching behaviors is misplaced.

The supervisor helping teachers evaluate themselves also runs into some real and often unexpressed fears of teachers, such worries as these:

- They will be exposed and their shortcomings, made known to the world.

- They will be subjected to ridicule if they make mistakes.

- Anything less than perfection will penalize them in terms of continued employment, salary, tenure, or promotion.

Consequently, the teaching profession has built into itself some potent avoidance behaviors. The profession has resisted merit pay plans by raising such questions as, "Who will do the evaluating?" "How do you allow for individuality?" "How can you identify merit in teaching?" As a result of public pressure, more state legislatures have passed laws that reward teachers for their teaching and their students' performance on academic tests. This topic is discussed in Chapter 14. Some teachers view their classrooms as their own territorial domains and the entrance of administrators, supervisors, and the public into those domains as an unwarranted intrusion. Academic freedom is mentioned as a reason to justify the teacher's performance. Some teachers maintain that if they pass the initial test of an interview, have the appropriate teaching credentials, and are hired by the administrator, they have demonstrated all the competence they need to demonstrate. If their professional skills are found to be less than might be desired, they view that situation as the administrator's problem, not theirs.

Because of these attitudes and fears toward evaluation, the supervisor's primary role in the evaluation of teacher competence should be one of helping teachers evaluate themselves rather than one of evaluating teachers. This subtle distinction is crucial to the problem of evaluation. The supervisor's role as teacher evaluator can set up barriers between the teacher and the supervisor and perpetuate the fears of teachers. In this evaluative role, the supervisor can be seen as a threat to the teacher rather than a help, and rapport between the supervisor and the teacher may be difficult to achieve.

The supervisor's role in evaluating teachers reveals the school system's concept of supervision—that is, whether supervision is conceived of as a function of administration or as a support service for teachers. A central theme of this text has been that supervision for today's schools is first of all a support service and secondarily an administrative function. Unfortunately, as school budgets continue to be limited, the separate role of supervisor is often transferred to the school building administrator. More and more principals are assuming the dual role that school principals must play—supervisor and administrator. In order for the relationship between the principal and the teachers to remain positive and cooperative and to yield results, a *positive, trusting* relationship must have been established.

Many school systems require supervisors to evaluate teachers, rate them on certain competencies, and complete annual reports of performance that are submitted to the administrator. Preferably, however, the administrator should assume the role of teacher-rater, removing this task from the shoulders of the supervisor and allowing the supervisor to concentrate on the role he or she should fulfill—*helping teachers improve their teaching skills.* If a supervisor must rate a teacher and report the ratings to the administrator—and this must be done in many school systems—the ratings themselves should be played down, teachers themselves should enter fully into the process of rating, ratings should be liberally interpreted, and emphasis throughout the process should be on helping teachers evaluate their own performance. Furthermore, the confidentiality of such evaluations must be preserved—only those who have the right to see them should see them.

Supervisors who are not the teachers' administrator and must rate teachers are walking a tightrope. They must build a *solid base of trust and confidence and a reputation for fairness* if their relationship with teachers is to withstand the trauma of rating. It would be preferable if the service-oriented supervisor never had to rate a teacher, but such an expectation would be unrealistic in the light of many administrators' expectations of supervisors. The challenge to the supervisor, therefore, is to make the system work to achieve the major goal being sought—improved achievement of learners through improved teacher competence.

Of course, ratings of teachers are necessary. Personnel decisions must be made on the basis of competence. Whenever possible, however, the administrator, not the supervisor, should bear the primary responsibility for making judgments about the competence of teachers. That is, the burden of formative evaluation should fall on staff persons identified as instructional supervisors, and the job of summative evaluation should go to the administrator. In some of the smallest school systems, and increasingly in larger districts as well, there are no instructional supervisors at either the district or individual school level. In those cases, both administrative and supervisory responsibilities will of necessity fall on the principal, who serves as the instructional leader of the school. Although some principals are adept at fulfilling what can be conflicting roles, the result is often an emphasis on summative evaluation for the purpose of making personnel decisions and deemphasis on formative evaluation for the purpose of improving instruction.

The principles of evaluation discussed in Chapter 10 and in this chapter are aimed at those persons who function as supervisors and as administrators when they are fulfilling the role of instructional supervisor. Chapter 13 is aimed at administrators when they are fulfilling their role as personnel managers.

The instructional supervisor should use every technique available to help teachers evaluate their own competencies with as little stress on rating as possible. An important part of the process of self-evaluation should be teachers' reflecting on the lessons they teach. Completing that task at the end of each lesson is the ideal, but realistically it is frequently done at the end of the school day. If a foundation of trust has been developed between the supervisor and/or administrator and the teacher, this process of reflection will be easier to establish. If it is the supervisor's duty to make an annual report on a teacher, the supervisor should make sure that such an evaluation becomes an exercise in teacher self-evaluation under his or her guidance. The evaluation should be a process of discussion between a teacher and supervisor and a means for the teacher to set his or her own goals for the future.

COMPETENCIES TO BE EVALUATED

Before considering how the supervisor can help teachers evaluate themselves, let us look at some of the competencies school systems believe are important enough to be evaluated. If teachers are to be evaluated, they should know well in advance the criteria on which assessments will be made.

School systems vary on teacher behaviors they consider important, but among the categories of behavior that most frequently appear on instruments for assessing teacher performance are (1) instructional skills, (2) personal traits, and (3) professional attributes. The Summative Evaluation Report form of the Webster Groves, Missouri, School District contains these categories, but they are listed under the four standards their plan contains: planning and preparation, classroom environment, instruction, and professional responsibility. The form, Figure 12.5, illustrates the categories of performance evaluated by the school system. The evaluator decides whether the teacher meets Webster Groves' expectations and, if not, whether the teacher has to work on certain goals or to undergo intensive assistance.

The form in Figure 12.5 serves the purpose of summative or annual evaluation (see Chapter 13), which includes assessment of professional and personal attributes as well as instructional skills. Without the inclusion of the professional and personal behaviors, the supervisor would have an instrument for classroom observation (see Chapter 10).

Administrators and supervisors must bring teachers in at the beginning of the process of identifying teacher competencies and attributes and developing the means of evaluating these competencies and attributes. Teacher participation in the development of evaluation

EVALUATION REPORT (SUMMATIVE)
WEBSTER GROVES SCHOOL DISTRICT

Teacher:	Date:	☐ Non-Tenured	☐ Tenured
Grade/Subject:	Dates of Formal Observations:		
Administrator/Supervisor:	School:		

Standard I: Planning and Preparation	Meets Expectation***	Approaching Expectation**	Does Not Meet Expectation*	Comments:
1A Demonstrates knowledge of content and instructional practices and methods				
1B Demonstrates knowledge of students				
1C Selects instructional goals and objectives				
1D Demonstrates knowledge of resources				
1E Designs coherent instruction				
1F Assesses student learning				

*** Expected level of performance for all teachers ** Documentation Required *PIP required

(continued)

FIGURE 12.5 Evaluation Report (Summative) Form. *Source*: Webster Groves School District, Webster Groves, Missouri. Reprinted with permission of the Webster Groves School District.

Standard 2: Classroom Environment	Meets Expectation***	Approaching Expectation**	Does Not Meet Expectation*	Comments:
2A Creates an environment of respect and rapport				
2B Establishes a culture for learning				
2C Manages classroom procedures				
2D Manages student behavior				
2E Organizes physical space				

Standard 3: Instruction	Meets Expectation***	Approaching Expectation**	Does Not Meet Expectation*	Comments:
3A Teaches the Board approved curriculum				
3B Communicates clearly and accurately				
3C Uses effective questioning and discussion techniques				
3D Engages students in learning				
3E Provides feedback to students				
3F Demonstrates flexibility and responsiveness				

*** Expected level of performance for all teachers ** Documentation Required * PIP required

(continued)

Standard 4: Professional Responsibility	Meets Expectation***	Approaching Expectation**	Does Not Meet Expectation**	Comments:
4A Communicates with families				
4B Contributes to the school and district				
4C Grows and develops professionally				
4D Demonstrates professional behavior				
4E Reflects on teaching				

*** Expected level of performance for all teachers **Documentation Required * PIP required

Teacher's comments:

Administrator's/Supervisor's comments:

Teacher's signature	Date	Teacher's signature	Date

Signature(s) indicates the above ahs been reviewed and discussed. Copies to teacher and administrator/supervisor.

FIGURE 12.5 *(continued)*

plans from the beginning is the best means of securing the teachers' commitment the evaluation process.

Among the numerous evaluation systems, two general categories of teacher behavior predominate: *instructional skills*, which lie more in the cognitive and performance areas, and *personal and professional attributes*, which lie more in the affective area. These two major categories of teacher behavior are assumed to be worthy of appraisal, and we will suggest ways in which the supervisor can help teachers evaluate themselves in these broad areas.

Evaluation of Instructional Skills

Previous chapters of this text have sought to describe instructional skills that are desirable for teachers to master while focusing the evaluative spotlight on learners and their performance. Now the spotlight is trained on the teachers' performance. The supervisor mulls the question, "How can I best go about helping teachers see and analyze their own performance?" Several approaches are possible, one or more of which may run into a dead end:

- The supervisor may enter the teacher's classroom unannounced and unexpected, sit down at the back of the room, observe the teacher's performance, take notes while the teacher is teaching, write up a summary, and hand it to the teacher.

- The supervisor may appear periodically, evaluate the teacher's performance by using a rating instrument, and deliver the instrument to the administrator.

- The supervisor may drop in informally several times to get acquainted and to learn whether the teacher needs help of any kind before turning to procedures for a more structured type of evaluation.

- The supervisor may set up in-service training programs designed to help teachers evaluate their own performance before entering into a more structured type of evaluation.

- The supervisor may be invited by the teacher to observe a lesson. If a level of trust has been established, a free exchange of words will flow regarding the lesson.

The supervisor must gain the teacher's confidence and trust before the two of them can together talk about evaluating the teacher's performance. Therefore, of the five approaches just described, only the last three are acceptable. *The first two approaches are not acceptable* because they are grading approaches that place the teacher under threat. To the fullest extent possible, provision must be made for discussion and analysis in a trusting, threat-free environment.

To institute teachers' examination of their own competence, the supervisor may take an approach that consists of the following three stages:

1. Examination of teacher performance in general terms—that is, analysis of the teaching act in a theoretical context. This is accomplished by study of the literature and other selected media on teaching.

2. Examination of the performance of other teachers both inside and outside the school system. This is accomplished by the use of audio and visual media and by teachers visiting each other's classrooms.

3. Examination of the teacher's own performance. This is accomplished through the use of both written materials and other selected media.

We identify the first two stages as *external analysis*. At these points, teachers look at teaching in general and at the performance of other teachers. As they make external analyses of teaching, they begin to internalize, drawing implications for their own teaching. They begin to develop certain understandings about teaching and start to see how they can improve themselves.

The third stage is *internal analysis*, at which time the teacher focuses on his or her own behaviors. Now the individual teacher comes to center stage and, instead of concentrating on the teaching act impersonally or on the performance of other teachers, is brought around to evaluating his or her own performance.

This three-stage sequence from external to internal analysis allows time for the supervisor to help teachers build a positive mind-set toward evaluation, equip them with skills for evaluating themselves, and develop confidence in their own abilities.

The literature on teacher behavior is already vast and still growing. Many studies of teacher performance have been conducted, and numerous training programs have been developed that permit teachers to look at teaching and at their own performance. The next section offers the prospective supervisor several strategies for developing skills of self-evaluation, briefly describes the nature of these strategies, and directs the supervisor to a number of sources and programs.

Models of Teaching   There is no single best point of departure for the evaluation of teacher competence, but a productive route to external analysis is the study of teaching models. By looking at various models of teaching, the teacher can identify the model or models he or she either makes use of or can make use of. Bruce Joyce, Marsha Weil, and Beverly Showers defined a model of teaching as "a plan or pattern that we can use to design face-to-face teaching in classrooms or tutorial settings and to shape instructional materials—including books, films, tapes, computer-mediated programs, and curricula (long-term courses of studies)."[1]

In the sixth edition of their book, Joyce, Weil, and Showers described sixteen models of teaching grouped into four families: social families, information-processing families, personal families, and behavioral systems families.[2] Some models of teaching are more evident than others. The following models can be identified among many that are followed by teachers:

1. *The teacher as lecturer.* This historic model conceives of the teacher as a conveyor of information from his or her mind to the minds of the learners, primarily through the medium of oral language.

2. *The teacher as expert resource person.* The teacher who follows this model is available to share information about content and sources whenever learners need help.

3. *The teacher as facilitator.* Following this model, the teacher does everything possible to provide resources and direction to learners so that they may go about their studies and continuously guides their learning in the process of study.

4. *The teacher as counselor.* The teacher who adopts this model sees the personal development of the learner as more important than the content, advises students, encourages them, and, more important, listens to learners' problems.

5. *The teacher as a leader of group meetings.* This teacher is the master of ceremonies, the group's chairperson, who promotes the work of the group, directs its activities, and encourages participation from all group members.

6. *The teacher as tutor.* The teacher following this model engages in instruction on a one-to-one basis, and in so doing may employ a variety of techniques, including contractual-type arrangements that provide for independent study.

7. *The teacher as manager of mediated instruction.* Various media, including television and computers, play a primary role in the presentation of instruction via this model. The teacher selects the necessary media, arranges for their use, and follows up the mediated presentations with discussion and evaluation.

8. *The teacher as laboratory supervisor.* This model requires the establishment of a laboratory approach to instruction—experimenting, constructing, researching activities, which learners carry out under the supervision of the teacher.

9. *The teacher as programmer.* Derived from the fields of programmed instruction and computer-assisted instruction, this model directs the teacher to write specific programs, which learners then work through either individually or in groups.

10. *The teacher as manipulator of the learning environment.* This behavioristic model calls for the teacher to manipulate the stimuli in the classroom environment. The teacher gives and withholds reinforcement for specific kinds of learning that the students are attempting.

Research does not identify any single model as preferable to all others. Often the model(s) of teaching that a teacher uses are determined by the subject taught, the grade level, resources available, and the ages and/or makeup of the students in a particular class. Experienced teachers are often more able to "explore" the use of various teaching models than less experienced teachers who are still mastering the basics of teaching. The study of models of teaching also serves the worthwhile function of causing supervisors and teachers to realize that a number of models of teacher behavior are possible and that the use of particular models may be dictated by particular teaching situations.

In some respects a model of teaching resembles a style of teaching. The concept of style injects a very personal, individualized dimension, for it includes elements of the teacher's personality—facial expressions, gestures, kinesthetic movements, choice of vocabulary, dramatic flare, wit—the total personal delivery system.

As research into learning and teacher behavior continues, new models and adaptations of old models may be expected. A productive in-service program could involve the identification and analysis of various models of teaching. The purpose of such an in-service program would not be to have teachers select one of the models and adopt it for exclusive use but to give them some basis for identifying their own pattern(s) and adding new models to their repertoire. The choice of a model or models is a function of the grade level, discipline, instructional objectives, and the teacher's own personality. Some models have general applicability at all grade levels and in all disciplines; others are more suited to particular grade levels and disciplines. Effective teachers demonstrate competence in several models of teaching. After a study of models of teaching, the supervisor may turn the external analysis of models into an internal analysis by asking teachers to describe and classify their own models.

Protocol Materials   Protocol materials are brief taped or filmed incidents of actual classroom situations. They have been described as

> vignettes of behavior which illustrate key concepts that enable the teacher to better
> interpret behavior in the classroom and the school. The main purpose of Protocol
> Materials is to develop conceptual knowledge through concept analysis and to link
> specific behavior to a conceptual basis.[3]

Classroom behavior captured on tape or film lets teachers study and restudy the behavior. Protocol materials differ from ordinary taping and filming of classroom situations in that the producers of protocol materials zero in on the concepts they wish to illustrate. They may be looking for examples of focusing, probing questions, verbal interaction, behavior modification, teacher enthusiasm, or other teaching skills. They capture the performance of a particular skill on tape or film so that it can be studied at a future time.

Supervisors may seek protocol materials from other school systems or educational agencies. However, with today's videorecording equipment and with the help of media support personnel, the supervisor can produce a library of local protocol materials— videorecorded situations in the local schools. Locally produced protocol materials will have heightened meaning for teachers in the system who use the materials. Of course, classroom teachers would have to give their permission for recording to take place in their classrooms and would have to fully cooperate in the process. Only the most confident teachers will probably be willing—at least at first—for themselves and their classes to be recorded and for the protocols to be studied by other teachers in the system. Some school districts are involving National Board Certified Teachers in the preparation of protocol materials to be used with local teachers. Distance learning strategies are being implemented in several rural school districts. Protocol materials, instructional modules, videorecorded field trips, and other enrichment materials are used. Viewing recordings of excellent teachers as they teach, followed by discussion, can be a very useful method of external analysis.

B. Othanel Smith, Saul B. Cohen, and Arthur Pearl spoke about the purpose of protocol materials, which they called "samples of behavior to be studied":

> The study of protocol materials will not only result in the prospective teacher's
> ability to understand and to interpret situations he will face in the classroom, school,
> and community; it will also increase the teacher's interest in theory, for he will see
> clearly for the first time that it is useful.[4]

We would add that not only the prospective teacher but also the in-service teacher can profit from the use of protocol materials. Smith, Cohen, and Pearl give examples of types of factors that protocols can point up: interference of concepts, conflict situations, self-image, self-fulfillment, differential reinforcement, and vicarious reinforcement.

Smith, Cohen, and Pearl also recommended using protocol materials for the purpose of expanding the teacher's theoretical knowledge:

> Apart from situational instruction, theoretical knowledge is apt to remain
> pedagogically useless. Protocol materials should not be used merely to illustrate
> points in education courses. The whole procedure should be turned about so that the
> principles of the psychological, sociological, and philosophical studies, as well as
> those of pedagogy, are brought to the analysis of protocol materials, not the other way
> around. These materials suggest the knowledge that is relevant to the teacher's work.[5]

A school system that contemplates the purchase or production of protocols will need to develop a system for classifying and cataloging behaviors to make effective use of these materials. Smith, Cohen, and Pearl suggested a simple classification system:

1. Classroom situations
   a. Instructional situations
   b. Situations of classroom management and control
2. Extraclassroom situations
   a. Situations that arise in planning school programs, working with peers and the administration
   b. Situations that occur in working with parents and other members of the community
   c. Situations that occur in working in professional organizations[6]

Because we are concerned at this time with the evaluation of instructional skills, we are interested primarily in classroom situations, but keep in mind that protocol materials do not have to be confined exclusively to classroom behaviors. To aid in establishing a bank of protocol materials, the supervisor might well appoint a protocols development committee composed of teachers and other specialists in the school system. Although interest in the development of protocol materials was more pronounced in the 1970s, the technique has much to recommend it to supervisors seeking ways to help teachers improve instruction.

Electronically Recorded Lessons   Teachers may examine other teachers' performance by watching videotapes or digital camera recordings of their lessons. Such recordings resemble protocol materials. However, protocol tapes and films depict brief episodes highlighting key concepts, whereas the recorded lessons capture complete lessons, running anywhere from thirty minutes to an hour or more. Thus, teachers can follow a lesson as it unfolds and witness skillful teachers in action. Supervisors and teachers can watch those lessons together and discuss what they have seen.

Possible sources of lessons taped or on DVD are educational associations and teacher-training institutions. However, rather than depend on locating lessons from outside sources, the supervisor could easily build a library of recordings of effective teaching within the system. As in the case of protocol materials, the teachers whose lessons are to be recorded would need to give their consent and feel comfortable with having their colleagues view and discuss their performance. The former Commissioner of Education in Florida recommended that National Board Certified Teachers and other senior teachers be involved in leading other teachers in these and other professional development and school improvement activities.[7] Florida teachers who are National Board Certified receive monetary rewards if they mentor other teachers who are seeking National Board Certification and/or serve as mentors for new teachers.

Teacher-Training Modules   Over the years, teacher-training institutions, state departments of education, and other educational agencies have produced training packages known in the profession as *teacher-training modules*, consisting of printed materials often accompanied by other media. A large number were developed in past years for use in preservice and in-service teacher training. Each module focuses on the development of a particular competency. The modular approach is an individualized process of training, and though modules may be used in a group setting, each individual teacher must work through his or her own module.

At one time or another the following organizations were engaged in the development of teacher-training modules: Brigham Young University, Dade County (Florida) Public Schools, Florida Department of Education, Florida State University, the University of Georgia, Northwest Regional Laboratory, Southwest Minnesota State College, State University College of Buffalo, Thiokol Chemical Corporation, University of Toledo, University of Houston, Weber State College (Utah), and Western Washington State College. The development of teacher-training modules reflected the interest of institutions and states in a competency-based approach to teacher education.

One of the better-known, but now unavailable, sets of teacher-training modules was the Weber State College *WILKITS*.[8] The *WILKITS* (Weber State College, Utah, *Individualized Learning Kits*) were produced for Weber State College's preservice training program. Weber State, one of the early developers of competency-based teacher education programs, developed eighty-five modules to train teachers in various phases of professional education. Titles of some of these modules are:

- Classroom Management and Discipline
- Self-Concept
- Motivation and Learning
- Professional Relationships
- Purposes and Methods of Classroom Evaluation
- Reading Study Techniques
- Classroom Strategies Inquiry

Although interest in the competency-based approach to teacher education and activity in developing teacher-training modules has declined in recent years, use of the teacher-training module approach to staff development is still worthy of consideration. Teacher-training modules provide a way for teachers to examine some of the dimensions of teaching. The supervisor may wish to select teachers to work with on developing modules for their own school system. The Association for Supervision and Curriculum Development (ASCD) has training materials that emulate a training-module approach.

Laboratory Approaches   Several approaches to the evaluation of teacher behavior that are followed to a large extent in preservice programs are equally suitable to in-service training programs, although in the latter case they pose special operational and motivational problems. Referred to as *laboratory* or *clinical approaches*, they include peer teaching and microteaching, both with and without videos.

Microteaching is central to the laboratory approach. In microteaching, a teacher or prospective teacher demonstrates in a clinical setting a particular teaching skill before a small group of students (preferably not his or her own) or peers. The purpose of micro-teaching is to give teachers feedback about their teaching so they may make improvements. The process of microteaching calls for a presentation of a very short (mini) lesson, after which the teacher's performance is critiqued on the basis of an instrument or a prespecified set of criteria. Many teacher preparation programs include courses that require students to prepare and present lessons to small groups of students in a controlled environment. After the critique, the teacher repeats the lesson and it is again analyzed. When the subjects are students, it is preferable for the repetition to be conducted with a different group of students. The critique of the lesson may be directed by the supervisor or other consultant, by a peer, or by the teacher if the lesson is videorecorded.

When the microteaching session is conducted with colleagues serving as students, it is called *peer teaching*. Although microteaching and peer teaching can be carried out in a clinic that is not outfitted with videorecording equipment, they gain added impact when recorded. Videorecording permits the teacher to view his or her own performance and allows repeated analysis.

The supervisor also should take the initiative to establish a microteaching laboratory in the school or school system. Microteaching laboratories give students opportunities to "practice" teaching while they are still learning. Space and equipment needed are minimal. The laboratory, a small room reasonably free from external noise, is usually equipped with a desk, chalkboard, and technology for the teacher to use while teaching: camcorder, VCR, television monitor, CD and DVD players, computer, and other media.

The laboratory approach establishes an artificial, simulated, controlled situation, but it provides an opportunity for development or refinement of a particular technique or skill that the teacher may use in a real classroom. A possible problem may be the teacher's willingness to be placed in a learner-type situation, to appear before colleagues and/or students, and to face constructive criticism of his or her performance. Another problem could arise with regard to finding suitable space, providing necessary equipment, and finding a convenient time for everyone involved—teachers, students, peers, observers, and media personnel. However, none of these problems will be insurmountable if the laboratory is an accepted and voluntary part of a total in-service program or has been offered to teachers who need to improve their instruction. A special incentive, such as released time, additional pay, or university credit, may make the use of a laboratory approach more attractive to teachers.

Observation Systems The intensive research into teaching performance has launched a number of systems for studying, analyzing, and recording teacher behavior in the classroom. These systems provide a means by which trained observers may record the actual performance of a teacher and by which teachers may evaluate their own performance through the use of videorecordings. The ultimate purpose of an observation system is to give teachers opportunities to analyze their own teaching systematically to make improvements. An observation system structures the teacher's evaluation by enabling him or her to look for prespecified aspects of teaching.

A few systems of observation analysis are very well known to the profession, but many existing systems are not as well known. The number of observation instruments is quite large, as many school systems have now developed their own instruments.

The aspects of teacher performance that the numerous instruments choose for observation vary somewhat from system to system. Some focus on the teacher, others on the student, and still others on teacher–student interaction. Some stress cognitive learning, whereas others look at affective behavior. Some emphasize verbal behavior, others nonverbal behavior. Some instruments are refinements of previously created instruments, capitalizing on the research that has taken place.

"The question naturally arises," said Smith, Cohen, and Pearl,

> as to which of the many observation systems should be used for the training of teachers. But a review of the literature indicates that the analyses differ more in the labels used than in the substance of the categories themselves. In other words, there is not as much variation among the analyses as the terminology seems to indicate.[9]

A viable procedure for selecting an observation instrument is for the supervisor to appoint a committee of teachers to study various systems and choose an instrument they would be willing to use (alternatively, the teachers might even wish to develop their own instrument). The process of selecting or developing an instrument would be valuable in-service training for those participating on the committee, and the instrument would gain support for its use because of the involvement of teachers. The supervisor and the committee might begin their work by sending for copies of instruments and accompanying explanatory literature of systems in which they may have a particular interest.

The kinds of behavior the developers of observation instruments consider important enough to be observed and analyzed—and possibly to be improved—are illustrated by two instruments: Ned A. Flanders's pioneering Flanders Interaction Analysis Categories (FIAC) (Figure 12.6) and Bruce W. Tuckman's Tuckman Teacher Feedback Form (Figure 12.7).

Observation analysis has been introduced in this chapter with the Flanders and Tuckman instruments to point out that teachers can use a systematic form of observation in analyzing their own performance.

Flanders's system concentrates on verbal interaction, whereas Tuckman's instrument assesses certain personal characteristics of teachers that can affect classroom climate and instruction. Flanders's system prescribes a tally every three seconds, and Tuckman's system uses a simple checklist. Both instruments may be used for either self-appraisal or appraisal of teachers' performance on items assessed by these instruments. When teachers apply the Flanders instrument to assess their own performance, they may do so by reviewing a transcript, audiotape, or videorecording of their lessons. The Tuckman instrument may be converted from an appraisal form to a teacher preference or self-appraisal form by changing the data at the top of the instrument shown from "Person Observed," "Observer," and "Date" to "Name," "Date," and "My Preference for."

Observation analysis can be implemented in a number of ways. Proceeding from an external approach to an internal approach, let's examine several ways to use observation instruments:

- Following a technique employed in many teacher-training institutions, the teacher may view videorecordings of classroom sessions showing other teachers in action and apply an instrument to these recordings of teacher performance. The Association for Supervision and Curriculum Development offers helpful videotapes and DVDs of classroom episodes. The teacher may analyze the performance of teachers on these recordings and make recommendations for that teacher. At the same time, the teacher will also be making self-recommendations.

- The teacher may permit an observation of his or her teaching to be made live in the classroom—without videorecording—by an outside, trained observer; by a colleague; or by the supervisor who will employ an observation instrument and review the observation with the teacher. This approach is, perhaps, the most threatening of all

Teacher Talk	Response	1.	*Accepts feeling.* Accepts and clarifies an attitude or the feeling tone of a student in a nonthreatening manner. Feelings may be positive or negative. Predicting and recalling feelings are included.
		2.	*Praises or encourages.* Praises or encourages students; says "um hum" or "go on"; makes jokes that release tension, but not at the expense of a student.
		3.	*Accepts or uses ideas of students.* Acknowledges student talk. Clari es, builds on, or asks questions based on student ideas.
		4.	*Asks questions.* Asks questions about content or procedure, based on teacher ideas, with the intent that a student will answer.
	Initiation	5.	*Lectures.* Offers facts or opinions about content or procedures; expresses his or her own ideas, gives his or her own explanation, or cites an authority other than a student.
		6.	*Gives directions.* Gives directions, commands, or orders with which a student is expected to comply.
		7.	*Criticizes student or justifies authority.* Makes statements intended to change student behavior from nonacceptable to acceptable patterns; arbitrarily corrects student answers; bawls someone out. Or states why the teacher is doing what he or she is doing; uses extreme self-reference.
Student Talk	Response	8.	*Student talk—response.* Student talk in response to a teacher contact that structures or limits the situation. Freedom to express own ideas is limited.
	Initiation	9.	*Student talk—initiation.* Student initiates or expresses his or her own ideas, either spontaneously or in response to the teacher's solicitation. Freedom to develop opinions and a line of thought; going beyond existing structure.
Silence		10.	*Silence or confusion.* Pauses, short periods of silence, and periods of confusion in which communication cannot be understood by the observer.

FIGURE 12.6 Flanders Interaction Analysis Categories (FIAC). Based on Ned A. Flanders, *Analyzing Teaching Behavior,* 1970. No scale is implied by these numbers. Each number is classificatory; it designates a particular kind of communication event. To write these numbers down during observation is to enumerate, not to judge, a position on a scale. *Source*: Ned A. Flanders, *Interaction Analysis: Teacher Handbook* (San Francisco: Far West Laboratory for Educational Research and Development, 1972), p. 5.

approaches and one that some teachers find difficult to accept. It requires real confidence for a teacher to ask for and receive what amounts to feedback, even in the most positive terms, of his or her teaching, especially in the face-to-face arrangement of this approach.

- Some teachers may allow their teaching to be videorecorded and may ask a trained observer, colleague, or supervisor to apply an observation instrument to the recorded session and then review the analysis with the individual teacher. The element of threat is still present, but it is softened by the relative remoteness of the videorecording. It is less threatening because the teacher is not undergoing analytical observation while teaching; this comes afterward when the observer views the recording.

Person Observed _____ Observer _____

Date: _____

1.	Original	—:—:—:—:—:—	Conventional
2.	Patient	—:—:—:—:—:—	Impatient
3.	Cold	—:—:—:—:—:—	Warm
4.	Hostile	—:—:—:—:—:—	Amiable
5.	Creative	—:—:—:—:—:—	Routinized
6.	Inhibited	—:—:—:—:—:—	Uninhibited
7.	Iconoclastic	—:—:—:—:—:—	Ritualistic
8.	Gentle	—:—:—:—:—:—	Harsh
9.	Unfair	—:—:—:—:—:—	Fair
10.	Capricious	—:—:—:—:—:—	Purposeful
11.	Cautious	—:—:—:—:—:—	Experimenting
12.	Disorganized	—:—:—:—:—:—	Organized
13.	Unfriendly	—:—:—:—:—:—	Sociable
14.	Resourceful	—:—:—:—:—:—	Uncertain
15.	Reserved	—:—:—:—:—:—	Outspoken
16.	Imaginative	—:—:—:—:—:—	Exacting
17.	Erratic	—:—:—:—:—:—	Systematic
18.	Aggressive	—:—:—:—:—:—	Passive
19.	Accepting (People)	—:—:—:—:—:—	Critical
20.	Quiet	—:—:—:—:—:—	Bubbly
21.	Outgoing	—:—:—:—:—:—	Withdrawn
22.	In Control	—:—:—:—:—:—	On the Run
23.	Flighty	—:—:—:—:—:—	Conscientious
24.	Dominant	—:—:—:—:—:—	Submissive
25.	Observant	—:—:—:—:—:—	Preoccupied
26.	Introverted	—:—:—:—:—:—	Extraverted
27.	Assertive	—:—:—:—:—:—	Soft-Spoken
28.	Timid	—:—:—:—:—:—	Adventurous

FIGURE 12.7 Tuckman Teacher Feedback Form (Short Form). *Source*: Bruce Wayne Tuckman, "New Instrument: The Tuckman Teacher Feedback Form (TTFF)," *Journal of Educational Measurement* 13, no. 3 (Fall 1976): 234. Reprinted with permission of Bruce W. Tuckman.

- The teacher may arrange to have his or her teaching videorecorded and then personally use an observation instrument to critique his or her own performance. Except in the case of research studies in which observations must be carried out by trained members of a research staff, this approach holds the most promise for lasting change and continuous improvement in teaching performance. This threat-free approach encourages teachers to look at their own teaching, knowing that no one is present to criticize them for poor performance.

To achieve reliable observation, the observer (who may actually be the teacher) must be thoroughly familiar with the categories of behavior to be observed and the procedures for recording and interpreting the data. The observer should undergo a training period and a number of practice sessions to gain skill in using the instrument. Because the supervisor will want each teacher to develop proficiency in analyzing his or her own behavior, in-service training in the observation system must precede actual use of the system.

Access to videorecording equipment is a must if teachers are ever going to see themselves in action and be able to study their own performance. No matter how helpful an observer may be to a teacher, nothing can replace a teacher's viewing his or her own teaching performance.

Faculties considering the use of observation instruments might wish to create and try out a simplified, even rough or crude instrument to become familiar with the concept of observation analysis. Their initial efforts at creating an instrument might result in a simple tool, such as the one below, on which an observer would make tallies of each evidence of the specified behaviors of the teacher and students:

TEACHER BEHAVIOR	TALLY	STUDENT BEHAVIOR	TALLY
• Lecturing _____		• Responding to teacher's questions _____	
• Leading discussion _____		• Asking questions of the teacher _____	
• Questioning orally _____		• Participation in class discussion _____	
• Reinforcing student responses _____		• Participating in work activities _____	
• Directing/facilitating class activities _____		• Performing leadership role _____	
• Moving about the classroom _____		• Misbehaving _____	
• Other (identify) _____		• Other (identify) _____	

When using an instrument of this nature, the observer—who could be the teacher employing videorecordings of his or her own classes—makes a tally mark every time the teacher shows any of the specified teacher behaviors and every time any pupil shows any of the behaviors in the student behavior column. Such a simplified instrument may be used as an introduction to more sophisticated, validated instruments. Observation analysis through the use of coding instruments offers a productive route for helping teachers evaluate themselves.

Teacher performance can be evaluated through the study of teaching models, the use of selected media and training packages, the use of laboratories, and the application of observation systems. With videorecording equipment in the classroom and laboratory, teachers can be helped to appraise and improve their own teaching.

Evaluation of Personal and Professional Attributes

Moving from the evaluation of cognitive and instructional skills to the areas of personal and professional attributes presents different problems. Not only is it difficult to agree on and define the personal and professional attributes teachers ought to possess, but it is also difficult to assess such attributes and, if they are found to be lacking, to effect a change in the teacher.

How does one judge relationships with administrators, for example? Should subservience be rewarded over outspokenness? How do you rate appearance? Are the teacher's memberships and participation in professional organizations of concern to administrators? If so, should the teacher be evaluated by number of memberships or by degree of participation? Is membership in a professional organization today a plus or a minus?

If teachers are to be evaluated by someone else—or by themselves—on personal and professional attributes, these traits must be clearly spelled out, and instances of behavior demonstrating the attributes must be described. The democratic approach to supervision means that teachers should be involved in deciding what personal and professional attributes will be evaluated and what evidences of these traits will be recorded. Personal and professional attributes are the most difficult to document, except in extreme cases, such as insubordination and criminal and moral offenses.

Certain personality characteristics and certain human-relations skills are necessary for success in any field, or in life as a whole, and are among the personal and professional attributes essential to successful teacher performance:

- Sense of humor.
- Ability to relate to students, other teachers, administrators, parents, and the public.
- Positive self-concept.
- Open personality.
- Use of appropriate verbal and nonverbal language.
- Respect for the individual.
- Respect for cultural differences.
- Absence of prejudice.
- Expectation for excellence.
- Respect for the confidentiality of school matters.
- Well-modulated voice.
- Cooperative attitude.
- Appropriate clothing.
- Industriousness, high energy level.
- Varied outside interests.
- Well read on current trends and issues.

The problem for the supervisor trying to help teachers evaluate their own personal and professional attributes is to find ways for teachers to reflect on their own traits, agree that there is need for improvement, and make changes accordingly. Personality traits are especially difficult to change because they are embedded in the individual's history, lifestyle, and philosophy of life.

The supervisor may once again begin with an external approach—an intellectual discussion about traits that most educators feel teachers should possess. The process of identifying these traits and agreeing on ways they can be observed are the first hurdles to be cleared. The supervisor might direct teachers to some of the literature on the development of the individual's self-concept and the meaning of the term *self-actualizing personality*, as found in the writings of Arthur W. Combs,[10] Earl C. Kelley,[11] and Abraham H. Maslow.[12]

It is in the area of personal development that consultants may be helpful to groups of teachers, if only for the purpose of bringing them inspirational messages. The use of certain personality inventories and attitude instruments, such as William C. Schutz's FIRO-B and Katherine C. Briggs and Isabel Briggs Myers's Myers-Briggs Type Indicator, may lead teachers into greater awareness of their personal traits.[13] Whereas FIRO-B explores ways individuals interact with other people, the Myers-Briggs Type Indicator focuses on the traits of extroversion versus introversion, sensation versus intuition, thinking versus feeling, and judgment versus perception.

One school of thought warmly endorses encounter groups or sensitivity training—"touchy-feely," in the vernacular—as the way for individuals to change their behavior. We have reservations about these methods because sensitivity training may have negative effects on some participants. Such training must be on a voluntary basis, free of pressure to participate, and stringently controlled and conducted by trained leaders.

This discussion of the issue of evaluating personal and professional attributes leads to two conclusions:

1. The attributes to be evaluated should cover a very limited, specifically defined, and observable set of characteristics agreed on in advance by teachers.

2. Lasting change can come about only as teachers evaluate their own behavior and internalize the necessity for change.

USING EVALUATION INSTRUMENTS

If the instructional supervisor is required to evaluate teachers periodically (e.g., annually) for reporting purposes, teachers should enter fully into the evaluation process. What some people call "goal-oriented supervision" is a valuable approach. With this approach, the teacher and supervisor agree on the areas of performance the teacher will work on during the year. When it is time for an evaluation at the end of the year, the supervisor and teacher meet and assess whether and to what degree the teacher has improved in the performance areas.

More school districts are adopting this approach to teacher observation and evaluation, which accomplishes the goal of bringing the teacher into the evaluation process. Furthermore, not requiring the teacher to demonstrate improvement across the board is much more realistic than expecting improvement in many or all performance areas.[14]

The School Board of Brevard County, Florida, has developed an in-depth instructional personnel appraisal system that is designed to incorporate and comply with provisions of Florida Statute 231.29. That system consists of observations of a teacher's performance for the purposes of formal evaluation by school administrators, district-level administrators, or other qualified persons,[15] either singularly or in combination:

- If an observer/evaluator is used who is not regularly assigned to work in the same school as the teacher being observed/evaluated, such observer/evaluator shall be identified to the teacher prior to the observation/evaluation.

- All of the formal observations shall be conducted with the knowledge of the teacher. Any observations shall be no less than twenty consecutive minutes in length and no longer than the period of time that the particular class or activity is in session, and shall be reduced to writing. The observation shall be discussed with the teacher within ten workdays following the observation and a copy of the observation record shall be given to the employee.

- The purpose of the discussions shall be for the observer/evaluator and teacher to examine the teacher's strengths and weaknesses and possible assistance to be given and means for improvement of the weaknesses and strengths. Teachers are provided a copy of all written observation records and shall be given the opportunity to submit written comments to be attached to the observation within fifteen workdays.[16]

To gather, report, and record the data required by the evaluation process, the Brevard County Schools have created instruments or forms that are reproduced here in a reduced format. The forms are available as files for use with word processors, which allows observers to enlarge the indicated spaces for comments for each of the various categories:

1. *Professional Performance Standards—Brevard County Schools.* This form (Figure 12.8) is completed during the observation and shared with the teacher. A narrative summary and comments may be attached by the observer along with comments from the teacher who was observed. Similar observation forms are available for Teachers Resource, Student Services, and Library Media. Figure 12.9 presents the form used when educators of exceptional students are observed and evaluated.

2. *Instructional Personnel Performance Appraisal System—Summary Form.* This form (Figure 12.10) is completed for all teachers on annual contract status and once every three years for all teachers who hold a continuing contract or professional services contract. The form will be used to help identify teachers who qualify for a 5 percent salary bonus under the state of Florida's Special Teachers Are Rewarded (STAR) Program (pay for performance). Instructional personnel are evaluated on the three strands of Instruction, Professional Standards, and Student Response. Teachers' uses of technology in the classroom are noted in the Instructional Organization and Development section.

3. *Instructional Personnel Performance Appraisal System—Summary Form.* This form (Figure 12.11) is used for instructional personnel who hold a continuing contract or professional services contract; it is used if the two-page form (Figure 12.10) is not required.

PROFESSIONAL PERFORMANCE STANDARDS—BREVARD COUNTY SCHOOLS

Name_____ Date_____

Name of Observer_____ Time_____

Basic Education

	Obs.
PLANNING	

a. Selected content at appropriate level of difficulty based on student's needs
b. Task-analyzed content
c. Stated learner objective and related objective to activity
d. Selected appropriate and relevant materials, activities and models
e. Selected, sequenced, organized and paced appropriate activities
f. Provided for evaluation of objective

MANAGEMENT OF STUDENT CONDUCT

a. Stops misconduct
b. Poses questions—selects one reciter from nonvolunteers as well as volunteers (manages group attention)
c. Maintains instructional momentum
d. Praises appropriate behavior

INSTRUCTIONAL ORGANIZATION AND DEVELOPMENT

a. Uses time wisely
b. Begins instruction promptly
c. Provides activities and attends students
d. Handles materials in an orderly manner
Lesson Review Summary
e. Conducts beginning review
f. Conducts topic summary within the lesson
g. Conducts ending review
Lesson Development
h. Orients student to classwork
i. Specifies objective, purpose, and activities
j. Talks on subject matter
k. Provides appropriate models as needed
Checking for Understanding
l. Uses varied questioning techniques
m. Single factual questions (input)
n. Requires analysis/reasons (process)
o. Requires speculation/predicts (output)
p. Pauses before soliciting answers to complex questions (think time)
Teacher Treatment of Student Responses
q. Recognizes response/amplifies/gives correct feedback
r. Gives corrective feedback for incorrect response
Effective Practice
s. Provides for practice
t. Gives directions/checks comprehension of homework/seatwork directions
u. Circulates and assists
v. Gives feedback on homework/seatwork

PRESENTATION OF SUBJECT MATTER

a. Treats concepts—definition, critical attributes/examples, nonexamples
b. Discusses cause-effect/uses linking words/applies law or principles
c. States and applies academic rule
d. Develops criteria and evidence for value judgment

COMMUNICATION: VERBAL/NONVERBAL

a. Speaks and uses appropriate verbal expression
b. Emphasizes important points
c. Expresses enthusiasm verbally/challenges students
d. Smiles, eye contact, body behavior that shows interest, excitement

STUDENT EVALUATION

Test Preparation
a. States purpose, importance, and use of test results
b. States content to be tested
c. Reviews test content
d. Gives test taking directions/strategies
e. Provides practice
Test Administration
f. Controls test environment (lights, temperature, noise, space)
g. Monitors while taking test
h. Attends to student needs
i. Reviews test results with students

RESPONSIBILITIES

a. Is attentive to punctuality, attendance, records, reports, and plans
b. Performs assigned duties
c. Complies with approved policies, procedures, and programs
d. Exercises professional judgment
e. Maintains appropriate classroom appearance

RELATIONSHIPS

a. Maintains a professional attitude
b. Accepts constructive criticism
c. Communicates effectively with students, parents, and staff

KNOWLEDGE OF SUBJECT MATTER

a. Demonstrates knowledge of subject matter
b. Participates in inservice
c. Seeks opportunities for professional growth
d. Shares professional knowledge and expertise with others
e. Is open to utilizing new ideas

Observation Summary:

FIGURE 12.8 Professional Performance Standards Form—Basic Education. *Source*: School Board of Brevard County, Florida, Instructional Personnel Performance Appraisal System (Brevard County, Fla.: Human Resources Services, April 2000), p. 45. Reprinted with permission of the Brevard County Schools.

PROFESSIONAL PERFORMANCE STANDARDS—BREVARD COUNTY SCHOOLS

Name_____ Date_____

Name of Observer_____ Time_____

Exceptional Student Education

PLANNING   Obs.

a. Selects and uses assessment instruments to develop student profiles and write objectives
b. Incorporates the goals of other professionals (OT,PPT,S/L,VI,HI) in the daily schedule
c. Schedules for classroom, group, and individual
d. Provides for physical management of a medically fragile student
e. Uses a curriculum guide to determine instructional objectives that are both developmentally appropriate and functionally useful
f. Lesson plans are reflective of the IEP objectives

MANAGEMENT OF STUDENT CONDUCT

a. Classroom rules and consequences are posted
b. Stops misconduct
c. Maintains instructional momentum
d. Uses a behavior management plan for controlling aberrant behavior
e. Attends to two instructional tasks simultaneously
f. Gives short, clear, nonacademic directions
g. Reinforces appropriate performance through specific praise statements

INSTRUCTIONAL ORGANIZATION

a. Begins instruction promptly
b. Handles materials in an orderly manner
c. Orients students to classwork/maintains academic focus
d. Conducts beginning and ending review
e. Questions: single factual
f. Pauses before soliciting answers
g. Recognizes response/amplifies/gives correct feedback
h. Gives specific academic praise
i. Circulates and assists students
j. Uses a range or sequence of instructional cueing and prompting in a hierarchical fashion
k. Maximizes time in instruction by continually scheduling students in direct instruction

PRESENTATION OF SUBJECT MATTER   Obs.

a. Instructs, supervises, provides feedback, orchestrates use of teacher assistance in the classroom.
b. States concept and definition
c. Points out distinctive features of new concepts
d. Models a behavioral response or steps of a procedure in procedural learning
e. Provides for practice
f. Uses error correction procedure (prompts or models) rather than tell answer
g. Follows correct academic response with specific praise

COMMUNICATION

a. Repeats important points
b. Expresses verbal enthusiasm
c. States single question
d. Smiles, eye contact, body behavior that shows interest, excitement

STUDENT EVALUATION

a. Maintains records or graphs of student progress
b. Uses assessment instruments that would analyze both developmental levels and functional abilities
c. Performance appraisal on report cards are directly related to classroom records of progress

RESPONSIBILITIES

a. Is attentive to punctuality, attendance, records, reports and plans
b. Performs assigned duties
c. Complies with approved policies, procedures, and programs
d. Exercises professional judgment
e. Maintains appropriate classroom appearance

RELATIONSHIPS

a. Maintains a professional attitude
b. Accepts constructive criticism
c. Communicates effectively with students, parents, and staff

KNOWLEDGE OF SUBJECT MATTER

a. Demonstrates knowledge of subject matter
b. Participates in inservice
c. Seeks opportunities for professional growth
d. Shares professional knowledge and expertise with others
e. Is open to utilizing new ideas

Observation Summary:

FIGURE 12.9 Professional Performance Standards Form—Exceptional Student Education. *Source*: School Board of Brevard County, Florida, Instructional Personnel Performance Appraisal System (Brevard County, Fla.: Human Resources Services, April 2000), p. 49. Reprinted with permission of the Brevard County Schools.

SCHOOL BOARD OF BREVARD COUNTY
INSTRUCTIONAL PERSONNEL PERFORMANCE APPRAISAL SYSTEM
SUMMARY FORM 2006-2007

Name _____ **School/Dept** _____
        Last   First   MI   Name   Number

Assignment _____ **School Year** **2006-2007** **Contract Status** AC ☐ CC or PSC ☐

Principal/Department Head _____ **Type of Evaluation** Interim ☐ Annual ☐

PERFORMANCE AREAS	RATINGS

A. INSTRUCTIONAL STRAND (*Must be completed for all certificated employees*):

1. Planning

Pre-classroom activities that develop schemata for classroom activities. (Content coverage, utilization of materials, activity structure, goal focusing, and diagnosis)

Unsatisfactory ☐   Needs Improvement ☐   Satisfactory ☐   High Performing ☐   Outstanding ☐

2. Instructional Organization and Development

Teacher performance that provides for conservation of class time. organization and delivery of instruction, use of technology in the classroom. and teacher-student interaction. (Efficient use of time, review, lesson development, treatment of student talk. feedback, and management of seatwork/homework)

Unsatisfactory ☐   Needs Improvement ☐   Satisfactory ☐   High Performing ☐   Outstanding ☐

3. Presentation of Subject Matter

Developing the content of instruction to influence learning; using and documenting ESOL strategies, when appropriate. (Presenting concepts, laws or law-like principles, academic rules, and value knowledge)

Unsatisfactory ☐   Needs Improvement ☐   Satisfactory ☐   High Performing ☐   Outstanding ☐

4. Instructional Communication

Verbal, nonverbal, and written behavior that evokes and expresses information. (Control of discourse, emphasis, task attraction, and challenge; speech and body language)

Unsatisfactory ☐   Needs Improvement ☐   Satisfactory ☐   High Performing ☐   Outstanding ☐

B. PROFESSIONAL STANDARDS STRAND (*Must be completed for all certificated employees*):

1. Knowledge of Subject Matter

Demonstrates an acceptable level of knowledge and willingness to actively participate in staff development activities; is open to and shares new ideas; shows evidence of growth.

Unsatisfactory ☐   Needs Improvement ☐   Satisfactory ☐   High Performing ☐   Outstanding ☐

2. Responsibilities

Teacher actions that demonstrate attention to punctuality, attendance, records, and reports; performance of assigned duties, compliance with policies, procedures, programs, and the Code of Ethics; is dependable and exercises appropriate professional judgment; develops and implements an appropriate Professional Development Plan.

Unsatisfactory ☐   Needs Improvement ☐   Satisfactory ☐   High Performing ☐   Outstanding ☐

3. Relationships

Maintains professional relations and attitude; communicates effectively with students, parents, and staff: accepts constructive criticism; establishes and maintains a positive, collaborative relationship with students' families to increase student achievement.

Unsatisfactory ☐   Needs Improvement ☐   Satisfactory ☐   High Performing ☐   Outstanding ☐

Initials: Administrator _____ **Employee** _____

(continued)

FIGURE 12.10 Professional Performance Standards Form—Summary Form. *Source*: School Board of Brevard County, Florida, Instructional Personnel Performance Appraisal System (Brevard County, Fla.: Human Resources Services, August 2006), pp. 40–41. Reprinted with permission of the Brevard County Schools.

C. STUDENT RESPONSE STRAND *(Must be completed for classroom teachers and other professionals who are responsible for providing direct instruction to students)*:

1. Management of Student Conduct

Teacher actions that minimize the frequency of disruptive student behavior. (Rules, teacher awareness, quality of desist, group alert, movement, smoothness/slowdown, and praise)

Unsatisfactory ☐   **Needs Improvement** ☐   **Satisfactory** ☐   **High Performing** ☐   **Outstanding** ☐

2. Student Evaluation

Development and maintenance of an environment in which student can validly demonstrate knowledge, skills, etc. and receive adequate information about the quality of their test performance; makes data-driven decisions regarding student performance. (Test preparation, administration, and formative feedback).

Unsatisfactory ☐   **Needs Improvement** ☐   **Satisfactory** ☐   **High Performing** ☐   **Outstanding** ☐

D. OVERALL EVALUATION *(Comments Required)*:

Unsatisfactory ☐   **Needs Improvement** ☐   **Satisfactory** ☐   **High Performing** ☐   **Outstanding** ☐

_____ / _____

Signature of Principal/Administrative Supervisor (Required) (Blue Ink Only)   Date

_____ / _____

Signature of Assistant Principal (Blue Ink Only)   Date

Teacher Comments *(Optional)*:

_____

_____

_____

My signature indicates that this evaluation has been discussed with me:

_____ / _____

Signature of Employee (Blue Ink Only)   Date

FIGURE 12.10 *(continued)*

    4. *Professional Development Assistance Form.* This form (Figure 12.12) is required when any of the ratings in the performance areas are unsatisfactory. This form is designed to provide specific strategies and suggestions for improvement in the areas noted as deficient. Specific teaching behaviors that are to be acquired, improved, or deleted are recorded.[17]

    The last performance area of each of the respective summative forms is an overall rating. Consistent with the requirement of law or rule, any individual whose performance is rated overall unsatisfactory for two consecutive years is referred to the Professional Practices Services for their review. In cases where the rating of instructional performance of an employee is deficient enough to affect the employee's contract status, the N.E.A.T. Procedures (Figure 12.13) are applied, reflecting management's recognition that dismissal may be necessary and, accordingly, due process must be followed. The district feels that every case is unique and must be evaluated on its own merit; thus, a defined series of forms is not used. Instead, a series of management communication documents is required. The

SCHOOL BOARD OF BREVARD COUNTY
INSTRUCTIONAL PERSONNEL PERFORMANCE APPRAISAL SYSTEM
SUMMARY FORM

Name _____ School Year _____
Last   First   MI

Department/School _____ Principal/Department Head _____
Name   Number

Assignment _____

Instructional personnel who hold a **Continuing Contract or Professional Services Contract** shall be evaluated on the standard, two-page summary form once every three years as a minimum. This summary form may be used when the two-page form is not required. Performance area ratings are based on the standard, two-page form.

_____ has rendered overall effective performance.

Summary Statement (*Required*):

_____ / _____
Signature of Principal/Administrative Supervisor (Required)   Date

_____ / _____
Signature of Assistant Principal   Date

Teacher Comments (*Optional*):
_____
_____
_____
_____

My signature indicates that this evaluation has been discussed with me:

_____ / _____
Signature of Employee   Date

FIGURE 12.11   Professional Performance Standards Form—Summary Form. *Source*: School Board of Brevard County, Florida, Instructional Personnel Performance Appraisal System (Brevard County, Fla.: Human Resources Services, April 2000), p. 44. Reprinted with permission of the Brevard County Schools.

employee's rights of procedural due process are guaranteed when the steps in Figure 12.13 are followed.

The overall purpose of the Brevard County Personnel Performance Appraisal System is to ensure that educational excellence is provided through quality instructional performance. The district views the employee appraisal system as a year-long planned sequence of activities designed to assist individuals in identifying and reaching their individual goals and aspirations through goal setting and feedback components. Through this process, the district hopes to support the continuing growth of high morale and effective instruction.

SCHOOL BOARD OF BREVARD COUNTY

PROFESSIONAL DEVELOPMENT ASSISTANCE FORM

Teacher's Name _____

Principal/Supervising Administrator's Name _____

Performance Area

Specific Behaviors

Strategies for Improvement

Assistance

Date for Follow Up Review _____   Completion Date _____

_____/_____   _____/_____
Teacher's Signature   Date   Administrator's Signature   Date

---

FIGURE 12.12 Professional Development Assistance Form. *Source*: School Board of Brevard County, Florida, Instructional Personnel Performance Appraisal System (Brevard County, Fla.: Human Resources Services, April 2000), p. 50. Reprinted with permission of the Brevard County Schools.

N.E.A.T. Procedures

N - Notice	Written *notice* to the individual that specific deficiencies exist which, if not corrected, would lead to dismissal procedures.
E - Explanation	Full and complete *explanation* of the specific performance deficiencies with suggested methods of correction.
A - Assistance	A written description of the management *assistance* which is to be offered and provided.
T - Time	A written, specific *time* frame which is reasonable in nature to provide for the correction of identified deficiencies.

FIGURE 12.13 N.E.A.T. Procedures. *Source*: School Board of Brevard County, Florida, Instructional Performance Appraisal System (Brevard County, Fla.: Human Resources Services, April 2000), p. 4. Reprinted with permission of the Brevard County Schools.

STUDENT EVALUATIONS

More frequently than in days gone by, the recipients of instruction—the learners—are being asked to give their reactions to the teacher's performance. Learners can provide insights into instruction that cannot be gained otherwise.

Conscientious teachers seek the counsel of their students about the effectiveness of their instruction. They want to know whether students perceive that they have learned. Student evaluations of the instructor and the instruction provide one more source of data about the effectiveness of teaching. These evaluations may become more important as the multicultural makeup of many classrooms continues to be the norm in many school districts.

Teachers at all levels should be encouraged by their supervisors to solicit student reactions to their performance. Student evaluations should be gathered anonymously (or as anonymously as possible, given the teacher's intimate knowledge of the students' handwriting). The use of forms that have students mark their choices of responses from a list would keep the responses anonymous.

Supervisors should help teachers fashion student evaluation instruments if the teachers feel the need for such help. Instruments may be simple checklists or rating scales. A place for comments can allow for observations that students may wish to make. The comments section, if handwritten, however, is where the learners are most likely to reveal their identity by the distinctiveness of their writing. If possible, the handwritten responses can be typed on a summary sheet to reduce the possibility of identifying remarks from individual students. Teachers must be professional enough not to retaliate for negative comments they are able to ascribe to a particular student. To reduce the potential threat implicit in student evaluations, the results should be available to the teacher only for his or her own guidance and should be revealed to others only if the teacher decides to do so.

The results should be given close attention, but at the same time, teachers should realize that student evaluations represent the learners' perceptions of instruction and not their actual achievement. Perceptions, however, are extremely important and must be dealt with. Thus, if the majority of learners feel, for example, that the teacher's grading system is unfair, the teacher needs to decide whether there is merit to the criticism. If the teacher agrees that the students have justification for their beliefs, he or she can modify the system. If the teacher finds that criticisms are not accurate, he or she should spend some time explaining the rationale for the grading procedures.

Institutions of higher education have gathered student evaluations of faculty performance for years. In colleges and universities, the results of student evaluations are regularly shared with the faculty member and his or her administrative superiors and become a part of the documentation required for decisions on merit increases in salary, promotion, and tenure.

Following the movements for student rights, teacher accountability, and student participation in governance, the public schools have begun to establish procedures for collecting student reactions to instruction. Student input about teacher performance is being sought at all school levels.

MIAMI SOUTHRIDGE SENIOR HIGH SCHOOL

Student Evaluation of Classroom Instruction

PURPOSE: To provide your teachers with information that will be useful in improving classroom instruction.

Directions: Check the space that you feel best describes the classroom atmosphere. Be fair and honest. You do <u>not</u> have to sign your name. (This is a voluntary exercise.)

	Always	Often	Seldom	Never
1. The classroom atmosphere is free from bias and prejudice.	_____	_____	_____	_____
2. The lessons are clear and well organized.	_____	_____	_____	_____
3. The lessons and assignments have meaning and are purposeful.	_____	_____	_____	_____
4. Student participation in class discussions is encouraged.	_____	_____	_____	_____
5. Individual help is available when needed.	_____	_____	_____	_____
6. The students have the right to express their own opinions on controversial issues without jeopardizing relations with the teacher.	_____	_____	_____	_____
7. My personal rights as a student are respected.	_____	_____	_____	_____
8. All tests are graded and reviewed. Questions regarding the test are answered.	_____	_____	_____	_____
9. The classroom discipline is fair, consistent, and encourages learning.	_____	_____	_____	_____
10. The test schedule is announced and adhered to.	_____	_____	_____	_____
11. A variety of teaching methods is used in classroom instruction.	_____	_____	_____	_____

12. The attendance procedures and classroom policies are clearly explained at the beginning of the semester.   Yes _____   No _____

13. The grading policy is explained at the beginning of each semester.   Yes _____   No _____

14. The students are notified of unsatisfactory progress with sufficient time for corrective action.   Yes _____   No _____

COMMENTS: _____

_____

THANK YOU!

FIGURE 12.14 Student Evaluation of Classroom Instruction. *Source*: Dade County Public Schools, Student Evaluation of Classroom Instruction (Miami, Fla.: Miami Southridge Senior High School). Reprinted with permission of the Dade County Public Schools.

A sample student evaluation form is shown in Figure 12.14. This checklist was formerly used by senior high school students from Miami Southridge Senior High School, in Miami, Florida, but could serve as a starting point for others to consider.

Students can provide valuable insights about the course, the instruction, and the instructor. Though somewhat threatening to teachers at first, student evaluations can become a valuable tool in the improvement of instruction.

Students may already be rating their teachers through the online site "Rate My Teacher."[18] Caution should be exerted in frequenting this site because the student evaluations are usually done away from the school setting and often result in negative comments.

PARENT EVALUATIONS

Schools involve parents in a variety of ways, such as serving on School Advisory Committees (SACs), School Improvement Committees (SICs), and PTAs, working as volunteer aides, and expressing their views on curricular needs, but schools rarely seek parents' feedback about teacher performance in any systematic fashion. Many schools are required to poll parents about what they think about the instructional skills of their children's teachers, and such polls could take the form of questionnaires modeled on student questionnaires, with such items as:

- My child's teacher enjoys teaching.
- My child's teacher is patient and understanding.
- My child's teacher is fair when students misbehave.
- My child's teacher gives clear directions and explanations.
- My child's teacher seeks my advice concerning my child.
- My child's teacher keeps me informed about my child's progress.
- My child's teacher is available to discuss my child's progress.

This dimension of evaluation is lacking in many school systems, but this situation is changing as the impact of accountability on state evaluation of schools increases. As technology continues to play a more prominent part in a school's total operation, school administrators may begin to include online surveys for parents to complete. One such secure survey type (SurveyMonkey) is used by advanced graduate students as they complete their thesis or dissertation.[19] The solicitation of anonymous parent evaluations about teacher performance is a path lightly trod in the evaluation of instruction. In seeking parents' opinions, we must keep in mind, as in the case of student evaluations, that parent evaluations are perceptions that may or may not be accurate. Nevertheless, both student and parent evaluations can help teachers evaluate themselves.

SUMMARY

Supervisors effect changes in instruction as they help teachers evaluate themselves. The supervisor must master a variety of techniques for getting teachers to look at their own behavior. An external approach is recommended as a step to be taken prior to an internal approach—the provision of opportunities for teachers to analyze their own performances. Teacher evaluation systems should include three components: self-appraisal, formative evaluation during the year, and summative or annual evaluation.

Competencies that school systems consider important enough to be evaluated tend to fall within two major categories: instructional skills and personal and professional attributes. Techniques for evaluating instructional skills include an examination of models of teaching; the use of protocol materials, videorecordings, and teacher-training packages; and the application of observational analysis systems.

Teacher self-appraisal should be the goal of efforts to evaluate teaching competency. Self-appraisal can be realized through videorecording in the classroom or clinic. Clinical approaches—peer teaching and microteaching—offer the opportunity to try out new techniques and skills in a controlled learning situation.

Personal and professional attributes are difficult to identify and evaluate. Agreement of the faculty on the personal and professional traits that should be evaluated, and how they will be assessed is essential. Self-evaluation of personal and professional characteristics may be initiated by a review of the literature on personality development and by the use of selected personal attitude inventories.

In addition to teachers' appraisals of their own performance, student and parent evaluations of instruction can aid teachers in analyzing their own behavior and making needed improvements.

Many school systems require supervisors to evaluate teachers periodically. The supervisor is advised to institute a goal-oriented evaluative process whereby the supervisor and teacher agree on the teacher's job targets for the year and also agree to monitor and evaluate these jointly. Although the supervisor may evaluate *teachers*, his or her primary role should be helping teachers to evaluate *themselves*. Changes in behavior, whether in instructional skills or in personal and professional attributes, can come about only if the teacher sees the need for change and agrees to try to improve.

QUESTIONS FOR DISCUSSION

1. How would you work with teachers to be sure there is a teacher in every classroom who cares that every student, every day, learns and grows and feels like a real human being?

2. Which of the ten models of teaching presented in this chapter do you use most frequently and also advocate? Be ready to discuss your choice.

3. Which of the observation systems presented in this chapter do you think would yield the most information for a supervisor and teachers? Why?

4. What would you include in a teacher self-appraisal form you would use with teachers?

5. What use can supervisors make of protocol materials?

ACTIVITIES FOR FURTHER STUDY

REFLECTIVE

1. Choose one of the models of teaching found in Bruce Joyce, Marsha Weil, and Emily Calhoun, *Models of Teaching*, 7th ed., and describe its characteristics and uses.

2. Write a paper analyzing the model of teaching you use most frequently. Include the type of teaching setting you work in and the type(s) of students in your classroom.

3. Preview a protocol material and write a brief evaluation of its effectiveness in bringing out the particular point it aims to portray.

4. Draft a proposal describing personal and professional attributes that you feel should be evaluated and how they would be assessed.

5. Obtain samples of teacher-training packages and analyze their suitability as materials for studying the teaching act.

APPLICATION

1. Create a classification system for retrieval of protocol materials.

2. Employ videorecording equipment and create a protocol, identifying the behavior shown in the protocol.

3. Develop a plan for a clinical laboratory, with complete specifications for equipment, including costs.

4. Prepare a five-minute lesson to demonstrate one generic teaching skill, have it videorecorded, watch the recording of your performance, select and apply an observation instrument, and present a critique of your own performance.

5. Select an observation instrument and train a teacher to use it to analyze (a) a film or videorecording of another teacher teaching and (b) a recording of the teacher instructing students.

6. Using appropriate visual materials, prepare a presentation on the Flanders Interaction Analysis Categories.

7. Create and, if you are teaching, use an instrument for student evaluation of your teaching performance.

8. Create and, if you are teaching, use an instrument for parent evaluation of your teaching performance.

NOTES

1. Bruce Joyce and Marsha Weil with Beverly Showers, *Models of Teaching*, 6th ed. (Boston: Allyn and Bacon, 1999).
2. Ibid.
3. National Resource and Dissemination Center, *Protocol Materials for Use in Preservice and Inservice Teacher Education*, Tampa, Fla., n.d., unnumbered page 1. Center is no longer operating.
4. B. Othanel Smith, Saul B. Cohen, and Arthur Pearl, *Teachers for the Real World* (Washington, D.C.: American Association of Colleges for Teacher Education, 1969), p. 63.
5. Ibid.
6. Ibid., pp. 51–52.
7. Jim Horne, Commissioner of Education, Florida, online document available at www.flboe.org.
8. *WILKITS* (Ogden, Utah: Weber State College).
9. Smith, Cohen, and Pearl, *Teachers for the Real World*, p. 55.
10. Arthur W. Combs, *Individual Behavior: A Perceptual Approach*, rev. ed. (New York: Harper and Row, 1959).
11. Earl C. Kelley, *Education for What Is Real* (New York: Harper and Row, 1947).
12. Abraham H. Maslow, *Motivation and Personality*, 2nd ed. (New York: Harper and Row, 1970).
13. William C. Schutz, *FIRO-B* (Palo Alto, Calif.: Consulting Psychologists Press, 1957). See also William C. Schutz, *FIRO: A Three Dimensional Theory of Interpersonal Behavior* (New York: Holt, Rinehart and Winston, 1958); Katherine C. Briggs and Isabel Briggs Myers, *Myers-Briggs Type Indicator* (Palo Alto, Calif.: Consulting Psychologists Press, 1983).
14. For specification of the objectives of the individual within the framework of the objectives of the institution, see some of the literature on management by objectives, such as John William Humble, ed., *Management by Objectives in Action* (New York: McGraw-Hill, 1970); George S. Odiorne, *Management by Objectives: A System of Managerial Leadership* (New York: Pitman, 1965); and Robert O. Riggs, "Management by Objectives: Its Utilization in the Management of Administrative Performance," *Contemporary Education* 63 (January 1972): 129–33. See also Robert E. Boston and David A. Spencer, *Management by Objectives* (Minneapolis, Minn.: Amidon, 1973).
15. School Board of Brevard County, Florida, *Instructional Personnel Performance Appraisal System* (Brevard County, Fla.: Human Resources Services, revised September, 1999).

16. Ibid., p. 3.
17. Ibid., p. 37.
18. Rate My Teacher Web site: www.ratemyteacher.com.
19. SurveyMonkey Web site: www.surveymonkey.com.

BIBLIOGRAPHY

AIRASIAN, PETER W., and ARLEN R. GULLICKSON. *Teacher Self-Evaluation Tool Kit*. Thousand Oaks, Calif.: Corwin Press, 1997.

ALLEN, DWIGHT, and KEVIN RYAN. *Microteaching*. Reading, Mass.: Addison-Wesley, 1969.

ALLEN, PAUL M., WILLIAM D. BARNES, JERALD L. REECE, and E. WAYNE ROBERSON. *Teacher Self-Appraisal: A Way of Looking over Your Own Shoulder*. Worthington, Ohio: C. A. Jones, 1970.

AMIDON, EDMUND J., and NED A. FLANDERS. *The Role of the Teacher in the Classroom: A Manual for Understanding and Improving Classroom Behavior*, rev. ed. Minneapolis. Minn.: Association for Productive Teaching, 1971.

AMIDON, EDMUND J., and JOHN B. HOUGH, eds. *Interaction Analysis: Theory, Research, and Application*. Reading, Mass.: Addison-Wesley, 1967.

AMIDON, EDMUND J., and ELIZABETH HUNTER. *Improving Teaching: The Analysis of Classroom Verbal Interaction*. New York: Holt, Rinehart and Winston, 1966.

BELLACK, ARNO A., H. M. KLIEBARD, R. T. HYMAN, and F. L. SMITH Jr. *The Language of the Classroom*. New York: Teachers College Press, 1966.

BOSTON, ROBERT E., and DAVID A. SPENCER. *Management by Objectives*. Minneapolis, Minn.: Amidon, 1973.

Brevard Public Schools. *Instructional Personnel Performance Appraisal System*. Brevard County, Fla.: Human Resources Services, 1999.

BRIGGS, KATHERINE C., and ISABEL BRIGGS MYERS. *Myers-Briggs Type Indicator*. Palo Alto, Calif.: Consulting Psychologists Press, 1983.

BRIGGS, LESLIE J. *The Use and Evaluation of "Protocol" Materials in Teacher Education Program*. Tallahassee, Fla.: State Department of Education, 1971.

BROPHY, JERE E., and THOMAS L. GOOD. *Teacher-Child Dyadic Interaction: A Manual for Coding Classroom Behavior*. Austin: University of Texas, 1969.

COMBS, ARTHUR W. *The Professional Education of Teachers: A Perceptual View of Teacher Preparation*. Boston: Allyn and Bacon, 1965.

———, ed. *Perceiving, Behaving, Becoming: A New Focus for Education*, 1962 Yearbook. Alexandria, Va.: Association for Supervision and Curriculum Development, 1962.

COSTA, ARTHUR L., and ROBERT J. GAMSTON. *Cognitive Coaching: A Foundation for Renaissance Schools*, 2nd ed. Norwood, Mass.: Christopher-Gordon, 2002.

DIETZ, MARY E. "Using Portfolios as a Framework for Professional Development." *Journal of Staff Development* 16 (Spring 1995): 40–43.

FLANDERS, NED A. *Analyzing Teaching Behavior*. Reading, Mass.: Addison-Wesley, 1970.

———. *Interaction Analysis: Teacher Handbook*. San Francisco: Far West Laboratory for Educational Research and Development, 1972.

Florida Department of Education. *B-2 Teacher Education Modules*. Chipley, Fla.: Panhandle Area Educational Cooperative, n.d.

HARTZELL, GARY N. "Helping Administrators Learn to Avoid Seven Common Employee Appraisal Errors." *Journal of Staff Development* 16 (Spring 1995): 32–37.

HUMBLE, JOHN WILLIAM, ed. *Management by Objectives in Action*. New York: McGraw-Hill, 1970.

HUNTER, MADELINE. "Teacher Competency: Problem, Theory, and Practice." *Theory into Practice* 15 (April 1976): 162–71.

JENSEN, RUSSELL N., DARLEEN VIDEEN, and CHARLES F. GRUBBS. *Teacher Self-Appraisal Program, 1967–68*. Tucson, Ariz.: Research and Development, Tucson Public Schools, July 1968.

JOYCE, BRUCE R., and MARSHA WEIL, with EMILY CALHOUN. *Models of Teaching*, 7th ed. Boston: Allyn and Bacon, 2004.

KELLEY, EARL C. *Education for What Is Real*. New York: Harper, 1947.

MARTIN-KNIEP, GISELLE O. *Becoming a Better Teacher: Eight Innovations That Work*. Alexandria, Va.: Association for Supervision and Curriculum Development, 2000.

MASLOW, ABRAHAM H. *Motivation and Personality*, 3rd ed. New York: Harper and Row, 1987.

———. *Toward a Psychology of Being*, 3rd ed. New York: Wiley, 1999.

National Resource and Dissemination Center. *Protocol Materials for Use in Preservice and Inservice Teacher Education*. Tampa, Fla.: National Resource and Dissemination Center, n.d. (Center is no longer operating.)

ODIORNE, GEORGE S. *Management by Objectives: A System of Managerial Leadership*. New York: Pitman, 1965.

PAJAK, EDWARD. *Approaches to Clinical Supervision: Alternatives for Improving Instruction*, 2nd ed. Norwood, Mass.: Christopher-Gordon, 2000.

PETERSON, PENELOPE L., and HERBERT J. WALBERG, eds. *Research on Teaching: Concepts, Findings, and Implications*. Berkeley, Calif.: McCutchan, 1979.

RIGGS, ROBERT O. "Management by Objectives: Its Utilization in the Management of Administrative Performance." *Contemporary Education* 63 (January 1972): 129–33.

ROBERSON, E. WAYNE. *A Manual for Utilizing the Teacher Self-Appraisal Observation System*. Tucson, Ariz.: Educational Innovators Press, 1973.

———. *The Preparation of an Instrument for the Analysis of Teacher Classroom Behavior*. Tucson: University of Arizona, 1967.

SCHUTZ, WILLIAM C. *FIRO-B*. Palo Alto, Calif.: Consulting Psychologists Press, 1957.

———. *FIRO: A Three Dimensional Theory of Interpersonal Behavior*, 3rd ed. Muir Beach, Calif.: WSA (Will Schutz Associates), 1998.

SIMON, ANITA, and E. GIL BOYER. *Mirrors for Behavior III: An Anthology of Observation Instruments*, 3rd ed. Philadelphia: Research for Better Schools, 1974.

SMITH, B. OTHANEL, SAUL B. COHEN, and ARTHUR PEARL. *Teachers for the Real World*. Washington, D.C.: American Association of Colleges for Teacher Education, 1970.

STANLEY, SARAH J., and JAMES W. POPHAM, eds. *Teacher Evaluation: Six Prescriptions for Success*. Alexandria, Va.: Association for Supervision and Curriculum Development, 1988.

WITTROCK, MERLIN C., ed. *Handbook of Research on Teaching*, 3rd ed. New York: Macmillan, 1986.

INVENTORIES

KATHERINE C. BRIGGS and ISABEL BRIGGS MYERS. Myers-Briggs Type Indicator. 1983. Inventory of traits of extroversion versus introversion, sensation versus intuition, thinking versus feeling, and judgment versus perception. CPP, Inc., 1055 Joaquin Road, 2nd Floor, Mountain View, CA 94043.(800) 624–1765.

WILLIAM C. SCHUTZ, *FIRO-B*. 1957. Survey of interpersonal skills. CPP, Inc., 1055 Joaquin Road, 2nd Floor, Mountain View, CA 94043.(800) 624–1765.

VIDEOTAPE

The Teacher Series. 2001. The six videotapes are a comprehensive resource for providing new and experienced teachers in all grade levels the guidance and support they need to meet the complex and ever-changing challenges of the teaching profession. Association for Supervision and Curriculum Development, 1703 N. Beauregard Street, Alexandria, Va. 22311–1714, (800) 933–2723;www.ascd.org.

PART V

THE SUMMATIVE DIMENSION OF TEACHER EVALUATION

Robert Kalman/The Image Works

CHAPTER 13

SUMMATIVE ASSESSMENT OF TEACHER PERFORMANCE

OBJECTIVES

After studying Chapter 13 you should be able to accomplish the following objectives:

1. Define summative evaluation as applied to teacher performance.
2. Distinguish between administrative assessment and clinical supervision.
3. Describe the principal's role in summative evaluation.
4. Describe the instructional supervisor's role, if any, in summative evaluation.
5. Describe how to collect data for purposes of summative evaluation.
6. State what teacher behaviors should be administratively assessed. Defend your choice of behaviors.
7. Describe how you would assess each behavior that you believe should be assessed.
8. Distinguish between and write competencies, indicators, and descriptors.
9. Select or create and apply, if required by the job, an instrument by which the administrator may assess teacher performance.

SUMMATIVE EVALUATION

Summative evaluation, as the term is used in this chapter, is the overall assessment of teacher performance made by the administrator (or the administrator and others) that culminates in a comprehensive appraisal either annually or as otherwise required by the state or locality. Included within the concept of summative evaluation are the periodic (some would say formative) evaluations made during the year for the purpose of collecting data with which to make the summative appraisal at the end of the year. Jerry J. Bellon and Elner C. Bellon, for example, postulated three formative observational phases of classroom supervision (see Chapter 10). They also called attention to a fourth phase of the supervisory process: the Evaluation Program, during which the data from periodic formative evaluations form the basis for the annual or summative evaluation.[1]

We considered titling this chapter "Helping Teachers through Assessment of Performance." Yet in reality, there is some question about the degree to which teachers benefit from summative evaluations, even though some educators claim that the purpose of summative assessment is the improvement of instruction. On receipt of their "report cards" (copies of the principal's written reports of the periodic and summative appraisals), if they have earned "passing grades," many teachers simply file the reports away and wait for the next one.

Some educators attribute the lack of help in evaluation systems to misuse of the process. Arthur Shaw took this position when he said, "Evaluation is often dreaded by principals, feared by teachers, and seldom utilized by school districts for the purposes for which it was intended—the improvement of instruction and the subsequent facilitation of learning."[2]

Actually, effective, conscientious, professional teachers will try out the administrator's recommendations if they feel the suggestions are sound. Ineffective teachers who receive low ratings are forced to attempt to make improvements in their teaching if they wish to maintain their positions. Thus, summative or administrative assessment does have as a goal the improvement of instruction. It might be said that the system succeeds in this goal to some degree despite itself.

The major purpose of administrative assessment of teachers, however, lies in another direction. *Summative evaluation* is essentially a necessary exercise in personnel, not instructional, management. Whereas the primary purpose of *formative evaluation* as carried out in clinical supervision, for example, is to improve the teacher's instructional skills, the main purpose of summative evaluation is to provide input for making decisions about personnel. Both formative and summative evaluation have as their ultimate purpose improvement in student learning.

On the college level, annual evaluations of faculty are made for the purpose of deciding on tenure, promotion, and salary increments. On the public school level, the decisions to be made primarily concern retention, including tenure or continuation of contract and dismissal or termination of contract. Occasionally, summative evaluations are used for making decisions about transferring teachers to other schools or assigning them other responsibilities—for example, team leader, grade coordinator, lead teacher, department head, teacher on special assignment, and workshop staff.

Although almost any evaluation system has to some degree the improvement of instruction as its purpose, summative evaluation ultimately aims to rid the profession of incompetent teachers. As such, summative evaluation is a necessary function of administration. True, effective (however defined) teachers may take to heart suggestions made in the evaluation for improving instruction. True, ineffective (however defined) teachers may be pressured by the administrator to undergo some remedial training to remedy deficiencies. But the bottom line—which gives summative evaluation an aura of threat—is the potential for dismissal. Even the mere existence of written evaluations that are good to excellent but less than perfect is cause for concern to teachers who know that personnel files can dog them the same way cumulative records can hound students. A careless, inaccurate, or biased comment by an evaluator can be a source of both professional and psychological harm to the teacher.

You may well ask why, if summative assessment is a personnel rather than an instructional matter, a chapter on the subject is included in this textbook. We offer the following reasons:

1. In some schools, particularly small ones, the principal is the instructional supervisor. He or she takes on responsibilities for both formative and summative evaluation, combining the functions—a difficult assignment!

2. In some school systems the instructional (staff) supervisor is either charged with the responsibility for both formative and summative evaluation, even though the administrator may actually sign the year-end assessment report or is called on to participate with the administrator and/or others in the summative evaluation process.

3. Instructional supervisors and administrators must be able to distinguish between the purposes and processes of formative and summative evaluation of teachers.

4. Both staff and line supervisors owe it to the profession, to teachers, to students, to the public, and to themselves, to make the summative assessment of teachers as fair, meaningful, and constructive as possible, basing it on the evidence presented by the formative evaluations.

5. The summative evaluation process should be coordinated with the processes of teacher self-appraisal and formative evaluation.

In evaluating teachers for personnel purposes, school systems must provide answers to the following questions:

- Who should be evaluated?
- Who should do the evaluating?
- What should be evaluated?
- How should the evaluations be done?
- How should the data be used?

Answers to these questions at first appear deceptively simple, but they are not. Our decentralized system of education has produced a variety of answers; we provide our own answer later in this chapter as we examine each of these questions.

Perry A. Zirkel reported that, as early as 1980, "fewer than half ($n = 23$) of the states have statutes or administrative regulations directly dealing with the evaluation of public school teachers."[3] Zirkel's later research revealed that thirty-four states had enacted either legislation or regulations dealing with the evaluation of public school teachers.[4] It comes as a surprise to learn that some states have no established regulations to control a process so fundamental to education as the evaluation of teachers. Zirkel noted that even in the majority of states with teacher evaluation laws, the local level is "the primary locus for establishing the policies and procedures for teacher evaluation."[5] As a result, the responsibility for establishing policies about teacher evaluation falls on the local boards of education. In some states "the input of local teachers is provided for in the form of either advice (Arizona, California), consultation (Nevada, Oklahoma), or negotiation (Connecticut)."[6] In contrast, the state of Georgia, for example, has mandated annual evaluation of performance of all school personnel and has developed model instruments, model processes, and technical assistance for local units of administration.[7] Thus, responsibility for establishing procedures for the evaluation of school personnel is shared by the state and local levels.

Zirkel pointed out that local regulations must conform to state minimum statutory standards and that both state and local regulations must abide by federal constitutional and statutory provisions. These include the First and Fourteenth Amendments, the Civil Rights Act of 1964, Section 504 of the Rehabilitation Act of 1973, and the Age Discrimination in Employment Amendments of 1978.[8]

Who Should Be Evaluated?

Teachers, of course, should be evaluated, but the answer is not that simple. A great diversity of practice exists in the assessment of school personnel. Some states (e.g., Florida and Georgia) require evaluation of all certificated personnel. Some states (e.g., Arizona) limit evaluation to certificated *teachers*. Other states (e.g., Kansas and West Virginia) require that all employees be evaluated. Some states (e.g., Florida, Louisiana, and Nevada) list the personnel to be evaluated by category, as teachers, counselors, librarians, and so on. Some states (e.g.,

Massachusetts and Michigan) call for the evaluation of nontenured teachers only, whereas others (e.g., Florida) stipulate that both tenured and nontenured teachers be evaluated.[9]

One might argue that after teachers have gone through their probationary period and have been accorded tenure, they are fully competent and need no further supervision or evaluation. The argument might be pushed back even further and a case made that if teachers were carefully selected, once on the job there would be no need for continuing supervision and evaluation. If so, instruction would be superb and school administration would be child's play. We all know, however, that the existence of ineffective teachers makes that argument untenable. Although much can be said in defense of tenure, and we would not advocate giving it up, on the negative side is the presence of tenured teachers who perform poorly, lack motivation, barely meet minimum professional standards, or are actually incompetent. Tenure is no guarantee of teaching ability. Consequently, evaluation of teacher performance is necessary. The evaluation of all teachers (though not necessarily every teacher every year, nor even on the same cycle), tenured and nontenured, appears to be the prevailing practice.

Who Should Evaluate Teachers?

You would probably answer the question "Who should evaluate teachers?" with "the principal." But this answer is not universal. Zirkel observed that Florida, Hawaii, New Jersey, New Mexico, and Wyoming specify that the evaluation of teachers be performed by the principal or immediate supervisor.[10] In most states that have addressed teacher evaluation, the choice of evaluator is left to the local board of education.[11] In some states (Connecticut and Pennsylvania, for example), the decision on who will do the evaluating is left to the superintendent.[12] A unique process is followed by Massachusetts, where a committee of three people does the evaluating; one person is selected by the teacher to be evaluated, one by the local school board, and one by those two together.[13]

Generally, either by state mandate, local board regulations, or just tradition—or we might add, by reasonable administrative practice—responsibility for evaluating school personnel falls to the principal. Most principals regard this task as their responsibility and their prerogative. Whether they carry out that responsibility themselves is another matter. In some cases in which principals bear the responsibility, they delegate to their assistant principals the task of collecting data and reporting to them. The principal in these instances evaluates teachers on data that are not firsthand.

Some persons believe that the principal should not perform the task of evaluating teachers. Shaw, for example, voiced this sentiment, which applies equally well today:

> The answer to the problem lies not so much in changing the attitudes of the administrators who now do the bulk of the evaluation, but with teachers who must somehow wrest the privilege away from administrative personnel in order to come full cycle as a viable profession and emerge as the leaders of instruction. As the Texas Federation of Teachers proposes: "Control and entry into and egress from the teaching profession should be in the hands of the practicing professionals."
>
> As long as teachers allow themselves to be capriciously evaluated, the teaching profession will not assume its proper role in the educational world. A profession sets its own standards and requires members to adhere to these standards. Improved teacher evaluation techniques may be the key to realizing these standards.[14]

Shaw's proposal is not too likely to be implemented in the immediate future—though it would certainly take teachers a long way down the road to empowerment.

Who may do the evaluating is bound not only by state and local board regulations but also by contracts negotiated between school boards and teachers' organizations. The contracts usually specify who may do the evaluating, how often, how the data will be used, and what records will be kept.

Controversy swirls around the issue of whether staff supervisors from the central office or individual school should be involved in the summative evaluation of teachers. In some school systems that have negotiated contracts, department chairpersons are forbidden to do any formal evaluating of teachers because the chairpersons are considered members of the bargaining unit—that is, teachers—and summative evaluations (and formative evaluations as well, which are for the purpose of making a summative evaluation) must be done by management—that is, administrators.

Many of us in supervision believe that instructional supervisors should be as far removed from summative evaluation as possible. They should try to avoid summative assessments that require the data to be furnished to the administrator for personnel action. They should become involved only under the following conditions:

1. If such evaluations are standard practice agreed on by the teachers when the evaluation process was set up.
2. If a teacher requests the supervisor to do his or her evaluation.
3. If the principal requests the supervisor to do so *and the teacher consents.*
4. If a teacher is facing dismissal for incompetence and an expert judgment is needed.
5. If so ordered by the superintendent.
6. If doing so does not violate the state law, school board policy, or terms of a negotiated contract.

Generally, the principal is responsible for the summative evaluation of teachers; this, we believe, is as it should be. The principal should personally observe all teachers a sufficient number of times in their classrooms in order to form a judgment about their performance and provide a basis for a written annual assessment. In the Brevard County, Florida, public schools, the school principal's signature must be included on the two summary forms, although other administrators or supervisors may have observed teachers (refer back to Figures 12.10 and 12.11). In this process, the principal engages in both formative and summative evaluation. The principal may, if he or she chooses, seek additional evaluation by assistant administrators as supplementary to but not in place of the principal's own evaluation. Principals are charged with many duties and must delegate certain tasks, but the task of teacher evaluation should not be one of them. It is the principal who should possess the highest degree of competence in evaluating personnel and should therefore be the one to put those skills to use. We believe teachers have the right to expect an evaluation of their performance, if it is done at all, from their status leader—the principal. Keep in mind, however, that none of the principal's activity in formative or summative evaluation obviates the formative evaluation carried on by instructional supervisors.

What Should Be Evaluated?

There is no simple answer to the question "What should be evaluated?" Some would say teacher competence, which is both a simple answer and a simplistic one. The response made by some evaluators to how they know good teaching is like the response that is given to the question "How do you know a good painting?" The answer, "I know it when I see it," does not tell us very much. Teaching is often judged in the same way. To some extent, we can all identify good teachers and good teaching. Unfortunately, there often is disagreement on who the good teachers are and what good teaching is. John D. McNeil, referring to A. S. Barr's summary of studies of teaching effectiveness, observed that the problem is common:

> He [Barr] correctly saw that the problem that needs clarifying before all others is the criterion of teaching effectiveness. Different people employ different criteria and approaches to the evaluation of teachers. Some prefer to approach effectiveness from the point of view of personal prerequisites; some from teacher-pupil behaviors; some from basic knowledge, attitudes, and skill; and some from the point of view of results or products. These different approaches give different answers to the question, "Is this teacher an effective teacher?"[15]

Teaching effectiveness, like beauty, can be in the eye of the beholder. We need to come to grips with the basic question, "What is effectiveness in teaching?" We may arrive at an answer to this question in a number of ways. First, we may accept what the experts—for example, professors of education—tell us is good or effective teaching. We find, however, that lacking hard data, the experts disagree. Some look for a heavy affective orientation in teaching; others advocate a heavy cognitive load. Some professors have a fondness for particular methods and feel that other methods are inferior. For example, some champion inquiry learning, cooperative learning, and small-group instruction. Others favor didactic teaching and the use of large groups.[16]

Despite such disagreements, however, there is also considerable uniformity of thought about teaching effectiveness. We know that teachers who like children are more effective instructors than those who do not. We know that student achievement is higher when teachers reinforce correct responses. We know that as a rule, if students are to be motivated, the teacher must be motivated. We know that a teacher cannot teach what he or she does not know. Many educators follow what Allen R. Warner and Dora H. Scott referred to as "the contemporary conventional wisdom of teaching."[17] Both the experts and the not-so-expert rely heavily on conventional wisdom, which itself is derived from research, personal and vicarious experience, and common sense.

Second, we can base a definition of teacher effectiveness on descriptions of what teachers actually do. We can observe what most teachers do and try to describe effective teaching on the basis of those observations. We could sharpen our observations by first identifying good teachers and poor teachers and then studying what good teachers do. But that could put us in a catch-22 situation, for the good teachers must be identified, and we will probably find it difficult to achieve consensus among the identifiers as to what good teaching is.

Third, we can gather empirical data about teaching behaviors that are related to certain learner variables—for example, student achievement. We can try to find out which behaviors have a positive effect on student achievement so that teachers may repeat those behaviors. The research on effective teaching mentioned in Chapter 4 establishes some generally accepted principles to guide us.

Fourth, we can ask a group of teachers or a mixed group of professional educators to describe effective teaching behaviors. Many professional educators have been involved in identifying generic competencies in their states. Although the lists of competencies vary from state to state, which once again reveals the uncertainty in the profession concerning what good teaching is, nevertheless the competencies are uniform within those states that have undertaken the task and thus provide some direction for the evaluation of teachers.

In the absence of recommended or mandated systemwide or statewide processes, which have already specified the teaching competencies to be evaluated or even as supplementary to state and local systems of evaluation, the faculty of each school should reach consensus on what it believes is good teaching. No exercise could be more valuable in-service activity than the production of a description of what is effective teaching as perceived by local teachers and administrators.

Richard P. Manatt's report on the School Improvement Model, a system of teacher and administrator evaluation in five school organizations in Iowa and Minnesota, furnishes an example of specification of competencies.[18] In describing the model, Manatt listed a composite of performance criteria assessed by one or more of the five organizations, as shown in Figure 13.1.

---

1. Maintains an effective relationship with students' families.
2. Provides instruction appropriate for capabilities, rates of learning styles of students.
3. Prepares appropriate evaluation activities.
4. Communicates effectively with students.
5. Monitors seatwork closely.
6. Demonstrates sensitivity in relating to students.
7. Promotes positive self-concept in students.
8. Promotes students' self-discipline and responsibility.
9. Uses a variety of teaching techniques.
10. Spends time at the beginning of the learning demonstrating processes to the student (cueing).
11. Uses controlled (guided) practice before assigning homework (independent practice).
12. Organizes students for effective instruction.
13. Provides students with specific evaluative feedback.
14. Selects and uses appropriate lesson content, learning activities, and materials.
15. Demonstrates ability to monitor student behavior.
16. Writes effective lesson plans.
17. Demonstrates a willingness to keep curriculum and instructional practices current.
18. Has high expectations.
19. Organizes resources and materials for effective instruction.
20. Models and gives concrete examples.

This list is a composite of discriminating criteria used by one or more of the five SIM school organizations.

FIGURE 13.1 Discriminating Teacher Performance Criteria in Rank Order. *Source*: Richard P. Manatt, "Lessons from a Comprehensive Performance Appraisal Project," *Educational Leadership* 44, no. 7 (April 1987): 10. Reprinted with permission of the Association for Supervision and Curriculum Development and Richard P. Manatt. Copyright 1987 by the Association for Supervision and Curriculum Development. All rights reserved.

Because the principal, who is a generalist, will ordinarily be the person doing the evaluating, he or she will evaluate teacher performance in relation to specified generic competencies. The principal's major purpose in observing and evaluating is to gather reliable data for annual assessment and making personnel decisions, so his or her observations will usually be of the global variety. The principal will evaluate teachers each time he or she observes them on all the specified competencies.

Ben M. Harris and his colleagues suggested that competencies possess the following characteristics:

1. There should be relatively few *important* competencies that are demonstrably related to effective teaching and learning.

2. The competencies should be sufficiently specific so that they are clearly definable.

3. The competencies should be amenable to reliable measurement.

4. For formative evaluation purposes, the performance manifestation of the competencies should be subject to change through school-sponsored, in-service programs and instructional supervision.[19]

We would amend the fourth characteristic to read "for both formative and summative evaluation purposes."

Studies of personnel evaluation as carried out in the schools reveal that administrators seek to evaluate more than teaching competencies. The process extends beyond the classroom into personal and professional attributes of teachers. Harris and colleagues observed that "basically, there are three approaches to the evaluation of personnel: (1) the characteristics of the individual, sometimes called 'presage criteria,' (2) the products attributed to the individual, and (3) the processes used by the individual."[20]

Let's take a quick look at these three approaches.

Characteristics of the Teacher The personal characteristics of the teacher do make a difference to the learners, to the school, and to the community. In earlier eras, administrators and school boards prescribed in detail, for example, how a teacher would dress. Male teachers in all schools were once required to wear suits; female teachers were prohibited from wearing cosmetics; both male and female teachers were required to teach Sunday school. Of course, neither could imbibe alcoholic beverages or use tobacco.

The number of restrictions on personal behavior has diminished in recent years. General statements are found in school board policies about clean and appropriate dress and grooming and general decorum in behavior. Some school district policies are written so loosely that the decision about what teachers can or should wear to school is left for the school principal or a committee of teachers in conjunction with the principal to make. In response to growing concerns about teachers' clothing, several North Texas school districts implemented detailed dress codes for teachers and staff.[21] This is not to say that personal and professional characteristics are not important—they are; nor that they should not be evaluated—they should be. John C. Reynolds commented, "Four factors generally differentiate effective teachers from ineffective teachers—superior personality organization, good judgment/reasoning, capacity to relate to others, and a knowledge of basic content and instructional methods."[22]

The first three factors are largely personal. Faculties can and should draw up their own lists—if it is not already a part of the evaluation system—of personal and professional characteristics they deem essential to the teacher, such as warmth, enthusiasm, communication skills, concern for cultural differences, and so on. The tough responsibility is in the assessment of these traits.

Process and Product Prevailing practice in teacher evaluation seeks to assess teacher performance in terms of process, personal characteristics, and professional attributes. For formative purposes, teachers are judged on process, the effectiveness with which they demonstrate generic teaching skills in the classroom. For summative purposes, personal characteristics and professional attributes are often assessed in addition to process skills. The typical classroom observation instrument describes teacher effectiveness in terms of competencies that the teacher must possess. If you look at a typical summative evaluation instrument, you will see teacher performance judged in relation to classroom competencies as well as personal and professional traits. In current practice the majority of items on evaluation instruments focus on process or methods used by the teacher. As a rule, processes are easier to observe and evaluate than personal and professional characteristics or products of teaching.

The belief is growing that teacher performance should be assessed, at least in part, on the school's products—that is, the performance of students. The accountability movement aims to discover what success teachers have had in promoting student achievement. National, state, and local assessments of student achievement have evolved to determine whether students have mastered the content with which they have been confronted. Test data reveal one dimension of product evaluation. They do not disclose, however, less observable behaviors, particularly those in the affective domain. An assessment of the product of teaching should be built into the teacher evaluation system. As Shaw said, "At least some of the evaluation should center on whether the teacher has changed any student behavior; has the teacher taught the student anything?"[23] Increasingly, school districts are including in their systems of evaluation of both teachers and administrators the degree of success of the students as measured by criterion-referenced and norm-referenced tests that meet state and federal standards and laws.

Processes, personal and professional characteristics, and products are all elements to be evaluated. Whether an element is to be evaluated, however, should be agreed on by both the evaluators and the evaluatees. Together, representatives of the administrators and teachers should create a system that gains general consensus, that does not conflict with state or federal laws and constitutional provisions, and that, of course, the local school board endorses.

How Should the Evaluations Be Done?

Sampling of Behavior The evaluator should make enough visits to a teacher's classroom and observe long enough each time to obtain a generous sampling of the teacher's performance. The principal or other evaluator must decide how many times he or she will visit, observe, and evaluate each teacher at the school, but those decisions may be dictated by state laws and local school district master contracts or agreements with teachers. Practice varies widely; the states offer no uniform answer to this problem. Zirkel wrote, "A few states

($n = 3$) answer this question with a weasel word—'continuously' in Connecticut, 'on a regular basis' in West Virginia, and 'periodically' in Wyoming. What such continual evaluation means is left immediately to professional discretion and ultimately to judicial determination."[24]

Some states (Alaska, Florida, Michigan, Oregon, and Washington, for example) specify that evaluations be conducted annually. Some states require more frequent evaluations for nontenured teachers than for tenured ones. California and Louisiana, for example, require an evaluation every year for nontenured teachers but every two years for tenured teachers. In Oklahoma and South Dakota, nontenured teachers are evaluated twice a year, tenured teachers every three years. Nontenured teachers in New Jersey are evaluated three times a year, tenured teachers once.[25]

Hawaii takes into consideration the teacher's experience, requiring evaluations four times the first year, twice the second year, and annually each year thereafter. Kansas follows a different pattern, requiring evaluations twice during the first and second years, annually during the third and fourth years, and once every three years thereafter.[26]

Which pattern is best? Who can say? Some argue that the more frequently an administrator observes a teacher, the better he or she is able to judge that teacher's performance and the fairer will be any personnel decisions made as a result. There is some evidence that the more frequently administrators visit teachers, the more readily teachers accept the evaluation process.[27]

We have neglected to mention one of the purposes of administrative evaluation besides evaluation of the teacher—that is, to keep the administrator apprised of what is going on in the school. The principal who does nothing but sit in his or her office has no idea of what is being taught, what delivery methods are being used, whether lesson plans are being followed, and whether students and teachers are using their time wisely.

The number of visits to observe the teacher must be adjusted to the size of the staff and the number of evaluators. We know administrators who make a classroom observation visit to each teacher once a month. We know others who visit all teachers five times a year and still others who visit teachers on annual contract (nontenured) four times a year and tenured teachers twice a year. There is no magic number.

Certainly, the administrator should observe a teacher often enough to gather sufficient data on which to make judgments about the teacher's performance. Gene Huddle concluded, "Teacher observation in any form occurs infrequently for most teachers."[28] Huddle supported this statement by citing a study of more than 400 secondary school administrators and 10,000 teachers conducted by the National Institute of Education. The study found that 26 percent of the teachers who responded reported that they had not been visited by an administrator at all during the previous year; 27 percent had been visited once; and 23 percent twice.[29] Kim Marshall also contends that a principal who formally observes a teacher for one full class period a year (which he says is a "fairly typical scenario") sees less than 0.1 percent of the teacher's instruction. He based those statements on the premise a teacher has five classes a day, which is 900 periods each school year. Marshall concluded that even if a principal made three full-class observations a year, that would still leave the teacher unobserved with students 99.7 percent of the school year.[30]

When the principal sums up his or her observations in an end-of-year report for each teacher, he or she should have observed each teacher a sufficient number of times to complete the report accurately and fairly. Furthermore, if the principal begins to detect evidence of a teacher's incompetence, the principal would do well to visit that teacher often enough that if the time came to build a case for dismissal, he or she would have the necessary documentation. Included in that documentation should be evidence that due-process procedures were followed and that support was provided to the teacher.

As far as length of each visit is concerned, the principal or other evaluator should remain in the classroom long enough to obtain a fair appraisal of the teacher's performance. If possible, the administrator, or evaluator, should plan to enter the classroom during the transition times between subjects. The teacher can be observed as the transition from one subject to another is made. Also, the time needed to begin the next subject can be observed. Unfortunately, that is rather vague advice. Thus, we suggest the following for formative clinical observations: at least thirty minutes at the elementary school level and one class period at the secondary school level.

Announced versus Unannounced Visits

We believe the clinical supervisor should always schedule visits in advance at a time agreeable to the teacher; the summative evaluator, however, may find it desirable to make a combination of announced and unannounced visits. Because entrapment is not the name of the game, a sufficient number of prearranged visits should be made. The teacher should be seen at his or her best. On the other hand, unannounced or drop-in visits can confirm whether the observations made at announced times revealed the teacher's typical performance. They can introduce an element of simple control, tacitly advising the teacher that he or she is expected to be prepared to teach all day, every day. They can let the teacher know that the principal is on the job and is interested in what is happening in the school. Some agreements or contracts negotiated annually by teachers and school boards establish the beginning date for principals to be allowed to enter classrooms to observe. Ending dates by which these observations, and subsequent evaluations, must be completed are often established by state statute.

Some administrators make casual, brief, frequent (even daily) drop-in visits to each teacher. We should distinguish these brief appearances of the administrator, during which he or she makes only the most perfunctory observations, from significant classroom observation of the teacher's instruction. The short drop-in visit, though useful, is more of a monitoring or even social procedure than instructional supervision. Principals sometimes refer to these brief classroom visits as "5 × 5s." By that they mean they visit five classrooms a day for five minutes each. Most principals leave a note with brief comments either on the teacher's desk on exiting the room or in the teacher's mailbox. Tom Peters and Robert Waterman Jr. in *In Search of Excellence*, referred to this high-visibility management style as "managing by wandering around" or "managing by walking about (MBWA)."[31]

Collecting and Recording the Data

If an evaluation system is not already in place, the faculty and administrators will need to decide what data they want collected and how the data will be gathered. They will need to select or create instruments for recording both the periodic observations and the final appraisal.

For periodic observations in the teacher's classroom, a global instrument such as the ones described in the preceding chapter is desirable. These classroom observation forms are designed to help the evaluator assess what is occurring in the classroom. Occasionally, these forms include items for which evidence must be found by means other than classroom observation.

The summative evaluation instrument, which some call the *teacher appraisal form*, must bear some relationship to both the classroom observation form and any teacher self-appraisal form in use. In some cases, the teacher appraisal form is identical to the classroom observation form. The classroom observation form should be limited to *only* those items that can be observed in the classroom. The teacher appraisal form then could include all the items on the classroom observation form plus items for which data must be obtained in other ways—for example, certain personal and professional characteristics, products, and processes in outside-of-class activities.

Some of the data to be collected will come from classroom observations. Other data will result from examination of the teacher's lesson and unit plans. Some data will be derived from conferences with the teacher. Student work samples and test data will furnish clues to teacher performance. Comments from students, parents, teachers, and even other administrators about a given teacher should be, as the cliché goes, treated with a grain of salt until firsthand evidence confirms or refutes the statement made either on behalf of or in criticism of the teacher.

Personnel evaluation calls for the rating of teachers. The administrator, not the supervisor, should bear the primary responsibility for making judgments about the competence or incompetence of teachers. It appears appropriate and timely for the profession as well to set up some mechanism for monitoring itself. Other professions, notably medicine and law, have devised ways to warn or remove members of the profession deemed unsuitable. In rebuttal, it is often said that teaching is not a profession, that teachers' salaries are not comparable to those of the medical and legal professions, and therefore that such monitoring would be out of line. Perhaps one of the reasons some members of the public do not regard teaching as a profession is the inability or unwillingness of the profession itself to spell out and monitor standards of performance. The development of state and national standards is a move in the direction of identifying elements of teaching effectiveness.

Harris and colleagues underscored the care that must be taken in rating personnel: "It is crucial that the decisions concerning ratings be based on relevant, descriptive, and verifiable data."[32] Furthermore, they cautioned, "Every effort should be made to reassure teachers through processes that are assistance-oriented and through instruments that are objective, descriptive, and diagnostic."[33] The evaluator must have firm evidence for each behavior rated, or else he or she should not rate that behavior.

After each evaluation, periodic and final, the evaluator should confer with the teacher. The administrator hopes that the periodic evaluations will result in improvement in instruction during the year and that the summative appraisal will work the same way for instruction during the ensuing year. It is customary for both the administrator and the teacher to sign the summative evaluation report. The teacher's signature does not necessarily signify agreement with the administrator's rating; rather it signifies that the teacher has seen the evaluation, acknowledges it, and has received a copy. Some school districts have included a section where the teacher may add comments or reactions.

It is of interest to note the evolution of some evaluation systems on both a state and local/district level. The metamorphoses undergone by the Georgia system provide an example of a state constantly seeking to perfect its personnel evaluation system. In the early 1980s, Georgia mandated and conducted a statewide assessment system for permanent certification of beginning teachers by means of the Teacher Performance Assessment Instruments (TPAI), a process that was exported to some school systems outside Georgia.[34] With the TPAI evaluations, agencies outside the school systems, known as Regional Assessment Centers (RACs), conducted assessments using three independent assessors: an RAC employee, an administrator, and a peer teacher, all of whom had been trained in the use of the instruments.

Teachers prepared for their assessments by creating a set of lesson plans, known as a portfolio. During the period when the planned lessons were taught, assessors visited— observing for at least thirty minutes and rating the teacher's performance. Follow-up visits were often necessary.

As you might guess, controversy swirled around such questions as interrater reliability and the validity of some of the items on the instrument. Nevertheless, determinations of eligibility for permanent state certification were made on the basis of scores assigned by the raters. As a rule, the RAC assessments were not conducted primarily for the purpose of improving instruction, which might be incidental to the assessments, but rather for certification purposes.

In 1989, after considerable investment, Georgia abolished the TPAI process, partly because the state was awash in the development of evaluation systems for all types of school personnel. In the case of teacher evaluation, duplication of processes, assessor time, and costs were factors in the decision to cease using the TPAI. That same year, the state switched to the Georgia Teacher Evaluation Program to accomplish the dual purpose of permanent certification and summative evaluation.

Assessment in Georgia is now the responsibility of district-level and school-based administrators and supervisors. Until 1995, the state mandated the use of four instruments: the Georgia Teacher Observation Instrument (GTOI), consisting of three forms, the Standard, the Formative, and the Extended, which follow the classroom teacher's job description; an instrument for assessing Georgia Teacher Duties and Responsibilities (GTDR); the Georgia Teacher Evaluation Program Annual Evaluation Summary Report, which summarizes both the observation and duties and responsibilities assessments; and the Professional Development Plan.[35]

Like the states, school districts have engaged in studying and revising their evaluation systems. Littleton Public Schools in Colorado furnishes an excellent illustration of the evolution of district appraisal systems. The school system uses a comprehensive teacher appraisal rating scale that measures personal qualifications, professional attitudes, and personal and professional relationships in addition to teaching effectiveness. Currently, the district employs, on an annual basis and for teachers, a rating scale with spaces for comments about each competency (Figure 13.2). The school district utilizes an interim review process after an initial year of comprehensive assessment or every few years for a teacher who has had successful years of teaching.

Littleton Public Schools

SUMMATIVE EVALUATION REPORT
Teacher

School Year: _____

Name: _____ Position: _____ School: _____

Evaluator: _____ Date of Evaluation Conference: _____

This evaluation is based. in part. on formal observations conducted on the following dates:

Observation Date(s)	Conference Date(s)
_____	_____
_____	_____
_____	_____
_____	_____
_____	_____

In addition to observations, relevant sources of documentation of performance may be cited.

OTHER SOURCES OF DATA: _____

Proficient Performance, means the teacher meets performance criteria in each Category of Responsibility. Unsatisfactory Performance means that the teacher does not meet one or more performance criteria in a Category of Responsibility.

SUMMARY OF PERFORMANCE (Refer to Performance Criteria):

PERFORMANCE EVALUATION

	Meets Performance Standards	Does Not Meet Performance Standards
Categories of Responsibility		
Instructional Planning	☐	☐
Delivery of Instruction	☐	☐
Assessment of Student Learning	☐	☐
Management of the Learning Environment	☐	☐
Professional Growth	☐	☐
Professional Responsibilities	☐	☐

Revised September 9, 2003

Teacher Initials _____
Evaluator Initials _____

(continued)

FIGURE 13.2 Summative Evaluation Report Form (multiple pages). *Source*: Littleton Public Schools, Littleton, Colorado. Reprinted with permission of the Littleton Public Schools.

Summative Evaluation Report (Teacher)
Page 2

Name: _____

A teacher on regular contract and in good standing receives a comprehensive rating on all performance standards. Comments and ratings related to performance on individual criteria are provided at the discretion of the evaluator. However, comments must be provided in any area of standards or criteria where concerns exist.

Performance Standards (Narrative of Strengths and Weaknesses)

1. INSTRUCTIONAL PLANNING

1.1 Plans instruction consistent with State Model Content Standards, district approved curricular learning objectives and embedded district technology standards for assigned subject area(s)/grade levels.
1.2 Plans instruction based on formal and informal assessment of student abilities and needs.
1.3 Plans effective use of class time.

Comments:

2. DELIVERY OF INSTRUCTION

2.1 Implements an instructional design to reach learning objectives.
2.2 Applies principles of teaching/learning to enhance student achievement.
2.3 Modifies instruction to meet student needs.
2.4 Communicates effectively with learners.
2.5 Provides for and maintains student involvement during instruction.
2.6 Integrates available technology as a tool to enhance student achievement.

Comments:

3. ASSESSMENT OF STUDENT LEARNING

3.1 Demonstrates appropriate selection, development and use of quality assessment practices, processes, and instruments.
3.2 Evaluates the quality of assessment information and use, when appropriate.
3.3 Provides effective communications about student learning and achievement that are based on defensible and consistent grading practices and relevant, accurate assessment information.
3.4 Assists students to engage in quality self-assessment of learning and to gain a sense of responsibility for monitoring their own learning.
3.5 Describes student achievement in terms of performance levels associated with the State Model Content Standards.

Comments:

4. MANAGEMENT OF THE LEARNING ENVIRONMENT

4.1 Establishes a climate for learning.

Teacher Initials _____
Evaluator Initials _____

(continued)

FIGURE 13.2 *(continued)*

Summative Evaluation Report (Teacher)
Page 3

4.2   Manages classroom procedures in a manner that maximizes instruction.
4.3   Organizes classroom space and materials for safe and effective use by all students.
4.4   Establishes clear expectations for student behavior.
4.5   Establishes consequences for inappropriate behavior.
4.6   Identifies students displaying serious behavioral or personal problems and refers them to administrators or school counselors.
4.7   Maintains required federal, state, district student records in an accurate and thorough manner and according to established guidelines.

Comments:

5. RESPONSIBILITY FOR PROFESSIONAL GROWTH

5.1   Accepts responsibility for the professional growth plan consistent with the format of evaluation.
5.2   Thinks systematically about teaching practice and learns from experience.
5.3   Participates in collaborative efforts to improve the effectiveness of school staff.
5.4   Demonstrates learning from participation in professional growth activities.

Comments:

6. PROFESSIONAL RESPONSIBILITIES

6.1   Demonstrates consistent positive communication with parents.
6.2   Collaborates with others to fulfill responsibilities related to building and district vision, mission, priorities and goals.
6.3   Recognizes problems within the school and actively contributes to their solution.
6.4   Accepts and fulfills assigned responsibilities and duties in a prompt and efficient manner.
6.5   Accepts a reasonable responsibility for contributing to the total school program.
6.6   Follows Board of Education Policies, building procedures, and any other rules, regulations or procedures that may be established by the central or building administration.
6.7   Performs other reasonable duties as may be assigned by the building principal.

Comments:

PROGRESS ON PROFESSIONAL GROWTH PLAN:

☐ Satisfactory

☐ Unsatisfactory

Comments:

Teacher Initials _____
Evaluator Initials _____

(continued)

FIGURE 13.2   *(continued)*

Summative Evaluation Report (Teacher)

Page 4

Name: _____

RECOMMENDATIONS:

Teacher Initials _____
Evaluator Initials _____

(continued)

FIGURE 13.2 (*continued*)

Name: _____

OVERALL PERFORMANCE EVALUATION

☐ At this time, the teacher demonstrates proficient performance.

☐ At this time, the teacher meets performance standards and will continue at Level I.

☐ At this time, the teacher meets performance standards at Level I and will pursue a differentiated evaluation format.

☐ At this time, the teacher does not meet performance standards and needs improvement. Provide assistance at Level II.

☐ Following assistance at Level II, the teacher has made required improvement and will be placed at Level I.

☐ Following assistance at Level II, the teacher has not made required improvement and will be placed at Level III.

_____   _____
Teacher Signature   **Date**

_____   _____
Evaluator Signature   **Date**

The teacher's signature on this form represents neither acceptance nor approval of the report. It indicates that the teacher has reviewed the report in conference with the evaluator. The teacher may reply, in writing, within seven (7) working days of the date the report is signed by the evaluator. The teacher's statement should be in duplicate and attached to this form.

Comments attached: ☐ Yes ☐ No

_____   _____
Supervisor Signature   **Date**

The Supervisor's signature on this form verifies that the report has been reviewed and that the proper process and procedure appear to have been followed.

Summ_Eval_Rept_Tcher.dot
Licensed
(05/11/00)

Original: Personnel File
Copy: Evaluator
Copy: Teacher

Teacher Initials _____
Evaluator Initials _____

FIGURE 13.2 (*continued*)

Rating Scales versus Open-Ended Instruments   Both rating scales and open-ended instruments have their advantages and disadvantages. A rating scale is easier to fill out, it focuses on specific behaviors, and the data can be treated quantitatively, if one prefers to do so. An open-ended instrument gives the evaluator greater flexibility; it is a more personal, individualized approach that avoids quantification of the data.

Rating scales are used by school systems with a teacher evaluation form that requires quantification of the data. Using a rating scale with, for example, a low of 1 and a high of 5, principals rate a set of generic competencies and average them. If the teacher's average score falls below 3.5, he or she is considered to be performing unsatisfactorily and might expect to suffer any consequences that follow unsatisfactory work.

With an evaluation system of this type, principals encounter the same type of difficulty as teachers who must decide whether a student has earned a 78 or an 82, a C+ or a B−. When a cutoff score signals the boundary between satisfactory and unsatisfactory performance, the sagacious principal, aware of his or her own fallibility in judgment, tends to inflate the "grades" and give the benefit of the doubt to the teacher. The open-ended system eliminates this problem but introduces other problems of its own.

A binary rating system—a checklist, for example—reduces the necessity for making fine numerical distinctions, but because behavior is reported with only two symbols—for example, S (Satisfactory) and U (Unsatisfactory) or A (Acceptable) and U (Unacceptable)—a wide range of behavior is encompassed by each of the two symbols. The binary rating system takes a great deal of pressure off the administrator because decisions about teachers' competencies do not have to be as carefully deliberated. Although many teachers prefer the broader symbols, some teachers feel that terms like *satisfactory* and *acceptable* do not do justice to those teachers who are performing at a high level. In this respect, teachers who reject the binary approach emulate those students who object to satisfactory–unsatisfactory, pass–fail, credit–no credit systems and demand A through F letter grades, which allow for distinctions in achievement along with commensurate rewards.

Professional Portfolios   In recent years, some school districts have provided alternative forms of evaluation to tenured teachers on continuing contracts and/or professional services contracts. The professional development portfolio (PDP) provides teachers with a framework for initiating, planning, and facilitating their own personal growth while building connections between their professional goals and those of the school.

A portfolio may be in the form of a folder, notebook, video, or computer file. Artifacts and other evidences, such as samples of work, achievement records, in-service participation and leadership, new curriculum development, instructional strategies, and the use of technology may be included.

Mary E. Dietz (1995) supported the use of PDPs. She suggested that the portfolios should be designed with the following assumptions in mind:

1. Professional development activities are most effective when professionals set their own goals, determine their preferred method for learning, and make decisions about how to integrate new learnings.

2. A continuous learning environment can result if adults design the environment for the learners and themselves.

3. Adult learners will engage in learning if they are encouraged to question current assumptions, explore new findings, and gain expertise.

4. Professional growth for teachers is critical to the process of change in schools.[36]

The PDP differs from traditional assessment because it is not administrator-directed. The PDP teacher is responsible for both directing and carrying out professional growth using the model. The administrator becomes a facilitator, collaborator, and supporter in the process. The behaviors of teachers and administrators involved in PDP activities are those encouraged by advocates of enhanced professionalism in schools.

The Webster Groves, Missouri, School District's professional development plan has eight options for a teacher or a small group of teachers to engage in professional activities such as: issues concerning new teachers; exploration of various methods of instruction; individual areas of interest explored and approved for one teacher; creation or update of curriculum; work to benefit building or district goals; personal professional reflection to grow professionally; teacher leadership activities; and research and development of evaluation standards. The Individual Professional Development Plan form used in the school district is reproduced as Figure 13.3.

Competencies, Indicators, and Descriptors If you incline toward the use of instruments that detail specific competencies, as we do, you should collect data using instruments that break the competencies into more specific indicators and, if desired, into descriptors of the indicators.

We may define a competency as a particular teaching behavior or skill. The Georgia State Department of Education defined a competency as follows: "A generic *teacher competency* is a conceptualization of a responsible and purposeful performance essential to the effective professional conduct of all teachers."[37] The Georgia Department notes, however, that "this definition results in statements which are too broad for assessment purposes."[38]

Planning for instruction, using student responses, and managing the classroom are examples of generic competencies. We make a mistake if we try to evaluate these competencies without detailing what they mean. We need some indicators to guide us in gathering evidence that the teacher possesses the competency. The Georgia State Department of Education explained indicators in the following way: "Competency *indicators* . . . define behaviors representative of the competency. The more indicators a person demonstrates proficiently, the more likely it is that that person is demonstrating the target competency."[39]

Most of the evaluation instruments we have seen divide the competencies no further than the indicator level. The Georgia Teacher Assessment program, however, broke indicators into *descriptors*. In defining descriptors, the Georgia Department stated, "They are more specific than either competencies or indicators, and are used to describe the quality of a teacher's performance relevant to a competency indicator."[40]

Webster Groves School District
Individual Professional Development Plan

Teacher(s) Signature(s)_____

Building: _____ Date: _____ Principal's Signature: _____

District Goal

Question/Objective: What is desired?

Action Plan: What are the steps and/or activities for achieving the objective and what is the calendar for completion?

Assessment: What methods will you use to measure results?

Results of Actions: What was the impact on student achievement?

Reflections: What are your thoughts about this experience?

FIGURE 13.3 Individual Professional Development Plan Form. *Source:* Webster Groves School District, Missouri. Reprinted with permission of the Webster Groves School District.

An example of a competency with one of its indicators and descriptors for that indicator, taken from the TPAI used in Georgia in the 1980s, follows:

Competency VI: Uses Instructional Techniques, Methods, and Media Related to the Objectives

Indicator 12: Uses procedures which get learners initially involved in lessons.

Descriptors:

a. Helps learners recall past experiences or knowledge.

b. Uses existing interests of learners as a link to new activities.

c. Stimulates new interests in activities with techniques such as discrepant events or thought-provoking questions.

d. Helps learners understand what they may achieve by participating in the activities.[41]

Indicators and descriptors are helpful in refining a competency. They serve as guides for the evaluator's observations and provide a basis for assessment. When a teacher asks, "What do you mean by this competency?" the evaluator can easily reply, "It means these indicators" or "It means these indicators and descriptors." Georgia itself has moved away from the use of the terms *indicators*, *descriptors*, and *competencies* and instead uses the terms *tasks*, *dimensions*, *subdimensions*, and *effective practices*.[42]

The terminology of competencies and indicators stems from the broader concept of competency-based education—particularly popular in the 1970s. Although the terminology may differ among school systems (for example, competency may be *objective* or *skill* and indicator may be *subobjective* or *subskill*), the practice of specifying competencies, objectives, and skills in performance terms remains strong and is, we believe, essential.

Georgia's experience demonstrates well the power of state mandating because the Georgia Teacher Assessment Program was designed for purposes of certifying beginning teachers. However, many school districts of the state simply adapted the state's assessment model and established that model as its summative and, in some cases, formative evaluation process.

How Should the Data Be Used?

The administrator uses the data collected on a teacher's performance for (1) conferences with the teacher, (2) creation of a professional development assistance plan, and (3) personnel decisions, including decisions about merit pay, career ladder, change of assignment or increased responsibilities, retention, and dismissal.

Conferences Conferences should be held with the teacher after each observation and for the summative evaluation and are often mandated to be held in a specific time period by school district policy. When the administrator is making global assessments, preobservation conferences are less important and may be transacted in a few minutes (e.g., to schedule a visit or to obtain any special information the administrator would need to know about the class).

Conferences between the teacher and administrator serve two purposes. First, they offer an opportunity for the administrator to gather data about factors not witnessed during a classroom visit, and they give the teacher an opportunity to describe or interpret some of the events the administrator viewed. Second, they form the setting for an evaluation. Although the administrator's periodic observations are or can be formative, they are also evaluations.

Each conference with the administrator, then, is evaluative in nature. The administrator is simply not the same person, nor should he or she be, as the staff instructional supervisor. Consequently, the administrator should not and, because of legal responsibilities, cannot avoid the evaluative dimension of observations and conferences.

The rules of the game are different for the line administrator and the staff supervisor. The staff supervisor divulges to persons other than the teacher only what he or she deems necessary or is required to tell about a teacher's performance. The line administrator tells everything, in writing, and forwards it to the superintendent's office. In the case of teachers charged with incompetence, the data go beyond the superintendent's office. The staff supervisor does not have to make the hard personnel decisions; the line administrator does. The staff supervisor relies on the authority of persuasion and expertise, the line administrator on the authority of the office.

Administrators or supervisors who must simultaneously function as evaluator and instructional supervisor have a difficult role. Their observations and conferences must be both formative and summative. Although they diagnose and prescribe, they must also rate. Although they may try to minimize the element of threat, they cannot erase all teacher anxiety.

Administrators cannot, and should not if they could, obliterate all traces of status. Although we believe protocol is overdone in many cases, a modicum of protocol is essential to the efficient operation of the program. Teachers want and expect their administrators to maintain some semblance of status. Thus, although we would argue that the clinical supervisor should confer with a teacher in the teacher's classroom or on neutral territory, we would take the position that it is proper for evaluative conferences to be held in the administrator's office or in the administrator's conference room. The administrator can ease the tension by coming out from behind the desk and conferring with the teacher while sitting at a table or in comfortable chairs.

During each of the postobservation conferences, the administrator should make and record suggestions for improvements that he or she feels are necessary for the teacher to make. Refer to the Recommendations section of the Summative Evaluation Report form from the Littleton Public Schools. At the summative conference, which is scheduled toward the end of the school year, the administrator brings together all of the data he or she has gathered during the year pertaining to the various criteria on which teachers in that school are evaluated.

Madeline Hunter referred to the summative conference as the *evaluative conference* and made it clear that it should be based on previous classroom observations conferences during the year, which she called *instructional conferences*. She described an evaluative conference as follows:

> The objective of an *evaluative conference* is that a teacher's placement on a
> continuum from "unsatisfactory" to "outstanding" will be established and the
> teacher will have the opportunity to examine the evidence used. ... An evaluative
> conference should be the summation of what has occurred in and resulted from a
> series of instructional conferences. Information given and conclusions reached in an
> evaluative conference should come as no surprise to the teacher because the
> supporting evidence has been discussed in previous instructional conferences. As a
> result, the evaluative conference has high probability for being perceived as fair,
> just, and supportable by objective evidence rather than based on subjective opinion.
> This conference is the culmination of a year's diagnostic, prescriptive, collaborative
> work with a teacher and supervisor who shared responsibility for the teacher's
> continuous professional growth.[43]

Although the teacher may offer opinions, it is incumbent on the administrator to make suggestions for improvement if he or she feels the teacher needs to improve certain behaviors. The general perception and legal expectation is that the administrator, not the teacher, has the responsibility to recommend remedial measures for a teacher who shows deficiencies. If the principal seeks to dismiss a teacher for incompetence, the first question that will be asked under due-process expectations, is "What did you do to help the teacher overcome the deficiencies?" Thus, rating a teacher is not enough. The principal must propose actions the teacher can take if deficiencies are noted. Furthermore, the principal has the obligation to monitor the teacher's progress in overcoming the deficiencies.

Professional Development Assistance Plans As a part of summative evaluation, administrators typically draw up a professional development assistance plan for teachers, showing areas that need improving or that could be enhanced. For those teachers demonstrating deficiencies, the administrator includes means of overcoming the deficiencies, states how evaluation of the improvement will be carried out, and establishes timelines. The School Board of Brevard County (Florida) Professional Development Assistance form (Figure 13.4) and the Webster Groves School District Professional Improvement Plan form (Figure 13.5) are examples of forms the administrator would fill out and that both the teacher and administrator would sign.

SCHOOL BOARD OF BREVARD COUNTY

PROFESSIONAL DEVELOPMENT ASSISTANCE FORM

Teacher's Name _____

Principal/Supervising Administrator's Name _____

Performance Area

Specific Behaviors

Strategies for Improvement

Assistance

Date for Follow-Up Review _____ Completion Date _____

_____/_____   _____/_____
Teacher's Signature   Date   Administrator's Signature   Date

---

FIGURE 13.4 Professional Development Assistance Form. *Source*: School Board of Brevard County, Fla. Reprinted with permission of the Brevard County Public Schools.

PROFESSIONAL IMPROVEMENT PLAN (PIP) WEBSTER GROVES SCHOOL DISTRICT		
Teacher	☐ **Non-Tenured**	☐ **Tenured**
Grade/Subject/Course		**Date**
Administrator/Supervisor		**School**
Standard and Criterion Where Deficiency is Noted:		
Performance Indicators:		
Strategies/Steps To Be Taken:		
Resources/Support Structures:		
Data Collection Method and Sources:		
Timelines/Deadlines:		
Teacher's signature Date Administrator's/Supervisor's signature Date Signature(s) indicates the above has been reviewed and discussed. Copies to teacher and administrator / supervisor.		
Evidence of Progress		

Teacher's signature   Date   Administrator's/Supervisor's signature   Date
Signature(s) indicates the above has been reviewed and discussed. Copies to teacher, administrator/supervisor and Department of Human Resources.

FIGURE 13.5 Professional Improvement Plan Form. *Source*: Webster Groves School District, Missouri. Reprinted with permission of the Webster Groves School District.

Improvement activities commonly suggested for the teacher are a college course, a staff-development activity in the local system, visits to peers' classes, working with a colleague or mentor, and reading the professional literature. Manatt has advocated the use of a three-person intensive assistance team composed of administrators and supervisors to help marginal teachers—that is, those who are not effective but might improve with help.[44]

When the summative conference is terminated and recommendations for improvement have been made, copies of the completed evaluation instrument and professional development plan, duly signed by both the administrator and teacher, should be placed on file. Normally, the teacher would receive a copy, the principal would retain a copy, and a copy would be sent to the appropriate official at the central office.

Harris and others noted the importance of selection, formative evaluation, and summative evaluation in making personnel decisions:

> If formative evaluation is well done, most summative evaluation decisions should be routine (e.g., continuation on the job for the majority of the teachers) or nonthreatening (e.g., transfer, change of function, or placement in a tenure status). Recommendations for termination of contract or other unpleasant eventualities are and should be relatively rare. They should be extremely rare if initial selection of personnel is carefully done and if formative evaluation and follow-up growth activities are carried out.[45]

Personnel Decisions Administrators will have to make a number of decisions on the basis of their evaluation of the teacher's performance. They will often have to make decisions about changes of assignment from one group of students to another, from one grade to another, from their school to another school, from present position to special assignment, and from a teaching position to an administrative position. If their district operates a merit pay system or career ladder, they will have to decide which teachers should receive these incentives. They will also have to deal with questions of retention and dismissal.

The decision to retain a teacher is much easier to make than a decision for dismissal. The dismissal of a teacher is stressful both for the administrator and, of course, for the teacher to be dismissed. It is particularly stressful if the administrator was the person who hired the teacher in the first place, because this can reflect on that administrator's judgment in initially selecting people.

Retention decisions become more difficult at the point when a teacher is being considered for a continuing contract, professional services contract, or tenure, usually at the end of three years of teaching in a school system. The administrator knows that a decision to retain will mean that the teacher will be employed in the school system for a long time, possibly a lifetime. The administrator also knows that it is far easier to dismiss a nontenured teacher than a tenured one. Although there may be moral and ethical reasons for informing a nontenured teacher of causes of nonretention, usually there are no legal reasons compelling an administrator to do so.

Dismissal of a teacher after the teacher has earned tenure is much more difficult. In some cases, teachers may be discharged if their positions are abolished, but the major grounds for dismissal are what some people call the three I's: insubordination, immorality, and incompetence. Proving insubordinate and immoral behavior is relatively easy, although immorality is becoming an increasingly difficult question as standards of behavior differ greatly from community to community. Dealing with incompetent teachers is a bear for administrators because of the time and energy it takes and the resultant need to be absent from other teachers' classrooms. Some incompetent teachers are deficient in their knowledge of subject matter, in their use of English, in their teaching skills, and in their interpersonal skills. Yet it is difficult to prove incompetence. How incompetent does one have to be for removal from the teaching profession? Neither teachers' organizations nor the profession in general has fully come to grips with this question. The major burden for removing an incompetent teacher is placed on the shoulders of the principal.

Dismissal for incompetence requires a great deal—some principals would say an excessive amount—of documentation. The principal must build a case carefully, citing chapter and verse, to remove a teacher who is tenured. State laws and local policies have set certain specific procedures concerning notices to be given to the teacher, hearings provided for, and appeals that may be taken before a teacher can be discharged. Many educators believe that if a state has a strong due-process law, tenure is not an essential provision. Teachers, however, somewhat distrustful of administration in general, still lean toward preservation of the principle of tenure.

To some degree, the profession regulates standards of professional competence through professional practices commissions established in some states. The Professional Practices Commission of Georgia, for example, "was established for the purpose of setting and enforcing standards of competent professional performance and ethical conduct for educators in Georgia."[46] In 1998, the Georgia legislature transferred all cases pending before the Professional Practices Commission to the Professional Standards Commission. The commission, composed of seventeen practicing members of the education profession, advises in matters of school law; counsels members of the profession; investigates complaints brought against educators; holds hearings to adjudicate matters brought before a local board of education; conducts professional, on-site reviews of the services of an educator whose performance has been questioned; and makes recommendations to the state board of education or the department of education in matters concerning denial, suspension, or revocation of teaching certificates.[47] A state professional practices commission can be of help to teachers, administrators, and the profession by setting standards of competence and assisting schools in maintaining those standards. Standards set by the National Board for Professional Teaching Standards (NBPTS) have guided states and administrators in determining the competence of teachers.

PROBLEMS IN SUMMATIVE EVALUATION

We are sure you know teachers who, having received their summative appraisal reports, declare, "How can the principal know how well I am doing? He (she) has spent hardly any time in my classroom." Even when they receive glowing reports from the administrators, the teachers resent this type of administrative behavior. A variation on this theme is the comment voiced by numerous teachers, "But he (she) has been to visit me only once this year and then he (she) stayed only ten minutes." One of the scandals of summative evaluation practices is the failure of the administrator to obtain an adequate sampling of a teacher's performance. The teacher should be visited, observed, and evaluated several times during the year. We can find examples of administrators who limit their visits to a few minutes once or twice during the year. We have even heard of administrators who render summative judgments without a single visit to the teacher's classroom!

Many principals delegate teacher evaluation to their assistant principals. In fact, this is accepted practice in some school systems. There is nothing inherently wrong with such a process, but if principals are required to sign their names to evaluation reports, if principals must make personnel decisions or recommendations to the superintendent about personnel, and if principals must document teaching performance, they should want better than secondhand information. Otherwise, the process should be turned over completely to the assistant principal, who would not only do the observing, the conferencing, and the evaluating but also sign the appraisal reports and defend them if challenged.

Principals err in evaluating personnel when they skew their ratings to the high side of the scale. The easy rater may be compensating for failure to gather enough data to make accurate evaluations, may feel that the whole process is burdensome and unnecessary, may be striving to maintain rapport with teachers, or may simply feel that teachers need positive reinforcement for their efforts. Overrating a teacher's performance is, therefore, a much more common error than is underrating it. Permit us to generalize: If we were to analyze the administrative evaluations of both public school and college faculties, we would conclude that almost all our teachers have reached a state of perfection. Giving high ratings is an easy way out for the administrator who wishes to avoid the stress that comes from conflicts with teachers over low ratings. High, even satisfactory ratings of less-than-competent teachers have come back to haunt administrators when they attempted to dismiss a teacher who had routinely received acceptable appraisals.

Ratings should be as objective as possible. We all have room for growth, so suggestions should be made that will lead to improvement. Teachers have reason to be concerned about the lack of consistency among evaluators. Teachers are confused and resentful when one evaluator rates a teacher's performance high, whereas another rates the same teacher's performance low. Evaluators must take care not to let their own biases about teaching and about individual teachers affect their ratings.

Still another problem sometimes encountered is the lack of specific feedback to the teacher. If teachers are to profit from an assessment, they must know what they need to do to be more effective. Personal conferences between the teacher and evaluator are essential to the process. Sufficient time must be allocated for each conference so the teachers feel they have had adequate opportunity to express themselves and understand what the administrator expects.

As administrators and/or supervisors work with teachers during a school year and complete the required formative and summative forms, they must keep in mind the life cycle of career teachers. The six basic phases that career teachers experience are novice, apprentice, professional, expert, distinguished, and emeritus.[48] If predictions of teacher turnover become reality, the efforts of supervisors initially will be focused on working with many novice teachers—those in their first few years of teaching. At the same time, they should provide encouragement and support for the teachers at the other end of the life cycle—the professional, expert, and distinguished teachers. The summative evaluations of these teachers may be focused appropriately on professional development plans rather than on regular classroom observations and the subsequent evaluation form. The expertise, knowledge, and skills these career professionals possess should be used to help the apprentice teachers as they grow and mature in skill development.

The bipolar nature of supervision in future years should be viewed as a source of professional growth for all who are involved.

Many of the problems associated with summative evaluation can be alleviated through appropriate in-service training of the evaluators. Administrators are in as great a need of in-service education as are the teachers they supervise.

SUMMARY

Summative evaluation of teacher performance is the assessment administrators make toward the end of the year for purposes of arriving at personnel decisions. The summative appraisal is based on periodic or formative evaluations conducted during the year. All teachers should be evaluated periodically. The frequency and length of visits to the classroom vary greatly from school to school and from school system to school system. In practice, nontenured teachers are evaluated more frequently than are tenured teachers. The frequency of summative appraisals varies from state to state.

Principals are expected to and should evaluate the teachers of their school. They may call for help from assistants as needed. Administrators and teachers should be in agreement about what should be evaluated. Generally, administrators collect data concerning processes, personal and professional characteristics of teachers, and products and outcomes of teaching.

Administrators normally use a classroom observation instrument to make periodic or formative evaluations during the year. This type of instrument permits a comprehensive assessment of teacher competencies. Competencies are best evaluated if defined with indicators and, if desired, descriptors of the indicators. The year-end summative appraisal is based on the periodic evaluations made during the year and any additional data required by the instrument in use. The summative instrument is usually correlated with the classroom observation form and with any teacher self-appraisal instrument.

If teachers are expected to make improvements in their teaching, the administrator must give them specific feedback. This means at the very least a conference following each formative evaluation and the summative appraisal conference. Administrators will develop or co-develop a professional improvement plan for teachers.

Copies of the written evaluations and improvement plans should be given to the teacher and placed on file in the principal's office and in the appropriate office of the central administration. Evaluative data are used for administrative decisions on merit pay, career ladder, change of assignment, increased responsibilities, retention, and dismissal. In presenting a case for dismissal of a teacher, the administrator must adhere to due process. Administrators must make their ratings of teachers as fair and objective as possible. If a teacher is found to be deficient in some way, it is the administrator's responsibility to recommend and monitor measures that may assist the teacher in overcoming the deficiencies.

QUESTIONS FOR DISCUSSION

1. What problems were identified with summative evaluations? How would you correct them?
2. Should instructional supervisors be engaged in preparing summative assessments of teachers? Why or why not?
3. How should administrators use summative assessments?
4. Should supervisors make announced or unannounced classroom visits?
5. What impact do professional improvement plans (PIPs) have on the assessment of teacher performance?

ACTIVITIES FOR FURTHER STUDY

REFLECTIVE

1. Distinguish between summative evaluation and formative evaluation of teacher performance.

2. Report (if the data can be obtained) on the performance of a faculty as a group (not as individuals) on annual ratings of competence in one school by percentages of faculty on each category rated.

3. Report (if data are available) on the number of dismissals or terminations of contract in a particular school system for the past five years. Classify the data according to reasons for dismissal and whether each teacher was tenured or nontenured.

4. Report on a principal's perceptions of teacher evaluation, describing processes, difficulties, and suggestions for prospective evaluators.

5. Of the following types of summative instruments, tell which you prefer and why:
   a. Rating scale with numbers, as 1 to 5.
   b. Checklist with two categories, as satisfactory and unsatisfactory.
   c. Open-ended, narrative.
   d. Other (specify).

6. Show your positions on the following:
   a. How often should a principal visit and observe each teacher?
   b. How long should a principal remain in the classroom when observing?
   c. Should the principal's formal observations be (1) all announced, (2) all unannounced, or (3) a combination of announced and unannounced? If (3), what percentage of each?

7. Reply to the following questions:
   a. Is annual evaluation of each teacher necessary?
   b. If you believe an annual evaluation of each teacher is not necessary, how often should a summative appraisal be made for each teacher?
   c. Should the frequency of summative evaluation be varied on the basis of tenured and nontenured status of the teachers?

8. Prepare a position statement on this question: Should the principal delegate responsibility for teacher evaluation to an assistant principal?

9. Show your position on this question: Can the principal serve as a clinical supervisor?

10. Describe some observable symptoms of teacher incompetence.

11. Report on the work of the professional practices commission or similar body if there is one in your state.

12. Prepare a statement on what you believe the profession should do to weed out incompetent teachers. Be specific about persons or groups within the profession whom you believe should take responsibility for this task.

13. Suggest procedures for selection of teachers that would help ensure the employment of competent teachers. Specify the school personnel you feel should be involved in the selection of teachers.

14. Show your position on this question: Should states mandate a uniform teacher evaluation process to be followed by all school systems of the state?

15. Report on the work of the National Board for Professional Teaching Standards.

APPLICATION

1. Create a set of correlated instruments for (a) teacher self-appraisal, (b) classroom observation, and (c) summative evaluation of teachers.

2. Interview and report on the views of at least three teachers regarding administrative ratings of teacher competence concerning categories rated and procedures.

3. Locate samples of summative evaluation instruments used by school systems to evaluate teacher competencies and compare them in respect to similarities and differences. Which one would you prefer, and why?

4. Interview several teachers and determine (a) whether recommendations for improving instruction are regularly made by evaluators, (b) whether the teachers try to follow the recommendations, and (c) whether the evaluator monitors their progress in implementing the recommendations.

5. Write several indicators for each of the following competencies:

   a. The teacher demonstrates the ability to communicate clearly to learners.

   b. The teacher demonstrates the ability to motivate the learners.

   c. The teacher demonstrates skill in classroom management.

   d. The teacher demonstrates professional behavior.

   e. The teacher demonstrates enthusiasm.

6. For each of the following indicators, suggest a competency of which it might be indicative:

   a. The teacher uses strategies appropriate to learners.

   b. The teacher uses evaluation techniques that relate to the objectives.

   c. The teacher varies the stimuli.

   d. The teacher uses English correctly.

   e. The teacher shows personal interest in the learners.

7. For each indicator in Activity 6, write two descriptors.

NOTES

1. Jerry J. Bellon and Elner C. Bellon, *Classroom Supervision and Instructional Improvement: A Synergetic Process*, 2nd ed. (Dubuque, Iowa: Kendall/Hunt, 1982), p. 32.

2. Arthur Shaw, "Improving Instruction through Evaluation: One Teacher's View," *Action in Teacher Education* 2 (Winter 1979–80): 1.

3. Perry A. Zirkel, "Teacher Evaluation: A Legal Overview," *Action in Teacher Education* 2 (Winter 1979–80): 19.

4. Perry A. Zirkel, *The Law of Teacher Evaluation: A Self-Assessment Handbook* (Bloomington, Ind.: Phi Delta Kappa Educational Foundation, 1996).

5. Zirkel, "Teacher Evaluation," p. 19.

6. Ibid.

7. *Georgia's Quality Basic Education Act*, Part 6 Personnel, Subpart 2, 20–2-210, "Performance Evaluations," 1985 and Georgia Teacher Evaluation Program, 1989.

8. Zirkel, "Teacher Evaluation," pp. 17, 19.

9. Some of the data are from Zirkel, "Teacher Evaluation," p. 19.

10. Ibid.

11. Ibid.

12. Ibid.

13. Ibid.

14. Shaw, "Improving Instruction," p. 4.

15. John D. McNeil, "A Scientific Approach to Supervision," in *Supervision of Teaching*, 1982 Yearbook, ed. Thomas J. Sergiovanni (Alexandria, Va.: Association for Supervision and Curriculum Development, 1982), p. 23.

16. See Peter F. Oliva and Kenneth T. Henson, "The Expert Syndrome," *Contemporary Education* 53 (Winter 1982): 61–64.

17. Allen R. Warner and Dora H. Scott, "Evaluating Teacher Effectiveness: Professional Dimensions," *Action in Teacher Education* 2 (Winter 1979–1980): 30.

18. Richard P. Manatt, "Lessons from a Comprehensive Performance Appraisal Project," *Educational Leadership* 44 (April 1987): 8–14.

19. Ben M. Harris et al., *Personnel Administration in Education: Leadership for Instructional Improvement*, 2nd ed. (Boston: Allyn and Bacon, 1985), p. 226.

20. Ibid., p. 234

21. Kristine Hughes, "Districts on Teacher Dress: Have Some Class," *DallasNews.com*. Retrieved September 15, 2006, from http://www.dallasnews.com/sharedcontent/dws/dn/latestnews/stories/0915dnmetteacherdress.325d576.html.

22. John C. Reynolds, "In Search of Mr. (Ms.) Goodteacher," *Action in Teacher Education* 2 (Winter 1979–80): 37.

23. Shaw, "Improving Instruction," p. 4.

24. Zirkel, "Teacher Evaluation," pp. 19–20.

25. Ibid., p. 20.

26. Ibid.

27. Gary Natriello, *Evaluation Frequency, Teacher Influence, and the Internalization of Evaluation Processes* (Eugene: Center for Educational Policy and Management, College of Education, University of Oregon, 1983).

28. Gene Huddle, "Teacher Evaluation—How Important for Effective Schools? Eight Messages from Research," *NASSP Bulletin* 69 (March 1985): 58.

29. Ibid., 58–59

30. Kim Marshall, "It's Time to Rethink Teacher Supervision and Evaluation," *Phi Delta Kappan* 86 (June 2005): 727–35.

31. Tom Peters and Robert Waterman Jr., *In Search of Excellence* (New York: Warner Books, 1982), p. 122.

32. Harris et al., *Personnel Administration in Education*, p. 240.

33. Ibid., p. 241.

34. Georgia Department of Education, *Teacher Performance Assessment Instruments: A Handbook for Interpretation* (Atlanta: Georgia Department of Education, 1980). Formerly used for on-the-job assessment of beginning teachers for the purpose of certification, these instruments were revised in 1985 and discontinued in 1989.

35. Ibid.

36. Mary E. Dietz, "Using Portfolios as a Framework for Professional Development," *Journal of Staff Development* 16 (1995): 40–43.

37. Georgia Department of Education, *Teacher Performance Assessment Instruments*, p. 3.

38. Ibid.

39. Ibid.

40. Ibid., p. 4.

41. Ibid., p. 87.

42. Georgia Department of Education, *Georgia Teacher Evaluation Program*.

43. Madeline Hunter, "Six Types of Supervisory Conferences," *Educational Leadership* 37 (February 1980): 408, 412.

44. See Richard P. Manatt, narrator of videotape, *Supervising the Marginal Teacher* (Alexandria, Va.: Association for Supervision and Curriculum Development, 1983).

45. Harris et al., *Personnel Administration in Education*, p. 240.

46. Professional Practices Commission, *Professional Practices Commission: Serving Education in Georgia* (brochure), Atlanta, Ga. For an illustration of the rules of a Professional Practices Council, see Florida Administrative Code: Chapter 6, *The Code of Ethics of the Education Profession in Florida*, and Chapter 6, *Standards of Competent Professional Performance*.

47. Ibid.

48. Betty E. Steffy and Michael P. Wolfe, *The Life Cycle of the Career Teacher* (West Lafayette, Ind.: Kappa Delta Pi, 1997).

BIBLIOGRAPHY

ACHESON, KEITH A., and MEREDITH DAMIEN GALL. *Clinical Supervision and Teacher Development: Preservice and Inservice Applications*, 5th ed. New York: Wiley, 2003.

BARTH, ROLAND S. *Improving Schools from Within: Teachers, Parents, and Principals Can Make the Difference.* San Francisco: Jossey-Bass, 1990.

BELLON, JERRY J., and ELNER C. BELLON. *Classroom Supervision and Instructional Improvement: A Synergetic Process*, 2nd ed. Dubuque, Iowa: Kendall/Hunt, 1982.

BOWMAN, MICHAEL L. "Using Peers in Teacher Evaluation." *School Administrator* 56 (October 1999): 36.

BRIDGES, EDWARD M. *Managing the Incompetent Teacher.* Eugene, Ore.: ERIC Clearinghouse on Educational Management, 1984.

DIETZ, MARY E. "Using Portfolios as a Framework for Professional Development." *Journal of Staff Development* 16 (1995): 40–43.

EVERTSON, CAROLYN, and FREDA M. HOLLEY. "Classroom Observation." In *Handbook of Teacher Evaluation*, ed. Jason Millman Beverly Hills, Calif.: Sage, 1981.

FLANDERS, NED A. *Analyzing Teaching Behavior.* Reading, Mass.: Addison-Wesley, 1970.

GAGE, N. L. *The Scientific Basis of the Art of Teaching.* New York: Teachers College Press, 1978.

———, ed. *Handbook of Research on Teaching.* Chicago: Rand McNally, 1963.

Georgia Department of Education. *Georgia Teacher Evaluation Program: Evaluation Manual.* Atlanta: Georgia Department of Education, 1989.

———. *Teacher Performance Assessment Instruments: A Handbook for Interpretation.* Atlanta: Georgia Department of Education, 1980.

GIBSON, JANE WHITNEY. *The Supervisory Challenge: Principles and Practices*, 2nd ed. Englewood Cliffs, N.J.: Prentice Hall, 1995.

GLANZ, JEFFREY, and RICHARD F. NEVILLE. *Educational Supervision: Perspectives, Issues, and Controversies.* Norwood, Mass.: Christopher-Gordon, 1997.

GLASS, GENE. "Teacher Effectiveness." In *Evaluating Educational Performance: A Sourcebook of Methods, Instruments, and Examples*, Herbert J. Walberg, ed. Berkeley, Calif.: McCutchan, 1974.

GLATTHORN, ALLAN A. *Differentiated Supervision*, 2nd ed. Alexandria, Va.: Association for Supervision and Curriculum Development, 1997.

HARRIS, BEN M. *Developmental Teacher Evaluation.* Boston: Allyn and Bacon, 1986.

HARRIS, BEN M., KENNETH E. MCINTYRE, VANCE C. LITTLETON Jr., and DANIEL F. LONG. *Personnel Administration in Education: Leadership for Instructional Improvement*, 3rd ed. Boston: Allyn and Bacon, 1992.

HUGHES, KRISTINE. "Districts on Teacher Dress: Have Some Class." Retrieved September 15, 2006, from http://www.dallasnews.com/sharedcontent/dws/dn/latestnews/stories/0915dnmetteacherdress.325d576.html.

HUNTER, MADELINE. "Appraising Teaching Performance: One Approach." *National Elementary Principal* 52 (February 1973): 62–63.

———. "Six Types of Supervisory Conferences." *Educational Leadership* 37 (February 1980): 408–12.

KYTE, GEORGE C. *The Principal at Work*, rev. ed. Boston: Ginn, 1952.

LEVIN, BENJY. "Teacher Evaluation: A Review of the Research." *Educational Leadership* 37 (December 1979): 240–45. (See bibliography at end of article.)

MANATT, RICHARD P. "Lessons from a Comprehensive Performance Appraisal Project." *Educational Leadership* 44 (April 1987): 8–14.

———. "Feedback from 360 Degrees: Client-Driven Evaluation of School Personnel." *School Administrator* 54 (March 1997): 8–11, 13.

MANN, LARRY. "New Goals for Teacher Evaluation." *ASCD Education Update* 41 (March 1999): 1, 4.

MARSHALL, KIM. "How I Confronted HSPS (Hyperactive Superficial Principal Syndrome) and Began to Deal with the Problem." *Phi Delta Kappan* 77 (January 1996): 336–345.

———. "It's Time to Rethink Teacher Supervision and Evaluation." *Phi Delta Kappan* 80 (June 2005): 727–35.

MCGREAL, THOMAS L. *Successful Teacher Evaluation.* Alexandria, Va.: Association for Supervision and Curriculum Development, 1983.

MCLAUGHLIN, MILBREY WALLIN, and R. SCOTT PFEIFER. *Teacher Evaluation: Improvement, Accountability, and Effective Learning.* New York: Teachers College Press, 1988.

McNeil, John D. "A Scientific Approach to Supervision." In *Supervision of Teaching*, 1982 Yearbook, ed. Thomas J. Sergiovanni. Alexandria, Va.: Association for Supervision and Curriculum Development, 1982.

McNeil, John D., and W. James Popham. "The Assessment of Teacher Competence." In *Second Handbook of Research on Teaching*, ed. Robert M. W. Travers. Chicago: Rand McNally, 1973.

Medley, Donald M. "The Effectiveness of Teachers." In *Research on Teaching: Concepts, Findings, and Implications*, eds. Penelope L. Peterson and Herbert J. Walberg. Berkeley, Calif.: McCutchan, 1979.

Medley, Donald M., Homer Coker, and Robert S. Soar. *Measurement-Based Evaluation of Teacher Performance: An Empirical Approach*. White Plains, N.Y.: Longman, 1984.

Millman, Jason, ed. *Handbook of Teacher Evaluation*. Beverly Hills, Calif.: Sage, 1981.

Millman, Jason, and Linda Darling-Hammond. *The New Handbook of Teacher Evaluation: Assessing Elementary and Secondary School Teachers*. Newbury Park, Calif.: Sage, 1990.

Natriello, Gary. *Evaluation Frequency, Teacher Influence, and the Internalization of Evaluation Processes*. Eugene: Center for Educational Policy and Management, College of Education, University of Oregon, 1983.

Oliva, Peter F., and Kenneth T. Henson. "The Expert Syndrome." *Contemporary Education* 53 (Winter 1982): 61–64.

Peterson, Donovan, and Kathryn Peterson. "A Research-Based Approach to Teacher Evaluation." *NASSP Bulletin* 68 (February 1984): 39–46.

Professional Practices Commission. *Professional Practices Commission: Serving Education in Georgia*. Atlanta: Georgia Department of Education, Professional Practices Commission, n.d.

"Progress in Evaluating Teaching." *Educational Leadership* 44 (April 1987): 3–80.

Reiman, Alan J., and Lois Thies-Sprinthall. *Mentoring and Supervision for Teacher Development*. New York: Longman, 1998.

Reynolds, John C. "In Search of Mr. (Ms.) Goodteacher." *Action in Teacher Education* 2 (Winter 1979–1980): 35–38.

Rosenshine, Barak V. "Academic Engaged Time, Content Covered, and Direct Instruction." *Journal of Education* 160 (August 1978): 38–66.

———. "Classroom Instruction." In *The Psychology of Teaching Methods*, ed. N. L. Gage. Chicago: National Society for the Study of Education, 1976.

———. "Content, Time, and Direct Instruction." In *Research on Teaching: Concepts, Findings, and Implications*. eds. Penelope L. Peterson and Herbert J. Walberg. Berkeley, Calif.: McCutchan, 1979.

Rosenshine, Barak V., and Norma Furst. "The Use of Direct Observation to Study Teaching." In *Second Handbook of Research on Teaching*, ed. Robert M. W. Travers. Chicago: Rand McNally, 1973.

Sergiovanni, Thomas J., and Robert J. Starratt. *Supervision: A Redefinition*, 8th ed. Boston: McGraw-Hill, 2007.

Shaw, Arthur. "Improving Instruction through Evaluation: One Teacher's View." *Action in Teacher Education* 2 (Winter 1979–1980): 1–4.

Steffy, Betty E., Michael P. Wolfe, Susanne H. Pasch, and Bllie J. Enz. *Life Cycle of the Career Teacher*. Thousand Oaks, Calif.: Kappa Delta Pi and Corwin Press, 2000.

Strike, Kenneth A., and Barry Bull. "Fairness and the Legal Context of Teacher Evaluation." In *Handbook of Teacher Evaluation*, ed. Jason Millman. Beverly Hills, Calif.: Sage, 1981.

Sweeney, Jim, and Dick Manatt. "A Team Approach to Supervising the Marginal Teacher." *Educational Leadership* 41 (April 1984): 25–27.

Teacher Performance Assessment Instruments: A Handbook for Interpretation. Atlanta: Georgia State Department of Education, 1980.

Wilen, William, Margaret Ishler Bosse, Janice Hutchison, and Richard Kindsvatter. *Dynamics of Effective Secondary Teaching*, 5th ed. New York: Longman, 2004.

Wise, Arthur, Linda Darlinge Hammond, Milbry McLaughlin, and Harriet Bernstein. *Teacher Evaluation: A Study of Effective Practices*. Santa Monica, Calif.: Rand Corporation, 1984.

Wittrock, Merlin C., ed. *Handbook of Research on Teaching*, 3rd ed. New York: Macmillan, 1986.

Zirkel, Perry A. "Teacher Evaluation: A Legal Overview." *Action in Teacher Education* 2 (Winter 1979–80): 17–25.

———. *The Law of Teacher Education: A Self-Assessment Handbook*. Bloomington, Ind.: Phi Delta Kappa Educational Foundation, 1996.

PART VI

INSTRUCTIONAL SUPERVISION: EVALUTION AND CHANGE

Michael Newman/PhotoEdit

CHAPTER 14

IMPROVING INSTRUCTIONAL SUPERVISION

OBJECTIVES

After studying Chapter 14 you should be able to accomplish the following objectives:

1. Design an instrument by which administrators can evaluate supervisors.
2. Design an instrument for self-evaluation of the supervisor.
3. Design an instrument for evaluation of the supervisor by the teachers.
4. Design a plan for evaluating the supervisory program.
5. Predict likely developments in supervision in the future.

ROLE OF THE SUPERVISOR: A REPRISE

Throughout this text, the supervisor has been seen performing a variety of roles. This staff person has been conceptualized as an individual whose primary role is to foster the improvement of instruction and the curriculum through individual and group assistance to teachers. The instructional supervisor is a service-oriented staff person who would be more effective if freed of administrative responsibilities.

As noted at the beginning of this text, there are many types of supervisors: generalists, specialists, supervisor-administrators, building supervisors, district supervisors, department heads, team leaders, grade coordinators, and state supervisors. The role and function of each of these positions differ to some extent, though their primary roles are similar—the improvement of programs for young people through the professional development of teachers. Consequently, the principles of supervision that have been discussed in this text have relevance for all supervisors. Specific practices and procedures, however, will need to be modified to fit the various types of supervisor roles.

All supervisors have certain common interests, such as helping teachers with planning, selection of strategies and resources, and evaluation. Some supervisors—for example, those on the state level—are more remote from the firing line than local supervisors, but they still follow similar principles of supervision in somewhat modified ways. The supervisors at each higher level of the educational hierarchy may aid supervisors below them as well as teachers; therefore, they must be thoroughly conversant with the duties and responsibilities of supervisors at lower levels of the echelon.

The responsibilities of the supervisor imply a number of roles, four of which were conceptualized in the model of supervision in Chapter 1. The supervisor is

- A coordinator, who seeks to achieve articulation between programs and levels and helps teachers become aware of each other's problems.
- A consultant, who shares his or her expertise with individual teachers and groups.
- A group leader, who knows how to work with groups and help them develop.
- An evaluator, who assists teachers in evaluating instruction, the curriculum, and themselves.

In addition, the supervisor is

- An expert on instruction, who is knowledgeable about the latest and best methods.
- A curriculum expert, who is knowledgeable about the curriculum and ways to improve it.
- A communicator, who can relate information and ideas to teachers and is a good listener.
- An organizer, who is skillful in establishing various kinds of programs of value to teachers.
- A stimulator, who suggests ideas for teachers to consider.
- An orienter, who takes responsibility for helping teachers who are new to the system and community to become acquainted.
- A public relations person, who may be invited to interpret the school's curriculum to the public, either in written communications or in talks to lay groups.
- A researcher, who instigates research studies, particularly action research.
- A change agent, who is a catalyst for helping teachers change and improve.
- A master teacher, who can describe and demonstrate effective teaching.

Although supervisors have other tasks, these roles show the scope of their job in today's schools. Obviously, a special kind of person is required to be a supervisor, one with extended training and experience.

Once appointed, the supervisor must not assume that the training period is over. It may be unrealistic to assume that supervisors will excel in every role. Nevertheless, supervisors need to develop and demonstrate some degree of proficiency in each of the roles called for in their own school setting. As with the teachers they supervise, supervisors must keep up with developments in the fields of supervision, curriculum, and instruction. To remain up-to-date and maintain effectiveness, supervisors should (1) participate in in-service activities for professional development, (2) regularly and systematically evaluate themselves, and (3) regularly and systematically request teachers and others to evaluate their effectiveness.

Supervisors can improve themselves by participating in some of the workshops, institutes, and conferences sponsored by both teacher education institutions and professional associations. They can take part in the activities of state and national organizations of particular service to supervisors, such as the Association for Supervision and Curriculum Development and the National Staff Development Council. In large school systems, supervisors can meet periodically to discuss problems. Formal course work during the year or during the summer at a teacher education institution is another means of self-improvement. Supervisors can keep up with current developments by establishing their own professional libraries, regularly reading the professional journals that have the most significance for them and the teachers they supervise, and consulting the Web sites of pertinent professional organizations.

Supervisors may learn some of the skills of supervision through on-the-job training. For example, they may become adept at writing curriculum guides by participating with a group of teachers in that activity. They may polish their research skills by participating in a research study under the direction of a specialist. They may develop the skills of organizing in-service activities by drafting plans for specific activities and putting them to the test. Nothing can be more incongruous in a school system than a faculty experiencing professional growth while the supervisory staff remains stagnant. The supervisor must continue to develop professionally if for no other reason than to set an example for teachers, thus communicating to them that professional growth is an expected part of the life of a professional.

EVALUATION OF THE SUPERVISOR

Supervisors should continuously seek to evaluate their effectiveness. In seeking evaluation, supervisors serve as models to teachers, demonstrating a personal need for continuous evaluation of their performance. Feedback on performance is necessary for all professionals if they are to grow and develop. Supervisors can gain feedback on their performance in three ways. First, they are ordinarily evaluated by their administrators. Second, they can evaluate their own performance. Third, they can survey the perceptions of teachers about their work.

Evaluation by Superordinates

It is rather general practice for administrators and supervisors to be evaluated by their superordinates. Central-office supervisors and principals are evaluated by their supervisors in the central administration. Principals assess the performance of assistant principals, lead teachers, department heads, grade coordinators, team leaders, and other supervisory personnel of the school.

Administrators and supervisors who rise through the ranks often hold continuing contracts as teachers. They do not, as a rule, have tenure in administrative or supervisory positions. They serve in leadership positions at the discretion of their superordinates. Even the superintendent is evaluated one way or another by his or her superordinates: the public. If the superintendent is elected to office, the people may vote for a rival candidate at the next election. An appointed superintendent, which most superintendents are, serves at the pleasure of the people's representatives, the local board of education. If the board is dissatisfied with the performance of the superintendent, it may refuse to renew a contract. If the board becomes dissatisfied enough with the superintendent during the period of the contract, it may buy up the remaining time of the contract and discharge the administrator.

Thus, school personnel are evaluated by their superordinates. Administrators and supervisors are evaluated for two purposes: (1) to provide them with feedback so they can improve their performance, and (2) to provide their superiors with data on which to base personnel decisions, such as retention in their administrative or supervisory positions or change in assignment.

Many school systems rate their administrative and supervisory personnel through instruments that detail the specific criteria considered important in those systems. Some school systems use the same instrument to rate both administrators and supervisors without distinguishing between these two types of personnel. In that respect, they emulate those preservice training programs of professional education institutions that stipulate the same course requirements for administrators and supervisors.

The evaluation instrument of the Ridgefield, Connecticut, public schools, shown in Figure 14.1, provides an illustration of the kinds of support and characteristics supervisory personnel are expected to demonstrate. Prospective administrators and supervisors should examine the criteria on which they will be evaluated before accepting a leadership position, so they can decide whether they wish to or could fulfill the requirements of the position.

In selecting people for administrative or supervisory positions, especially those with no previous track record in administration or supervision, the employing officials need to gather as much evidence as they can to predict whether the applicants will be successful in the job. They should be sure that prospective administrators and supervisors were not only successful but superior teachers. They should learn something of their philosophy of education, their organizational and problem-solving skills, and especially their skills in communicating and working with people.

Self-Evaluation

A conscientious supervisor will stop periodically for self-assessment, raising questions about the effectiveness of the help he or she provides teachers, looking for evidence of the kind of assistance rendered, and gauging his or her competencies against some standards of performance, such as those described in the literature on supervision. Supervisors should look at the objectives they have specified for the year or other period of time and determine whether the objectives have been met. Not only should they assess the effectiveness of the supervisory program per se, but they should also evaluate how well they have played each of their roles in that supervisory program. While encouraging teachers to evaluate themselves, supervisors can do no less than practice what they preach—evaluate their own traits and accomplishments, and make changes as a result of self-discovery. A checklist or inventory, such as the one shown in Figure 14.2, can be helpful in directing a self-appraisal.

Ridgefield Public Schools
Ridgefield, Connecticut

Department Chairperson-Department Leader : Professional Evaluation

School Year: 20___ to 20___

Name: _____   School: _____   Assignment: _____

Evaluate and describe how the chairperson/leader demonstrated competence in each of the professional responsibilities listed below. Include, if appropriate, exemplary practices used and/or areas of performance that need improvement.

	EVALUATION KEY
U	Unsatisfactory performance; improvement required.
A	Acceptable professional performance, compatible with the standards of the Ridgefield Public Schools.

	Observe, counsel and assist in the evaluation of department teachers.
	Provide leadership for a continuous program of curriculum improvement and development.
	Assist in the development of the departmental schedule.
	Recommend a departmental budget and requisition instructional materials.
	Maintain an accurate inventory of textbooks, equipment and supplies and provide for maintenance of equipment.
	Interview and make recommendations for the hiring of department teachers.
	Provide orientation and assistance to new department member and to substitutes.
	Provide assistance to the Assistant Superintendent for Curriculum and Instruction and to building administrators in matters relating to the system-wide departmental curriculum and assist in explaining matters of curriculum.
	Carry out such other reasonable duties and responsibilities designated by the Principal consistent with the position and in accordance with the contract between the Board of Education and the N.E.A.-Ridgefield.

Evaluator's Comments:

Professional Staff Member's Comments:

I HAVE READ THIS REPORT.

Date: _____   Date: _____

_____   _____
Evaluator's Signature   *Professional Staff Member's Signature*

FIGURE 14.1   Ridgefield Public Schools Department Chairperson-Department Leader: Professional Evaluation. *Source:* Ridgefield Public Schools, Ridgefield, Connecticut. Reprinted with permission of Ridgefield Public Schools.

Rate yourself on each of the tems below by checking the appropriate number. 5 is the highest and 1 is the dwest. NA means not appliable.

Characteristics	5	4	3	2	1	NA
1. I provide assistance as needed.						
2. I am open to communication.						
3. I show concern for the individual teacher.						
4. I transmit pertinent information.						
5. I am receptive to others' ideas.						
6. I interact effectively with teachers.						
7. I communicate clearly.						
8. I provide leadership in curriculum development.						
9. I am up-to-date on curriculum developments.						
10. I am effective as a demonstration teacher.						
11. I am skillful in diagnosing instructional difficulties.						
12. I am skillful in prescribing measures for instructional improvement.						
13. I am effective as a group leader.						
14. I involve teachers in decision making.						
15. I am skillful in conducting conferences with teachers.						
16. I plan in-service activities in response to teachers' needs.						
17. I perceive my primary role as a helper to teachers.						

FIGURE 14.2 Self-Assessment Instrument.

Instead of following a checklist, the supervisor could keep in mind a few basic questions to which he or she could periodically and privately respond:

- Am I meeting my objectives?
- Am I providing any real help and service to teachers?
- Where are the gaps in my help?
- Am I using my time wisely?
- In what areas do I need in-service education?
- Am I behaving like a supervisor or like an administrator?

Professional supervisors evaluate their own performance continuously.

Evaluation by Teachers

Although supervisors are commonly evaluated by their superiors in the educational hierarchy, much rarer but obviously necessary are opportunities for teachers to evaluate administrators and supervisors. Administrative and supervisory personnel at all levels of the educational spectrum commonly omit what could be a vital source of feedback—evaluation by "the troops."

Evaluation of superiors by subordinates is a relatively recent development, but there is a growing movement toward having teachers evaluate the performance of those who administer and supervise their work. The traditional and commonly held point of view has been that administrators and supervisors are immune from evaluation by those lower on the table of organization. Historically, the bureaucratic approach to administration and supervision has dominated most formal organizations. Authority and communication in bureaucratic organizations usually proceed from the top down, with no upward flow.

With a growing emphasis on the democratic or collegial approach to administration, however, and the move toward empowerment of teachers, superordinates have begun to permit and encourage subordinates to participate in the administration of the organization. In school settings, the evaluation of administrators and supervisors by the subordinates, the teachers, is analogous to the evaluation of teachers by their students and by their students' parents. As administrators and supervisors suggest or require student evaluations and often recommend parents' evaluations of teachers, they should set an example by seeking teachers' perceptions of their performance.

The accountability movement, which has rubbed off not only on teachers but also on their administrators and supervisors, and the power of teachers' organizations have also contributed to the notion that administrators and supervisors are accountable to their subordinates as well as to their superiors. New supervisors can forge a strong link in the chain of rapport with teachers by promptly and voluntarily instituting a process by which the teachers supervised can periodically—at least annually—evaluate their performance. Feedback from teachers is the best way for supervisors to learn whether they are accomplishing the mission. The teachers whom the supervisors serve are in a real sense the consumers of the product brought to them, and they are in the best position to judge whether that product is effective.

With the assistance of teachers, the supervisor may design an instrument that teachers can fill out toward the end of the year. To obtain valid results, the instrument should be administered in a threat-free environment. The best way to accomplish this is to have teachers fill out the instrument anonymously and turn it in to an elected committee of their colleagues. This committee will tabulate the data and furnish the supervisor with a summary of the data, after which the original evaluations will be destroyed.

With some minor changes, the supervisor's self-evaluation instrument in Figure 14.2 can be transformed into an instrument by which teachers can evaluate the performance of the supervisor (Figure 14.3). Descriptive terms are used in place of numbers. A space is provided for the response "No information" if teachers feel they have inadequate data on which to base a judgment. Appropriate directions on how to complete the instrument and who would collect it would accompany the evaluation form.

Please rate your supervisor on the following characteristics.

Characteristics	Outstanding	Very Good	Good	Fair	Poor	No information
1. Provides assistance as needed.						
2. Is open to communication.						
3. Shows concern for the individual teacher.						
4. Transmits pertinent information.						
5. Is receptive to others' ideas.						
6. Interacts effectively with teachers.						
7. Communicates clearly.						
8. Provides leadership in curriculum development.						
9. Is up-to-date on curriculum developments.						
10. Is effective as a demonstration teacher.						
11. Is skillful in diagnosing instructional dif culties.						
12. Is skillful in prescribing measures for instructional improvement						
13. Is effective as a group leader.						
14. Involves teachers in decision making.						
15. Is skillful in conducting conferences with teachers.						
16. Plans in-service activities in response to teachers' needs.						
17. Perceives his or her primary role as a helper to teachers.						

FIGURE 14.3 Teacher Evaluation of the Supervisor.

EVALUATION OF THE SUPERVISORY PROGRAM

In addition to assessing their success in fulfilling prescribed roles, supervisors should assess the results of the supervisory program. Evaluation should reveal not only how well the supervisor functions but also what results have been achieved. Two approaches to evaluation of the supervisory program have proved helpful. We call them (1) evaluation by objectives and (2) evaluative questioning.

Evaluation by Objectives

In keeping with the approach to administration referred to as management by objectives, supervision by objectives requires the supervisor to establish at the beginning of the year specific objectives that are to be pursued during the year. Just as the specification of instructional (behavioral) objectives simplifies the task of evaluating student achievement, the specification of supervisory objectives does the same for evaluating the success of the supervisory program.

Assume for the moment the role of assistant principal for curriculum and instruction in an elementary school. In this school, the principal, assistant principal, grade coordinators, and central-office supervisors regularly visit and observe teachers. During the summer, the assistant principal drafts the following objectives, which will become the supervisory job targets for the ensuing academic year:

- By September 30, times and dates of staff-development workshops based on last year's survey of teachers will have been scheduled.
- By December 1, a videorecording system will have been put in place for teachers to evaluate their own performances.
- By January 1, each tenured teacher will have been visited once and each nontenured teacher twice; conferences will have been held with each teacher.
- By February 1, assessment tests in the basic skills of fifth graders will have been completed.
- By March 1, a curriculum mapping study will have been completed at each grade level.
- By April 1, curriculum guides in social studies and science will have been completed.
- By May 1, the in-service needs of teachers will have been surveyed for purposes of planning next year's staff-development program.
- By May 31, the workshops scheduled in September will have been offered.
- By June 5, each teacher will have had the opportunity to visit and observe for one day another teacher in the school system.

The foregoing objectives are typical of those that might be specified by a school-based supervisor. In evaluating the supervisory program, the supervisor can readily determine which objectives have been achieved. Establishing the objectives in advance is an earmark of sound planning. Specifying objectives clarifies the program directions in the supervisor's own mind, communicates the targets to others, and simplifies the process of evaluating the program.

Evaluative Questioning

The supervisor who employs evaluative questioning uses it to assess the results achieved. John T. Lovell and Kimball Wiles illustrated this approach by suggesting the following questions, which might be asked by the supervisor:

1. How many more teachers are experimenting?
2. Has there been an increase in the calls for help in thinking through problems?
3. Has there been a change in the nature of the problems presented?
4. Is there an increased demand in the staff for professional materials?

5. Is there more sharing of materials among members of the staff?

6. Is the faculty identifying the problems it has to face further ahead, so that it isn't confronted with so many emergencies?

7. Is there a greater use of evidence in deciding issues?

8. Is there within the faculty a greater acceptance of differences?

9. How many more parents are involved in the school?

10. How many rooms are attractive?

11. How many more teachers are active in professional organizations?

12. How many more teachers are seeking in-service experience?

13. How many more teachers are planning with other teachers?

14. How many more pupils are being included in planning and evaluating?

15. Is a larger percentage of the staff assuming responsibility for the improvement of the program?

16. Are staff meetings becoming more faculty directed?

17. How many more teachers are using a wider range of materials?

18. How are students scoring on achievement tests?[1]

Answers to questions like these will reveal a great deal about the effectiveness of the supervisory program. If the two approaches to program evaluation are both followed—that is, if prespecified objectives are assessed and if probing, evaluative questions are answered—a thorough assessment of the program may be made. Where deficiencies are uncovered, the supervisor must make plans to overcome them.

FUTURE DIRECTIONS IN SUPERVISION

It is almost pro forma for the authors of an education textbook to gaze into a crystal ball and prophesy what they see for the future. We have seen the emergence of an academic specialty called Futurism. It has its own organization composed of Futurists, whose writings appear in the organization's journal, *The Futurist*,[2] a magazine of forecasts, trends, and ideas about the future. We can identify any number of books and films that predict what life will be like in the future. The beauty of prophesying is that no one can prove the prophet wrong. Not until the future arrives can the prophecies be pronounced "right" or "wrong," or perhaps judged on the scale employed by some of those tough standardized-test items, "more right than wrong" or "more wrong than right."

So we cannot resist becoming a bit delphic and very briefly playing the game Prophecy. We'd like to consider this question with you: What will supervision be like ten years from now?

Domains of Supervision

Supervisory tasks will continue to fall in the three domains: instructional, curriculum, and staff development. In some cases, one supervisor may fulfill roles in all three domains. In other cases, separate supervisors will be charged with responsibility in one or two domains. School systems will continue to employ a part-time or full-time person to coordinate staff-development activities and a limited number of generalist and specialist coordinators.

Clarification of Approaches, Functions, and Roles

The first edition of this textbook (1976) optimistically predicted that the supervisor's role would be clarified in ten years. That prediction fell far short of complete realization. Supervision remains even yet in a state of uncertainty and flux. Would that we could say the many issues discussed in Chapter 2 have been resolved!

A lack of clarity about the functions, roles, and practices of supervision permeates the field. The Association for Supervision and Curriculum Development, for example, devoted its 1992 Yearbook to *Supervision in Transition*.[3] Thomas J. Sergiovanni and Robert J. Starratt[4] and Carl D. Glickman and colleagues[5] called for redefinition of supervision. In fact, Sergiovanni, in speaking of "the regeneration of supervision," expressed the hope that as we enter the twenty-first century, schools will be "learning communities" where "supervision will no longer be needed."[6]

In seeking clarification of the function, roles, and practices of supervision, both practitioners and theorists face a number of conflicting approaches that command their attention. Multiple questions remain to be answered, for example:

- To which approach shall we subscribe: the scientific? the human relations? the human-resources development? the artistic? the hermeneutic? the ecological-cultural?
- Shall supervisors work primarily with individual teachers? with groups? with neither, serving instead as broker-impresarios?
- Shall supervisors be primarily colleagues and teaching mentors, or shall they be drawn from the central-office staff or regional educational service agencies?

Perhaps no national resolution of the issues can ever be made. Instead, issues will be addressed locality by locality, school system by school system, school by school. By the very nature of the task, we may never see complete and unequivocal clarification.

For the immediate future, supervision in its clinical mode will continue to follow the scientific approach, with primary emphasis on helping individual teachers and secondarily working with groups. Emphasis is shifting from service provided by supervisors from outside the school to help from staff members within the school.

Instructional supervisors will continue to put into practice the results of more than thirty years' research on teacher evaluation, generic teaching skills, objective data collection, conferencing based on observable data, effective teaching practices, and instrumentation.

We can expect to see some synthesis of the scientific and artistic, interpretive, and ecological approaches. Elements of qualitative analysis of what goes on in the classroom will accompany quantitative analysis of observable teaching behaviors. We will see a heightened concern with the multicultural nature of teaching and learning and increased sensitivity to the school's culture and to the ecology of the classroom.

Supervisors will encourage teachers to perfect strategies, try out different models of teaching, and examine their teaching styles. They will lead teachers toward achieving loyalty to the group, commitment to the organization, positive attitudes toward themselves and their job, mutual trust, and effective communications within the system. They will become more perceptive of the goal of teacher satisfaction as expressed in the human resources approach to supervision. They will be concerned about the effectiveness and health of both the organization and the individuals who make up the organization.

Balanced Supervision

Eclecticism is almost a way of life in the field of education. More and more, we are beginning to realize that no single approach to supervision guarantees success under all conditions. Therefore, we expect to see the best features of the scientific and other approaches selected, combined, and implemented. Were we to coin a term for this approach, we might call it *balanced supervision.*

James Nolan and Pam Francis set forth several principles defining a "new mindscape on supervision":

> The primary purpose of supervision is to provide a mechanism for teachers and supervisors to increase their understanding of the learning-teaching process through collaborative inquiry with other professionals.
>
> Teachers should not be viewed only as consumers of research but as generators of knowledge about learning and teaching.
>
> Supervisors must see themselves not as critics of teaching performance, but rather as collaborators with teachers in attempting to understand the problems, issues, and dilemmas that are inherent in the process of learning and teaching.
>
> Acquiring an understanding of the learning-teaching process demands the collection of many types of data over extended periods of time.
>
> The focus for supervision needs to be expanded to include content-specific as well as general issues and questions.
>
> Supervision should focus not only on individual teachers but also on groups of teachers who are engaged in ongoing inquiry concerning problems, issues, and questions.[7]

With the exception of those supervisors who reject one approach or the other outright, most supervisors will likely adopt a combination of approaches. Some will follow a scientific approach with added artistic, interpretive, ecological, and qualitative dimensions; others will adopt artistic, interpretive, ecological, and/or qualitative approaches with added scientific and quantitative dimensions.

Clearly stating the premises undergirding an ecological approach to teaching with its implications for supervision, C. A. Bowers and David J. Flinders left some room for other ways of working:

> Our purpose is to help establish a new conceptual foundation for thinking about effective classroom practices, effective in the sense of being justified on sound pedagogical and political grounds. We shall thus incorporate the insights and classroom practices from other paradigms, including classroom management, when they can be reconciled with our more culture- and language-sensitive orientation.[8]

A new mindscape for or redefinition of supervision should allow for multiple approaches within a given setting.

Some clarification, however, has taken place. We can be optimistic and predict that the profession will continue to clarify supervisory roles and responsibilities. Typically, school districts have written job descriptions for supervisors (as they have for all school personnel), delineating duties and differentiating responsibilities among various types of supervisors. We anticipate that school systems that have not yet developed job descriptions will certainly do so in the near future.

Unfortunately, as has been the case for many years, supervision still resides between teaching and administration. Some sharpening of focus for both supervision and administration is taking place and will continue. In all but the smallest schools, we will see two types of supervisors: the staff specialist whose role is to help teachers improve instruction, and the line administrator, or school principal, whose task is to evaluate teachers for the purpose of making personnel decisions.

Institutions will continue to develop training programs for staff specialists, better tailored to the needs of those who see their careers as instructional supervisors, not administrators-in-waiting or teachers-once-removed. Training components for instructional specialists will emphasize such areas as curriculum development, instructional design, microteaching, human relations (to include multiculturalism), communications skills, measurement and evaluation, and use of technology, in addition to the more general background needed by professional personnel.

Instructional supervision will become increasingly important for the line supervisor. "The principal as instructional leader" has already become a cliché, implying that today's school administrators must give instructional supervision a higher priority. School administrators must be skilled in evaluating teacher performance for the purpose of making personnel decisions. To be effective, school administrators must have sufficient training in the techniques of instructional supervision.

Teacher Empowerment

Teachers will play an increasingly vital role in the operation of the school's programs. As noted in Chapter 9, their choices for staff-development activities, for example, will take preference over supervisors' and administrators' wishes. As control of schools becomes more decentralized, continuing a current trend, school faculties will be charged with greater responsibility for making curricular and instructional decisions. If parental choice of school becomes universal practice, administrators, supervisors, and teachers will be forced to work even more closely together and share decision making to ensure successful programs that will attract and retain students.

In the not-too-distant future, we should see teachers playing key roles in selecting administrators, supervisors, and new teachers for their schools. Although they may not have the final say on hiring, their input will be sought and heeded through a formalized process. It is a paradox of the educational system that higher educational institutions have long involved faculty (and even students) in hiring both faculty members and college administrators, yet public school teachers have little or no say in the hiring of superintendents, principals, supervisors, or faculty. Employment of personnel remains largely the highly guarded prerogative of school principals, the superintendent, and, of course, the school board.

School-Based Supervision

The companion movements of school- or site-based management and shared decision making or shared governance will continue to spread and grow. As detailed state mandating holds constant or possibly diminishes and as the empowerment movement grows in strength, school-based management will increase in intensity. Some school districts have for years granted principals a degree of authority over their own budgets, although the amount of the actual budget involved may not be large. The public schools in North Carolina, for example, are expected to utilize components of school-based management in the improvement of student performance.[9]

Although states and the federal government have been promoting accountability through testing, the individual school has made progress in becoming the locus of school reform; states and districts have been encouraging the formation of councils composed of teachers, parents, and other laypeople to work with principals and staffs to determine the goals of the school and the means for achieving those goals. Chicago made news in 1989 with its efforts to grant considerable decision-making authority to eleven-member school councils made up of the principal, two teachers from the school, six parents of children in the school, and two laypeople without children in the school.[10] Chicago's efforts have not been without conflict and litigation, some of which have come from within the educational system. Salt Lake City's practice of shared governance dates back to the 1970s.[11]

Both Florida and Kentucky have mandated shared decision making. In 1976, the Florida legislature required school boards to establish a district "advisory committee . . . composed of teachers, students, parents, and other citizens" and allowed similar committees for each school. In 1991, the legislature more specifically mandated school boards to "establish an advisory council for each school in the district composed of teachers, students, parents, and other citizens who are representative of the ethnic, racial, and economic community served by the school." Although it encouraged the creation of advisory councils at every school, the legislature permitted districts with 10,000 or fewer students to "establish a district advisory council comprised of a representative of each school in the district." The advisory councils assist the principal and staff in preparing and evaluating plans for school improvement.[12] The Kentucky Education Reform Act of 1990 (KERA) made provision for school-based decision making; professional development of school employees, including administrators; and statewide assessment of student achievement, among other reforms.[13]

Site-based management, an often-desired goal of school-district administrators, has experienced stress and strain as well as success in student achievement, teachers' perceptions, group morale, parental participation, and administrative efficiency.[14] School-based management and shared decision making, however, are natural concomitants of efforts to empower teachers, students, parents, and other members of the community. As a result of the thrust toward school-based management, individual schools will assume increased responsibility for providing instructional supervision for their faculties. Schools will seek to develop teachers' supervisory skills so they may aid each other. A significant portion of curriculum and instructional leadership is now performed by persons in the individual schools, namely, lead teachers, assistant principals for curriculum and instruction, resource specialists, peers, coaches, and mentors. More of the day-to-day, one-on-one supervision conducted for improving instruction will become the province of school-based supervisors.

With greater responsibility placed on the individual school, the role of the central-office supervisor will change. Typically, the services of central-office supervisors have been spread thin throughout the system. These personnel have tried, with varying degrees of success, to meet the supervisory needs of all the schools in their districts. As school-based personnel take over some of the tasks of instructional supervision, central-office supervisors will be able to give more attention to facilitating and coordinating programs among the various schools and providing back-up help to school-based supervisory personnel who encounter problems. They will be consultants to teachers in some of the specialized subject areas. They will be staff-development organizers and/or presenters. They will serve as trainers of lead teachers, team leaders, department heads, grade coordinators, peer supervisors, coaches, and mentors. They will keep teachers informed of significant developments in curriculum and instruction. They will serve as third-party evaluators of teacher performance. They will be a liaison between the school district and the state and nation on curricular and instructional matters.

Peers, Coaches, and Mentors

Whether they are called supervisors, coaches, mentors, or master teachers, peers will be more engaged in helping each other with the improvement of instruction. Master teachers and mentors will help induct beginning teachers into the profession. Generally, teachers are favorably predisposed toward accepting help from their colleagues, so the use of peers in the supervisory process may be expected to increase. Programs in which peers assist each other eliminate or minimize the difference in status between the supervisor and teacher and allow schools to provide human resources beyond their current supervisory staffs.

The peer supervision movement responds to teachers' preference for turning to colleagues for help before looking elsewhere. School-based supervisors will work with central-office supervisors in training classroom teachers, team leaders, grade coordinators, and department heads to analyze their own performance and the performance of other teachers so they can assist colleagues. We will see a greater camaraderie developing among faculty members when they work together in a supportive manner, effecting true learning communities.

Teachers within departments, grades, and teams will develop the skills and attitudes needed to help each other. More school systems will be willing to place some of their supervisory dollars into training teachers and providing released time for them to help their peers, especially assisting those peers who may be having difficulties.

Schools may institute coaching models in which teams of two teachers help each other develop new teaching strategies, as advocated by Bruce Joyce and Beverly Showers, among others.[15] They may establish mentoring programs, as various states and districts have done, providing stipends and released time for experienced teachers ("mentors") to assist beginning teachers.

Problems abound in establishing and operating mentoring, coaching, and peer supervisory programs. Among these are funding and provision of released time for supervisory duties. Mentors should not be expected to perform supervisory tasks on top of a full teaching load, even if there is additional pay for mentoring responsibilities. Although some school-based supervisors—for example, lead teachers—may serve full-time in supervisory roles, mentor teachers, as a rule, should maintain responsibility for teaching some classes, thereby preserving their peer status and continuing to demonstrate their forte—effective teaching.

Teacher Incentives, Career Ladder, and Merit Pay

Schools will constantly seek to identify incentives for teachers that promote pupil learning and staff growth. Rewarding teachers for outstanding performance in the classroom gained momentum during the 1980s as some two-thirds of the states, including Arizona, California, Florida, Georgia, Iowa, North Carolina, Tennessee, Texas, and Virginia, either adopted or considered incentive programs in the form of career ladders or merit pay.[16]

The Governor's Review Commission of Georgia, for example, stated the intention of a career ladder program as follows: "It is intended that a professionally competitive base salary coupled with career development incentives will provide a framework for a balanced and comprehensive system of teacher compensation that will recognize proficient and productive performance of teachers and reward them for it."[17]

Tennessee gained considerable recognition in the 1980s for its career ladder program consisting of five levels.[18] Through a combination of state and local assessments, the Tennessee plan called for evaluation of teachers on six basic areas of competence ("domains"):

- Planning for instruction
- Delivery of instruction (teaching strategy)
- Evaluation of student progress
- Classroom management
- Professional leadership
- Basic communication skills[19]

Data came from seven sources:

- Observation of classroom performance
- Students
- Supervisors (principals or immediate supervisors)
- Peers
- The teacher being evaluated
- Materials created by and for the teacher
- Test results[20]

The Tennessee plan made use of state-appointed peer evaluators with at least twelve years of experience to conduct the state's evaluations and submit the results of their evaluations to the State Testing and Evaluation Center for scoring. Through provisions of the career ladder, Tennessee's teachers could become eligible for extended eleven- and twelve-month contracts and, depending on the level of the ladder, could earn substantial additional compensation. Mississippi, Oklahoma, and North Carolina tied incentives to certification by the National Board for Professional Teaching Standards, which began to certify teacher attainment of national standards in 1994–1995.[21]

The profession has flirted with teacher incentive programs in the form of merit pay systems in the past, as in New York State in the 1940s. Rewarding individual teachers with additional compensation for performance deemed outstanding has been attempted off and on in various states and localities from the early 1900s to the present. The concept regained popularity in the 1980s as states engaged in school-reform movements to improve student achievement and the image of public education.

Neither career ladders nor merit pay systems have proved particularly popular with teachers. In recent years, states have rescinded incentive programs and abandoned efforts to implement them. Criticisms of both career ladders and merit pay programs center on competitiveness and divisiveness, which lower a group's morale. Although the public overwhelmingly endorses the concept of merit pay, surveys of teachers' attitudes toward the public schools reveal widespread disapproval of such systems.[22]

Once again we see arising the controversial issue of awarding bonuses to individual teachers for meritorious performance as a concomitant of the search for, and retention of, "highly qualified teachers" whose students demonstrate proficiency on state tests.

Distrust of administration is rampant in the merit pay issue. Teachers' groups raise the questions of subjectivity and unreliability in evaluation of teacher performance. They question whether teachers can be evaluated fairly. They object to plans that impose quotas on the numbers of teachers who can be rewarded, thus eliminating some deserving teachers. They frown on the efforts they must make to apply for and participate in the incentive programs. They view the customary small salary increments as just enough to exacerbate the situation. Faculty in institutions of higher education where merit pay systems have long been in effect wrestle with the same problems identified by public school teachers.

At this time, the movement toward career ladders has crested. Speaking of career ladder plans, Lynn M. Cornett observed, "With the exception of Arizona, Missouri, Tennessee, and Utah, states with such plans never implemented all of the career levels their plans called for."[23] Although extrinsic incentives like career ladders and merit pay provide recognition and status to a limited number of teachers, whether these systems enhance student achievement is debatable and doubted by many teachers.[24]

A further deficiency of many career ladder and merit plans, especially the early ones, is the exclusive focus on teacher performance without assessment of student achievement. Several states, including Kentucky, South Carolina, Tennessee, and Texas, did give some consideration to student achievement, although not all retained student achievement as a criterion. "Only Arizona," said Cornett, "made student achievement an integral part of its comprehensive career ladder system."[25] Plans in Kentucky, South Carolina, Tennessee, and Texas, however, factored student progress into decisions on individual or school merit.[26]

Newer directions in teacher incentives will include group merit pay systems that reward schools and faculty as a group on the basis of student achievement, creating competition among schools as opposed to competition among *individuals*. Rewarding the faculty as a whole is more palatable to most teachers than attempting to attribute superior merit to individual teachers. Pay-for-performance plans are in effect in a few locations. Minnesota legislators approved a voluntary teacher pay plan in 2005. That same year, Denver voters approved a plan that rewards teachers based on student achievement, training, and working in high-needs schools and positions. The state of Texas, in 2006, implemented a $10 million pilot teacher incentive plan to reward top-performing teachers who work in schools attended by lower-income students. The Houston School Board implemented a

$14.5 million plan to pay teachers more for raising student scores on state and national exams.[27]

In 2006, the Florida legislature passed a new teacher performance pay plan, Special Teachers Are Rewarded (STAR). Under the provisions of the STAR program, school districts will establish performance pay plans through negotiations with local union leaders. Student testing results must be a factor in the STAR pay plans.[28]

Other incentives, like nonmonetary professional recognition and acclaim for work well done, will appeal to teachers' intrinsic motivation. Extrinsic rewards for all teachers will consist of opportunities for teachers to observe each other and work together, to participate in professional development activities designed around their individual needs and interests, and to receive administrative logistical support in the form of books, equipment, and supplies necessary for promoting student achievement.

A distinction should be made between teacher incentive programs in the form of merit pay and career ladders versus master teacher and mentoring programs that do offer some recognition, status, and additional pay to a limited number of teachers. The purposes of these two types of programs are far different—the former, a means of rewarding teachers who do their job well; the latter, a means of offering supervisory help to teachers.

In the evaluation of teachers for merit pay and position on the career ladder, the role of the instructional supervisor, as opposed to the role of the administrator, needs to be carefully defined. Because application for advancement on the ladder is a choice for teachers to make, the teacher choosing to apply may want the instructional supervisor to participate in the evaluation process.

Emphasis on Observable Teaching Competencies

Despite some educators' recommendations to the contrary, continuing emphasis will be placed on the identification and development of specified, measurable, and observable competencies of teachers. Supervisors at the state and local levels will work with teachers to identify those competencies and devise strategies for achieving and evaluating them.

The principle of accountability will continue taking root with joint efforts by teachers and supervisors to ascertain whether the demonstrated instructional competencies of the teacher make a difference in the product of instruction—the students. In this respect, teacher competency will be considered effective when teachers succeed in helping learners reach instructional objectives.

Distinction will be made between the competencies to be evaluated for formative purposes and those to be assessed for summative purposes. In working with teachers in a formative setting, supervisors will collect and interpret data exclusively on classroom performance. Those supervisors charged with the responsibility of making summative evaluations will expand the range of assessed competencies to include not only classroom performance but also personal and professional attributes. In all cases, competencies will be assessed on the basis of observable indicators of the teacher behaviors considered to be important to a school system. Teachers will have agreed in advance with school administrators on which behaviors will be assessed, how they will be measured, and how the results will be used.

Increasingly, school systems, frequently with pressure from the state and national levels, will give attention in teacher evaluations to product—that is, the achievement of learners. Incorporating some way to relate teacher success to pupil success is not likely to displace completely current efforts to judge teaching process and selected teacher characteristics. Enough momentum has been generated throughout the country for the assessment of teachers on process criteria that this approach to teacher evaluation is not likely to disappear in the immediate future. Some judicious mixture of assessment of process, product, and attributes will no doubt be the key to successful teacher evaluation.

The advent and growth of online or virtual schools could pose another challenge for supervisors as they supervise and evaluate teachers. For example, the Virtual High School (VHS) of a national nonprofit provider of virtual instruction has begun providing free access to online courses to long-term hospitalized children at three hospitals. These opportunities present teachers and their supervisors with "out-of-the-box" changes for the supervision and evaluation of the involved teachers.[29]

The profession may even make a breakthrough in answering this question: "What is effective teaching?" The advent of national standards for teachers will heighten the debate on what constitutes effective teaching.

Clinical Supervision

Clinical supervision will continue to play an important role in the total supervisory program. Instructional supervisors will increase the help they give individual teachers in their classrooms. We believe the prevailing model for delivery of classroom supervision will continue to be the clinical model of supervisor and teacher working on a one-to-one basis. Supervisors and teachers working together will identify specific behaviors with which the teacher would like assistance. They will collect ample data, following a cycle of supervision that includes observation and pre- and postobservation conferences. Clinical supervisors will focus on the improvement of instruction and will avoid rating teachers for personnel purposes. Teachers named to assist their peers will be trained in clinical techniques of supervision. Supervisors may explore with teachers linguistic, social, and cultural patterns in their classrooms. They may engage in discussion with teachers on the learning–teaching process.

The one-to-one model does not, of course, eliminate staff-development activities in which a supervisor or group of supervisors works with groups of teachers.

Goal-Oriented Supervision

Goal-oriented supervision will be a viable alternative to or a supplement to across-the-board or global evaluation of teacher competencies. Supervisors and teachers will identify specific job targets on which the teachers will focus during a particular period of time, usually a year. The supervisor will help the teacher delimit areas in which they agree the teacher needs improvement. Teacher self-appraisal will be increasingly used as a technique for identifying areas needing improvement and for selecting job targets.

Supervisory Teams

Some teachers will be aided by supervisory teams. Although we do not see school systems deploying teams of supervisors to work with individual teachers generally throughout the system, we do see increased use of teams to help teachers who are having serious instructional difficulties. At least one member of each supervisory team will be a professional colleague trained and experienced in the teacher's field of specialization. The other members of the team may be school administrators, central-office supervisors, or regional educational service agency specialists. Furthermore, the teacher to be assisted will have some say in the composition of the supervisory team.

Increased Use of Technology

More teachers will be willing to have their lessons videorecorded so they and their supervisors may carefully analyze the teachers' performance. Media will become more of an aid in the supervisory process. Teachers will feel less threatened and students less distracted by the repeated appearance of videorecording equipment and digital cameras in the classroom.

Enterprising school systems will create a professional library of protocol materials on tape or disks to be used for the analysis of teaching. Supervisors will need sophistication in the use of computers not only to carry out their own work but also to assist teachers in doing their jobs. Supervisors will be able to keep records, produce materials, and conduct training sessions using the computer. They will assist teachers in helping students achieve skill in using computers in all subject areas and to do research via the Internet. Supervisors will aid teachers in using technology to prepare tests and other instructional materials for classroom use, to carry out their own research, and to maintain their own classroom records. Some school administrators are using technology, such as "The Administrative Observer" software, to help them prepare classroom observation summaries, performance appraisals, and other staff evaluations.[30]

Needed Research

The supervisory profession needs continuing and repeated research on all three of the major domains of supervision: instructional, curriculum, and staff development. Supervisors must sharpen their knowledge and skills for performing their various roles.

Beyond conducting or examining research on improving knowledge and skills, supervisors should frequently survey teachers' perceptions about the supervisory program and processes. They should seek answers to questions such as these:

- What type of supervision do teachers want?
- Which do teachers prefer: individual help or help in collaborative groups?
- Are teachers, already hard-pressed to keep up with demands on their time, willing to allocate the time necessary for group deliberations?
- Do "most teachers," as Sergiovanni states, "consider supervision to be a nonevent—a ritual they participate in according to well-established scripts without much consequence"?[31]
- What kinds of help from supervisors would make supervision a meaningful event?

Kim Marshall's personal experiences as a school administrator, along with those of other school administrators, served as the basis for his article on rethinking teacher supervision and evaluation. After discussing ten reasons why the conventional supervision and evaluation process is ineffective for improving teaching and learning, he presented twelve steps to linking supervision and evaluation to improved school improvement.[32]

Professional Education

Training programs for instructional specialists have been modified to a limited extent by professional education institutions. However, many programs for supervisors still reflect a heavy orientation toward administration. Previous editions of this text contained the prediction that preparation for instructional supervisors would become more distinguishable from programs designed for the preparation of administrators. Perhaps that was wishful thinking. We have seen few efforts (except at the doctoral level) to distinguish programs for training administrators from programs for training instructional supervisors. Supervisory programs are often lumped together under the rubric of educational leadership. In fact, a set of guidelines developed for the National Council for Accreditation of Teacher Education (NCATE) encompasses both administration and supervision. Proposed by the National Policy Board for Educational Administration, on which ten prestigious educational associations are represented, these guidelines consist of eleven domains in five areas. Entitled *NCATE Curriculum Guidelines: Advanced Programs in Educational Leadership for Principals, Superintendents, Curriculum Directors, and Supervisors*, the guidelines were adopted by NCATE in October 1995.[33] Professional education institutions that seek accreditation from NCATE will be required to tailor their programs so that those in training for administrative and supervisory positions will achieve competence in the eleven domains of the five areas presented in the guidelines.

It is our hope, if not prophecy, that preparation programs for instructional supervisors will become more distinguishable from programs designed for the preparation of administrators. Prospective supervisors need to gain greater depth in curriculum, instruction, and staff development. The National Policy Board's guidelines leave an opening for some differentiation of programs while at the same time calling for uniformity of programs:

> While the emphasis in preparation programs may shift among the domains depending upon specific leadership roles (i.e., potential superintendents may focus more on finance and policy development while potential principals may focus more on instructional programs and student personnel), it is important for all school leaders to be familiar with all eleven domains presented in the Guidelines as well as to participate in an extensive internship.[34]

Training in understanding the ecology of the classroom with its social and cultural patterns and the cultural dimension of language—oral, written, and nonverbal—will become a part of the teacher education curriculum. Bowers and Flinders, for example, addressed the necessity of training in cultural and language processes of the classroom.[35] We may expect teacher education programs to increase efforts to develop an awareness of cultural, ethnic, and gender biases in the classroom. In so doing, programs will enable teachers to sense their own biases, attitudes, values, and cultural patterns.

Proposals for the reform of teacher education made in the late 1980s by the Holmes Group[36] and the Carnegie Forum on Education and the Economy's Task Force on Teaching as a Profession[37] contained a number of implications for supervision. Wholesale adoption of their recommendations would have impacted undergraduate and graduate education of teachers, induction of new teachers into the profession, staff development of in-service teachers, and certification.

The Holmes Group, for example, would have eliminated majors in education at the undergraduate level. In addition to gaining a background in general education, prospective secondary school teachers would pursue a major in an academic field; prospective elementary school teachers would engage in multiple areas of concentration in subject fields. Prospective teachers would earn a master's degree in education and would be required to complete successfully a year's internship in a school. "Supervised by clinical faculty, interns teach children half of their time, engage in action research, and study curriculum."[38]

The Task Force on Teaching as a Profession recommended that prospective teachers obtain a bachelor's degree in the arts and sciences as "a prerequisite for the professional study of teaching"[39] and a Master in Teaching degree with an internship in the schools. It recommended employment of lead teachers to take leadership in redesigning schools and in exercising instructional supervisory functions. The task force's agenda included the restructuring of the schools to grant teachers more autonomy and enhance their professionalism while at the same time holding them accountable for student achievement.

One of the task force's more controversial proposals was its recommendation for establishing a National Board for Professional Teaching Standards whose "primary function would be to establish standards for high professional teaching competence and issue certificates to people who meet those standards."[40] Created in 1987 by the Carnegie Forum on Education and the Economy, the National Board for Professional Teaching Standards offered a voluntary means of certification that would not supplant state licensing.

The board called for assessment of teachers on the standards, using newer measures, such as interviews, portfolios, and videorecording of teacher performance, after they have earned a bachelor's degree and have at least three years of teaching experience. Rather than control the entry into the profession as does state licensing, the national certificate bestows a mark of distinction on experienced teachers and recognition that they demonstrate high and rigorous standards.[41]

Changes in restructuring the schools and reforming teacher education are bound to affect the roles, responsibilities, and training programs of the instructional supervisor.

SUMMARY

Today's supervisor plays a number of varied roles. Throughout this text, his or her primary role is presented as that of a service-oriented helper to teachers in the areas of curriculum, instruction, and staff development. While giving attention to the in-service needs of teachers, supervisors must not neglect their own in-service training.

Supervisors are regularly evaluated by their supervisors. Conscientious supervisors regularly engage in self-evaluation and seek evaluation of their performance by the teachers being served. The supervisory program may be evaluated by determining whether objectives have been met and by responding to searching questions about the effects of the program.

The field of supervision is undergoing numerous changes. Among developments that might be predicted are the following:

- Supervisors will continue to work in three domains: curriculum, instruction, and staff development.
- Supervisory roles will be clarified and differentiated.
- Teachers will assume more responsibility in decision making in their schools.

- School-based supervisors will assume primary responsibility for day-to-day instructional supervision.
- Colleagues, in the roles of coaches and mentors, will be instrumental in helping each other.
- In place of individual merit pay programs, schools will resort to more group-oriented merit systems and appeal to intrinsic motives.
- Emphasis will continue on observable teaching competencies with some added attention to product.
- Clinical supervision will be widely practiced.
- Goal-oriented supervision will be an alternative to, or supplement to, global assessment of teaching performance.
- Supervisory teams will evaluate and assist teachers who are experiencing difficulties.
- Supervisors will make greater use of technological aids.
- There will be some synthesis of scientific and other approaches to supervision.
- Teacher education will continue to undergo modifications that will in turn affect the roles and responsibilities as well as the training programs of instructional supervisors.
- Supervisors will encourage teachers to obtain certification from the National Board for Professional Teaching Standards.

QUESTIONS FOR DISCUSSION

1. How will instructional supervision change in the next ten years?
2. How can schools reward effective teachers?
3. What social forces may change the tasks of the supervisor?
4. How will training programs for supervisors differ in the next ten years?
5. What do you see as the main problems with instructional supervision?

ACTIVITIES FOR FURTHER STUDY

REFLECTIVE

1. Locate and report on one or more self-evaluation instruments for supervisors that are in use in school systems.
2. Locate and report on one or more instruments in use in school systems by which administrators rate their supervisors' performance.
3. Locate and report on one or more instruments in use in school systems by which teachers may evaluate supervisors' performance.
4. Obtain and analyze a set of objectives for a year that have been drawn up by one or more of the following:
   a. Assistant principal
   b. Department head
   c. Grade coordinator
   d. Lead teacher

    e. Team leader

    f. Central-office supervisor (coordinator)

5. Obtain and analyze a set of objectives for a year that have been drawn up by a principal. Identify which objectives pertain to instructional supervision.

6. Make a list of probable questions you would ask as a supervisor to assess the results of your supervisory program.

7. Write a paper or make a PowerPoint® presentation on how computers might be used in the field of supervision.

8. Draw up your own list of prophecies concerning what developments are likely to take place in the field of supervision within the next ten years.

9. Analyze the future directions in supervision discussed in this chapter and state whether you agree or disagree with each position and why.

10. Locate and report on several articles or books that make predictions about changes that may occur within the next ten years in curriculum and instruction.

11. Identify professional organizations and their major publications that are of special significance to the development and growth of the supervisor.

12. Compile a bibliography of books on supervision copyrighted within the past five years that would be suitable as the nucleus of a professional library for supervisors.

13. Defend or rebut this proposition: Teacher salary schedules should make provision for salary increments based on merit. If you take the affirmative side of this issue, suggest how merit will be defined and determined.

14. Describe a merit pay system that is in place. If your state or school system has a merit pay plan, tell how teachers are selected for merit increments.

15. Prepare a report on the pros and cons of a system of national certification of teachers. State your position.

16. Prepare a report on the extent of national certification of teachers in your state. For state-by-state data, see the Web site www.nbpts.org.

17. Critique the following reports showing the implications for instructional supervision:

    a. The Holmes Group, *Tomorrow's Teachers: A Report of the Holmes Group*

    b. National Board for Professional Teaching Standards, *Toward High and Rigorous Standards for the Teaching Profession*

    c. Task Force on Teaching as a Profession, *A Nation Prepared: Teachers for the 21st Century*

APPLICATION

1. Create a self-evaluation instrument for supervisors.

2. Create an instrument by which administrators can evaluate supervisors' performance.

3. Create an instrument by which teachers can evaluate supervisors' performance.

4. Interview a supervisor (preferably in the type of position to which you aspire) and construct a job analysis of that supervisor's duties.

5. Survey at least ten teachers to learn whether they have ever had the opportunity to evaluate an administrator or supervisor.

6. Talk with a number of supervisors and report on in-service activities in which they have participated for their own professional development in the past twelve months.

NOTES

1. John T. Lovell and Kimball Wiles, *Supervision for Better Schools*, 5th ed. (Englewood Cliffs, N.J.: Prentice Hall, 1983), pp. 287–90.
2. See *The Futurist*. Published by World Future Society, 7910 Woodmont Avenue, Suite 450, Bethesda, MD 20814.
3. Carl D. Glickman, ed., *Supervision in Transition*, 1992 Yearbook (Alexandria, Va.: Association for Supervision and Curriculum Development, 1992).
4. Thomas J. Sergiovanni and Robert J. Starratt, *Supervision: A Redefinition*, 8th ed. (Boston: McGraw-Hill, 2007).
5. Carl D. Glickman, Stephen P. Gordon, and Jovita M. Ross-Gordon, *SuperVision and Instructional Leadership: A Developmental Approach*, 7th ed. (Boston: Allyn and Bacon, 2007).
6. Thomas J. Sergiovanni, "Moral Authority and the Regeneration of Supervision," in *Supervision in Transition*, 1992 Yearbook, ed. Carl D. Glickman (Alexandria, Va.: Association for Supervision and Curriculum Development, 1992), pp. 211–12.
7. James Nolan and Pam Francis, "Changing Perspectives in Curriculum and Instruction," in *Supervision in Transition*, 1992 Yearbook, ed. Glickman, (Alexandria, Va.: Association for Supervision and Curriculum Development, 1992), p. 58.
8. C. A. Bowers and David J. Flinders, *Responsive Teaching: An Ecological Approach to Classroom Patterns of Language, Culture, and Thought* (New York: Teachers College Press, 1990), p. 29.
9. North Carolina Department of Public Instruction. Retrieved September 28, 2006, from http://www.ncpublicschools.org/docs/schoolimprovement/2004abcmanual.pdf.
10. Maxey Bacchus and Bruce Marchiafava, "Implementing School Reform in Chicago: The System Perspective" (Paper presented at the annual meeting of the American Educational Research Association, Chicago, 1991), ERIC Document ED 331 887 TM 016 473.
11. Betty Malen and Rodney T. Ogawa, *The Implementation of the Salt Lake City School District's Shared Governance Policy: A Study of School-Site Councils* (Salt Lake City, Utah: Salt Lake City School District, 1985), ERIC Document ED 274 099 EA 018 864.
12. See *Florida Statutes*, Section 229.58 (1976 and 1991).
13. Mary Helen Miller et al., *A Guide to the Kentucky Education Reform Act of 1990* (Frankfort: Kentucky Legislative Research Commission, 1990), ERIC Document ED 327 352 RC 017 896. See also Eddy J. Van Meter, "The Kentucky Mandate: School-Based Decision Making," *NASSP Bulletin* 75 (February 1991): 52–62; Wallace G. Wilkinson, "Kentucky Education Reform: Schools Held Responsible and Accountable," *Appalachia* 23 (Summer 1990): 7–9.
14. Patsy E. Johnson and Joyce Logan, "Efficacy and Productivity: The Future of School-Based Decision-Making Councils in Kentucky," *Journal of Student Leadership* 10, no. 4 (July 2000): 311–31. Contains fifty-nine references. ERIC Document EJ 612 864.
15. See Bruce Joyce and Beverly Showers, "The Coaching of Teaching," *Educational Leadership* 40 (October 1982): 4–10; and Beverly Showers, "Teachers Coaching Teachers," *Educational Leadership* 42 (April 1985): 43–48.
16. Larry E. Frase and William K. Poston Jr., "Teacher Incentive Programs: Diversity and Effectiveness without State Funding," *Clearing House* 64 (November–December 1990): 95–98.
17. Georgia Department of Education, *The Georgia Career Ladder for Public Elementary and Secondary School Professional Personnel* (Atlanta: Georgia Department of Education, 1987), p. 1.
18. Tennessee Department of Education, *Tennessee Career Ladder: Better Schools Program: Teacher Orientation Manual, 1984–85* (Nashville: Tennessee Department of Education, 1984), pp. 1, 4–7.
19. Ibid., p. 13.
20. Ibid., p. 19.
21. Lynn M. Cornett, "Lessons from 10 Years of Teacher Improvement Reforms," *Educational Leadership* 52, no. 5 (February 1995): 29.
22. See, for example, Stanley M. Elam, "The Second Gallup/Phi Delta Kappa Poll of Teachers' Attitudes toward the Public Schools," *Phi Delta Kappan* 70 (June 1989): 790.
23. Cornett, "Lessons," p. 29.
24. See Mark A. Smylie and John C. Smart, "Teacher Support for Career Enhancement Initiatives: Program Characteristics and Effects on Work," *Educational Evaluation and Policy Analysis* 12 (Summer 1990): 139–55.
25. Cornett, "Lessons," p. 29.
26. Ibid.

27. Holly K. Hacker and Terrence Stutz, "Incentive Pay Enters Classroom," DallasNews.com. Retrieved September 28, 2006, from http://www.dallasnews.com/sharedcontent/dws/dn/education/stories/061206dnmetpayplan.dabdea3.html.

28. "Teachers Union: State's Performance Pay Rules are Invalid," OrlandoSentinel.com. Retrieved September 28, 2006, from http://www.orlandosentinel.com/news/education/orl-bk-teacherpay091806,0,3219511.story.

29. Dennis Pierce, "Free Online Instruction for Hospitalized Kids," *eSchoolNewsonline*. Retrieved September 21, 2006, from http://www.eschoolnews.com/news/showStory.cfm?ArticleID=6602.

30. "The Administrative Observer" staff evaluation software. Perferred Educational Software, Cherry Valley, Ill.

31. Sergiovanni, "Moral Authority," p. 203.

32. Kim Marshall, "It's Time to Rethink Teacher Supervision and Evaluation," *Phi Delta Kappan* 86 (June 2005): 727–35.

33. The Educational Leadership Constituent Council (c/o Association for Supervision and Curriculum Development, 1703 North Beauregard Street, Alexandria, Va. 22311–1714), *NCATE Curriculum Guidelines: Advanced Programs in Educational Leadership for Principals, Superintendents, Curriculum Directors, and Supervisors*, 1995.

34. Ibid., p. F-1.

35. Bowers and Flinders, *Responsive Teaching*, p. 22.

36. The Holmes Group, *Tomorrow's Teachers: A Report of the Holmes Group* (East Lansing, Mich.: Holmes Group, 1986).

37. Task Force on Teaching as a Profession, *A Nation Prepared: Teachers for the 21st Century* (Washington, D.C.: Carnegie Forum on Education and the Economy, 1986).

38. The Holmes Group, *Tomorrow's Teachers*, p. 95.

39. Task Force on Teaching as a Profession, *A Nation Prepared*, p. 55.

40. Ibid., p. 66.

41. National Board for Professional Teaching Standards, *Toward High and Rigorous Standards for the Teaching Profession* (Detroit, Mich.: National Board for Professional Teaching Standards, 1989). See discussion of national standards as an issue in Chapter 2.

BIBLIOGRAPHY

ALFONSO, ROBERT J., and LEE GOLDSBERRY. "Colleagueship in Supervision." In *Supervision of Teaching*. 1982 Year book, ed. Thomas J. Sergiovanni. Alexandria, Va.: Association for Supervision and Curriculum Development, 1982.

BACCHUS, MAXEY, and BRUCE MARCHIAFAVA. "Implementing School Reform in Chicago: The System Perspective." Paper presented at the annual meeting of the American Educational Research Association, Chicago, 1991. ERIC Document ED 331 887 TM 016 473.

BANG-JENSEN, VALERIE. "The View from Next Door: A Look at Peer 'Supervision.'" In *Improving Teaching*. 1986 Yearbook, ed. Karen K. Zumwalt. Alexandria, Va.: Association for Supervision and Curriculum Development, 1986.

BOWERS, C. A., and DAVID J. FLINDERS. *Culturally Responsive Teaching and Supervision: A Handbook for Staff Development*. New York: Teachers College Press, 1991.

———. *Responsive Teaching: An Ecological Approach to Classroom Patterns of Language, Culture, and Thought*. New York: Teachers College Press, 1990.

BRANDT, RONALD S. "On Teachers Coaching Teachers: A Conversation with Bruce Joyce." *Educational Leadership* 44 (February 1987): 12–17.

COLLINS, ROBERT A., and MARJORIE K. HANSON. *School-Based Management/Shared Decision Making Project 1987–88 through 1989–90, Summative Evaluation Report*. Miami, Fla.: Dade County Public Schools, 1991. ERIC Document ED 331 922 UD 028 023.

CORNETT, LYNN M. "Lessons from 10 Years of Teacher Improvement Reforms." *Educational Leadership* 52, no. 5 (February 1995): 26–30.

———. " Trends and Emerging Issues in Career Ladder Plans." *Educational Leadership* 43 (November 1985): 6–10.

CORNETT, LYNN M., and G. GAINES. *Reflecting on Ten Years of Incentive Programs*. Atlanta: Southern Regional Education Board, 1994.

DeBevoise, Wynn. "Synthesis of Research on the Principal as Instructional Leader." *Educational Leadership* 41 (February 1984): 14–20.

Edelfelt, Roy A. "Career Ladders: Then and Now." *Educational Leadership* 43 (November 1985): 62–66.

Frase, Larry E., and William K. Poston Jr. "Teacher Incentive Programs: Diversity and Effectiveness without State Funding." *Clearing House* 64 (November–December 1990): 95–98.

Furtwengler, Carol. "Tennessee's Career Ladder Plan." *Educational Leadership* 43 (November 1985): 50–56.

Georgia Department of Education. *The Georgia Career Ladder for Public Elementary and Secondary School Professional Personnel.* Atlanta: Georgia Department of Education, 1987.

Glatthorn, Allan A. *Differentiated Supervision*, 2nd ed. Alexandria, Va.: Association for Supervision and Curriculum Development, 1997.

Glickman, Carl D., ed. *Supervision in Transition.* 1992 Yearbook. Alexandria, Va.: Association for Supervision and Curriculum Development, 1992.

Glickman, Carl D., Stephen P. Gordon, and Jovita M. Ross-Gordon. *SuperVision and Instructional Leadership: A Developmental Approach*, 7th ed. Boston: Pearson/Allyn and Bacon, 2007.

Gray, William A., and Marilynne M. Gray. "Synthesis of Research on Mentoring Teachers." *Educational Leadership* 43 (November 1985): 37–43.

Grimmett, Peter P., Olaf P. Rostad, and Blake Ford. "The Transformation of Supervision." In *Supervision in Transition.* 1992 Yearbook, ed. Carl D. Glickman, pp. 185–202. Alexandria, Va.: Association for Supervision and Curriculum Development, 1992.

Hawley, Willis. "Designing and Implementing Performance-Based Career Ladder Plans." *Educational Leadership* 43 (November 1985): 57–61.

The Holmes Group. *Tomorrow's Teachers: A Report of the Holmes Group.* East Lansing, Mich.: Holmes Group, 1986.

Johnson, Patsy E., and Joyce Logan. "Efficacy and Productivity: The Future of School-Based Decision-Making Councils in Kentucky." *Journal of Student Leadership* 10, no. 4 (July 2000).

Joyce, Bruce, and Beverly Showers. "The Coaching of Teaching." *Educational Leadership* 40 (October 1982): 4–10.

Langdon, Carol A. "The Sixth Phi Delta Kappa Poll of Teachers' Attitudes toward the Public Schools." *Phi Delta Kappan* 81 (April 2000): 607–11.

Lavely, Carolyn, et al. "Role and Duties of Lead Teachers in Career Ladder Programs." *Education* 110 (Spring 1990): 388–96.

Malen, Betty, and Rodney T. Ogawa. *The Implementation of the Salt Lake City School District's Shared Governance Policy: A Study of School-Site Councils.* Salt Lake City, Utah: Salt Lake City School District, 1985. ERIC Document ED 274 099 EA 018 864.

Mann, Larry. "New Goals for Teacher Evaluation." *ASCD Education Update* 41 (March 1999): 1, 4, 5, 8.

Marshall, Kim. "It's Time to Rethink Teacher Supervision and Evaluation." *Phi Delta Kappan* 86 (June 2005): 727–35.

McIntyre, Kenneth E. "The Merits and Demerits of Merit Pay." *NASSP Bulletin* 68 (November 1984): 100–104.

Miller, Mary Helen, et al. *A Guide to the Kentucky Education Reform Act of 1990.* Frankfort: Kentucky Legislative Research Commission, 1990. ERIC Document ED 327 352 RC 017 896.

Moffett, Kenneth L., Jane St. John, and Jo Ann Isken. "Training and Coaching Beginning Teachers: An Antidote to Reality Shock." *Educational Leadership* 44 (February 1987): 34–36.

National Board for Professional Teaching Standards. *Toward High and Rigorous Standards for the Teaching Profession.* Washington, D.C.: National Board for Professional Teaching Standards, 1989.

Neubert, Gloria A., and Elizabeth C. Bratton. "Team Coaching: Staff Development Side by Side." *Educational Leadership* 44 (February 1987): 29–32.

Nolan, James, and Pam Francis. "Changing Perspectives in Curriculum and Instruction." In *Supervision in Transition.* 1992 Yearbook, ed. Carl D., Glickman. Alexandria, Va.: Association for Supervision and Curriculum Development, 1992.

Peterson, Ken, and Anthony, Mitchell. "Teacher-Controlled Evaluation in a Career Ladder Program." *Educational Leadership* 43 (November 1985): 44–47.

"Redefining Supervision." *Educational Leadership* 46, no. 8 (May 1989): 2–64.

Rettig, Perry R. "Differentiated Supervision: A New Approach." *Principal* 78 (January 1999): 36–39.

Rooney, Joanne. "Teacher Supervision: If It Ain't Working . . ." *Educational Leadership* 63 (November 2005): 88–89.

SCHLECHTY, PHILLIP C. "Evaluation Procedures in the Charlotte-Mecklenburg Career Ladder Plan." *Educational Leadership* 43 (November 1985): 14–19.

SERGIOVANNI, THOMAS J. "Moral Authority and the Regeneration of Supervision." In *Supervision in Transition.* 1992 Yearbook, ed. Carl D. Glickman, pp. 203–14. Alexandria, Va.: Association for Supervision and Curriculum Development, 1992.

———, ed. *Supervision of Teaching.* 1982 Yearbook. Alexandria, Va.: Association for Supervision and Curriculum Development, 1992.

SERGIOVANNI, THOMAS J., and ROBERT J. STARRATT. *Supervision: A Redefinition,* 8th ed. Boston: McGraw-Hill, 2007.

SHOWERS, BEVERLY. "Teachers Coaching Teachers." *Educational Leadership* 42 (April 1985): 43–48.

STEVENSON, ZOLLIE Jr. *Local School-Based Management in the District of Columbia Public Schools: First Impressions of Pilot Sites.* Washington, D.C.: District of Columbia Public Schools, 1990. ERIC Document ED 331 188 EA 022 974.

Task Force on Teaching as a Profession. *A Nation Prepared: Teachers for the 21st Century.* Washington, D.C.: Carnegie Forum on Education and the Economy, 1986.

Tennessee Department of Education. *Tennessee Career Ladder: Better Schools Program: Teacher Orientation Manual, 1984–85.* Nashville: Tennessee Department of Education, 1984.

THOMPSON, J. C. *On Models of Supervision in General and on Peer Clinical Supervision in Particular.* 1979. ERIC Document Reproduction Service No. ED 192 462.

VAN METER, EDDY J. "The Kentucky Mandate: School-Based Decision Making." *NASSP Bulletin* 75 (February 1991): 52–62.

WILES, JON, and JOSEPH BONDI. *Supervision: A Guide to Practice,* 6th ed. Upper Saddle River, N.J.: Merrill/Prentice Hall, 2004.

ZEPEDA, SALLY J. *Instructional Supervision: Applying Tools and Concepts.* Larchmont, N.Y.: Eye on Education, 2003.

ZEPEDA, SALLY J., and R. STEWART MAYERS. *Supervision Across the Content Areas.* Larchmont, N.Y.: Eye on Education, 2004.

WILKINSON, WALLACE G. "Kentucky Education Reform: Schools Held Responsible and Accountable." *Appalachia* 23 (Summer 1990): 7–9.

ZUMWALT, KAREN K., ed. *Improving Teaching.* 1986 Yearbook. Alexandria, Va.: Association for Supervision and Curriculum Development, 1986.

WEB SITES

Association for Supervision and Curriculum Development: www.ascd.org

National Board for Professional Teaching Standards: www.nbpts.org

National Staff Development Council: www.nsdc.org

World Future Society: www.wfs.org

CREDITS

NAME INDEX

A

Acheson, Keith, 135, 146, 368, 373, 375, 379, 380, 382
Alexander, Lawrence T., 98, 106
Alexander, William M., 350
Alfonso, Robert J., 10, 26, 45, 369, 386, 387, 409, 412, 420, 422
Allen, Dwight, 143, 150, 151
Anderson, Robert H., 367, 385, 386
Anglin, Joyce Shanahan, 7
Anglin, Leo W., 7

B

Baker, Eva L., 286
Barker, Roger G., 175
Barnard, Henry, 6
Barr, A. S., 486
Barth, Roland, 335
Beach, Don M., 10
Beane, James A., 300
Becker, Wesley C., 190
Bell, Cecil H., Jr., 413
Bellon, Elner C., 373, 481
Bellon, Jerry J., 373, 481
Benne, Kenneth D., 8, 429, 430, 431, 432
Bennis, Warren G., 8
Beyer, Barry K., 112
Blanchard, Kenneth H., 405
Bloom, Benjamin S., 99, 100–102, 112, 147, 148, 180, 216, 217, 219, 221, 236, 238, 248
Blumberg, Arthur, 14, 67
Bondi, Joseph, 11
Bowers, C. A., 378, 421, 528, 537
Briggs, Katherine C., 463
Brooks, David, 196
Brueckner, Leo J., 10, 46
Bruner, Jerome S., 287
Bryan, Joy, 173
Burbach, Harold J., 47, 48
Burke, Peter J., 11
Burns, Robert, 444
Burrello, Leonard C., 340
Burton, William H., 10, 19, 46
Bush, George H. W., 178, 221, 273, 302, 321
Bush, George W., 222, 273, 302

C

Carter, Jimmy, 419
Champagne, David W., 335
Chase, Stuart, 429
Checkley, Kathy, 173
Clanton, Marsha T., 41
Clarizio, Harvey F., 166, 184, 185
Clinton, Bill, 221, 273, 321
Cogan, Morris, 53, 368, 373
Cohen, Saul B., 176, 454–455, 458
Coleman, James S., 177
Coleman, Joyce B., 386
Combs, Arthur W., 178, 180, 463
Corbia, Joyce, 173
Cornett, Lynn M., 533
Costa, Arthur, 112
Cowley, W. H., 404
Cunningham, Luverne L., 60

D

Daresh, John C., 11, 55
Davis, Allison, 172
Davis, Ed, 41
Davis, Robert H., 98, 106
De Bruyn, Robert L., 404
Deming, W. Edwards, 8, 415
Dewey, John, 34, 183, 335
Dietz, Mary, 499
Dobbs, Susan, 112
Dull, Lloyd W., 51, 332, 358
Dunn, Kenneth J., 182
Dunn, Rita S., 182

E

Edelfelt, Roy A., 336
Einstein, Albert, 113
Eisner, Elliot W., 377
Elfman, Julia A., 342
Embretson, Gary, 54
Englemann, Siegfried, 190
English, Fenwick W., 318
Esposito, James P., 47, 48
Evans, N. Dean, 10, 39, 40, 61
Eye, Glen G., 47

F

Fast, Julius, 421
Ferber, Ellen, 54

F (continued)

Feyereisen, Kathryn V., 53
Fiedler, Fred E., 406
Fiorino, A. John, 53
Firth, Gerald R., 10, 26, 45, 369, 409, 412, 420, 422
Fischer, Barbara Bree, 180
Fischer, Louis, 180
Flanders, Ned A., 381, 458, 459
Flinders, David J., 378, 421, 528, 537
Follett, Mary Parker, 8
Forsyth, Patrick B., 45, 47
Foster, Garrett, 342
Francis, Pam, 528
Franklin, Benjamin, 6
Franseth, Jane, 10
Fredrich, G. H., 54, 55
French, Wendell L., 413
Friedenberg, Edgar Z., 175

G

Gagné, Robert M., 109–112
Gall, Meredith Damien, 135, 136, 145, 146, 368, 373, 375, 379, 380, 382
Galloway, Charles M., 381, 421
Gardner, Howard, 114, 133
Garman, Noreen, 369, 370, 387
Garmston, Robert J., 386
Getzels, Jacob W., 413, 414
Giammatteo, Dolores M., 417–418
Giammatteo, Michael C., 417–418
Glasser, William, 170, 173, 175, 176, 177
Glatthorn, Allan A., 389
Glickman, Carl D., 11, 68, 403, 527
Gold, Hilary A., 176
Goldhammer, Robert, 367, 373, 375, 379, 385, 386, 388
Golding, William, 283
Goldman, Richard, 7
Goldsberry, Lee, 369, 386, 387
Goodlad, John I., 64, 342
Gordon, Stephen P., 11, 403
Guba, Egon, 413, 414
Gump, Paul V., 175

H

Hall, Edward T., 422, 423
Hall, Gene E., 340

Hamachek, Don E., 170, 171, 179
Harris, Ben M., 4, 20, 50, 333, 488, 492, 506
Harrow, Anita, 104
Hastings, J. Thomas, 216, 219, 221, 248
Hayes, Andrew E., 343
Hersey, Paul, 405
Hines, Vynce A., 350
Hirsh, Stephanie, 334
Hollins, Etta R., 336
Homans, George C., 429
Hord, Shirley M., 411
Hoy, Wayne K., 45, 47
Huddle, Gene, 490
Hunter, Madeline, 139, 143, 375, 380, 382, 383, 388, 503

J
Jacobs, Heidi Hayes, 318
Jacobson, L., 179
Jamison, Patricia J., 340
Johns, Roe L., 406
Johnson, Russell E., 60
Jones, Fredric, 166, 197
Jones, Linda L., 343
Joyce, Bruce, 333, 386, 452–453, 531

K
Kelley, Earl C., 171, 463
Kells, Patricia, 340
Kim, Peter, 178, 212
Kinsey, Alfred, 212
Kounin, Jacob S., 183, 381
Krajewski, Robert J., 367, 385, 386
Krathwohl, David R., 99, 102–104
Krey, Robert, 11
Kyte, George C., 370–373, 383

L
Lambert, Linda, 403
Langager, Terry, 54
Lewin, Kurt, 8, 406, 429
Lewis, Arthur J., 63
Lightfoot, Sarah Lawrence, 175
Lipham, James M., 403
Lippitt, Ronald, 8, 406, 429
Lovell, John T., 10, 26, 53, 64, 334, 335, 525
Lucio, William H., 8, 45, 53
Luthans, Fred, 414
Lutz, Jay, 342

M
MacNaughton, Robert H., 389
Madaus, George F., 216, 219, 221, 248

Manatt, Richard P., 487, 586
Mann, Floyd C., 22
Mann, Horace, 6
Marshall, Kim, 490, 536
Marczely, Bernadette, 22
Marzano, Robert J., 112–113
Masia, Bertram B., 100
Maslow, Abraham H., 170, 463
Maughan, Barbara, 174
Mayo, Elton, 8
McGregor, Douglas M., 406
McNeil, John, 8, 45, 53, 486
Medley, Donald M., 126
Miel, Alice, 63
Morphet, Edgar L., 406
Morris, Desmond, 421
Mortimore, Peter, 174
Mosher, Ralph L., 10, 12, 369, 373, 380, 383, 385
Mudrey, James E., 185
Myers, Isabel Briggs, 463

N
Neagley, Ross L., 10, 39, 61
Netzer, Lanore A., 47
Neville, Richard F., 10, 26, 45, 369, 409, 412, 420, 422
Nicholson, George, 196
Nolan, James, 528
Nordstrom, Carl, 175
Nowak, Arlene T., 53
Noyce, Pendred, 334

O
Oakes, Jeannie, 77
Oliva, Peter, 169, 241, 242, 244, 245, 266, 433
Omotani, Les M., 179
Orbaugh, Tim, 340
Orlich, Donald C., 50, 333
Ouchi, William G., 415
Ouston, Janet, 174

P
Pajak, Edward, 22, 56, 63, 368
Palardy, J. Michael, 179, 185
Patterson, Jim, 178, 212
Pavan, Barbara Nelson, 385
Pavlov, Ivan, 109
Pawlas, George, 245
Pearl, Arthur, 454–455, 458
Peters, Tom, 491
Petrie, Thomas A., 54
Playko, Marsha A., 11
Poole, Bernie, 75
Popham, W. James, 286

Portner, Hal, 387
Purpel, David E., 10, 12, 369, 373, 380, 383, 385

R
Rafferty, Max, 60
Reinhartz, Judy, 10
Reller, Theodore L., 406
Reynolds, John C., 488
Riley, Richard W., 169
Rogers, Carl R., 170
Rosenshine, Barak V., 126
Rosenthal, R., 179
Ross-Gordon, Jovita M., 11, 403
Russell, Douglas, 139, 143
Russell, Sister Francis, 338
Rutter, Michael, 174, 175
Ryan, Kevin, 143, 150, 151

S
Sarason, Seymour B., 176
Schlesinger, Arthur M., Jr., 77
Schutz, William C., 463
Scott, Dora H., 486
Scriven, Michael, 218
Seaver, Burleigh, 179
Sergiovanni, Thomas J., 11, 333, 407, 527, 536
Sharma, Toni, 337
Shaw, Arthur, 489
Sheats, Paul, 8, 429, 430, 431, 432
Showers, Beverly, 333, 386, 452–453, 531
Silberman, Charles E., 175, 182
Simpson, Elizabeth Jane, 100, 104–105
Sizer, Theodore R., 175
Slavin, Robert E., 151
Small, Walter Herbert, 5
Smith, B. Othanel, 177, 454–455, 458
Smith, Gary E., 47, 48
Snyder, Karolyn J., 20, 381, 386
Sparks, Dennis, 334
Spears, Harold, 47
Starratt, Robert J., 11, 333, 407, 527
Stein, Gertrude, 51, 301
Stogdill, Ralph M., 405
Stoops, Emery, 60
Stufflebeam, Daniel L., 310

T
Tanner, Daniel, 286
Tanner, Laurel N., 184, 286
Taylor, Frederick W., 8
Thelen, Herbert A., 414

Thomas, Don R., 190
Thompson, Steven R., 335, 338, 348
Tocqueville, Alexis de, 399
Tracy, Saundra J., 389
Trimble, Susan, 41
Truman, Harry S, 407, 458
Tuckman, Bruce W., 458, 460
Tyler, Ralph W., 285, 286, 320, 411

V
Villani, Susan, 386, 387

W
Walton, Izaak, 15
Warner, Allen R., 486
Waterman, Robert, Jr., 491
Waugh, Alec, 283
Webb, Nettie, 74
Weber, Barbara J., 179
Weber, Max, 8
Weber, Wilford A., 184
Weil, Marsha, 452–453
Weldy, Gilbert, 417
White, Ralph K., 8, 406, 429
Wiles, John, 11

Wiles, Kimball, 10, 26, 53, 525
Williamson, Peter A., 342
Wolfe, Patricia, 112
Wolfgang, Charles H., 186
Wood, Fred H., 335, 338, 348

Y
Yelon, Stephen L., 98, 106

Z
Zachary, Lois, 386
Zirkel, Perry A., 483–484, 489

SUBJECT INDEX

A

Academic freedom, 38
Affective domain. *See* Taxonomies,
    affective domain
Age Discrimination Act of 1978, 483
Aims, statements of, 272–273
Alaska, state of, 489
America 2000, 273, 302, 321
American Association of School
    Administrators, 74
American Educational Research
    Association, 320
*American Educational Research
    Journal*, 320
American Federation of Teachers, 73
Anticipatory set, 138–142
Arizona, state of, 483, 531, 532
Artistic approach to supervision, 9, 376–
    377
Assessments. *See also* Needs
    assessment
        international, 321
        local, 322
        national, 222–223, 320
        state, 222, 321
Assignment making, 154–156
Association for Supervision and
    Curriculum Development (ASCD),
    22, 35, 113, 173, 351, 352, 353, 354,
    433, 456, 519, 527
        Working Group on Supervisory
        Practices, 35–36

B

Balance in the curriculum, 288–290
Behavior modification, 184–187
Behavior problems
    causes of
        originating in the larger
            social order, 178–179
        originating with the child,
            169–171
        originating with the
            child's group,
            171–172
        originating with the home
            and community, 177
        originating with the
            school, 174–177

originating with the
    teacher, 172–174
correction of, 187–198
    corporal punishment,
        197–198
    detention, 193
    expulsion, 196–197
    isolation within a class,
        194
    referral to security guards
        or police, 195–196
    restitution and reparation,
        192
    sending students to office,
        193
    suspension, 194
    taking away school
        privileges, 192
    transfer to special school,
        197
prevention of, 179–187
Behavior systems, 34
Behavioral objectives, 95–98, 138
Behavioral settings, 176
Bloom Taxonomy, 100–102, 148, 217,
    226, 236–238
Board of Cooperative Educational
    Services (BOCES), New York, 60
Boston (Massachusetts), 6
Brain, hemispheres of, 112
Brevard County (Florida) School
    District, 61, 62, 342, 344, 351, 355,
    464, 465–470, 485, 504
*Brown v. Board of Education of Topeka,
    Kansas*, 292
Buffalo (New York), 6
Bureaucratic management, 8
Burnout, teacher, 42–43

C

California, state of, 483, 490,
    532
Carbondale (Illinois) Community High
    School, 271–272
Career ladder, 532
Carnegie Corporation, 320
Carnegie Forum on Education and the
    Economy's Task Force on Teaching
    as a Profession, 73, 537

Carnegie Foundation for the
    Advancement of Teaching, 341
Carnegie unit, 284–285
Centres Régionaux de Documentation
    Pédagogique, 357
Chicago (Illinois) Public Schools, 530
Child abuse, 177
CIPP Evaluation Model, 309–311, 408
Civil Rights Act of 1964, 177, 483
Classroom management, 164–207. *See
    also* Discipline
Climate of the school, 176
Clinical supervision, 11, 12, 370–389,
    535
Closure, 154–156
Coaching, 386, 531–532
Cognitive domain. *See* Taxonomies,
    cognitive domain
Columbine High School, 166
Commission on the Reorganization of
    Secondary Education, 272
Committee on Assessing the Progress of
    Education, 320
Communication skills. *See* Leadership,
    communication
Competencies, generic. *See* Generic
    teaching competencies (skills)
Competency-based education, 135
Concerns-Based Adoption Model
    (CBAM), 340
Conditions (types) of learning,
    108–111
Conference
    postobservation, 382–384
    preobservation, 373–375
    summative, 507–509
Connecticut, state of, 483, 484
    State Board of Education, 6
Cooperative learning, 151–152,
    243–244
Cooperative (regional) educational
    service agencies, 59, 60–61
Corporal punishment, 197–198
Council of Chief State School Officers,
    73
County superintendents, 59–60
Criterion-referenced measurement, 135,
    215–216
CSE Evaluation Model, 311–312

Culture of the school, 174–177
Curricular reform, 291
Curriculum
    courses of study, 279
    defined, 262–265
    evaluation of, 298–328
    goals, 272–273, 290
    guides, 277–278
    mapping, 318
    needs assessment, 311,
        312–314
    plans, design of, 280–281
    relevance, 176
    resource unit, 279
    syllabus, 279
Curriculum development, 21, 51–53,
    261–295
    approaches to, 261–295
        comprehensive,
            266–278
        problem-centered,
            278–280
    defined, 261–263
    models for, 261–263
    supervision as, 52–54
    supervisor in, 265–266
Curriculum evaluation, 292, 298–328
    formative, 309
    summative, 309
    supervisor's role in, 301–302
Curriculum goals, 273–275
Curriculum mapping, 318
Curriculum objectives, 275–277
Curriculum organization,
    290–291
Curriculum problems
    continuing
        balance, 288–290
        scope, 282–286
        sequence, 286–288
    controversial, 291–292

D
Dade County (Florida) Public Schools,
    59, 222, 456, 472, 529
Decision making, 407–409
Delphi Technique, 315–316, 410
Department heads, 65
Discipline, 164–199
    approaches to, 184–187
    defined, 165–167
    models of, 186–187
    self-discipline, 168
Dissertation Abstracts International,
    319
Domains
    of learning. *See* Taxonomies
    of supervision, 20–23, 526–527

E
Early Reading First, 273
Ecological approach to supervision, 9,
    377–378, 528
Ecology of the school, 174–177
Education Commission of the States,
    320–321
Education Index, 319
Educational Policies Commission,
    111–112
Educational Researcher, 320
Educational Resources Information
    Center (ERIC), 319
Educational Testing Service, 320–321
    International Assessment of
        Educational Progress (IAEP),
        321
Effective teaching research, 125–127
Elementary and Secondary Education
    Act (ESEA), 221–222
Empowerment of teachers, 64, 335–336,
    529
Ethos of the school, 174–177
Evaluation
    of affective objectives, 239–240
    of the curriculum. *See* Curricu-
        lum evaluation
    of instruction, 208–257
        continuing assessment,
            210–211
        formative evaluation, 53,
            218–219, 442
        self evaluation, 442
        summative evaluation, 54,
            218–219, 442
    marking practices, 246–248
    of materials and studies,
        318–321
    models of, 309–312, 408–409
    of objectives. *See* Tests
    preassessment, 209–210
    reporting practices, 249–250
    supervision as, 53–55
    of supervisors, 519–524
    of supervisory program, 524–
        525, 557–560
    of teacher performance, 53–55,
        442–448, 449–477
        formative evaluation, 53,
            218–219, 365–366,
            442, 482
        instructional skills,
            449–452
        laboratory approaches,
            456–457. *See also*
            Microteaching
        observation systems,
            457–461

    parent evaluations,
        473
    personal-professional
        attributes, 449, 462–
        463
    portfolios, 242, 538
    self-evaluation, 442,
        520–522
    student evaluations,
        471–473
    summative evaluation,
        54, 442, 481–514
    using evaluation instru-
        ments, 463–471,
        491–498
    techniques other than testing,
        240–246
    types of, 309–312
        context, 310
        implementation, 311
        input, 310
        outcome, 311
        process, 311
        product, 311
        progress, 312
Evaluation techniques, other,
    240–246
    Creative assignments, 243
    Group work, 243
    Observation of class participa-
        tion, 240
    Oral reports, 240–242
    Portfolio assessments, 242–243,
        538
    Self Evaluation and Joint Eva-
        luation, 243–246
    Written assignments, 242
Evaluative Criteria, 316–318
Expulsion, 196–197

F
Federal Bureau of Investigation, 178
FIRO-B, 464
First Amendment (to the U.S.
    Constitution), 483
First International Assessment of
    Educational Progress (IAEP), 321
*Flanders Interaction Analysis
    Categories (FIAC)*, 381, 458, 459
Florida, state of, 59, 63, 64, 73, 223, 274,
    322, 332, 348, 357, 386, 456, 483,
    484, 490, 530, 532
Formative evaluation
    of the curriculum, 309
    of instruction, 53, 219–220, 482
Fourteenth Amendment (to the U.S.
    Constitution), 483
Futurist, The, 526

G

Gallup polls, 166
General information processing skills, 113
Generic teaching competencies (skills), 8, 142–153, 519–520, 534–535
assignment making 154–156
closure, 154–156
conducting a discussion, 145
focusing, 150
gestures, 150
individualizing instruction, 152–153
lecturing, 144–145
movement, 150
pausing, 150
providing for variation, 149–153
questioning, 147–149
set induction (anticipatory set), 138–142
shifting sensory channels, 149–150
silence and nonverbal cues, 147, 149–150
Georgia, state of, 58, 59, 386, 483, 502, 532
Department of Education, 314, 500
Georgia Teacher Assessment Program, 500, 502
Georgia Teacher Duties and Responsibilities Instrument (GTDR), 493
Georgia Teacher Observation Instrument (GTOI), 493
Governor's Review Commission, 532
Professional Practices Commission, 507
Professional Standards Commission, 507
Regional Assessment Centers (RACs), 493
Teacher Performance Assessment Instruments (TPAI), 493, 502
Goals, instructional, 93–95
writing, 93–95
Grade coordinators, 63
Group dynamics, 9–10
Group interaction, 428–430
interaction skills, 430–433
Group process, 426–428
process-oriented, 426
task-oriented, 426
Group therapy, 430–433

H

Harrison (South Dakota) Board of Education, 6, 7
Harvard University, 366
Hawaii, state of, 59, 484, 489
Hawthorne effect, 429
Holmes County (Florida) Public Schools, 59
Holmes Group, 537
Human relations approach to supervision, 5, 9
Human resources approach to supervision, 5, 9

I

Illinois, state of, 59
Implementation of instruction. *See* Presentation of instruction
Indicators, 500–502
Individualizing instruction, 152–153
In-service education, 50–51, 331–364, 409–412
assumptions about, 338–339
characteristics of effective programs, 340–341
consultants, 350–351
control of, 356
defined, 332–334
evaluation of, 341
funding, 349–350
implementation, 341, 345–348
incentives, 348–349
individual school plans, 345
key elements, 340–341
master plans, 343–344
model, 341
needs assessment, 341–342
planning, 341–342
posttraining and application, 351
supervisor's role in, 334–338
teacher-training modules, 345–348, 455–456
technology, 339
writing components, 345. *See also* Staff development
Instruction
direct, 127–128
evaluation, 209–256
formative, 219–220
summative, 219–220
goals, 93–95
lesson plans, 115–118
model, 89, 92–93
objectives. *See* Objectives, instructional
planning. *See* Planning for instruction
presentation. *See* Presentation of instruction
unit plans, 116–117
Instructional development, 21, 50–51
Instructional goals, 93–95
Instructional objectives, 95–105
Instructional plans, 114–118
lesson plans, 115–118
unit plans, 114–115
Intensive assistance team, 506
Intermediate level, 58–61
cooperative (regional) educational service agencies, 60–61
county superintendents, 59–60
International Assessment of Educational Progress (IAEP), 321
International Association for the Evaluation of Educational Achievement (IEA), 321
Interpretive approach to supervision, 9, 377–378, 527
Iowa, state of, 487, 532
Issues in supervision, 32–84

J

Joint Committee on Standards for Educational Evaluation, 312
Jones High School (Orlando, Florida), 348
Journal of Staff Development, 433

K

Kalamazoo, Michigan, 6
Kansas, state of, 483, 490
Kentucky, state of, 530, 533
Kentucky Education Reform Act of 1990, 530
Krathwohl Taxonomy, The, 102–104

L

Latin grammar schools, 6, 167, 410
Lead teacher, 63
Leadership
body language, 421–422
gestures, 421–423
nonverbal language, 421–422
oral language, 419–420
silent language, 422–423
written language, 420–421
communication, 419–423
decision making, 407–409
defined, 403–404
effecting change, 409–412

Leadership (*continued*)
  change agent, 409–412
  intervention strategies, 411
  group process in, 423–426
  organization development, 412–415
  situational, 35
  styles, 406–407
  traits, 404–406
  value-added, 407
Learning resource systems, 58
Lecturing, 144–145
Lesson plans. *See* Instructional plans
Lesson presentation, 137–158
  checklist on, 156–158
  generic competencies (skills) in. *See* Generic teaching competencies (skills)
Littleton (Colorado) Public Schools, 442, 443, 445, 503
Louisiana, state of, 483, 490
Louisville, Kentucky, 6

M
Management
  bureaucratic, 8
  by objectives/results (MBO or MBO/R), 416
  scientific, 8
Mandate, state, 13, 64
Marking practices, 246–249
Marking student achievement, 246–249
Massachusetts, Commonwealth (state) of, 484
  State Board of Education, 6
MBWA (Management by Walking About), 491
Measurement
  criterion-referenced, 215–216
  defined, 212–216
  norm-referenced, 213–214
Mental Measurements Yearbook, The, 223
Mentoring, 531–532
Merit pay, 531–533
Metacognition, 112
Metropolitan Life, 173
Miami, Florida, 59
Miami (Florida) Southridge Senior High School, 472
Michigan, state of, 484, 490
Microteaching, 456–457
Minnesota, state of, 487
Mississippi, state of, 532
Missouri, state of, 533

Models of
  clinical supervision, 366–385, 388–389
  curriculum development, 259–265
  curriculum evaluation, 309–312
    CIPP model, 309–311
    CSE model, 311–312
  disciplinary
    behavior modification, 185–186
    group dynamics, 184
    personal-social growth, 184
    psychodynamics, 184
    training, 184–185
  in-service education, 341
  instruction, 87–93
  supervision, 21
  teacher concerns, 341–342
    Concerns-Based Adoption Model (CBAM), 340
  teaching, 452–453
Modules, teacher-training, 346, 456–457
  Weber State College (Utah), WILKITS, 456
Monograph Series on Evaluation: Perspectives of Curriculum Evaluation, 320
Motivation, place of, 153–154
Multiculturism, 76–77
Multiple intelligences, 113–114
Myers-Briggs Type Indicator, 463

N
Nation at Risk, A, 273
National Assessment of Educational Progress (NAEP), 266, 320–321
National Association of Elementary School Principals (NAESP), 73
National Association of Secondary School Principals (NASSP), 73
National Board for Professional Teaching Standards (NBPTS), 52, 72–74, 435, 507, 532, 538
National Center for Education Statistics, 168
National Council for Accreditation of Teacher Education (NCATE), 537
National Education Association, 73, 274
National examinations, 301–302
National goals, 273, 321
National Governors' Association, 221, 273
National Institute of Education, 195, 490
National Policy Board of Educational Administration, 537

National School Safety Center, 196
National Staff Development Council, 433, 518, 552
National Study of School Evaluation (NSSE), 270–271, 317–318
Needs assessment
  curriculum, 312–314
  in-service, 341
Needs of youth, ten imperative, 274
Nevada, state of, 483
Newington (Connecticut) Public Schools, 335
New Jersey, state of, 59, 484
New Mexico, state of, 484
New York, state of, 59, 60, 532
No Child Left Behind Act, 13, 33, 58, 221–222, 273, 302, 321, 332, 338
Nonverbal cues, 147, 150
Nonverbal language, 421–422
Norm-referenced measurement, 135, 213–214, 306
North Carolina, state of, 531, 532

O
Objectives, behavioral. *See* Objectives, instructional
Objectives, instructional, 92, 95–100
  taxonomies of, 99–100
  teaching to objectives (T2O), 142–154
  writing, 95–99
Observation, classroom, 375–382
  global approach, 376, 381
  how to record, 378–379
    note taking, 379
    selective verbatim, 380
    verbatim, 379
  instruments, 381–382, 457–462
    competencies. *See* Generic teaching competencies (skills)
    descriptors, 517–518
  specific approach, 380–381, 382
  techniques other than instrumentation, 382
Office of Educational Research and Improvement, 320
Oklahoma, state of, 483, 490, 532
"Old Deluder Law" of 1647, 5
Oregon, state of, 490
Organization development, 412–415

P
Peer supervision, 12, 386, 531–532
Pennsylvania, state of, 484
Perceptual psychology, 170–171

Personnel evaluation, 53–55, 445, 465, 472–473
Perspectives of Curriculum Evaluation, 320
Phi Delta Kappa, 166
Philadelphia Academy and Charitable School, 6
Philosophy, writing a school's, 268–272
Planning for instruction, 87–124. *See also* Instructional plans
Portfolio assessment, 242–243, 499–500
Postobservation conference, 382–384
Preassessment, 209–210
Preobservation conference, 376–378
Presentation of instruction, 125–163. *See also* Lesson presentation
Primary Message Systems, 423
Process-product
     in research, 127
     in teacher evaluation, 489, 534–535
Professional improvement (development) assistance plans, 504–506
Professional portfolios, 499–500
Protocol materials, 454–455
Providing for variation, 149–153
Psychomotor domain. *See* Taxonomies, psychomotor domain
Punishment. *See* Behavior problems, correction of

Q
Questioning, 147–149
Quality-control circles, 415

R
Rand Corporation, 179–180
Reader's Guide to Periodical Literature, 319
Reading First, 273
Regional (cooperative) educational service agencies, 60–61
     in New York, 60
Rehabilitation Act of 1973, Section 504, 483
Reporting practices, 249–250
Reporting student achievement, 249–250
Research
     concepts of. *See* Research concepts
     teacher participation in, 308–309
     types of, 307–308
          action, 308
          applied, 307, 308

basic, 307
          descriptive, 308
          experimental, 308
          fundamental, 307
          process, 309
          pure, 307
Research and Development Utilization Project, 314
Research concepts, 303
     coefficient of correlation, 305
     mean, 304
     median, 304–305
     mode, 307
     normal curve, 303–304
     norms, 306–307
     percentile, 304, 307
     reliability, 305
     standard deviation, 304, 305, 306
     standard scores, 306
     validity, 305
Resources, selection of, 128–130
Resource unit, 279–280
Ressentiment, 178
Review of Educational Research, 320
Review of Research in Education, 320
Roles of supervisors, 23–24

S
Salt Lake City (Utah) Public Schools, 530
School- (site-) based management, 64, 342–343, 563–564
School Improvement: Focusing on Student Performance, 317–318
School Improvement Model, Manatt's, 487
Scientific approach to supervision, 8, 528–529
Scientific management, 8
Scientific method, 408
Scope of curriculum, 282–286
Self-concept, 170–171
Self-fulfilling prophecy, 171
Self-pacing, 135
Sequence of curriculum, 286–288
Set induction, 137–142
Seven Cardinal Principles, 272
Simpson taxonomy, 104–105
Skill-mix, 22
South Carolina, state of, 533
South Dakota, state of, 490
Staff development, 21, 50–51, 331–364
     defined, 332–334
     key elements, 340–341
     supervision as, 50–51. *See also* In-service education
     technology, 339
STAR (pay for performance), 464, 534

State departments of education, 57–58
Strategies, selection of, 130–137
Stress management, 416–419
Styles
     of learning, 180–181
     of teaching, 181–182, 451–452
Summative evaluation
     of the curriculum, 298–328
     of instruction, 54, 218–219
     of teacher performance, 54, 442, 481–514
Sunshine State Standards, 322
Supervision
     approaches
          administrative, 11, 53–55, 64
          artistic, 5, 9, 376–377, 528
          authoritarian-inspectorial, 9
          bureaucratic, 5
          clinical, 5, 12, 366–389, 535
          collaborative, 5, 9, 68, 370
          collegial, 385–386, 531–532
          consultative, 9, 12, 53
          cooperative, 9
          democratic, 5, 9, 10
          developmental, 12
          differentiated, 12, 389
          ecological, 5, 9, 377–378, 528
          educational, 12, 55
          formative, 54
          general, 12, 368
          goal-oriented, 463, 535
          group dynamics, 9
          historical, 4–9
          human relations, 5, 9
          human resources, 5, 9
          inspection, 5, 6–7
          instructional, 12
          interpretive, 5, 9, 377–378, 528
          laissez-faire, 9
          peer, 12, 385–388, 531–532
          qualitative, 528
          quantitative, 528
          scientific, 5, 9, 528
          summative, 53–55
          supportive, 9
          synthesis of, 527–528
     as curriculum development, 51–53
     defined, 3–4, 10–11
     differing conceptions of, 12

Supervision (*continued*)
    domains of, 20–23, 526–527
    as evaluation, 53–55
    foundations of, 22–26
    future directions, 526–538
    of groups, 55–57
    individualized, 55–57
    issues in, 32–84
    knowledge and skills of, 25–26
    model of, 20–22
    multiculturism as a focus, 76–77
    proficiencies of, 22–24
    school-based, 63–65, 530–531
    situational, 35
    as staff development, 50–51
    tasks of, 19–20
    technology in, 74–76, 536
Supervisors
    as change agents, 409–412
    evaluation of, 519–524
    expertise, 44–46
    as group leaders, 403–426
    knowledge and skills of,
        25–26
    need for, 38–40
    personal traits, 24–25
    roles of, 23–24
    status, 45–46
    taxonomy of supervisory role, 48
    teams of, 534–535. *See also*
        Intensive assistance team
    types
        central office, 61–65
        collaborative, 68, 409
        continuum, 15
        directive, 65–68
        district, 17–18
        generalists, 16, 69–73,
            384–385
        local, 17–19, 61–65
        nondirective (indirect),
            65–68
        school-based, 18–19
        specialists, 17, 68–72,
            384–385
        state, 17, 58–59
SurveyMonkey, 473
Suspension, 194–195

Syllabus, 277
System, four major behavior, 34

T
Task analysis, 106, 108–113
Task description, 105–108
Taxonomies
    affective domain, 95, 97–98,
        102–104, 116, 213, 239–240
    cognitive domain, 95, 100–102,
        116, 214
    psychomotor domain, 95, 102–
        104, 116
Taxonomy of supervisory role, 48
Teacher Behavior Continuum, 186
Teacher centers, 356–357
    British, 357
    Centres Régionaux de Docu-
        mentation Pédagogique, 357.
        See also Teacher education
        centers
Teacher Education Center Act of 1973
    (Florida), 357
Teacher education centers, 356–357
Teacher efficacy, 181–182
Teacher-training modules, 345–348,
    455–456
Teaching competencies. *See* Generic
    teaching competencies (skills)
Teaching, effective, 12
Team leaders, 63
Ten Imperative Needs of Youth, 274
Tennessee, state of, 532–533
    career ladder program, 532–533
    State Testing and Evaluation
        Center, 532
Tenth Amendment (to the U.S.
    Constitution), 57
Testing, 219–238. *See also* Tests
Tests
    essay, 224–227
    objective, 227–228
        alternate response, 232–
            234
        matching, 234–236
        multiple choice,
            229–232

        rearrangement,
            234–236
        recall, 228–229
        teacher-made, 223–224
    performance, 223–224
    standardized, 219–223
Texas, state of, 532, 533
Theory X, 406
Theory Y, 406
Theory Z, 415
Thesaurus of ERIC Descriptors, 319
Thinking skills, 112
    metacognition, 112
Time management, 416–419
Trends in International Mathematics and
    Science Study (TIMSS), 321
Tuckman Teacher Feedback Form, 458,
    460
Tyler Rationale, 285–286

U
U.S. Department of Education, 6, 196,
    319
U.S. Department of Justice, 196
U.S. Supreme Court, 192, 195
Unit plans, 114–115
University of Chicago, 411
University of Texas, 340
Utah, state of, 533

V
Virginia, state of, 532

W
Washington, state of, 490
Weber State College (Utah), 456
Webster Groves (Missouri) Public
    Schools, 443, 444, 446, 449, 500,
    501, 504, 505
Western Electric research, 429
    Hawthorne Effect, 429
West Virginia, state of, 483, 490
White House Cabinet Council,
    196
WILKITS, 456
Wyoming, state of, 484, 490